Communications
in Computer and Information Science 2009

Rationale

The CCIS series is devoted to the publication of proceedings of computer science conferences. Its aim is to efficiently disseminate original research results in informatics in printed and electronic form. While the focus is on publication of peer-reviewed full papers presenting mature work, inclusion of reviewed short papers reporting on work in progress is welcome, too. Besides globally relevant meetings with internationally representative program committees guaranteeing a strict peer-reviewing and paper selection process, conferences run by societies or of high regional or national relevance are also considered for publication.

Topics

The topical scope of CCIS spans the entire spectrum of informatics ranging from foundational topics in the theory of computing to information and communications science and technology and a broad variety of interdisciplinary application fields.

Information for Volume Editors and Authors

Publication in CCIS is free of charge. No royalties are paid, however, we offer registered conference participants temporary free access to the online version of the conference proceedings on SpringerLink (http://link.springer.com) by means of an http referrer from the conference website and/or a number of complimentary printed copies, as specified in the official acceptance email of the event.

CCIS proceedings can be published in time for distribution at conferences or as post-proceedings, and delivered in the form of printed books and/or electronically as USBs and/or e-content licenses for accessing proceedings at SpringerLink. Furthermore, CCIS proceedings are included in the CCIS electronic book series hosted in the SpringerLink digital library at http://link.springer.com/bookseries/7899. Conferences publishing in CCIS are allowed to use Online Conference Service (OCS) for managing the whole proceedings lifecycle (from submission and reviewing to preparing for publication) free of charge.

Publication process

The language of publication is exclusively English. Authors publishing in CCIS have to sign the Springer CCIS copyright transfer form, however, they are free to use their material published in CCIS for substantially changed, more elaborate subsequent publications elsewhere. For the preparation of the camera-ready papers/files, authors have to strictly adhere to the Springer CCIS Authors' Instructions and are strongly encouraged to use the CCIS LaTeX style files or templates.

Abstracting/Indexing

CCIS is abstracted/indexed in DBLP, Google Scholar, EI-Compendex, Mathematical Reviews, SCImago, Scopus. CCIS volumes are also submitted for the inclusion in ISI Proceedings.

How to start

To start the evaluation of your proposal for inclusion in the CCIS series, please send an e-mail to ccis@springer.com.

Harkeerat Kaur · Vinit Jakhetiya · Puneet Goyal ·
Pritee Khanna · Balasubramanian Raman ·
Sanjeev Kumar
Editors

Computer Vision and Image Processing

8th International Conference, CVIP 2023
Jammu, India, November 3–5, 2023
Revised Selected Papers, Part I

 Springer

Editors
Harkeerat Kaur
Indian Institute of Technology
Jammu, India

Vinit Jakhetiya
Indian Institute of Technology
Jammu, India

Puneet Goyal
Indian Institute of Technology
Ropar, India

Pritee Khanna
Indian Institute of Information Technology
Jabalpur, India

Balasubramanian Raman
Indian Institute of Technology
Roorkee, Uttarakhand, India

Sanjeev Kumar
Indian Institute of Technology
Roorkee, Uttarakhand, India

ISSN 1865-0929　　　　　　　ISSN 1865-0937 (electronic)
Communications in Computer and Information Science
ISBN 978-3-031-58180-9　　　　ISBN 978-3-031-58181-6 (eBook)
https://doi.org/10.1007/978-3-031-58181-6

Preface

The 8th International Conference on Computer Vision & Image Processing (CVIP 2023), a premier annual conference focused on Computer Vision and Image Processing, was held during November 3–5, 2023 at Indian Institute of Technology Jammu (IIT Jammu), India. CVIP provides a great platform for students, academics, researchers and industry persons. Previous editions of CVIP were held at VNIT Nagpur (CVIP 2022), IIT Ropar (CVIP 2021), IIIT Allahabad (CVIP 2020), MNIT Jaipur (CVIP 2019), IIIT Jabalpur (CVIP 2018), and IIT Roorkee (CVIP 2017 and CVIP 2016). All editions of CVIP have been endorsed by the International Association for Pattern Recognition (IAPR).

This year we had paper submissions in two rounds. We received a total of 467 submissions, out of which 140 were accepted. CVIP 2023 set a benchmark as receiving the highest number of submissions in CVIP history till now. Submissions were received from almost all premier Indian institutions including IIT Kharagpur, IIT Guwahati, IIT Roorkee, IIT Delhi, IIT Bombay, IIT Kanpur, IIT Patna, IIT Goa, IIT Tirupati, IIT Varanasi, IIT Ropar, IIT Pallakad, IISC, ISI, IIIT Allahabad, IIIT Delhi, IIIT Gwalior, IIIT Jabalpur, IIIT Kanchipuram, and various NITs (Calicut, Warangal, Silchar, Delhi, Agartala) and various internationally renowned institutes such as Norwegian University of Science and Technology, Trinity College Dublin, NTU Singapore, New York University, etc. spanning over 10 different countries. A single-blind review policy was used with a minimum of three reviews per manuscript to decide acceptance or rejection. The selected papers cover various important and emerging aspects of image processing, computer vision applications and advance deep learning and machine learning techniques in the domain. The selected publications also address various practical and life-touching scenarios in the domain.

The technical program committee was led by Puneet Goyal, Pritee Khanna, Aparajita Ojha, Santosh Kumar Vipparthi (IIT Guwahati), Deepak Mishra (IIST Trivandrum), Ananda S. Chowdhury (Jadavpur University), Gaurav Bhatanagar (IIT Jodhpur), Deep Gupta (VNIT Nagpur), Ranjeet Kumar Rout (NIT Srinagar), Nidhi Goel (IGDTUW, Delhi), Rama Krishna Sai Gorthi (IIT Tirupati), Shiv Ram Dubey (IIIT Allahabad), Arvind Selwal (Central University Jammu) and Jagadeesh Kakarla (IIIT Kanchipuram). Apart from their roles as TPC members, their significant contribution along with IIT Jammu faculty members Karan Nathwani, Badri S. Subudhi, Yamuna Prasad, Ambika Shah, Gaurav Varshney, Shaifu Gupta, Samaresh Bera, Quleen Bijral, and Subhasis Bhattacharjee under the mentorship of Manoj Singh Gaur (General Chair and Director IIT Jammu) led to successful completion of the event.

CVIP 2023 was an incredible concoction of Academia, Industry and Entrepreneurship. Keynotes talks were delivered by Santanu Chaudhury (IIT Jodhpur), D. Ram Rajak (ISRO), Amal Chaturvedi (Roche), Tsachy Weissman (Stanford University), and Isao Echizen (University of Tokyo). For the first time in CVIP history a special session on Women in Computer Vision with keynote talks was given by Sushmita Mitra (ISI

Kolkata), Devi Parikh (Georgia Tech) and Geetha Manjunath (Niramai Health analytics), who have distinguished themselves in top research and entrepreneurial positions. The practical and real-life aspects of computer vision were demonstrated in special stalls set up by UNITY AR/VR, Niramai Health Analytics (a breast cancer detection device using AI and image processing), Asterbyte (emotion detection) and a special stall by IHUB Drishti (IIT Jodhpur). A challenge was also organized, Automatic Detection and Classification of Bleeding and Non-Bleeding frames in Wireless Capsule Endoscopy, with over 150 participants who took this challenge. Several technical workshops were also organized by Mathworks and UNITY AR/VR and a special tutorial on Learned Image Compression was delivered by Pulkit Tandon (Grancia) and Animesh Chaturvedi (Amazon).

CVIP 2023 presented high-quality research works with innovative ideas. To acknowledge and promote the spirit of research and participation, five different awards were announced: IAPR Best Paper Award, IAPR Best Student Paper, CVIP 2023 Best Paper Award, CVIP 2023 Best Student Paper Award and CVIP 2023 Best Poster Award. Three prizes were awarded to the challenge winners who secured first, second and third positions. Moreover, to celebrate outstanding work the committee nominated Umapada Pal, ISI Kolkata, for the CVIP 2023 Lifetime Achievement Award for his remarkable research in the field of Image Processing and Computer Vision. Also 75 travel grants were offered to partially support the travel of various participants who travelled to Jammu from near and far places.

We wish the CVIP conference series a grand success as the baton is passed to IIIT Kanchipuram for CVIP 2024 in high spirits!

November 2023

Harkeerat Kaur
Vinit Jakhetiya
Puneet Goyal
Pritee Khanna
Balasubramanian Raman
Sanjeev Kumar

Organization

Patron

B. B. Chaudhuri   ISI Kolkata, India

General Chairs

Manoj Singh Gaur   IIT Jammu, India
Santanu Choudhary   IIT Jodhpur, India
Isao Echizen   National Institute of Informatics, Japan

General Co-chairs

R. Balasubramanian   IIT Roorkee, India
Pritee Khanna   IIITDM Jabalpur, India
Yudong Zhang   University of Leicester, UK

Conference Chairs

Harkeerat Kaur   IIT Jammu, India
Vinit Jakhetiya   IIT Jammu, India
Puneet Goyal   IIT Ropar, India
Deep Gupta   VNIT Nagpur, India
Aparajita Ojha   IIITDM Jabalpur, India

Conference Co-chairs

Sanjeev Malik   IIT Roorkee, India
Partha Pritam Roy   IIT Roorkee, India
Naoufel Werghi   Khalifa University, UAE

Conference Conveners

Gaurav Bhatnagar	IIT Jodhpur, India
Subrahmanyam Murala	IIT Ropar, India
Satish K. Singh	IIIT Allahabad, India
Shiv Ram Dubey	IIIT Allahabad, India
Santosh Vipparthi	IIT Guwahati, India

Publicity Chairs

Jagadeesh Kakarla	IIITDM Kancheepuram, India
Arvind Selwal	Central University Jammu, India
Gaurav Varshney	IIT Jammu, India

Local Organization Committee

Yamuna Prasad	IIT Jammu, India
Shaifu Gupta	IIT Jammu, India
Badri Subudhi	IIT Jammu, India
Karan Nathwani	IIT Jammu, India
Samaresh Bera	IIT Jammu, India
Ambika Prasad Shah	IIT Jammu, India
Subhasis Bhattacharjee	IIT Jammu, India

Technical Program Committee

M. K. Bajpai	IIITDM Jabalpur, India
Deepak Mishra	IIST Trivandrum, India
Ananda S. Chowdhury	Jadavpur University, India
Rama Krishna Sai Gorthi	IIT Tirupati, India
M. V. Joshi	DA-IICT, India
Priyanka Singh	DA-IICT India
Ayan Seal	IIITDM Jabalpur, India
Abhinav Dhall	IIT Ropar, India
Durgesh Singh	IIITDM Jabalpur, India
Shreelekha Pandey	Thapar University, India
Nidhi Gupta	NIT Kurukshetra, India
Amal Chaturvedi	Roche, USA
Pulkit Tandon	Grancia, USA

Debashis Sen	IIT Kharagpur, India
M. Tanveer	IIT Indore, India
Surya Prakash	IIT Indore, India
Deepak Mishra	IIT Jodhpur, India
Basant Kumar	MNNIT Allahabad, India
Shubham Chandak	Amazon, USA
Ajay Mittal	UIET, Panjab University, India
Sumam David S.	NITK Surathkal, India
Shitala Prasad	IIT Goa, India
Anuj Mahajan	SMVDU Jammu, India
Mahesh R. Panicker	IIT Palakkad, India
Indukala Naladala	Apple Inc., India
Pankaj Pratap Singh	CIT Kokrajhar, India
Vishwas Rathi	NIT Kurukshetra, India

International Advisory Committee

Iman Behesti	University of Manitoba, Canada
Anil K. Jain	Michigan State University, USA
Kiran Raja	Nanyang Technological University, Singapore
Raghavendra Ramachandra	NTNU, Norway
Ondrej Krejcar	University of Hradec Kralove, Czech Republic
Bharat Biswal	New Jersey Institute of Technology, USA
Fabio Dell'Acqua	University of Pavia, Italy
K. P. Subbalakshmi	Stevens Institute of Technology, USA
Waleed H. Abdulla	University of Auckland, New Zealand
Yasushi Yamaguchi	University of Tokyo, Japan
Petia Radeva	Universitat de Barcelona, Spain
R. Venkatesh Babu	IISC Bangalore, India
Sharath Chandra Guntuku	University of Pennsylvania, USA
Shou Li	Case Western Reserve, University, USA
Gaurav Sharma	University of Rochester, USA
Rangaraj M. Rangayyan	University of Calgary, Canada
Yongmin Li	Brunel University London, UK
Phalguni Gupta	IIT Kanpur, India

Reviewers

Aashish Kumar	IIT Jammu, India
Abhimanyu Sahu	Motilal Nehru National Institute of Technology, India
Abhishek Singh Sambyal	Indian Institute of Technology Ropar, India
Aditi Palit	Indian Institute of Technology Tirupati, India
Ajay Mittal	Panjab University, India
Ajeet Verma	IIT Jammu, India
Amardeep Gupta	Amity University, India
Ambreen Sabha	Central University of Jammu, India
Amit Bhati	Indian Institute of Information Technology, Design and Manufacturing, Jabalpur, India
Amit Kumar	Indian Institute of Information Technology Kota, India
Amit Vishwakarma	Indian Institute of Information Technology, Design and Manufacturing, Jabalpur, India
Amitesh Rajput	Birla Institute of Technology & Science, Pilani, India
Angshuman Paul	Indian Institute of Technology Jodhpur, India
Anjali Gautam	Indian Institute of Technology Jodhpur, India
Ankit Bhurane	Visvesvaraya National Institute of Technology, India
Ankit Jain	National Institute of Technology Kurukshetra, India
Anuj Mahajan	Shri Mata Vaishno Devi University, India
Anuj Rai	Indian Institute of Technology Indore, India
Aravinda P. N.	Indian Institute of Technology Kharagpur, India
Arif Ahmed Sekh	XIM University, India
Arijit De	Jadavpur University, India
Arindam Sikdar	Jadavpur University, India
Arnav Bhavsar	IIT Mandi, India
Aroof Aimen	Indian Institute Of Technology Ropar, India
Arun Kumar Sivapuram	Indian Institute of Technology Tirupati, India
Ashish Gupta	Thapar University, India
Ashish Mishra	Indian Institute of Technology Madras, India
Ashish Phophalia	Indian Institute of Information Technology Vadodara, India
Ashish Tripathi	Malaviya National Institute of Technology Jaipur, India
Ashutosh Kulkarni	Indian Institute of Technology Ropar, India
Bala Venkateswarlu Isunuri	IIITDM, India

Basant Kumar | Motilal Nehru National Institute of Technology, India

Bharat Singh | Indian Institute of Information Technology Ranchi, India

Bhaskar Mukhoty | Mohamed bin Zayed University of Artificial Intelligence, UAE

Bhavana Singh | Maulana Azad National Institute of Technology Bhopal, India

Bhukya Krishna Priya | IIITDM Kancheepuram, India

Bindu Avadhani | IIITDM Kancheepuram, India

Bindu Avadhani | Amrita Vishwa Vidyapeetham, India

Chandranath Adak | Indian Institute of Technology Patna, India

Chinmaya Panigrahy | Thapar University, India

Debasis Samanta | Indian Institute of Technology Kharagpur, India

Deebha Mumtaz | IIT Jammu, India

Deep Gupta | Visvesvaraya National Institute of Technology, India

Deepak Mishra | Indian Institute of Space Science and Technology, India

Deepak Ranjan Nayak | Malaviya National Institute of Technology Jaipur, India

Deval Verma | Bennett University, India

Jagadeesh Kakarla | IIITDM Kancheepuram, India

Krishan Kumar | National Institute of Technology Kurukshetra, India

Mukesh Kumar | Indian Institute of Technology Patna, India

Palak Mahajan | Central University of Jammu, India

Rahul Nijhawan | Thapar University, India

Shiwangi Mishra | Asterbyte Software Systems Ltd., India

Soubhagya Barpanda | Vellore Institute of Technology, India

Arvind Selwal | Central University of Jammu, India

B. Surendiran | National Institute of Technology Puducherry, India

Chandra Prakash | National Institute of Technology Delhi, India

Debanjan Sadhya | Atal Bihari Vajpayee - Indian Institute of Information Technology & Management, India

Irshad Ahmad Ansari | Atal Bihari Vajpayee - Indian Institute of Information Technology & Management, India

Kirti Raj Bhatele | Rustamji Institute of Technology, India

Mohammed Javed | Indian Institute of Information Technology Allahabad, India

Parveen Kumar | National Institute of Technology Kurukshetra, India

Soumendu Chakraborty	Indian Institute of Information Technology Lucknow, India
Tusar Kanti Mishra	Manipal Institute of Technology, Manipal Academy of Higher Education, India
Vikram Pudi	Indian Institute of Technology Tirupati, India
Vishwas Rathi	Thapar University, India
Ayan Seal	IIITDM Jabalpur, India
Durgesh Singh	IIITDM Jabalpur, India
Gaurav Bhatnagar	Indian Institute of Technology Jodhpur, India
Gian Luca Foresti	University of Udine, Italy
Gorthi Rama Krishna Sai Subrahmanyam	Indian Institute Of Technology Tirupati, India
Gourav Siddhad	IIT Roorkee, India
Gulshan Sharma	Indian Institute of Technology Ropar, India
Gurinder Singh	Cleveland State University, USA
Gyan Singh Yadav	IIIT Kota, India
Hadia Kawoosa	Indian Institute of Technology Ropar, India
Harkeerat Kaur	Indian Institute of Technology Jammu, India
Indukala Naladala	Apple Co., USA
Ishrat Nazeer	National Institute of Technology Srinagar, India
Jagannath Sethi	Jadavpur University, India
Jasdeep Singh	Indian Institute of Technology Ropar, India
Jayant Mahawar	Indian Institute of Technology Jodhpur, India
Joohi Chauhan	Indian Institute of Technology Ropar, India
Joy Dhar	Indian Institute of Technology Ropar, India
Kailash Kalare	Motilal Nehru National Institute of Technology Allahabad, India
Kanchan Kashyap	VIT Bhopal University, India
Kanishka Tyagi	UHV Technologies Inc., USA
Kapil Rana	Indian Institute of Technology Ropar, India
Karan Nathwani	Indian Institute of Technology Jammu, India
Katta Ranjith	Indian Institute of Technology Ropar, India
Komuravelli Prashanth	Indian Institute of Technology Tirupati, India
Krishan Sharma	Scaledge India Pvt. Ltd., India
Krishna Kumar Mohbey	Central University of Rajasthan, India
Krishna Sumanth Vengala	Indian Institute of Technology Tirupati, India
Kushall Singh	Malaviya National Institute of Technology Jaipur, India
K. V. Sridhar	National Institute of Technology Warangal, India
Lalit Kane	MIT World Peace University, India
Mahapara Khurshid	IIT Jodhpur, India
Mahendra Gurve	Indian Institute of Technology Jammu, India

Mahesh Raveendranatha Panicker	Indian Institute of Technology Palakkad, India
Manisha Sawant	Visvesvaraya National Institute of Technology Nagpur, India
Manjunath Joshi	Dhirubhai Ambani Institute of Information and Communication Technology, India
Manoj Kumar	GLA University, India
Massimo Tistarelli	University of Sassari, Italy
Mayank Sharma	IIT Jammu, India
Meghna Kapoor	Indian Institute of Technology Jammu, India
Mohit Dua	National Institute of Technology Kurukshetra, India
Monika Khandelwal	National Institute of Technology Srinagar, India
Monika Mathur	IGDTUW, India
Monu Verma	University of Miami, USA
Mrinal Kanti Bhowmik	Tripura University, India
Muhammad Kanroo	Indian Institute of Technology Ropar, India
Mukesh Mann	Indian Institute of Information Technology Sonepat, India
Muzammil Khan	Maulana Azad National Institute of Technology, India
Nand Yadav	Indian Institute of Information Technology Allahabad, India
Neeru Rathee	MSIT, India
Neha Gour	Indian Institute of Information Technology, Design and Manufacturing, Jabalpur, India
Nidhi Goel	IGDTUW, India
Nidhi Gupta	National Institute of Technology Kurukshetra, India
Nikita Yadav	Maulana Azad National Institute of Technology, India
Nirmala Murali	IIST, India
Nitigya Sambyal	Thapar University, India
Nitin Kumar	Punjab Engineering College Chandigarh, India
Nitin Kumar	National Institute of Technology Uttarakhand, India
Nitish Kumar Mahala	Maulana Azad National Institute of Technology, India
Palak H.	Delhi Technological University, India
Palak Verma	IIT Jammu, India
Pankaj Kumar Sa	National Institute of Technology Rourkela, India
Pankaj P. Singh	Central Institute of Technology Kokrajhar, India
Partha Pratim Das	Indian Institute of Technology Kharagpur, India

Pisharody Harikrishnan Gopalakrishnan	Indian Institute of Technology Palakkad, India
Poonam Kainthura	University of Petroleum and Energy Studies, India
Poornima Thakur	Indian Institute of Information Technology, Design and Manufacturing, Jabalpur, India
Pournami P. N.	National Institute of Technology Calicut, India
Prashant Patil	Deakin University, India
Prashant Patil	Indian Institute of Technology Ropar, India
Pritee Khanna	Indian Institute of Information Technology, Design and Manufacturing, Jabalpur, India
Priyanka Kokil	Indian Institute of Information Technology, Design and Manufacturing, Jabalpur, India
Priyanka Mishra	Indian Institute of Technology Ropar, India
Protyay Dey	Indian Institute of Technology Ropar, India
Puneet Goyal	Indian Institute of Technology Ropar, India
Pushpendra Kumar	Maulana Azad National Institute of Technology Bhopal, India
R. Malmathanraj	NIT Tiruchirappalli, India
Rahul Raman	IIITDM Kancheepuram, India
Rakesh Sanodiya	Indian Institute of Information Technology Sri City, India
Ram Padhy	IIITDM Kancheepuram, India
Ramesh Kumar Mohapatra	National Institute of Technology Rourkela, India
Rameswar Panda	MIT-IBM Watson AI Lab, USA
Randheer Bagi	Thapar University, India
Ranjeet Rout	National Institute of Technology Srinagar, India
Raqib Khan	Indian Institute of Technology, India
Ravi Shanker	Indian Institute of Information Technology Ranchi, India
Ridhi Arora	IIT Roorkee, India
Rishabh Shukla	Indian Institute of Technology Jammu, India
Rohit Kumar	The Captury, Germany
Rukhmini Bandyopadhyay	University of Texas MD Anderson Cancer Center, India
S. N. Tazi	RTU, India
S. H. Shabbeer Basha	Indian Institute of Information Technology Sri City, India
Sachin Kansal	Thapar Institute of Engineering Technology, India
Sadbhawna	Indian Institute of Technology Jammu, India
Sadbhawna Thakur	Indian Institute of Technology Jammu, India
Samir Jain	IIITDM Jabalpur, India
Samridhi Singh	NIT Hamirpur, India
Sandeep Kumar	National Institute of Technology Delhi, India

Sania Bano	Indian Institute of Technology Ropar, India
Sanjay Kuanar	GIET University, India
Sankar Behera	Indian Institute of Technology Jammu, India
Santosh Vipparthi	Indian Institute of Technology Ropar, India
Santosh Mishra	Indian Institute of Technology Patna, India
Saquib Mazhar	IIT Guwahati, India
Sevakram Kumbhare	Jadavpur University, India
Shanti Chandra	Indian Institute of Information Technology Allahabad, India
Shehla Rafiq	Islamic University of Science & Technology, India
Shitala Prasad	NTU, Singapore
Shiv Ram Dubey	Indian Institute of Information Technology Allahabad, India
Shounak Chakraborty	Indian Institute of Information Technology Design and Manufacturing Kurnool, India
Shree Prakash	IIITDM Kancheepuram, India
Shruti Phutke	Indian Institute of Technology Ropar, India
Shubham Chandak	Amazon, USA
Snehasis Mukherjee	Shiv Nadar University, India
Soumi Dhar	NIT Silchar, India
Sree Rama Vamsidhar S.	Indian Institute of Technology Tirupati, India
Subin Sahayam	Shiv Nadar University, India
Sukrit Gupta	Hasso Plattner Institute, Germany
Sumam David S.	National Institute of Technology Karnataka, India
Surabhi Narayan	PES University, India
Surbhi Madan	Indian Institute of Technology Ropar, India
Surinder Singh	Central University of Jammu, India
Sushanta Sahu	Jadavpur University
Swalpa Kumar Roy	Alipurduar Government Engineering and Management College, India
Tajamul Ashraf	Indian Institute of Technology Delhi, India
Tanisha Gupta	Central University of Jammu, India
Tasneem Ahmed	Integral University Lucknow, India
Usma Bhat	Indian Institute of Technology Ropar, India
Vaishnavi Ravi	Indian Institute of Technology Tirupati, India
Vinayak Nageli	DRDO, India
Vipin Kamble	Visvesvaraya National Institute of Technology Nagpur, India
Vishal Satpute	VNIT Nagpur, India
Vishnu Srinivasa Murthy Yarlagadda	Manipal Institute of Technology Bengaluru, India

Vivekraj K.   Indian Institute of Information Technology
                                   Dharwad, India
Watanabe Osamu   Takushoku University, Japan
Ximi Hoque   Indian Institute of Technology Ropar, India

Contents – Part I

Contents – Part II

Contents – Part III

WSD: Wild Selfie Dataset for Face Recognition in Selfie Images

Laxman Kumarapu[1], Shiv Ram Dubey[2], Snehasis Mukherjee[3(⊠)], Parkhi Mohan[4],
Sree Pragna Vinnakoti[5], and Subhash Karthikeya[6]

[1] New York University, New York, USA
[2] Computer Vision and Biometrics Lab, Indian Institute of Information Technology,
Allahabad, Jhalwa, UP, India
[3] Department of Computer Science and Engineering, School of Engineering,
Shiv Nadar Institute of Eminence, Delhi NCR, Greater Noida, India
snehasis.mukherjee@snu.edu.in
[4] Indian Institute of Management, Lucknow, Lucknow, India
[5] Arizona State University, Tempe, USA
[6] Indian Institute of Information Technology, Sri City, Chittoor, India

Abstract. With the rise of handy smart phones in the recent years, the trend of capturing selfie images is observed. Due to the different visual effects offered by the selfie apps, face recognition becomes more challenging with existing approaches. We develop a challenging Wild Selfie Dataset (WSD) where the images are captured from the selfie cameras of different smart phones. The WSD dataset contains 45,424 images from 42 individuals (i.e., 24 female and 18 male subjects), which are divided into 40,862 training and 4,562 test images. The average number of images per subject is 1,082 with minimum and maximum number of images for any subject are 518 and 2,634, respectively. The proposed dataset consists of several challenges, including but not limited to augmented reality filtering, mirrored images, occlusion, illumination, scale, expressions, view-point, aspect ratio, blur, partial faces, rotation, and alignment. We compare the proposed dataset with existing benchmark datasets in terms of different characteristics. The complexity of WSD dataset is also observed experimentally as compared to the existing face datasets. The dataset can be obtained from https://github.com/shivram1987/WildSelfieDataset.

Keywords: Wild Selfie Images · Face Detection · Face Recognition · Selfie Dataset · Deep Learning · MTCNN · Facenet

1 Introduction

Face recognition has been a challenging problem for computer vision researchers during the past few years. The recent advancements in face recognition research, with the help of deep learning methods, can be observed from the outstanding performance of deep learning models [20], such as VGGFace [3, 15] and FaceNet [17]. So far, several deep

---

All authors were affiliated to IIIT Sri City at the time of dataset creation.

H. Kaur et al. (Eds.): CVIP 2023, CCIS 2009, pp. 1–12, 2024.
https://doi.org/10.1007/978-3-031-58181-6_1

learning models have been developed by the researchers for face [21,23]. The recent progress in deep learning based face recognition technology is heavily governed by the large-scale face datasets. The popular face datasets include Labelled Faces in Wild [7], CASIA WebFace [30], VGGFace [15], VGGFace2 [3], UMDFace [1], Microsoft Celeb (MS-Celeb-1M) [4] and WebFace [33]. Some other face datasets include YouTube Face Dataset [27], CelebFaces Attributes Dataset (CelebA) [13], etc. These existing datasets were generally developed by mining the images of celebrities from the public domain. The major focus of these datasets is on more samples. Hence, some of these datasets are noisy and does not contain the scenarios where users take their selfies using mobiles.

Some researchers have tried to come across the datasets which include the selfie images, such as Selfie Dataset[1] by Kalayeh et al. [9], DocFace [18] & DocFace+ [19] by Shi and Jan, and SelfieCity[2]. The images in Selfie Dataset [9] is collected from Instagram and annotated with different attributes. Hence the Selfie Dataset [9] is used for analyzing "How to Take a Good Selfie" instead of face recognition. However, we aim to develop a wild selfie dataset, which poses a great challenge by avoiding any environmental constrains while taking the selfies. Further, the proposed dataset should be useful for face recognition in selfie images. The DocFace performs the matching of ID photos with live face photos/selfies [18]. The DocFace+ supports multiple ID/selfie per class for ID-Selfie matching [19]. The SelfieCity dataset is collected from Instagram and labelled based on the Cities. This dataset is also not available publicly for the research purposes. The effect of selfie beautification filters is analyzed in [6].

The existing selfie datasets are either not available publicly or not suitable for face recognition in selfie images. Thus, through this paper, we propose a selfie dataset for face recognition. Following are the contributions of this paper:

- A wild selfie dataset (WSD) containing more than 45K images from 42 individuals is collected for face recognition in selfie images captured using smartphones.
- The proposed dataset poses a great challenge in terms of severe variability in image characteristics, such as aspect ratio, partial faces, occlusion, illumination, scale, expression, viewpoint, blur, reflection and augmented reality.
- We test the performance of existing deep learning based face recognition models to show the complexity of the proposed WSD dataset.

2   Proposed Wild Selfie Dataset

This section describes the proposed Wild Selfie Dataset (WSD) including the selfie image collection process, dataset characteristics, different challenges and a comparison with the existing face datasets. The challenges in WSD include combinations of diverse and difficult real-world selfie image scenarios that humans click selfies in, like augmented reality (AR) filters, blurred and occluded images, mirrored reflections, etc. The sample images depicting different challenges in the dataset are shown in Fig. 1. The dataset comprises of a total of 45,424 selfie images from 42 participants including 24 females and 18 males of 18–31 years age group. The average number of samples

---

[1] https://www.crcv.ucf.edu/data/Selfie/.

[2] https://selfiecity.net/.

Fig. 1. Sample images depicting the challenges in WSD dataset. Rows from top to bottom: Images having effect of AR Filters, Mirrored Reflections, Blurred Images, Partial Faces, Occlusions, Illumination Changes, Scaling, Different Expressions and Emotions, Different Alignments, View Point Variation and Different Aspect Ratios.

in each category is 1,082 with minimum and maximum number of samples in a category as 518 and 2,634, respectively. The labelling is performed manually in terms of the bounding box annotations, subject class levels, and gender of subjects. The dataset is divided into training and test sets with 40,862 and 4,562 images, respectively. The category-wise number of training and test images is summarized in Fig. 2. It can be seen that the dataset is split in the training and test sets uniformly.

2.1 WSD Dataset Creation

The procedure of creation of the proposed WSD Dataset consists of the following steps: Raw data collection, Pre-processing raw data, Near duplicate elimination, Face detection and bounding box annotation, Manual Filtering and Human Annotation, and Labelling the faces. Next we describe each step in detail. *Raw Data Collection:* Participants were asked to contribute to the Wild Selfie Dataset by submitting selfie images and self-recorded videos. A selfie is a photograph that a person takes of himself/ herself, captured through the front or rear camera of the phone. The selfie videos were strictly restricted to be taken through the front camera of a smartphone to capture the face. *Pre-Processing Raw Data:* After collection of the raw data of selfie images and videos, the unsupported file formats and corrupted images are removed from the dataset. Then, the images are extracted from video frames using the multimedia framework FFmpeg[3] For each individual video, different number of images are extracted depending on expression, illumination, surrounding background, etc. *Near Duplicate Elimination:* After extracting images from video frames, all data are in the form of images. At this stage duplicate elimination is imperative to reduce the undue bias during training. A duplicate image in the Wild Selfie Dataset collection is defined as one which is an exact (duplicate) or almost exact (near duplicate) pixel-to-pixel match to an identical image or is obtained from another image through cropping or rescaling techniques. There exist image pairs in the final WSD dataset, that are similar, but not the exact same. A clear distinction is visible in variations that may be present in the face position, orientation, illumination or expression of the person. *Face Detection and Bounding Box Annotation:* Following near duplicate image removal, unique selfies of each participant are obtained. The annotation of the WSD Dataset is performed by generating the face bounding boxes. The Dlib [10] general-purpose cross-platform software library is used to detect the faces and to obtain the top-left and bottom-right facial bounding box coordinates. The coordinates are used to compute the width and height of the bounding box. Thus, the final bounding box annotations include the top-left coordinates (X, Y), the width (W), and the height (H). Upon human evaluation of the generated bounding boxes, we find the following issues: 1) not all bounding boxes contain faces, 2) some bounding boxes include the faces having severe occlusion with others, and 3) some faces remain undetected by Dlib. *Manual Filtering and Human Annotation:* As mentioned above, the manual checking and human annotation are performed to fix the discrepancies caused by Dlib face detection. For each image, the bounding boxes generated through Dlib are manually verified and corrected using the following three criteria: 1) if the image contains a bounding box having a face of the corresponding person then the same is retained, 2) if the image contains a bounding box having a face of a person other than the labeled person, then that bounding box is removed and the bounding box of the corresponding individual is then manually computed, and 3) if Dlib is unable to detect a face in the selfie then the bounding box is manually computed. *Labelling the Faces:* We also provide the face identities of the subjects, for use in face recognition task. We provide the face identities using the unique codes, such as WSDXX, where XX is from 01 to 42 for all 42 persons participated in data collection. The gender of all participants are also labelled.

2.2 Dataset Distribution

To analyse the camera movement, the distribution of the WSD dataset is calculated through head pose estimation. The head pose is determined by the position of the human

---

[3] FFmpeg Developers: http://ffmpeg.org/.

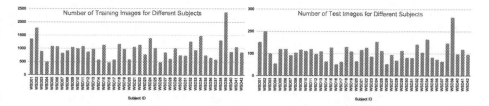

Fig. 2. Subject-wise number of samples in WSD dataset in training and test sets.

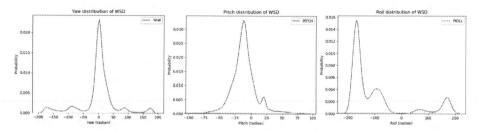

Fig. 3. Histogram of Yaw angles (left), Pitch angles (middle), and Roll angles (right) of faces in the WSD dataset.

face and it's alignment. A camera can be rotated in three ways: side-to-side, up-and-down, and around the optical axis with three corresponding angles, i.e., Yaw, Pitch, and Roll, respectively. OpenCV tool [2] and 6 key landmark points are used to estimate the 3D head pose of images. The six landmarks used are: Left-Eye-Left-Corner, Right-Eye-Right-Corner, Mouth-Left-Corner, Mouth-Right-Corner, Nose-Center-Tip, and Chin-Center-Tip. Yaw angles vary around the perpendicular axis. Yaw positive values depict the right side positions and negative values depict the left side positions. Pitch angles vary across the lateral axis. Pitch positive values depict the upward direction and negative values depict the downward direction. Roll angles vary around the longitudinal axis. Roll positive values depict clockwise rotation and negative values depict counter-clockwise rotation. The yaw, pitch and roll distributions of the proposed WSD dataset are illustrated in Fig. 3. The yaw distribution shows that more people are inclined towards a slight right profile, though variation is throughout visible. The pitch distribution shows that people tilt their head more towards the bottom in comparison to top while clicking the pictures. The roll distribution shows that the left head rotation is present heavily than the right counterpart. It is also interesting to note that no image head is exactly straight.

2.3   WSD Dataset Characteristics and Challenges

The proposed WSD dataset poses multiple not-available-before challenges in a single dataset that mimic real-world selfie data. The major challenges included in WSD dataset are augmented reality (AR) filters, mirrored reflections, blur, partial faces, occlusions, illumination changes, scaling variations, different expressions, variation in alignments, view Point variation, and different aspect ratios. *AR Filters:* Augmented Reality (AR)

Table 1. Comparison of challenges in the proposed WSD dataset vs the existing face datasets. Here, ✓: Present, ✗: Absent, and P: Partial.

A comparison of challenges among different face datasets										
Dataset Name	View-point Variation	Different Alignments	Different Expressions & Emotions	Scaling Changes	Illumination Changes	Occlusions	Partial Faces	Blur Images	Mirror Reflections	AR Filters
LFW [7]	✓	✗	P	✗	P	✗	✗	✗	✗	✗
CASIA Web-Face [30]	✓	✗	✗	✗	P	✗	✗	✗	✗	✗
VGG Face [15]	✓	✓	✓	✗	P	✗	P	✗	✗	✗
UMDFace [1]	✓	✓	✓	✓	✓	P	P	✗	✗	✗
WSD (Ours)	✓	✓	✓	✓	✓	✓	✓	✓	✓	✓

is the technology which superimposes a computer-generated image on the user's view of the real-world. There are many smartphone inbuilt applications that provide AR filters like Snapchat, Instagram, B612, etc. that are used by the contributors of the WSD dataset. The AR filters transform the user's image using a wide range of accessories and combinations of special effects, e.g., the Snapchat application transforms the human face into a dog or zombie using animated tricks. While people play with filters for entertainment, the human face still remains visible, and can be both detected and recognized. It makes the dataset more challenging and mimics the selfie clicking behaviour of young population. *Mirrored Reflections:* In the WSD dataset, there are two kinds of mirrored selfies. The first one is due to the pictures taken while standing in front of a mirror by the rear camera of smartphones. The second one is due to the capturing of images through the mobile camera with the reflected selfies. *Blurred Images:* There are two kinds of blurred images present in the WSD dataset. While some blurred pictures are clicked with the moving camera, others are captured with blur filters 'on' in the smartphone. The faces in the selfies are detectable and easily recognizable by the human beings. *Partial Faces:* Many selfies present in WSD contain only partial visible faces and do not include the complete face. Some selfies contain only the left/right half or only the top/bottom portion of the face. A human glance can be easily detected and recognised in these images. Some images are also tilted with multiple alignments in addition to partial faces, adding the diversity and severe challenges in the WSD dataset. *Occlusions:* The occlusions and obstructions are present in several images of the WSD dataset. Multiple variations of such obstructions such as a facial regions being covered by hand, pen covering the nose tip, AR filters hiding the mouth region, etc. have been included in WSD. *Illumination Changes:* The WSD dataset incorporates multiple natural and artificial lighting conditions in an unconstrained way. Selfies are clicked during dawn, noon, afternoon, dusk, late evening, and even at night. Some images contain lighting variation from natural light falling on faces from slits through vents or window panes, are present. *Scaling Variations:* Participators clicked selfies in different poses consisting of different sizes of their faces, by changing the camera positions and angles with respect to their faces. Some are full close-up shots covering the facial region from the eyebrows to the chin, while others are shots from far containing the full face along with

Table 2. A comparison of the proposed WSD dataset with existing face datasets.

Dataset Name	#Subjects	#Images	Availability	Annotation Properties
LFW [7]	5,749	13,233	Public	Several Annotation Attributes
CelebFaces [22]	10,177	202,599	Private	5 Landmarks and 40 Binary Attributes
CASIA WebFace [30]	10,575	494,414	Public	–
VGG Face [15]	2,622	2,600,000	Public	Face bounding boxes and Coarse pose
UMDFace [1]	8,501	367,920	Public	Face bounding boxes, 21 keypoints, Gender and 3D pose
Proposed WSD	42	45,426	Public	Selfie images, Class labels, Face bounding boxes, and Gender of subjects

high degree of background regions. ***Different Expressions and Emotions:*** The images in the WSD dataset contain different expressions and emotions of the subjects. Some facial sentiments present include sad, angry, happy, sleepy, excited, irritated, pouting, sulking, crying, smiling, fearful, laughing, yawning, winking, disgusting, and surprised. ***Different Poses and Alignments:*** The geometric alignment of selfies also differ greatly in the WSD dataset. As mentioned above, Roll angles in the dataset are diversely varied with no image being strictly vertically aligned leading to different poses and alignments in the WSD dataset. ***View Point Variation:*** Multiple profiles of candidates are included in the WSD dataset as analyzed above using Yaw characteristics which represent the variations in the view point. ***Different Aspect Ratios:*** Since all candidates used the front or back camera of their smartphones and/or mobile devices to click the selfies and videos, the aspect ratios obtained are diverse. While data collection, no restriction on aspect ratio is kept. Some common aspect ratios in the WSD dataset are 1:1, 5:4, 4:3, 3:2, and 16:9. We use the dataset after resizing the images to a fixed size.

2.4 Comparison with Existing Datasets

Table 1 compares the proposed WSD dataset with the existing face datasets, on the basis of the various challenges present in WSD. We can observe from the existing face datasets that though some challenges like profile variation are present in all the existing datasets, few challenges like scaling, occlusion and partial faces together are present only in a few datasets. The proposed WSD dataset is the only dataset to contain selfies with blurred images, mirrored reflections and AR filters. All the challenges present in the proposed dataset make it highly relevant depicting the real-world scenario. Table 2 presents a statistical comparison of the proposed WSD dataset with the existing face datasets. Though the number of subjects and samples are less in the proposed dataset, the images in WSD are collected by the subjects themselves in an unconstrained environment. Whereas the existing datasets are mostly crawled from internet. The existing face datasets do not contain the selfie images which pose its own challenges. More-over, the proposed dataset contains only the selfie images which have become popular among young population to capture the images. Further, as mentioned earlier, there is no publicly available selfie dataset for face detection and recognition in selfies.

3   Methodology and Experimental Setup

In this paper, we adopt the standard face detection (i.e., face region localization) and face recognition methodology for the experiments. Specifically, we consider the existing deep learning based face detection and face recognition approaches to judge their performance on the proposed WSD dataset. The results of two face detection models and three face recognition models are computed by training the models using the WSD training set and evaluating using the WSD test set. Networks are trained/fine-tuned for about 100 epochs on training set using Tesla T4 GPU and evaluated on test set.

Before using the WSD for face recognition task, we perform face detection using WSD dataset. The state-of-the-art You Only Look Once - v3 (YOLOv3) [16] and Multitask Cascade Convolutional Neural Network (MTCNN) [31] models are used to test the face detection performance on the proposed WSD dataset. The YOLOv3 model [16] is a real-time object detection CNN model by utilizing a fast Darknet module as compared to previous versions of YOLO. The MTCNN model [31] consists of three separate convolutional networks, including P-net, R-net and O-net. The MTCNN model first resizes the input to create the image pyramid followed by non-maximum suppression and bounding box regression for every scaled image to find the face regions in the image. In both cases of YOLOv3 and MTCNN, we use the pretrained models and fine-tune it using our WSD training set and evaluate the model performance on the WSD test set in terms of the mean average precision (mAP). For YOLOv3, we use batch size of 16, learning rate of 0.0001, and batch normalization after each convolution layer for regularization. In case of MTCNN model, we use batch size of 32, learning rate of 0.001, and batch normalization after each convolution layer for regularization.

Next we perform the experiments for face recognition on the proposed selfie dataset with three state-of-the-art face recognition models, namely VGGFace [15], VGGFace2 [3] and FaceNet [17]. The VGGFace model [15] uses CNN descriptors for face recognition. The CNN descriptors are obtained using the VGG-Very-Deep-16 CNN architecture. The VGGFace model is trained on VGGFace dataset consisting of 2,622 identities over 2.6 million images. We use the pretrained VGGFace model and fine-tune it using the WSD training set to evaluate the performance of VGGFace on the WSD test set. In case of VGGFace model, training/fine-tuning on the WSD dataset is done by stochastic gradient descent with 0.9 momentum coefficient using mini-batches of 64 samples and learning rate of 0.01. The VGGFace model is regularised using dropout and weight decay factor of 5×10^{-4}. The VGGFace2 model [3] also uses the CNN descriptors for face recognition similar to VGGFace, however, the CNN descriptors are computed using ResNet-50 model [5] rather than VGG CNN architecture. The VGGFace2 model is trained on VGGFace2 dataset that consists of 9,131 identities and 3.31 million images. We use the pretrained VGGFace2 model and fine-tune it using the WSD training set to evaluate its performance on the WSD test set. The training configuration of VGGFace2 model is similar to VGGFace, except the Adamax optimizer with learning rate of 0.001 is used for VGGFace2 model. FaceNet model [17] uses face embeddings generated using deep CNN like Inception network followed by Triplet loss layer for face recognition and verification. We evaluate the performance of the FaceNet model on the proposed WSD test set by fine tuning the face embeddings of FaceNet model using the

Table 3. Face detection results using YOLOv3 [16] and MTCNN [31] models on WSD dataset in terms of mean average precision (mAP) metric.

Dataset	YOLOv3	MTCNN
FDDB [8]	93.90 [12]	90.20 [12]
Wider Face (Easy) [29]	87.60 [24]	85.10 [31]
Wider Face (Medium) [29]	85.80 [24]	82.00 [31]
Wider Face (Hard) [29]	72.90 [24]	60.70 [31]
WSD (Ours)	96.92	95.77

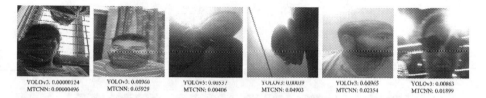

YOLOv3: 0.00000124   YOLOv3: 0.00968   YOLOv3: 0.00557   YOLOv3: 0.00039   YOLOv3: 0.60965   YOLOv3: 0.00863
MTCNN: 0.00000496   MTCNN: 0.05929   MTCNN: 0.00406   MTCNN: 0.04903   MTCNN: 0.02354   MTCNN: 0.01899

Fig. 4. The sample face images for which both the YOLOv3 and MTCNN fail to detect the faces along with the score to have a face.

WSD training set with triplet loss. In case of FaceNet model, a batch size of 16, learning rate of 0.001 and L2 Regularization are used while fine-tuning face embeddings.

4   Experimental Results

Face Detection Results: Table 3 shows the face detection results on WSD and other face datasets, in terms of mAP by using the YOLOv3 [16] and MTCNN [31] CNN models. The results on the WSD dataset are depicted in the first row. The publicaly available results on benchmark face detection datasets, such as ace Detection Data Set and Benchmark (FDDB) [8] and WIDER FACE [29] are also included in the table for a comparison. It can be noticed that the performance of both the models on the WSD dataset is higher as compared to FDDB and WIDER FACE dataset. This is due to the nature of images in the proposed and existing datasets. Specifically, the selfie images are generally captured from a camera placed within a limited distance from the subject. This leads to significantly higher facial regions in selfie images as compared to the non-selfie images. Moreover, the majority of the images in the proposed WSD dataset consist of images with single face. Hence, the face detection in the proposed dataset is easier as compared to large-scale non-selfie face datasets. However, the real challenges in the proposed dataset are observed for face recognition as described next. We report some failure cases where both the YOLOv3 and MTCNN models are not able to detect the face regions in Fig. 4 alongwith the score of having the face. It can be seen that the score to detect a face in the images is very low using both the models, which indicate the complexity of the images for face detection. Upon analysis with the failure cases, we notice that the selfies with severe background illumination changes

Table 4. Face recognition results (in % of accuracy) using VGGFace, VGGFace2 and FaceNet models on WSD dataset in terms of validation accuracy metric. The existing results on LFW [7], CASIA WebFace [30], VGGFace2 [3], YouTube Faces [27] and IJB-A [11], IJB-B [25], and IJB-C [14] face datasets are also included for a comparison.

Dataset	VGGFace	VGGFace2	FaceNet
LFW	98.95 [15]	–	99.63 [17]
CASIA WebFace	90.7 [32]	–	99.05 [26,28]
VGGFace2	89.4 [3]	96.1 [3]	99.65 [26,28]
YouTube Faces	97.3 [15]	–	95.12 [17]
IJB-A	95.4 [3]	98.0 [3]	–
IJB-B	85.0 [3]	93.8 [3]	–
IJB-C	–	95.0 [3]	–
WSD (Ours)	88.53	92.78	93.98

Fig. 5. Few sample of failed cases, where all the models misclassify the face to some other person. The correct class with score and incorrect class with score are mentioned in Green and Red color, respectively. (Color figure online)

are not being detected, irrespective of whether the face is clearly visible or challenging. In addition to this, people having occlusions near the eye are harder to detect. Partial images are another difficulty to detect and in many cases, images containing AR filters had incorrect detections. In such cases bounding box does not contain the face, but other regions. These are the challenges for the face detection task in selfie images.

Face Recognition Results: Table 4 shows the results of applying VGGFace [15], VGGFace2 [3] and FaceNet [17] face recognition techniques on different face reginition datasets including the WSD. The first row depicts the face recognition results on the proposed WSD dataset. In order to perform the results comparison, the existing results on the benchmark datasets, such as LFW [7], CASIA WebFace [30], VGGFace2 [3], YouTube Faces [27], Iarpa Janus Benchmark-A (IJB-A) [11], IJB-B [25] and IJB-C [14], are also reported. It is quite clear from the face recognition results that the performance of the face recognition models is significantly lower on the proposed WSD dataset as compared to the existing face datasets. The lower face recognition performance on the proposed WSD dataset is due to the inherent challenges present in the dataset, such as illumination changes, occlusion, scale changes, blur, pose variations, and many more. Sample images are shown in Fig. 5 where all the classification models fail to classify the faces into correct class. The correct class alongwith score for each model is shown in Green color. Whereas, the incorrectly recognized classes alongwith score for each model is shown in Red color. It can be seen that the class score for correct class is very low for all the models. On the other hand, the class score for incorrect class is very high. The complexity level of the images and the experimental results confirm that the proposed WSD dataset is challenging for face recognition in selfie images.

5   Conclusion

A wild selfie dataset (WSD) is proposed in this paper, for face recognition in selfie images. The WSD dataset is very challenging in terms of AR filters, mirrored reflections, blur, partial faces, occlusions, illumination changes, scaling, different expressions and emotions, different alignments, view point variation and different aspect ratios. The proposed WSD dataset is tested for face detection and face recognition tasks. The face detection results using YOLOv3 and MTCNN models are satisfactory on the WSD dataset as the images are captured from a limited distance. However, the presence of severe illumination changes and occlusions pose significant challenges to the face detection models. The face recognition results using VGGFace, VGGFace2 and FaceNet models are significantly lower as compared to the existing face datasets. The face recognition results confirm the complexity of the proposed WSD dataset.

References

1. Bansal, A., Nanduri, A., Castillo, C.D., Ranjan, R., Chellappa, R.: UMDFaces: an annotated face dataset for training deep networks. In: Proceedings of the IJCB, pp. 464–473 (2017)
2. Bradski, G.: The OpenCV library. Dr. Dobb's J. Softw. Tools (2000)
3. Cao, Q., Shen, L., Xie, W., Parkhi, O.M., Zisserman, A.: VGGFace2: a dataset for recognising faces across pose and age. In: Proceedings of the FG, pp. 67–74 (2018)
4. Guo, Y., Zhang, L., Hu, Y., He, X., Gao, J.: MS-Celeb-1M: a dataset and benchmark for large-scale face recognition. In: Leibe, B., Matas, J., Sebe, N., Welling, M. (eds.) ECCV 2016. LNCS, vol. 9907, pp. 87–102. Springer, Cham (2016). https://doi.org/10.1007/978-3-319-46487-9_6
5. He, K., Zhang, X., Ren, S., Sun, J.: Deep residual learning for image recognition. In: Proceedings of the CVPR, pp. 770–778 (2016)
6. Hedman, P., Skepetzis, V., Hernandez-Diaz, K., Bigun, J., Alonso-Fernandez, F.: On the effect of selfie beautification filters on face detection and recognition. Pattern Recogn. Lett. **163**, 104–111 (2022)
7. Huang, G.B., Mattar, M., Berg, T., Learned-Miller, E.: Labeled faces in the wild: a database for studying face recognition in unconstrained environments. In: Workshop on faces in 'Real-Life' Images: Detection, Alignment, and Recognition (2008)
8. Jain, V., Learned-Miller, E.: FDDB: a benchmark for face detection in unconstrained settings. Technical report, UMass Amherst Technical report (2010)
9. Kalayeh, M.M., Seifu, M., LaLanne, W., Shah, M.: How to take a good selfie? In: Proceedings of the ACMMM, pp. 923–926 (2015)

10. King, D.E.: Dlib-ml: a machine learning toolkit. J. Mach. Learn. Res. **10**, 1755–1758 (2009)
11. Klare, B.F., et al.: Pushing the frontiers of unconstrained face detection and recognition: IARPA Janus benchmark A. In: Proceedings of the CVPR, pp. 1931–1939 (2015)
12. Li, C., Wang, R., Li, J., Fei, L.: Face detection based on YOLOv3. In: Recent Trends in Intelligent Computing, Communication and Devices, pp. 277–284 (2020)
13. Liu, Z., Luo, P., Wang, X., Tang, X.: Deep learning face attributes in the wild. In: Proceedings of the ICCV (2015)
14. Maze, B., et al.: IARPA Janus benchmark-C: face dataset and protocol. In: Proceedings of the International Conference on Biometrics, pp. 158–165 (2018)
15. Parkhi, O.M., Vedaldi, A., Zisserman, A., et al.: Deep face recognition. In: Proceedings of the BMVC, vol. 1, p. 6 (2015)
16. Redmon, J., Farhadi, A.: YOLOv3: an incremental improvement. arXiv preprint arXiv:1804.02767 (2018)
17. Schroff, F., Kalenichenko, D., Philbin, J.: FaceNet: a unified embedding for face recognition and clustering. In: Proceedings of the CVPR, pp. 815–823 (2015)
18. Shi, Y., Jain, A.K.: DocFace: matching id document photos to selfies. In: Proceedings of the International Conference on Biometrics Theory, Applications and Systems, pp. 1–8 (2018)
19. Shi, Y., Jain, A.K.: DocFace+: ID document to selfie matching. IEEE Trans. Biometr. Behavior Identity Sci. **1**(1), 56–67 (2019)
20. Srivastava, Y., Murali, V., Dubey, S.R.: A performance evaluation of loss functions for deep face recognition. In: Proceedings of the NCVPRIPG, pp. 322–332 (2019)
21. Srivastava, Y., Murali, V., Dubey, S.R.: Hard-mining loss based convolutional neural network for face recognition. In: Proceedings of the CVIP, pp. 70–80 (2020)
22. Sun, Y., Wang, X., Tang, X.: Deep learning face representation from predicting 10,000 classes. In: Proceedings of the CVPR, pp. 1891–1898 (2014)
23. Taigman, Y., Yang, M., Ranzato, M., Wolf, L.: DeepFace: closing the gap to human-level performance in face verification. In: Proceedings of the CVPR, pp. 1701–1708 (2014)
24. Tuli, S.H., Mao, A., Liu, W.: A novel face detector based on YOLOv3. In: Australasian Joint Conference on AI, pp. 55–68 (2020)
25. Whitelam, C., et al.: IARPA Janus benchmark-b face dataset. In: Proceedings of the CVPR Workshops, pp. 90–98 (2017)
26. William, I., Rachmawanto, E.H., Santoso, H.A., Sari, C.A., et al.: Face recognition using FaceNet (survey, performance test, and comparison). In: International Conference on Informatics and Computing (ICIC), pp. 1–6 (2019)
27. Wolf, L., Hassner, T., Maoz, I.: Face recognition in unconstrained videos with matched background similarity. In: Proceedings of the CVPR, pp. 529–534 (2011)
28. Xu, X., Du, M., Guo, H., Chang, J., Zhao, X.: Lightweight FaceNet based on MobileNet. Int. J. Intell. Sci. **11**(1), 1–16 (2020)
29. Yang, S., Luo, P., Loy, C.C., Tang, X.: Wider face: a face detection benchmark. In: Proceedings of the CVPR, pp. 5525–5533 (2016)
30. Yi, D., Lei, Z., Liao, S., Li, S.Z.: Learning face representation from scratch. arXiv preprint arXiv:1411.7923 (2014)
31. Zhang, K., Zhang, Z., Li, Z., Qiao, Y.: Joint face detection and alignment using multitask cascaded convolutional networks. IEEE Signal Process. Lett. **23**(10), 1499–1503 (2016)
32. Zhang, L., Kakadiaris, I.A.: Local classifier chains for deep face recognition. In: Proceedings of the IJCB, pp. 158–167 (2017)
33. Zhu, Z., et al.: WebFace260M: a benchmark unveiling the power of million-scale deep face recognition. In: Proceedings of the CVPR, pp. 10492–10502 (2021)

PoseWatch: Advancing Real Time Human Pose Tracking and Juxtaposition with Deep Learning

Tajamul Ashraf[1]($\boxtimes$) iD, B. V. Balaji Prabu[2],
and Omkar Subbaram Jois Narasipura[3] iD

[1] Indian Institute of Technology Delhi, New Delhi, India
tajamul@sit.iitd.ac.in
[2] Malnad College of Enginnering, Hassan, India
[3] Indian Institute of Science, Bangalore 560012, India

Abstract. Human pose estimation is the process of continuously monitoring a person's action and movement to track and monitor the activity of a person or an object. Human pose estimation is usually done by capturing the key points which describe the pose of a person. A guiding practicing framework that enables people to learn and exercise activities like yoga, fitness, dancing, etc., might be built using human posture recognition remotely and accurately without the help of a personal trainer. This work has proposed a framework to detect and recognize various yoga and exercise poses to help the individual practice the same correctly. A popular Blaze-pose model extracts key points from the student end and compares the same with the instructor pose. The extracted key points are fed to the Human Pose Juxtaposition model (HPJT) to compare the student pose with the instructor. The model will assess the correctness of the pose by comparing the extracted key points and give feedback to students if any corrections need to be made. The proposed model is trained with 40+ yoga and exercise poses, and evaluated the model's performance with the mAP, and the model achieved an accuracy of 99.04%. The results proved that any person could use the proposed framework in real-time to practice exercise, yoga, dance, etc. At their respective location without the help of a physical instructor with precision and accuracy, leading to a healthy life.

Keywords: Human Pose Estimation · Deep learning · client server model

1 Introduction

A long-standing issue in computer vision, human posture estimate has presented several difficulties. Pose estimation anticipates and extracts the key-point position of a person or item to follow the activities taken by the individual while executing any activity to draw insights. Many industries, including video surveillance, biometrics, assisted living, at-home health monitoring, helping yoga and

H. Kaur et al. (Eds.): CVIP 2023, CCIS 2009, pp. 13–24, 2024.
https://doi.org/10.1007/978-3-031-58181-6_2

exercise, etc., can benefit from human activity analysis. In today's fast-paced society, people choose to exercise at home by copying the teacher through online video chats or YouTube videos. Humans are prone to making mistakes while mimicking the virtual world when there is no one to guide them. Therefore they feel the need for an instructor to grade their activities. A self-learning system can be created using human posture recognition [18].

Due to the complexity of the human body, pose estimation has been a challenging issue and a topic of current research [4]. Although not all motions between joints are visible, the human body contains 244 degrees of freedom and 230 joints.

20 degrees of freedom and 10 big components, according to [6]. Deep learning has tremendously aided human posture estimation recently, and enormous performance improvements have been made. [13]. This paper presents a novel and state-of-the-art Human Pose Tracking and Juxtaposition(HPTJ) Model to aid students in practicing the exercise properly in a remote place with proper guidance. It is the first of its kind where we propose an Instructor Based Model, which gives proper instructions to the user through feedback at each step of the exercise to practice it properly. The developed model lays the foundation for building a system that can recognize human poses on both pre-recorded videos and live to stream. The model can autonomously teach proper workout regimes, sports techniques, and dance activities. Also, it can be used to understand full-body sign language, motion Capture and augmented reality, and Training Robots. The present work considers Yoga postures for implementing the model, which could recognize and assist the users in practicing all yoga postures correctly by following a pre- recorded video or a live class.

The rest of the paper is organized as follows. Section 2 highlights the previous works done on pose estimation. Section 3 discusses the proposed model and implementation for the same. Section 4 discusses the results obtained and the evaluation of the proposed model. Future research directions are provided in Sect. 5 of the paper.

2   Related Work

Many research employs a variety of methods, including posture estimation using the thiazepine model and posture identification through machine learning and deep learning techniques. Human position detection plays a significant part in these investigations [9].

Prior until now, numerous people's poses were classified using machine learning for real-time posture recognition utilizing posture estimation using a 3D posture from the camera [17]. In those models, basically, we compared the poses of two people in general, it can be an instructor and a student, captured by a webcam camera. Several businesses have created a range of tech related goods for sports and fitness using this methodology. For instance, the Company offered the NADI X-Smart Yoga Pants as a wearable product (which could guide exercise form via a mobile application) [11], Smart Mat developed an intelligent yoga mat with a sophisticated sensor to detect the pressure node of stance on the mat and deliver real-time feedback on how the user has executed the yoga posture, i.e., properly or wrongly, via a mobile application [5]. Yoga Notch came up with a yoga wearable device guide, placed on the body, which provides audio feedback on alignments when the user imitates instruction at home [20]. We tend to observe that all the existing systems use a sensor-based system which is not only expensive but hard to realize in real-life scenarios with sensors all around our bodies [19]. Since the invention of the deep pose, approaches based on deep learning have replaced the classic skeletonization approach [2]. It directly applies deep neural network-based regressors on joint coordinates. It predicts a person's behavior and the location of concealed bodily components. Using OpenPose and long short-term memory networks, researchers have devised a way to detect human behaviors in real-time [14]. This method is based on screenshots that are timed and taken from real-time photographs that are obtained by attaching the camera. OpenPose is a real-time, open-source project that aims to jointly identify the human body with hands, faces, and legs on a single picture [12]. The output of body features is split into sub-sequence called windows using a sliding window approach. Whereas Long Short- term Memory is an RNN (Recurrent Neural Network) [10] different from feed-forward Neural Networks. It can handle both the sequence of data and a single data point thanks to its feedback links. Long Short Term Memory (LSTM) model is suitable for this scenario and provides good results [16]. It efficiently learns the key point features and returns an activity class. Although OpenPose, LTSM methodology became quite revolutionary, it was also filled with many flaws. A new topology employing 33 points on the human body was created by taking the superset of the points utilised by Blaze Face, Blaze Palm, and Coco in order to fix the flaw in the prior technique. We are able to maintain consistency with the relevant datasets and inference networks as a result. As opposed to OpenPose and Kinect [15] topologies, We estimate the rotation, size, and position of the region of interest for the subsequent model using just a few critical points on the hands, feet, and face. [8]. Blaze pose estimation is a real-time multi-person system presented to detect a human body, hand, facial, and foot key points on single images [1]. Convolutional neural networks (CNN)-based architecture is used to provide the positions of the human body's joints, which represents a significant advancement in the field of pose recognition. The goal of this project was to create a coaching system for human posture detection based on transfer learning. In this methodology, eight joint angles are calculated, and the students; joint angles are compared with the instructors. This method removed the deficiency of sensor-based pose identification as well as improved the time lag faced in open pose estimation methods as well as LTSM [3]. For comparison, an earlier segment was constructed across the two images, and through histogram, a comparison was done, which was prone to many errors as image normalization was very difficult to obtain in that case [7]. To improve these shortcomings, In this project, we used angle comparison techniques between different points and transferred calculated angles between two servers that easily detect errors with greater accuracy. We have also added commands which constantly tell users if they are making any mistakes. What lagged in the previous model was real-time comparison and giving feedback at the same time. Each segment will be extremely quick, taking only a few milliseconds per frame, thanks to the real-time speed of a comprehensive ML pipeline that integrates positioning and tracking models. The proposed system can recognize a complete human pose in real-time and from pre- recorded videos as well while performing real-time comparisons on poses concerning an instructors pose to enable an appropriate mimicking mechanism.

3   Methodology

This section discusses model development, validation, and implementation of the proposed model. The architecture of the proposed model is shown in Fig. 1 and is divided into three main stages namely 1) Pose Extraction 2) Real-time angle transfer and Comparison 3) Evaluation metrics and user feedback. In the pose estimation phase, input from both users and instructors is considered as frames and each frame is processed using the BlazePose model to extract the key-points. The extracted key points from both the user and instructor are used as input in phase 2 and the angles between them are computed to check the similarity between them. The final stage computes the error and accuracy of the user's pose and appropriate feedback is given to the user to correct the pose on par with the instructors.

3.1   Pose Extraction

The Blazepose model is used to extract the crucial details that aid in pose detection. A Blaze posture is a real-time pose recognition method that can identify human poses in an image or video by identifying various body components, including elbows, hips, wrists, knees, and ankles. By connecting these points, the method creates a pose's skeletal structure. The user's stream is recorded using a camera and fed into the BlazePose model in order to extract the critical points. As illustrated in Fig. 2, the BlazePose model estimates the person's posture using 33 important points, including the person's ears, eyes, nose, neck, shoulders, buttocks, knees, ankles, elbows, and wrists. To extract the human posture, BlazePose employs two machine learning models, a Detector and an Estimator. The Estimator calculates the important locations while the detector determines the human area from the supplied image. The detector runs on each frame when the frame is supplied to the Blazepose model, locating the region of interest (ROI) to detect a person. The tracker is used to monitor the individual in consecutive frames once they have been spotted, and it predicts all 33 posture key-points from this ROI. When it comes to movies, the detector is only performed on the first frame and the ROI is derived from the key-points of the preceding frame. The pipeline's pose estimation component forecasts the locations of each of the 33 essential points with three degrees of freedom (x, y location, and visibility). The detector may be used in either box mode or alignment mode. Box mode uses its location (x, y) and size to establish the bounding

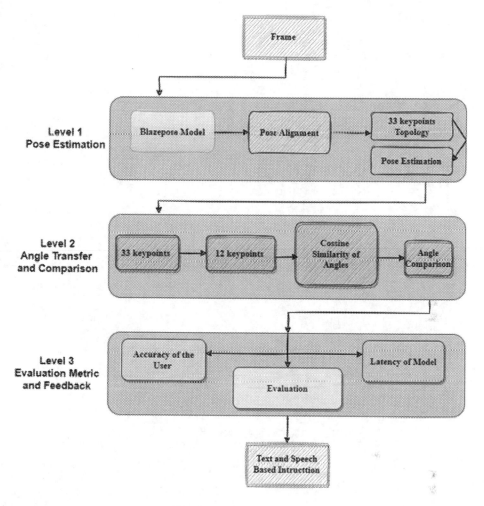

Fig. 1. Model Structure

box (w, h). While in alignment mode, the bounding box with rotation may be anticipated and the scale and angle are derived from (kp1x, kp1y) and (kp2x, kp2y). The suggested model detects the human area in box mode. The model's first output is a set of landmarks, which total 165 components and have (x, y, z, visibility, and presence) for every 33 key-points. A sigmoid function is used to transform the visibility and presence from key point values in the [min to max] range to probability. The visibility function returns the likelihood that any key points are present in the frame and unobstructed by other objects. The likelihood of important points existing in the frame is returned by presence. The attribute of visibility describes whether a key-point is visible, not visible, or not labelled.

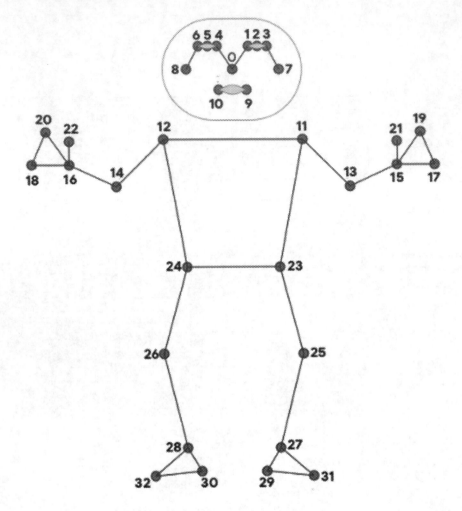

Fig. 2. BlazPose Keypoint Model

3.2 Real-Time Angle Transfer and Comparison

Once the key points are identified, the next step is to compute the angles between them. As mentioned earlier, BlazePose uses 33 key points for human pose estimation but all 33 key points are not necessary for identifying a human pose. Based on the type of posture interested to detect, selected key points could be used. The proposed model uses 12 key points namely: 16, 14, 12, 24, 26, 28, 15, 13, 11, 23, 25 and 27. The x and y coordinates from those points are used to calculate the angle using the 2-argument arc tangent function as shown in Eq. 1, which returns a value between $-180°$ and $180°$. After this step, the radian is calculated and finally, it is converted to an angle using NumPy's abs [27].

$$\theta = \tan^{-1}\left(\frac{Perpendicular}{Base}\right) \tag{1}$$

Here, θ is the angle between the hypotenuse and the base of a right-angled triangle.

If the measured angle was greater than 180, then the new angle was obtained by subtracting the obtained angle by 360 as the input to the function is defined from -180 to 180. Likewise using 12 points, 8 angles were determined. Once the angles for student and instructor frames are computed, they need to be transferred to the server for comparison. This work uses sockets for transferring the angles These angles are calculated simultaneously on the server and client side and then transmitted from the server to clients using socket links.

3.3 Evaluation Metrics and User Feedback

The error between the teachers' angles and students' angles can be stated as the performance of the student to the teacher. Per frame, accuracy was calculated for both real-time and recorded videos and the average mean of all the frames by total frames was taken as the overall accuracy of the student. To calculate the latency i.e. time taken by the algorithm to detect the key points on both teacher's and students' sides and transferring through sockets and doing the comparison and instructing the students about his/her pose. To efficiently take the latency, timeit.timeit() library was used and per instruction, latency was calculated. At the end of the session, the average mean latency of all the instructions, and the no of times the key points were compared were taken to get the overall latency of the algorithm. The pose and model evaluation metrics were calculated on the client side. The pose accuracy was calculated to angles from the server script and the overall performance of the user was determined using object key-point similarity (OKS) based mAP. It is defined as

$$\sum_i \frac{(-d_i^2/2\,s^2 k_i^2)\sigma(v_i > 0)}{\sum_i \sigma(v_i > 0)} \tag{2}$$

where,
The euclidean distance between the projected keypoint and the ground reality is di (Fig. 3).
S is the object segment area's square root.
The per-keypoint constant known as k regulates fall off.
Vi is regarded as a visibility flag that may be set to 0 for not labelled, 1 for labelled but not visible, or 2 for both labelled and visible.

OKS is used to calculate the distance (0–1), it shows how close a predicted keypoint is to the true keypoint. The pose error between the 8 corresponding calculated angles was determined and compared to certain predetermined threshold values which assisted in building an audio feedback mechanism for the user to correct their pose with respect to the instructors. The algorithm latency

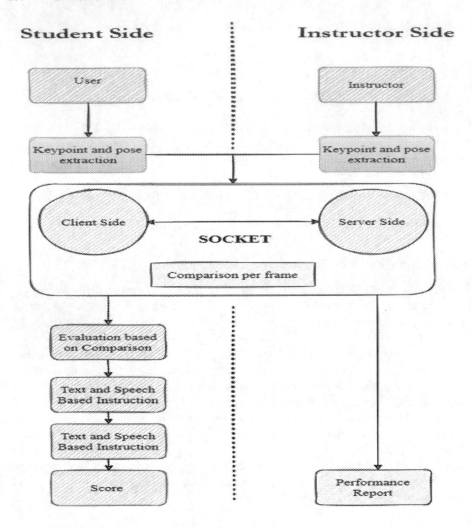

Fig. 3. Socket Architecture

was calculated between each error calculation which aided in finding the overall algorithm latency and efficiency.

4   Results

Input video is passed to the system as frames. First the frames are taken as input from student and teacher side. Detection model is performed on the teacher and student frames. From both these sides, the poses is extracted as shown in Fig. 4 the points are detected and send to the client side(teacher side).

It should be emphasised that our method may be used with input from a normal RGB camera, eliminating the requirement for Kinect or any other specialist

Teacher

Extracted Pose of Teacher

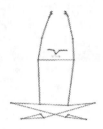

Student

Extracted Pose of Student

Fig. 4. Initial Input and output frame

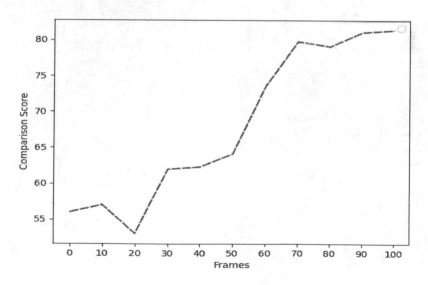

Fig. 5. Frame wise accuracy of the client side wrt to teacher side

Teacher Student

Instructions sent to student to correct the pose

Fig. 6. Client and server side keypoint comparison

gear for Yoga position detection. After the pose is detected, the comparison is calculated and the instrcutions are sent to the student using text and speech, so as to correct the pose. With each frame a comparison score is calculated, which is used to evaluate the student performance. Figure 5 shows the comparison accuracy for 100 frames.

The graph showing the per frame accuracy is shown in Fig. 5. The model was able to use the information gained from client and server side at each frame in order to compare the actions performed by two people. The results are shown in Fig. 6

Additionally, the system may be put into use on a portable device for self-training and real-time forecasts. For practical applications like yoga, this study serves as a demonstration of activity recognition systems. For posture recognition in a variety of applications, including surveillance, sports, healthcare, picture classification, etc., a similar method may be employed.

5   Conclusion

An integrated system for the localization of points and the recognition of human body positions, followed by a procedure for error identification, has been established in this study. With the use of this approach, people will be able to practice yoga correctly on their own and avoid injuries that could result from improper technique. The proposed model uses the student pose and compares the correctness with teachers through key point extraction. Appropriate feedback is given to students when the pose performing is not on par with the teacher. The proposed model helps people to practice yoga at their places without the help of a physical instructor with precision and accuracy, leading to a healthy life. A mobile application with voice feedback could be developed in the future to help people to access the system easily. Also, the system could be extended to practice any exercise any time.

Disclosure of Interests.. The authors have no competing interests to declare that are relevant to the content of this article.

References

1. Bazarevsky, V., Grishchenko, I., Raveendran, K., Zhu, T., Zhang, F., Grundmann, M.: BlazePose: on-device real-time body pose tracking. arXiv preprint arXiv:2006.10204 (2020)
2. Chen, Y., Tian, Y., He, M.: Monocular human pose estimation: a survey of deep learning-based methods. Comput. Vis. Image Underst. **192**, 102897 (2020)
3. Chong Loo, K.B.K., et al.: Detection of violent behavior in open environments using pose estimation and neural networks (2020)
4. Erol, A., Bebis, G., Nicolescu, M., Boyle, R.D., Twombly, X.: Vision-based hand pose estimation: a review. Comput. Vis. Image Underst. **108**(1–2), 52–73 (2007)
5. Kasman, K., Moshnyaga, V.G.: New technique for posture identification in smart prayer mat. Electronics **6**(3), 61 (2017)

6. Koolstra, J.H.: Dynamics of the human masticatory system. Crit. Rev. Oral Biol. Med. **13**(4), 366–376 (2002)
7. Koprinska, I., Carrato, S.: Temporal video segmentation: a survey. Signal Process.: Image Commun. **16**(5), 477–500 (2001)
8. LaViola Jr., J.J., Feliz, D.A., Keefe, D.F., Zeleznik, R.C.: Hands-free multi-scale navigation in virtual environments. In: Proceedings of the 2001 Symposium on Interactive 3D Graphics, pp. 9–15 (2001)
9. Liu, Z., Zhu, J., Bu, J., Chen, C.: A survey of human pose estimation: the body parts parsing based methods. J. Vis. Commun. Image Represent. **32**, 10–19 (2015)
10. Mikolov, T., Karafiát, M., Burget, L., Cernocký, J., Khudanpur, S.: Recurrent neural network based language model. In: Interspeech, vol. 2, pp. 1045–1048. Makuhari (2010)
11. Muhammad Sayem, A.S., Hon Teay, S., Shahariar, H., Luise Fink, P., Albarbar, A.: Review on smart electro-clothing systems (SeCSs). Sensors **20**(3), 587 (2020)
12. Osokin, D.: Real-time 2D multi-person pose estimation on CPU: lightweight openpose. arXiv preprint arXiv:1811.12004 (2018)
13. Rafi, U., Leibe, B., Gall, J., Kostrikov, I.: An efficient convolutional network for human pose estimation. In: BMVC, vol. 1, p. 2 (2016)
14. Sawant, C.: Human activity recognition with OpenPose and long short-term memory on real time images. EasyChair Preprint (2297) (2020)
15. Smisek, J., Jancosek, M., Pajdla, T.: 3D with kinect. In: Fossati, A., Gall, J., Grabner, H., Ren, X., Konolige, K. (eds.) Consumer Depth Cameras for Computer Vision. Advances in Computer Vision and Pattern Recognition, pp. 3–25. Springer, London (2013). https://doi.org/10.1007/978-1-4471-4640-7_1
16. Staudemeyer, R.C., Morris, E.R.: Understanding LSTM–a tutorial into long short-term memory recurrent neural networks. arXiv preprint arXiv:1909.09586 (2019)
17. Takahashi, K., Sakaguchi, T., Ohya, J.: Remarks on a real-time 3D human body posture estimation method using trinocular images. In: Proceedings 15th International Conference on Pattern Recognition. ICPR-2000, vol. 4, pp. 693–697. IEEE (2000)
18. Tawar, R., Jagtap, S., Hirve, D., Gundgal, T., Kale, N.: Real-time yoga pose detection
19. Xu, T., Zhou, Y., Zhu, J.: New advances and challenges of fall detection systems: a survey. Appl. Sci. **8**(3), 418 (2018)
20. Yoshida, K., Murao, K.: Load position estimation method for wearable devices based on difference in pulse wave arrival time. Sensors **22**(3), 1090 (2022)

Diabetic Retinopathy Detection Using Novel Loss Function in Deep Learning

Saurabh Singh[iD], B. Annappa[iD], and Shubham Dodia[✉][iD]

Department of Computer Science and Engineering, National Institute of Technology
Karnataka, Surathkal, Mangaluru, India
saurabhsingh.212is028@nitk.edu.in, annappa@ieee.org,
shubham.dodia8@gmail.com

Abstract. Globally, the number of diabetics has significantly increased
in recent years. Several age groups are affected. Diabetic Retinopathy
(DR) affects those with diabetes for a long time. DR is a side effect of
diabetes that affects the retina's blood vessels and is caused by high blood
sugar levels. Therefore, early detection and treatment are preferred. Manual recognition concerns and a lack of technology support for ophthalmologists are the most complex problems. Nowadays, Deep Learning (DL)
based approaches are used significantly for creating DR detection systems because of the ongoing development of Artificial Intelligence (AI)
techniques. This paper uses the APTOS dataset of retina images to train
four deep Convolution Neural Network (CNN) models using a novel loss
function. The four DL models used are VGG16, Resnet50, DenseNet121,
and DenseNet169 to explain their rich properties and improve the classification for different phases of DR. The experimental results of this
study demonstrate that VGG16 produced the lowest accuracy of 73.26%
on the APTOS dataset, while DenseNet169 based detection gives the
most significant result of 96.68% accuracy among the four approaches.

Keywords: Diabetic Retinopathy · Convolution Neural Network ·
VGG16 · DenseNet169 · Ophthalmologists

1 Introduction

The most severe form of diabetes, classified as Diabetic Retinopathy (DR), causes
substantial retinal damage and vision loss. It damages the veins in the retinal
tissue, leading to fluid leaks and vision loss. Along with vision-related disorders like glaucoma and waterfall, DR is among the most prevalent diseases. The
two primary kinds of DR are Proliferative Diabetic Retinopathy (PDR) and
Non-Proliferative Diabetic Retinopathy (NPDR) [1]. Early-stage DR is also categorized into Mild, Moderate, and Severe stages and is referred to as NPDR.
The mild stage includes a micro-aneurysm, which is a little red dot at the end
of a blood vessel. During the moderate phases, the micro-aneurysms rip into the
deeper layers of the retina, causing bleeding that resembles a flame. Neovascularization, or the expansion of functional microvascular networks on the retina's

© The Author(s), under exclusive license to Springer Nature Switzerland AG 2024
H. Kaur et al. (Eds.): CVIP 2023, CCIS 2009, pp. 25–37, 2024.
https://doi.org/10.1007/978-3-031-58181-6_3

inner surface, is a more severe form of DR called PDR. Neovascularization is a normal process that produces new blood vessels [2]. Figure 1 shows the various DR stages [26]. The provided figure shows that the Normal and Moderate levels match one another. As a result, it can be challenging to distinguish between the Mild stage.

Fig. 1. The different stages of Diabetic Retinopathy

Currently, 382 million individuals over the world are Diabetic patients. By 2025, there will probably be 592 million Diabetic patients globally [4]. About 77 million people in India currently have diabetes, and by 2045, that figure is expected to reach 125 million [5]. In India, it is estimated that one in five adults has diabetes. Type two diabetes is typically detected in people while they are still in their working years. Some, though, are not discovered until complications arise. If Diabetic Retinopathy screening and treatment options are not given crucial priority, it is anticipated that the risk of blindness due to DR will increase at the same time that the prevalence of diabetes in the nation is exponentially increasing [5,6].

Additionally, since current methods for diagnosing take a long time, the treatment may need to be more effective. Doctors use a fundus camera to diagnose retinopathy, which captures images of the veins and nerves behind the retina. It is challenging to diagnose this disease in its early stages because there are no symptoms of DR in the early stages. Multiple Convolutional Neural Network (CNN) algorithms have been used to make early diagnoses so medical professionals can start the right treatment. The "Aravind Eye Hospital" have provided the dataset that was used in this study, and it is publicly available for the research under the name "APTOS (Asia Pacific Tele-Ophthalmology Society)". The outcomes of four CNN architectures, namely ResNet50, DenseNet121, VGG16, and DenseNet169 are presented in this work.

The following sections comprise the remaining portions of the paper: The DR image classification is reviewed in Sect. 2. Section 3, in particular, discusses the dataset in detail. Section 4 contains information on the DL architecture methodology. In Sect. 5, the study's main finding is discussed. Finally, Sect. 6 illustrates the conclusion.

2   Literature Review

The work of Diabetic Retinopathy Detection has been reviewed in this section. Different studies try to address this problem with different levels of performance. To get a deep understanding of previous progress, several papers have been reviewed and summarized datasets, methods, and results obtained. J. R. Dinesh Kumar et al. [7] proposed CNN model-based classification of DR diagnosis. They employ the Dry-yard dataset, which includes 5500 images and three classifications: Normal Retina, Non-proliferative DR, and Proliferative DR (NR). YOLO (You Only Look Once) and ResNet152 architectures were used and this work yielded an accuracy of 93%. The system evaluates the three stages of DR and predicts outcomes based on picture categorization. P. N. Nasir et al. [8], created the IDRID dataset using actual clinical examinations from an eye clinic in Nanded, M.S. Focusing on the macula, retinal images of diabetes individuals were taken using the Kowa VX10 fundus camera. The final dataset's 516 subjects were divided up into five DR (0–4) groups. There were professional opinions on typical DR lesions and healthy retinal components. In this study, they achieved a test accuracy of 96.5% accuracy. S. Mishra et al. [9] used the APTOS dataset, which consists of an image of 224 * 224 pixels, three RGB channels, and five classes. The dataset consists of 1928 test images and 3662 train images. They compare two CNN models, VGG16 and DenseNet121, whose accuracy is 73.25% and 94.11%, respectively. Tymchenko et al. [10], used the image data in this study which was compiled from numerous sources. They used a readily available dataset from the 2015 Kaggle Diabetic Retinopathy Detection Challenge (EyePACs, 2015) to train the CNNs. This is the most significant freely available dataset. It contains 35126 images of the left and right fundus from Americans with diabetic retinopathy. Additionally, the APTOS 2019 and IDRid data sets from India were also used. Furthermore, they employed hybrid models, including Ensemble of 3 CNN architectures, EfficientNet-B4, EfficientNet-B5, and SE-ResNeXt50 (380 * 380 and 512 * 512), achieving an accuracy of 90.4%, 90.78%, and 92.40%, respectively.

BERBAR et al. [11] proposed two models that were trained and tested using standard datasets such as Messidor-1, Messidor-2, and Kaggle EyePACS. The training images gathered have been rendered in resolutions as low as 224 * 224 pixels and as high as 512 * 512 pixels. If a fund image falls into DR class 0, 1, 2, 3, or 4, its DR grade is positive; if not, it is considered negative. They tested several machine learning models developed with data-driven methods throughout the project. The Alex-Net, Google-Net, VG19-Net, and ResNet50 pre-trained CNN models have been utilized twice as direct classifiers and feature extraction methods. They then applied AlexNet and GoogleNet, and their results for the testing data were 74% and 68.8% accuracy, respectively. S. Taufiqurrahman et al. [17] proposed two models that were trained and tested using the APTOS dataset. The APTOS dataset contains 3662 images for training and 1928 images for testing purposes. Using bilinear interpolation, the color retinal images are resized to 224×224 pixels. They used MobileNetV2 and MobileNetV2-SVM for training purposes. They used quadratic weighted kappa (QWK) score to measure the performance. Using MobileNetV2, they got an average QWK of 0.903, an average accuracy of 78%, and an f1 score is 0.62, and using MobileNetV2-SVM, they got an average QWK of 0.905, an average accuracy of 82%, and an f1 score is 0.67.

Guanghui Yue et al. [13]. They made use of the Kaggle-available APTOS and EyePACS datasets. APTOS was made available for the 2019 Kaggle competition for blindness detection by the Asian Pacific Tele-Ophthalmology Society. It contains 3662 fundus images classified by severity level 0 to 4. There are 35,126 fundus images in the EyePACS dataset, also created for the DR detection competition on Kaggle (only available training sets are counted here). It has 25,810 photos and covers the first five DR phases. Furthermore, this study used ResNet50, DenseNet121, MobileNetV2, Res2Net, and ADCNET for both datasets to perform binary and multiclass classification. This study only employed the APTOS dataset for binary-class classification, with DensNet121 having the lowest accuracy (97.99%) and ADCNET having the greatest (99.18% accuracy). Both the APTOS and EyePACS datasets were used for multiclass categorization. ResNet50 yields the APTOS dataset's lowest accuracy and ADC-NET's highest accuracy, 83.40%. For EyePACS, MobileNetV2 provides the lowest accuracy (68.02%), whereas ADCNET provides the best (72.44%).

Md Robiul Islam, et al. [14]. APTOS 2019 and Messidor-2 are the two datasets that were used in this study. Contrast Limited Adaptive Histogram Equalization (CLAHE) was used to improve the image quality, and the pretrained Xception CNN model was used as the encoder using transfer learning. Cross-entropy loss is a popular loss function used for training in supervised learning for classification tasks. For multi-class classification using APTOS 2019, the overall performance evaluation of supervised contrastive learning (SCL) and end-to-end approaches is 84.36% and 82% accuracy, respectively. SCL and end-to-end techniques for binary class classification with APTOS2019 have overall performance evaluations of 98.90% and 98.10% accuracy, respectively. For multi-class classification with Messidor-2, the overall performance evaluation of supervised contrastive learning (SCL) and end-to-end approaches is 74.21% and 72.80% accuracy, respectively. For multi-class classification with Messidor-2, the overall performance evaluation of supervised contrastive learning (SCL) and end-to-end approaches is 80.52% and 79.90% accuracy, respectively.

3   Dataset

A dataset, an accessible resource that anybody may use, was used to collect the image data. The 2019 APTOS (Asia Pacific Tele-Ophthalmology Society) 4th Blindness Detection was open to the public. Figure 2 illustrates sample images from APTOS dataset. The most recent publicly available Kaggle dataset from the APTOS Blindness Detection competition on Kaggle for Diabetic Retinopathy Detection. This dataset contains many high-resolution retinal images collected under various imaging circumstances. Fundus images of the DR are produced by the fundus camera used to collect images. The DR status was recorded using a fundus camera, a magnifying lens with an integrated camera that can take pictures of the inside surface of the eye. The clinicians divided DR into five categories. This depicts the DR stages are classes. The composition of these 3562 images is listed in Table 1.

Table 1. Class-wise description of the APTOS dataset

Class	Name	No. of images
0	No DR	1805
1	Mild DR	370
2	Moderate DR	999
3	Severe DR	193
4	Proliferative DR	295

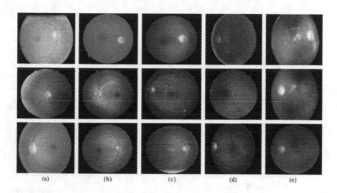

(a)   (b)   (c)   (d)   (e)

Fig. 2. Sample images from APTOS dataset; (a) no DR, (b) mild, (c) moderate, (d) severe, and (e) proliferative

4   Proposed Methodology

4.1   Preprocessing

Detecting diabetic retinopathy, a consequence of diabetes that can result in blindness if left untreated, involves examining retinal images for their characteristic indications. Pre-processing retinal images is a crucial step in this procedure which improves the quality of the images and this boosts the visibility of characteristics which in turn helps in detecting diabetic retinopathy.

The initial step is to crop the region of interest in the image to focus on the crucial region. As a result, noise is decreased, and feature detection is more accurate. The training images that could not be used instantly for training were then downsized due to the non-standard image resolutions. The images were scaled down to 224 * 224 pixels of constant resolution to give a consistent dataset. Further, contrast enhancement techniques were utilized to increase the visibility of minute indications that could indicate diabetic retinopathy. After that, image normalization was necessary for this study since these procedures can be used to fix disparities in image brightness and contrast brought on by changes in lighting and other circumstances. After normalization, it might be easier to identify features consistently across images because factors like camera noise or patient movement during image acquisition could cause retinal pictures to be noisy. The steps of data preprocessing are shown in Fig. 3.

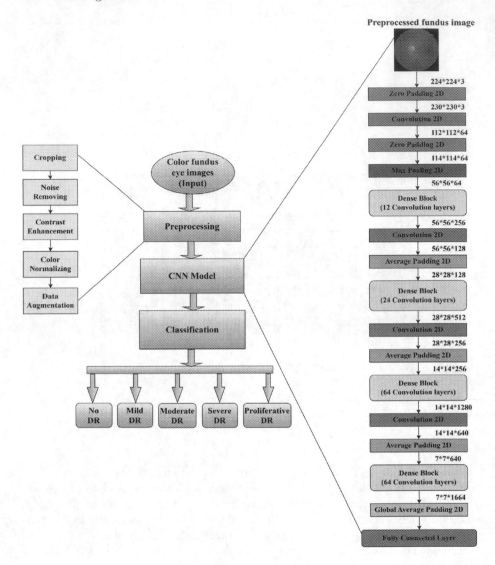

Fig. 3. Architecture of Proposed model

Data augmentation is a more advanced method of data variation that incorporates a variety of image alteration operations, including random shifts, flips, rotations, zooms, and more. Table 2 displays the data augmentation arguments along with their parameter values chosen.

Table 2. Data Augmentation used in proposed model

Argument	Parameter
Zoom Range	0.10
Width Shift Range	0.20
Rotation Range	30
Horizontal Flip	True
Vertical Flip	True
Fill Mode	Constant

4.2   Evaluation Matrix

In this study, our primary metric was the quadratic weighted Cohen's kappa score. The kappa value measures the agreement between the two ratings. Between the ratings provided by the human rating scale and the predicted ratings, the quadratic weighted kappa (QWK) is calculated. This metric's values range from -1 (complete rater disagreement) to 1. (complete agreement between raters). The definition of κ is given in Eq. 1.

$$\kappa = 1 - \frac{\sum_{i=1}^{k} \sum_{j=1}^{k} w_{ij} O_{ij}}{\sum_{i=1}^{k} \sum_{j=1}^{k} w_{ij} E_{ij}} \tag{1}$$

where O_{ij}, E_{ij}, κ and w_{ij} are the observed agreement between raters for category 'i' and 'j', expected agreement between raters for category 'i' and 'j', number of categories, and the weight assigned to each combination, respectively.

Equation 2 explains the calculation of w_{ij}

$$w_{ij} = \frac{(i-j)^2}{(N-1)^2} \tag{2}$$

where, N is the number of instances.

Researchers must evaluate this ratio cautiously because of Cohen's Kappa's characteristics. For instance, one should be aware that the Kappa ratio will be significantly impacted if we compare two pairs of raters with the same degree of agreement but different ratings proportions. To not have access to test dataset labels is the primary justification for using the Kappa ratio.

4.3   VGG16

In the VGG16 [15] architecture there are 16 layers. The input for the conv1 layer is an RGB image with the exact same dimensions of 224 * 224. The image is processed through one or more convolutional layers using filters. For 3 * 3 convolutional layers, the padding of the input is one pixel, preserving the spatial resolution after convolution. The five max-pooling layers that come after a few conv layers are responsible for spatial pooling. Stride two is used by max-pooling with only a window larger than 2 * 2 pixels. After some layer of convolutional layers, the final layer is a fully connected (FC) layer. Each of the completely connected levels has 4096 channels.

4.4　ResNet50 Model

The 50 layers of the commonly used ResNet50 [20] CNN design are grouped in what is known as residual blocks. It is well known for eventually solving the vanishing gradient problem using a skip connection method. ResNet50 consists of 48 convolutional layers, one MaxPool layer, and one AveragePool layer. Because it allows the subsequent layers to pick up on less important data recorded in the previous layers, this was wanted in our approach for diabetic retinopathy. A 3 * 3 filter was used to perform the spatial convolution, and the max-pooling method was used to reduce it.

4.5　DenseNet121 Model

DenseNet121 [16] is a 121-layer deep, densely connected convolutional network. The DenseNet121 architecture is found in the left portion of the DesneNet121, whereas the DenseBlock, convBlock, and transition layers are located in the right section. Three different types of blocks are utilized by DenseNet121. Here, the initial convolutional block is a simple block of dense blocks. Similar to this Convolution block, the identity block in the ResNet. The second dense block is created by convolving and densely coupling these convolution blocks. The majority of the DenseNet is formed of these dense pieces. The topmost layer is the transition layer, which links two nearby dense blocks. The transition layer reduces the feature map's dimensions as the convolutional feature sizes remain constant throughout the dense block. All of the blocks use the bottleneck method.

4.6　DenseNet169 Model

DenseNet169 [21] model was an important model that was taken into consideration. It has more layers than the ResNet50 model. The dense block, similar to skip connections, is included throughout. The model can learn more distinctive traits as the number of layers increases. As seen in Fig. 3, the architecture comprises four dense blocks with various amounts of levels. With no top or bottom layer and direct weight loading into the network, we employed a DenseNet-169. The final layer does not exist at first while modelling the network. A Dropout layer with a value of 0.2 and Global Average Pooling 2D are used to build this layer with five nodes for each class. Global Average Pooling 2D counts the total size of the input blocks as the pool size, in contrast to 2D average pooling. A dropout layer is used to deal with overfitting. The weights that were utilised to train this model are optimized using the Adam algorithm. In this paper, we propose a modified Categorical cross-entropy loss function and use it in the final architecture.

4.7 Loss Function

The result ranges have lower load levels when DL models are confident in their predictions. The models may, however, become overconfident in the dominant class under class-imbalanced training settings and incorrectly classify the majority of the samples as belonging to that class. This could result in model overfitting and have a negative effect on generalization effectiveness. In these conditions, a penalty that penalises peaked distributions could be added in the form of a regularisation term, lowering overfitting and enhancing generalisation. A model creates a conditional distribution p(y|x) across a set of classes y given an input x through using the Softmax function. This conditional distribution's entropy is given in Eq. 3.

$$E(p_\Omega(y|x)) = -\sum_m p_\Omega(y_m|x) log\,(p_\Omega(y_m|x)) \tag{3}$$

Here, E is the Entropy. An addition of the negative entropy to the continuous random variable is proposed as a regularisation factor to prevent overconfident output distributions. This can be observed in Eq. 4.

$$Entropy - Reg(\Omega) = -\sum log\,p_\Omega(y|x) - \beta E(p_\Omega(y|x)) \tag{4}$$

In this case, β regulates the severity of the punishment. Using observational analyses, the value of $\beta = 3$ was determined. Model was trained to reduce the categorical cross-entropy loss. In the final dense layer, this regularisation term was used as an activity regularizer. In this study, β is not set to 3 at random; instead, apply the brute-force method, checking β values from 1 to 9; and find that $\beta = 3$ gives the highest accuracy.

5 Result and Discussion

This section discusses the experiments carried out and the results obtained, demonstrating the project's accuracy. For the APTOS dataset, four different architectures were tested and compared in terms of their accuracies. As is shown in the Table 3 below, ResNet50, ResNet121, and DenseNet169 are used ImageNet and quadratic weighted kappa (QWK), while VGG16 is used alone. As a result, DenseNet169 performed better than others and VGG16 displayed least accuracy.

Table 3. Comparision of the proposed model with existing deep learning models

Architecture	QWK	Loss	ACC (in %)
VGG16	Not Used	0.7874	73.26
ResNet50	0.8219	0.4375	84.72
DenseNet121	0.8725	0.1840	87.58
DenseNet169 + novel loss fn	**0.9421**	**0.1040**	**96.68**

Our proposed model has a training accuracy of 99.06%, a validation accuracy of 96.68%, and a QWK of 94.21 after being trained for 25 epochs. Every epoch of the model's training took an average of 45 s on Google Colab. The model training process lasted about 19 min. Figure 4 represent the confusion matrix of our proposed model. The model was able to predict 97.0%, 97.5%, 96.6%, 96.4%, and 95.9% class-wise accuracies. The overall accuracy is 96.68%.

Figures 5 and 6 show the validation and training accuracy as well as the validation and training loss respectively for the proposed model. An observation can be drawn from both graphs that the proposed model does not have either overfitting or underfitting.

Table 4. Class wise performance evaluation for proposed model

Class	Precision	Recall	f1-score
0	0.9870	0.9660	0.9880
1	0.9690	0.8759	0.9179
2	0.9830	0.9659	0.9339
3	0.9924	0.9767	0.9338
4	0.9443	0.9577	0.8979

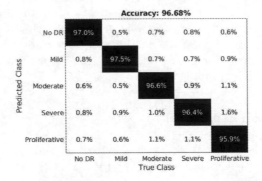

Fig. 4. Confusion matrix of our proposed model

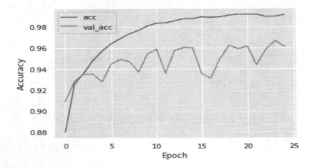

Fig. 5. Accuracy curve of our proposed model

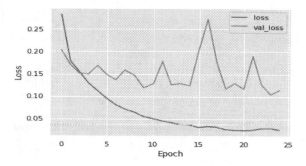

Fig. 6. Loss curve of our proposed model

Table 4 illustrates the comparison of the proposed model with state-of-the-art approaches. In 2019, Niloy Sikder et al. [23] used the Ensemble ML algorithm technique and obtained 90% accuracy. In 2020, S. Mishra et al. [9] used a transfer learning technique with the DenseNet121 model and obtained 96.11% accuracy. In 2020, Shidqie Taufiqurrahman et al. [24] used the Hybrid and Efficient MobileNetV2-SVM Model and got 85% accuracy. In 2021, Gazala Mushtaq et al. [22] used DenseNet169 and got 91% accuracy. In 2021, Chaymaa Lahmar et al. [25] used MobileNet-V2 architecture and obtained 93.09% accuracy. The current study used DenseNet169 and a novel loss function, which outperformed existing works with an accuracy of 96.68% using just 1.2 million parameters (Table 5).

Table 5. Comparison of the proposed model with state-of-the-art approaches on APTOS dataset

Ref.	Year	Methods	ACC (in %)
[23]	2019	Ensemble ML Algorithm	91
[9]	2020	DenseNet121	96.11
[24]	2020	MobileNetV2-SVM	85
[22]	2021	DenseNet169	91
[25]	2021	MobileNetV2	93.09
Current study	**2023**	**DenseNet169 + novel loss function**	**96.68**

6   Conclusion

A patient with diabetes has about 30% risk of getting diabetic retinopathy, according to several surveys. There are many stages of DR, from mild to severe, and Proliferative Diabetic Retinopathy. Since diabetic retinopathy (DR) is a significant concern for those with the disease, manually detecting DR takes a lot of time. To detect DR automatically, this work aimed to develop an architecture using a novel loss function. The experiments were also carried out on four different architectures to determine which architecture performed better in each case. The four architectures accuracy rates are 73.26%, 84.72%, 87.58%, and 96.68% for VGG16, ResNet50, DenseNet121, and the proposed model. This research is pertinent to fundus images; in future research, we aim to develop a model that can be used to evaluate images taken with a regular camera.

References

1. Memon, W.R., Lal, B., Sahto, A.A.: Diabetic retinopathy frequency at level of hba1c greater than 6.5 (2017)
2. Ophthalmoscopy, Dilated, and E. T. D. R. S. Levels: International clinical diabetic retinopathy disease severity scale detailed table (2002)
3. Vora, P., Shrestha, S.: Detecting diabetic retinopathy using embedded computer vision. Appl. Sci. **10**(20), 7274 (2020)
4. Jan, S., Ahmad, I., Karim, S., Shah, M.A.: Status of diabetic retinopathy and its presentation patterns in diabetics at ophthalomogy clinics. J. Postgraduate Med. Inst. **32**(1) (2018)
5. Federation, I.D.: IDF Diabetes Atlas tenth. International Diabetes (2021)
6. Teo, Z.L., Tham, Y.-C., Yu, M., Lu, Y.: Global prevalence of diabetic retinopathy and projection of burden through 2045 systematic review and meta-analysis. Ophthalmology **128**(11), 1580–1591 (2021)
7. Kumar, J.R.D., Priyadharsini, K.: Analysis of CNN model based classification of diabetic retinopathy diagnosis. In: 2nd ICSCCC. IEEE (2021)
8. Nasir, N., Oswald, P., Al-Shammaa, A.: Deep DR: detection of diabetic retinopathy using a convolutional neural network. In 2022 ASET (2022)
9. Mishra, S., Seema, H., Zia, S.: Diabetic retinopathy detection using deep learning. In: 2020 ICSTCEE. IEEE (2020)
10. Tymchenko, B., Marchenko, P., Spodarets, D.: Deep learning approach to diabetic retinopathy detection. arXiv preprint arXiv:2003.02261 (2020)
11. Berbar, M.A.: Diabetic retinopathy detection and grading using deep learning. Menoufia J. Electron. Eng. Res. (2022)
12. Wang, X., Lu, Y., Wang, Y., Chen, W.-B.: Diabetic retinopathy stage classification using convolutional neural networks. In: 2018 IEEE International Conference on IRI, pp. 465–471. IEEE (2018)
13. Yue, G., Li, Y., Zhou, T., Wang, T.: Attention-driven cascaded network for diabetic retinopathy grading from fundus images. J. Biomed. Signal Process. Control 1746–8094 (2023)
14. Islam, M.R., et al.: Applying supervised contrastive learning for the detection of diabetic retinopathy and its severity levels from fundus images. J. Comput. Biol. Med. 0010–4825 (2022)
15. Rezende, E., Ruppert, G., Carvalho, T., Theophilo, A., Ramos, F., Geus, P.: Malicious software classification using VGG16 deep neural network's bottleneck features. In: Latifi, S. (ed.) Information Technology - New Generations. AISC, vol. 738, pp. 51–59. Springer, Cham (2018). https://doi.org/10.1007/978-3-319-77028-4_9

16. Odusami, M., Maskeliūnas, R., Damaševičius, R., Misra, S.: ResD hybrid model based on resnet18 and densenet121 for early Alzheimer disease classification. In: Abraham, A., Gandhi, N., Hanne, T., Hong, T.-P., Nogueira Rios, T., Ding, W. (eds.) ISDA 2021. LNNS, vol. 418, pp. 296–305. Springer, Cham (2022). https://doi.org/10.1007/978-3-030-96308-8_27

17. Taufiqurrahman, S., Handayani, A., Hermanto, B.R.: Diabetic retinopathy classification using a hybrid and efficient MobileNetV2-SVM model. In: 2020 TENCON, pp. 235–240. IEEE (2020)

18. APTOS 2019 diabetic retinopathy dataset. https://www.kaggle.com/c/aptos2019-blindness-detection/data

19. He, K., Zhang, X., Ren, S., Sun, J.: Deep residual learning for image recognition. arXiv preprint arxiv:1512.03385 (2015)

20. He, K., Zhang, X., Ren, S., Sun, J.: Deep residual learning for image recognition. In: CVPR, pp. 770–778 (2016)

21. Huang, G., Liu, Z., Van Der Maaten, L., Weinberger, K.Q.: Densely connected convolutional networks. In: CVPR, pp. 4700–4708 (2017)

22. Mushtaq, G., Farheen, S.: Detection of diabetic retinopathy using deep learning methodology. In: IOP Conference Series: Materials Science and Engineering, vol. 1070, no. 1, p. 012049. IOP Publishing (2021)

23. Sikder, N., Sanaullah, M., Nahid, A.-A.: Early blindness detection based on retinal images using ensemble learning. In: 22nd ICCIT, pp. 1–6. IEEE (2019)

24. Taufiqurrahman, S., Handayani, A., Hermanto, B.R., Mengko, T.L.E.R.: Diabetic retinopathy classification using a hybrid and efficient MobileNetV2-SVM model. In: IEEE TENCON, pp. 235–240. IEEE (2020)

25. Lahmar, C., Idri, A.: On the value of deep learning for diagnosing diabetic retinopathy. Health Technol. 1–17 (2021)

26. Hossain, I., Puppala, S., Talukder, S.: Collaborative differentially private federated learning framework for the prediction of diabetic retinopathy. In: 2nd ICAIC. IEEE (2023)

A Novel Dual Watermarking for ECG Signals with Improved Payload

Jyoti Rani[✉], Ashima Anand, and Shivendra Shivani

CSED, Thapar Institute of Engineering and Technology, Patiala, Punjab, India
{jrani60_phd20,ashima.anand,shivendra.shivani}@thapar.edu

Abstract. The requirement to safeguard the integrity and validity of ECG signals drives the adoption of watermarking in these signals. Any tampering with or manipulation of ECG signals can result in inaccurate diagnosis or treatment because these signals are crucial for identifying and monitoring cardiovascular illnesses. Also, these signals are frequently sent via the internet, raising the possibility of unwanted access and manipulation. Hence, ECG signal watermarking is crucial for maintaining the reliability and accuracy of these signals in both clinical and research environments. This paper presents a novel ECG signal-based dual watermarking framework using a combination of two medical images: chest X-ray and PET image. A hybrid of DTCWT (Dual-Tree Complex Wavelet Transforms), HD (Hessenberg Decomposition), and MSVD (Multi-resolution singular valued decomposition) is used to embed the dual watermark. This hybrid method represented a significant enhancement not just in aspects of retrieving hidden data from the watermarked ECG signals but also in terms of its resistance to several attacks. To demonstrate the effectiveness of the watermarked ECG signal, we have evaluated the efficacy of the suggested technique using the PSNR, NC, KL, PRD and SSIM parameters. The recovered dual watermark is tested and found to be resistant to various attacks. The simulation results also show that the proposed methodology provided the best results of performance parameters, even when the size of the payload is large.

Keywords: ECG Signal · Dual Watermarking · MVMD · Pan Tompkins · DTCWT · MSVD · NSCT · Hessenberg Decomposition

1 Introduction

In the recent years, the transmission and distribution of multimedia information including speech, images, audio, and signals has been transformed by the development of information technology [1,13]. Evidently, this advancement broadens the scope for illegally copying, modifying, and spreading of multimedia content [13,15]. In consideration of these risks, watermarking has become a popular method for ensuring the originality, stability, and intellectual property rights of multimedia data. ECG signal watermarking is utilized in telemedicine, where

H. Kaur et al. (Eds.): CVIP 2023, CCIS 2009, pp. 38–49, 2024.
https://doi.org/10.1007/978-3-031-58181-6_4

patients can send their ECG signals to healthcare providers for remote diagnosis and monitoring. This maintains the validity and integrity of the ECG signals delivered, preventing unwanted alterations or manipulation. Large ECG databases are also frequently utilized in biomedical research for developing and testing novel algorithms and models. Watermarking can be used to protect these ECG datasets from unlawful copying and distribution, as well as to track their usage and ownership. This paper investigates the efficacy of ECG-based Dual watermarking as a technique for preserving multimedia data and discusses its potential applications in a wide range of fields.

In recent years, many experts have sought to build strong watermarking to authenticate the integrity and authenticity of ECG signals. Sharma et al. presented an ECG signal-based watermarking using RDWT and SVD technique which is employed to suppress patient information and logo inside the original signal [11]. Using an RDWT and GSVD, a robust watermarking system that efficiently combines multiple markings into ECG signals is developed the authors of Ref. [12]. This technique incorporates multiple marks into the signal to enable copyright protection and avoid ownership issues.

Table 1. List of abbreviations

Symbol	Description
MVMD	Multivariate Variational Mode Decomposition
DTCWT	Dual-Tree Complex Wavelet Transforms
NSCT	Non-subsampled contourlet transform
MSVD	Multi-resolution singular valued decomposition
W1, W2	ChestX-Ray Image, PET Image
$\alpha 2$	Scaling factor for ECG Signal
$\alpha 1$	Scaling factor for Dual watermark
[Yl, Yh]	Low pass and high pass filter of DTCWT
[P, H]	Hessenberg and Unitary Matrix
[cY, cU]	Components of ECG signal
[wY, wU]	Components of Dual watermark image
[CY, CU]	Components of ChestXray image
[WY, WU]	Components of PET image
Ecg_psnr	Peak Signal to Noise ratio of Ecg Signal
Img_psnr	Peak Signal to Noise ratio of Dual watermark
NC1	Normalized co-relation of Dual Watermark
NC2	Normalized co-relation of PET Image
PRD	Percentage Residual difference
Img_ssim	Structural Similarity Index Measure of Dual Watermark
Ecg_ssim	Structural Similarity Index Measure of Dual Watermark
KL divergence	Kullback leibler

Further, Ref. [13] introduced a FDCT and SVD for extracting the dominant coefficients of an ECG signal, which is used for watermarking to avoid false positives. The logistic chaotic map was also used to embed the watermark for enhancing security. An imperceptible and robust watermarking technique is presented by the author, which is used a combination of RDWT-DCT-SVD and HD in the YCbCr color space [4]. The suggested method uses two distinct sub-bands to represent two additional color areas. To further strengthen the safety of the proposed method, the author employs two watermark logos. The YCbCr model is preferred for watermarking. A. Anand et al. proposed a hybrid approach that uses the RDWT-HD-MSVD technique to covertly embed the dual watermarks into enhanced CT scan images [3]. The noise is removed from the recovered mark image using a DNN-based method after the marked image has been encrypted.

In this work, we present a novel dual watermarking approach based on ECG signals [8] where two medical images are concealed inside the carrier ECG signal. The wavelet transform is used in combination with the HD and MSVD transform to improve the visual quality and overall efficiency of medical watermarking. Existing schemes based on individual DTCWT suffer from a major shortcoming as they fail to strike a balance between robustness and imperceptibility. To overcome this limitation, a new watermarking technique that combines DTCWT, HD, and MSVD has been developed. This combination improves the invisibility and capacity and makes it more resistant to common watermarking assaults. Following are the special features of the proposed scheme:

- **Noise removal using MVMD:-** MVMD is a signal processing technique used for noise removal [10]. This algorithm decomposes a multivariate signal into a set of intrinsic mode functions (IMFs) and generates a noiseless signal.
- **Conversion using Pan Tompkins:-** After getting a noiseless signal, Pan tompkins algorithm is used to convert the 1D ECG signal to 2D ECG matrix.
- **Enhanced capacity using Dual Watermarking:-** To increase the payload, we generated a final watermark using two medical image. The mark is obtained by concealing the image using NSCT and MSVD techniques [2].

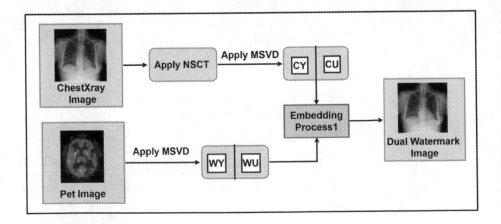

Fig. 1. Flow diagram of generation of Dual watermark

- **Improved Imperceptibility and robustness:-** In the proposed scheme, the dual watermark is embedded into the singular component of selected cover signal coefficients, increasing the visual quality and robustness of the proposed scheme against different attacks [14].
- **Experimental results and analysis:-** Extensive evaluation of the proposed methodology is done and it marks the proposed method as not only robust but also imperceptible and has high embedding capacity.
- **Comparative analysis:-** The proposed method achieves better NC results than existing methods when subjected to the Median attack, salt and pepper noise attack, and speckle noise attack. In terms of capacity, it conceals 131072 bits inside the ECG signal, which is best when compared to the previous method.

This paper is structured as follows: Sect. 2 gives a detailed explanation of the proposed scheme. Section 3 presents experimental results and analysis. Finally, Sect. 4 concludes the paper.

2   Proposed Methodology

This section comprises two parts. Section 2.1 demonstrates the generation of the dual watermark, and Sect. 2.2 outlines the embedding process for the proposed methodology. Table 1 gives details of those symbols which we used in this work.

Algorithm 1: Generation of dual watermark Using NSCT_MSVD

Input   : ChestX-ray Image(W1), PET Image(W2), Scaling Factor $\alpha 1$
Output: Dual watermark Image(dual_mark)
// Step:1 Apply NSCT on ChestX-ray image size '$W1$' of 256 × 256
1     $coef \leftarrow NSCT(W1)$;
// Step:2 Apply MSVD on coefficient 'coef' of '$W1$'
2     $[CY, CU] \leftarrow MSVD(coef\{1, 2\}\{1, 1\})$;
// Step:3 Apply MSVD on PET Image '$W2$' size of 256 × 256
3     $[WY, WU] \leftarrow MSVD(W2)$;
// Step:4 embed 'WY' component of '$W2$' inside 'CYv component of '$W1$' using $\alpha 1$ =0.5
4     $embed\_coef \leftarrow CY.HL + \alpha 1 \times WY.HL$;
5     $temp \leftarrow CY.HL$;
6     $CY.HL \leftarrow embed\_coef$;
// Step:5 Apply Inverse MSVD on Embedding image coefficient '$embed\_coef$'
7     $embed\_coef \leftarrow IMSVD(CY, CU)$;
8     $coef\{1, 2\}\{1, 1\} \leftarrow embed\_coef$;
// Step:6 Apply Inverse NSCT on coef
9     $dual\_mark \leftarrow Inverse\_NSCT(coef)$;
10   return $Dualwatermark Image$

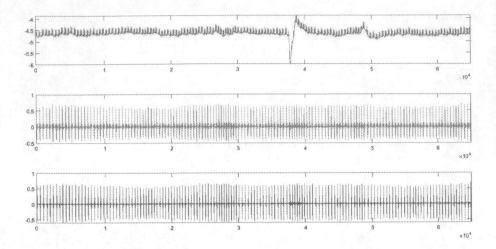

Fig. 2. Diagram of MVMD

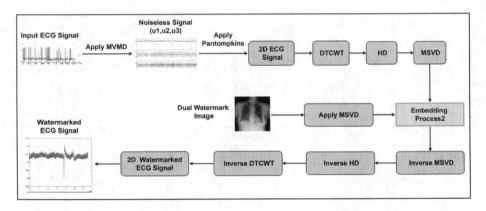

Fig. 3. Embedding Process of Dual watermarking

2.1 Generation of Dual Watermark

The major motivation for developing a dual watermark was to improve patient privacy while simultaneously decreasing the watermark's size. During this phase, we applied the NSCT technique to the ChestXray Image represented by '$W1$' of size 256 × 256. After that, MSVD method is applied on selected coefficients '$coef\{1,2\}\{1,1\}$' and creates components 'CY' and 'CU'. Further, MSVD is applied on the PET Image denoted as '$W2$' of size 256×256 and generates 'WY' and 'WU'. The singular component of '$W2$', i.e., 'WY' is concealed inside the singular component of '$W1$', i.e., 'CY' by taking a suitable Scaling factor of 0.5. Finally, the inverse MSVD and NSCT are employed on embedding coefficients '*embed_coef*', which gives a resultant dual watermark image as illustrated in Fig. 1. Algorithm 1 describes the algorithmic steps necessary to create the dual watermark.

2.2   Embedding Process

The dual mark generated by the Algorithm 2 is integrated into the ECG Signal as shown in Fig. 3. Initially,The cover ECG signal is decomposed by MVMD technique for reducing the MA noise and generates three modes of ECG signal i.e. u1, u2, u3 as shown in Fig. 2. The pan-tompkins algorithm is then used to transform the resulting noiseless signal into a 2-D ECG matrix.The ECG matrix is divided into the subbands 'Yl' and 'Yh' using the DTCWT method. The HD technique is applied on the selected subband 'Yh', followed by MSVD method to produce two components, 'cY' and 'cU'.

Algorithm 2: DTCWT_HD_MSVD based ECG Signal Watermarking (Embedding Process)

Input   : ECG signal(ecg_sig), Dual watermarked image (Dual_watermark), Scaling factor ($\alpha2$)

Output: watermarked ECG signal(marked_ecg)

// Step:1 Apply MVMD for denoising the ecg signal
1        $denoised\_sig \leftarrow MVMD(ecg\_sig)$;

// Step:2 Apply pantompkins for converting 1D to 2D denoised signal
2        $Ecg\_2D \leftarrow PAN\_TOMPKINS(denoised\_sig)$;

// Step:3 Apply DTCWT on 2D Ecg signal size of 512 by 512
3        $[YlYh] \leftarrow DTCWT(Ecg\_2D)$;

// Step:4 Apply HD on coefficient of 'Yh' Subband of 2D Ecg signal
4        $[P, H] \leftarrow HD(Yh\{1,1\}(:,:,1))$;

// Step:4 Apply MSVD on 'H' Subband of HD matrix
5        $[cY, cU] \leftarrow MSVD(H)$;

// Step:6 Apply MSVD on Dual Watermarked image
6        $[wY, wU] \leftarrow MSVD(Dual\_watermark)$;

// Step:7 embed 'wY' component of final dual watermark inside 'cY' component of 2D Ecg signal
7        $watHL \leftarrow cY.HL + \alpha_2 \times wY.HL$;
8        $temp \leftarrow cY.HL$;
9        $cY.HL \leftarrow watHL$;

// Step:8 Apply Inverse MSVD on embedding signal coefficient
10       $watHL \leftarrow IMSVD(cY, cU)$;

// Step:9 Apply Inverse HD on embedding signal coefficient
11       $Yh\{1,1\}(:,:,1) = P * watHL * P'$;
12       $watHL \leftarrow IMSVD(cY, cU)$;

// Step:10 Apply Inverse DTCWT
13       $watermarked\_ecg \leftarrow IDTCWT(YlYh)$;

// Step:11 Reshape 1D watermarked_ecg to 2D Watermarked ECG Signal
14       $marked\_ecg \leftarrow reshape(watermarked\_ecg)$;

15   return $watermarkedECGsignal$;

The dual watermark is then decomposed by using MSVD, and produced 'CY' and 'CU' components. Following this, the specific component 'CY' is embedded into the resultant singular component of ECG signal 'cY' using SF of 0.07. The final 2D watermarked signal '*marked_ecg*' is obtained by applying the inverse of MSVD, HD, and DTCWT method as described in Algorithm 2, and the entire embedding process is depicted in Fig. 3. The extraction process is the opposite of the embedding process.

3   Result and Analysis

This section of the article thoroughly evaluates the proposed technique, starting with the experimental configurations and then by performance evaluation utilizing various cover images and dual watermarks. At the conclusion, the comparative study of the proposed technique is presented.

In our experiments, we embed two 256×256 watermark images, comprising the patient's chest X-ray '$W1$' and PET image '$W2$', within a 512×512 2D-ECG signal. The suggested method is validated using a variety of parameters, such as PSNR, PRD, KL distance, and NC. PSNR evaluates how difficult it is to distinguish between the unaltered signal and the watermarked one. PRD is used to check the authenticity of an ECG signal before and after it has been marked. Moreover, KL divergence evaluates the gap between the original and marked ECG signals' probability density functions. NC enables a quantitative assessment of the concealed watermark's robustness against a variety of attacks on the watermarked signal.

The effectiveness of the technique used to hide the watermark is proportional to a scaling factor known as α. Table 2 displays the results of a range of *alpha* values from 0.01 to 0.5 in evaluating the effectiveness of the current method. It is observed that the scaling factor of 0.07 gives best results in terms of PSNR, SSIM, PRD, and NC. Moreover, the human eye cannot distinguish between the unaltered and watermarked ECG signals.

Table 2. Performance evaluation using different scaling facor

Alpha	Ecg_psnr	Ecg_ssim	Ecg_prd	Ecg_kl	NC1	NC2
0.01	82.5594	1	0.0369	−0.5591	0.9993	1
0.03	73.017	1	0.1107	−0.5693	0.9994	1
0.05	68.58	1	0.1845	−0.1571	0.9994	1
0.07	**65.6575**	**1**	**0.2583**	**0.4814**	**0.9994**	**1**
0.09	63.4746	0.9999	0.3321	1.2134	0.9994	1
0.1	62.5594	0.9999	0.369	1.6348	0.9994	1
0.3	53.017	0.9994	1.107	12.0801	0.9994	1
0.5	48.58	0.9984	1.8449	21.7545	0.9994	1

Table 3. Average results of different evaluation parameters using 50 images

Image	Img_psnr	Img_ssim	Img_nc	Ecg_psnr	Ecg_ssim	Ecg_prd	Ecg_kl	Sig_nc
	57.80081	0.99974	0.99997	65.26466	0.99997	0.27024	0.48826	0.99923
	60.12786	0.99984	0.99998	65.26775	0.99997	0.27014	0.36633	0.99935
	59.38127	0.99989	0.99995	65.21901	0.99996	0.27166	0.46227	0.99909
	59.55115	0.99989	0.99997	65.67325	0.99997	0.25782	0.40178	0.99865
	65.77258	0.99991	0.99999	71.14435	0.99999	0.13733	-0.36759	0.99912
	60.19040	0.99973	0.99998	65.96420	0.99997	0.24933	0.36957	0.99942
Avg of 50 images	59.48394	0.99970	0.99997	64.86494	0.99996	0.29157	0.76823	0.99874

Many experiments are included in order to verify the stealthiness, durability, and practicability of the proposed method. Average results for 50 chestX-ray images in aspects of imperceptibility and robustness are shown in Table 3 [16]. Also, the average findings on performance metrics employing 45 various ECG signals were displayed in Table 4 [8]. The best PSNR achieved is 65.6575 dB, which is consistent with a significant amount of imperceptibility. The NC value for the dual watermark is 0.999378 and watermark 'W2' is approximately one, which shows strong robustness. Also, the best value of PRD is 0.2582. These low PRD values indicate that the suggested approach successfully masks the original signal without degradation. The SSIM(Structural Similarity Index) considers an image's brightness, contrast, and structure. These comparisons determine the degree of resemblance between the original image and the watermarked image. The index ranges from −1 to 1, with a value of 1 indicating flawless similarity and a value of −1 representing complete dissimilarity. In this proposed work, value of Img_ssim and Ecg_ssim is approximately one. It is observed that in most cases, we are getting the best results.

Table 5 shows the robustness of both watermarks against different attacks. Compared to the existing scheme, the proposed scheme gives the best NC result in many cases Table 6. In our experiments, we used a dual watermark of 131072 bits. In Table 7, the proposed method gives better results in terms of PSNR

Table 4. Performance evaluation of different parameters on various ECG signal

Signal	Ecg_psnr	Ecg_ssim	Ecg_prd	Sig_nc	Img_nc
100 m	64.76256	0.999968	0.319372	0.999379	0.999982
101 m	68.59371	0.999968	0.357913	0.999378	0.999982
103 m	65.48152	0.999967	0.220795	0.999379	0.999982
106 m	65.69216	0.999968	0.279953	0.999381	0.999982
107 m	65.79884	0.999967	0.424197	0.99938	0.999982
108 m	68.3727	0.999968	0.699392	0.999381	0.999982
109 m	66.39637	0.999967	0.68533	0.999379	0.999982
111 m	67.72389	0.999968	0.432422	0.999381	0.999982
112 m	71.53058	0.999969	0.251427	0.99938	0.999982
113 m	66.73183	0.999968	0.214526	0.999378	0.999982
114 m	63.53639	0.999968	0.372825	0.99938	0.999982
115 m	64.67258	0.999969	0.225787	0.999375	0.999982
116 m	64.09057	0.999967	0.402932	0.999379	0.999982
117 m	66.41996	0.999968	0.212114	0.999374	0.999982
118 m	65.87182	0.999967	0.615779	0.99938	0.999982
119 m	63.99581	0.999968	0.234628	0.999378	0.999982
121 m	73.13196	0.999968	0.654885	0.999384	0.999982
122 m	66.98256	0.999968	0.278447	0.999378	0.999982
123 m	**65.65746**	**0.999968**	**0.258291**	**0.999378**	**0.999982**
124 m	64.33857	0.999967	0.39951	0.99938	0.999982
Avg of 45 signals	**66.05937**	**0.999968**	**0.356727**	**0.999379**	**0.999982**

Table 5. Robustness evaluation on the basis of different Attack

Attacks	NC1	NC2
Speckle Noise	0.9974	1
Histogram Attack	0.9991	1
Median Filter Attack (3 3) (2 2)	0.9994 0.9994	1 1
Sharpening Mask attack	0.9992	1
Gaussian low-pass filter	0.9994	1
Rotate Attack	0.7157	0.9993
Scaling Attack	0.9994	1
Gaussian Noise Attack (.001)	0.9782	1
Salt and Pepper Noise Attack (.01) (.001)	0.8305 0.9653	0.9997 0.9999
JPEG Compression Attack (10) (5)	0.9994 0.9994	1 1

Table 6. Robustness comparison of proposed with existing technique

Attack	Noise density	Ref [11]		Proposed	
		NC1	NC2	NC1	NC2
Gaussian Noise	0.001	0.9841	0.9354	0.9782	1
	0.01	0.6627	0.5841	0.8504	0.9997
	0.1	0.3828	0.4302	0.4829	0.9978
Salt and Pepper	0.001	0.9577	0.7514	0.9653	0.9999
	0.01	0.6691	0.4583	0.8305	0.9997
	0.1	0.4075	0.424	0.45	0.9974
Speckle Noise	0.001	0.9908	0.977	0.9992	1
	0.01	0.9982	0.9692	0.9974	1
	0.1	0.9726	0.8849	0.9805	1
Rotation	1	0.9922	0.4156	0.7157	0.9993
Median Filter	[1]	0.9905	0.976	0.9994	1

Table 7. Analysis of Performance parameters of the proposed method with other existing techniques

Methods	PSNR	SSIM	PRD	KL distance	NC1	NC2
Ref [5]	38.06	/	2.45	0.119	/	/
Ref [6]	43.44	/	1.32	0.1448	/	/
Ref [7]	57.43	/	0.246		/	/
Ref [9]	48.33	/	/	/	/	/
Ref [11]	65.6154	/	0.291	0.0025	0.9906	0.9791
Proposed	65.65746	0.999968	0.258291	0.481373	0.999378	0.999982

Table 8. Comparison of payload Analysis of proposed work with other existing methods

Methods	Watermark Size (W1, W2)	Cover Image	Payload (bit/Pixel)
Ref [1]	256 * 256, 12 Characters	512 * 512	0.2505
Ref [3]	256 * 256, 343 bits	512 * 512	0.2539
Ref [14]	256 * 256, 12 Characters	512 * 512	0.2505
Ref [15]	60 * 60	480 * 680	0.011
Proposed	256 * 256, 256 * 256	512 * 512	0.5

and NC. In the case of PRD, it gives better results as compared to Ref [5,6,11]. Table 8 provides the comparison of embedding the capacity of the suggested algorithm with some existing techniques. This method yields a capacity of 0.5 bits per pixel. Compared to other existing study, the outcomes of payload analysis using this proposed technique is realistic and satisfactory.

4   Conclusion

In this research, we develop dual watermarking strategy based on ECG signal that makes use of DTCWT-HD-MSVD.We have employed scaling factor to increase both stealth and robustness. A novel dual watermarking algorithm utilizing an ECG signal is developed to embed dual watermarks(a combination of a ChestX-ray Image '$W1$' and a PET Image '$W2$') into a selected decomposition mode (u1) of a noiseless ECG signal. This was achieved through a combination of DTCWT-HD-MSVD, resulting in a watermarked ECG signal that provides information security. The watermarks were still robust even with standard attacks, including speckle noise, Salt and pepper noise, and median filtering. Quantitative results showed that the extracted watermarks, dual watermark and PET image watermark '$W2$', were of high quality due to using less significant regions of the host ECG. However, caution should be used when using these features due to their potential diagnostic significance. The proposed algorithm enables practitioners to easily access different medical images of patients as it combines different information. The experimental results demonstrated that the suggested technique provides excellent resilience and payload with optimum imperceptibility. Compared to other existing work, Excellent results are discovered in terms of its imperceptibility, resilience, and payload capacity.

References

1. Anand, A., Singh, A.K.: An improved DWT-SVD domain watermarking for medical information security. Comput. Commun. **152**, 72–80 (2020)
2. Anand, A., Singh, A.K.: RDWT-SVD-firefly based dual watermarking technique for medical images (workshop paper). In: 2020 IEEE Sixth International Conference on Multimedia Big Data (BigMM), pp. 366–372. IEEE (2020)
3. Anand, A., Singh, A.K.: Dual watermarking for security of COVID-19 patient record. IEEE Trans. Dependable Secure Comput. (2022)
4. Awasthi, D., Srivastava, V.K.: Dual image watermarking using Hessenberg decomposition and RDWT-DCT-SVD in YCbCr color space. In: 2022 International Conference on Computing, Communication, and Intelligent Systems (ICCCIS), pp. 1–6. IEEE (2022)
5. Jero, S.E., Ramu, P.: Curvelets-based ECG steganography for data security. Electron. Lett. **52**(4), 283–285 (2016)
6. Jero, S.E., Ramu, P., Ramakrishnan, S.: ECG steganography using curvelet transform. Biomed. Signal Process. Control **22**, 161–169 (2015)
7. Mathivanan, P., Edward Jero, S., Ramu, P., Balaji Ganesh, A.: QR code based patient data protection in ECG steganography. Aust. Phys. Eng. Sci. Med. **41**, 1057–1068 (2018)
8. Moody, G.B., Mark, R.G.: The impact of the MIT-BIH arrhythmia database. IEEE Eng. Med. Biol. Mag. **20**(3), 45–50 (2001)
9. Nambakhsh, M.S., Ahmadian, A., Zaidi, H.: A contextual based double watermarking of pet images by patient id and ECG signal. Comput. Methods Programs Biomed. **104**(3), 418–425 (2011)
10. ur Rehman, N., Aftab, H.: Multivariate variational mode decomposition. IEEE Trans. Signal Process. **67**(23), 6039–6052 (2019)

11. Sharma, N., Anand, A., Singh, A., Agrawal, A.: Optimization based ECG watermarking in RDWT-SVD domain. Multimed. Tools Appl. 1–17 (2021)
12. Sharma, N., Singh, O.P., Anand, A., Singh, A.K.: Improved method of optimization-based ECG signal watermarking. J. Electron. Imaging **31**(4), 041207 (2022)
13. Sharma, N.K., Kumar, S., Kumar, N.: HGSmark: an efficient ECG watermarking scheme using hunger games search and Bayesian regularization BPNN. Biomed. Signal Process. Control **83**, 104633 (2023)
14. Thakur, S., Singh, A.K., Kumar, B., Ghrera, S.P.: Improved DWT-SVD-based medical image watermarking through hamming code and chaotic encryption. In: Dutta, D., Kar, H., Kumar, C., Bhadauria, V. (eds.) Advances in VLSI, Communication, and Signal Processing. LNEE, vol. 587, pp. 897–905. Springer, Singapore (2020). https://doi.org/10.1007/978-981-32-9775-3_80
15. Thanki, R., Kothari, A., Borra, S.: Hybrid, blind and robust image watermarking: RDWT-NSCT based secure approach for telemedicine applications. Multimed. Tools Appl. **80**(18), 27593–27613 (2021)
16. Wang, X., Peng, Y., Lu, L., Lu, Z., Bagheri, M., Summers, R.: ChestX-ray8: hospital-scale chest X-ray database and benchmarks on weakly-supervised classification and localization of common thorax diseases. In: 2017 IEEE Conference on Computer Vision and Pattern Recognition (CVPR), pp. 3462–3471 (2017)

Near-Infrared Image Colorization Using Unsupervised Contrastive Learning

Devesh Rao, P. B. Jayaraj, and P. N. Pournami[✉]

Department of Computer Science and Engineering, National Institute of Technology
Calicut, Kozhikode 673601, Kerala, India
{jayarajpb,pournamipn}@nitc.ac.in

Abstract. Near-Infrared (NIR) images are widely used in a variety of
low-light situations for security and safety applications. A colorised version of NIR images provide better image understanding and interpretation of features. Because the number of NIR-RGB paired datasets is
limited and often unavailable, a method to convert a given NIR image to
an RGB image is highly desirable. The present work proposes an unsupervised image to image translation technique for generating colorized
images (*UGCI*) for transforming an input NIR image to an RGB image.
UGCI outperforms present NIR-RGB colorizing models and have shown
approximately 57% improvement in terms of Fréchet inception distance
(FID) with reduced training time and less memory usage. Finally, a thorough comparative study based on different datasets is carried out to confirm superiority over leading colorization approaches in qualitative and
quantitative assessments.

Keywords: near-infrared images · colorization · unsupervised learning

1 Introduction

The goal of "Image to Image translation", a class of computer vision and image
processing problems, is to identify the relationship between an input image and
an output image in order to transform the image into the desired domain. Near-
Infrared (NIR) Imaging is a technique for imaging using the infrared band of
the electromagnetic spectrum, covering the wavelengths ranging from 700 nm
to 1400 nm. This wavelength is outside the human visible spectrum (400 nm to
700 nm). As the NIR spectral band is dependent on the material, most of the
material colors are transparent to NIR, as shown in Fig. 1. It is observed that the
red and white band pattern, which is depicted in the center of the image with a
green arrow, vanishes in the near-infrared view. On the other hand, the two black
objects - yellow arrows on the left side of the image - have significantly distinct
appearances. This implies that the difference in NIR intensities is related to
the material's natural hue and the dye's absorption and coefficient of reflection.
Since the human sensory system is sensitive to wavelengths between 400 and
700 nm, the traditional RGB illustration is favored when providing information
to the end-user.

H. Kaur et al. (Eds.): CVIP 2023, CCIS 2009, pp. 50–61, 2024.
https://doi.org/10.1007/978-3-031-58181-6_5

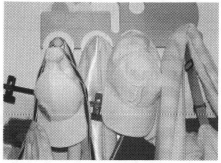

Fig. 1. RGB-NIR Comparison [5]

NIR imaging is used to capture images in low lighting conditions as NIR wavelength comes outside the visible spectrum (380 nm–700 nm). NIR can be used for quantitative analysis and process control. NIR can be used for process control, qualitative analysis (identification of finished products and raw materials) and quantitative analysis (determination of substance concentrations). It has various applications in military fields, including video surveillance, medical imaging, food detection, remote sensing, and Advanced Driver Assistance Systems. Also, its demand is increasing in Veterinary Science and Medicine for detecting diseases, faulty equipment detection in the industry, and for inspection of buildings.

The longer wavelengths of NIR spectrum makes it more effectively pass through haze, light fog, smoke, and other atmospheric conditions than visible light. This frequently produces an image that is sharper, less distorted and has higher contrast for long-distance imaging than what can be seen in visible light. Due to the lack of color information in the image, NIR images are not adequate for human interpretation. However, because the NIR image is transparent to haze, more features such as mountains are easily noticeable in the infrared image. Furthermore, since humans are more comfortable with RGB images, if there is a means to colorize the infrared image, end users will be able to extract more useful information from the captured pictures.

2 Related Works

The traditional approach of colorizing images relies on histogram algorithms, which store pixel information in databases to train models and require human intervention (semi-automatic) to estimate the color of objects and other details. Recently, Deep Convolutional Neural Networks (DCNN) replaced the semi-automatic approaches with a fully automatic approach by predicting the color of different objects like cars, trees, etc. from the image automatically using the probability of the pixel from histogram like in work done by Welsh et al. [25]. The primary issue with this type of architecture is that the reference images should have some common regions so that the model can observe similar patterns and predict the target image's color; otherwise, the model will perform inefficiently. Now with the help of neural networks, there are a number of methods to colorize grayscale images, for image translation, and to increase the resolution of images using supervised and unsupervised techniques such as Pix2pix [10]. The study given in FusionGAN [16] suggests a technique to preserve the texture details of the image using the fusion of infrared thermal features and visible real image with the help of generative adversarial networks (GANs).

Recently, Generative Adversarial Network (GAN) [6] has been able to generate better composite images than previous generative models and has become one of the most popular areas of research in the meantime. In recent years many improved GANs has been introduced which outperforms many traditional and state-of-the-art approaches by giving impressive results such as PCSGAN [3], FVGAN [27], LBP-BEGAN [26], DualGAN [28]. CycleGAN [29] used ResNet architecture [7] as a part of the generator in CycleGAN, demonstrating that it is quite capable of transforming one image into another and achieving acceptable results using cycle consistency loss in image improvement, style transfer and other applications. The cycle consistency loss has also been used in many recent works for image to image translation [13]. CycleGAN, however, was unable to achieve satisfactory results in learning the color between domains and transferring the learned color without changing the shape of the samples because the network stops learning the color after a certain number of epochs and also because networks need a lot of data in the RGB domains. Based on the SPADE generator a method for NIR colcorization is proposed in [22]. The generator has spatial adaptive denormalization (SPADE) as the encoder with takes multiscale NIR images as input and extracts the texture from the NIR images and effectively preserves the RGB color of the synthesized image.

3   Materials and Methods

3.1   Dataset Description

The proposed *UGCI* model is trained using the images from the dataset by published by Brown et al. [4]. This dataset has 477 registered colour (RGB) and near-infrared (NIR) image pairs. From this dataset, 180 RGB images are chosen and 726 images were downloaded from the internet, making a total of 906 images from the categories Mountains, Sky, and Fields.

3.2   Proposed Unsupervised Generation of Colorized NIR Images (*UGCI*)

The proposed model, Unsupervised Generation of Colorized NIR Images (*UGCI*) is an extension of Contrastive Learning for Unpaired Image-to-Image Translation method [19]. In order to understand the fundamental characteristics of a dataset without labels, Contrastive Learning teaches the model which data points are identical and which are distinct. The proposed method has been trained to convert an input NIR image $X \subset R^{H \times W \times C}$ to an output RGB image $Y \subset R^{H \times W \times 3}$ with unaligned instances of X and Y.

Initially, the input images in the training dataset are pre-processed and resized to 256×256 pixel patches, and the first half of the generator is used as encoder to project the patches into the embedding space and GAN discriminator to generate the colored output. The paired input and output patch at the same location are considered to ensure that the pair's embeddings are similar referred as positive pair. On the other hand, the patches from the different locations should be mapped far from the positive pairs, which is formulated as contrastive loss [12]. The model architecture of UGCI is given in Fig. 2.

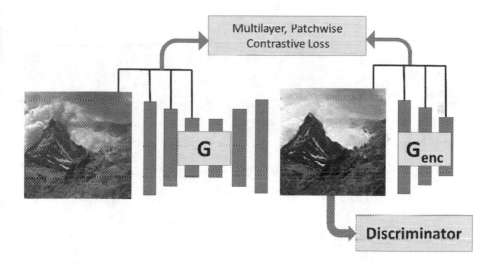

Fig. 2. Proposed UGCI Model Architecture

The sample from the colorized image is mapped with the corresponding input patch with a similar embedding space which refers to the positive pair, and all other N patches form the negative patch, which is placed far from the positive pairs. In short, positive pairs are formed by corresponding input and output patches, while negative pairs are formed by patches from other locations. Cosine similarity is used to improve the similarity between positive patches while minimizing that of negative patches, and this is done by formulating a classification task with the target class of positive pairs; such formulation is called InfoNCE [18] was introduced and used in representation learning.

3.3   Generator Architecture

The *UGCI* model's generator encoder is a ResNet-18 neural network with 18 deep residual blocks [7]. The Residual Network solves the issue of degrading accuracy with the increase in number of layers of the network after the model accuracy is saturated in the traditional neural networks. It also solves the issue of vanishing gradient. Both the 18-layer and the 34-layer plain networks have a comparable shape. The results reveal that the shallower 18-layer plain network has a smaller validation error than the 34-layer plain network. Therefore, ResNet18 was chosen as the *UGCI* generator as opposed to ResNet34. In *UGCI*, every block of the ResNet-18 neural network is similar to the architecture illustrated in Fig. 3. The sequential layers are Reflection pad [15], Conv2d [2], Instance Norm [23], ReLU [1] and Dropout [21].

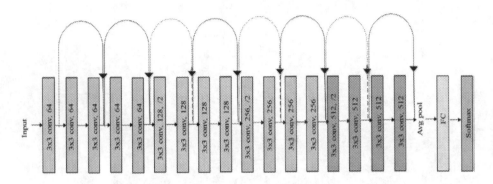

Fig. 3. ResNET-18 Architecture [7]

3.4   Discriminator Architecture

An NxN PatchGAN [10] is used as the classifier in the discriminator. Sample architecture is given in Fig. 4. The classifier gives the $N \times N$ patch as output from the discriminators and classifies it by giving the probability that the image is from fake data distribution or real data distribution. In the discriminator of *UGCI*, a 70×70 PatchGAN is used which gives a 70×70 vector as output.

3.5   Evaluation Metrics

The propsoed *UGCI* model has been evaluated using the following standard metrics.

– **The Fréchet inception distance (FID)** [8] is very popular for evaluating the results of generative models. If X and Y are real and fake embeddings, Tr is the trace of the matrix, Σ_X and Σ_Y are the covariance of the matrices X and Y respectively, FID is computed as given below. A lower FID score indicates the credibility of the generated images.

$$FID(X,Y) = \|\mu_X - \mu_Y\|_2^2 + \text{Tr}\left(\Sigma_X + \Sigma_Y - 2\left(\Sigma_X \Sigma_Y\right)^{\frac{1}{2}}\right) \quad (1)$$

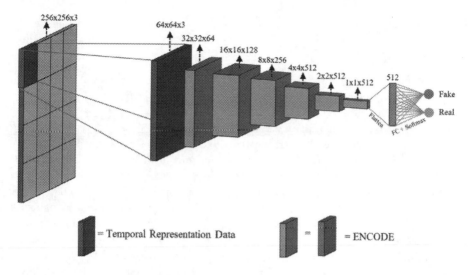

Fig. 4. Discriminator Architecture

– **Angular Error (AE)**, θ, is the average angular distance between every pixel of the generated image and the groundtruth image and is calculated as given below.

$$\theta = \sum_{i=0}^{H} \sum_{j=0}^{W} \cos^{-1} \left[\frac{\vec{X}_{ij}\vec{Y}_{ij}}{|\vec{X}_{ij}||\vec{Y}_{ij}|} \right] \qquad (2)$$

where H and W represents the dimension of the image(in our expreiment H = 256, W = 256). In theory, the closer an image is to the ground truth, the smaller the angle between images.
– **Structural Similarity Index (SSIM)** [24] measures the perpetual differ-ence between two similar structures. It compares the image similarity using luminance, structure and contrast.
– **Peak signal-to-noise ratio (PSNR)** [9] is the ratio of a signal's maxi-mum possible value(in out case image pixels has values (0,255) to the noise distortion that affects the quality of representation.

It has been observed that computing the contrastive loss at multiple layers is important for stable training. Therefore, the feature stack of multiple layers has been considered to train the model with more stability. This method replaces the fixed pixel-based cycle loss and does not require a generator and discriminator in the inverse direction as used in CycleGAN [6] for cycle consistency loss, so it can be trained faster and uses less memory compared to CycleGAN. This model used ResNet18 network model as the generator and patchGAN is used as classifier in the discriminator. Our generator function G is divided into two parts, an encoder G_{enc} and a decoder G_{dec}, which are used in order to create the output image Y. Loss function, $L_{GAN}(G, D, X, Y)$ for the proposed model is computed as in Eq. (3).

$$L_{GAN}(G, D, X, Y) = E_{Y \sim p_{data}(y)}[log D(Y)] + E_{X \sim p_{data}(X)}[1 - log D(G(X))] \quad (3)$$

The formulation in Eq. 3 is the adversarial loss [6] for the mapping function $G : X \rightarrow Y$ where generator G seeks to produce images that resemble or mimics images from the target domain Y, whereas discriminator D tries to tell the difference between real samples y and translated samples $G(x)$. G is attempting to limit this goal whereas D is trying to maximize it. Using a noise contrastive estimation framework, we aim to optimise the mutual information between the input and output patches. In contrast to other patches, the goal of contrastive learning is to link the output patch to the appropriate input patch referred as positive pair. An $(N + 1)$-way classification problem is formulated using N negative patches from separate locations in the input image. A two-layer multi-layer perceptron (ML) network is then built and reuse the generator's encoder portion G_{enc}. The input and output patches are both projected by this network to a common embedding space. The chance of choosing the positive example over the negative examples is computed as the cross-entropy loss as given in Eq. (4).

$$l(v, v^+, v^-) = -log \left[\frac{\exp (\boldsymbol{v} \cdot \boldsymbol{v}^+/\tau)}{\sum_{n=1}^{N}(\exp (\boldsymbol{v} \cdot \boldsymbol{v}_n^-/\tau) + \exp(\boldsymbol{v} \cdot \boldsymbol{v}^+/\tau)} \right] \quad (4)$$

where $v, v^+ \in \mathbb{R}^K$ represent the positive pair, $\boldsymbol{v}^- \in \mathbb{R}^{N*K}$ represent negatives and $\boldsymbol{v}_n^-$ represents n_{th} negative. Lastly, the result is then wrapped in $-log()$ so that increasing the likelihood that the two augmented images are similar corresponds to decreasing this loss function. In order to create a feature stack, we pass the feature maps through a multi-layer perceptron (MLP) network with L layers of interest.

As the generator encoder feature stack is available after image translation, the layer and spatial location represent a patch of the input image, with deeper layers corresponding to larger patches. At a specific point, we try to match input-output patches that coincide. We can use the additional patches in the input as negatives. For instance, a colorful picture mountain peak needs to be more strongly related to an input NIR mountain peak than other patches of the same input, like other mountainous regions or the grass and sky in the backdrop. It is known as the PatchNCE loss and is computed as in Eq. (5).

$$L_{PatchNCE}(G, H, X) = \mathbb{E}_{x \sim X} \sum_{l=1}^{L} \sum_{s=1}^{S_l} l(z_l^s, z_l^s, z_l^{S \backslash s}) \quad (5)$$

where L represents the layers chosen to pass from MLP network, S_l denotes the spatial locations in a layer with z^{s_l} as the corresponding feature where $s \in 1, 2, ..., S_l$, $\hat{z}_l^s \in \mathbb{R}^{C_l}$ is the output of two-layer MLP network(H_l) by taking the feature stacks of selected NCE layers as input $\{\hat{z}_l^s\}_L = \{H_l(G_{enc}^l(x))\}_L$ and C_l is channels in layer l, and $z_l^{S \backslash s} \in \mathbb{R}^{(S_l-1) \times C_l}$ denotes the features of other layers except the one currently selected. The overall loss for the proposed $UGCI$ model is computed as per Eq. (6).

$$GAN(G, D, X, Y) + \lambda_X \mathcal{L}_{PatchNCE}(G, H, X) + \lambda_Y \mathcal{L}_{PatchNCE}(G, H, Y) \quad (6)$$

4   Results and Discussion

The proposed UGCI model's discriminator is trained using 477 NIR images were used during training, while the corresponding ground truth was not used in training or testing. All the images have been resized to 256 × 256 pixels before training. The training has been done using Nvidia Tesla V100-PCIE-3 2GB. It took around 10 h to train the model for 200 epochs.

At the time of training, the ADAM stochastic optimizer has been used, and the model hyperparameters were as follows: For generators and discriminators, the learning rate was 0.0002; 100 epochs to linearly decay the learning rate to zero; beta1 and beta2 momentum were 0.5 and 0.999, respectively; and dropout had a probability of 0.5. The feature stack of layers 0, 4, 8, 16, 20, 24, 28, and 32 have been used to calculate Noise-cross entropy loss. UGCI results have been compared with the baseline models CycleGAN and Colorizing Near-Infrared Images through a cyclic Adversarial. The qualitative and quantitative results are presented in the following section.

4.1   Qualitative Analysis

Unpaired images were used to test the model; these images were not used during training. In Fig. 5, the visual outcomes in comparison to the baseline models are shown, which contain the NIR image, Ground truth and outputs from $UGCI$, CycleGAN (UNET-based), and CycleGAN. Compared to the output of other models, the color and structure of $UGCI$ output images are closer to the ground truth. Color details are more accurate in our output, whereas the outputs of other models are brighter and more colorful. Compared to CycleGAN, $UGCI$ is quicker and more memory-efficient because it substitutes patchNCE loss for cycle consistency loss, negating the need for the extra generator and discriminator.

Extensive experiments were performed with different generator architectures such as StyleGAN2 [11], U-NET [20], ResNet(four blocks, six blocks, and nine blocks), and different datasets to analyze the capability of the contrastive learning on datasets having different categories like country, mountain, field, buildings, forest, etc. It is observed that f the model is trained on internal data, which refers to the dataset containing images of a single domain, it performs much better than the dataset containing images of the external domain (i.e., consists of images from different categories). $UGCI$ degrades the quality of output if trained with the external dataset because the external dataset consists of many false positives.

NIR   GROUNDTRUTH   UGCI   CycleGAN(UNET)[16]   CYCLEGAN

Fig. 5. Colorized images from different models

4.2   Quantitative Analysis

The loss curve for *UGCI* is given in Fig. 6.

Table 1 displays the evaluation findings.

According to these results, the proposed method, *UGCI*, outperforms the CycleGAN (UNET) [17] in terms of FID by 57% and Angular Error by 42%. Our proposed method exhibits better performance compared to DualGAN by Wei Liang et al. [14], in terms of PSNR and SSIM. From the results, it is visible that the proposed model, UGCI, is faster compared to the present NIR-RGB colorizing models as it uses only patchwise loss and GAN adversarial loss while training the model. In the CycleGAN, the cycle consistency loss has been added both in forward and backward translation.

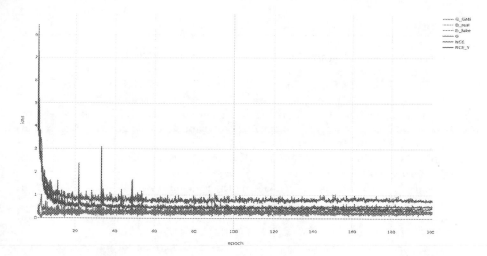

Fig. 6. Model Loss Curve

Table 1. Evaluation Results

Method	FID↓	AE↓	SSIM	PSNR
CycleGAN	146.77	13.77	0.869	38.84
CycleGAN (UNET)	105.21	9.18	0.908	40.11
UGCI* (Proposed)	**67.04**	**6.45**	**0.912**	**40.57**

5   Conclusion

Near-Infrared images are primarily used in low or no light conditions using rays outside the visible spectral range. Absence of color information in NIR images poses difficulties for analysis by human beings. An automated, unsupervised NIR image colorization technique (*UGCI*) is proposed in this work. Based on the qualitative and quantitative results, *UGCI* outperforms state-of-the-art methods for colorizing unpaired NIR datasets, and the visual results obtained from *UGCI* are very close to real-world scenarios. When training the model with images from the same domain, *UGCI* produces excellent results; however, the output degrades when there are many external patches, as the external patches produce false negatives; thus, we used the internal dataset for training. Overall, *UGCI* is very efficient in terms of training time and memory usage, and it meets our requirement that the end-user be able to extract discriminant features from the image easily.

References

1. Agarap, A.F.: Deep learning using rectified linear units (ReLU) (2018)
2. Albawi, S., Mohammed, T.A., Al-Zawi, S.: Understanding of a convolutional neural network. In: 2017 International Conference on Engineering and Technology (ICET), pp. 1–6 (2017). https://doi.org/10.1109/ICEngTechnol.2017.8308186
3. Babu, K.K., Dubey, S.R.: PCSGAN: perceptual cyclic-synthesized generative adversarial networks for thermal and NIR to visible image transformation. Neurocomputing **413**, 41–50 (2020)
4. Brown, M., Süsstrunk, S.: Multi-spectral sift for scene category recognition. In: CVPR 2011, pp. 177–184 (2011)
5. Fredembach, C., Süsstrunk, S.: Colouring the near-infrared. In: International Conference on Communications in Computing (2008)
6. Goodfellow, I., et al.: Generative adversarial networks. In: Advances in Neural Information Processing Systems, vol. 3 (2014)
7. He, K., Zhang, X., Ren, S., Sun, J.: Deep residual learning for image recognition (2015)
8. Heusel, M., Ramsauer, H., Unterthiner, T., Nessler, B., Hochreiter, S.: GANs trained by a two time-scale update rule converge to a local nash equilibrium (2017)
9. Horé, A., Ziou, D.: Image quality metrics: PSNR vs. SSIM. In: 2010 20th International Conference on Pattern Recognition, pp. 2366–2369 (2010). https://doi.org/10.1109/ICPR.2010.579
10. Isola, P., Zhu, J.Y., Zhou, T., Efros, A.A.: Image-to-image translation with conditional adversarial networks (2016)
11. Karras, T., Laine, S., Aittala, M., Hellsten, J., Lehtinen, J., Aila, T.: Analyzing and improving the image quality of StyleGAN (2019)
12. Khosla, P., et al.: Supervised contrastive learning. In: Larochelle, H., Ranzato, M., Hadsell, R., Balcan, M., Lin, H. (eds.) Advances in Neural Information Processing Systems, vol. 33, pp. 18661–18673. Curran Associates, Inc. (2020)
13. Lee, H.Y., et al.: DRIT++: diverse image-to-image translation via disentangled representations (2019)
14. Liang, W., Ding, D., Wei, G.: An improved DualGAN for near-infrared image colorization. Infrared Phys. Technol. **116**, 103764 (2021)
15. Liu, G., et al.: Partial convolution based padding (2018)
16. Ma, J., Yu, W., Liang, P., Li, C., Jiang, J.: FusionGAN: a generative adversarial network for infrared and visible image fusion. Inf. Fusion **48**, 11–26 (2019)
17. Mehri, A., Sappa, A.D.: Colorizing near infrared images through a cyclic adversarial approach of unpaired samples. In: 2019 IEEE/CVF Conference on Computer Vision and Pattern Recognition Workshops (CVPRW), pp. 971–979 (2019)
18. Oord, A.v.d., Li, Y., Vinyals, O.: Representation learning with contrastive predictive coding (2018)
19. Park, T., Efros, A.A., Zhang, R., Zhu, J.-Y.: Contrastive learning for unpaired image-to-image translation. In: Vedaldi, A., Bischof, H., Brox, T., Frahm, J.-M. (eds.) ECCV 2020. LNCS, vol. 12354, pp. 319–345. Springer, Cham (2020). https://doi.org/10.1007/978-3-030-58545-7_19
20. Ronneberger, O., Fischer, P., Brox, T.: U-net: convolutional networks for biomedical image segmentation. In: Navab, N., Hornegger, J., Wells, W.M., Frangi, A.F. (eds.) MICCAI 2015. LNCS, vol. 9351, pp. 234–241. Springer, Cham (2015). https://doi.org/10.1007/978-3-319-24574-4_28

21. Srivastava, N., Hinton, G., Krizhevsky, A., Sutskever, I., Salakhutdinov, R.: Dropout: a simple way to prevent neural networks from overfitting. J. Mach. Learn. Res. **15**(56), 1929–1958 (2014)
22. Sun, T., Jung, C.: Nir image colorization using spade generator and grayscale approximated self-reconstruction. In: 2020 IEEE International Conference on Visual Communications and Image Processing (VCIP), pp. 463–466 (2020)
23. Ulyanov, D., Vedaldi, A., Lempitsky, V.: Instance normalization: the missing ingredient for fast stylization (2016)
24. Wang, Z., Bovik, A., Sheikh, H., Simoncelli, E.: Image quality assessment: from error visibility to structural similarity. IEEE Trans. Image Process. **13**(4), 600–612 (2004)
25. Welsh, T., Ashikhmin, M., Mueller, K.: Transferring color to greyscale images. ACM Trans. Graph. **21**(3), 277–280 (2002)
26. Xu, J., Shi, X., Qin, S., Lu, K., Wang, H., Ma, J.: LBP-BEGAN: a generative adversarial network architecture for infrared and visible image fusion. Infrared Phys. Technol. **104**, 103144 (2020)
27. Yang, W., Hui, C., Chen, Z., Xue, J.H., Liao, Q.: FV-GAN: finger vein representation using generative adversarial networks. IEEE Trans. Inf. Forensics Secur. **14**(9), 2512–2524 (2019)
28. Yi, Z., Zhang, H., Tan, P., Gong, M.: DualGAN: unsupervised dual learning for image-to-image translation. In: Proceedings of the IEEE International Conference on Computer Vision (ICCV) (2017)
29. Zhu, J.Y., Park, T., Isola, P., Efros, A.A.: Unpaired image-to-image translation using cycle-consistent adversarial networks. In: 2017 IEEE International Conference on Computer Vision (ICCV), pp. 2242–2251 (2017)

CoreDeep: Improving Crack Detection Algorithms Using Width Stochasticity

Ramkrishna Pandey⑩ and Akshit Achara$^{(\boxtimes)}$⑩

GE Research, Bangalore, India
ramp@alum.iisc.ac.in, f2016953p@alumni.bits-pilani.ac.in

Abstract. Automatically detecting or segmenting cracks in images can help in reducing the cost of maintenance or operations. Detecting, measuring and quantifying cracks for distress analysis in challenging background scenarios is a difficult task as there is no clear boundary that separates cracks from the background. Some of the other perceptually noted challenges with the images are variations in color, intensity, depth, blur, motion-blur, orientation, region of interest (ROI) for the defect, scale, illumination, backgrounds, etc. These variations occur across (crack inter-class) and within images (crack intra-class variabilities). In this work, we have proposed a stochastic width (SW) approach to reduce the effect of these variations. Our proposed approach improves detectability and significantly reduces false positives and negatives. We have measured the performance of our algorithm objectively in terms of mean intersection over union (mIoU) and subjectively in terms of perceptual quality.

Keywords: Crack Segmentation · Uncertainty · Deep Learning

1 Introduction

Cracks are a common defect category in many distress analysis tasks ranging from road inspection to estimating the remaining useful life of the material, object, surface or machine parts. They develop in structures that are subjected to cyclic load and fatigue stress over time. Crack detection in civil engineering structures is an essential aspect of ensuring the safety and longevity of infrastructure.

There are various methods for crack detection, including visual inspection, acoustic emission testing, ultrasonic testing, infrared thermography, and ground penetrating radar. However, the proposed work is focused on visual inspection.

Visual inspection is the most commonly used method for crack detection, where trained personnel visually inspect the structure for visible cracks, and the severity of the crack is evaluated based on the thickness, length, and location of the crack.

In most of the cases, experts are needed to perform the visual inspection of cracks. This manual process is very tedious, challenging and error prone. Early detection of cracks allows us to take preventive measures for possible failures [1]. Numerous computer vision methods have been applied to detect cracks in an

© The Author(s), under exclusive license to Springer Nature Switzerland AG 2024
H. Kaur et al. (Eds.): CVIP 2023, CCIS 2009, pp. 62–73, 2024.
https://doi.org/10.1007/978-3-031-58181-6_6

image. These algorithms can be broadly categorized into thresholding based [2], handcrafted feature based such as local binary pattern [3], histogram of oriented gradients [4], wavelets [5] and gabor filters [6]. These approaches capture the local information but miss the global context. Crack detection using global view [7] takes in account geometric and photo-metric characteristics that help in better connectivity. However, the performance drops significantly in challenging backgrounds.

Recently, deep learning techniques have shown promising results in various computer vision tasks such as semantic segmentation, object detection and classification. These algorithms extract features in hierarchical form from a low level to a high level representation. These features are extracted from data to capture local as well as global feature representation of an image that helps in solving many challenging problems. In [8], the authors have shown that the performance of algorithms can be improved at three different levels i.e. input, architecture, and the objective followed by post-processing. In [9], the authors have shown randomly dropping character pixels in input image can help better connecting strokes thereby improving OCR performance. In this work, we have explored input with better augmentation strategy [10], used two different backbones [11,12] as the encoder of U-Net [13]. We have used binary cross entropy [14] and binary focal dice loss [15] (objective exploration), to improve the performance of our crack detection algorithm by a significant margin.

1.1 Contributions

Following are our key contributions :

1. We advocate the use of stochastic dilation (also referred as stochastic width, see Fig. 2) to improve the crack detectability and connectivity (see results shown in Fig. 4a and 4b).
2. We use binary focal dice loss [15] and random augmentation [10] to improve the performance over our own baseline by a significant margin.
3. We have analyzed the prediction probabilities and grouped the predictions with different probability ranges to obtain a threshold cutoff probability (see Subsect. 3.1) that further refines the predictions and improves the mIoU.
4. Our method significantly reduces false positives (FP) and false negatives (FN) (refer Sect. 3.3 for details on the computation) by a significant margin (see Tables 1a and 1b).

2 Datasets Used for Study

We have used Kaggle crack segmentation dataset [7,16–21] that has around 11298 images. These images are obtained after merging 12 crack segmentation datasets. including some 'noncrack' images (images that have no cracks). All the images are resized to a fixed size of (448, 448). Dataset is split into a train and test folders. The train folder contains 9603 images and test folder contains 1695 images. The splitting is stratified so that the proportion of each datasets in the train and test folder are similar.

2.1   Training and Validation

For all our experiments, we have further divided the train split of the dataset into train and validation splits. We created the validation set from the overall train set by aggregating 20 percent of the images from each of the 12 crack segmentation datasets. The validation set remains fixed for all the experiments.

The model trained on overall dataset using the binary cross-entropy loss function [14] is hereafter referred as 'Baseline' and model trained on overall dataset with random augmentations during the training process using binary focal dice loss function [15] is hereafter referred as 'Baseline+'.

2.2   Stochastic Width (SW)

We perform augmentation on the training data by taking each input ground truth mask and performing augmentations of 3×3, 5×5 and 8×8 incrementally as shown in Fig. 1. Figure 2 shows the different masks obtained for an input image in the stochastic width approach.

We trained a model on the above mentioned augmented dataset which is hereafter referred as 'SW'. The loss function used here is binary focal dice loss [15].

We assume that (a) there is fuzziness in the boundaries of crack which can easily result in human error while marking the crack pixels, and (b) there is a variability in the width of the crack which is seen across different datasets (e.g. see image (i) in Figs. 4a and 4b taken from two different datasets. Figure 4a has thinner cracks as compared to 4b and within each image (e.g. top right portion of the crack the image (a) in Fig. 4a is thin and faint compared to other cracks in the same image). Therefore, we incorporate width stochasticity to allow the model to learn the width variabilities across and within multiple datasets.

3   Experiments

We have performed all the experiments using the 2D Unet architectures initialised with resnet50 [11] and efficientnet [12] backbones trained on imagenet [22] dataset.

We also perform runtime augmentations during our training process by selecting two augmentations randomly [10] from flip, rotate, brightness contrast, shiftScaleRotate, shear, scale, translate, multiplicativeNoise, randomGamma, downScale, HueSaturationValue, CLAHE, channel dropout, coarse dropout [23], color jitter, gaussian blur, median blur, grid dropout and maskDropout and, applying them incrementally(one after the other) on each input. We have used a batch size of 8 for training all our models. The optimizer used is adam [24] with an initial learning rate of 1e−3. We used the ReduceLROnPlateau [25] learning rate callback to adjust the learning rate based on the change in validation loss. After every 50 epochs, the learning rate was reduced by 0.5 with a minimum possible learning rate of 1e−6.

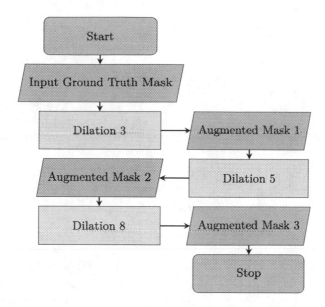

Fig. 1. The flowchart shows the process stochastic width augmentation. The input ground truth mask is augmented multiple times using Dilation 3, Dilation 5 and Dilation 8 incrementally. The augmented dataset will include 4 masks (Input Ground Truth Mask, Augmented Mask 1, Augmented Mask 2 and Augmented Mask 3) for each input.

3.1   Threshold Selection

We have used the numpy [26] implementation of argmax function for calculating the labels from prediction probabilities. We have also analyzed the prediction probabilities from the model to obtain the predictions with high probabilities (strong candidate pixels for cracks) and the predictions with low probability (weak candidate pixels for cracks). We have performed an experiment on the validation dataset where we obtain the crack probabilities for all the pixels in an image. For each validation image prediction, the pixel crack probabilties are divided into ten equally sized bins which are created using the hist function from

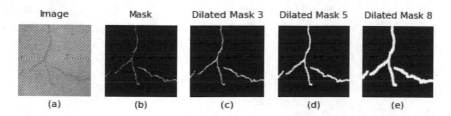

Fig. 2. Shows (a) original image, (b) ground truth, (c) dilated with mask 3×3, (d) dilated (c) mask 5×5 and (e) dilated (d) mask 8×8.

matplotlib [27]. The bins are arranged in ascending order of probabilities. We start from minimum probability value and keep increasing the threshold (to the maximum probability of the next bin) till the number of connected components (cracks) is more than the number of connected components in the initial prediction. Once the number of connected components in the thresholded prediction are more than the original prediction, the current bin is further divided into 10 bins and the threshold is reduced from the maximum probability of the last bin to the first bin until the number of connected components is same as in the original prediction.

Finally, we created 10 bins from all the thresholds and found that the most common threshold values lie in the 10th bin, so we chose the middle value of 0.95 from the last bin boundaries (0.899 and 0.999). Figure 3 shows a flowchart for calculating the thresholds for each validation image. The overall idea here is to remove the pixels along the crack boundaries and avoid disconnectivity of the cracks.

The threshold values of 0.90 to 0.98 with a step size of 0.01 were used on the test image predictions and it was observed that the weaker predictions were removed resulting in a significant increase in the mean IoU as shown in the Tables 1a, 2a, 1b and 2b. The thresold value of 0.95 resulted in the highest increase in the IoU.

3.2   Naming Conventions

The SW outputs post thresholding will hereafter be referred as $SW <T>$ where T is the *threshold applied* $\times 100$. For Example, SW 95 means the output is obtained using the model trained on the augmented dataset on which a threshold of 0.95 is applied.

3.3   Image Level False Positives and False Negatives

The approach to compute false positives and false negatives listed in the Tables 1a and 1b are as follows; if the model predicts a crack even if there was no crack in the true mask and the image is FP. So, we count the number of 'noncrack' datasets images for which there was a crack predicted. The false negatives are computed by counting non crack predictions (misses) when there was actually a crack in the true mask and the image. FP and FN computation can be considered an alternative metric to access the performance of the algorithms in practical scenarios.

4   Results and Discussions

The results reported in the Tables 1a, 2a, 1b and 2b and Figs. 4a and 4b are obtained on the test split of the kaggle crack segmentation dataset [16] (for more details, see Sect. 2).

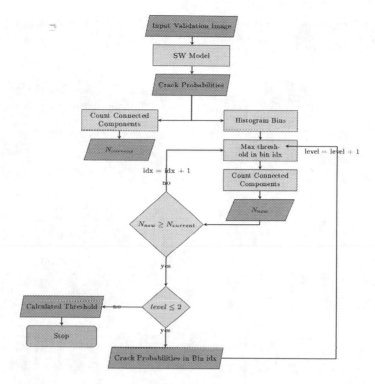

Fig. 3. The flowchart shows the process of calculating the threshold probability for each validation image as discussed in Sect. 3.1. *idx* is the bin index (0 to 9) and *level* is the number of times (maximum of 2 times) binning is done. $N\_current$ is the number of connected components in the original prediction and $N\ new$ is the number of connected components after applying a threshold on the original prediction. The calculated thresholds are analyzed to get the final threshold to use on test data (see Sect. 3.1).

Table 1a shows the quantitative results obtained by the models trained with different approaches utilizing resnet50 [11] backbone. The SW approach shows a significant improvement in terms of all the metrics (except FN, which increases slightly) on applying thresholding (see the approaches SW 94, SW 95 and SW 96). The false positives have significantly reduced from 32 to 2 for SW 95 approach.

Table 1b shows the quantitative results obtained by the models trained with different approaches utilizing efficientnetb4 [12] backbone. It can be observed that these approaches have significantly less false positives as compared to the approaches in Table 2a which utilize resnet50 [11] backbone. Thresholding on SW results in an improvement in all metrics except for false negatives which is similar to the pattern in Table 1a.

Note that a false positive here is calculated with respect to an image i.e. a prediction is called as false positive if it containts crack pixels and the ground

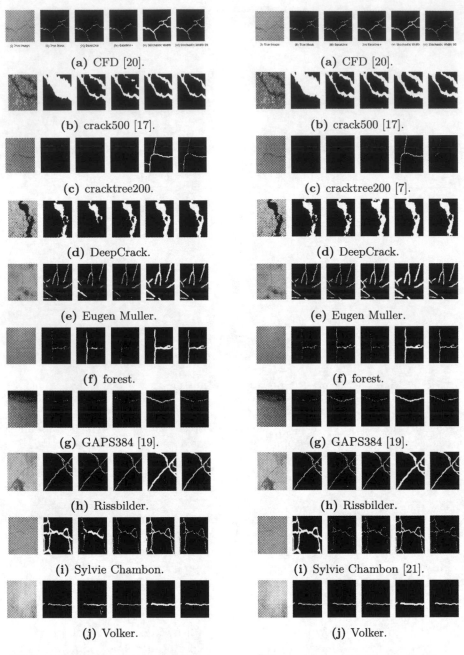

All approaches here are trained using resnet50 backbone and test split of each dataset was used for predictions.

All approaches here are trained using efficientnetb4 backbone and test split of each dataset was used for predictions.

Fig. 4. Figures show an example image from each dataset; from left to right: (a) original image, (b) ground truth, (c) Baseline, (d) Baseline+ and (e) SW (f) SW 95 (see Sect. 3.2 for details on naming). Zoom to see details.

Table 1. The tables show a comparison of our proposed approaches using multiple metrics. mIoU is mean IoU, mF1 is mean F1 score, FN is the count of false negative images, FP is the count of false positive images, C_IoU is crack IoU, C_P is crack precision, C_R is crack recall, C_F1 is crack F1 score and B_F1 is background F1 score.

(a) The results here are obtained using the 2D Unet models with an resnet50 [11] backbone as the encoder.

Approach	mIoU	mF1	FN	FP	C_IoU	B_IoU	C_P	C_R	C_F1	B_F1
Baseline	0.73	0.82	20	32	0.485	0.98	0.73	0.60	0.640	0.99
Baseline+	0.75	0.83	22	30	0.515	0.98	0.72	0.65	0.676	0.99
SW	0.71	0.80	16	11	0.464	0.96	0.51	0.89	0.624	0.98
SW 94	0.75	0.83	21	2	0.526	0.98	0.67	0.76	0.680	0.99
SW 95	0.75	0.83	22	2	0.526	0.98	0.68	0.74	0.680	0.99
SW 96	0.75	0.83	22	1	0.525	0.98	0.70	0.71	0.678	0.99

(b) The results here are obtained using the 2D Unet models with an efficientnetb4 [12] backbone as the encoder.

Approach	mIoU	mF1	FN	FP	C_IoU	B_IoU	C_P	C_R	C_F1	B_F1
BaseLine	0.76	0.84	5	2	0.543	0.98	0.78	0.65	0.689	0.99
BaseLine+	0.77	0.85	15	6	0.557	0.98	0.73	0.71	0.705	0.99
SW	0.71	0.80	8	4	0.458	0.96	0.49	0.93	0.615	0.98
SW 94	0.76	0.84	11	2	0.550	0.98	0.66	0.81	0.699	0.99
SW 95	0.76	0.84	12	1	0.553	0.98	0.68	0.78	0.701	0.99
SW 96	0.77	0.84	11	1	0.552	0.98	0.70	0.75	0.700	0.99

truth has no crack pixles (there are 'noncrack' images in the dataset which do not have any cracks). Similarly, FN (false negative) in Tables 2a and 2b is calculated with respect to an image i.e. a prediction is called as false negative if it contains no crack pixels and the ground truth contains crack pixels.

Overall, the SW 95 approach has the highest crack IoU and crack F1 amongst all the approaches.

Table 2. The tables show a comparison of the crack IoU of all the methods on various datasets.

(a) The results here are obtained on multiple test datasets using the 2D Unet models with n resnet50 [11] backbone as the encoder.

Dataset	BaseLine	BaseLine+	SW	SW 94	SW 95	SW 96
Sylvie Chambon	0.262	0.165	0.495	0.298	0.278	0.254
Eugen Muller	0.342	0.548	0.531	0.626	0.625	0.619
CRACK500	0.552	0.584	0.578	0.555	0.547	0.534
cracktree200	0.109	0.04	0.059	0.113	0.121	0.131
Volker	0.585	0.601	0.548	0.66	0.664	0.666
DeepCrack	0.669	0.684	0.491	0.625	0.634	0.645
forest	0.253	0.467	0.212	0.322	0.334	0.349
Rissbilder	0.474	0.503	0.395	0.525	0.533	0.54
GAPS384	0.282	0.331	0.366	0.333	0.315	0.29
CFD	0.276	0.459	0.186	0.287	0.299	0.315

(b) The results are obtained on multiple test datasets using the 2D Unet models with an efficientnetb4 [12] backbone as the encoder.

Dataset	BaseLine	BaseLine+	SW	SW 94	SW 95	SW 96
Sylvic Chambon	0.229	0.401	0.452	0.277	0.256	0.24
Eugen Muller	0.602	0.612	0.496	0.618	0.625	0.631
CRACK500	0.591	0.625	0.574	0.609	0.604	0.596
cracktree200	0.076	0.028	0.079	0.176	0.179	0.169
Volker	0.65	0.66	0.527	0.656	0.663	0.67
DeepCrack	0.747	0.726	0.511	0.685	0.696	0.705
forest	0.432	0.317	0.231	0.381	0.398	0.415
Rissbilder	0.51	0.524	0.381	0.52	0.529	0.536
GAPS384	0.41	0.413	0.365	0.374	0.356	0.327
CFD	0.401	0.301	0.212	0.356	0.373	0.39

Tables 2a and 2b show the crack IoU of our approaches over multiple datasets. It can be observed that thresholding results in a higher crack IoU as compared to SW over all datasets except Sylive Chambon where it reduces.

4.1   Observations

The images in Figs. 4a and 4b compare the Baseline, Baseline+, SW and SW <T> methods. Figures 4a(b), 4b(b), 4a(c) and 4b(c) show that our predictions are better than that of the ground truth mask. Figure 4b(j) shows that the left side portion of the crack is captured better in stochastic width experiment compared to the other methods.

It can be observed in the Figs. 4a and 4b that the boundary pixels in the thicker crack predictions from SW have been improved in SW 95 which is more precise. However, it is to be noted that there are some cases of disconnectivity in cracks in SW 95 predictions. The SW method captures the crack randomness effectively resulting in the least misses, thereby obtaining better connected cracks than other methods.

Figures 5a and 5b show the frequency plot all the crack images in the validation dataset having thresholds above 0.899 using the models trained with efficientnetb4 [12] and resnet50 [11] backbones respectively. Figures 5c and 5d show the frequency plot all the crack images in the validation dataset over all

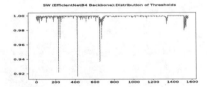

(a) Shows that the threshold distribution (from the bin: 0.899 to 0.999) of pixels in the prediction mask using the SW model trained using efficientnetb4 backbone

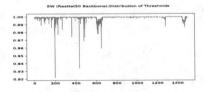

(b) Shows that the threshold distribution (from all bins: 0.899 to 0.999) of pixels in the prediction mask using the SW model trained using resnet50 backbone

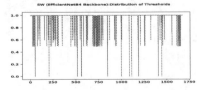

(c) Shows that the threshold distribution (from the bin: 0 to 0.999) of pixels in the prediction mask using the SW model trained using efficientnetb4 backbone

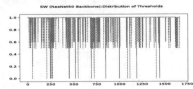

(d) Shows that the threshold distribution (from all bins: 0 to 0.999) of pixels in the prediction mask using the SW model trained using resnet50 backbone

Fig. 5. Shows the plot of threshold for each image in the val set (crack images)

thresholds using the models trained with efficientnetb4 [12] and resnet50 [11] backbones respectively.

It can be observed that most of the crack probabilities are above 0.899 and efficientnetb4 model has around 1600 images while resnet50 model has around 1450 images above threshold 0.899. This implies that efficient net model is better compared to the resnet50 model. The plot also visually validates the idea of binning discussed in Sect. 3.1.

5 Conclusion

We have shown that judiciously combining traditional approaches in a deep learning framework can result in significant boost in the performance of the crack detection algorithms. The proposed SW method results in better crack connectivity, reduces false positives and improves the crack detactability by a significant margin (see results in the Figs. 4a and 4b and Tables 1a, 1b). We have further refined the predictions based on the probabilities of each pixel in predicted masks. The thresholded masks obtain better estimates of "crack width" which further refines the predictions, improves the perceptual quality (shown in Figs. 4a and 4b), reduces the number of false positives (in terms of pixels), and improves the mIoU by a significant margin as listed in the Tables 1a and 2b.

Acknowledgements. We would like to thank GE Research for supporting our work. We would also like to thank the publishers of the kaggle crack segmentation dataset [16] which enabled us to conduct this study.

References

1. Dhital, D., Lee, J.R.: A fully non-contact ultrasonic propagation imaging system for closed surface crack evaluation. Exp. Mech. **52**(8), 1111–1122 (2012)
2. Liu, F., Xu, G., Yang, Y., Niu, X., Pan, Y.: Novel approach to pavement cracking automatic detection based on segment extending. In: 2008 International Symposium on Knowledge Acquisition and Modeling, pp. 610–614. IEEE (2008)
3. Hu, Y., Zhao, C.: A novel LBP based methods for pavement crack detection. J. Pattern Recogn. Res. **5**(1), 140–147 (2010)
4. Kapela, R., et al.: Asphalt surfaced pavement cracks detection based on histograms of oriented gradients. In: 2015 22nd International Conference Mixed Design of Integrated Circuits & Systems (MIXDES), pp. 579–584. IEEE (2015)
5. Zhou, J., Huang, P.S., Chiang, F.-P.: Wavelet-based pavement distress detection and evaluation. Opt. Eng. **45**(2), 027007 (2006)
6. Xu, H., Xiu, S., Wang, Y., Cai, H., Cui, K., Chen, X.: Automatic bridge crack detection using a convolutional neural network. Appl. Sci. **9**(14), 2867 (2019)
7. Zou, Q., Cao, Yu., Li, Q., Mao, Q., Wang, S.: CrackTree: automatic crack detection from pavement images. Pattern Recogn. Lett. **33**(3), 227–238 (2012)

8. Pandey, R.K., Ramakrishnan, A.G., Karmakar, S.: Effects of modifying the input features and the loss function on improving emotion classification. In: TENCON 2019-2019 IEEE Region 10 Conference (TENCON), pp. 1159–1162. IEEE (2019)

9. Pandey, R.K., Vignesh, K., Ramakrishnan, A.G.: Binary document image super resolution for improved readability and OCR performance. arXiv preprint arXiv:1812.02475 (2018)

10. Cubuk, E.D., Zoph, B., Shlens, J., Le, Q.V.: RandAugment: practical automated data augmentation with a reduced search space. In: Proceedings of the IEEE/CVF Conference on Computer Vision and Pattern Recognition Workshops, pp. 702–703 (2020)

11. He, K., Zhang, X., Ren, S., Sun, J.: Deep residual learning for image recognition. In: Proceedings of the IEEE Conference on Computer Vision and Pattern Recognition, pp. 770–778 (2016)

12. Tan, M., Le, Q.: EfficientNet: rethinking model scaling for convolutional neural networks. In: International Conference on Machine Learning, pp. 6105–6114. PMLR (2019)

13. Ronneberger, O., Fischer, P., Brox, T.: U-net: convolutional networks for biomedical image segmentation. In: Navab, N., Hornegger, J., Wells, W.M., Frangi, A.F. (eds.) MICCAI 2015. LNCS, vol. 9351, pp. 234–241. Springer, Cham (2015). https://doi.org/10.1007/978-3-319-24574-4_28

14. Zhang, Z., Sabuncu, M.: Generalized cross entropy loss for training deep neural networks with noisy labels. In: Advances in Neural Information Processing Systems, vol. 31 (2018)

15. Iakubovskii, P.: Segmentation models. GitHub. GitHub repository (2019). https://github.com/qubvel/segmentation_models

16. Kaggle Crack Segmentation Dataset. https://www.kaggle.com/datasets/lakshaymiddha/crack-segmentation-dataset. Accessed 2020

17. Zhang, L., Yang, F., Zhang, Y.D., Zhu, Y.J.: Road crack detection using deep convolutional neural network. In: 2016 IEEE International Conference on Image Processing (ICIP), pp. 3708–3712. IEEE (2016)

18. Yang, F., Zhang, L., Yu, S., Prokhorov, D., Mei, X., Ling, H.: Feature pyramid and hierarchical boosting network for pavement crack detection. IEEE Trans. Intell. Transp. Syst. 21(4), 1525–1535 (2019)

19. Eisenbach, M., et al.: How to get pavement distress detection ready for deep learning? A systematic approach. In: 2017 International Joint Conference on Neural Networks (IJCNN), pp. 2039–2047. IEEE (2017)

20. Shi, Y., Cui, L., Qi, Z., Meng, F., Chen, Z.: Automatic road crack detection using random structured forests. IEEE Trans. Intell. Transp. Syst. 17(12), 3434–3445 (2016)

21. Amhaz, R., Chambon, S., Idier, J., Baltazart, V.: Automatic crack detection on two-dimensional pavement images: An algorithm based on minimal path selection. IEEE Trans. Intell. Transp. Syst. 17(10), 2718–2729 (2016)

22. Deng, J., Dong, W., Socher, R., Li, L.-J., Li, K., Fei-Fei, L.: ImageNet: a large-scale hierarchical image database. In: 2009 IEEE Conference on Computer Vision and Pattern Recognition, pp. 248–255. IEEE (2009)

23. DeVries, T., Taylor, G.W.: Improved regularization of convolutional neural networks with cutout. arXiv preprint arXiv:1708.04552 (2017)

24. Kingma, D.P., Ba, J.: Adam: a method for stochastic optimization. arXiv preprint arXiv:1412.6980 (2014)

25. Chollet, F., et al.: Keras. GitHub (2015). https://github.com/fchollet/keras

26. Harris, C.R., et al.: Array programming with NumPy. Nature **585**(7825), 357–362 (2020)
27. Hunter, J.D.: Matplotlib: a 2D graphics environment. Comput. Sci. Eng. **9**(03), 90–95 (2007)
28. Buslaev, A., Iglovikov, V.I., Khvedchenya, E., Parinov, A., Druzhinin, M., Kalinin, A.A.: Albumentations: fast and flexible image augmentations. Information **11**(2), 125 (2020)

A Blockchain and Steganography Based Approach for Storing and Accessing Medical Images

Rohit Malik$^{(\boxtimes)}$ (ID), Parth (ID), Ishan Chourasia (ID), and Raghav Pande (ID)

Department of Electronics and Communication Engineering, Netaji Subhas University of Technology, New Delhi, India
rohit.ec19@nsut.ac.in

Abstract. In today's heavily digitalised world, cyber security is essential when it comes to safeguarding data and networks from malware attacks. Blockchain technology presents a data structure that is inherently secure. This paper extrapolates the concept of a blockchain to create an imagechain where the image itself acts as a block. The idea of an imagechain when combined with the technique of steganography enables us to hide data within an image. This study also addresses the difficulty in accessing medical images remotely, as in the current paradigm, patients usually have to rely on carrying a physical copy. The proposed imagechain creates a distributed network, allowing the concerned figure to access and retrieve the medical image from any node in the network. In essence, this study intends to improve the way medical images are shared across various stakeholders in a healthcare ecosystem and aims to provide a safe and secure model for the same using a combination of blockchain and image steganography.

Keywords: Blockchain · Steganography · Imagechain ·
Decentralization · DICOM · Medical Images

1 Introduction

With the world around us getting heavily digitalised, instances of cyber crimes have increased exponentially. All the industries are falling victim to cyber threats and the healthcare industry is no exception. A cyber attack on a healthcare centre could hamper the day-to-day functioning as well as compromise a huge amount of confidential patient data. While there could be numerous vulnerable points in the entire network concerning the healthcare industry, this study is centred around the vulnerability in the DICOM (Digital Imaging and Communications in Medicine) framework used to share medical images.

DICOM is an international standard for medical images and related information [1]. A DICOM file is made up of a header and image data sets that are all placed together in a single file. The file header consists of a 128-byte Preamble

H. Kaur et al. (Eds.): CVIP 2023, CCIS 2009, pp. 74–85, 2024.
https://doi.org/10.1007/978-3-031-58181-6_7

which helps in accessing the images and other data stored in the DICOM file. The data sets contain a multitude of information ranging from patient data to information about the image itself.

A paper titled 'DICOM Images Have Been Hacked! Now What?' [2] explains why DICOM file format preambles are a major flaw in design because they can be used to embed executable files and malicious software. The security lapse here is that there are no limitations to the data that can be inserted into the preamble, thus any 128-byte sequence can be placed there [3]. Hence, by altering the preamble, it is straightforward for hackers to piggyback malicious files along with the DICOM file without altering the image contained within.

The fact that these modifications are harder to detect by anti-malware software makes matters worse as it can lead to a huge spread of the malware in the entire healthcare system. Since these images are also shared between different hospitals, the spread of the malware is not bound to geography and can infect remote servers too, leading to a possible full-blown attack on the global healthcare system.

Also, the sensitive information contained in the data sets can be easily altered through any DICOM browser or dedicated editing software. Thus, it may lead to corruption and hence misuse of data.

Further medical images are currently stored in centralised networks such as medical institutions or third-party service databases, with heavy reliance on printed records and physical copies for transmitting them to different hospitals and healthcare providers for diagnostic purposes. Dependence on physical copies exposes patients to potential delays in their care pathway and erroneous research transcription due to their degradation over time.

Addressing the disadvantages and vulnerabilities in the present system as discussed above, it is prudent to look for alternatives. This paper proposes a two-pronged solution that eliminates the disadvantages of printed records via using digital non-DICOM images, and at the same time provides a novel method of transmitting patient data and other associated information within the image itself through the process of steganography. It further puts forward that the vulnerabilities of a centralised system to access images can be overcome by shifting to a decentralised network, ensuring the integrity of the data.

The paper is organized in 5 sections. Various terminologies associated with the ideas discussed in the paper are described in Sect. 2. Algorithms, their implementation and trade-offs between different image formats that could be used for the platform are discussed in Sect. 3. A description of the platform and simulation results can be found in Sect. 4. Section 5 summarizes the paper.

2   Key Terms

2.1   Blockchain

The simplest definition of the blockchain is a distributed ledger technology that is decentralised and allows for community sharing of information [4]. Due to the distributed nature of blockchain technology, it is very hard to hack or compromise the entire system. Blockchain, as a result, is a tamper-proof technology. The previous transactions cannot be modified or destroyed [5]. The network is robust in its unstructured simplicity [6] and offers all previous transactions transparency and immutability.

2.2 Blockchain in Healthcare and Medical Imaging

A blockchain can be used as a digitalized and distributed cryptographic database where medical data can be securely stored and controlled [7]. Further, it can provide radiology departments with a platform for efficient data management, that includes clinical activities for educational and research use cases. Also, medical imaging data is susceptible to malicious alteration. Patel in his paper outlined a blockchain system that allows patients to be the owner of their imaging data and regulate access privileges to healthcare providers without the requirement for a mediator [8].

2.3 Imagechain

The motivation for this paper is to link together related digital images with each other, providing ease of access to a record of images all across the network, without any centralized intervention. For this reason, this work aims to create a blockchain-based model in which images are directly linked and no additional files are required.

A paper by Katarzyna Koptyra and Marek R. Ogiela [9] proposes a new method of chaining digital images which is based on the blockchain. A key feature that sets imagechain apart from existing solutions is that the images are directly linked, i.e. a separate chain for storing only metadata or URL to the image is not required. Rather, the image itself becomes the building block in the chain. This is achieved by inserting blocks of data in the image(through the manipulation of its metadata). Further, joining is done using the hash values of the images.

2.4 Steganography

The practice of steganography involves concealing information (message) in another digital information medium or carrier (such as image, video or audio). It is done in a way that prevents an intrusive party or undesirable personnel from recognising the embedded information's presence. Steganography techniques can be implemented either in the transform domain or in the spatial domain of the carrier. As the size of the message to be encoded increases, the number of variations from the original image (artefacts) that are produced in the steganographed image increases.

Since we are working with medical images, it is crucial that the steganographic version of the image achieves the highest level of clinical reading clarity with minimal perceptual variation from the original to avoid any potential misdiagnosis.

Referring to [10], we have opted for a steganographic algorithm that first requires dividing the image into blocks of size 8×8. The message is then embedded in the LSB of the DCT coefficients of the blocks. Inverse DCT is then performed on each of the blocks and combined together to form the steganographic image. This method requires knowledge of the length of the message embedded at the receiver side for decoding.

To improve the robustness of the steganography process(to attacks such as compression), the message is embedded in the lower frequency regions of the DCT block. While this comes at the cost of reduced capacity as compared to the middle frequency region, the capacity is sufficient for a typical medical report(usually around 1–1.5 kB) (Fig. 1).

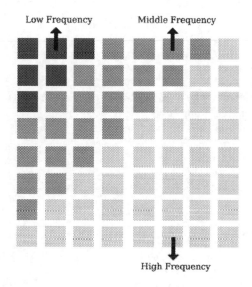

Fig. 1. Frequency Region of DCT Coefficients

3   Implementation

3.1   Working of Imagechain

Imagechain works in the same way as a blockchain i.e. a chain of images instead of blocks, with each image consisting of three components: data, hash, and the previous image's hash. The stitching of these images is done on hash values (set-length digests of variable-sized inputs). Each image stores information which includes the hash of the previous image and further roots to all its predecessors in a reverse linked list fashion.

To generate independent imagechain blocks and comprehend them, the steps are as follows:

1. The Embedding function, to add the hash information in the image file
2. The Extracting function

Their roles are inverse of each other and both the methods are public to all the participants running the blockchain nodes. Each image has the embedded data in the format - Block number, Timestamp, previous hash.

3.2   Imagechain Algorithm

Algorithm 1. Imagechain Algorithm

1: **procedure** INITIALIZE CHAIN
2:      $TailNode \leftarrow$ latest block in the imagechain
3:      $JSON\ File \leftarrow$ keeps track of the state of the chain
4:      **if** $TailNode$ is $NULL$ **then**
5:          Chain initialized with a genesis image
6:      **else**
7:          Generate SHA-256 hash of the new image(tail of the chain)
8:          Get current timestamp in yyyy-mm-dd hh:mm:ss.microSeconds format
9:          Add Timestamp and the hash of the previous block to the current image metadata
10:         Save the updated image
11:         Update the $TailNode$
12:         Update the $JSON\ File$ to record the changes
13:     **end if**
14: **end procedure**

3.3   Steganography Algorithm

Embedding Algorithm: The input image is first divided into blocks of size 8×8 and the message to be embedded, patient's data, is converted into a stream of bits. Going block by block, first their DCT coefficients are computed and then their LSBs are replaced by the bits of the message bit stream (Fig. 3).

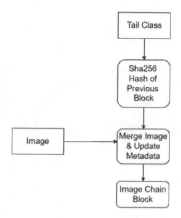

Fig. 2. Imagechain Algorithm

Algorithm 2. Embedding Process

Input: Medical image scan, Message bit stream
Output: Steganographic image
1: *Initialisation* : Image divided into 8x8 blocks (*blocks*), Message bit stream (*m*),
     $i = 0$, Length of $m(N)$
2: **while** *block* in *blocks* **do**
3:     compute DCT coefficients of *block*
4:     **for** $x = 0$ to 7 **do**
5:         **for** $y = 0$ to 7 **do**   ▷ replace LSB of coefficients with message bit stream
6:             **if** $i < N$ **then**
7:                 $b \leftarrow m[i]$
8:                 $block[x, y] \leftarrow block[x, y] \oplus b$
9:                 $i \leftarrow i + 1$
10:             **else**
11:                 **break**
12:             **end if**
13:         **end for**
14:     **end for**
15:     compute IDCT of *block* and insert into steganographic image
16: **end while**
17: insert remaining blocks into the steganographic image as is

---

Extraction Algorithm: The message, the patient's data or report in this case, is extracted from the steganographic image using the prior information about the length of the embedded message (Fig. 4).

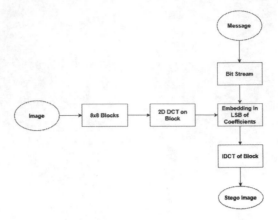

Fig. 3. Embedding Process of Steganography

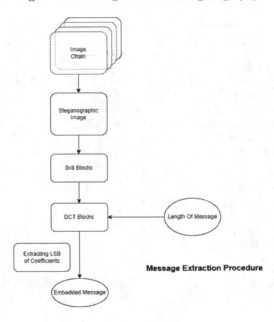

Fig. 4. Extraction Process of Steganography

3.4   Steganography Based Imagechain

The entire discussion till now has led up to this novel idea of combining the technologies behind steganography and imagechain. This approach combines the previously mentioned algorithms of steganography and imagechain. The entire algorithm is described as follows -

---

Algorithm 3. Extraction Process

Input: Steganographic Image, Length of message(N)
Output: Message
1: *Initialisation* : Image divided into 8x8 blocks (*blocks*), Message array(m), $i = 0$
2: **while** *block* in *blocks* **do**
3:      compute DCT coefficients of *block*
4:      **for** $x = 0$ to 7 **do**
5:          **for** $y = 0$ to 7 **do**
6:              **if** $i < N$ **then**
7:                  $m[i] \leftarrow block[x, y]$ **mod** 2
8:                  $i \leftarrow i + 1$
9:              **else**
10:                     **break**
11:              **end if**
12:          **end for**
13:      **end for**
14: **end while**
15: construct message from bitstream array m

Algorithm 4. Combined Algorithm

1: **procedure** UPDATING CHAIN
2:      Encrypted message(report/patient data) bit stream is generated
3:      Message embedded within the image using the steganography algorithm
4:      **if** *patient (unique id)* does not *exist* **then**
5:          Initialize chain
6:      **end if**
7:      Add hash of the previous image to the metadata of the current image
8:      Image is now part of the *patient's chain*
9: **end procedure**
10: **procedure** READING IMAGE
11:      Embedded message retrieved using the extraction algorithm
12:      Message decrypted
13:      Patient data can be viewed alongside the medical scan
14: **end procedure**

3.5   Choice of Image Format

Initially, PNG was chosen as the format for the Medical Images. However, after the steganography process, there were instances where the output image had floating-point pixel values. This was a result of embedding the information in the DCT coefficients and then taking an inverse transform to generate the output image. TIFF, or Tagged Image File Format provides a lossless way to store raster images. TIFF can handle floating point values as it uses up to 32 bits per pixel as opposed to 8 bits per pixel in the case of a PNG file, which can only handle integral pixel values. This ensured the correct decoding of the hidden message. Further, TIFF provides an easy way to manipulate metadata through Tags. Different tags were used to store imagechain data in the image file.

4 Simulations

4.1 Steganography Domain Comparison

Sample images used for the simulations are 512×512 TIFF files of MRI Scans (converted from DICOM format), sourced from the Patient Contributed Image Repository (PCIR). A 20 kB dummy text was embedded into the image through steganography in different domains(roughly 61.23% image is altered).

Both - steganography in the frequency as well as the spatial domain, generated excellent results in terms of SSIM values and didn't produce any significant artefacts, but overall steganography in the frequency domain performed better, producing images that were almost identical to the original with no discernible differences (Table 1).

Table 1. Quality comparison of Steganography in Spatial and Frequency domain with different sample medical images

Image	SSIM	PSNR
a) Sample image 1		
Spatial domain	0.9903	70.6412 dB
Frequency domain	0.9999	121.864 dB
b) Sample image 2		
Spatial domain	0.9769	61.5736 dB
Frequency domain	0.9999	122.3464 dB
c) Sample image 3		
Spatial domain	0.9945	79.011 dB
Frequency domain	0.9999	122.1387 dB

With respect to PSNR values, the results were heavily skewed in favour of frequency domain Steganography, producing a 75% higher PSNR value on average as compared to the spatial domain.

4.2 Platform

Using an image of a Brain MRI scan from Masoudi, Mojtaba; Saadatmand-Tarzjan, Mahdi (2018) Collection and a typical MRI report, we ran a simulation of how we envision the platform to look (Fig. 5).

At the time of creation of a new user/patient, a unique ID has to be entered. In a real-world scenario, this unique ID will be issued by the government, which can even be an existing identification document/number.

Patients will have restricted view-only access to their reports. The ability to add and update records will lie with the healthcare centres and medical professionals. Patients can view their reports by putting in their unique ID along with a password set by them. Healthcare stakeholders will have their own government issued unique ID that lets them log in to the platform to make changes.

Adding and updating records to the patient's chain will require a two-factor approval. One by the healthcare centre or medical professional and the other by the patient. If the patient is unable to grant the approval, it must be given by a previously approved medical practitioner who has worked on the patient's prior cases or by a person the patient designates.

Using the option menu, new scans and reports can be added or the previous ones be updated. If a certain patient was previously in the system, all files relevant to that patient that were already there would be displayed. Opening a particular scan displays the steganogrpahic image alongside the report embedded in it.

Tampering with the patient data will set off an alert, indicating the corruption of the blockchain. When this happens, the last correct version of the chain would be fetched. Till then any new uploads or changes will be blocked, protecting the integrity of data on the platform.

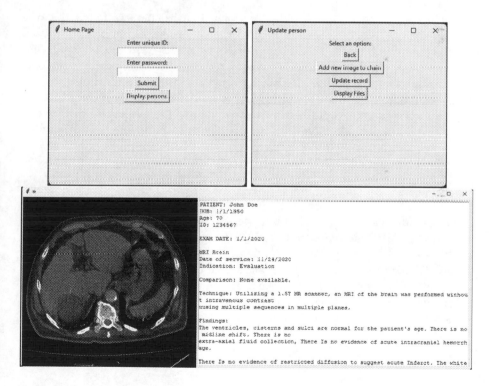

Fig. 5. Screenshots of the work-in-progress platform

5   Conclusion

Through our literature survey, we were able to identify problems with the current system of sharing Medical Images and further develop a plan to mitigate them with our proposed solution. We used an extension of the blockchain concept to create an imagechain and we explored the idea of a decentralised network of medical images.

We implemented steganography to embed the relevant patient information as well as the corresponding medical report, which removes the dependency on DICOM images. We were also able to perform testing with an initial algorithm chosen for steganography which produced satisfactory results. Two approaches - steganography in the spatial and the frequency domains were implemented, and the latter was preferred as it produced higher PSNR and SSIM values.

Addressing the disadvantages and vulnerabilities of DICOM, we believe that it is essential to consider alternative image formats for medical images. Increased use of soft copies over physical copies will by default eliminate the disadvantages of printed records as mentioned previously.

Further, as demonstrated in later sections of this paper, we found that the transmission of patient data and other relevant information can be done within the image itself through the process of steganography. We also showed that the vulnerabilities of a centralised system to access images can be overcome by shifting to a decentralised network, based on the novel technology of an imagechain. Since it is built upon the foundation of blockchain technology, the proposed imagechain network becomes a lot more secure by definition. Unlike a centralised network, where tampering with a file might go unnoticed, the network proposed by us is tamper-proof.

Appendix

- Sample Medical Images: Masoudi, Mojtaba; Saadatmand-Tarzjan, Mahdi (2018): FUMPE. figshare. Collection. https://doi.org/10.6084/m9.figshare.c.4107803.v1
- Sample Medical Images: Patient Contributed Image Repository(PCIR), Available at: http://www.pcir.org/researchers/downloads_available.html
- MicroDicom: https://www.microdicom.com/
- Flow Charts: https://app.diagrams.net/

References

1. About DICOM. https://www.dicomstandard.org/about-home. Accessed 3 Dec 2022
2. Desjardins, B., Mirsky, Y., Ortiz, M.P., et al.: DICOM images have been hacked! now what? AJR Am. J. Roentgenol. **214**(4), 727–735 (2020). https://doi.org/10.2214/AJR.19.21958

3. HIPAA-Protected Malware? Exploiting DICOM Flaw to Embed Malware in CT/MRI Imagery. https://www.gisconsulting.in/hipaa-protected-malware-misusing-dicom-flaw-to-embed-malware-in-ct-mri-imagery/. Accessed 5 Sept 2022
4. Suman, Kumar, A., Patel, M.: An Introduction to Blockchain Technology and Its Application in Libraries, 28 December 2021. SSRN: https://ssrn.com/abstract=4019394 or https://doi.org/10.2139/ssrn.4019394
5. Forsström S.: Blockchain Research Report (2019)
6. Nakamoto S.: Bitcoin: a peer-to-peer electronic cash system, 2009, 2012. http://www.bitcoin.org/bitcoin.pdf
7. Kuo, T.T., Kim, H.E., Ohno-Machado, L.: Blockchain distributed ledger technologies for biomedical and health care applications. J. Am. Med. Inform. Assoc. **24**(6), 1211–1220 (2017). https://doi.org/10.1093/jamia/ocx068
8. Patel, V.: A framework for secure and decentralized sharing of medical imaging data via blockchain consensus. Health Inform. J. **25**(4), 1398–1411 (2019). https://doi.org/10.1177/1460458218769699
9. Koptyra, K., Ogiela, M.R.: Imagechain-application of blockchain technology for images. Sensors (Basel) **21**(1), 82 (2020). https://doi.org/10.3390/s21010082. PMID: 33375606; PMCID: PMC7796195
10. Mahesh, K., Munesh, Y.: Image steganography using frequency domain. Int. J. Sci. Technol. Res. **3**(9) (2014). ISSN 2277-8616

Enhanced On-Device Video Summarization Using Audio and Visual Features

Lokesh kumar Thandaga Nagaraju$^{(\boxtimes)}$, Ranjitha B, and Jani Basha Shaik

Samsung R and D Institute India - Bangalore, Bangalore, Karnataka, India
{nagaraju,b.ranjitha,jani.sk}@samsung.com

Abstract. Video Summarization is gaining popularity, as there is lot of content available. Video Summarization is about determining the key or primary moments in the video. Hence, the most important step in a video summarization technique is identifying the key moments. While most of the related works are based on generating video summaries using only visual features, few recent studies have explored a better approach that utilizes the audio of the video along with the visual features. While considering the use of audio, it is very crucial to understand the correlation between the visual and audio features. However, while dealing with a constrained environment like embedded devices and smartphones, one has to consider the limitations of the resources available as well. Though using audio is found to improve the summary generated of the video, the resources of a mobile environment are hard constraints and one has to leverage the resources wisely. In this paper, we present a novel approach which demonstrates a different method to make use of audio features along with visual cues in video summarization. The proposed approach uses different models for inferencing from audio and visual features and provides an exhaustive approach on engineering both the features intelligently. Using different neural network models for audio and visual features makes it feasible to use in a mobile environment.

Keywords: Video Summarization · Embedded Devices · AudioVisual Analysis

1 Introduction

In the era of technology, where content generation either in the form of video or image is being used on a daily basis, video summarization is gaining popularity ever so increasingly. The use of video summarization is not only limited to get an overview of the original video, but it can also be used in content storage, video retrieval and indexing. Due to the huge volume of media available at the disposal of the end users, most of the users are more likely to be interested in watching a glimpse of the contents in the video before watching the full video. Therefore, it becomes even more important to provide a meaningful and complete summary of the original video.

Since video summarization is very subjective to each individual and everyone might have their own, often contradictory, opinion of what a summarization of a video should contain, it becomes crucial to define video summarization before dwelling in detail. Most

H. Kaur et al. (Eds.): CVIP 2023, CCIS 2009, pp. 86–98, 2024.
https://doi.org/10.1007/978-3-031-58181-6_8

of the existing works define "video summarization" as extracting the key moments and most important part of the video. However, as one can observe this is not a very definitive definition of video summarization, as the important parts of the video are subjected to differ based on individual's perspective. So defining the key moments and important parts of the video will be crucial in order to remove the subjective part to some extent, if not completely. The key moments of the video are defined as that part of video which when watched by a user, should be able to dissect or grasp an idea as to what might have happened in the remaining parts of the video. However, the idea that the user gets after watching the summarized video might be wrong, due to the unforeseen variability of the video, but the summarized video should be sufficient to generate a possible sequence of events in the full video. The primary purpose of the presented video summarization technique is not in correctness of the stated sequence, but in-fact in the generation of the sequence that is expected by the end users. A summary of the video is complete if the summary is able to give the possibility of all the events present in the video. Again, the summary should present the idea of the event though it might be wrong. However, it should not be an addition of an event that the end user could think of, but rather a correction.

Lot of efforts have been done in order to generate the most comprehensive summary automatically. Most of the research presented so far, can be broadly classified into two methods.

- The first method mainly focuses on dividing the whole video into a sequence of segments and scoring each segments based on its interestingness. The final video summary is then generated by picking the segments that have high interestingness score.
- The second method focuses on scoring individual frames and selecting the best sequence of frames for generation of video summary.

However, in both the approaches the use of audio is kept to minimal. In-fact, though researchers have been trying different approaches for generation of the best summary, audio feature of media was not explored until recent.

In recent studies in the video summarization field, the approaches that has explored audio as a feature for summary generation, use the audio in its raw format in-conjunction with visual features. Using audio along with visual feature gives the complete ownership of engineering the correlation between audio and visual features to the model. However, in such cases, it is difficult to disentangle the importance of visual and audio features. Also, such complex models are difficult to be used in mobile devices due to hardware constraints [1]. Therefore, the proposed approach uses audio class labels instead of raw audio features. The audio class label denotes the class to which the audio belongs to (such as speech, clapping, etc.). The model is queried for the class of the audio at a constant interval of every 1 s. The audio class is then used to update the score of the segment accordingly.

In the proposed methodology module, a detailed information on the solution to effectively make use of audio in video summarization are discussed.

Key contributions:

- We proposed an enhanced approach that enables the use of audio in video summarization technique for mobile devices. The novelty is introduced by considering the use of audio as a catalyst rather than a core component for scoring the segments.
- The proposed methodology has also contributed in personalization of generation of video summaries based on user interests.
- We have achieved an f-measure score of 0.739 while the adopted method achieved 0.672.

2 Literature Survey

Among the existing works in the field of video summarization, some of the works that we found unique are described in this section. Munukutla et al. [2] presents a real-time video analysis technique for mobile platform, which aims to generate video summary instantaneously by analyzing the video during live camera. The novelty in the proposed system is carried in, by employing the camera activity information along with the frame data of the video, for generation of the video summary. The performance of the proposed system was compared with several other algorithms and results depicted the superiority of the proposed system's performance along with higher average f-measure score. But this approach does not consider audio features in the video summarization, which when used improves the quality of video summary generated. Zhao et al. [3] has proposed a Deep Learning based Video Summarization system called Audio Visual Recurrent Network, which utilizes both audio and visual information for generating the video summary. The system uses a GoogleNet based model and a VGG-based model for extraction of visual and audio features from the video respectively. Along with these, the proposed system is constructed with three important modules, which includes, two stream LSTM, fusion LSTM and a self attention video encoder module. It was concluded that the proposed system is dominantly better than the others because of its novelty in considering the audio features along with visual information.

Psallidas et al. [4] describes about the adopted machine learning based multimodal video summarization technique to produce dynamic summaries of the videos. The dynamic summaries of the videos are generated by selecting significant parts of the video while preserving its temporal order. The supervised binary classifier as machine learning model plays its role in selecting the significant parts of the video. After evaluating several algorithms using various metrics, it was concluded that Random Forest algorithm outperformed the other algorithms and has the best AUC score and F1 score. Haopeng et.al. [5] has proposed a multimodal self-supervised progressive video summarization framework to generate semantic representations of the videos. The modalities considered for self-supervised learning of semantic consistency in the videos are visual modality and text. The semantic consistency between the visual modality and texts are explored in both coarse-grained and fine-grained fashions. The multimodal network was designed with two unimodal encoders, text encoder and visual data encoders. It was inferred that the performance of the self-supervised pre-training improves significantly with increase in number of stages.

Though these approaches have been successful in developing better video summarization techniques, the use of complex deep learning models restricts its use on embedded systems such as mobile devices. To overcome this drawback and to be able to make use of camera activity information, our approach adopts the technique used in [2], while considering the use of audio features. The proposed system as brought in the novelty by engineering audio and visual features independently and leveraging the correlation between them.

3 Methodology

The proposed methodology primarily focuses on the effect of usage of audio in video summarization. For visual analysis of video, it was observed from literature survey that using camera activity information along with other visual features gives better results. So to incorporate the same and to showcase the effectiveness of audio features, the findings of the paper [2] has been adopted for extracting the visual features. Figure 1. Depicts the revised architecture of the system, which is adopted from [2]. The novelty of the disclosed architecture are highlighted in the same.

Given a video for summarization, the video is first divided into small clips called shots. A shot is defined as that smallest part of the video which when seen in isolation, the user does not feel that the video started or ended abruptly. When a shot ends, a new shot starts from the same timestamp. In other words, we define that a video is a continuous sequence of shots, where each shot itself has the potential to be an independent video without abrupt start or end. Each shot is an atomic unit, implying that a shot when further split at any point, neither of the two shots thus generated, satisfy the characteristics of a shot. A shot is further divided into segments of equal durations except for the last segment. Each segment is then scored based on the video and audio features present in that segment. This score is a measure of aesthetics present in the segment, usually referred to as interestingness score [2]. Visual score comprises of motion score, face score, event detection and camera activity information. Motion score captures the motion activity through histogram difference of the adjacent frames in the segment. Face score is the measure of number of human count present in the frame. The scenario in the frame, if present, such as jumping, dancing, etc., are detected through event detection module. Camera activity information refers to the came movement performed while capturing the video, such zoom, focus, etc. The audio score is based on the audio class labels. The audio class labels obtained from the audio classifier [1] every second, are stored for each segment along with its respective scores. These scores are later used in calculating the total interestingness score of the segments along with the total visual score of the segment. The same can be seen in Fig. 2.

A summary of the video is then generated by selecting the segments having high interestingness score across all the shots of the video, for the given duration of summary. Dividing the shots further into segments enables the ability to pick the best parts of the shots rather than the whole shot. Keeping the whole shot in the summary of a video is not a good choice as the interestingness score of a shot might be misleading. The interestingness score of a shot does not take the variability of the score within the shot, and hence would require localization of high scoring part of the shot. Further, scoring shots instead of segments would mean that either a whole shot is selected in the summary generated, or the whole shot is not. A summary thus selected would not be complete as discussed above.

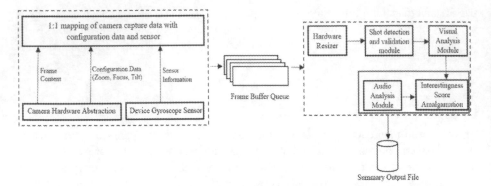

Fig. 1. High level Architecture.

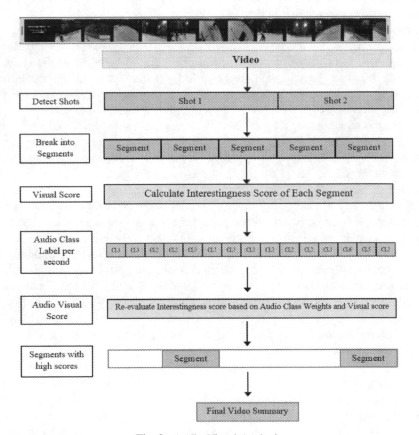

Fig. 2. Audio-Visual Analysis.

3.1 Audio as a Catalyst

The features used in the scoring criteria of a segment are broadly classified into two components: core and catalyst. A core component is the component that has some significance without any external factor. It can exist on its own and is unaffected by the presence or absence of any other feature. On the other hand, a catalyst is the component that enhances a core feature. It does not hold much significance when used independently but glorifies the core component and enhances its importance. Through the experimental results, the proposed work argues that audio features should be used as a catalyst and not a core. That is, the audio should be used as a feature that enhances the aesthetics of visual features rather than using it independently.

For the audio feature, rather than using the intermediate latent vectors [3] the class labels of the audio are used [6–9]. The incoming audio stream is passed through a audio classifier model. The audio classifier model [1] is polled every second to obtain the class label of the previous one-second content. The interval for polling the network is strategically opted to be one-second, as it is an optimal duration to obtain the class to that the audio belongs to, and thereby the need for localization is eliminated. Polling the model every one second for an audio class gives little scope for multiple audio classes to be present. However, it is to be noted that the scope of the proposed methodology is to emphasize on the usage of the audio class label in video summarization, and does not include the development of audio classifier itself.

The interestingness score of every segment is initially calculated based on its visual features [10, 11]. Later, the class of the audio is used to enhance the interestingness score of each segment. Each class 'c' of the audio class label set is given a pre-fixed weight, W_c, based on its significance. The classes that are more specific, such as 'flute', are given higher weightage than a generic class such as 'music'. The reason behind this is that the chances of finding specific class label in the video are less as compared to finding the generic class label. Thus, a generic class can be formed by any combination of specific classes, and the same is not true when the model predicts a specific class label. Hence, it becomes important to differentiate between the audio content that has a specific class label and a generic class label. For this reason, the classes that are more specific, are given higher weightage than the generic classes.

The interestingness score, S_i, is calculated as

$$S_i = \left[S_v \times \sum_{i=0}^{n} (W_{c_i}) \right] + S_v$$

where, n is the number of audio class labels in the segment, S_v is the interestingness score of the segment formed due to visual features and W_{c_i} is the audio class label weight for the ith audio class label of the segment.

It is to be noted that the interestingness score is a sum of core and catalyst component. The core component is represented through the visual features interestingness score, The catalyst component is a product of audio class weight and interestingness score obtained based on visual features. This implies that the scores of each segment will be enhanced by audio based on the interestingness of visual features, and audio class label alone cannot add to the value of the final interestingness score.

3.2 Diversity Over Consistency for Video Summarization

Another observation made was that using audio feature as a catalyst at all times was not a good option. For example, considering that a segment has 5 s of content and the audio classifier is polled every second for the audio class, then each segment will have 5 audio classes. Using all the five audio class labels did not prove to be efficient. Suppose a segment has the sequence of audio class labels as ['speech', 'speech', 'speech', 'speech', 'speech'], and another segment has ['speech', 'speech', 'clap', 'cheer', 'clap']. It can be observed that the second segment has the content of audience clapping and cheering to the speech of a person, while the first segment has only speech. Thus the second segment can be called the *happening* segment of the shot as the next event of the shot starts from the next segment. For the summary generation, the segment that represents all the segments in the shot has to be selected. In order to do so, it is important to differentiate between the *happening* segments from the *consistent* segments. This is done by enhancing the segment's interestingness score only once by a particular audio class. So the final segment scores, S_i, will now be calculated as,

$$S_i = \left[S_v \times \sum_{i=0}^{n} \left(W_{o_i} \times W_{c_i} \right) \right] + S_v$$

where, n is the number of audio class labels in the segment, W_{o_i} is 1 if audio class label is not found previously in the segment, else 0, W_{c_i} is the audio class label weight for the ith audio class label of the segment and S_v is the interestingness score of the segment formed due to visual features.

A summary of the video is complete when the summary contains segments of all the shots present in the video. One has to keep a check on the segment interestingness scores which has higher weight audio class labels, so that the segments of other shots stand a chance to get selected in the final summary generated. If not, the generated summary might contain segments of only few shots and the rest of the shots will be ignored. Deciding to use every audio class label only once per segment not only increases the chances of *happening* segments getting selected in the final summary but also improved the chances of a complete summary being generated, as every shot has only a small portion of their segments which qualify as *happening*.

3.3 Personalization Using User Perspective Weights

Due to the highly subjective nature of summary generation, it is hard for a single algorithm to satisfy every user. The summary generated by one algorithm might appear better for one person while the other might chose a different opinion. In order to satisfy all users, an algorithm has to be open to changes so that it can learn different perspectives of end users. The algorithm should try to learn what a particular user feels is the right combination for a perfect summary. The end users experiences the algorithm through the final selected segments and not through the interestingness score of the individual segments. The end user is not concerned with the interestingness score of the segment as long as the segment that the user feels is important, is present in the final summary generated. Hence, the algorithm is designed to learn the adaptive weights based on user preferences by taking a feedback through a rating, of how satisfied the user is with the generated summary. Based on the rating provided, the algorithm learns itself to generate different summaries that matches to the user's interests. In the subsequent usage, these learnings from the user perspective are adopted for generation of summarized videos.

Since the aim is to understand the user interests and deliver the summary satisfactory to the user. A mechanism to generate different summaries of the same video has been developed. Since, the segments that has high interestingness scores are selected for the summary of a video, a mechanism to change the interestingness score of the segments based on user's perspective is required. Therefore, an additional weight, W_u, which represents the user's perspective has been introduced. W_u represents the balance between a core and catalyst component of the interestingness score. Higher value of catalyst component means that more happening segments are prioritized. However, a user might be interested in some consistent segment as well. The weight of the core component is kept as constant at 1, while we modified the weight of the catalyst component. Changing the value of W_u, changes the scores of the segments, while still retaining high interestingness scores to the key segments. This enables the other segments with competing high interestingness scores, that were discarded in the current summary, to be selected. So the interestingness score, S_i, of a segment is now calculated as

$$ S_i = \left[W_u \times S_v \times \sum_{i=0}^{n} (W_{o_i} \times W_{c_i}) \right] + S_v $$

where, n is the number of audio class labels in the segment, W_u is the user perspective of the summary, W_{o_i} is 1 if audio class label is not found previously in the segment, else 0, W_{c_i} is the audio class label weight for the ith audio class label of the segment and S_v is the interestingness score of the segment formed due to visual features.

4 Experimental Setup

The proposed methodology has experimented the efficient way of using audio features in the video summarization technique for mobile devices. In order to verify the effectiveness of audio features, the proposed algorithm is compared with the adopted Video Summarization technique on Mobile Platform algorithm [2]. Along with this primary comparison, few experiments are performed to identify the efficient way of using audio in the video summarization technique and the results of the same are compared for inference. As previously proposed various algorithms were compared over SumMe dataset [12] using the F-measure score, the current methodology has also followed the same for evaluating the algorithms. This way it is made sure that the performance of all algorithms are compared using same dataset and metrics. Further, TVSum dataset is used to evaluate the effects of user perspective weights on unseen dataset.

As the proposed work has experimented different ways of using audio features, evaluation has been performed to compare the performance differences between the algorithms. The main two comparisons are, the audio being used as a core component vs as a catalyst for calculating the interesting score of the segments and another comparison is done between the algorithm which focuses on considering the diversity of audio class labels in a segment vs consistency of audio class labels.

For the comparison of the experimented methods, 12 videos from SumMe dataset, considered as test data and the TVSum dataset [13] are used to generate video summaries. The generated summaries were analyzed to obtained information of the segments that were selected from the original video to form a summary. Using the analyzed data, average f-measure was measured between the generated summary data and the ground truths obtained from a set of different users on those videos.

Another experiment that was performed was the use of user perspective weight in scoring criteria. Different users can have different perspectives of expecting the video summary. In order to make sure the generated video summaries are satisfactory for a particular user, an additional weight that represents the user's perspective was trained and experimented. Using SumMe dataset, different video summaries were generated based on different impact scales representing user's perspective. Based on the heuristics and experiments, five different values of W_u were selected to verify the similarities between the summaries generated using these weights. The analyzed data of generated summaries were used to calculate the similarity score using IOU [Intersection Over Union] value [14]. Closer the value is to one, more similar is the summaries generated. This way it can be observed on how similar/ varying the summaries obtained are to each other.

The primary focus of the proposed method is to develop an enhanced video summarization technique for mobile platforms. In order to measure the performance metrics for the same, an average battery consumption for generating summary of a video is calculated on a mobile device. It was inferred that the battery consumption for generating a summary for a video with an average duration of 3:20 min is 2.34 mAh.

5 Inference and Conclusion

Table 1, depicts the f-measure scores for 12 videos of SumMe dataset for comparison of the experimented methods that uses audio and the adopted method that does not use audio for the video summarization. All columns are numbered in the order, for easy inference. (1) and (2) represents the comparative results between the adopted method that uses only visual features and the proposed model that uses audio as a catalyst along with visual features, while considering the importance of diversity of audio class labels. The proposed method signifying the use of audio, out-performed the adopted method with an f-measure value of 0.74. From the average f-measure values of both the methods, it can be concluded that, the proposed method generates better summaries than that, which does not uses audio.

Similarly, (2) and (3), compares the methods that use audio as a catalyst in scoring the segments is significantly better than audio being used as a core component to the scores of the segments. This proves the importance of considering the correlation between the visual and audio features in the video. This helps in reducing the false-positive segments in the summaries that can be caused due to the redundant background noise in the videos. (2) and (4), contains the f-measure scores of all videos generated for the methods considering the importance of diversity and consistency of audio class labels in each segment respectively. The method considering the importance of diversity of audio class labels in a segment has an average f-measure score of 0.74, which is greater than the method that does not consider it. This explains another way of reducing false positives

Table 1. Comparative results of the proposed method and other experimented methods (SumMe dataset)

Videos	Only Visual Features(1)	Visual and audio features [Diversity*](2)	Visual and Audio features as Core(3)	Video and Audio features [Consistency#](4)
Air Force One	0.871	1.416	0.871	1.071
Base jumping	0.464	1.111	0.464	0.605
Bearpark climbing	0.879	1.146	0.879	1.288
Bus in Rock Tunnel	0.436	0.819	0.436	0.921
Cockpit Landing	0.543	0.609	0.543	0.552
Kids playing in leaves	0.510	0.320	0.510	0.344
Playing on water slide	0.362	0.276	0.362	0.512
Saving dolphines	1.271	0.601	1.271	0.703
Scuba	0.550	1.012	0.550	1.012
Statue of Liberty	0.823	0.409	0.823	0.291
Uncut Evening Flight	0.629	0.409	0.629	0.172
Valparaiso Downhill	0.730	0.747	0.730	0.904
Average	**0.672**	**0.739**	**0.672**	**0.698**

* Diversity: In each segment, audio class labels are considered only once for scoring, even if it occurs multiple times.

#Consistency: In each segment, audio class labels are considered for scoring including repetitions.

by not giving more importance to those segments with same audio class of higher score, than the segments with different audio classes, which represents the segments to be more happening with several events.

Table 2, is the tabulated results for analyzing the usage of user perspective weight. The table clearly indicates how the summaries are varying over different values. It can be observed that the closer the impact scale values or weights are, closer the similarity between the summaries, while still being different from each other. This indicates the possibility of tuning the user perspective weight according to the user edits on the generated summary. This way, better video summaries that are personalized based on user's interests can be generated. Figure 3, depicts that as the user perspective weights increases, the segments with more diverse audio class labels are selected for the summary. For each user perspective weight, the solid uniform colored lines represents the segments selected along the duration of the video(Legend Segments: Weights) and the doted continuous lines represents the audio class labels in the segment, where each dot represents audio class at that second(Legend: Audio Class Labels).

Similar to Table 1 and Table 3 tabulates the F-measure score over the TVSum dataset to compare the efficiency of the summaries generated. The table compares the results for the approach that uses only visual features (1) with the proposed approach that uses both audio and visual features (2). Using the proposed approach, the results are captured for different user perspective weights for comparison of the efficiency and to analyze how the weights affect the F-measure score. From the table, it can be clearly concluded that the proposed method outperforms the adopted approach. It can be seen that varying the user perspective weight produces different but competitive F-measure score. This seconds our observation, that user perspective weight can be used to generate qualitative summaries based on the interests of a user.

Table 2. Intersection over Union score of video summaries for different user perspective weights

User Perspective Weights	0.8	1.4	2.2	3.5	4.5
0.8	1	0.867	0.759	0.673	0.662
1.4	0.867	1	0.867	0.749	0.735
2.2	0.759	0.867	1	0.824	0.810
3.5	0.673	0.749	0.824	1	0.961
4.5	0.662	0.735	0.810	0.961	1

Table 3. Comparative results of the proposed method with different weights and the adopted method using only visual features over TVSum dataset

User Perspective Weights	F-measure Score
Only Visual Feature [1]	0.489
(Audio + Visual) 0.8	0.510
(Audio + Visual) 1.4	0.509
(Audio + Visual) 2.2	0.520
(Audio + Visual) 3.5	0.523
(Audio + Visual) 4.5	0.531
(Audio + Visual) 5.5	0.532

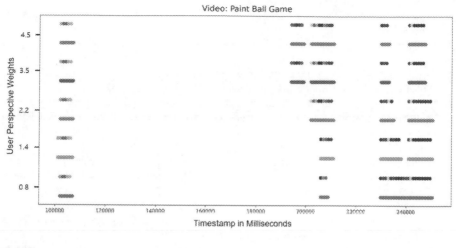

Fig. 3. Impact of user perspective weights on segment selection and their audio classes.

6 Conclusion

Audio feature was not explored until recently in the video summarization technique. But, the recent the literatures has proved that using audio feature in video summarization enhances the quality of the summarized video. However, these systems were not designed to be feasible in mobile environment. Therefore, in this paper, we provide a technique to overcome these challenges. Based on our results, we conclude that audio can play a major role in video summarization. The paper not only brings out an efficient approach to make use of audio in video summarization but also introduces personalized video summarization based on user interests in a mobile environment. Our results prove that the proposed system efficiency is over the existing prior arts. The suggested approach of personalization can further be explored in video edits such as auto background music genre selection.

References

1. Choudhary, S.: LEAN: Light and Efficient Audio Classification Network. In: 2022 IEEE 19th India Council International Conference (INDICON), pp. 1–6 (2022)
2. Choudhary, P.: Real time video summarization on mobile platform. In: IEEE International Conference on Multimedia and Expo (ICME), 1045–1050 (2017)

3. Zhao, B.: Audiovisual video summarization. IEEE Trans. Neural Network Learn. Syst. **34**(8), 5181–5188 (2021)
4. Psallidas, T.: Multimodal summarization of user-generated videos. Appl. Sci. **11**(11), 5260 (2021)
5. Li, H.: Progressive video summarization visa multimodal self-supervised learning. IEEE/CVF Winter Conference on Applications of Computer Vision, pp. 5584–5593 (2023)
6. Wang, Y.: Audio-based multimedia event detection using deep recurrent neural networks In: IEEE International Conference on Acoustics, Speech and Signal Processing (ICASSP), pp. 2742–2746 (2016)
7. Veluri, B.: Real-Time target sound extraction. arXiv:2211.02250 (2022)
8. Bahmei, B.: CNN-RNN and data augmentation using deep convolution generative adversarial network for environmental sound classification. IEEE Signal Process. Lett. **29**, 682–686 (2022)
9. Delcroxic, M.: Soundbeam: target sound extraction conditioned on sound-class labels and enrollment clues for increased performance and continuous learning. IEEE/ACM Trans. Audio, Speech Lang. Process. **31**, 121–136 (2022)
10. Veerakumar, T.: Shot Boundary detection from lecture video sequences using histogram of oriented gradients and radiometric correlation. Smart computer vision. Springer international publishing, 35–59 (2023) https://doi.org/10.1007/978-3-031-20541-5_2
11. Sheena, C.V.: Key-frame extraction by analysis of histograms of video frames using statistical methods. Proc. Comput. Sci. **70**, 36–40 (2015)
12. Gygli, M., Grabner, H., Riemenschneider, H., Van Gool, L.: Creating Summaries from User Videos. In: Fleet, D., Pajdla, T., Schiele, B., Tuytelaars, T. (eds.) ECCV 2014. LNCS, vol. 8695, pp. 505–520. Springer, Cham (2014). https://doi.org/10.1007/978-3-319-10584-0_33
13. Yale, S.: TVSum: summarizing web videos using titles, In: IEEE Conference on Computer Vision and Pattern Recognition, pp. 5179–5187 (2015)
14. Eric Hofesmann, IoU a better detection evaluation metric, https://towardsdatascience.com/iou-a-better-detection-evaluation-metric-45a511185be1, Accessed 30 Mar 2023

Fractal-Based Approach to Secure Key Generation from Fingerprint and Iris Biometrics

Priyabrata Dash[1]([✉]) [iD], Monalisa Sarma[2] [iD], and Debasis Samanta[3] [iD]

[1] Advanced Technology Development Center, Indian Institute of Technology Kharagpur, Kharagpur, India
priya.fav67@iitkgp.ac.in

[2] Subir Chowdhury School of Quality and Reliability, Indian Institute of Technology Kharagpur, Kharagpur, India
monalisa@iitkgp.ac.in

[3] Department of Computer Science and Engineering, Indian Institute of Technology Kharagpur, Kharagpur, India
dsamanta@iitkgp.ac.in

Abstract. The generation of keys from users' biometric data is gaining popularity in biometric-based cryptography systems. In such a system, managing keys and maintaining the security of biometric data are two challenging tasks. Existing methods, in general, use direct application of biometric templates, which can reveal the user's biometric data and thus useless for future applications once it is compromised. To address this issue, researchers advocate multimodal biometrics combining two or more traits. This work aims generating a key from a person's multimodal biometric traits with two modes: fingerprint, and iris. The work proposes a representation learning-based feature extraction for robust features from the reconstructed and latent image spaces. It utilizes a locally invariant segmented-based fractal texture descriptor to extract scale, rotation, and translation-invariant features from the regions of interest (ROIs) in fingerprint and iris images. The feature vectors from two modalities are then fused to form a single feature vector. A quantization mechanism is applied to generate a stable and unique key. The efficacy of the proposed method was evaluated through a number of experiments with multimodal datasets. The uniqueness, dissimilarity, and randomness analyses revealed the usefulness of the proposed approach against several security threats. Indeed, the proposed method offers a promising solution for generating secure keys from multimodal biometric traits.

Keywords: Multimodal biometrics · Biometric cryptosystem · Key generation from biometric · Fractal-based texture extraction

H. Kaur et al. (Eds.): CVIP 2023, CCIS 2009, pp. 99–111, 2024.
https://doi.org/10.1007/978-3-031-58181-6_9

1   Introduction

Advancements in big data, Cloud computing, IoT, and Blockchain have transformed society, but information security and digital identity must be prioritized for sustainable growth. Recently, biometric information has emerged as a favored form of identity information, given its inherent uniqueness. However, unimodal systems are vulnerable. Multimodal biometric systems offer better accuracy and security. However, they still have flaws that could lead to biometric information leakage. Biometric cryptosystems merge biometrics and cryptography to address these concerns. The aim is to leverage the benefits of both techniques while compensating for their limitations. This approach can help overcome the challenges of securing biometric information against malicious use.

The most crucial element in a cryptographic algorithm is the cryptographic key, also known as the secret key. Current static key generation mechanisms, such as fuzzy commitment or fuzzy vault techniques [8], have been used, but there is a growing need for dynamic key generation from biometric data for online authentication while avoiding the storage of biometric data [9]. Generating secret keys from biometric data has gained significant attention in recent years, with a focus on addressing two primary issues. Firstly, ensuring the accuracy of the biometric key and preventing unauthorized access or leakage of users' biometric data. Secondly, developing fault-tolerant generation techniques that reduce intra-variations and inter-similarity of the keys. Additionally, for increased security and efficiency, the use of multimodal biometric keys has been explored. However, the generation technique for multimodal keys should also address the issues of revocability, unlinkability, privacy preservation, and dimensional reduction of the keys [8].

In this paper, we propose a novel technique for generating secret keys using an individual's fingerprint and iris, which can be used for various cryptographic applications. The proposed technique involves several steps. First, the acquired biometric images are pre-processed to enhance their quality. Then, regions of interest (ROIs) are selected from the latent and reconstructed images of the individual's fingerprints and irises, following a segmented-based fractal texture analysis (SFTA) approach (proposed by Costa et al. [4]). To further process the ROIs, we utilize an Extreme Learning Machine-based Auto-Encoder (ELM-AE) [15]to create latent and reconstructed representations of the ROIs in the image data. Subsequently, quantization and encoding techniques are applied to the extracted feature vectors to generate a secret key. The major contributions of this work are as follows:

- A unified system for generating cryptography keys from multimodal biometric data is proposed. The generated keys satisfy randomness, unlinkability, and revocability properties.
- The proposed method of SFTA-based features extraction from reconstructed and latent image space of a user's multimodal qualities outperforms the previous techniques of creating irreversible and stable keys.
- The proposed method is applicable to images with wavelengths in the near-infrared and visible ranges thus give a more widespread applications of it.

The rest of the paper is organized as follows: The existing key generation strategies based on various biometric features are discussed in Sect. 2. In Sect. 3, the proposed approach is presented. Experiments and experimental results are included in Sect. 4. Finally, Sect. 5 offers the conclusions.

2 Literature Survey

In biometric cryptosystems (BC), several mechanisms have been proposed in the literature for generating cryptographic keys (also known as users' identities or UIDs) from biometric data. Some approaches use one-way hash functions or user-defined algorithms, while others use key-binding systems. These mechanisms have been developed using various biometric modalities such as iris [5,14], facial features [2], and fingerprint minutiae [9,10,16]. Some key generation techniques include selecting stable bits in iris codes [14], using fuzzy commitment [8] and error-correcting codes [10,16] to generate random keys, and adopting unique encoding techniques [10]. Other methods involve utilizing feature encoding, and machine learning algorithms to generate biometric-based keys [2]. Some approaches also use multiple biometric features, such as iris codes, binary features of iris and face, binary strings, and point-set templates, and employ fuzzy commitment and bit selection techniques for securing the keys [7]. While there are many techniques for generating keys or UIDs from biometric data, each method has pros and cons. Some methods may suffer from issues such as leakage of biometric data, limited applicability to certain types of images, or reliance on specific biometric modalities. Further research is needed to investigate discriminative dynamic UID generation from multi-modal biometric templates, such as fingerprint and iris, to develop robust and secure biometric cryptosystems. In this research, we propose a method for creating biometric keys using multimodal biometric data. Section 3 illustrates the suggested scheme.

3 Proposed Method

This section discusses the proposed method of key generation from multimodal biometric traits. This work considered fingerprint and iris biometric data for the purpose. An overview of the work is shown in Fig. 1. The key generation steps have the following sub steps: ROI extraction, segmented-based fractal texture features extraction from reconstructed and latent image space and key generation from multimodal biometric.

3.1 ROI Extraction

For stable feature extraction, the entire region of every biometric trait is not used. As a result, an acceptable area is chosen in order to calculate the feature. According to the biometric trait, the suggested ROI extraction comprises of multiple sub-processes. The ROI is extracted separately from both the fingerprint and the iris in this scheme.

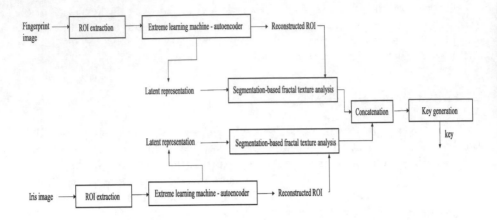

Fig. 1. The schematic diagram for key generation.

ROI Extraction from Fingerprint: The fingerprint is first given a basic pre-processing and enhancement. The pre-processing methods include robust and accurate segmentation as in approach, vertical alignment of the segmented fingerprint using the singular value decomposition method proposed in [11] and enhancement using Gabor filters as described in [11]. Finally, Walking Directional Fields (WDFs) are used to identify a singular point in an improved fingerprint image, as detailed in [18]. For feature extraction, a consistent region of size 64×64 is chosen around it.

ROI Extraction from Iris: There are various processes in the ROI extraction procedure. The Single Scale Retinex (SSR) strategy to normalizing an eye picture and reducing noisy pixels with a median filter [17] is used. Then, using the relative total variation model presented in [17], the iris structure is retrieved. In addition, a two-phase circular Hough transform is used to identify pupil and iris circle [17]. After that, a post-processing technique is used to accurately detect the iris region. Finally, Daugman's rubber sheet normalization is applied to the segmented iris image. Normalizing the iris region mitigates pupil size variations, but the entire region isn't conducive to feature extraction. Hence, a consistent iris region of 64×64 is obtained using the method proposed in [5].

3.2 Feature Extraction Using Representation Learning

This scheme extracts features from the fingerprint and iris's reconstructed and latent (abstract representation) ROI images. The latent and reconstructed ROI is generated using an Extreme Learning Machine-based Auto-Encoder(ELM-AE) [15]. Further, fractal features (i.e., from fingerprint F_{FIN} and from iris F_{IR}) are extracted from them. An overview of the work is shown in Fig. 2.

ELM-AE, or Extreme Learning Machine with autoencoder, exhibits remarkable training speed, surpassing that of backpropagation-based learning methods,

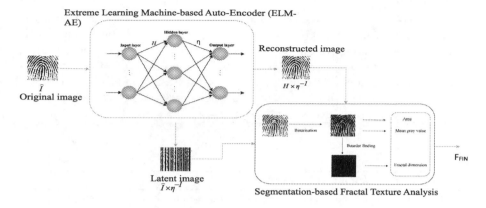

Fig. 2. The schematic diagram for representation learning based feature extraction

while also demonstrating superior pattern reconstruction capability. The ELM-AE mechanism to produce latent and reconstructed ROI image is depicted in the following paragraph. It is used to minimize the reconstruction error of input $\hat{I}$. Thus the objective function of ELM-AE with L2-norm is,

$$\min_{\eta} \frac{1}{2} \|\eta\|^2 + c\frac{1}{2} \left\|\hat{I} - H\eta\right\|^2 \tag{1}$$

where c is the regularization factor, η is output weight vector, and hidden layer output matrix $H = g(\text{input weight}(W) * \hat{I})$, where g is a sigmoid activation function. Then the gradient of above equation with respect to η is,

$$\nabla \eta = \eta - cH^T(\hat{I} - H\eta) \tag{2}$$

by setting gradient to zero, the optimal solution is obtained as:

$$\eta = \left(\frac{I}{c} + H^T H\right)^{-1} H^T \hat{I} \tag{3}$$

where I is an identity matrix. According to [15], $\eta = (H^T H)^{-1} H^T \hat{I}$. Thus the reconstructed ROI image $\hat{I}_r$ is $H \times \eta^{-1}$ and the latent ROI image $\hat{I}_{new}$ is $\hat{I} \times \eta^T$.

To get the optimal value of η, we have trained a model by splitting the dataset using the person split approach. In this case, two instances of each person are used for training, and all the remaining instances for testing. We used the root mean square error (RMSE) to analyze the proposed algorithm's performance. The optimal η calculation is given in Algorithm 1. The proposed approach obtained the optimal performance, i.e., root mean square error (RMSE) (in the range of 2.6372×10^{-12} to $7.5838\times^{-15}$) for maximum N=100 number of hidden nodes. Further, using the optimal η, the reconstructed and latent ROI images are calculated. Furthermore, fractal features are calculate from these ROI images.

In the Segmentation-based Fractal Texture Analysis(SFTA), the ROI image is decomposed into a set of binary images using Two Threshold Binary Decomposition(TTBD) through multi otsu algorithm [4]. Then fractal dimensions of the regions' borders are computed. From each binary image, three sets of feature such as fractal dimension using Box counting algorithm [4], mean gray level, and the area is calculated. From ROI images of fingerprint and iris reconstructed images $\hat{I}_{Fr}$, $\hat{I}_{Fnew}$, and $\hat{I}_{ir}$, $\hat{I}_{inew}$ are derived using ELM-AE. Then SFTA features are extracted from all four ROI images using the p threshold and normalized. All feature vectors are concatenated to form a single feature vector F of length 228, where each SFTA feature is of length 57(i.e., $6 * p - 3 = 6 * 10 - 3 = 57$, p is the number of threshold) [4].

Algorithm 1: Optimal η calculation

Input : Data $X = x_i$, where $i = 1...l$, number of epochs $E(100)$, stopping criteria $S = \dfrac{\|X - H * \eta\|}{\|X\|} < \epsilon$, where $\epsilon \in \{1 \times 10^{-14}$ to $1 \times 10^{-17}\}$ for different datasets, number of hidden neurons N.

Output: Optimal η.

1　Assign the weights W and biases b in the hidden layer randomly and orthogonally.
2　Calculate the output matrix of hidden node $H = g(W.x_i) + b$.
3　Calculate the output weights as follows $\eta = H^{-1}X$, where H^{-1} is calculated using the Moore-Penrose generalized inverse .
4　**while** S *or* E *does not occur* **do**
5　$\quad\lfloor$ Increase the number of hidden neurons and goto step 1.

Key Generation In this module, a key Bk is generated from the feature vector F. This module consists of two sub-steps, i.e., quantization parameter and auxiliary vector generation, and key generation. From the feature vectors of t instances of the user quantization parameter θ and auxiliary vector V are generated. In the key generation phase, key is generated using θ and V from the query feature vector. In Algorithms 2 and 3 quantization parameter and auxiliary vector generation, and key generation are depicted respectively.

4　Experiment and Experimental Results

In this section, the performance of the feature descriptor derived through segmented-based fractal texture features on different multimodal datasets(fingerprint, iris) is analyzed. The multimodal datasets are prepared by combining the publicly available fingerprint dataset and iris dataset.

4.1　Objectives of the Experiments

The objectives of the experiments on different multimodal datasets(fingerprint and iris) are mentioned below.

Algorithm 2: Quantization parameter and auxiliary vector generation

---

Input : Feature vectors F_j (t-instances per individual) , feature vector of reference instance(F_r), threshold(th).

`/* Each` F_j `contains z components.` $1 \leq j \leq t$ `*/`

Output: Auxiliary vector(V) and quantization threshold(θ).

1   $j \leftarrow 1$

2   $tempvec(1:z,1) \leftarrow F_r$ `// Feature vector of reference instance`

3   **for** $i \leftarrow 2$ to t **do**

4      $tempvec(1:z,2) \leftarrow F_i$

5      $tempvec(1:z,3) \leftarrow norm((tempvec(1:z,1) - tempvec(1:z,2)))/(norm(tempvec(1:z,1)) + norm(tempvec(1:z,2)))$

6      $max - val = max(tempvec(1:z,3))$ `// Maximum value of feature components`

7   **if** $max - val \leq th$ **then**

8         $j \leftarrow j + 1$

9         $featuretemp(1:z,j) \leftarrow tempvec(1:z,2)$

10   **for** $k \leftarrow 1$ to z **do**

11      $f_m(1,k)$=mean(featuretemp(k,1:j))   `// Mean vector of features`

12   temp(k,1)=max(feature(k,1:j))

13   temp(k,2)=min(feature(k,1:j))

14   temp(k,3)=mean(feature(k,1:j))

15   mx=temp(k,1)-temp(k,3)

16   mn=temp(k,2)-temp(k,3)

17      $\theta = max(mx, mn)$ `// Qunatization threshold parameter`

18   **Quantization:** The scalar equalized mean feature is quantized to f_q using following equation:

$$f_q = b \quad if \ (b-1)*\theta \leq f_m < b*\theta \tag{4}$$

where $b = 1, 2, ...$ is the quantized interval and positive integer. $q = 1, 2, ..., z$

19   **Auxiliary vector generation:** A 2-bit auxiliary information V_1 is calculated for each quantized feature component of f_q using following equation:

$$[v_1 \ v_2] = (f_q - 1)mod \ 4 \tag{5}$$

Finally, auxillary feature vector V is calculated using equation.

$$V = [V_1 \ || \ V_2 \ || \ ... \ || \ V_z] \tag{6}$$

Algorithm 3: Key generation

Input : Query feature vector $\vec{F}$, auxillary feature vector V, and quantization threshold(θ).

`/*` $\vec{F}$ `contains z components.`   `*/`

Output: Key Bk.

1   **Step-1:** Let $\vec{F}$ query feature vector. Then find the quantized feature $\vec{f_q}$ and auxiliary vector $\vec{V}$ from it using equations 4 and 5 respectively.

2   **Step-2:** In the key generation, if there is some variation of query feature vector $\vec{F}$ then distortion variant feature vector calculation is done using following equations 7 and 8:

$$\vec{g_q} = \begin{cases} 0 & if \ [\vec{v_1} \ \vec{v_2}] = ([v_1 \ v_2] - 1)mod \ 4 \\ 1 & if \ [\vec{v_1} \ \vec{v_2}] = ([v_1 \ v_2] + 1)mod \ 4 \\ 2 & otherwise \end{cases} \tag{7}$$

$$\vec{F}1 = \begin{cases} \vec{F} + \theta & if \ \vec{g_q} = 0 \\ \vec{F} - \theta & if \ \vec{g_q} = 1 \\ \vec{F} & otherwise \end{cases} \tag{8}$$

Step-3: The modified feature vector $\vec{F}1$ quantized using equation 4. The quantized feature vector is termed as final key Bk of length 456 bits.

Key Generation:

- To assess the randomness of the key, NIST statistical test suite is used.
- Analyzing the uniqueness, dynamicity and dissimilarity of keys generated using the suggested method.
- The computational time to reconstruct the key and key strength is investigated.
- A comparative analysis is performed to verify the novelty of the proposed scheme compared to state-of-the-art methods.

4.2 Multimodal Dataset Preparation

The multimodal dataset is prepared in the combination of fingerprint and iris datasets. In experiments, noisy visible wavelength iris image databases (UBIRIS.v1 [13], along with near-infrared iris image datasets like (MMU [1], ATVS-FIr DB [6], is used. Similarly, publicly available fingerprint datasets like FVC 2006(DB2-A) [3], FVC 2006(DB3-A) [3] are used to create multimodal datasets. We have designed four multimodal datasets : **Set-1** (UBIRIS.v1& FVC 2006(DB2-A)), **Set-2** (UBIRIS.v1& FVC 2006(DB3-A)), **Set-3** (MMU-ATVS-FIr & FVC 2006(DB2-A)), **Set-4** (MMU-ATVS-FIr & FVC 2006(DB3-A)). These datasets consist of heterogeneous number of users. Thus from each dataset, 5 instances of 140 user's biometric modality are considered (Table 1).

Table 1. Datasets information details.

Dataset	Spectrum	Number of images(classes)	Resolution
MMU.v1	NIR	450(90)	320×240
ATVS-FIr	NIR	800(50)	640×480
UBIRIS. V1	VW	1877(241)	200×150
FVC 2006 DB2-A	–	1680(140)	400×560
FVC 2006 DB3-A	–	1680(140)	400×500

4.3 Experimental Environment

Experiments were carried out with Intel(R) Core(TM) i7-9750H CPU @ 2.60 GHz dual core processor. MATLAB R2018a was used to develop all programs in Windows 10 OS.

4.4 Dissimilarity of Keys

Generally, Hamming distance is used to calculate dissimilarity among keys. For this purpose, a key was generated from a multimodal instance of a user and the keys from inter-instances of all other users. Further, Hamming distances among keys were evaluated. The dissimilarity between different keys 300–340 bits out of 456 bits. From this analysis, it is evident that intruder cannot guess the key. Dissimilarity analysis for the feature descriptor is illustrated in Fig. 3.

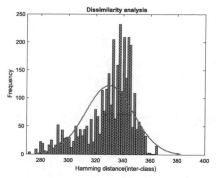

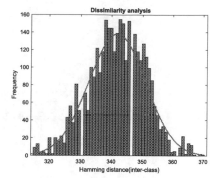

(a) Multimodal dataset(MMU-ATVS-FIr (b) Multimodal dataset(UBIRIS(VW)
& FVC 2006).   & FVC 2006).

Fig. 3. Dissimilarity analysis.

4.5 Distinctiveness Analysis of Keys

In this experiment, the performance of the proposed method is analyzed through key regeneration rate for the proposed descriptor on different multimodal datasets. The key regeneration rate (bkgr) is number of times the key is generated for successful authentication. The key regeneration rate for the proposed descriptor on different datasets is shown in Table 2. The missing key scenario would be the worst, it means that either the user has missed the secret key or the intruder knows the secret key. A new key can be generated by changing the quantization scheme as described in Algorithms 2, 3. So, the proposed method ensures the revocability of key which is not dependent on the missing one.

Table 2. Key regeneration rate of the proposed descriptor.

Dataset	bkgr
UBIRIS.v1& FVC 2006(DB2-A)	97.78%
UBIRIS.v1& FVC 2006(DB3-A)	96.44%
MMU-ATVS-FIr & FVC 2006(DB2-A)	97.33%
MMU-ATVS-FIr & FVC 2006(DB3-A)	95.56%

4.6 Computational Complexity to Generate Key

The proposed method can be used to generate key for cryptographic application's requirements. The breakdown of time complexity for different sub-steps are depicted in Table 3.

Table 3. Computational complexity analysis.

Sub-steps	Computational time(in ms)
ROI extraction(Fingerprint)	0.4326
ROI extraction(Iris)	0.8456
Feature extraction(Fingerprint)	100.2345
Feature extraction(Iris)	102.2542
Key generation	70.2468

4.7   Comparisons with Other Recent Key Generation Methods

The proposed method is compared with other recent key generation methods with respect to trait used(T), key regeneration rate(bkgr), revocability(R), key size(S) and cost(C). The comparison with other key generation schemes is shown in Table 4. The proposed approach's key length is more significant than other multimodal bio-cryptosystems. Further, the proposed system uses a dynamic process compared to the static method(fuzzy vault and fuzzy commitment) applied in Nandakumar et al. [8] Moreover, it has achieved FAR of 0% compared to 1.80% in [8].

Table 4. Comparisons with others with respect to T, bkgr, R, S, and C

Method	Trait used	bkgr	R	S	C
Proposed	Multimodal(Fingerprint+Iris)	97.78(highest) %	Yes	456	274 ms
Wang et al. [16]	Fingerprint	92.92%	Yes	120–168	51.1 ms
Anees et al. [2]	Face	89.98%	Yes	256	23.1 ms
Panchal et al. [10]	Fingerprint	93.52%	Yes	1274	1040.71
Panchal et al. [9]	Fingerprint	99.27%	No	1024	930
Dash et al. [5]	Iris	95.59 %	Yes	333–1120	191–322

The proposed SFTA-based feature extraction was replaced with Gabor and Haralick feature extraction techniques. Further, the computational efficiency and key generation accuracy were analyzed for SFTA and other state-of-the-art texture methods. It is evident from the Table 5 that the proposed SFTA feature extraction technique outperforms Gabor and Haralick-based methods.

Table 5. Comparisons with others feature extraction methods

Features	Time complexity(in ms)	Key generation accuracy(bkgr)
Proposed (SFTA)	274 ms	97.78 (highest) %
Gabor feature	382 ms	93.92 %
Haralick feature	292 ms	90.84 %

4.8   Security Analysis

The security of biometric key generation is assessed based on two primary attributes: correctness (which is evaluated through key generation accuracy (bkgr)) and security, which is assessed via key randomness, biometric privacy, and entropy analysis.

Key Randomness: The randomness of the generated keys has been checked using the NIST test suite [12]. More than 10^6 bits were generated using the proposed approach. NIST tests result is presented in Table 6. Therefore, the results obtained ensure the randomness of the keys for cryptographic applications. **Biometric privacy:** In case of theft or loss, the adversary must not extract any pertinent biometric information from the provided auxiliary feature vector V. Let $V_q = (f_q - 1) mod \ 4$ is a 2-bit value, where q=1,2...228. Hence, the quantized feature vector $f_q = 2 * b - 1$, and b can be any positive integer. The total number of combination of 2-bit auxiliary information is $(2 * b - 1)^{228}$. Therefore, it is impossible to derive fractal feature vector information from V_1. Further, the auxiliary vector V is resistant to brute-force attack. Our method has $b = 20$ unique quantized intervals, and the fractal feature vector length for each ROI image is 57. Thus, the total number of combinations of auxiliary information is 20^{57}. Hence, it is impossible to brute force all the combinations to get the biometric information. **Entropy analysis:** In this study, the generated keys' entropy has been computed using a statistical technique called Discrimination Entropy, which measures the number of uncorrelated bits U among inter-subject key distributions. $U = (\mu * (1 - \mu))/\sigma^2$, where μ, σ are the mean and standard deviation of the distribution. It is observed that $\mu \in \{0.4987, 0.5041\}$ and

Table 6. Randomness checking of key with NIST test suite

Statistical test	p-value	Conclusion
Frequency	0.214325	PASSED
Block frequency	0.852618	PASSED
Runs	0.852618	PASSED
Longest run	0.214325	PASSED
Rank	0.076862	PASSED
FFT	0.076862	PASSED
Non-overlapping template	0.755146	PASSED
Overlapping template	0.473685	PASSED
Universal	0.473685	PASSED
Linear complexity	0.732618	PASSED
Serial (1)	0.018812	PASSED
Serial (2)	0.463166	PASSED
Approximate entropy	0.473685	PASSED
Cumulative sums (1)	0.951324	PASSED
Cumulative sums (2)	0.852618	PASSED

$\sigma \in \{0.0307, 0.0301\}$ for MMU-ATVS-FVC 2006 and UBIRIS-FVC 2006 dataset respectively. Further, the entropy ranges from 264 to 275 out of 456 bits.

5   Conclusions

The proposed technique for generating secret keys from biometric data is unique in that it utilizes texture information for fingerprint data and minutiae point information for iris data, which is different from traditional approaches. The use of the SFTA (Scale and Translation Invariant Feature Transform) feature descriptor has shown promise as an effective technique for feature extraction. Experimental results have shown that SFTA outperforms other features reported in the literature. Notably, SFTA features are rotation, scale, and translation invariant, making them suitable for both fingerprint and iris biometric data. Furthermore, the proposed approach has been shown to work effectively with both near-infrared (NIR) and visible wavelength (VW) iris images. Statistical randomness tests have demonstrated the robustness and uniqueness of the generated keys. The proposed key generation technique has potential applications in various biometric cryptosystem scenarios, including storage security, network communication, remote authentication, and cryptography. Future research could explore the use of other scale and rotation-invariant features from fingerprint and iris data for key generation, as well as extend the proposed texture-based method to other biometric modalities for recognition and key generation tasks.

References

1. Multimedia university (MMU) iris dataset (2007). http://pesona.mmu.edu.my/~ccteo/
2. Anees, A., Chen, Y.P.P.: Discriminative binary feature learning and quantization in biometric key generation. Pattern Recogn. **77**, 289–305 (2018)
3. Cappelli, R., Ferrara, M., Franco, A., Maltoni, D.: Fingerprint verification competition 2006. Biometric Technol. Today **15**(7–8), 7–9 (2007)
4. Costa, A.F., Humpire-Mamani, G., Traina, A.J.M.: An efficient algorithm for fractal analysis of textures. In: 2012 25th SIBGRAPI Conference on Graphics, Patterns and Images, pp. 39–46. IEEE (2012)
5. Dash, P., Pandey, F., Sarma, M., Samanta, D.: Efficient private key generation from iris data for privacy and security applications. J. Inf. Security Appl. **75**, 103506 (2023)
6. Fierrez, J., Ortega-Garcia, J., Toledano, D.T., Gonzalez-Rodriguez, J.: Biosec baseline corpus: a multimodal biometric database. Pattern Recogn. **40**(4), 1389–1392 (2007)
7. Nagar, A., Nandakumar, K., Jain, A.K.: Multibiometric cryptosystems based on feature-level fusion. IEEE Trans. Inf. Forensics Secur. **7**(1), 255–268 (2011)
8. Nandakumar, K., Jain, A.K.: Multibiometric template security using fuzzy vault. In: 2008 IEEE Second International Conference on Biometrics: Theory, Applications and Systems, pp. 1–6. IEEE (2008)

9. Panchal, G., Samanta, D.: A novel approach to fingerprint biometric-based cryptographic key generation and its applications to storage security. Comput. Electr. Eng. **69**, 461–478 (2018)
10. Panchal, G., Samanta, D., Barman, S.: Biometric-based cryptography for digital content protection without any key storage. Multimed. Tools Appl. 1–22 (2019)
11. Pandey, F., Dash, P., Samanta, D., Sarma, M.: ASRA: automatic singular value decomposition-based robust fingerprint image alignment. Multimed. Tools Appl. **20**(5), e0154160 (2020)
12. Pareschi, F., Rovatti, R., Setti, G.: On statistical tests for randomness included in the NIST SP800-22 test suite and based on the binomial distribution. IEEE Trans. Inf. Forensics Secur. **7**(2), 491–505 (2012)
13. Proenca, H., Alexandre, L.A.: Ubiris iris image database (2004). http://irisdi.ubi.pl. Accessed 15 Jan 2011
14. Rathgeb, C., Uhl, A.: Context-based biometric key generation for iris. IET Comput. Vis. 5(6), 389–397 (2011)
15. Wang, L., Ding, S.: Multi-view spectral clustering via ELM-AE ensemble features representations learning. IEEE Access **8**, 198679–198690 (2020)
16. Wang, P., You, L., Hu, G., Hu, L., Jian, Z., Xing, C.: Biometric key generation based on generated intervals and two-layer error correcting technique. Pattern Recogn. **111**, 107733 (2021)
17. Zhao, Z., Ajay, K.: An accurate iris segmentation framework under relaxed imaging constraints using total variation model. In: Proceedings of the IEEE International Conference on Computer Vision, pp. 3828–3836 (2015)
18. Zhu, E., Guo, X., Yin, J.: Walking to singular points of fingerprints. Pattern Recogn. **56**, 116–128 (2016)

Cross View and Cross Walking Gait Recognition Using a Convolutional Neural Network

Sonam Nahar[✉], Sagar Narsingani, and Yash Patel

Pandit Deendayal Energy University, Gandhinagar, Gujarat, India
{sonam.nahar,sagar.nce19,yash.pce19}@sot.pdpu.ac.in

Abstract. In this paper, we propose a gait recognition method using a convolutional neural network (CNN). A CNN architecture is designed and trained to learn an efficient representation with which walking patterns i.e., gait can be disentangled from the visual appearance of the subjects caused by covariate factors such as variation in view angles, clothing and carrying conditions. Since dynamic areas contain the most informative part of the human gait and are insensitive to changes in various covariate conditions, we feed the gait entropy images as input to CNN model to capture mostly the motion information. The learned gait features from CNN are then fed into a K-NN classifier to identify individuals based on their unique gait patterns. Experiments are carried out for cross-view and cross-walking gait recognition using the CASIA-B dataset. Our experimental results demonstrate the effectiveness of the proposed method.

Keywords: Gait Recognition · CNN · Cross View · Cross Walking

1 Introduction

'Gait' is defined as the way people walk and is used as a behavioral biometric [9]. The gait pattern can be captured and perceived from a distance in an unconstrained background. It does not require subject cooperation and can operate without interrupting or interfering with the subject's activity unlike other kinds of biometric features such as face, ear, iris, and fingerprint. Gait recognition is a relatively new and rapidly evolving field in computer vision and biometric research community [11,13]. However, for vision-based gait recognition, one of the biggest challenges is to disentangle the covariate factors which can alter gait appearances drastically and make the recognition process difficult. It is essential that gait recognition is more robust against these covariates. In this work, we consider the covariates such as view angles, walking with carrying a bag and walking with wearing a coat, and propose a novel gait feature extraction method which can automatically select gait features invariant to these covariates for subject recognition.

© The Author(s), under exclusive license to Springer Nature Switzerland AG 2024
H. Kaur et al. (Eds.): CVIP 2023, CCIS 2009, pp. 112–123, 2024.
https://doi.org/10.1007/978-3-031-58181-6_10

In general, silhouettes are used to represent the human gait. However, gait silhouettes are sensitive to changes in the appearance of the subject and to overcome this problem, several state-of-art gait recognition methods have proposed gait representations which are invariant to different covariate conditions [1,4,6,7,15]. Even though these strategies have provided relatively satisfactory results in the past years, they are usually constrained to hand-crafted features and have limited capacity for learning intrinsic patterns in data.

Recently, deep learning has become popular in gait recognition task because of it's ability to learn the gait features from the large amount of gait data [11]. In particular, convolutional neural networks (CNN) has been mostly used in gait recognition, especially as feature extractor [2,12,17]. CNNs use convolutional layers to extract local features, pooling layers to reduce dimensionality, and fully connected layers to classify images based on learned features. Our work is similar to the method presented in [12]. In the method entitled as GEINet [12], a CNN was trained in order to learn the gait features, given gait energy images as input. For recognition, a simple Euclidean distance measure was used between the gallery and probe features. While authors in [12] reported that their method outperformed on the benchmark dataset for cross view gait recognition, we find few limitations: (1) they used gait energy images as input to the CNN because GEI can efficiently capture both the static (e.g., head, torso) and dynamic parts (e.g., lower parts of legs and arms) of the human silhouette. However, since GEI mainly contain body shape information, they are sensitive to changes in various covariate conditions, and hence is not an appropriate representation to feed in a CNN for learning robust gait features, (2) The method has shown the results in cross view settings only. Gait recognition should also be tested in cross walking scenarios where the same person walks with different carrying and clothing conditions, (3) they have chosen the CNN architecture based on empirical results, no systematic hyperparameter tuning was performed. (4) The gallery and probe gait features extracted from CNN were used as templates and the gait recognition problem was solved by measuring the distance between templates directly. However, direct template matching is susceptible to noise.

We therefore propose a gait recognition method using CNN that learns suitable representations with which walking patterns i.e., gait can be disentangled from the visual appearance of the subjects and subsequently used for recognition, and also demonstrate its effectiveness in the settings of cross view and cross walking using the benchmark dataset [18]. Here, cross-view means the probe gait sequences are with different view angles as angles in gallery sequences. In cross-walking setting, the subjects have walking sequences either with a coat or with a bag, while subjects in the gallery are under the normal walking condition. The key contributions of the paper are summarized as follows:

1. We propose to use gait entropy images [1] to be fed as input to our CNN model to capture mostly the motion information because gait entropy image captures the dynamic areas (motion) of the human body as dynamic areas contain the most informative part of the human gait and are insensitive to changes in various covariate conditions.

2. We design our CNN model consisting of two sets of convolutions, batch normalization and pooling layers followed by two fully connected layers and employ a method of cross-validation for tuning the hyperparameters such as number of filters, size of filters, number of epochs, dropout rate and batch size.
3. With the learned gait features in gallery and probe set, K-NN classifier is used to recognize the subject uniquely.
4. We present extensive experimental results for cross-view and cross-walking gait recognition using the CASIA-B benchmark dataset [18].

The rest of the paper is organized as follows: in Sect. 2, related work is reviewed. The proposed gait recognition method is detailed in Sect. 3. Experimental results and conclusion are presented in Sect. 4 and Sect. 5, respectively.

2   Related Work

In general, model-free gait recognition approaches represent gait based on silhouettes extracted from the human walking sequences. Gait energy image (GEI) is proven to be an effective gait representation which is obtained by averaging the silhouette value pixel-by-pixel over the gait period [4]. However, GEI loses information in a gait sequence which affects performance due to changes caused by covariate conditions such as clothing, carrying conditions and view variations. To mitigate these affects, gait entropy image is proposed [1] which focus on dynamic regions and is computed as pixel-by-pixel entropy of the GEI. In another variant of GEI, to preserve the temporal information from loss, Chrono-Gait Image (CGI) is proposed which is based on multi-channel temporal encoding scheme [15]. A gait flow image (GFI) focuses more directly on the dynamic components, where the optical flow lengths observed on the silhouette contour are averaged over the gait period [6]. Frequency domain gait features are proposed by considering the periodic property of gait [7]. [5]. In such frequency-based methods cross-view projections are learned with which one can normalize gait features from one view to another, and hence one can compare the normalized gait features extracted from any two videos in order to compute their similarity.

The state-of-the-art methods based on such gait representations have shown promising results in cross-view and cross-walking scenarios [11,13]. However, these methods use gait features which are hand-crafted and have limited capacity for learning intrinsic patterns in data. In addition, these image-based gait features are transformed into a feature vector and the techniques such as linear discriminant analysis (LDA) [4], primal rank support vector machines [3], multi-view discriminant analysis (MvDA) [8] are applied to extract the relevant gait features that are invariant to various covariate conditions. However, each dimension in the feature vector corresponds to each pixel for further classification/recognition, and the spatial proximity in the gait image is not captured which results in overtraining.

Recently, gait recognition methods based on deep learning have dominated the state of the art in the field through the ability to automatically learn discriminative gait representations. In particular, a CNN is mostly used because it considers spatial proximity in the image using a convolutional operation and improve the recognition accuracy significantly. The work termed as GEI-Net [12] learns gait representations from GEI via convolutional neural networks directly. Authors in [17] proposed a deep convolutional neural network based cross-view and cross-walk gait recognition framework which learns similarities between pairs of GEIs. Another recent work is GaitSet [2] makes an assumption that appearance of a silhouette contains its position information and thus regards gait as a set to extract temporal information using CNN.

In addition to CNN, recently several other deep architectures [11] have also been designed to solve the gait recognition problems, for example, deep belief networks (DBN), long short-term memory (LSTM) - a type of recurrent neural network (RNN) architecture, deep autoencoders (DAE), generative adversarial networks (GAN), capsule network, and hybrid networks that combines one or more of these architectures. Though, these methods have shown excellent results in the challenging cross-view and cross-walking scenarios, they form a very complex network and require huge amount of labeled data during training. In contrast, we present a simple CNN architecture which can learn efficient gait features using a moderate size of training data.

3   Proposed Method

3.1   Generation of Gait Entropy Images

Given a human walking sequence, a silhouette is extracted from each frame using the background subtraction [10]. The height of the silhouettes is then normalized followed by the center alignment. Gait cycles are then estimated using the method of autocorrelation presented in [7]. The gait cycle is defined as the time interval between the same repetitive events of walking that generally starts when one foot is in contact with the ground. Since, the walking of a person is periodic, it is sufficient to consider only one gait cycle from the whole gait sequence.

Given a gait cycle of size-normalized and center aligned silhouettes, a gait entropy image (GEnI) is computed by calculating the Shannon entropy for each pixel in the silhouette images over a complete gait cycle as given in [1]:

$$GEnI = I(x, y) = \sum_{k=1}^{K} p_k(x, y) \log_2 p_k(x, y), \qquad (1)$$

where x, y are the pixel coordinates and $p_k(x, y)$ is the probability that the pixel takes on the kth value in a complete gait cycle. In our case, the silhouettes are binary images and we thus have K = 2. Figure 1 shows some examples of gait gntropy images along with gait energy images from the CASIA-B dataset. One can clearly see that dynamic areas such as legs and arms are represented by higher intensity values whilst the static areas such as head, torso have low values in the GEnIs. This is because silhouette pixel values in the dynamic areas

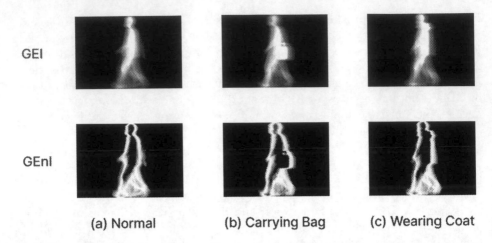

GEI

GEnI

(a) Normal   (b) Carrying Bag   (c) Wearing Coat

Fig. 1. Examples of Gait Energy Images (GEI) and Gait Entropy Images (GEnI) from the CASIA-B dataset [18] with different walking conditions. Columns (a) Normal Walking, (b) Carrying a bag, and (c) Wearing a coat.

are more uncertain and thus more informative, leading to higher entropy values. It can also be observed that the effect of appearance changes caused by carrying a bag and wearing a coat is significant in GEIs whereas it is clearly reduced in GEnIs and shown only in the outer contour of the human body. In our proposed method, we feed GEnI as input to our CNN architecture.

3.2   Convolutional Neural Network Architecture

Our CNN architecture consists of eight layers, where the leading six layers are the two sets of convolutions, batch normalization and pooling layers. The last two layers are the fully connected (FC) layers where the first FC layer has 1024 units followed by another FC layer consisting of M units where SoftMax function is applied at each output unit. Let us assume that there are M number of subjects in the training set and each subject is denoted by number ranging from 1, 2, ..., M.

More specifically, the ith unit of the last layer ideally outputs 1 for the input belonging to subject i, otherwise, it outputs 0. Figure 2 shows our CNN architecture. Dropout for regularization and ReLU activation function for non-linearity is applied at every layer of the network except at the last layer. We consider number of filters, size of filters, number of epochs, dropout rate and batch size as set of hyperparameters for our CNN model and choose their optimal values using cross validation. The configuration for each convolution and pooling layer with optimal set of hyperparameters is illustrated in Table 1. We consider this configuration for learning relevant gait features for the test data.

Though our CNN architecture is not very deep, it learns robust gait representations based on input GEnI. This is due to the fact that input gait data

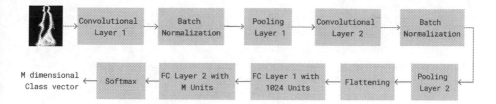

Fig. 2. The CNN Architecture

Table 1. CNN Configuration with Optimal Hyperparameters

Hyperparameters		
Conv Layer 1	# Filters	40
	Size of Filters	3×3
	Stride	2
Max Pooling Layer 1	Size of Filters	2×2
	Stride	2
Conv Layer 2	# Filters	32
	Size of Filters	5×5
	Stride	3
Max Pooling Layer 2	Size of Filters	3×3
	Stride	2
Number of Epochs	100	
Learning Rate	0.001	
Dropout Rate	40%	
Batch Size	64	

in form of silhouettes (for e.g., GEnI) do not present considerable complexity in terms of texture information. Hence, a shallow CNN architecture is sufficient for encoding gait data. This is contrary to many other domains such as face [14] or activity [16] recognition, where very deep networks are used to learn highly discriminative features. Moreover, through preliminary experiments, we have confirmed that additional convolutional layers following two existing sets of convolution, batch normalization and pooling in our network do not help in improving the significant gait recognition accuracy.

3.3   Feature Learning

Let the training set contains N number of gait sequences belonging to M number of subjects. We first compute a gait entropy image for every gait sequence and obtain a set of training GEnIs as $\{I_1, I_2, \ldots, I_N\}$ with their corresponding ground truth label vectors as $\{y_1, y_2, \ldots, y_N\}$. For an input I_i belonging to subject j, it's label is denoted as M dimensional vector, $y_i = [y_{i1}, y_{i2}, \ldots, y_{iM}]$ where $y_{ij} = 1$ and the other entries are equal to 0.

Given an input image I_i and set of weighting parameters w, we define the output $\hat{z}_i$ of last layer as a function of I_i and w using forward propagation as:

$$\hat{z}_i = f(I_i, w), \tag{2}$$

where $\hat{z}_i$ is denoted as a M dimensional vector. We subsequently apply the SoftMax function on every element of $\hat{z}_i$ and obtain the final class probability vector $\hat{y}_i$ where each jth element in $\hat{y}_i$ is computed using the softmax function as follows,

$$\hat{y}_{ij} = \frac{e^{\hat{z}_{ij}}}{\sum_{j=1}^{M} e^{\hat{z}_{ij}}} \quad for \ j = 1, 2, \ldots, M \tag{3}$$

Given a training set: $\{I_1, I_2, \ldots, I_N\}$, we train our CNN network by minimizing the following cross-entropy loss function L using the stochastic gradient descent algorithm:

$$L(w) = \sum_{i=1}^{N} \sum_{j=1}^{M} y_{ij} \log \hat{y}_{ij} \tag{4}$$

In this learning phase, we obtain an optimal set of weighting parameters w.

3.4   Gait Recognition

A GEnI is fed as an input to the trained network and the output computed at the fully connected layer (FC1), which is the layer immediately preceding the last year, is considered as a feature vector to represent the gait in our work. Since the FC1 layer consists of 1024 units, we obtain 1024-dimensional feature vector. For a given gallery and probe gait sequences with their corresponding gait entropy images, we extract the gait features from our trained CNN architecture and use K-NN classifier for gait recognition. The K-NN classifier is trained using the features of gait sequences in gallery set and the subject/class is recognized for every gait sequence in probe set.

4   Experimental Results

4.1   Datasets and Test Protocol

We use CASIA-B dataset [18] for our experiments. CASIA-B is one of the most widely used and publicly available gait database which contains gait sequences of 124 subjects with 11 different views ranging from $0°$ to $180°$ (with $18°$ increments). The dataset considers three different walking conditions namely normal walking (NM), walking with a coat (CL), and walking with a bag (BG), respectively with 6, 2, and 2 gait sequences per subject per view.

In order to test the performance of our proposed method, we use the subject independent testing protocol. In subject independent testing protocol, the subjects in the training set are disjoint from the subjects in test set. We choose randomly 74 subjects for training and the remaining 50 subjects for testing. Training set consists of $11 * 10 = 110$ gait sequences per subject i.e., total $110 * 74 = 8140$ sequences. We compute the gait entropy image for every gait sequence in the training set and obtain a fixed size GEnIs of 88×128 pixels. Example GEnIs extracted from this dataset can be found in Fig. 1. Since our training set is moderate in size and hence to reduce the problem of overfitting, we perform the cross validation by randomly splitting the training set into train (70%) and validation (30%) set, and choose the hyperparameters that reduce the variance error, for instance, we consider those set of hyperparameters where both the train and validation errors are low and the difference between these errors are also low as well. With the training GEnIs and best set of hyperparameters (see Table 1), we train our CNN model and learn the parameters (w) of the model. Since our model is trained using normal walking, carrying bag and wearing coat gait sequences captured using different view angles, it can learn the reliable gait features invariant to these covariates.

The test set consisting of 50 subjects is further divided into a gallery set including the first four gait sequences from the NM gait data and the probe set consists of the rest of the sequences namely, the remaining 2 NM (probe subset-NM), 2 CL (probe subset-CL), and 2 BG (probe subset-BG) sequences, per each subject per each view. This testing scenario is named as cross-walking because here the subjects in the gallery are under the normal walking conditions while probe contains the walking sequences with coat or bag. We perform the experiments for gait recognition in cross walking along with cross view settings where the probe gait sequences are with different view angles from the view angles in gallery sequences. Note that we have used TensorFlow for training the CNN and all experiments were conducted on machine with 11th Gen Intel(R) Core(TM) i7-1165G7, 2.80 GHz frequency, SSD - 512 MB, RAM - 8 GB and System Type - 64-bit operating system.

4.2   Results

We learn the gallery and probe features using the trained CNN model and use K-NN classifier (with K = 1) to compare the probe features with the gallery ones in order to identify most similar gait patterns and label them as being from the same subject. Results are measured and presented using rank-1 recognition accuracy. Table 2 shows the results for cross view scenario where both the gallery and probe gait sequences belong to same walking conditions (4 NM in gallery and 2 NM in probe) with different view angles. Table 3 and Table 4 demonstrate the cross-view recognition accuracies when probe contains bag and coat sequences, respectively.

Cross view and cross walking gait recognition is challenging. Our method has obtained promising results on the NM probe subset, when the cross-view angle is not larger than 18° as shown in Table 2. The results are better with probe angles

Table 2. Cross-View recognition accuracies when both gallery and probe contains normal walking sequences.

		Probe Angles (Normal Walking: NM # 5-6)										
		0°	18°	36°	54°	72°	90°	108°	126°	144°	162°	180°
Gallery Angles: NM #1-4	0°	86.73	57.9	31	17	9	4.04	6.06	13	12	19	28
	18°	66.32	84	69	20	19	12.12	8.08	11	15	28.9	37
	36°	27.55	51	76	66	16	6.06	5.05	8	15	26	21
	54°	13.26	21	36	76	30	19.2	17.2	17	18	15	12
	72°	8.16	13	16	23	97	71.71	49.5	43	28	14	7
	90°	6.12	12	9	10	81	96.97	91.91	53	19	9	10
	108°	6.12	4	7	10	46	90.9	93.93	74	31	12	6
	126°	6.12	9	9	14	57.9	71.71	86.86	94	67	21	11
	144°	9.18	12	18	20	41	33.33	43.43	78	93	59	24
	162°	17.34	23	19	18	21	16.17	13.13	19	55	96	60
	180°	24.48	18	13	6	9	5.05	3.03	9	15	44	97

Table 3. Cross-View recognition accuracies when gallery contains normal and probe with bag sequences.

		Probe Angles (Bag: BG #1-2)										
		0°	18°	36°	54°	72°	90°	108°	126°	144°	162°	180°
Gallery Angles: NM #1-4	0°	54.08	51.02	26.26	10.20	7.14	3.06	1.02	5	8	10.1	16
	18°	26.53	53.06	28.28	9.18	9.18	4.08	5.10	6	6	12.12	18
	36°	16.32	34.69	43.43	23.46	8.16	3.06	3.06	5	10	12.12	12
	54°	12.24	17.34	21.21	42.85	19	12.24	13.26	14	14	16.16	11
	72°	6.12	12.24	10.10	13.26	68.36	37.75	23.46	21	16	11.11	10
	90°	5.10	9.18	7.07	11.22	52.04	69.38	59.18	31	17	3.03	8
	108°	4.08	6.12	5.05	7.14	38.77	67.34	62.24	39	19	10.10	6
	126°	8.16	3.06	8.08	8.16	35.71	51.02	48.97	61	30	15.15	11
	144°	10.20	9.18	11.11	13.26	25.51	20.40	21.42	37	66	28.28	16
	162°	14.28	16.32	12.12	16.32	21.42	6.12	3.06	6	28	66.67	40
	180°	15.30	19.38	16.16	8.16	5.10	5.10	3.06	6	5	31.31	67

72°, 90°, 108° and 126° because most of the gait information is visible in these viewpoints. Especially, with cross view of 90° and 108° angles, we obtain more than 90% accuracy on the NM probe set. Even though the silhouettes in frontal and back viewpoints such as 0°, 18°, 162° and 180° carry little gait information, our method works well with more than 60% accuracy with the NM probe subset and the cross-view angle less than 18° as shown in Table 2. As for the BG probe subset, our method still performs well (see Table 3). However, the performance degrades for the CL probe subset even when the cross-view angle is not larger than 18° as depicted on Table 4. The cause behind these results is that carrying a bag only affects a small part of a gait silhouette, while wearing a coat can greatly change the appearance. Another possible reason for the performance degradation may be the lack of training data. Due to larger appearance variations, the CL

Table 4. Cross-View recognition accuracies when gallery contains normal and probe with coat sequences.

		Probe Angles (Coat: CL #1-2)										
		0°	18°	36°	54°	72°	90°	108°	126°	144°	162°	180°
Gallery Angles: NM #1-4	0°	24.48	19.38	13.26	10.10	10	2	4	5.05	8.08	12.24	7
	18°	23.46	24.48	21.42	11.11	14	6	6	11.11	10.10	14.28	8
	36°	8.16	18.36	29.59	22.22	15	6	6	6.06	7.07	13.26	8
	54°	7.14	12.24	20.40	36.36	12	9	8	12.12	9.09	17.34	11
	72°	4.08	11.22	7.14	14.14	43	42	16	26.26	14.14	8.16	5
	90°	5.10	5.10	7.07	24	41	43	22.22	13.13	4.08	1	3.06
	108°	3.06	1.02	3.06	10.10	14	40	46	25.25	17.17	7.14	4
	126°	3.06	7.14	5.10	8.08	17	28	32	37.37	30.3	12.24	4
	144°	3.06	11.22	3.06	20,20	19	19	17	26.26	40.4	19.38	15
	162°	6.12	15.30	11.22	13.13	8	11	8	13.13	20.2	43.87	19
	180°	7.14	9.18	6.12	4.04	4	1	3	7.07	9.09	19.38	36

subset is harder than the NM and BG subsets. Networks may easily over-fit if the training set is not big enough. For all the three probe subsets: NM, BG, and CL, our method needs further improvements when the cross-view angle is larger than 18°.

Table 5. Comparison of cross-view methods on CASIA-B in terms of Rank-1 mean accuracy (%). Here, '-' denotes that results are not reported.

Gallery (NM #1-4): 0°–180°

Probe		0°	18°	36°	54°	72°	90°	108°	126°	144°	162°	180°	Mean
NM #5-6	GEI	9.14	14.87	15.03	16.07	23.75	22.5	23.91	17.2	12.44	13.40	9.02	16.13
	GEnI	12.45	16.12	13.1	12.38	15.02	23.62	23.21	21.10	15.20	15.57	16.18	16.72
	CMCC [5]	46.3	–	–	52.4	–	48.3	–	56.9	–	–	–	-
	GEINet [12]	45.8	57.6	67.1	66.9	56.3	48.3	58.3	68.4	69.4	59	46.5	58.5
	CNN-LB [17]	79.1	88.4	95.7	92.8	89.1	87	89.3	92.1	94.4	89.4	75.4	88.4
	GaitSet [2]	90.8	97.9	99.4	96.9	93.6	91.7	95	97.8	98.9	96.8	85.8	95
	Proposed	24.67	27.72	25.73	22.73	36.99	38.84	38.02	38.09	33.45	30.35	28.45	31.37
BG #1-2	GEI	6.44	9.91	11.61	9.32	15.32	12.21	11.65	11.97	8.26	8.94	6.37	10.18
	GEnI	7.64	9.82	7.31	7.08	9.81	13.63	12.37	12.59	7.27	7.26	7.97	9.34
	CMCC [5]	–	–	–	–	–	–	–	–	–	–	–	-
	GEINet [12]	–	–	–	–	–	–	–	–	–	–	–	-
	CNN-LB [17]	64.2	80.6	82.7	76.9	64.8	63.1	68	76.9	82.2	75.4	61.3	72.4
	GaitSet [2]	83.8	91.2	91.8	88.8	83.3	81	84.1	90	92.2	94.4	79	87.2
	Proposed	17.11	21.05	17.17	14.84	26.4	25.41	22.17	21	19.91	19.65	19.55	20.39
CL #1-2	GEI	2.57	4.27	6.23	6.32	6.28	7.01	6.6	6.97	5.18	4.62	2.54	5.33
	GEnI	3.02	5.01	4.61	4.52	6.44	8.24	8.06	8.64	6.36	5.33	4.42	5.88
	CMCC [5]	–	–	–	–	–	–	–	–	–	–	–	-
	GEINet [12]	–	–	–	–	–	–	–	–	–	–	–	-
	CNN-LB [17]	37.7	57.2	66.6	61.1	55.2	54.6	55.2	59.1	58.9	48.8	39.4	54
	GaitSet [2]	61.4	75.4	80.7	77.3	72.1	70.1	71.5	73.5	73.5	68.4	50	70.4
	Proposed	8.62	12.24	11.59	15.77	17.55	17.91	5.45	16.62	15.43	15.3	10.91	13.4

The comparison of our proposed method with those in the literature is presented in Table 5. Note that each of these identification accuracies is the average score for a given probe view angle with different gallery view angles ($0°$–$180°$). These methods are listed because they are the most recent and are evaluated under cross-view and cross-walking scenarios, and their scores are directly taken from the original papers. We also include two traditional methods (non deep) such as GEI and GEnI for fair comparison. These methods use GEI and GEnI as features, respectively and perform gait recognition in cross walking and cross view scenarios by direct template matching (Euclidean distance) between gallery and probe set. There are little results reported under cross-walking where probe set belongs to BG and CL. Our method performs better than the traditional methods such as GEI and GEnI with significant margins. This shows the advantage of using the learned features from CNN as compared to handcrafted features in gait recognition. In the case of experimental setting where both the gallery and probe set contains the NM sequences, our method shows comparable performance when compared to the methods CMCC [5] and GEINET [12], especially, when the probe angle is $90°$. The proposed method does not show significant improvements when compared to the recent deep learning based gait recognition methods, GaitSet [2] and CNN-LB [17] because these recent methods use the view transformation models and are trained using a large dataset. Overall, our method outperforms the traditional gait recognition method in cross view setting under the 3 different cross walking scenarios such as probe with NM, BG and CL, respectively.

5   Conclusion

This paper presents a gait recognition method using CNN. Given gait entropy images, the CNN is trained to learn the gait features invariant to viewpoints, clothing and carrying conditions. Finally, a K-NN classifier is used to compare the probe features with the gallery ones in order to identify most similar gait patterns. The experimental results show the effectiveness of our approach in cross-view and cross-walking scenarios and comparison with state of the art traditional and deep learning-based gait recognition methods.

References

1. Bashir, K., Xiang, T., Gong, S.: Gait recognition using gait entropy image. In: 3rd International Conference on Imaging for Crime Detection and Prevention (ICDP 2009), pp. 1–6 (2009)
2. Chao, H., He, Y., Zhang, J., Feng, J.: Gaitset: regarding gait as a set for cross-view gait recognition. CoRR abs/1811.06186 (2018)
3. Chen, X., Xu, J.: Uncooperative gait recognition. Pattern Recogn. **53**(C), 116–129 (2016)
4. Han, J., Bhanu, B.: Individual recognition using gait energy image. IEEE Trans. Pattern Anal. Mach. Intell. **28**(2), 316–322 (2006)

5. Kusakunniran, W., Wu, Q., Zhang, J., Li, H., Wang, L.: Recognizing gaits across views through correlated motion co-clustering. IEEE Trans. Image Process. **23**(2), 696–709 (2014)
6. Lam, T., Cheung, K., Liu, J.: Gait flow image: a silhouette-based gait representation for human identification. Pattern Recogn. **44**, 973–987 (2011)
7. Makihara, Y., Sagawa, R., Mukaigawa, Y., Echigo, T., Yagi, Y.: Gait recognition using a view transformation model in the frequency domain. In: Leonardis, A., Bischof, H., Pinz, A. (eds.) ECCV 2006. LNCS, vol. 3953, pp. 151–163. Springer, Heidelberg (2006). https://doi.org/10.1007/11744078_12
8. Mansur, A., Makihara, Y., Muramatsu, D., Yagi, Y.: Cross-view gait recognition using view-dependent discriminative analysis. In: IEEE International Joint Conference on Biometrics, pp. 1–8 (2014)
9. Murray, M.: Gait as a total pattern of movement (1967)
10. Sarkar, S., Phillips, P., Liu, Z., Vega, I., Grother, P., Bowyer, K.: The humanid gait challenge problem: data sets, performance, and analysis. IEEE Trans. Pattern Anal. Mach. Intell. **27**(2), 162–177 (2005)
11. Sepas-Moghaddam, A., Etemad, A.: Deep gait recognition: A survey. IEEE Trans. Pattern Anal. Mach. Intell. **45**(1), 264–284 (2023)
12. Shiraga, K., Makihara, Y., Muramatsu, D., Echigo, T., Yagi, Y.: Geinet: view-invariant gait recognition using a convolutional neural network. In: 2016 International Conference on Biometrics (ICB), pp. 1–8 (2016)
13. Singh, J.P., Jain, S., Arora, S., Singh, U.P.: Vision-based gait recognition: a survey. IEEE Access **6**, 70497–70527 (2018)
14. Taigman, Y., Yang, M., Ranzato, M., Wolf, L.: Deepface: closing the gap to human-level performance in face verification. In: 2014 IEEE Conference on Computer Vision and Pattern Recognition, pp. 1701–1708 (2014)
15. Wang, C., Zhang, J., Wang, L., Pu, J., Yuan, X.: Human identification using temporal information preserving gait template. IEEE Trans. Pattern Anal. Mach. Intell. **34**(11), 2164–2176 (2012)
16. Wang, J., Chen, Y., Hao, S., Peng, X., Hu, L.: Deep learning for sensor-based activity recognition: a survey. CoRR abs/1707.03502 (2017)
17. Wu, Z., Huang, Y., Wang, L., Wang, X., Tan, T.: A comprehensive study on cross-view gait based human identification with deep CNNs. IEEE Trans. Pattern Anal. Mach. Intell. **39**(2), 209–226 (2017)
18. Yu, S., Tan, D., Tan, T.: A framework for evaluating the effect of view angle, clothing and carrying condition on gait recognition. In: 18th International Conference on Pattern Recognition (ICPR 2006), vol. 4, pp. 441–444 (2006)

Is Grad-CAM Explainable in Medical Images?

Subhashis Suara, Aayush Jha, Pratik Sinha, and Arif Ahmed Sekh[✉]

XIM University, Bhubaneswar, India
skarifahmed@gmail.com

Abstract. Explainable Deep Learning has gained significant attention in the field of artificial intelligence (AI), particularly in domains such as medical imaging, where accurate and interpretable machine learning models are crucial for effective diagnosis and treatment planning. Grad-CAM is a baseline that highlights the most critical regions of an image used in a deep learning model's decision-making process, increasing interpretability and trust in the results. It is applied in many computer vision (CV) tasks such as classification and explanation. This study explores the principles of Explainable Deep Learning and its relevance to medical imaging, discusses various explainability techniques and their limitations, and examines medical imaging applications of Grad-CAM. The findings highlight the potential of Explainable Deep Learning and Grad-CAM in improving the accuracy and interpretability of deep learning models in medical imaging. The code is available in (https://github.com/beasthunter758/GradEML).

Keywords: Explainable Deep Learning · Gradient-weighted Class Activation Mapping (Grad-CAM) · Medical Image Analysis

1 Introduction

Medical imaging, such as X-ray, CT, MRI, and ultrasound, plays a crucial role in the diagnosis and treatment of various diseases. With the increasing availability of medical imaging data, there is a growing interest in using machine learning techniques to aid in image analysis and interpretation. Figure 1 shows a typical setup for explainable medical image analysis.

Deep learning has shown remarkable success in medical image analysis tasks, but one challenge with deep learning models is their lack of interpretability, which is a major concern in the medical domain. Explainable Deep Learning is an emerging area of research that seeks to address this issue by providing interpretable models without sacrificing accuracy. Explainable Deep Learning techniques aim to explain how a model arrived at its decision by providing saliency maps or highlighting the most relevant features in the input image

---

S. Suara, A. Jha, P. Sinha, and A. A. Sekh—All authors are having equal contributions.

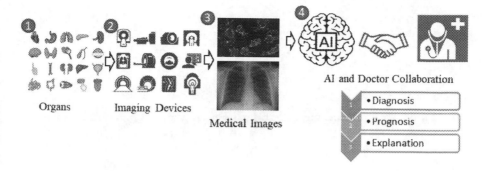

Fig. 1. A typical setup for explainable medical image analysis.

that contributed to the model's output. One popular Explainable Deep Learning technique is Gradient-weighted Class Activation Mapping (Grad-CAM), which visualizes the regions of an image that contribute most to the model's decision-making process. Grad-CAM has been successfully used in various medical imaging applications, such as detecting lung cancer [1], breast cancer [2], and brain tumors, to enhance the interpretability of deep learning models and improve trust in their results [3]. This paper explores the use of Grad-CAM as an Explainable Deep Learning technique in medical imaging applications, discussing its underlying principles, how it works, and recent studies that have used Grad-CAM to improve the interpretability of deep learning models in medical imaging. Deep learning models lack transparency in their decision-making process, which is crucial for ensuring patient safety in the medical domain. The study proposes using Gradient-weighted Class Activation Mapping (Grad-CAM) as an Explainable Deep Learning technique to enhance interpretability. Grad-CAM allows clinicians to visualize the regions of an image that contribute most to the model's decision-making process, enabling better understanding and trust in the model's results.

The specific objectives of this paper are:

- To review the literature on medical imaging and deep learning, explainable deep learning, and Grad-CAM in medical imaging such as the articles reported in [4–6].
- To develop and compare state-of-the-art deep learning model for medical image interpretation [7].
- To critically analyze Grad-CAM as an Explainable Deep Learning technique, evaluate its performance that can lead towards enhancing the interpretability.
- To discuss the implications and potential future applications of the Grad-CAM in different clinical settings such as [8,9].

This paper contributes to the ongoing effort to address the lack of interpretability in deep learning models, particularly in the medical domain. By improving the interpretability of deep learning models, clinicians can better understand and trust the decision-making process of these models, which can improve patient safety and lead to more efficient and effective diagnosis and treatment of various diseases. The proposed pipeline can also potentially be applied in other fields where deep learning is used for image analysis.

2   Literature Review

2.1   Medical Imaging and Deep Learning

A branch of machine learning called deep learning (DL) is able to learn to use its own computational strategy. Similar to how people make judgments, a deep learning model is employed to consistently organize data into a homogeneous framework [10]. This is accomplished using deep learning, which layers a number of algorithms into a structure known as an Artificial Neural Network (ANN). Medical imaging produces vast amounts of data, making it challenging and time-consuming for human radiologists to analyze effectively. Deep learning techniques can recognize patterns in medical images, identify anomalies, and categorize structures such as tumors or lesions, leading to faster and more accurate diagnoses and improved patient treatment regimens. However, the lack of annotated medical images for deep learning algorithm training and the potential for over-fitting are significant challenges. Deep learning algorithms have been successful in diagnosing Alzheimer's and Parkinson's, locating malignant tumors, and find anomalies in MRI scans. In one study, deep learning algorithms outperformed human radiologists in detecting breast cancer in mammograms, with an accuracy rate of 94.5% [11].

2.2   Explainable Deep Learning

Deep learning models are based on neural networks that are composed of multiple layers of interconnected artificial neurons [12]. These models are trained on large amounts of data and can learn complex patterns and relationships. However, these models can be considered as black boxes since their decision-making process is not transparent, and it is challenging to understand how they arrive at their predictions or decisions [13].

Explainable deep learning techniques provide transparency and interpretability to complex deep learning models. In medical imaging, these techniques allow clinicians to understand how models make decisions, improving accuracy and efficiency. Explainable deep learning is promising in cancer detection and personalized medicine, identifying patterns and relationships that predict treatment effectiveness.

Explainable deep learning techniques provide transparency, trust, and fairness in deep learning models, increasing their effectiveness and reliability [14]. Activation maps, LIME, SHAP, and decision trees are commonly used techniques. However, these techniques can increase complexity, training time, and cost, and may compromise performance for interpretability. Some models, such as those using unsupervised or reinforcement learning, may be challenging to interpret. It is essential to consider the specific requirements of the model before deciding to use explainable deep learning techniques to make informed decisions and achieve optimal results [15].

2.3   Gradient-Weighted Class Activation Mapping (Grad-CAM)

Class Activation Mapping (CAM) is a method for visualizing the regions in an image that are important for a given classification task. It was first introduced by Zhou et al. in 2016 [16] and has since become a popular tool for interpreting the predictions of deep convolutional neural networks (CNNs). Since the introduction of CAM, there has been a large amount of subsequent work in this field. Researchers have proposed a number of modifications and extensions to the original method, including the use of Grad-CAM (Gradient-weighted Class Activation Mapping), which uses the gradient of the output of the network with respect to the activations of the feature maps to generate the heatmap [3] (Fig. 2).

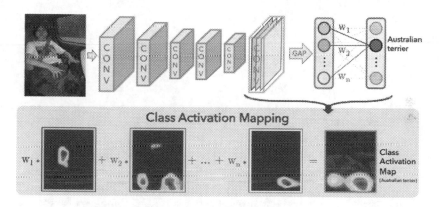

Fig. 2. Class Activation Mapping

Grad-CAM is a technique for visualizing where a CNN model is looking. It is class-specific and can produce a separate visualization for every class present in the image. It uses "alpha values" computed based on gradients to weight feature maps to create a heatmap. Grad-CAM has been used for cancer detection, and studies have shown that it improves accuracy and interpretability of results. However, limitations include lack of robustness to changes in input image and unclear explanation of the basis for prediction in complex images.

In recent years, there have been numerous efforts to improve the accuracy and interpretability of Grad-CAM for cancer detection [17]. One of the main focuses has been on improving the robustness of Grad-CAM to changes in the input image, as well as incorporating prior knowledge into the method to reduce the risk of misdiagnosis. One approach to improve the robustness of Grad-CAM is to use more sophisticated methods for computing the gradients used in the method [18].

Incorporating prior knowledge into Grad-CAM is another approach to improving the interpretability of the results. For example, Li et al. proposed a method for incorporating prior knowledge into Grad-CAM that improved the accuracy of cancer detection in biopsy images. The authors showed that their proposed method reduced the risk of misdiagnosis and improved the interpretability of the results [19].

In addition to these efforts to improve Grad-CAM for cancer detection, there have also been efforts to extend the method to other medical imaging modalities, such as magnetic resonance imaging (MRI) and positron emission tomography (PET) scans. For example, Wang et al. proposed a method for using Grad-CAM for cancer detection in MRI scans, which showed promising results in a preliminary study [20].

Overall, the recent advances in improving Grad-CAM for cancer detection demonstrate the potential of the method for improving the accuracy and interpretability of cancer detection in medical imaging. By addressing the limitations of the current methods and incorporating prior knowledge into the method, researchers are working towards making Grad-CAM a more reliable tool for cancer detection and diagnosis.

3   Methodology

We present the methodology used in our research to develop an accurate and interpretable model for the binary image classification task of identifying the presence of metastases from 96×96 px digital histopathology images.

Lymph nodes are crucial in cancer diagnosis and staging, but the current diagnostic procedure for pathologists is tedious and time-consuming. However, ongoing advancements in technology and techniques offer hope for more accurate and efficient assessments in the future. Histopathological images of lymph nodes are essential for the diagnosis of various diseases, including cancer. The dataset used in this study comprises of 220,000 training images and 57,000 evaluation images, which is a carefully curated subset of the PCam dataset [21, 22] derived from a comprehensive collection of H&E stained whole slide images. The quality of the data is ensured through manual inspection by experienced technicians and consultation with pathologist. Specifically, there are 130,000 negative images and only 90,000 positive images, resulting in a ratio closer to 60/40. Overall, the quality, quantity, and recency of the data are sufficient, and the dataset meets our expectations. These advancements will benefit pathologists and improve patient outcomes by enabling earlier detection and more targeted treatment.

Identifying metastases in lymph nodes is a challenging task, even for trained pathologists. It can be especially difficult for untrained individuals due to the varied features that metastases exhibit. Irregular nuclear shapes, sizes, and staining shades are some of the indications of metastases. To train a model for classification, we must consider the optimal crop size for the images. We can avoid overfitting by increasing the amount of data, using augmentation techniques, implementing regularization, and simplifying model architectures. We can incorporate augmentation techniques like random rotation, crop, flip, lighting, and Gaussian blur into the image loader function to improve data quality. We must also examine samples with extremely low or high pixel intensities to ensure data quality. All bright images in the dataset have been labeled as negative, but we are unsure about the dark images. Hence, removing these dark images (outliers) from a large dataset is unlikely to affect prediction performance.

When building a machine learning (ML) production pipeline, it's best to start with a simple model to identify any issues, such as poor data quality, before tuning further. Maintaining equal ratios of negative and positive labels in training and validation sets is important to prevent under representation of rare classes. Selecting the ideal model architecture requires considering various factors, including the risk of overfitting with a deeper architecture. A pre-trained convnet model, densenet169, with transfer learning, is an effective approach for this problem. We use the one cycle policy for disciplined hyperparameter selection, which can save time spent training suboptimal hyperparameters.

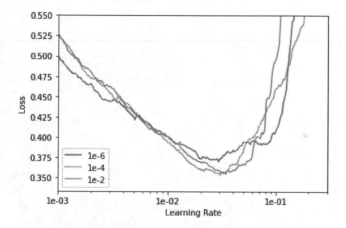

Fig. 3. Weight Decay Comparison

First, we determine the optimal learning rate and weight decay values. The ideal learning rate is found just before the loss plateaus and divergence occurs, and it should be selected at a point where the loss is still decreasing. For weight decay, we conduct a small grid search using values of 1e−2, 1e−4, and 1e−6 (Fig. 3). Our goal is to find the highest weight decay that results in a low loss and allows us to use the maximum learning rate before it spikes. Based on experimentation, we found that 1e−4 is the largest weight decay that enables us to train with the maximum learning rate. We select a learning rate of around 2e−2, which is close to the bottom but still descending. A two-step training approach, beginning with the heads and freezing remaining parts, is used to optimize model performance. Unfreezing all trainable parameters allows fine-tuning the pre-trained bottom layers to detect common shapes and patterns, avoiding overfitting, and achieving better accuracy and robustness.

Now we describe the implementation of Grad-CAM (Gradient-weighted Class Activation Mapping) for visualizing and localizing the image regions that contribute the most to the model's predictions. The Grad-CAM method is implemented using the fastai library's hooks feature, which allows us to attach functions to a model's forward and backward passes. First, we define the `hooked_backward` function that hooks into the convolutional part of the model and returns the activations and gradients. We use these activations and gradients to compute the Grad-CAM heatmap. To obtain the heatmap, we create a utility function `getHeatmap` that takes a validation set image and returns the activation map. This function hooks into the model's forward and backward passes using the `hooked_backward` function and computes the Grad-CAM map. The `getHeatmap` function uses OpenCV to convert the batch tensor image to a grayscale image, which is then overlaid with the Grad-CAM heatmap using matplotlib.

Finally, we plot the Grad-CAM heatmap for a few selected validation images as shown in Fig. 8 We use the `getHeatmap` function to obtain the heatmap and overlay it on top of the grayscale image. The resulting plots show the original image, the grayscale image, and the Grad-CAM heatmap overlaid on top. Hence, the Grad-CAM implementation provides a useful tool for understanding the decision-making process of a neural network and visualizing the image regions that contribute the most to its predictions as we will see in the next section.

4   Results and Discussion

4.1   Model Performance

In this section, we present the results of evaluating the performance of our proposed model.

Figure 4 displays the learning rate during the initial cycle of training. It starts at a low value and gradually increases to reach the maximum learning rate in the middle of the cycle, and then slows down towards the end. This approach uses a low warm-up learning rate initially, gradually increasing it to a higher value. The higher learning rate has a regularizing effect, preventing the model from settling for sharp and narrow local minima, and instead encouraging wider and more stable ones. As we approach the middle of the cycle, the learning rate is lowered to search for stable areas where minima may exist. This helps prevent overfitting and ensures the model can generalize well to new data.

In Fig. 5, we show the losses during the initial cycle of training. Upon analysis, we observe a slight increase in losses following the initial drop, which can be attributed to the escalating learning rate in the first half of the cycle. It is noteworthy that there is a temporary surge in losses when the maximum learning rate pushes the model out of local minima. However, this strategic move is expected to yield positive results as the learning rates are subsequently reduced.

In Fig. 6, we show the losses from training and validation for batches processed. Upon closer examination, we observe that the validation performance has diverged from the training performance towards the end of the cycle. This indicates that our model has begun to overfit during the small learning rates. Further training would result in the model solely memorizing features from the training set, leading to an increase in the validation set performance. Therefore, it is a good stopping point for the training process.

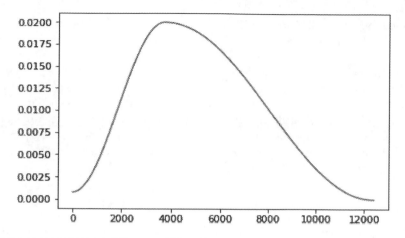

Fig. 4. Learning Rate of Initial Cycle

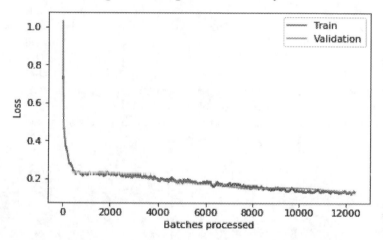

Fig. 5. Losses of Initial Cycle

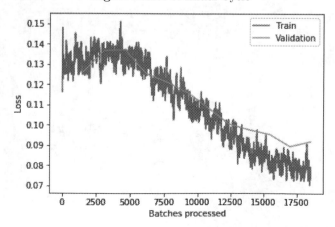

Fig. 6. Loss vs Batches Processed

Based on the validation set metrics, our model achieves an accuracy of 96.73%. In Fig. 7, we evaluate our model's performance on different types of image examples. Firstly, we randomly select samples to observe the overall accuracy of our model. Next, we focus on the most incorrectly labeled images with high confidence to identify patterns and areas for improvement. Finally, we explore the most accurately labeled images to gain insights into our model's strengths. This visualization provides valuable insights into challenging images for the model, and may uncover issues with the dataset. By analyzing these examples, we can improve the model's performance and gain a better understanding of the data.

4.2   Explainability of the Model with Grad-CAM

In this section, we explain the explainability of our model using Gradient-weighted Class Activation Mapping (Grad-CAM). Grad-CAM is a visualization technique that highlights important regions in the input image that contribute to the output class score. By applying Grad-CAM to our model, we gain insights into its decision-making process and identify important features for classification. To generate Grad-CAM visualizations, we select an image from the validation set, obtain the predicted class score, and compute gradients of the score with respect to feature maps. These gradients serve as importance weights for the feature maps, and we combine them to produce a heat map that highlights relevant regions in the input image. Figure 8 shows the Grad-CAM visualizations for

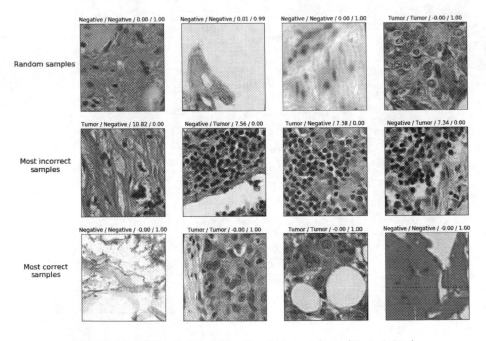

Fig. 7. Model Predictions (Predicted/Actual/Loss/Probability)

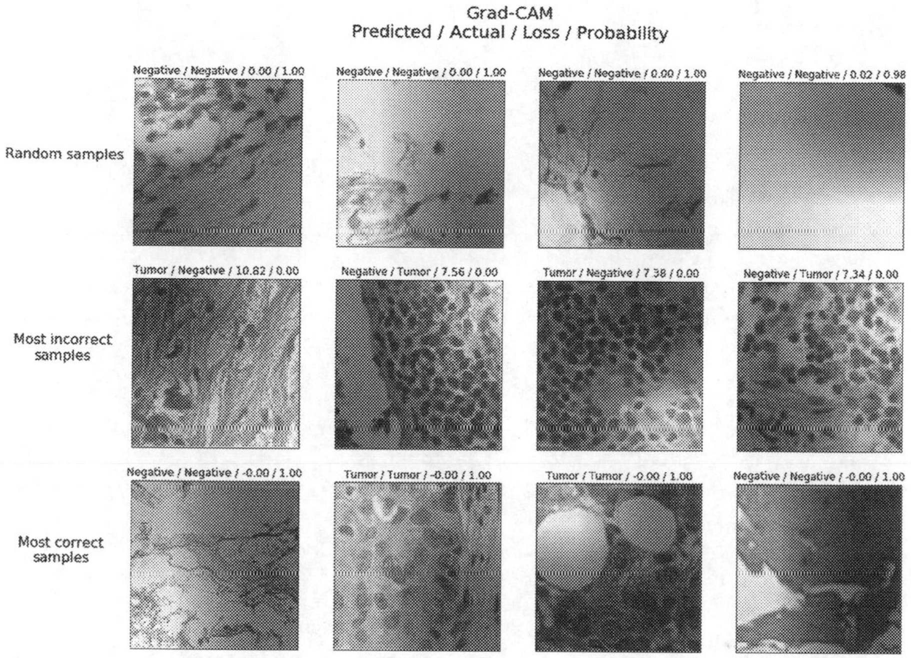

Fig. 8. Grad-CAM Results (Predicted/Actual/Loss/Probability)

different types of image examples. For instance, if the label is *tumor*, Grad-CAM will reveal all the locations where the model believes the tumor patterns exist.

5 Conclusion

In conclusion, this paper has explored the potential of using Grad-CAM as a technique for building explainable deep learning models in medical imaging, with a focus on cancer detection. While the findings are promising, there is still much work to be done in this field. Future research could focus on accuracy of Grad-CAM visualisations, extending it to other imaging modalities, and developing user interfaces that provide clinicians with intuitive and interpretable visualizations of the model's decision-making process. Overall, this paper highlights the importance of Explainable Deep Learning in medical imaging and the potential of Grad-CAM as a tool for enhancing interpretability and trust in deep learning models.

Funding. The Project funding including hardware resource (GPU) and other costs of the project is funded by the Science and Engineering Research Board (SERB), Govt. of India, Project No: SRG/2022/000122, executed in XIM University, Bhubaneswar, India, supervised by Arif Ahmed Sekh.

References

1. Wang, J., Wang, J., Zhao, H., Tong, L., Han, J., Wei, P.: A multi-scale convolutional neural network for lung cancer detection using a large dataset. Med. Biol. Eng. Comput. **59**, 2857–2866 (2021)
2. Wang, J., Sun, T., Zou, X., Cui, S., Han, J., Wei, P.: Exploring the interpretability of a deep learning-based system for breast cancer diagnosis using grad-cam and convolutional neural networks. J. Healthcare Eng. **1–9**, 2021 (2021)
3. Selvaraju, R.R., Cogswell, M., Das, A., Vedantam, R., Parikh, D., Batra, D.: Grad-CAM: visual explanations from deep networks via gradient-based localization. In: Proceedings of the IEEE International Conference on Computer Vision, pp. 618–626 (2017)
4. Shen, D., Wu, G., Suk, H.-I.: Deep learning in medical image analysis. Annu. Rev. Biomed. Eng. **22**, 223–256 (2020)
5. Zeiler, M.D., Fergus, R.: Visualizing and understanding convolutional networks. In: Fleet, D., Pajdla, T., Schiele, B., Tuytelaars, T. (eds.) ECCV 2014. LNCS, vol. 8689, pp. 818–833. Springer, Cham (2014). https://doi.org/10.1007/978-3-319-10590-1_53
6. Samek, W., Wiegand, T., Muller, K.-R.: Towards explainable artificial intelligence: concepts and methods. arXiv preprint arXiv:2001.06822 (2019)
7. Wang, X., Peng, Y., Lu, L., Lu, Z., Bagheri, M., Summers, R.M.: Deep learning in medical image analysis: a review. Engineering **7**, 935–949 (2021)
8. Rajpurkar, P., et al.: Deep learning for chest radiograph diagnosis: A retrospective comparison of the chexnext algorithm to practicing radiologists. PLoS Med. **15**(11), e1002686 (2018)
9. Beam, A.L., Kohane, I.S.: Clinical concept embeddings learned from massive sources. NPJ Digit. Med. **3**(1), 1–8 (2020)
10. Esteva, A., Robicquet, A., Ramsundar, B., et al.: A guide to deep learning in healthcare. Nat. Med. **25**(1), 24–29 (2019)
11. Shen, L., Margolies, L.R., Rothstein, J.H., Fluder, E., McBride, R., Sieh, W.: Deep learning to improve breast cancer detection on screening mammography. Sci. Rep. **9**(1), 12495 (2019). Nature Publishing Group UK London
12. Goodfellow, I., Bengio, Y., Courville, A.: Deep Learning. MIT Press, Cambridge (2016)
13. James Murdoch, W., Singh, C., Kumbier, K., Abbasi-Asl, R., Yu, B.: Interpretable machine learning: definitions, methods, and applications. arXiv preprint arXiv:1901.04592 (2019)
14. Samek, W., Wiegand, T., Muller, K.-R.: Explainable artificial intelligence: understanding, visualizing and interpreting deep learning models. arXiv preprint arXiv:1708.08296 (2017)
15. Ribeiro, M.T., Singh, S., Guestrin, C.: Why should I trust you?": explaining the predictions of any classifier. In: Proceedings of the 22nd ACM SIGKDD International Conference on Knowledge Discovery and Data Mining, pp. 1135–1144 (2016)
16. Zhou, B., Khosla, A., Lapedriza, A., et al.: Learning deep features for discriminative localization. In: Proceedings of the IEEE Conference on Computer Vision and Pattern Recognition, pp. 2921–2929. IEEE (2016)
17. Wang, Y., Wu, S., Zhang, Q., Zhang, J.: Robustness of grad-cam for multi-view mammogram classification. IEEE Access **9**, 13766–13774 (2021)
18. Qin, F., Wang, Y., Zhang, Q., Guo, Y.: Multi-scale deep neural network for lung nodule classification based on CT images. J. Xray Sci. Technol. **29**(4), 737–750 (2021)

19. Li, Z., Liu, W., Zhang, J., Shi, J., Wu, J.: Incorporating prior knowledge into grad-cam for improved interpretability and reduced misdiagnosis risk. Pattern Recogn. **119**, 108145 (2021)
20. Wang, H., Zhang, W., Wang, Y., Cai, Y.: Grad-cam based multiscale deep learning model for automatic MRI breast tumor detection and classification. J. Healthcare Eng. **1–11**, 2021 (2021)
21. Veeling, B.S., Linmans, J., Winkens, J., Cohen, T., Welling, M.: Rotation equivariant CNNs for digital pathology. GigaScience **7**(6) (2018)
22. Bejnordi, B.E., Veta, M., van Diest, P.J., et al.: Diagnostic assessment of deep learning algorithms for detection of lymph node metastases in women with breast cancer. JAMA, J. Am. Med. Assoc. **318**(22), 2199–2210 (2017)

Histogram Matching Based Data-Augmentation and Its Impact on CNN Model for Covid-19 and Pneumonia Detection from Radiology Images

Santanu Roy[1]($\boxtimes$) (iD) and Vibhuti Bansal[2] (iD)

[1] NIIT University, Neemrana, Rajasthan, India
santanuroy35@gmail.com
[2] Bharati Vidyapeeth's College of Engineering, New Delhi, India

Abstract. In this study, we present a Histogram-Matching based novel data augmentation method for Covid-19 and Pneumonia detection, from an imbalanced Radiology (Chest X-Ray) image dataset. Moreover, we have publicly shared a large augmented CXR dataset on the Kaggle site (https://www.kaggle.com/datasets/vibhuti25/histogram-matching-covid-cxr), which is more balanced than the original dataset. For data augmentation, we have incorporated the Histogram Matching technique, CLAHE 0.5, and CLAHE 0.75, in order to increase the number of images in the dataset. The number of images in the augmented dataset per class is chosen by a statistical formula which is computed from the dataset itself. We have implemented two existing Convolutional Neural Network (CNN) models for Covid-19 detection i.e., Covid Net and Covid-Lite models, on the proposed augmented dataset. We have achieved 3–5% and 7–9% improvement of testing accuracy, precision, recall and F1 score for Covid Net and Covid-Lite model respectively, after employing the proposed augmented dataset. Furthermore, we have implemented a popular CNN model i.e., VGG-16 and by the proposed data-augmentation we have achieved the best results of 95% accuracy, 96% F1 score, 96% precision and 96% recall.

Keywords: Covid-19 Detection · CXR images · Histogram Matching · CLAHE · CNN model

1 Introduction

Covid-19 disease has been affecting on mortality and health of the global population considerably [1], for the last two years. This disease is caused by Severe Acute Respiratory Syndrome-2 (SARS-2) [1] which is a very contagious virus

Supported by organization x.

and it spreads more with the physical contact of human beings. It caused death over 6 million people in the world for last two years. WHO already declared Covid-19 as a pandemic in March, 2020. However, in recent months (from April 2022 to January 2023), the influence of Covid-19 disease has slightly decayed [2] in terms of death. Nevertheless, distinguishing Covid-19 affected patients from other variants of patients like Pneumonia, Viral Pneumonia (VP), Lung Opacity, Tuberculosis (TB) etc. from Chest X-Ray images (or, radiology images) dataset, is a very challenging task for doctors and researchers. Diagnosing appropriate disease (whether it is VP or Covid) is very much necessary for further treatment of the patients. Therefore, an automatic diagnosis system for Pneumonia and Covid-19 detection from CXR images, is still a hot research topic, in recent advent.

1.1   Benchmark Methods for Covid-19 Detection

Numerous researchers [3–7] have proposed novel CNN architectures to detect Covid-19 and Pneumonia disease efficiently from CXR images. M. Shiddhartha et al. [3] proposed a very lightweight CNN model, they call this model Covid Lite. Unlike other standard CNN models, they utilized many Depth-Wise separable convolutional layers for reducing computational complexity. However, for this reason, this model has slight under-fitting on the employed CXR dataset. This model was only suitable for small dataset. L. Wang et al. [4] designed a novel CNN architecture, called as Covid-Net which is based on a human-machine collaborative design strategy. Despite their model become very popular, due to incorporating many layers in the model, Covid-Net often exhibits overfitting. Chiranjibi Sitaula et al. [5] have proposed an attention-based VGG-16 model in which they captured spatial relationship between pixels from CXR images, by incorporating an extra attention module. S.C. Ramirez et al. [8] have found that the impact of data imbalance on standard CNN models is considerably higher and they have further proposed a Mix-Match approach based semi-supervised learning model, in order to alleviate the data imbalance problem. M. Tyagi et al. [9] have recently proposed a Custom Weighted Balanced Categorical Cross Entropy (CWBCCE) loss function in order to overcome class imbalance problemem. This loss function was deployed in ResNet-18 model in which they employed transfer learning approach from ChexPert Dataset. S. Roy et al. [10] recently proposed Balanced Weighted Categorical Cross Entropy (BWCCE), in which they incorporated a probabilistic notion for assigning bias weight in each class (of loss function). However, we have found that over-sampling or data-augmentation [11] in minor class is the most suitable method, for resolving the class imbalance problem. Many of the researchers [9,12] have proposed over-sampling and modified Weighted CCE together, in order to overcome the class imbalance problem from the CXR dataset.

1.2   Contributions

The contributions of this paper are as follows:

1. In this research work, a very balanced augmented CXR dataset is made, by utilizing Histogram Matching (HM Min-Max Thresholding and HM Min-Max Normalization), CLAHE 0.5 and CLAHE 0.75 methods.
2. The number of images in the augmented dataset (in each class) is chosen by a statistical formula that is computed from the statistical inference of the dataset itself.
3. Existing CNN models Covid-Lite, Covid-Net and VGG-16 are implemented (trained from scratch) on the CXR dataset. Experimental results showed that there is considerable improvement in the performances of these models, after utilizing the proposed data augmentation method. Eventually, we have proposed the framework, i.e., VGG-16 model with proposed data-augmentation for Covid-19 detection from CXR images.
4. A recently invented loss function BWCCE [10] is also deployed on top of the proposed framework. There was slight improvement in the performances of Covid-Lite and Covid-Net model after incorporating BWCCE.

1.3   Employed CXR Dataset

A Chest X-Ray (CXR) dataset is taken from publicly available Kaggle website [13], in which there are four classes: Covid, Normal, Viral Pneumonia (VP) and Lung Opacity (LO). The researchers from Qatar University, Doha, Qatar, and the University of Dhaka, Bangladesh have created this dataset. They have combined the old Pneumonia datasets with Covid images. This dataset is highly imbalanced, since the number of images in Viral Pneumonia is only 1345 and for Covid it's only 3616, which is very much less than that of normal class (10,192) and lung opacity (6012) class. Thus, conventional CNN models have have not performed efficiently on this imbalanced dataset. The other challenges we found in this dataset are: (I) Intra-class variance is found very higher in the Covid class. (II) Inter-class variance between Normal and Lung Opacity is very less. These are further discussed in the methodology part.

2   Preparing Augmented CXR Dataset for Covid-19 and Pneumonia Detection

The proposed data-augmentation method is further divided into three parts: (I) Data-Augmentation by Histogram Matching method, (II) Data-Augmentation by CLAHE, (III) Schemes of Data-Augmentation.

2.1   Data-Augmentation Method by Histogram Matching

Histogram Matching (HM) is widely employed in medical image analysis by numerious researchers [14]. Unlike other HE techniques, in this method, the user first has to choose a reference image from the dataset that has decent contrast property. Thereafter, conventional Global HE stretching operation [15] is generally deployed of a poor contrast (source) image, until the histogram of the

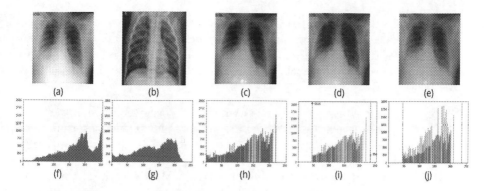

Fig. 1. Visualization of Histogram Matching methods for data-augmentation, (a) is an original image from dataset, (b) is the target image we choose from dataset, (c) is the processed image by conventional Histogram Matching, (d) is the processed image by HM Min-Max Truncated Thresholding, Fig. (e) is the processed image by HM Min-Max Normalization, f–j represents their corresponding histograms

processed image is very similar to the histogram of the reference image. From the theory of statistics, we know that, histogram is also a normalized Probability Density Function (PDF) [16] of an image. For simplicity of calculation, let's assume that PDF of the processed image is exactly equal to the PDF of the reference image after deploying HM method.

$$Thus, \quad p_t(t) = p_r(r) \tag{1}$$

where $p_t(t)$ is the PDF of the processed image, $p_r(r)$ is the PDF of the reference image. Now if $p_s(s)$ is the PDF of source image, from the statistical formula [16] we get from Eq. (2),

$$p_t(t) = \sum_{j=1}^{r} p_s(s_j)|\frac{ds_j}{dt}| \tag{2}$$

Here, in this Eq. (2), r is number of roots in the transformation function equation. Now considering the fact that transformation function of any Histogram Equalization has only one root, according to R. Gonzalez [15], we get,

$$p_t(t) = p_s(s)|\frac{ds}{dt}| \tag{3}$$

Substituting the value from Eq. (1) into (3) we get,

$$p_r(r) * \int dt = \int p_s(s)ds \tag{4}$$

$$or, \quad t = \frac{1}{p_r(r)} \int p_s(s)ds + k \tag{5}$$

Equation (3) reveals that transformation function 't' for HM technique is not exactly a linear transformation [17]. Thus, it often produces artefacts during pre-processing. For the employed CXR dataset, we have observed that often HM technique produces some processed images in which white and black patches generally appear in the form of artefacts. This can further be observed in Fig. 1(c). In order to remove those artefacts from the processed images, we have deployed further three steps:

(I) First, we deploy a reference image which has decent contrast rather than having the best contrast. This will prevent HM techniques from over-contrast enhancement. As a result, there will be less chance of appearing those artefacts.

(II) HM Min-Max Truncated Thresholding (HMMMTT) method is employed in order to reduce artefacts by HM method. We have observed that the main reason for getting those patches (or, artefacts), is that pixel intensity values in those images are either too higher or too lower. Therefore, we have incorporated a thresholding technique, in which a minimum threshold value 45 and a maximum threshold value of 235 are chosen empirically. Here, we have re-assigned all the pixels, having intensity value below 45 and greater than 235, to the intensity levels 45 and 235 respectively. This is further shown in Eq. (6)–(8). Hence, by utilizing HMMMTT method, it is likely that image pixel intensity values will not be extremely higher (>235) or not extremely lower (<45), thus, removing the artefacts effectively from the images.

$$t = Max(Th) \ \ if \ t > Max(Th) \tag{6}$$

$$t = t \ \ if \ Min(Th) < t < Max(Th) \tag{7}$$

$$t = Min(Th) \ \ if \ t < Min(Th) \tag{8}$$

(III) Although, this HMMMTT method avoids those white or black patches (artefacts) in the processed images to a large extent, however, mathematically the transformation function of HMMMTT is still a non-linear function which is noticed from Eq. (5). According to S.Roy et al. [17], a non-linear method is often prone to data loss. Therefore, we have come up with a second method, that is, normalizing or re-assigning pixel intensity values linearly in the range of intensity values $Min(Th)$ to $Max(Th)$, which we call HM Min-Max Normalization (HMMMN). This method has the ability to eliminate those artefacts entirely from the processed images. We have employed a by-default Open-CV library (cv2.normalize with norm type as min-max) in order to perform this HM Min-Max Normalization operation. This is to clarify that for oversampling CXR dataset, both of these methods HMMMTT and HMMMN are employed, this is further shown in Fig. 3.

2.2 Data-Augmentation Method by CLAHE

Contrast Limited Adaptive Histogram Equalization (CLAHE) [18] is an adaptive HE technique that performs Histogram Equalization operation in every local window. Moreover, the contrast enhancement is limited by a clipping value

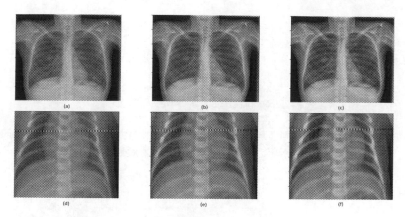

Fig. 2. (a) and (d) represents original images from normal and VP class respectively, (b) and (c) are processed images after applying CLAHE 0.5 and CLAHE 0.75 respectively on (a); whereas (e) and (f) are processed images on (d). The changes will be prominent, after zooming the image

in CLAHE method. This clipping value decides how much contrast should be enhanced for a particular image. In other words, it decides how much stretching of histograms should be done in the processed image. Thus, the performance of CLAHE is very much dependent on this contrast clipping value, which is generally chosen manually. Like Histogram Equalization and Histogram Matching, CLAHE method is also a non-linear method [17]. This is proved mathematically by S.Roy et al. [17] that CLAHE is prone to data loss, despite of deploying contrast clipping. Moreover, one experiment is done in our research, i.e., correlation coefficient [19] is computed between the processed image and the original images (for CLAHE 1.0 and CLAHE 2.0). It is found that mean of Pearson Correlation Coefficient (PCC) for CLAHE 1.0 and CLAHE 2.0 are 0.93 and 0.87 respectively. This indicates that there is 7–13% data loss [19] by CLAHE method. We have experimentally chosen CLAHE 0.5 and CLAHE 0.75 to over-sample the overall CXR dataset so that there will be less data loss (around 3–5%). This is to clarify that, we have chosen CLAHE techniques for data-augmentation, despite it is prone to data loss, because numerous researchers [3,20] have found that CLAHE method has the ability to extract prominent features, especially from CXR (or, from radiology) images (Fig. 2).

2.3   Scheme of Data-Augmentation

To decide the number of images of each class in the augmented dataset, we must formulate one mathematical formula. We have observed that this number of images (in a class) should not be always same per class for alleviating class imbalance problem. Rather it is dependent on two more factors: (a) It should be directly proportional to intra-class variance of a class. For example, if there is more statistical variance among images in a class (i.e. Covid), Deep Learning

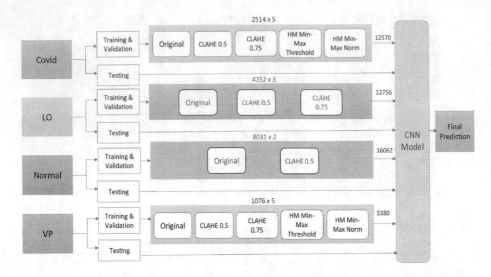

Fig. 3. Proposed framework by Data-Augmentation

model needs higher number of images from that class in order to achieve good accuracy. (b) It should be inversely proportional to this inter-class variance. For example, if the inter-class variance between some classes (e.g. Normal, Lung Opacity) is significantly less, Deep Neural network will need more number of such images from the corresponding class, so that it will have enough examples to study and distinguish the features between these classes. A factor γ_c is formulated whose value must lie between 0 to 1, given in Eq. (9). Thereafter, how many times the data should be increased per class, is chosen proportional to this factor γ_c.

$$\gamma_c = \frac{1}{K}(1 + \alpha * [1 - \frac{m_c}{\mu(m_c)}] + \beta * [\frac{\sigma_c(intra)}{\mu(\sigma_c(intra))} - 1] + \eta * [1 - \frac{\sigma_c(inter)}{\mu(\sigma_c(inter))}]) \quad (9)$$

Here, in Eq. (9), K is the total number of classes in the dataset, $\mu(m_c)$ is the mean of total number of images per class, $\mu(\sigma_c(intra))$ is the average intra-class variance computed per class, $\mu(\sigma_c(inter))$ is the average inter-class variance computed per class. This intra and inter-class variance have been computed by correlation coefficient [19], which is further explored in detail, in the supplementary material.

Lemma: If γ_c in each class is chosen as the formula given in Eq. (9), i.e., $\gamma_c = \frac{1}{K}(1 + \alpha * (1 - \frac{m_c}{\mu(m_c)}) + \beta * (\frac{\sigma_c(intra)}{\mu(\sigma_c(intra))} - 1) + \eta * (1 - \frac{\sigma_c(inter)}{\mu(\sigma_c(inter))}))$, where $\forall c = 1, 2, ..K$ and $(K > 1)$, then sum of γ_cs of all class will be equal to 1, i.e., $\sum_{c=1}^{K} \gamma_c = 1$, if $\alpha = \beta = \eta = 1$. This also reveals that, the number of images is assigned (in each class) based on probabilistic notion.

This *Lemma* is further proved in the supplementary material. We have chosen the value of $\alpha = 0.6, \beta = 0.7, \eta = 1.7$ empirically in the formula of Eq. (9), so that the variation of the values of intra-class variance and inter-class variance will be in the same range. This is to clarify that, here we maintain the average of sum of α, β and η to be 1, i.e., $\frac{\alpha+\beta+\eta}{3} = 1$, such that $\sum_{c=1}^{K} \gamma_c \approx 1$. Thus, assigning the number of images in the above way (which incorporates probabilistic notion), can alleviate class imbalance as well as intra and inter-class variance problems from the dataset considerably, to the best of our knowledge. The entire data-augmentation scheme is further shown in Fig. 3.

3   Results and Analysis

The Results and Analysis section is further divided into two parts: (a) Training Specifications, (b) Observation and Analysis.

3.1   Training Specification

All the models have been built using Keras sequential API, on the platform of Google Colab Pro service. Covid-Lite, Covid-Net and VGG-16 models are performed on the original Covid CXR dataset from the scratch, with the following specifications. All these models are trained from scratch, with almost same training specification, for fair comparisons.

1. Original CXR dataset is divided with 75–25% ratio of training and testing, 25% portion of the training images is chosen for the validation set.
2. Adams-optimizer is deployed as the preferred choice of optimizer for all the models with a learning rate of $1e^{-4}$.
3. A batch size of 8 is used while training all the CNN models.
4. Prior to feeding all the images into the CNN model, they are resized into 224×224. Moreover, their intensity is normalized from [0–255] to [0–1].
5. An early stopping call-back (of patience 5 epochs) is deployed which is monitored on the validation loss, in order to avoid overfitting.
6. For Covid-Lite model, 3 number of fully connected layers are employed, as it is mentioned in their paper [3]. For Covid-Net model only 1 fully connected layer is utilized as it is done in [4].
7. In contrast with conventional VGG-16 model, in the proposed VGG-16 model (trained from scratch), only 2 FC layers are deployed, to alleviate overfitting problem. Furthermore the number of neurons in those FC layers is chosen 128 and 32, thus, number of hyper-parameters is less.

3.2   Observations and Analysis

This is evident from the graph of Fig. 4, that there is no over-fitting by the VGG-16 model, implemented on the proposed augmented dataset. Because there is very little gap between training and validation graph, noticed from Fig. 4(a) and Fig. 4(b). Moreover, this can be observed that from Table 1, by VGG-16 model (incorporated on the proposed augmented dataset), the model has reached to

Table 1. Ablation Study and Comparison of several CNN models (trained from scratch), on testing dataset

Methodology	Accuracy	Precision	Recall	F1Score
Covid-Net on original dataset	0.87	0.88	0.86	0.87
Covid-Net on proposed augmented dataset	0.90	0.91	0.91	0.91
Covid-Net on proposed augmented dataset +BWCCE loss	0.92	0.93	0.91	0.93
Covid-Lite on original dataset	0.85	0.84	0.87	0.85
Covid-Lite on proposed augmented dataset	0.92	0.93	0.94	0.93
Covid-Lite on proposed augmented dataset +BWCCE loss	0.93	0.94	0.92	0.93
VGG-16 on original dataset	0.90	0.92	0.90	0.91
VGG-16 on proposed augmented dataset	**0.95**	**0.96**	**0.96**	**0.96**
VGG-16 on proposed augmented dataset +BWCCE loss	0.94	0.94	0.96	0.95

its optimal performance. Indeed, by utilizing VGG-16 model on the proposed framework, we have got the best results so far on this CXR dataset, i.e., 95% accuracy, 96% F1 score, 96% precision, 96% recall. Therefore, we eventually have proposed VGG-16 model on the proposed augmented dataset, for Covid-19 detection from CXR images. This is to clarify that, VGG-16 model performance is superior to other Covid-Lite and Covid-Net model, due to its simplicity of architecture. Covid-Net model has the most complex architecture, and 183 million number of hyper-parameters to train, therefore, Covid-Net model is prone to overfitting, to the best of our knowledge.

Table 1 also represents an ablation study of Covid-Lite, Covid-Net and VGG-16 on different frameworks. Table 1 reveals that Covid-Net and Covid-Lite, both of the models' performances have been significantly boosted after employing the proposed augmented dataset. Due to data-augmentation, Deep Learning model has many number of samples in minor class, thus, alleviating the problem of class imbalance. On top of this framework, a novel loss function BWCCE [10] is also incorporated in order to further alleviate class imbalance problem slightly. The

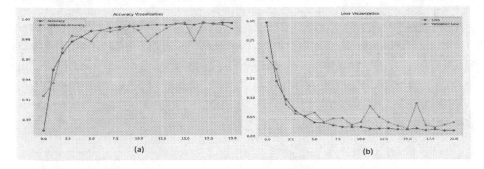

Fig. 4. Training (blue) vs Validation graph (Orange) comparison (a) Accuracy of VGG-16 model on proposedT augmented dataset, (b) Loss for VGG-16 model on proposed dataset (Color figure online)

exact mathematical formula of BWCCE along with one lemma, has already been shown in [10]. This is evident from the Table 1 that, BWCCE has enabled the Covid-Net model to achieve higher accuracy, precision and F1 score. Because Covid-Net model did not resolve the class imbalance problem appropriately. However, BWCCE has not caused significance changes in the performance of Covid-Lite model. Furthermore, BWCCE has decayed the performance of VGG-16 (trained from scratch) on the proposed augmented dataset. In fact, we believe that after utilizing VGG-16 on proposed augmented dataset, the model had already reached the saturation point (or, optimal performance) for this dataset. Further, on top of it, if any method is deployed, this will cause a decaying performance of the model instead of improving. He et al. [21] had already addressed this problem of degrading performance after reaching saturation point for CNN models.

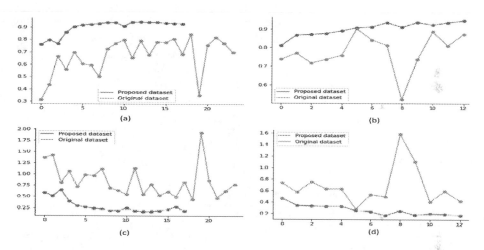

Fig. 5. Validation graph comparison for original dataset vs proposed augmented dataset (a) Accuracy for Covid-Lite model, (b) Accuracy for Covid-Net model, (c) Loss for Covid-Lite model, (d) Loss for Covid-Net model

Figure 5 represents a different kind of graph, that is, comparing the performance of original (Orange) vs proposed augmented dataset (blue) for only validation set. From the graph of Fig. 5 this can be observed that, on the proposed augmented dataset, the graph of both Covid-Lite and Covid-Net models have become considerably stable and converged faster than that of the original dataset. As a consequence, they have produced better performances in terms of accuracy, precision, recall and F1 score, as demonstrated in Table 1. Hence, this can be concluded that the proposed augmented dataset, has removed class imbalance as well as other challenges from the dataset significantly. Because our proposed data-augmentation method neither produced very different images (in terms of statistics) nor very similar images in the dataset and we have chosen the number of images in the augmented dataset based on statistical inference from the dataset, thus, we believe that after employing proposed data-augmentation method the CNN models almost reached its optimal performances. As a result, all three CNN models (shown in Table 1) have improved their performances considerably.

3.3   Conclusion

Histogram Matching based novel data-augmentation method was proposed for over-sampling an imbalanced Covid CXR dataset. Histogram Matching, CLAHE 0.5, CLAHE 0.75 are utilized for over-sampling the existing dataset. We made a large augmented dataset of 46,200 images. The proposed data-augmentation method was not only feature invariant for the final classification task, but also, it was able to generate synthetic images which had slightly different statistics, in terms of contrast and luminance. Moreover, the number of images in this augmented dataset was chosen based on some statistical computation from the dataset itself. Experimental results suggested that the performance of existing CNN models Covid-Lite, Covid-Net, VGG-16 had been significantly boosted after employing the proposed data-augmentation. Hence, our proposed framework outperformed the other benchmark methods. Furthermore, VGG-16 model on this proposed augmented dataset, was further proposed for automatic Covid-19 and Pneumonia detection from Chest X-Ray images.

References

1. Gorbalenya, A.E., et al.: The species Severe acute respiratory syndrome-related coronavirus: classifying 2019-nCoV and naming it SARS-CoV-2. Nat. Microbiol. **5**(4), 536–544 (2020)
2. Del Rio, C., Malani, P.N.: COVID-19 in 2022—the beginning of the end or the end of the beginning? JAMA **327**(24), 2389–2390 (2022)
3. Siddhartha, M., Santra, A.: COVIDLite: a depth-wise separable deep neural network with white balance and CLAHE for detection of Covid-19. arXiv preprint arXiv:2006.13873 (2020)
4. Wang, L., Lin, Z.Q., Wong, A.: Covid-net: a tailored deep convolutional neural network design for detection of Covid-19 cases from chest X-ray images. Sci. Rep. **10**(1), 1–12 (2020)
5. Sitaula, C., Hossain, M.B.: Attention-based VGG-16 model for Covid-19 chest X-ray image classification. Appl. Intell. **51**(5), 2850–2863 (2021)
6. Kumar, A., Tripathi, A.R., Satapathy, S.C., Zhang, Y.D.: SARS-Net: Covid-19 detection from chest X-rays by combining graph convolutional network and convolutional neural network. Pattern Recogn. **122**, 108255 (2022)
7. Xu, Y., Lam, H.K., Jia, G.: Manet: a two-stage deep learning method for classification of Covid-19 from chest X-ray images. Neurocomputing **443**, 96–105 (2021)
8. Calderon-Ramirez, et al.: Correcting data imbalance for semi-supervised Covid-19 detection using X-ray chest images. Appl. Soft Comput. **111**, 107692 (2021)
9. Tyagi, M., Roy, S., Bansal, V.: Custom weighted balanced loss function for Covid 19 detection from an imbalanced CXR dataset. In: 2022 26th International Conference on Pattern Recognition (ICPR), Montreal, Canada, pp. 2707–2713. IEEE (2022)

10. Roy, S., Tyagi, M., Bansal, V., Jain, V.: SVD-CLAHE boosting and balanced loss function for Covid-19 detection from an imbalanced chest X-ray dataset. Comput. Biol. Med. 106092 (2022)

11. Chandra, T.B., Verma, K., Singh, B.K., Jain, D., Netam, S.S.: Coronavirus disease (Covid-19) detection in chest X-ray images using majority voting based classifier ensemble. Expert Syst. Appl. **165**, 113909 (2021)

12. Chamseddine, E., Mansouri, N., Soui, M., Abed, M.: Handling class imbalance in Covid-19 chest X-ray images classification: using smote and weighted loss. Appl. Soft Comput. **129**, 109588 (2022)

13. Chowdhury, M.E., et al.: Can AI help in screening viral and Covid-19 pneumonia? IEEE Access **8**, 132665–132676 (2020)

14. Chen, X., et al.: Automatic histogram specification for glioma grading using multicenter data. J. Healthcare Eng. **2019** (2019)

15. Gonzalez, R.C.: Digital Image Processing. Pearson Education India (2009)

16. Papoulis, A., Unnikrishna Pillai, S.: Probability, random variables and stochastic processes (2002)

17. Roy, S., Bhalla, K., Patel, R.: Mathematical analysis of histogram equalization techniques for medical image enhancement: a tutorial from the perspective of data loss. Multimed. Tools Appl. 1–30 (2023)

18. Pizer, S.M.: Contrast-limited adaptive histogram equalization: speed and effectiveness Stephen M. Pizer, R. Eugene Johnston, James P. Ericksen, Bonnie C. Yankaskas, Keith E. Muller medical image display research group. In: Proceedings of the First Conference on Visualization in Biomedical Computing, Atlanta, Georgia, vol. 337, p. 1 (1990)

19. Roy, S., Panda, S., Jangid, M.: Modified reinhard algorithm for color normalization of colorectal cancer histopathology images. In: 29th European Signal Processing Conference (EUSIPCO), Dublin, Ireland, pp. 1231–1235. IEEE (2021)

20. Al-Waisy, A.S., et al.: COVID-CheXNet: hybrid deep learning framework for identifying COVID-19 virus in chest X-rays images. Soft. Comput. **27**(5), 2657–2672 (2023)

21. He, K., Zhang, X., Ren, S., Sun, J.: Deep residual learning for image recognition. In: Proceedings of the IEEE Conference on Computer Vision and Pattern Recognition, pp. 770–778 (2016)

DHFormer: A Vision Transformer-Based Attention Module for Image Dehazing

Abdul Wasi$^{(\boxtimes)}$ (iD) and O. Jeba Shiney (iD)

Chandigarh University, Mohali, India
`wasilone11@gmail.com`, `jeba.e10900@cumail.in`

Abstract. Images acquired in hazy conditions have degradations induced in them. Dehazing such images is a vexed and ill-posed problem. Scores of prior-based and learning-based approaches have been proposed to mitigate the effect of haze and generate haze-free images. Many conventional methods are constrained by their lack of awareness regarding scene depth and their incapacity to capture long-range dependencies. In this paper, a method that uses residual learning and vision transformers in an attention module is proposed. It essentially comprises two networks: In the first one, the network takes the ratio of a hazy image and the approximated transmission matrix to estimate a residual map. The second network takes this residual image as input and passes it through convolution layers before superposing it on the generated feature maps. It is then passed through global context and depth-aware transformer encoders to obtain channel attention. The attention module then infers the spatial attention map before generating the final haze-free image. Experimental results including several quantitative metrics demonstrate the efficiency and scalability of the suggested methodology.

Keywords: Residual Learning · Transmission Matrix · Vision Transformer · Attention Module

1 Introduction

In inclement weather, a commonly observed atmospheric phenomenon is haze, which impedes visibility in natural scenes (Fig. 1). It stems from the absorption or scattering of light when it passes through an assemblage of tiny, suspended particles. As a result, the observed scene has artifacts like subdued brightness and anomalous contrast, hue, and saturation. Moreover, this problem has gained widespread attention for the implications it has on a model's performance in complex vision tasks like satellite imagery and autonomous driving [1–3].

The objective behind this work is to approximate a dehazed image given its hazy equivalent. In general, the haze-free image is estimated utilizing the atmospheric scattering model. [4]. Mathematically:

$$I(x) = J(x)t(x) + A[1 - t(x)] \tag{1}$$

© The Author(s), under exclusive license to Springer Nature Switzerland AG 2024
H. Kaur et al. (Eds.): CVIP 2023, CCIS 2009, pp. 148–159, 2024.
https://doi.org/10.1007/978-3-031-58181-6_13

Here, for a pixel coordinate x, $I(x)$ is the observed image with haze, $J(x)$ is its haze-free equivalent, A equals the global atmospheric light and $t(x)$ is the medium's transmission matrix further put as:

$$t(x) = e^{-\beta d(x)} \qquad (2)$$

β being the coefficient of atmospheric scattering and $d(x)$ the depth of scene. Given the number of unknown parameters, the resultant problem is an ill-posed one. Traditionally, priors are used to approximate values for A and $t(x)$ [5–7] or in certain experiments, A is intuitively equated to a constant. Despite giving considerable results, the prior-based approaches are based on certain assumptions and estimations due to which, they at times do inadequate dehazing and introduce artifacts in the haze-free image such as unnatural contrast and color blockings.

Contrary to this, learning-based methods rely on a training process [8–10] where the model, rather than relying on self-curated priors to estimate A and $t(x)$, learns a mapping for the same, given a considerable number of hazy images and their dehazed equivalents. More recently, vision transformers (ViT) [11,12] have transcended most of the traditional learning-based networks in high-level vision tasks.

(a)   (b)

Fig. 1. (a) A hazy image. (b) Haze-free equivalent.

This work proposes an image-dehazing transformer in an attention network coupled with a CNN and a residual network that gives a haze-free image in the output. Input to the CNN is an image $I(x)$ affected by the haze. The network approximates a transmission matrix $t(x)$ as output whose ratio with the image affected by haze $(I(x)/t(x))$ goes into the residual network as input, the output being the residue between the hazy input and the potential haze-free image. Pertinent to mention is that this network does not need the approximation of the global atmospheric light A and so, is immune to the anomalies induced by it. Thereafter, an attention module employs transformer encoders that take into consideration both the global context and the scene depth of an image to infer the channel attributes of the residual image. Finally, the spatial attention is approximated, and the feature maps are concatenated to help estimate the final dehazed image.

2 Related Work

A concise overview of the methodologies relevant to Image dehazing are discussed in this section. It is broadly classified into methods that rely on priors and learning-based methods.

The prior-based methods focus on calculating the transmission matrix and global atmospheric light by making certain presumptions about the scene and using manually customized priors. Tang et al. [13] try to investigate the best features that help remove the haze. They reach the conclusion that the dark-channel features are the most important ones when it comes to haze removal. Despite being trained on patches of synthetic images, the model does well on real-world data. He et al. [5] estimate a dark-channel prior which, alongside an imaging model helps in estimating the depth of haze in a single image and its subsequent dehazing. Another key learning here is that one or a few color channels in a hazy image have pixels of low intensity. Also, the authors show how the patch size significantly alters the output. Fattal et al. [14] came up with a novel haze removal model which, in addition to the transmission map, takes into account the surface shading too, based on an assumption that they are orthogonal. A similar hypothesis is used to determine the hue of haze. Despite using images from different sources, the model gives a mean absolute error of less than 7% on dehazed output. Meng et al. [15] exploits the boundary limits of the transmission map along with the L1-norm-based contextual regularization to model an optimization problem for image dehazing. Also, this function is modeled on few assumptions about the scene making it more fault-tolerant. Zhao et al. [16] divide the hazy image into smaller blocks followed by a patch-wise estimation of the transmission maps. Further optimization results in refined details and well-defined edges in the output image. Pertinent to mention is that since these methods are dependent on hand-crafted priors and scene constraints, they exhibit less fault tolerance and flexibility.

The widespread application of deep learning in image dehazing tasks has given noticeable results. In these learning-based methods, a model learns a set of parameters and an input-output mapping when trained on images and uses the learned parameters to dehaze the rest, usually by estimating a medium transmission map. In, authors Ren et al. [17] learn a mapping from a single hazy input image to its corresponding transmission matrix using a coarse-scale network. Following this, another neural network helps refine the haze-free output. Cai et al. [18] use a trainable CNN-based module to approximate a transmission map, whose layers are crafted in a way that they extract features for which priors were used. Finally, a Bilateral Rectified Linear Unit is used for output quality enhancement. The work proposed by Zhang et al. in [19] has an end-to-end image dehazing module where a DenseNet-inspired encoder-decoder helps approximate the transmission matrix while the method jointly infers the atmospheric light and the dehazing task with it. Although further employing a discriminator improves the quality of the haze-free images, the output generated has low contrast. Li *et al.* [20] propose a residual learning-based network for haze removal. Here, the model first approximates a transmission map and then takes its ratio with the input image to generate the residual output. Also, the network functions without a need to estimate a value for the atmospheric light. Authors suggest it saves the model from the influence of invalid parameters. Despite this, the model is slow at processing and does inadequate dehazing of bright regions of the sky. In [21], Gao *et al.* uses a CNN and a vision transformer for dehazing images. They claim that although CNNs perform better than prior-based methods, they lag behind vision transformers when it comes to detailed information retrieval. However, it does not take into consideration the global features of the image and performs weakly on dark scenes and varying depth. Li [22] *et al.* propose a two-stage image dehazing module in which a Swin transformer along with a CNN is used in the first stage and the local features extracted in the second, while an attention mechanism is used between them. However, the computational cost to dehaze a real-world image is high. Also, the complexity of the network slows down the training too.

Even though learning-based methods outperform the prior-based ones, methods used to further improve the performance of learning-based networks add more depth to the network, resulting in adding more skip-connections, thereby increasing the network complexity and in certain cases, inducing noise too. As a result, by including a residual network, a scalable model is presented, which when used in conjunction with vision transformers, yields encouraging results.

3   Methodology

The overall network architecture of the proposed methodology is shown in Figs. 2 and 3. It dehazes the input image by passing it through two modules: the first one being a residual network and the other one a vision transformer-based attention module. Relevant to mention is that although the residual network alone can provide a dehazed image, the results are unsatisfactory since the output is not free of artifacts and color degradation. Also, it performs poorly on the quality metrics used in this work. Stacking it with an attention network enhances its dehazing performance, as will be evident from various quality metrics in the result section. The working of the two modules and the dataset description are discussed in this section.

3.1   Dataset

This work relies on the NYU2 depth dataset [23] for training the model and SOTS and HSTS datasets [24] for testing it. In practice, there is a shortage of pairs of hazy and dehazed images large enough to train a dehazing model efficiently. Pertinently, since the NYU2 dataset has clear haze-free images and their depth maps, we use these depth maps to get the transmission matrix and assign a constant value to the global atmospheric light to finally generate the required hazy dataset. We do this to 1000 such images from the NYU2 dataset, scaled down to $16 \times 16 \times 3$ for faster training. Although the train and test images have been captured in indoor scenes with varying luminescence, the model performs equally well in outdoor setups. For testing the model, we take 400 and 20 images from [24] respectively. Here, the images in SOTS are captured in indoor setups while the ones in HSTS are captured outdoors.

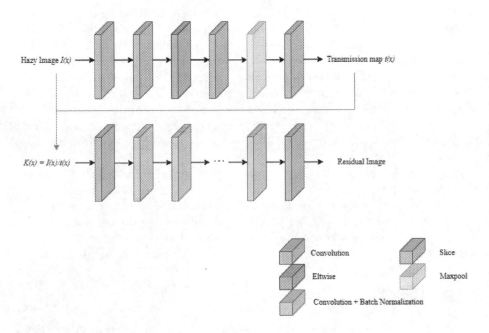

Fig. 2. Network architecture of the residual module. A description of the dimensions of these layers is given in Sect. 3.4.

3.2   The Residual Network

Previously, work done on image dehazing had an increased focus on approximating both the transmission matrix $t(x)$ and the global atmospheric light A to get $J(x)$. Erratic scene conditions make the estimation of these variables a tricky task. We solve Eq. (1) so that values for A and $t(x)$ are learned by the network. This helps in avoiding the abnormalities the misestimation of A causes to the network architecture. Also, the benefit of residual learning is that the impact is superior to direct learning when residual learning is used to characterize the approximate identity mapping. Dividing Eq. (1) by $t(x)$ on both sides, we have:

$$\frac{I(x)}{t(x)} = J(x) + \frac{A[1 - t(x)]}{t(x)} \tag{3}$$

Let $K(x) = \frac{I(x)}{t(x)}$ and $u(x) = \frac{A[1-t(x)]}{t(x)}$.

Equation (3) can be written as:

$$K(x) = J(x) + u(x) \tag{4}$$

In the proposed work, $I(x)$ passes through a CNN and the output is an approximation of the transmission matrix $t(x)$. Their ratio $K(x)$ is the input to the residual network with the aim to generate a residual image $(R'(K(x)))$. The haze-free image $J(x)$ can be given as:

$$J(x) = K(x) - R'(K(x)) \tag{5}$$

Here, $R'(K(x)) \approx u(x)$.

The loss function is described as:

$$l(\theta) = \frac{1}{2n} \sum_{i=1}^{n} \| R'(K(x_i)) - (K(x_i) - J(x_i)) \|_F^2 \tag{6}$$

This function trains θ to give the average squared error between the residual image estimated by the network $R'(K(x))$ and the expected one $(K(x) - J(x))$. The residual image simultaneously goes through two convolution layers with kernel sizes 3×3 and 5×5 giving 3 and 9 output channels respectively. These channels are concatenated with the residual image and the output generated goes into the attention module.

3.3   The Attention Module

The attention network proposed in this work takes inspiration from CBAM [25] which successively infers channel and spatial attention. However, in order to generate these attention maps, CBAM relies on operations such as max-pooling and average-pooling. We approach the task of inferring spatial attention with a vision transformer to demonstrate its effectiveness. The aim of using an attention module is to enhance and further dehaze the output $(R'(K(x))$ from the residual network in a way that takes into consideration both the global context and scene depth in an image.

The transformer here takes as input a sequence of one-dimensional tokens. The concatenated output in the previous step is divided into two-dimensional patches of resolution $m \times m$ which are then flattened into one-dimensional tokens. Mathematically, an image with C channels and dimensions $H \times W$ given by $x \in R^{C \times H \times W}$, is flattened into patches $x_m \in R^{N \times (m^2 \cdot C)}$ where N gives the total number of such patches. Since the latent vector size used here

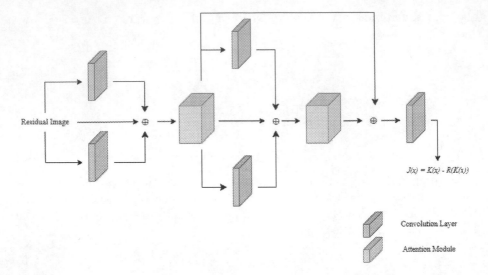

Fig. 3. Graphical overview of the proposed architecture. $\oplus$ denotes channel concatenation.

does not vary across layers, all these tokens are linearly projected to a constant dimension. Furthermore, to preserve the position information of these patches, learnable position embeddings E_t are used. The elaborated architecture of the transformer employed is given in Fig. 4. The final vector input to the transformer is:

$$T_i = x_m + E_t \tag{7}$$

The transformer encoder comprises multi-head attention (MHA) and multi-layer perceptron (MLP) blocks embedded between alternating layers of normalization (LN). For an nth transformer:

$$T'_{n-1} = MHA(LN(T_{n-1})) + T_{n-1}; n = 1 \dots N, \tag{8}$$

$$T_n = MLP(LN(T'_{n-1})) + T'_{n-1}, n = 1 \dots N. \tag{9}$$

Our approach utilizes global context self-attention modules in conjunction with conventional local self-attention mechanisms, enabling the effective and efficient modeling of spatial interactions across both long and short ranges. While doing so, it also learns to effectively dehaze at varying depth levels as well. As shown in Fig. 4, the local token embeddings are generated from the patch projections of the input feature map. For generating the global tokens, we take inspiration from [26]. The network then exploits the local queries for generic encoder operations with global keys and values. Finally, average pooling over the output tokens gives the output as a channel attention map. Further, max-pooling and average-pooling help generate the spatial attention map in a way similar to CBAM. The feature maps generated by channel and spatial attention modules are concatenated to obtain $(R(K(x))$ before a final convolution operation over

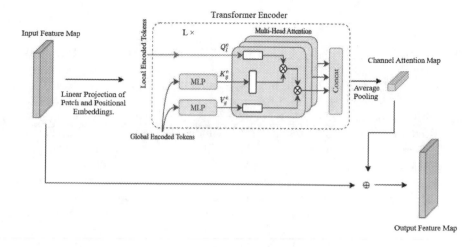

Fig. 4. The transformer-based channel attention module.

their feature maps. All convolution operations are performed as shown in Fig. 3. The output here ($R(K(x))$ is subtracted from $K(x)$ to get the final haze-free output ($J(x)$). Experimental results demonstrate the distinction of this method.

3.4 Implementation Details

Because of the dearth of a considerable number of hazy and haze-free image pairs, the NYU2 depth dataset was used to estimate hazy images from depth maps and haze-free images. A constant global atmospheric light value along with a transmission map approximated from scene depth helped with this estimation. Input to the model is a hazy image $I(x)$ of size $16 \times 16 \times 3$. The feature map obtained after passing through the first convolution layer is of size $14 \times 14 \times 16$. Further, the slice and eltwise layers convert it to feature maps of size $14 \times 14 \times 4 \times 4$ and $14 \times 14 \times 4$ respectively. A 7×7 max-pooling layer and ReLu activation is further applied to produce the transmission map $t(x)$. In the lower branch, ReLu is applied after every layer. 13 Convolution + Batch Normalization layers are used here, with 3×3 filters applied throughout. Output from the residual network is passed through convolution layers of kernel size 3×3 and 5×5 simultaneously, the feature maps concatenated with the residual image before being passed through the attention module, the detailed architecture of which can be found in Fig. 4. Output from the first transformer is further concatenated with layers that use 3×3 (same for the final layer) and 5×5 kernels. The final enhanced residual output is then subtracted from $K(x)$ to get the haze-free output.

4   Results

The proposed architecture is trained on 1000 images from the NYU2 dataset on a single Nvidia RTX 3090 Ti GPU for 150 epochs and a batch size of 16. A number of data augmentation techniques like random crop, horizontal flipping, and random rotation were applied to avoid overfitting. For testing the model, we take 400 and 20 images from SOTS and HSTS respectively. The outcomes are contrasted with various state-of-the-art image dehazing techniques like Fattal's [14], DehazeNet [18] and Gao *et al.* [21]. Along with the visual results, three metrics are used to evaluate the restored haze-free images' quality and compare the relative performance of different methods. These include PSNR [27], SSIM [28], and FSIM [29]. The better performance of a restoration method is judged by higher values of these spatial metrics. Mathematically, PSNR, SSIM, and FSIM are defined as follows:

$$PSNR(x,y) = 10\log_{10}(\frac{MAX^2}{MSE(x,y)}) \tag{10}$$

Here MSE is the mean squared error between images x and y and MAX equals the maximum possible value of the pixels in it.

$$SSIM(x,y) = l(x,y)c(x,y)s(x,y) \tag{11}$$

where, respectively, $l(x,y)$, $c(x,y)$, and $s(x,y)$ quantify the distance between the two images' mean luminance, mean contrast, and correlation coefficient.

$$FSIM = \frac{\sum a \in \omega S_L(a).PC_m(a)}{\sum a \in \omega PC_m(a)} \tag{12}$$

The maximum phase congruency for a location a is represented by the component $PC_m(a)$, and ω represents the spatial domain of the entire image. Tables 1 and 2 give the quantitative evaluation using the mean of PSNR, SSIM and FSIM over the SOTS and HSTS datasets respectively.

Table 1. Mean PSNR, SSIM, and FSIM of the given methods over the SOTS dataset.

Metrics	Fattal's	DehazeNet	Gao *et al.*	Proposed
MPSNR	16.74	15.49	20.86	22.93
MSSIM	0.705	0.739	0.874	0.903
MFSIM	0.946	0.884	0.949	0.933

Table 2. Mean PSNR, SSIM and FSIM of the given methods over the HSTS dataset.

Metrics	Fattal's	DehazeNet	Gao *et al.*	Proposed
MPSNR	17.74	22.39	23.26	26.83
MSSIM	0.803	0.817	0.917	0.924
MFSIM	0.901	0.952	0.921	0.978

4.1 Ablation Study

To corroborate the efficacy of the proposed network, an ablation study was designed in which the network was trained with and without the transformer-based attention module on the HSTS dataset. The test set was used to calculate the mean SSIM and PSNR of the architectures thus formed. The proposed module reported SSIM and PSNR that were 6.27% and 11.43% higher than the model which used just the residual module. This study thus demonstrates the importance of using an attention network alongside a residual module for effectual image dehazing (Fig. 5).

Fig. 5. Dehazing results on the HSTS Dataset. (a) Hazy Image; (b) Fattal's; (c) DehazeNet; (d) Gao *et al.*; (e) Proposed Network.

5   Conclusion and Future Scope

This work proposed a residual learning transformer in an attention module-based image dehazing network. Usually, work done on obtaining haze-free images relies on approximating the transmission matrix and atmospheric light out of the atmospheric scattering model equation. Estimating these variables in an ill-posed problem makes it prone to misestimation. In this paper, the residual module learns these variables. The channel attention network and the pooled spatial maps from the transformer further enhance the performance of the residual backbone. Experiments done on the NYU2, SOTS, and HSTS datasets demonstrate the robustness of the proposed methodology as can be validated by both visual results and quantitative evaluation given using PSNR, SSIM, and FSIM. Not only does the method estimate output with a high degree of similarity with the ground truth, but it also does so without inducing any artifacts. In the future, we intend to generate a large dataset captured in both indoor and outdoor setups with more diverse lighting conditions to train a network robust enough to do real-time image dehazing.

References

1. Zhu, Z., et al.: Atmospheric light estimation based remote sensing image dehazing. Remote Sens. **13**(13), 2432 (2021)
2. Yin, S., Wang, Y., Yang, Y.-H.: Attentive u-recurrent encoder-decoder network for image dehazing. Neurocomputing **437**, 143–156 (2021)
3. Shin, J., Paik, J.: Photo-realistic image dehazing and verifying networks via complementary adversarial learning. Sensors **21**(18), 6182 (2021)
4. McCartney, E.J.: Optics of the atmosphere: scattering by molecules and particles. New York (1976)
5. He, K., Sun, J., Tang, X.: Single image haze removal using dark channel prior. IEEE Trans. Pattern Anal. Mach. Intell. **33**(12), 2341–2353 (2010)
6. Fattal, R.: Dehazing using color-lines. ACM Trans. Graph. (TOG) **34**(1), 1–14 (2014)
7. Zhu, Q., Mai, J., Shao, L.: A fast single image haze removal algorithm using color attenuation prior. IEEE Trans. Image Process. **24**(11), 3522–3533 (2015)
8. Ren, W., et al.: Gated fusion network for single image dehazing. In: Proceedings of the IEEE Conference on Computer Vision and Pattern Recognition, pp. 3253–3261 (2018)
9. Dong, H., et al.: Multi-scale boosted dehazing network with dense feature fusion. In: Proceedings of the IEEE/CVF Conference on Computer Vision and Pattern Recognition, pp. 2157–2167 (2020)
10. Wang, C., et al.: EAA-Net: a novel edge assisted attention network for single image dehazing. Knowl.-Based Syst. **228**, 107279 (2021)
11. Vaswani, A., et al.: Attention is all you need. In: Advances in Neural Information Processing Systems, vol. 30 (2017)
12. Dosovitskiy, A., et al.: et al.: An image is worth 16×16 words: transformers for image recognition at scale. arXiv preprint arXiv:2010.11929 (2020)
13. Tang, K., Yang, J., Wang, J.: Investigating haze-relevant features in a learning framework for image dehazing. In: Proceedings of the IEEE Conference on Computer Vision and Pattern Recognition, pp. 2995–3000 (2014)
14. Fattal, R.: Single image dehazing. ACM Trans. Graph. (TOG) **27**(3), 1–9 (2008)
15. Meng, G., Wang, Y., Duan, J., Xiang, S., Pan, C.: Efficient image dehazing with boundary constraint and contextual regularization. In: Proceedings of the IEEE International Conference on Computer Vision, pp. 617–624 (2013)

16. Zhao, X.: Single image dehazing using bounded channel difference prior. In: Proceedings of the IEEE/CVF Conference on Computer Vision and Pattern Recognition, pp. 727–735 (2021)
17. Ren, W., Liu, S., Zhang, H., Pan, J., Cao, X., Yang, M.-H.: Single image dehazing via multi-scale convolutional neural networks. In: Leibe, B., Matas, J., Sebe, N., Welling, M. (eds.) ECCV 2016. LNCS, vol. 9906, pp. 154–169. Springer, Cham (2016). https://doi.org/10.1007/978-3-319-46475-6_10
18. Cai, B., Xu, X., Jia, K., Qing, C., Tao, D.: Dehazenet: an end-to-end system for single image haze removal. IEEE Trans. Image Process. 25(11), 5187–5198 (2016)
19. Zhang, H., Patel, V.M.: Densely connected pyramid dehazing network. In: Proceedings of the IEEE Conference on Computer Vision and Pattern Recognition, pp. 3194–3203 (2018)
20. Li, J., Li, G., Fan, H.: Image dehazing using residual-based deep CNN. IEEE Access 6, 26831–26842 (2018)
21. Gao, G., Cao, J., Bao, C., Hao, Q., Ma, A., Li, G.: A novel transformer-based attention network for image dehazing. Sensors 22(9), 3428 (2022)
22. Li, X., Hua, Z., Li, J.: Two-stage single image dehazing network using swin-transformer. IET Image Proc. 16(9), 2518–2534 (2022)
23. Silberman, N., Hoiem, D., Kohli, P., Fergus, R.: Indoor segmentation and support inference from RGBD images. In: Fitzgibbon, A., Lazebnik, S., Perona, P., Sato, Y., Schmid, C. (eds.) ECCV 2012. LNCS, vol. 7576, pp. 746–760. Springer, Heidelberg (2012). https://doi.org/10.1007/978-3-642-33715-4_54
24. Li, B., et al.: Benchmarking single-image dehazing and beyond. IEEE Trans. Image Process. 28(1), 492–505 (2018)
25. Woo, S., Park, J., Lee, J.-Y., Kweon, I.S.: CBAM: convolutional block attention module. In: Proceedings of the European Conference on Computer Vision (ECCV), pp. 3–19 (2018)
26. Hatamizadeh, A., Yin, H., Heinrich, G., Kautz, J., Molchanov, P.: Global context vision transformers. In: International Conference on Machine Learning, pp. 12633–12646. PMLR (2023)
27. Hore, A., Ziou, D.: Image quality metrics: PSNR vs. SSIM. In: 2010 20th International Conference on Pattern Recognition, pp. 2366–2369. IEEE (2010)
28. Wang, Z., Bovik, A.C., Sheikh, H.R., Simoncelli, E.P.: Image quality assessment: from error visibility to structural similarity. IEEE Trans. Image Process. 13(4), 600–612 (2004)
29. Zhang, L., Zhang, L., Mou, X., Zhang, D.: FSIM: a feature similarity index for image quality assessment. IEEE Trans. Image Process. 20(8), 2378–2386 (2011)

Swift Convergence: Federated Learning Enhanced with GMMs for Image Classification

Aditi Palit[(✉)][iD], Sai Pragna Nandanavanam[iD], and Kalidas Yeturu[iD]

Department of Computer Science and Engineering, Indian Institute of Technology Tirupati, Tirupati, India
{cs21d001,cs21m012,ykalidas}@iittp.ac.in

Abstract. In Federated learning (FL), *FederatedAveraging*(FedAvg) is widely used to compute the weighted mean of local models in the parametric space over time on a central server by exchanging intermediate updates over multiple rounds of communication. However, this approach requires many communication rounds for the central model to learn data generalization. Each local model updates the central model parameters in different directions of the multi-dimensional parameter space. To address this challenge, we propose *FedGMMinit: Federated Initialization with Gaussian Mixture Model*, which adjusts initial central model gradients by pre-training the model on synthetic data generated from a Gaussian Mixture Model (GMM). For each label in the client's dataset, a GMM is built. The pre-trained weights are then communicated to the selected clients to initialize FedAvg. To maintain data privacy, only the client's representation of the Gaussian is passed to the server. Our proposed approach is tested on MNIST digit datasets for image classification. It shows a reduction of 10–15 communication rounds required by the central model to achieve target accuracy for both IID and non-IID distributions. In the scope of the study, we also discovered that clustering clients and training them with global models also contributed to the overall improvement of convergence. We call this clustering method as FedGMMCluster.

Keywords: Communication rounds · Gaussian mixture model · Initialization · Proxy dataset · Clustering

1 Introduction

FL has gained significance recently as there is a need to maintain users' data privacy [1]. In FL, clients solve a common machine-learning problem under the supervision of a central server without revealing any information about each other's data. The global model is trained locally over the local dataset of a client without transferring raw data. To protect the information flow, FedAvg [2] uses gradient transfer to build a global model. However, for FedAvg, model

H. Kaur et al. (Eds.): CVIP 2023, CCIS 2009, pp. 160–172, 2024.
https://doi.org/10.1007/978-3-031-58181-6_14

weight convergence among different clients is a critical issue, significantly when the training data distribution and quantity can vary considerably across clients in non-IID settings [3].

Contribution Mechanism: In [4], to comprehend the downfall of model accuracy due to data heterogeneity, a regularization term is added to the FedAvg loss function to penalize weight updates that deviate from the central model update. In [5], a shared model adjusts the number of shared data assigned to users according to their data size, effectively alleviating data heterogeneity. An attention mechanism is introduced in the model aggregation phase, which assigns weights to users according to their contributions, thus improving the model performance.

Synthetic Data: In [6], the central concept revolves around gathering encoded data samples from various devices. These samples are deciphered using the exclusive OR (XOR) operations specific to each device's data. This decoding process generates synthetic yet credible samples, which are then utilized to create an independent and identically distributed (IID) dataset for training machine learning models. The encoding and decoding procedures employ bitwise XOR operations, deliberately introducing distortions to the original data to maintain its privacy intact.

In [7], statistics of the Batch Network (BN) layers are used to create synthetic data. A random data point is sampled from the normal distribution and fed to the model for training. To ensure that the synthetic data resembled the original data, the mean and variance of the BN distribution for both the synthetic and original data were minimized.

Clustering: In [8], the agglomerative clustering technique is used to group clients based on similar local model updates during the FL cycle. The similarity is measured using KL divergence. Subsequently, individual global models are created for each cluster. In [9], a full-pipeline expectation-maximization (EM) engine for GMMs is proposed. The scope is limited to EM implementations on FPGAs, and limitations include accuracy-speed trade-offs and hardware constraints.

Distillation: In [10], a data-free knowledge distillation approach for heterogeneous FL is proposed. The need for high-quality synthetic data and sensitivity to pre-trained model selection is a limitation. In [11], a practical data-free approach for one-shot FL with heterogeneity has been proposed. Synthetic data based on a pre-trained generative model is generated to simulate the heterogeneity of real-world data to produce a globally trained model. The drawbacks include the need for pre-trained generative models and the potential loss of privacy due to synthetic data generation.

Pre-initialization: Among few works on pre-initialization [12] proposed using fractals as a pre-training mechanism. Fractals are patterns that resemble patterns that occur in nature. A database of the fractals and corresponding categories is created, which is fed into the Neural network and then back propagated to reduce and optimize the loss function. As fractals do not resemble real data, data privacy is guaranteed. In [13], to protect the privacy of the client's local data, pre-training the central model with a public dataset instead of using the client's local data using four standard FL benchmark data sets has been discussed.

This paper tackles the convergence issue using GMM at the pre-initialization stage, which has not yet been discussed or explored in the FL literature. GMM provides more customized privacy settings than the prior works. By tweaking the number of GMM components, one can adjust the level of privacy needed. Fewer components can result in more non-homogeneous clusters and potentially more privacy. Moreover, GMM is commonly used for sampling due to its ease of computation and interoperability, making it better than the existing pre-initialization methods.

We thus propose FedGMMinit and FedGMMCluster. FedGMMinit focuses on pre-initializing the central model using GMMs. Whereas the Fedcluster approach groups clients into clusters and trains each cluster's clients with a global model using FedAvg.

2   Preliminary

In this section, we provide an overview of FedAvg, the GMM, and the importance of focusing on initialization.

2.1   FedAveraging

In FL, several clients participate in solving a common problem of interest without the clients exchanging or exposing their raw data. Fedavg uses an iterative approach where update and aggregation are the two primitive functions. In the update phase, clients run Stochastic Gradient Descent over their dataset to update the global model's parameter.

For aggregating, the client sends an updated version of the global model's parameter, and the server performs weighted aggregation.

The weighted average is set as the new weight of the central model. The new weights are sent to the clients for updates. This cycle repeats till convergence is attained (Algorithm 1). The objective is to minimize the empirical loss (Eqs. 1, 2, 3):

$$w^* = \arg \min_{w \in R^d} l(w) \tag{1}$$

where d is the dimension of the parameter space.

$$l(w) = \sum_{k=1}^{K} \frac{n_k}{n} L_k(w) \tag{2}$$

$$L_k(w) = \frac{1}{n_k} \sum_{i \in D_k} l_i(w) \tag{3}$$

$l_i(w)$ is the prediction loss for the sample $\{x_i, y_i\}$ by the model with parameter w, K is the number of clients, D_k is the dataset held with client $k \in K$, n_k and n are the datapoints belonging to the dataset D_k and total number of samples from all the participating parties.

Algorithm 1. Fedaveraging

1: **Server**
2: $\mathcal{K}$ *is the client set*
3: *initialize* ω_0;
4: **for** *each round* $t = 1, 2, \ldots$ **do**
5:     $S_t \leftarrow$ (*Sample a subset of clients from* $\mathcal{K}$)
6:     **for** *each client* $l \in S_t$ *in parallel* **do**
7:         $\omega^t \leftarrow ClientUpdate\,(l, \omega_t)$
8:     **end for**
9:     $\omega_{t+1} \leftarrow \sum_{i=1}^{n} \frac{n_k}{n} \omega_{t+1}$
10: **end for**
11: **ClientUpdate**(l, w) :
12: η *is the learning rate,* $\mathcal{D}_k$ *is the local dataset and* $\nabla\ell(\cdot)$ *is the local loss function.*
13: $\mathcal{B} \leftarrow$ (*split* $\mathcal{D}_k$ *into batches of size* B)
14: **for** *local epoch* e *from* 1 *to* E **do**
15:     **for** *batch* $b \in \mathcal{B}$ **do**
16:         $w \leftarrow w - \eta\nabla\ell(w)$
17:     **end for**
18: **end for**
19: **return** w **to server**

2.2 Gaussian Mixture Model

The normal distribution, commonly called the Gaussian distribution, is a well-known distribution. Any complex distribution can be approximated by combining multiple Gaussian distributions with different means, covariance, and weights. The goal of using GMMs is to estimate the parameters of these component distributions from the given data to model the underlying distribution of the data. They are particularly useful in scenarios where the data does not have clearly defined clusters or the boundaries between them are not well-defined.

The GMM is defined as $p(x) = \sum_{i=1}^{K'} \pi_i N(x|\mu_i, \Sigma_i)$, where x is a random variable, $p(x)$ is the PDF of the GMM for data point x, π_i represents the weight of the ith Gaussian component, μ_i is the mean of the ith Gaussian component, Σ_i is the covariance matrix of the ith Gaussian component, and K' is the number of Gaussian components in the mixture. The notation $\mathcal{N}(x|\mu_i, \Sigma_i)$ represents the probability density function of a Gaussian distribution with mean μ_i and covariance matrix Σ_i.

Overall, GMMs provide a flexible and powerful technique for modeling complex data distributions and resolving issues with unsupervised learning.

2.3 Initialization in FL

Since many FL methods employ neural networks for model training, initialization is a key component. The starting values of the deep neural network parameters significantly influence the model's performance. The convergence rate, precision, and stability of the training process can all be affected by the initialization approach chosen.

Each customer in FL only has access to a portion of the training data, which is split among several clients. Data distribution among clients may, therefore, differ, resulting in the spread of non-IID data. The initialization of the model becomes considerably more important in such circumstances. The impacts of non-IID data distribution can be lessened with an appropriate initialization approach, guaranteeing that the network can converge successfully. The privacy of user data may also be impacted by initialization quality. Poor initialization may force the model to contact the central server more frequently, exposing user data to an increased risk to their privacy.

Overall, FL's initialization process is crucial because it can have a big impact on both the model's performance and the training process.

3   Methods

The first section provides a detailed description of FedGMMinit. The following section highlights the workings of FedGMMCluster. The later section contains details about experiments.

3.1   FedGMMinit: Federated Learning with Gaussian Mixture Initialization

FedGMMinit uses GMMs to initialize the weights of the central model in an FL environment. Due to privacy concerns, raw data cannot be sent to the server for weight initialization. Instead, each client constructs label-specific GMMs for their data and sends them to the server. The server then samples a fixed number of data points from each GMM to build a corpus of proxy data, on which the global model is trained for a few epochs. The resulting weights are then used to initialize the local client models for further updates. This approach helps to safeguard the privacy of the client data while allowing for effective weight initialization using synthetic data. Once the initialization of the central model's weight is completed, FedAvg is carried out. Since only the GMMs from local clients go to the server, the client's data remains at the client's end only, thus safeguarding the privacy of the client. The empirical studies on FedGMMinit highlight the importance of initialization and how more tailored heuristics for initialization can drive a model to converge faster, reducing the number of federated cycles.

Let the data on the ith device be, $D_i = \{(x_i, y_i)\}_{i \in [1, \ldots, N]}$, where, $N = |D_i|$ is the cardinality of the set. Let there be K devices, the entire data set is $D = \bigcup_{i=1}^{i=K} D_i$. Let L be the set of labels, such that $(\forall i \in [1, \ldots, K])\{y | (x, y) \in D_i\} \subseteq L$. The proposed idea is to consider label-specific data subsets on each device. A representation generative model Γ is trained for each label-specific subset. Now, the idea is to sample data from each mixture model for all labels across devices in the central device. The synthetic dataset is given is denoted as $D_s = \bigcup_{i=1}^{K} \bigcup_{l \in L} s(\Gamma_{i,l}, n)$, where $s(\Gamma, n)$ is a function to sample data points n from Γ. The central model M^t, where $t = 0$, is then trained on the dataset D_s and sent to the clients as initial weights for FedAvg. For $t > 1$, the vanilla FedAvg is executed (Figs. 1 and 2).

Algorithm 2. FedGMMinit

1: **Client-end:**
2: *Input : $D, K, n, \mathcal{S}(\cdot)$ is a set operation, $t = 0$*
3: **for** *each client $i = 1 \ldots K$* **do**
4:     $L_i = \mathcal{S}(\{y | \forall (x, y) \in D_i\})$
5:     **for** *each label $l \in L_i$* **do**
6:         $D_{i,l} = \{x | y = l, \forall x \in D_i\}$
7:         $\Gamma_{i,l} = gmm(D_{i,l})$
8:     **end for**
9: **end for**
10: **Server-end:**
11: $L = \bigcup_{i=1}^{k} L_i$
12: **for** *each label $l \in L$* **do**
13:     $D_{o,l} = \bigcup_{i=1}^{k} s(\Gamma_{i,l}, n)$
14: **end for**
15: $D_s = \bigcup_{l \in L} D_{o,l}$
16: $M^t = train(D_s)$
17: *Each client receives M^t*
18: $t = t + 1$
19: **for** $t > 1$ **do**
20:     *FedAvg*
21: **end for**

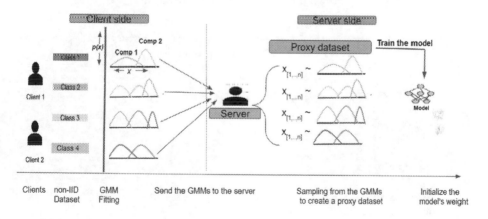

Fig. 1. A pictorial representation of FedGMMinit framework. Each client creates label-wise GMM from which proxy data is created for weight initialization of the central model.

Fig. 2. From left to right:(a) sample of private dataset,(b) sample from GMM of private dataset,(c) sample of public dataset,(d) sample from GMM of public dataset

3.2   FedGMMCluster: Federated Learning Clustering with Gaussian Mixture Model

The proposed approach suggests clustering of clients using GMMs. The clustering of clients is used in FL to group clients with similar data distributions, allowing for more efficient global model training. By clustering clients, we can reduce communication costs and speed up the learning process. Instead of having each client communicate with the central server at each iteration, clients within a cluster can communicate with each other and perform more local updates before sending their updated model weights to the central server. This reduces the number of times the central server needs to be updated and improves the convergence speed of the global model. Additionally, clustering helps to mitigate the effects of non-IID data distributions by ensuring that clients within a cluster have similar data distributions. Here, the algorithm starts by clustering 50 clients based on their local data distributed in non-IID form by taking the mean of samples from each client to form a list of 50 values. Each value represents the mean of the respective client's data and fits GMM on this list. Then, the clients are clustered using this GMM. For each cluster, the local models of clients are trained using FedAvg for a fixed number of iterations, and the resulting models are averaged to get a final model for that cluster. This process is repeated for multiple cycles. The final output is a set of central models, one for each cluster, trained on local data and averaged over multiple iterations.

Algorithm 3. Clustering the clients

1: **Clustering the clients**
2: *Input : D, K, n, nc is the number of clusters*
3: C_j *the set of clients in the jth cluster*
4: **for** *each $i \in 1, \ldots, K$* **do**
5:     $X_i = mean(x)_{\forall x \in D_i}$
6: **end for**
7: $X = \bigcup_{i=1}^{K} X_i$
8: $\Gamma = gmm(X)$
9: $C_j = \phi \, \forall \, j \in [nc]$
10: **for** *each cluster $j = 1, \ldots, nc$* **do**
11:     **for** *each datapoint $x \in X$* **do**
12:         **if** $j = \arg\max_{j \in 1, \ldots, nc} \rho(\Gamma(x_i))$ **then**
13:             $C_j = \bigcup i$
14:         **end if**
15:     **end for**
16: **end for**
17: **for** $j = 1, \ldots, nc$ **do**
18:     $M_j = Fedaveraging(\forall \, client \in C_j)$
19: **end for**
20: $M = Fedaveraging(M_1, \ldots, M_{nc})$

---

4   Experiments and Analysis

Experiments 1, 2, and 3 focus on investigating the number of cycles required for the central model to achieve a specified accuracy level. In Experiment 1, the central model's initial weights are set using the GMM proxy dataset, which is sampled from each client's private dataset. Experiment 2 conducts a comparative analysis between two initialization methods. It examines the performance when the central model's weights are initialized using a GMM constructed from publicly available data and contrasts it with initialization using a GMM constructed from a combination of private and public datasets. Experiment 3 studies the impact of different covariance metrics on the total iteration count, shedding light on how these metrics affect the convergence process. Experiment 4 studies the model accuracy with GMM initialization in a dynamic client selection scenario. Here, the central server dynamically chooses clients while averaging their models. This experiment operates in a non-iid setting using an MNIST dataset. Lastly, Experiment 5 explores the effects on the accuracy of the global model by clustering clients using GMMs. It calculates the mean of data samples from each client and fits a GMM on this aggregate data, providing valuable insights into the benefits of this clustering approach for accuracy enhancement.

4.1   Experimental Setup

For our preliminary experiments, we focused on the image classification problem using the MNIST dataset. The dataset includes 60,000 gray-scale training samples of dimensions 28×28, with ten labels.

IID Data Distribution: After shuffling the data, the 60,000 data points in the MNIST dataset are equally divided among the 100 clients, each holding a subset of the dataset with a carnality of 6000 in a random fashion.

non-IID Distribution: Each client has at least two different labels, and sample overlap between two sets is minimal. For MNIST, the data is shuffled and sorted according to the labels. Each class is divided into a group of 300 data points. The total number of sets so formed is 200.

Model: Due to the efficiency and state-of-the-art results of neural networks, we used Multi-layer perceptron (MLP) and convolutional neural networks (CNN) for the experiments. The architecture of the Multi-layer perceptron has 2-hidden layers having 200 nodes each using ReLu activation (199,210 total parameters) with batch size as 30 in 1 epoch. The CNN model has two 5×5 convolution layers. The first layer has 32 channels. The second layer is 64 channels. Both are followed by 2×2 max pooling. A fully connected layer with 512 units is followed by Relu activation, and the softmax operation is applied at the end with a batch size of 30 in 5 epochs. The central model, as well as the local clients, have identical model architecture.

4.2   Observations and Results

Experiments 1–4 were conducted using the initialization algorithm referenced as Algorithm 2, while Experiment 5 was executed following the procedure described in Algorithm 3. By default, the number of data points sampled from each GMM is 20.

1. GMM initialization reduces the number of cycles: The GMM initialization approach benefits both IID and non-IID datasets, as it helps the central server achieve the target accuracy faster than the random initialization (Table 1). This heuristic approach significantly reduces the number of communication cycles compared to the random initialization for both IID and non-IID distribution.

Table 1. Comparison between the number of training rounds required for a central model to achieve a target accuracy when it is initialized with random weights (RI) versus when it is initialized using a proxy dataset sampled from a GMM (Private).

Distribution	Model	Private	RI	Target
IID	CNN	9	11	96
IID	MLP	69	76	94
non-IID	CNN	34	45	96
non-IID	MLP	96	150	91

2. Gaussian samples of public dataset improve the central model's accuracy: To capitalize on the availability of publicly available data, one can pre-train the weights of the central model using this data. However, instead of solely relying on the public data, we augment it with GMM sampled from the same public data to introduce more variety into the dataset. In this paper, we used $fetch_{openml}('mnist_{784})$ dataset as a public dataset with 70,000 samples with labels between 0 to 9 on non-IID distribution. After importing the public dataset, the data is distributed among the 100 clients. Each client has samples of 2 different labels. 20 samples from each label in each client are collected to create a synthetic dataset with $20 * 2 * 100 = 4,000$ points to pre-train the central model. We also added Gaussian samples to these samples to improve the convergence of the central model. Our findings demonstrate that the accuracy of the augmented public dataset samples and GMM samples is high compared with public dataset samples (Table 2) and (Fig. 3).

3. Hyperparameter tuning can reduce the communication cycles: The performance of GMMs profoundly relies on the choice of hyperparameters, such as the covariance matrix. The selection of different variations of the covariance matrix can lead to significant variations in the number of cycles required by the central model to reach the targeted accuracy. We verify that tied GMM produces faster convergence and better results than the full covariance matrix (Table 3).

Table 2. The table compares the scenario where the central model's weights are initialized using Gaussian samples of public data to the situation where initialization is performed using Gaussian samples from both private and public datasets, particularly in non-IID for MLP model.

Cycles	Accuracy using GMM public data	Accuracy using GMM public and private samples
10	87	**90**
50	88	**91**
100	89	**91**

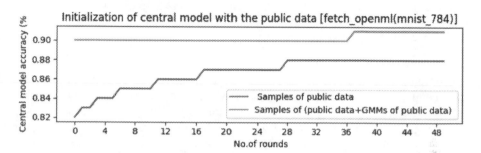

Fig. 3. The effect on the central model's accuracy when Gaussian data points sampled from public dataset versus when sampled from public and private dataset

4. Client selection via validation score: Instead of selecting clients randomly, we choose clients for averaging in each round based on their accuracy and F1 score on the validation dataset. When we randomly select ten clients among 50 clients, the accuracy fluctuates and is unstable. So, we are using dynamic client selection based on accuracy and F1 score. The results reveal that while using dynamic client selection, the accuracy is stable but not improving. This is because of the non-IID data distribution among clients since there is no assurance that clients with diverse datasets will be selected for aggregation (Fig. 4).

5. Clustering clients using GMM: Client clustering in FL helps clients with similar data distributions to reduce communication costs and improve global model convergence. Clients in a cluster can communicate with each other and perform local updates before sending the updated model weights to the central

Table 3. The table highlights how the choice of covariance matrix structure affects the required number of cycles to reach a target accuracy by the central model.

Distribution	Model	Cycles with Tied GMM	Cycles with Full GMM	Accuracy
IID	CNN	**10**	18	96
IID	MLP	**43**	68	94
non-IID	CNN	**27**	34	96
non-IID	MLP	**130**	150	91

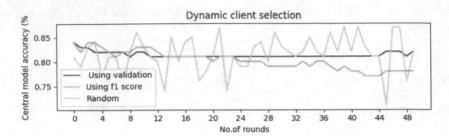

Fig. 4. Variation in the central model's accuracy when the participants for each FL round are selected (a) randomly (b) F1 score on the validation set (c) accuracy on the validation set in the non-IID environment.

server. This helps to reduce the impact of non-IID data distribution by ensuring that clients in the cluster have a similar data distribution. By experimenting with different numbers of clusters and iterations for each cluster, we found that fewer clusters resulted in more internal iterations for each cluster, resulting in higher accuracy compared to other clusters (Table 4). From Table 4, inter-rounds represent the number of communication rounds between the cluster central model and the clients. In contrast, intra-cycles represent the number of communication rounds between cluster-central and server-central models.

Table 4. The table presents the fluctuations in the accuracy of the central model as a function of various combinations of hyperparameters. These hyperparameters encompass the number of clusters used to group clients, the count of inter-cycles, and the count of intra-cycles

Clusters	Inter cycles	Intra cycles	Target
3	1	10	85
3	30	3	87
5	1	10	86
5	30	3	83

5   Conclusion and Future Work

From the above experiments on initialization, we observe that by pre-training the central model with private data GMMs, there is a reduction in the number of communication rounds required by the central model to reach a target accuracy compared to the random initialization. Thus, GMMs play a significant role in initializing the central model by training the model via a Gaussian sample taken from the private dataset as well as the public dataset.

Also, we note that by selecting clients to average the central model based on validation and F1 score, the accuracy of the central model is not improved much as the number of cycles increases. Due to this, the accuracy fluctuates. To overcome this problem, clustering of clients using GMMs is introduced. FedG-MMCluster reduces the number of communication rounds compared to selecting clients through validation score, as we are clustering clients based on similarity using GMMs.

While GMM is an effective initialization method, its drawback lies in its computational complexity, especially when dealing with high-dimensional data. Fitting a GMM in such scenarios can be computationally expensive, making it less practical.

As part of our future research, we plan to address this issue by exploring methods to reduce the complexity of GMM initialization, making it more suitable for higher-dimensional datasets. Furthermore, we intend to conduct a comparative study among other initialization methods and our proposed FedGMMinint methodology.

Acknowledgement. The authors acknowledge computational and funding support from the project numbered *CSE2122001FACEKALI* and titled *Design and Development of Disaster Response Dashboard for India* for carrying out the work.

References

1. Zhang, C., Xie, Y., Bai, H., Yu, B., Li, W., Gao, Y.: A survey on federated learning. Knowl.-Based Syst. **216**, 106775 (2021)
2. McMahan, B., Moore, E., Ramage, D., Hampson, S., Y Arcas, B.A.: Communication efficient learning of deep networks from decentralized data. In: Artificial Intelligence and Statistics, pp. 1273–1282. PMLR (2017)
3. Kairouz, P., et al.: Advances and open problems in federated learning. Found. Trends® Mach. Learn. **14**(1–2), 1–210 (2021)
4. Li, T., Sahu, A.K., Zaheer, M., Sanjabi, M., Talwalkar, A., Smith, V.: Federated optimization in heterogeneous networks. Proc. Mach. Learn. Syst. **2**, 429–450 (2020)
5. Chai, B., Liu, K., Yang, R.: Cross-domain federated data modeling on non-IID data. Comput. Intell. Neurosci. CIN **2022** (2022)
6. Shin, M., Hwang, C., Kim, J., Park, M., Bennis, J., Kim, S.L.: XOR Mixup: privacy-preserving data augmentation for one-shot federated learning. arXiv preprint arXiv:2006.05148 (2020)
7. Weituo, H., et al.: Towards fair federated learning with zero-shot data augmentation. In: Proceedings of the IEEE/CVF Conference on Computer Vision and Pattern Recognition, pp. 3310–3319 (2021)
8. Briggs, C., Fan, Z., Andras, P.: Federated learning with hierarchical clustering of local updates to improve training on non-IID data. In: 2020 International Joint Conference on Neural Networks (IJCNN), pp. 1–9. IEEE (2020)
9. Guo, C., Fu, H., Luk, W.: A fully-pipelined expectation-maximization engine for gaussian mixture models. In: 2012 International Conference on Field-Programmable Technology, pp. 182–189. IEEE (2012)

10. Zhu, Z., Hong, J., Zhou, J.: Data-free knowledge distillation for heterogeneous federated learning. In: International Conference on Machine Learning, pp. 12878–12889. PMLR (2021)
11. Jie, Z., et al.: A practical data-free approach to one-shot federated learning with heterogeneity. arXiv preprint arXiv:2112.12371 (2021)
12. Chen, H., Tu, C., Li, Z., Shen, H.W., Chao, W.L.: On the importance and applicability of pre-training for federated learning. In: The Eleventh International Conference on Learning Representations (2023)
13. Nguyen, J., Wang, J., Malik, K., Sanjabi, M., Rabbat, M.: Where to begin? On the impact of pre-training and initialization in federated learning. arXiv preprint arXiv:2210.08090 (2022)

Enhancing Video Surveillance with Deep Learning-Based Real-Time Handgun Detection and Tracking

Pavinder Yadav[1], Nidhi Gupta[2]([✉]), and Pawan Kumar Sharma[1]

[1] National Institute of Technology Hamirpur, Himachal Pradesh 177005, India
{pavinder_phdmath,psharma}@nith.ac.in
[2] National Institute of Technology Kurukshetra, Haryana 136119, India
nidhi.gupta@nitkkr.ac.in

Abstract. Handguns, pistols, and revolvers are commonly used in today's world for committing criminal acts, requiring the need for effective surveillance and control systems. However, despite the advancement of security systems, human monitoring and involvement are still necessary to effectively combat these crimes. This paper provides a robust automated handgun identification technique for recorded videos and live CCTV footage that may be used for both control and surveillance purposes. Automatic detection of firearms is crucial for improving people's protection and safety, however, it is a challenging task because of the numerous differences in design, size, and appearance of firearms. In recent years, object detectors have improved, yielding better findings and shorter inference times. The authors used cutting-edge object detector YOLOv7 for firearm detection. A varied and demanding dataset of 15,367 images for weapon identification is also proposed, which is carefully annotated for weapon localization and classification. After analysing the data, it is determined that the model achieves an accuracy rate of 96.80% and recall rate of 90.37%.

Keywords: Deep Learning · Machine Learning · Weapon Detection · Surveillance System · YOLO

1 Introduction

Dangerous weapons are utilised in criminal and terrorist actions. The Small Arms Survey statistics from 2017 [6] indicate that globally, the percentage of guns possessed by civilians was 84.6%, while the military held 13.1% and law enforcement held 2.2% as shown in Fig. 1. Consequently, implementing weapon detecting system in a security camera may increase security by automatically recognising weapons in the video stream. The current implementation of deep neural network for weapon identification delivers acceptable high accuracy but suffers from slow detection speed, making it unsuitable for real-time applications. The fundamental issue in implementing object recognition and localising in the real world, particularly for security concerns, is the trade-off between speed and precision. Automatic weapon detection is a critical need in surveillance video systems. However, the weapon identification system faces challenges in accurately detecting objects in low-quality surveillance footage. Furthermore, watching the surveillance footage for 24 hours a day needs a lot of manual labour, and certain security situations may be overlooked owing to human visual mistake.

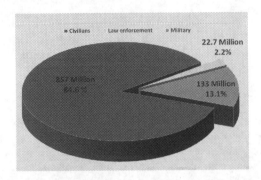

Fig. 1. Estimates of global firearm ownership in 2017 [6].

Automatic weapon detection in closed-circuit television systems (CCTV) can provide several benefits, including:

- **Early detection of potential threats:** Automatic weapon detection in CCTV systems can analyse video feeds in real-time and detect the presence of weapons, such as guns or knives, before a dangerous situation escalates.
- **Increased safety:** By detecting weapons early, automatic weapon detection in CCTV systems can help to prevent violence and protect the safety of individuals in the area.
- **Improved response time:** Automatic weapon detection in CCTV systems can alert security personnel or law enforcement quickly and accurately, allowing for a faster response to potential threats.
- **Decreased false alarms:** Weapon detection in CCTV systems can assist in the elimination of false alarms caused by other objects that resemble weapons.

Deep learning has made great progress during the previous decade, which is due to the availability of large datasets and advances in powerful technology. However, there are still obstacles to overcome, such as the need for more robust and efficient algorithms, as well as more interpretable models, in order to better understand the models' decisions. Overall, deep learning has shown to be a powerful tool for many applications, with its ability to learn from data and improve over time. As the field continues to evolve, It is predicted to have a substantial effect on many areas of science and technology. Deep learning is also highly adaptable and can be used in a variety of applications, such as self-driving cars [5], speech recognition [2], object detection [19], and so on.

The challenge of detecting firearms in real-time through surveillance is a complex issue because of modest size of the target object (handguns). Distinguishing it from other objects, especially those that could be mistaken for it, can be difficult in images. To address this challenge, scientists have been exploring the use of deep learning methods with two stages, such as the Region-based Convolutional Neural Network (R-CNN) series [3,15], and one-stage methods, including the Single Shot multibox Detector (SSD) [9] and You Only Look Once (YOLO) [13,14] series.

In this manuscript, the authors have proposed the use of a deep learning-based YOLOv7 model for weapon detection system to detect weapons in real-time, using surveillance cameras, recorded videos and, images as the input source. The idea of using advanced technology like deep learning for quickly identifying weapons is very important in today's society. With an increase in the number of mass shootings and terrorist activities, there is a growing need for efficient and accurate methods for detecting weapons in real-time.

The main contribution in the manuscript are following:

1. Collection of a large and diverse dataset: The authors of the manuscript collected a large dataset of 15,367 images and manually annotated them to ensure high quality training data for the deep learning model.
2. Utilization of Modified YOLOv7 Architecture: The authors used a modified YOLOv7 deep learning architecture, to train the model for handgun detection, which improved the performance of model compared to the original YOLOv7 architecture.
3. Real-time Weapon Tracking: The authors made the model compatible for real-time tracking of weapons, enabling the system to monitor the movement of weapons in video streams and alert relevant authorities if necessary.

The rest of the manuscript is organized as follows: In Sect. 2, related work in the field of weapon detection is discussed, including both traditional and deep learning-based approaches. In Sect. 3, the proposed system is described in detail, including the dataset used for training and the CNN architecture. In Sect. 4, results of the experiments are presented, which demonstrate the high accuracy and efficiency of the proposed system. Section 5 concludes the paper with a consideration on future research.

2 Related Work

The advent of improved CCTV, processing hardware, and deep learning models has brought forth the challenge of identifying and categorizing objects in real-time. Despite these advancements, there has been limited research on weapon detection, with most studies focusing on detecting concealed weapons [10].

Grega et al. [4] attempted to use CCTV footage to identify knives and handguns, but the use of the sliding window approach made the method slow for real-time detection, despite its good precision on the testing dataset. Kibria and Hasan [7] used different algorithms, such as Histogram of Oriented Gradients

(HOG) with Support Vector Machine (SVM), Convolutional Neural Network (CNN), Bag of Words (BoW) with linear SVM, and Speeded Up Robust Features (SURF), to detect knives from images. CNN was found to be the most accurate.

Olmos *et al.* [11] published a study on handgun detection using deep learning, where Faster R-CNN was trained on a dataset of 3,000 pistol images. The model managed to perform well on high-quality videos but generated a significant proportion of false positives and false negatives on low-quality videos. In a later study [12], an image fusion-based approach was used to identify potential regions from input images and a low-cost dual camera system was implemented. However, implementing this approach may not be feasible for many retail shops, as dual cameras are not commonly used in CCTV systems.

Singh *et al.* [17] used YOLOv4 and achieved a mean Average Precision (mAP) of 77.75%. Bhatti *et al.* [1] employed various algorithms, including YOLOv4, and found YOLOv4 to perform best with an F1 score of 91% and mAP of 91.73%. Lamas *et al.* [8] developed a top-down weapon detection method using Faster R-CNN and one-stage detectors such as SSD, EfficientDet, and CenterNet. EfficientDet performed well with a precision score of 94.4%. However, this method has only detected weapons which are handled by humans.

3   Proposed Methodology

3.1   Description of Dataset

The weapon detection dataset is a collection of 15,367 images, each of which has been manually annotated to identify the presence of a handgun. From the images gathered, 12,060 were utilised for training and 3307 for validation. The collection also includes 1719 negative samples that do not contain any weapon. Table 1 contains extensive description of the dataset that is being used.

Table 1. A detailed description of the collected dataset.

Classes	Images	Train	Intense in train	Validation	Intense in validation
Handgun	15,367	12,060	11,384	3307	3188

The images in the dataset were collected from various sources, including movies, social media, and other public domain sources. The images were chosen to span a broad variety of varied circumstances, such as indoor and outdoor locations, varying lighting conditions, and various weapon perspectives. Sample images from the constructed datasets are shown in Fig. 2. The images were then manually annotated by experts to identify the presence of a handgun, and to accurately label the location of the weapon in the image.

Fig. 2. Sample images from the generated dataset demonstrating the variety of weapons in a range of scenarios.

3.2 Architecture of YOLOv7

YOLOv7 [18] is a state-of-the-art computer vision model used for real-time object detection. In only a few milliseconds, the one-stage detector can precisely identify items in a video or image. This model operates on a CNN architecture and uses anchor boxes to predict the location of objects in an image. It also uses cross-class nms, dynamic anchor shapes, and a new Gaussian YOLO layer to improve its accuracy and performance. The YOLOv7 architecture as shown in Fig. 3, consists of several important components, including an input layer, a backbone network, a neck, a prediction head, an upsample layer, and an output layer.

The computation of target coordinates for bounding boxes in YOLOv7 is achieved through the following equation:

$$
\begin{aligned}
b_x &= (2 \cdot \sigma (t_x) - 0.5) + P_x \\
b_y &= (2 \cdot \sigma (t_y) - 0.5) + P_y \\
b_w &= p_w \cdot (2 \cdot \sigma (t_w))^2 \\
b_h &= p_h \cdot (2 \cdot \sigma (t_h))^2
\end{aligned}
\tag{1}
$$

where, P_x and P_y denote the positions of the grid. The bounding box positions are represented by the variables b_x and b_y., which is defined as (P_x, P_y)+delta and is constrained by $\sigma(t_x)$ and $\sigma(t_y)$. The values of p_w and p_h represent the anchor box obtained through clustering. The variables b_w and b_h represent the dimensions of the bounding box. The dimensions of (p_w, p_h) have been proportionally adjusted by a scaling factor of (t_w, t_h).

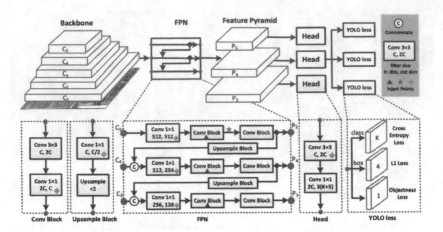

Fig. 3. An overview of the operational methodology that is utilised by YOLOv7 from a high-level perspective [18].

The loss function comprises three distinct components, namely the bounding box loss function denoted as l_{box}, the classification loss function referred to as l_{cls}, and the confidence loss function known as l_{obj}. These components can be mathematically expressed as follows:

$$Loss = l_{box} + l_{cls} + l_{obj} \tag{2}$$

The loss associated with the bounding box, which measures the discrepancy between the predicted and target box positions, can be expressed as follows:

$$l_{box} = L_{CIoU} = 1 - IoU + \frac{\rho^2\left(c, c^{gt}\right)}{b^2} + ..\alpha v$$

$$IoU = \frac{area\ of\ overlap}{area\ of\ union}$$

$$v = \frac{4}{\pi^2}\left(\arctan \frac{l^{gt}}{m^{gt}} - \arctan \frac{l}{m}\right)^2 \tag{3}$$

$$\alpha = \frac{v}{(1 - IoU) + v}$$

where, c and c_{gt} denote the centre of the projected box and target box, respectively. ρ is the Euclidean distance. b is the diagonal length of the minimal bounding box including two boxes. The two-variable trade-off is α. The metric v measures aspect ratio uniformity. l and m represent the boxes' width and height, respectively.

The loss function for classification is expressed as:

$$l_{cls} = \sum_{i=0}^{s^2} I_{i,j}^{obj} \sum_{C \in \text{Classes}} \left(\hat{x}_i(c) \log\left(x_i(c)\right) + (1 - \hat{x}_i(c)) \log\left(1 - x_i(c)\right)\right) \tag{4}$$

The confidence loss function is calculated as follows:

$$l_{obj} = \sum_{i=0}^{S^2} \sum_{j=0}^{B} I_{i,j}^{obj} = \left(\hat{P}_i \log(P_i) + \left(1 - \hat{P}_i\right) \log\left(1 - \hat{P}_i\right) \right)$$

$$- \lambda_{\text{noobj}} \sum_{i=0}^{S^2} \sum_{j=0}^{B} I_{i,j}^{noobj} \left(\hat{P}_i \log(P_i) + \left(1 - \hat{P}_i\right) \left(\log\left(1 - \hat{P}_i\right) \right) \right)$$

(5)

4 Result and Discussion

The deep learning model, modified YOLOv7, was utilised to effectively complete the weapon detection challenge. Furthermore, YOLOv7 provides the detection findings with the greatest potential. Four performance indicators, including accuracy, recall, mAP, and the F1-score, which analyses the balance between recall and precision, were used to assess the weapon detector's efficacy. Precision, recall, F1-score, and mAP are calculated using Eqs. 6–9 given below:

$$Precision = \frac{TP}{TP + FP}$$

(6)

$$Recall = \frac{TP}{TP + FN}$$

(7)

$$F1 - score = 2 * \frac{precision * recall}{precision + recall}$$

(8)

$$mAP = \frac{1}{N} \sum_{i=1}^{N} AP_i$$

(9)

where, True Positives (TP) corresponds to the overall number of images in which the existence of weapons has been confirmed. False Positives (FP) are the number of images of weapons produced by the model but containing no weapons. The False Negative (FN) is the number of images in which apparent weapons are present but the model fails to recognise them as such. Average Precision is denoted as AP.

The performance of YOLOv7 is enhanced by updating several components of the algorithm, such as the network architecture, anchor boxes, post-processing, data augmentation, and training technique. Various adjustments are done based on the nature of the issue as well as the dataset being used. This time, the detection results are improved since the model was able to recognise the weapons in a variety of conditions. The specific training outcomes are shown in Table 2, together with a number of other performance indicators like as accuracy, recall, F1-score, and mAP. According to the findings, the recall score for the class handgun reaches 90.37%, while the precision score for the handgun reaches 96.80%. Figure 4 shows several performance indicators for the training and validation sets over the epochs.

Table 2. Detailed training results obtained from YOLOv7, in terms of precision, recall, F1-score and mAP.

Class	Labels	Precision(%)	Recall(%)	F1-Score(%)	mAP@.5(%)
Handgun	3188	96.80	90.37	93.47	95.53

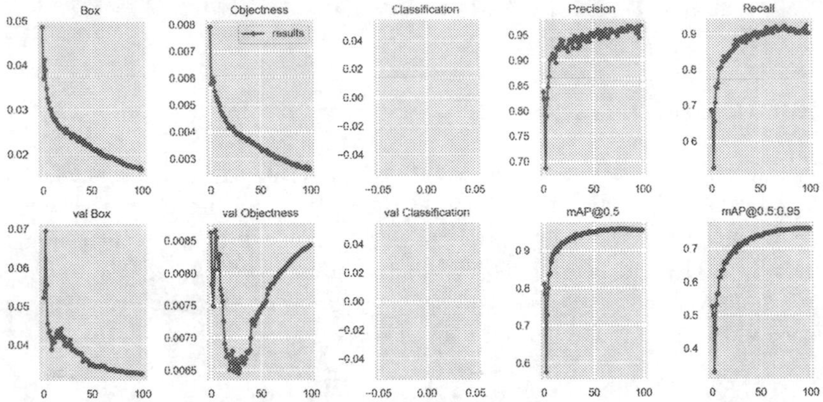

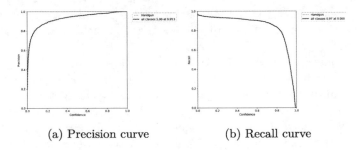

Fig. 4. Box loss, objectness loss, classification loss, precision, recall, and mAP plots over training epochs for the training and validation sets.

The precision and recall curves, together with the confidence score, that were obtained when the model was being trained are shown in Fig. 5. It is possible to draw the conclusion from the data that the model is functioning well if the confidence threshold value is 0.5. That is, the model will determine that there is a weapon present if the confidence score is greater than fifty percent. Figure 6 illustrates the trade-off between the accuracy and the recall, as well as the F1-curve with the confidences score.

(a) Precision curve   (b) Recall curve

Fig. 5. Precision and Recall curves generated during training.

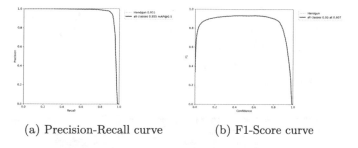

(a) Precision-Recall curve   (b) F1-Score curve

Fig. 6. Precision-Recall curve and F1-curve generated during training.

Table 3 compares the proposed model's Frame Per Second (FPS) at various video resolutions. The frames per second numbers represent the model's processing speed, which is critical in real-time applications like video surveillance and object recognition.

Table 3. Comparative Analysis of Frame Rates Across Different Video Resolutions.

Video Resolution	Frames Per Second
416 × 416	35
640 × 640	30
1024 × 1024	23

Figure 7 demonstrates the capability of identifying weapons based on images taken in various conditions. The trained model is capable of detecting weapons in scenarios such as multiple weapons in the same image, weapons at a distance, weapons in a blurry picture, and weapons located among other similar items, among others.

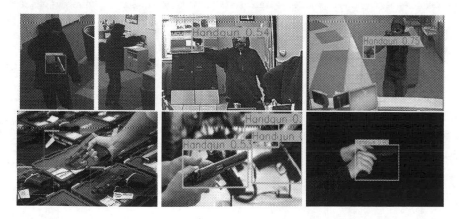

Fig. 7. Performance of YOLOv7 under a variety of testing situations with regard to the detection of weapons.

Figure 8 depicts the real-time tracking of a firearm in a video recording. The image depicts the real-time performance of the proposed deep learning-based weapon detection and tracking system utilising YOLOv7. The model correctly monitors the movement of a firearm in a recorded video, proving its use in real-world surveillance circumstances.

Fig. 8. Real-time tracking of a handgun in a recorded video using YOLOv7.

Table 4 shows a comparison of the findings from the present study to those published in other relevant studies. The table emphasises several metrics for handgun recognition, such as precision, recall, and F1-score, and offers a full assessment of the proposed deep learning-based weapon detection and tracking system utilising YOLOv7.

Table 4. Comparison of Handgun Detection Metrics: Results from Different Studies.

Authors	Precision (%)	Recall (%)	F1 - Score (%)
Olmos _et al._ (2018) [11]	84.21	100	91.43
Romero and Salamea (2019) [16]	86.00	86.00	86.00
Olmos _et al._ (2019) [12]	92.68	80.00	85.88
Bhatti _et al._ (2021) [1]	93.00	88.00	91.00
Lamas _et al._ (2022) [8]	94.40	91.50	92.90
Proposed Model	**96.80**	90.37	**93.47**

5   Conclusion

In this study, a deep learning-based real-time weapon detection and tracking system using a modified YOLOv7 model was presented. The method produced outstanding results when it came to recognising and tracking guns via video surveillance. detection under a range of circumstances. Precision, recall, and F1-score measurements were used to evaluate the model's performance, with the results confirming the model's ability to detect and track weapons in real-time video streams. The best precision and recall scores for handgun detection were 96.80% and 90.37% respectively. On average quality videos, the model could identify weapons at a rate of 30 frames per second.

References

1. Bhatti, M.T., Khan, M.G., Aslam, M., Fiaz, M.J.: Weapon detection in real-time CCTV videos using deep learning. IEEE Access **9**, 34366–34382 (2021). https://doi.org/10.1109/ACCESS.2021.3059170
2. Dokuz, Y., Tufekci, Z.: Mini-batch sample selection strategies for deep learning based speech recognition. Appl. Acoust. **171**, 107573 (2021). https://doi.org/10.1016/j.apacoust.2020.107573
3. Girshick, R., Donahue, J., Darrell, T., Malik, J.: Rich feature hierarchies for accurate object detection and semantic segmentation. In: Proceedings of the IEEE Conference on Computer Vision and Pattern Recognition, pp. 580–587 (2014). https://doi.org/10.1109/cvpr.2014.81
4. Grega, M., Matiolański, A., Guzik, P., Leszczuk, M.: Automated detection of firearms and knives in a CCTV image. Sensors **16**(1), 47 (2016). https://doi.org/10.3390/s16010047
5. Gupta, A., Anpalagan, A., Guan, L., Khwaja, A.S.: Deep learning for object detection and scene perception in self-driving cars: survey, challenges, and open issues. Array **10**, 100057 (2021)
6. Karp, A.: Estimating global civilian-held firearms numbers (2018). https://www.smallarmssurvey.org/resource/estimating-global-civilian-held-firearms-numbers. Accessed 29 Mar 2022
7. Kibria, S.B., Hasan, M.S.: An analysis of feature extraction and classification algorithms for dangerous object detection. In: 2017 2nd International Conference on Electrical & Electronic Engineering (ICEEE), pp. 1–4. IEEE (2017). https://doi.org/10.1109/ceee.2017.8412846
8. Lamas, A., et al.: Human pose estimation for mitigating false negatives in weapon detection in video-surveillance. Neurocomputing **489**, 488–503 (2022). https://doi.org/10.1016/j.neucom.2021.12.059
9. Liu, W., et al.: SSD: single shot MultiBox detector. In: Leibe, B., Matas, J., Sebe, N., Welling, M. (eds.) ECCV 2016. LNCS, vol. 9905, pp. 21–37. Springer, Cham (2016). https://doi.org/10.1007/978-3-319-46448-0_2
10. Mahajan, R., Padha, D.: Detection of concealed weapons using image processing techniques: a review. In: 2018 First International Conference on Secure Cyber Computing and Communication (ICSCCC), pp. 375–378. IEEE (2018)
11. Olmos, R., Tabik, S., Herrera, F.: Automatic handgun detection alarm in videos using deep learning. Neurocomputing **275**, 66–72 (2018). https://doi.org/10.1016/j.neucom.2017.05.012

12. Olmos, R., Tabik, S., Lamas, A., Perez-Hernandez, F., Herrera, F.: A binocular image fusion approach for minimizing false positives in handgun detection with deep learning. Inf. Fusion **49**, 271–280 (2019). https://doi.org/10.1016/j.inffus.2018.11.015

13. Redmon, J., Divvala, S., Girshick, R., Farhadi, A.: You only look once: unified, real-time object detection. In: Proceedings of the IEEE Conference on Computer Vision and Pattern Recognition, pp. 779–788 (2016). https://doi.org/10.1109/cvpr.2016.91

14. Redmon, J., Farhadi, A.: Yolo9000: better, faster, stronger. In: Proceedings of the IEEE Conference on Computer Vision and Pattern Recognition, pp. 7263–7271 (2017). https://doi.org/10.1109/cvpr.2017.690

15. Ren, S., He, K., Girshick, R., Sun, J.: Faster R-CNN: towards real-time object detection with region proposal networks. Adv. Neural Inf. Process. Syst. **28** (2015). https://doi.org/10.1109/tpami.2016.2577031

16. Romero, D., Salamea, C.: Convolutional models for the detection of firearms in surveillance videos. Appl. Sci. **9**(15), 2965 (2019)

17. Singh, A., Anand, T., Sharma, S., Singh, P.: IoT based weapons detection system for surveillance and security using yolov4. In: 2021 6th International Conference on Communication and Electronics Systems (ICCES), pp. 488–493 (2021). https://doi.org/10.1109/ICCES51350.2021.9489224

18. Wang, C.Y., Bochkovskiy, A., Liao, H.Y.M.: YOLOv7: trainable bag-of-freebies sets new state-of-the-art for real-time object detectors. arXiv preprint arXiv:2207.02696 (2022)

19. Yadav, P., Gupta, N., Sharma, P.K.: A comprehensive study towards high-level approaches for weapon detection using classical machine learning and deep learning methods. Expert Systems with Applications **212**, 118698 (2022). https://doi.org/10.1016/j.eswa.2022.118698

YOLORe-IDNet: An Efficient Multi-camera System for Person-Tracking

Vipin Gautam, Shitala Prasad$^{(\boxtimes)}$, and Sharad Sinha

School of Mathematics and Computer Science, Indian Institute of Technology Goa,
Farmagudi, India
{vipin2113106,shitala,sharad}@iitgoa.ac.in

Abstract. The growing need for video surveillance in public spaces has created a demand for systems that can track individuals across multiple camera feeds in real-time. While existing tracking systems have achieved impressive performance using deep learning (DL) models, they often rely on pre-existing images of suspects or historical data. However, this is not always feasible in cases where suspicious individuals are identified in real-time and without prior knowledge. We propose a person-tracking system that combines correlation filters and Intersection Over Union (IOU) constraints for robust tracking, along with a DL model for cross-camera person re-identification (Re-ID) on top of YOLOv5. The proposed system quickly identifies and tracks suspect in real-time across multiple cameras and recovers well after full or partial occlusion, making it suitable for security and surveillance applications. It is computationally efficient and achieves a high F1-Score of 79% and an IOU of 59% comparable to existing state-of-the-art algorithms, as demonstrated in our evaluation on a publicly available OTB-100 dataset. The proposed system offers a robust and efficient solution for the real-time tracking of individuals across multiple camera feeds. Its ability to track targets without prior knowledge or historical data is a significant improvement over existing systems, making it well-suited for public safety and surveillance applications.

Keywords: Realtime Systems · Person Tracking · Person Re-identification · Multi-camera tracking · Correlation filter tracking

1 Introduction

Visual security systems have become increasingly important in today's world from a surveillance and law and order point of view. Advancements in technology, such as high-definition images and artificial intelligence (AI) can be leveraged to create robust person and object identification and tracking systems. Traditional security approaches involve monitoring by human personnel, which can be challenging for large areas like malls, smart cities, and universities. Surveillance cameras are commonly used in public places, but it is difficult to compare different individuals manually. AI-powered surveillance systems [1] have been

© The Author(s), under exclusive license to Springer Nature Switzerland AG 2024
H. Kaur et al. (Eds.): CVIP 2023, CCIS 2009, pp. 185–197, 2024.
https://doi.org/10.1007/978-3-031-58181-6_16

developed to monitor suspects in real-time across multiple cameras, addressing these challenges.

Technically, intelligent surveillance systems [18] can be divided into two parts: intra-camera tracking and inter-camera tracking, which employs recognition strategies. There are various challenges in both strategies, such as viewpoint variation, occlusion, different aspect ratios and spatial sizes, lighting, and cluttered background, to name a few. In the case of intra-camera tracking, the difficulty is due to occlusion, which normally happens when people overlap each other or are overlapped by some other object, which leads a tracking algorithm to track the wrong target. In cases of inter-camera tracking, the difficulty is due to high intra-class variance due to variations in lighting conditions, angles, resolutions, and other factors. In addition to this, the task becomes more challenging when we have a large number of people to identify and a large number of non-overlapping cameras, as shown in Fig. 1 with high intra-class variance. In this work, we present YOLORe-IDNet. The YOLORe-IDNet combines Kernelized Correlation Filters (KCF) [7] with an IOU constraint and You Only Look Once (YOLOv5) [9] to form a more robust and efficient tracker for intra-camera tracking tasks. In order to reduce tracking errors and improve accuracy, an IOU-based occlusion assessment approach is introduced into our framework. For recognizing a person across multiple camera views, a DL based person Re-ID model has been used along with camera network information to reduce the latency. We make the following novel contributions:

Fig. 1. Person tracking in a real-world scenario, showcasing the challenges of high intra-class variability: (a) MCPT Dataset and (b) EPFL dataset.

- Creation of an open dataset using cameras placed at 9 different locations in the university campus (see Fig. 6), where the dataset consists of 81000 frames. The URL for the dataset is: https://www.kaggle.com/dsv/6369817.
- User defined real-time identification and selection of person of interest in a camera feed by a simple mouse gesture.
- A novel algorithm for intra-camera tracking that uses IOU-based novel occlusion assessment approach to effectively address occlusion and minimize tracking failures.

The rest of the paper is organized as follows: the related work on visual object tracking for intra- and inter-camera tracking is presented in Sect. 2, and Sect. 3 elaborates details of the methodology presented in this paper. Section 4 discusses the experimental setup and results using our dataset and comparison with some of the state-of-the-art (SOTA) tracking algorithms. Finally, in Sect. 5, we conclude the paper and discuss potential directions for future work.

2   Related Work

The field of Computer Vision (CV) has played a significant role in developing intelligent surveillance systems. Person tracking, in particular, is a critical component of these systems. In this section, we review the existing work on person-tracking methods and their strengths and weaknesses. Compared to conventional computer vision approaches, modern DL models have achieved significant progress in person tracking due to their ability to learn features and patterns in a data-driven manner. However, the existing models often require a large amount of labeled data for training and can be computationally expensive.

2.1   Intra-camera Tracking

Intra-camera object tracking refers to the process of tracking objects within a single video feed. Correlation filters [5] have been used for such a tracking exercise. These filters work by correlating a template with the target object in each frame of a video. One of the earliest approaches for single camera tracking used [4] MOSSE tracker. However, these trackers can be susceptible to distractors and are limited in their ability to handle occlusion and scale adaptation. Intersection over union (IOU) constraint-based tracking [3] is another approach that has been used to track individuals in real-time scenarios. This approach computes the IOU between the current frame and previous frames to predict the target's location. However, IOU-based tracking can be limited in its ability to handle complex scenarios with multiple objects.

The combination of a CNN based object detector and correlation filter can significantly enhance the robustness and tracking accuracy [17]. The detectors can quickly identify potential targets in a given scene, despite occlusions and scale variations. On the other hand, correlation filters are effective for tracking objects with stable appearances and minimal scale change but struggle when object undergoes significant changes in appearance. By integrating the strengths of both detectors and correlation filters, it is possible to leverage their complementary strengths and achieve improved tracker for challenging scenarios [17]. Our proposed approach incorporates YOLOv5 and correlation filter techniques, along with an occlusion detection module, to effectively mitigate tracking drifts. The selection of YOLOv5 and correlation filter, and the design of the occlusion detection module are done keeping in view real-time processing requirements.

2.2   Inter-camera Tracking

Inter-camera tracking tracks objects across multiple cameras, which is a challenging problem due to the differences in camera viewpoints, image quality, illumination conditions etc. In recent years, significant progress has been made in developing inter-camera tracking methods that are robust to these challenges. Several studies have investigated the use of camera networks for human tracking, including the review [8] on various tracking techniques and challenges. One common approach to inter-camera tracking is to use appearance-based methods such as person Re-ID [15]. Re-ID is a process of matching people across different cameras by using their appearance features such as color, texture, and shape. These models typically learn discriminative feature representations of people that are invariant to pose, illumination, and camera viewpoint changes. Therefore, we base our inter-camera tracking module upon AlignedReID++ [14] a person Re-ID model. It uses DMLI, a dynamically matching local information method, for person Re-ID and is effective at resolving pose misalignments or other challenging samples.

Another important aspect of inter-camera tracking is the use of camera network information. This includes the spatial relationships, the field of view (FOV), and the calibration parameters of each camera. By incorporating this information, inter-camera tracking methods can better estimate the trajectories of people across different cameras.

3   YOLORe-IDNet: Proposed Methodology

In this section we first present the algorithms in our methodology and then the implementation of the algorithms for real-time processing.

3.1   Proposed Algorithm

YOLORe-IDNet reads the Real Time Streaming Protocol (RTSP) URLs or paths of the video sources from a "txt" file. Upon identifying the target, the user of the system would input the camera number in the ROI selection field and be expected to draw a bounding box around the person who needs to be tracked. The system then encodes the target data and sends it to the cloud server via post request along with the camera number where the target was first seen. The cloud server then processes this request and validates whether or not the inter-camera tracking module needs to be activated, as illustrated in Fig. 2.

Inside the intra-camera tracking module, we first validate if this is the first request made to the server. If so, then the system performs feature extraction with the help of YOLO detections, finds a similarity score, and initializes the tracker with the coordinates of the person whose similarity score is highest with the target. This ensures the current location of the target is obtained since in real-time systems. Due to potential latency in the network and processing delays, the target may have moved from its original location by the time it is

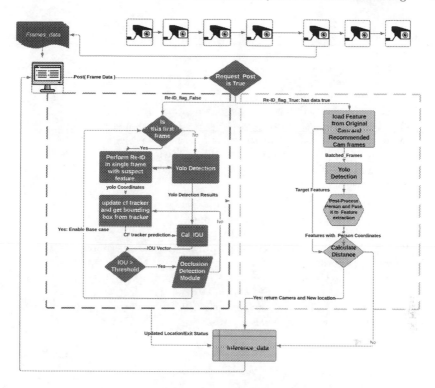

Fig. 2. Flow diagram with intra-camera tracking on left and inter-camera tracking on right.

found. Similarly, when the person exists from the camera's FOV, the cloud server sends the trigger to the client, and from there onwards the inter-camera tracking begins. In this way, the system continues to track the target and finally saves the trajectory map of the locations where the target visited, as shown in Fig. 6.

Intra-camera Tracking. The intra-camera tracking module consists of two stages. First, a base case is activated when the module is called for the first time or when occlusion is observed by the system in the current stream, as mentioned in the proposed Algorithm 1 (line 2). In the second stage of the algorithm (line 9), bounding box detections are obtained using YOLOv5 [9]. The correlation filter updates the target's new location, over which an IOU constraint is applied to select the bounding box with the highest IOU compared to a threshold of 30%, assuming that the movement of the target is limited. The system then applies the proposed Occlusion Detection Algorithm (Algorithm 2) to further assess whether the target has been occluded to overcome tracking errors. This reduces overall tracking errors that occur when the target is fully or partially occluded by other objects. If the occlusion is detected, the base case is activated. The features of the target are extracted along with the features of all the detected persons in the frame, and Re-ID is applied. The tracker is then updated with

---

Algorithm 1: Intra-camera tracking algorithm

Input: Image_frame, target
Output: yolo_bbox

1 $base\_case \leftarrow True$;
2 **if** $base\_case$ is $True$ **then**
3 | bboxes $\leftarrow$ run_yolo_detector(Image_frame); base_case = False;
4 | objects_features = extract_features(bboxes, Image_frame);
5 | target_features = extract_features(target);
6 | target_new_coords = perform_reid(objects_features, target_features);
7 | initialize_tracker(target_new_coords, Image_frame);
8 | **return** target_new_coords
9 **else**
10 | bboxes = run_yolo_detector(Image_frame);
11 | target_new_coords = update_tracker(Image_frame);
12 | IOU_vector, yolo_bbox, has_exit = apply_iou_constraint(bboxes, target_new_coords);
13 | **if** not has_exit **then**
14 | | **if** $max\_of(IOU\_vector) \geq Threshold$ **then**
15 | | | occlusion_flag = detect_occlusion(IOU_vector);
16 | | | **if** $occlusion\_flag$ is $True$ **then**
17 | | | | base_case = True;
18 | | | **else**
19 | | | | initialize_tracker(yolo_bbox, Image_frame);
20 | | | | **return** yolo_bbox;
21 | **else**
22 | | has_exit;

Algorithm 2: Occlusion Detection Algorithm

Input   : IOU_vector
Output: Boolean value indicating occlusion

1 $count \leftarrow 0$; $max\_iou \leftarrow$ max(IOU_vector);
2 **for** iou_score in IOU_vector **do**
3 | **if** $iou\_score > 0.1$ and $iou\_score \neq max\_iou$ **then**
4 | | $count \leftarrow count + 1$;
5 **if** $count > 1$ **then**
6 | **return** True;
7 **else**
8 | **return** False;

---

the coordinates of the person where the highest similarity is observed, else the system continues to track the target. Finally, the tracking module returns the target's location to the client, along with the camera ID, which is further stored

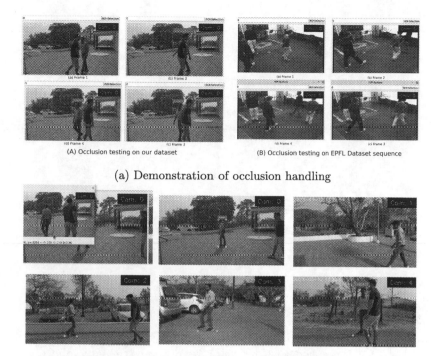

(a) Demonstration of occlusion handling

(b) Target location at different intervals: Capturing target movement

Fig. 3. System output on various video sequences.

to update the target's trajectory. The resulting trajectory map is stored as an output in Fig. 6.

To establish the exit of the target from the current stream, the IOU vector of the last three frames is observed. If the IOU vector is zero in the last three frames, the target is marked as exited, triggering the inter-camera tracking module. The system output shown in Fig. 3a demonstrates the performance of our occlusion detection algorithm on both our MCPT dataset and the EPFL dataset's test sequence [6]. Specifically, in subfigures (a) and (b), the targets were occluded in the second frame, but our algorithm was able to detect this and successfully recovered tracking from the third frame onwards.

Inter-camera Tracking. In the proposed work we make use of AlignedReID++ [14] for person Re-ID. The network uses the DMLI method that aligns horizontal stripes in person and learns global and local features. The local branch aligns local parts using the shortest path distance, which helps the global branch learn more discriminative features for robust Re-ID.

The main goal of the inter-camera tracking module is to conduct the search for the target, and after a successful search, return the camera-ID and bounding box coordinates of the target. As shown in Fig. 4 in the inter-camera tracking

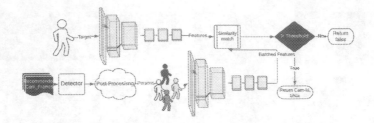

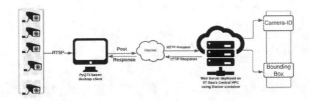

Fig. 4. Inter camera tracking flow diagram.

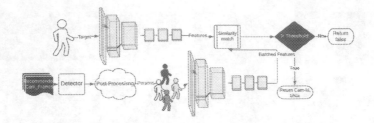

Fig. 5. System architecture for cloud-based application

module, initially target features are extracted using the Re-ID model, and the YOLO detector is applied to a batch of frames; subsequently, the bounding boxes are filtered to obtain person detections, which serve as candidates for Re-ID. Furthermore, post-processing is done to crop the images of all the persons in the frames, and another batch is formed and sent for Re-ID where the similarity match is performed with the original target features. In cases of success, the camera-ID and location are returned to the client; otherwise, the system continues the search with recommended cameras in the next iteration.

3.2 System Architecture and Implementation

Multithreading for Enhancing Execution Speed. To improve the client's performance during the I/O-blocking operation of reading from streaming cameras, we employed a multi-threading approach. Instead of relying on a single thread to grab frames sequentially and risking delays, we spawned an additional thread to handle grabbing frames in parallel. This enabled the continuous reading of frames from the I/O thread while allowing the root thread to process the current frame. In essence, by creating another thread to grab frames, we could enhance the execution of the client.

REST APIs for Inference Data. A REST (Representational State Transfer) API is an architectural style for building web services. REST APIs communicate over HTTP requests.

The complete architecture of the deployed system is shown in Fig. 5. The system architecture is based on a Flask server that receives video frames through HTTP requests. These frames are processed using object detection and tracking algorithms, as explained earlier. Once the cloud server generates inference data, a JSON response is prepared by the server, including bounding boxes and stream ID for the suspect. This response is then relayed back to the client as an HTTP response. Finally, the inference data is visualized on the client, allowing the generation of a target trajectory, as demonstrated in Fig. 3b and 6.

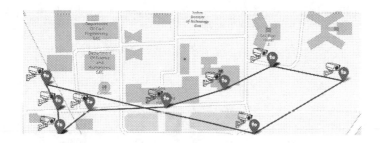

Fig. 6. Trajectory map saved by system as output

Multi-Camera Person Tracking (MCPT) Dataset. In general, person-tracking systems need datasets of the target's trajectory to be developed and evaluated. However, there is a shortage of such datasets that cover multiple cameras, making it difficult to evaluate tracking algorithms against obstacles like occlusions, scale and angle variations, and the movement of individuals in different zones.

To address this challenge, we created the MCPT dataset to evaluate person-tracking systems in real-world scenarios. The dataset consists of nine videos captured from non-overlapping cameras situated across the university campus, each of which is approximately 5 min long, resulting in a total of approximately 81,000 frames. Each camera was set to a resolution of 720×1280 and recorded at a frame rate of 30 frames per second (FPS). To generate suspicious trajectories that are representative of real-world scenarios, a target was recorded in each stream for a maximum of 30 s. The dataset captured the target amidst various intra-class variations, such as targets with varying angles, scale, and lighting variations, while also including instances of full and partial occlusion, providing a more realistic representation of real-world scenarios. The dataset is provided in a standard format, with each video stored as a sequence of frames in JPEG format and each frame labeled with the corresponding ground truth data in a separate "txt" file.

4   Experimental Results

Datasets and Evaluation Protocol: We evaluated the YOLORe-IDNet on MCPT dataset and Object Tracking Benchmark-100 (OTB-100) dataset. The

OTB-100 [16] dataset is a widely utilized benchmark dataset that is primarily used to evaluate the performance of visual object tracking algorithms. This dataset is composed of 100 video sequences, which present a wide range of visual challenges, including occlusion, motion blur, changes in lighting, scale variation, and background clutter. Moreover, this dataset features a diverse set of object classes, including humans, animals, vehicles, and other miscellaneous objects. Given that the primary objective of the YOLORe-IDNet is to track individuals, we deliberately selected 11 of the most challenging person sequences from this dataset for our evaluation.

Table 1. Results on MCPT dataset

	Cam0	Cam1	Cam2	Cam3	Cam4	Cam5	Cam6	Cam7	Cam8	Mean
Precision↑	1.00	1.00	1.00	1.00	1.00	1.00	1.00	1.00	1.00	1.00
Recall↑	0.82	0.81	0.78	0.70	0.75	0.91	0.73	0.93	0.85	0.81
IOU↑	0.91	0.90	0.89	0.93	0.92	0.92	0.91	0.92	0.90	0.91

Note: FPS for all camera feeds = 18.

Precision, Recall, F1Score, Intersection over union (IOU), and Overall precision error (OPE) are used as evaluation metrics.

$$Precision = \frac{TP}{TP+FP}, \ Recall = \frac{TP}{TP+FN}, \ F1Score = 2 * \frac{Precision * Recall}{Precision + Recall} \quad (1)$$

$$OPE = \frac{1}{N}\sum_{i=1}^{N} d_i, \ IOU = \frac{|GT \cap PD|}{|GT \cup PD|} \quad (2)$$

where N is the total number of matches for ground truth, d_i is the Euclidean distance between the center of the predicted bounding box (PD) and the center of the ground truth bounding box (GT) in the ith frame. IOU is the overlap between the PD and the GT box at frame f. True positives (TP) refer to the number of correctly identified GT matches, while false positives (FP) refer to the number of predicted matches that do not match GT. False negatives (FN) refer to the number of GT matches that are not identified by the tracker.

Evaluation on MCPT Dataset: As shown in Fig. 3b, the system is able to accurately track the targets in real-time. To assess the performance of our method, we computed Precision, Recall, and mean IOU for each camera, as reported in Table 1. During the experiments, the proposed system maintained an operational speed of 18 FPS, showcasing its capability to handle real-time feeds efficiently. Moreover, our method demonstrated high Precision and IOU values of 100% and 91% respectively, indicating its ability to provide accurate object localization across different camera views.

Ablation Study: As shown in Table 2 the ablation study was conducted to evaluate the effectiveness of the occlusion assessment module in improving the performance of the system. The results indicate that the inclusion of the occlusion assessment module led to a notable increase of 6% in F1Score and 5% in Recall, and 33.73 units decrease in OPE when compared to the system without the occlusion assessment module. The reason for this is that, when a target occludes, the tracker continues to track the wrong target in the absence of occlusion assessment and without any self-correcting mechanism.

Table 2. Ablation study on Occlusion assessment module.

	With occlusion assessment			Without occlusion assessment		
	F1Score↑	Recall↑	OPE↓	F1Score↑	Recall↑	OPE↓
Cam0	0.90	0.82	6.14	0.77	0.78	103.39
Cam1	0.89	0.81	7.75	0.90	0.82	7.22
Cam2	0.87	0.78	6.58	0.88	0.78	5.87
Cam3	0.82	0.70	5.68	0.85	0.74	5.98
Cam4	0.86	0.75	6.25	0.70	0.63	115.4
Cam5	0.95	0.91	6.21	0.77	0.72	104.8
Cam6	0.85	0.73	6.12	0.87	0.78	5.84
Cam7	0.96	0.93	5.94	0.87	0.78	5.55
Cam8	0.92	0.85	5.55	0.88	0.78	5.75
Mean	0.89	0.81	6.25	0.83	0.76	39.98

Upward arrow: Higher is desired; Downward arrow: Lower is desired.

Comparison with State-of-the-Art Methods: We selected several popular tracking algorithms for comparison, and our method achieved a high F1Score of 79%, second only to CSRT's 83%. However, our method outperformed CSRT's in terms of OPE (10.83 vs. 15.51) on OTB-100 Dataset, as shown in Table 3. Moreover, our algorithm achieved a relatively high mean IOU of 59%. We also compared these tracking algorithms on MCPT dataset, and our approach outperformed other tracking algorithms by a big margin. The reason for this high performance is the ability to recover from occlusions effectively.

Table 3. Comparison with SOTA methods on OTB-100 & MCPT dataset

Method	OTB-100 Dataset				MCPT dataset			
	F1Score↑	Recall↑	OPE↓	IOU↑	F1Score↑	Recall↑	OPE↓	IOU↑
Boosting [12]	0.50	0.40	53.05	0.29	0.50	0.37	198.76	0.30
CSRT [13]	**0.83**	**0.82**	<u>15.51</u>	**0.61**	0.33	0.27	363.89	0.23
KCF [7]	0.39	0.29	12.38	0.22	0.23	0.16	541.20	0.12
MFLOW [10]	0.35	0.26	65.13	0.21	0.13	0.07	319.87	0.11
MIL [2]	0.49	0.37	51.09	0.28	<u>0.55</u>	<u>0.43</u>	<u>146.48</u>	<u>0.33</u>
MOSSE [4]	0.23	0.19	22.81	0.24	0.40	0.28	327.36	0.20
TLD [11]	0.64	0.54	37.19	0.38	0.08	0.04	429.15	0.04
OURS	<u>0.79</u>	<u>0.69</u>	**10.83**	<u>0.59</u>	**0.89**	**0.81**	**6.25**	**0.91**

Bold: best; <u>Underlined</u>: second-best results.

5   Conclusion

In this study, we developed a person-tracking system that uses correlation filters and IOU constraints for reliable tracking and a DL model for cross-camera person Re-ID. Our experiments show that the proposed system is effective in detecting and tracking objects in multi-camera surveillance scenarios, achieving an F1Score of 89%, Recall of 81%, and a mean IOU of 91%, with a low OPE of 6.25. We also evaluated our system on the OTB-100 dataset and achieved competitive results with the least OPE of 10.83 and the second-highest F1Score of 79%, Recall of 69%, and mean IOU of 59% compared to SOTA tracking algorithms. In the future, we aim to explore additional techniques, such as apparel invariant Re-ID, to further enhance the accuracy and generalization of our system in real-world scenarios.

References

1. Ahmed, A.A., Echi, M.: Hawk-eye: an AI-powered threat detector for intelligent surveillance cameras. IEEE Access **9**, 63283–63293 (2021)
2. Babenko, B., Yang, M.H., Belongie, S.: Visual tracking with online multiple instance learning. In: CVPR, pp. 983–990. IEEE (2009)
3. Bochinski, E., Eiselein, V., Sikora, T.: High-speed tracking-by-detection without using image information. In: 2017 14th IEEE International Conference on Advanced Video and Signal Based Surveillance (AVSS), pp. 1–6 (2017)
4. Bolme, D.S., Beveridge, J.R., Draper, B.A., Lui, Y.M.: Visual object tracking using adaptive correlation filters. In: CVPR, pp. 2544–2550. IEEE (2010)
5. Chen, Z., Hong, Z., Tao, D.: An experimental survey on correlation filter-based tracking. CoRR **abs/1509.05520** (2015). http://arxiv.org/abs/1509.05520
6. Fleuret, F., Berclaz, J., Lengagne, R., Fua, P.: Multicamera people tracking with a probabilistic occupancy map. IEEE Trans. PAMI **30**(2), 267–282 (2007)
7. Henriques, J.F., Caseiro, R., Martins, P., Batista, J.: High-speed tracking with kernelized correlation filters. IEEE Trans. PAMI **37**(3), 583–596 (2015). https://doi.org/10.1109/TPAMI.2014.2345390

8. Hou, L., Wan, W., Hwang, J.N., Muhammad, R., Yang, M., Han, K.: Human tracking over camera networks: a review. EURASIP **2017**(1), 1–20 (2017)
9. Jocher, G., Chaurasia, A., Stoken, A., Borovec, J., Yonghye Kwon, E.A.: ultra-lytics/yolov5: v7.0 – YOLOv5 SOTA Realtime Instance Segmentation, November 2022. NanoCode012. https://doi.org/10.5281/zenodo.7347926
10. Kalal, Z., Mikolajczyk, K., Matas, J.: Forward-backward error: automatic detection of tracking failures. In: ICPR, pp. 2756–2759. IEEE (2010)
11. Kalal, Z., Mikolajczyk, K., Matas, J.: Tracking-learning-detection. IEEE Trans. PAMI **34**(7), 1409–1422 (2011)
12. Liu, R., Cheng, J., Lu, H.: A robust boosting tracker with minimum error bound in a co-training framework. In: ICCV, pp. 1459–1466. IEEE (2009)
13. Lukezic, A., Vojir, T., Cehovin Zajc, L., Matas, Jiri, A.K.M.: Discriminative correlation filter with channel and spatial reliability. In: CVPR, pp. 6309–6318 (2017)
14. Luo, H., Jiang, W., Zhang, X., Fan, X., Qian, J., Zhang, C.: Alignedreid++: dynamically matching local information for person re-identification. Pattern Recognit. **94**(C), 53–61 (2019). https://doi.org/10.1016/j.patcog.2019.05.028
15. Ming, Z., et al.: Deep learning-based person re-identification methods: a survey and outlook of recent works. Image Vis. Comput. **119**, 104394 (2022)
16. Wu, Y., Lim, J., Yang, M.H.: Object tracking benchmark. IEEE Trans. PAMI **37**(9), 1834–1848 (2015). https://doi.org/10.1109/TPAMI.2014.2388226
17. Yang, B., Tang, M., Chen, S., Wang, G., Tan, Y., Li, B.: A vehicle tracking algorithm combining detector and tracker. EURASIP **2020**(1), 1–20 (2020)
18. Zabłocki, M., Gościewska, K., Frejlichowski, D., Hofman, R.: Intelligent video surveillance systems for public spaces-a survey. J. Theor. Appl. Comput. Sci. **8**(4), 13–27 (2014)

Robust and Secure Dual Watermarking for Improved Protection and Preservation of Sensitive Healthcare Data

Nimit Gupta, Asmi Lakhani, and Ashima Anand[✉]

CSED, Thapar Institute of Engineering and Technology, Patiala, Punjab, India
ashima.anand@thapar.edu

Abstract. With the advancement of modern technology, the use of transmitting forms has increased. As a result, electronic patient records (EPRs) are transmitted throughout the Internet platform via wired and wireless communication routes. The frequent exchange of sensitive data across online platforms can pose a number of concerns, including security vulnerabilities, storage/bandwidth issues, noise distortion in transmission channels, and other issues. As a result, in the healthcare industry, EPR protection and preservation are key concerns. Digital watermarking is currently a feasible solution for providing digital image copyright protection. However, the effectiveness of invisible watermarking techniques in the face of malicious or unintentional attacks is still a challenge. Dual watermarking involves embedding robust and fragile watermarks in the same cover image, providing a way to integrate copyright protection and integrity verification into a single scheme. This paper proposes a method for detecting and recovering from image tampering using self-embedding dual watermarking. The dual watermarking is implemented by using NSST and SVD transforms to conceal one watermark image into the other. The dual watermark is then embedded into the cover image using NSST, BMEMD, and MSVD for improved imperceptibility and robustness compared to existing works. Encryption is applied to enhance the method's security and maintain the integrity of the information. Experimental results demonstrate that the proposed method performs better against various attacks and can withstand integrity attacks.

Keywords: Dual watermarking · BMEMD · Integrity · Security · Robust · Confidentiality

1 Introduction

In the globalized world, telemedicine services are widely used and recognized globally [1]. The ever-expanding health industry necessitates the most recent technological breakthroughs for optimum sustenance and keeping up with the needs of those in the health sector [2,3]. A poll on identity theft indicated that it is a severe crime and a significant source of fraud worldwide. Furthermore, patient/health data security is a significant concern in telecare implementations [4]. These applications necessitate tamper-resistant and authentic dispensing of health information, which is ensured by adding some visible/invisible piece of data (watermark) capable of resisting all attacks while remaining secure.

Researchers are interested in the ability of watermarking systems to endure attacks while maintaining security. Recently, researchers have combined encryption-decryption techniques with digital watermarking to address issues about health data management [3,5,6]. Watermarking methods are classified into domains such as transform and spatial methods. Analytic research has shown that transform domain methods outperform spatial methods. In addition, using multiple watermarks ensures security and decreases storage and bandwidth needs.

The article proposes a novel approach to embedding dual watermarks in cover images by combining the strengths of two existing methods: NSST-SVD transforms and NSST-BMEMD-MSVD. This new hybrid technique improves the embedded watermarks' integrity, security, and confidentiality. Although the reviewed data-hiding techniques provide authenticity and imperceptibility against common attacks, they are limited by lower security due to reduced computational complexity. The novelties of this paper are summarized as follows:

– Fusion of NSST-SVD [7]: NSST is a suitable option for watermarking due to its undetectable characteristics. Moreover, SVD is commonly used in watermarking applications due to its exceptional energy compaction properties and stability. When NSST and SVD are combined, their hybrid yields superior results compared to their application. The proposed paper employs a globally optimized algorithm to enhance the dual watermark's robustness and security.
– Improved embedding capacity: Our method involves imperceptibly embedding multiple watermarks into a cover image, enhancing security and minimizing the bandwidth requirement. To improve the visual quality of the resulting images, the final watermark is embedded directly into the subsampled area with the highest entropy. Before embedding, both the image and signature (text) watermarks are encoded using a hybrid of NSST-BMEMD-MSVD to provide extra robustness and security.
– High Security: To improve authentication and security at minimal computation, the sub-key for watermark encryption is calculated using FastMIE (Faster medical image encryption). The segmented component of the image is encrypted using a scrambled version of the segmented image and a key generated by RDWT and RSVD. We encrypt a sizable section of the original image to save processing costs rather than assessing it.
– The medical image dataset is selected, which includes MRI images, CT scans, X-Ray images, and standard images for analyzing the image quality. Thorough testing of the proposed approach is performed, and the results show that the proposed method is robust, undetectable, secure, and has high embedding capacity. When evaluated against various signal processing assaults, its performance also outperforms state-of-the-art approaches.

The article is structured as follows: Sect. 2 provides a review and summary of related literature. Section 3 delves into the details of the proposed framework. And the performance evaluation is covered in Sect. 4. The article concludes with a summary in Sect. 5.

2   Literature Review

This section summarizes some related watermarking techniques that employ dual watermarking and encryption.

Kumar et al. have developed a technique for dual watermarking that combines DWT, SVD and SPIHT. The host image is divided into various frequency components using second-level DWT in Ref. [8]. The chosen wavelet component is then modified using SVD. The logo watermark is protected using the Arnold transform, while the signature watermark is encoded using hamming code. The SPIHT method compresses the watermarked image and the location key to enable efficient data transmission. According to the experiment's results, the technique is secure, resilient to various attacks, and superior to alternative methods. This approach could be enhanced and adapted to other multimedia watermarking methods, such as audio and video.

Sharma et al. has introduced a new technique for dual watermarking, which helps maintain the authenticity and integrity of media, protecting identity and copyrights. Ref. [9] utilizes the owner's signature and fingerprint as watermarks. It employs DWT, DCT, and a novel median-based embedding block selection technique to select coefficients modified proportionally for watermark embedding. The flexible scheme can operate on continuous tone/greyscale and multitoned images, commonly used in electronic media and modern printing. The proposed method has been evaluated quantitatively and found invisible and secure, with excellent results regarding PSNR and NCC values. In the future, this approach could be further enhanced to achieve multiple copyright protection and authentication goals.

Husan et al. have proposed an encoding-based watermarking method that efficiently detects and locates tampering in any image compression standard in Ref. [10]. The block-based scheme performs well in imperceptibility, embedding capacity, fragility, and security. The cover image is initially divided into non-overlapping 4×4 blocks after setting LSBs to zero, and an Arithmetic Average (AA) is computed for each block to determine the tampered region. Huffman encoding is applied to the watermark to enhance imperceptibility, while DNA encryption is used to secure it. Both AA and the encrypted watermark are then embedded into the LSBs of pixels in the 4×4 block, and the watermarked image is obtained by embedding all the 4×4 blocks in the same manner. The data size has been reduced using Huffman encoding, achieving a compression ratio of 2.96. The experimental results show that the proposed method has lower computational complexity and can detect and localize tampering.

Kumar Mahto and Singh suggested an improved approach for capacity optimisation in color-image watermarking that employs both spatial and transformed domain techniques to embed three distinct marks in the carrier media's B-R-G channel. The algorithm improves the robustness and invisibility of the watermark and increases its capacity by combining the spatial approach of a magic cube with changed domain techniques such as CT, T-SVD, and DWT. Based on human visual perception, the suggested approach first embeds the encrypted image information into the blue channel, then the system MAC address into the red channel, then the Aadhaar number and hash value of the blue channel into the G channel. The optimal embedding strength factor is computed using the Firefly optimization algorithm to balance robustness and quality effectively. Compared to traditional schemes, Ref. [11] offers an 11% increase in robustness, highlighting its potential for secure media applications. The performance of the approach can be enhanced further by investigating the use of a computationally efficient encryption and optimisation algorithm for processing the watermark before embedding.

Sivananthamaitrey and Kumar have proposed an algorithm incorporating stationary wavelet transform and singular value decomposition to achieve tamper localization and copyright protection using a binary logo and a grayscale watermark. The green plane of the cover image is subjected to SWT and SVD, as well as the gray watermark in Ref. [12]. The transformed green plane of the cover image is then embedded with the gray watermark. The binary logo and blue plane B are divided into four sectors of equal size, and each sector of the logo is embedded into the corresponding sector of B using the LSB substitution method. Finally, the three planes are merged to create a dual watermarked image. Vision-based techniques may be implemented to achieve better perceptual quality and more accurate tamper localization.

Islam et al. has proposed a novel approach for watermarking images in audio with enhanced security and robustness. Ref. [13] involves encrypting the binary image using Arnold transform and BCH codes, followed by embedding using DTCWT, short-time Fourier transforms, and SVD. The proposed approach demonstrates superior security, robustness, embedding capacity, and imperceptibility performance compared to other existing methods. However, there is still room for further improvement in terms of efficiency. The accuracy of the approach is significantly influenced by choice of mother wavelet, order, and type of wavelet used, with various options available. Overall, the proposed scheme is highly effective in watermark detection, with the potential for further optimization.

3 Proposed Methodology

The proposed algorithm can be broken down into two main parts: embedding a dual watermark and embedding the dual mark into cover images. The algorithm is divided into three stages: creating the dual watermark, embedding it, extracting it, and encryption of the resultant watermarked image. The dual watermark

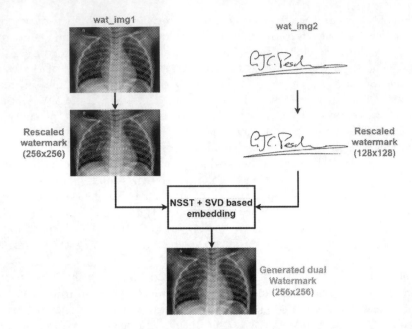

Fig. 1. Proposed embedding procedure for invisible dual watermark embedding

is created using NSST and SVD and is then placed in the cover images as given in Fig. 1. For final watermark embedding, the technique employs a variety of transforms, including NSST, BMEMD, and MSVD. The embedding diagram of the proposed approach is given in Fig. 2. The selection of specific transforms for digital watermarking is based on their ability to perform effective multi-scale and multi-direction analysis. Additionally, these transforms are chosen for their capacity to provide optimal approximations for piece-wise smooth functions, which leads to creating watermarks that are imperceptible to the human eye. By combining multiple transforms, the resulting watermark is more robust and secure, providing better results compared to using single transforms or other combinations. This approach improves the ability to detect unauthorized copying, manipulation, or distribution of the original digital media. The algorithm is discussed in further detail in the following subsections.

3.1   Robust Embedding of Dual Watermark

The given method aims to enhance the security of the input watermark image by integrating it into another watermark image of size 256×256. The watermark images undergo pre-processing, including resizing and determining their sub-images maximum entropy values. The sub-image with the highest entropy value is selected, and the input watermark is embedded into it using an embedding factor called emb_fac_wat. The embedding process is carried out using the equation W_embed = w2_s + emb_fac_wat * w1_S, that the resulting watermarked image appears visually imperceptible, i.e., without any noticeable distortion that could reduce its commercial value. The effectiveness of this method is judged by its ability to maintain robustness against attacks while ensuring high levels of imperceptibility. The algorithm for this method is described in detail below.

Algorithm 1: Dual Watermark embedding algorithm

Input : emb_fac as **alpha1**, $Watermark1$ as **wat_img1**, $Watermark2$ as **wat_img2**

Output: Dual watermarked image as **watermarked_img**

    // Phase 1: Sub-sampling of the wat_img2

1       $[F1, F2, F3, F4] \leftarrow$ **Img_Subsampling**(wat_img2);

    // Phase 2: Maximum entropy value of sub-images

2       $[E1, E2, E3, E4] \leftarrow$ **entropy**$(F1, F2, F3, F4)$;

3       $max\_F \leftarrow$ **Maximum**$(E1, E2, E3, E4)$;

    // Apply NSST and SVD on wat_img1

4       $[w1\_dst, wat1\_shear\_f] \leftarrow$ **NSST**$(double(wat\_img1)$;

5       $[w1\_U, w1\_S, w1\_V] \leftarrow$ **svd**$(w1\_dst1, 2(:, :, 2))$;

    // Apply NSST and SVD on wat_img2

6       $[w2\_dst, wat1\_shear\_f] \leftarrow$ **NSST**(max_F);

7       $[w2\_U, w2\_S, w2\_V] \leftarrow$ **svd**$(w2\_dst1, 2(:, :, 2))$;

    // Phase 3: Watermark embedding

8       $wat\_emb1 \leftarrow w2\_S + alpha1 * w1\_S$;

    // Phase 4: Inverse SVD and NSST

9       $w2\_w1\_nsst \leftarrow w2\_U * W\_emb1 * w2\_V^T$;

10     $w2\_dst1, 2(:, :, 2) \leftarrow w2\_w1\_nsst$;

11     $Watermarked\_F1 \leftarrow$ **Inverse_NSST**$(w2\_dst)$;

    // Phase 5: Applying inverse Sub-sampling

12

       $watermarked_img \leftarrow$ **iImg_Subsamplin**$(Watermarked\_F1, F2, F3, F4)$;

13   **return** $Watermarked_img$

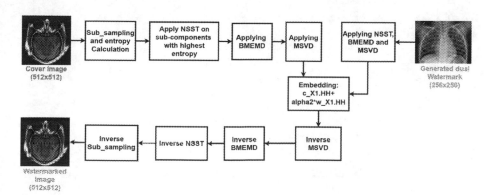

Fig. 2. Proposed embedding procedure for invisible final watermark embedding

3.2   Robust Embedding of Final Watermark

This method uses a hybrid optimal algorithm, NSST-BMEMD-MSVD, to embed a dual watermark into cover images. The cover image and watermark are resized and embedded into the subsampled image with the highest entropy. The final watermark is embedded using the equation W_embed2 ← c_X1.HH + emb_fac_cover× w_X1.HH, with the embedding factor emb_fac_cover used to achieve maximum imperceptibility so that no visible distortions appear in the image. The algorithm aims to maintain robustness while ensuring high imperceptibility to preserve the commercial value of the image.

Algorithm 2: Final watermark embedding algorithm

Input   : cover, emb_fac_cover as **alpha2**, Dual watermark
Output: Final generated watermarked image as **final_img**
// Phase 1: Sub-sampling of the cover image
1         $[F1, F2, F3, F4] \leftarrow$ **Img_Subsampling**$(cover)$;
// Phase 2: Maximum entropy value of sub-images
2        $[E1, E2, E3, E4] \leftarrow$ **entropy**$(F1, F2, F3, F4)$;
3        $max\_F \leftarrow$ **Maximum**$(E1, E2, E3, E4)$;
// Apply NSST, MSVD, and BMEMD on dual watermarked image
4        $[wat\_dst, wat1\_shear\_f] \leftarrow$ **NSST**$(watermarked_img)$;
5        $[im(:,:,1)] \leftarrow$ **wat_dst**$((1,2)(:,:,3))$;
6        $[im(:,:,2)] \leftarrow$ **wat_dst**$((1,2)(:,:,4))$;
7        $[imf1] \leftarrow$ **bmemd**$(im, 8)$;
8        $[w\_X1, w\_U1] \leftarrow$ **MSVD**$(imf11, 3(:,:,1))$;
// Apply NSST, MSVD, and BMEMD on cover image
9        $[C\_dst, wat2\_shear\_f] \leftarrow$ **NSST**(max_F);
10       $[im(:,:,1)] \leftarrow$ **C_dst**$((1,2)(:,:,3))$;
11       $[im(:,:,2)] \leftarrow$ **C_dst**$((1,2)(:,:,4))$;
12       $[imf2] \leftarrow$ **bmemd**$(im, 8)$;
13       $[c\_X1, c\_U1] \leftarrow$ **MSVD**$(imf21, 3(:,:,1))$;
// Phase 3: Watermark embedding
14       $wat\_embed2 \leftarrow c\_X1.HH + emb\_fac_cover * w\_X1.HH$;
// Phase 4: Inverse MSVD, BMEMD and NSST
15       $[imf21, 3(:,:,1)] \leftarrow Inverse\_MSVD(c\_X1, c\_U1)$;
16       $a \leftarrow imf21, 1(:,:,1) + imf21, 2(:,:,1) + imf21, 3(:,:,1) + imf21, 4(:,:,1) + imf21, 5(:,:,1)$;
17       $C\_dst1, 2(:,:,2) \leftarrow a$;
18       $Watermarked\_F2 \leftarrow$ **Inverse_NSST**(C_dst);
// Phase 7: Applying inverse Sub-sampling
19       $final\_img \leftarrow$ **Img_Subsampling**$(F1, F2, F3, Watermarked\_F2)$;
20   **return** $final\_img$

3.3 Encryption of the Final Marked Image Using a Hybrid of RDWT and RSVD

The random permutation functions are used to jumble up the segmented portion of the image. The segmented image is then processed using a combination of RDWT and RSVD transformed techniques to provide a secure key. Finally, the encrypted image is obtained using the produced encryption key and the scrambled picture. Also for reducing the computational cost only the significant part of the whole image is encrypted. It takes less time in encryption as compared to many other techniques.

Algorithm 3: Encryption of final marked carrier image

Input   : final_img
Output: F
// Phase 1:Generation of Encryption key
1       $[CA, CH, CV, CD] \leftarrow II[Xsegment]$;
2       $[U1, S1, V1] \leftarrow (??CA)$;
3   **for** $i \leftarrow 0 : m/2$ **do**;
4               $b1(:, i) \leftarrow U1(:, i)$;
5               $b2(:, i) \leftarrow V1(:, i)$;
6   **end**;
7       $W \leftarrow U1?V1$;
8       $U2, S2, V2 \leftarrow ??W$;
9       $K \leftarrow U2 * V2^T$;
10   **return** K
// Phase 2:Final Encryption
11          $E^{'} \leftarrow K * Xscrambled * K^T$;
12          $F \leftarrow Xoriginal?E^{'}$;

---

4   Result and Analysis

In this section, we discuss the detailed valuation of the techniques used in our study. We conducted experimental arrangements and evaluated the performance using different cover objects and watermarks. We performed various attacks to test the effectiveness of the techniques. Our initial trials involved using a chest X-ray image of size 256×256 as a cover watermark and a signature image as a watermark of size 128×128. We implemented these techniques on MATLAB R2021b using a system with an Intel Xeon(R) Gold processor and 256GB RAM. To assess the performance of our proposed technique, we used the following performance metrics - Peak Signal-to-Noise Ratio (PSNR), Normalized Correlation (NC), structural similarity index measure (SSIM), number of changing pixel rates (NPCR), and the unified averaged changed intensity (UACI). We

Table 1. Performance evaluation of the proposed method across a range of embedding factors

EF	PSNR	SSIM	NC	NPCR	UACI
0.1	68.6868	0.9998	0.9902	0.9968	0.4231
0.2	47.9308	0.9972	0.9904	0.9966	0.4228
0.3	44.4090	0.9940	0.9906	0.9970	0.4229
0.4	41.9012	0.9897	0.9908	0.9967	0.4230
0.5	39.9720	0.9844	0.9910	0.9968	0.4234

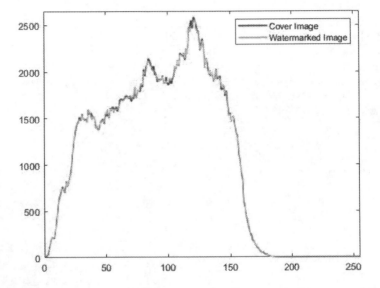

Fig. 3. Subjective evaluation of the proposed work using histogram comparison

compared the results obtained with these metrics to evaluate the effectiveness of our techniques.

Working of the proposed watermarking technique is examined for different values of embedding factor (EF), ranging from 0.1 to 0.5 (both embedding factors), and the results are summarized in Table 1. The highest PSNR score for emb_fac_wat is 68.6868 with the value of 'EF' as 0.1, while the highest 'NC' value achieved is 0.9910 at 'EF' as 0.5. We evaluated the impact of invisibility and robustness on different medical and non-medical, and standard images. We can see the results in Table 2 for medical [14] and standard images. The highest PSNR value for the proposed method is 68.6868 dB (for CT-Scan medical image), the highest SSIM and NC values are 0.9993 and 0.9995 (for MRI images), and the average PSNR, SSIM, and NC values are 57.0904, 0.9010, and 0.9987, respectively. Moreover, NPCR and UACI are more than 0.9960 and 0.3989 for all cases, indicating that the selected encryption can achieve high security.

Table 2. Objective evaluation of the proposed work on medical and standard images

Cover Images	PSNR(in dB)	SSIM	NC
CT Scan	68.6868	0.9992	0.9994
MRI	67.9339	0.9993	0.9995
X-ray	65.5258	0.9962	0.9994
Lenna	55.0953	0.9963	0.9993
Cameraman	56.9431	0.9971	0.9994
Peppers	54.9167	0.9648	0.9992
Barbara	57.5196	0.9985	0.9995
Average of CT scan images [14]	57.0904	0.9010	0.9987

Table 3. Robustness evaluation for different attacks

Attack	Noise	NC of Watermark1	NC of Watermark2
Salt & Pepper Noise	0.1	0.9908	0.9994
Gaussian Noise	0.1	0.9904	0.9993
JPEG compression	10	0.9908	0.9984
Cropping Attacks	[420 420 40 40]	0.9908	0.9972
Rotate	45	0.9908	0.9994
Gaussian low-pass filter	0.6	0.9908	0.9993
Sharpening Mask	0.1	0.9908	0.9993
Median Filter	[3 3]	0.9908	0.9993
Histogram equilization		0.9908	0.9994
Speckle Noise	0.5	0.9908	0.9993
Scaling	11	0.9921	0.9886
Translation attack	[7 7]	0.9908	0.9992
Average Filtering		0.9908	0.9992

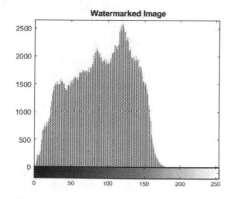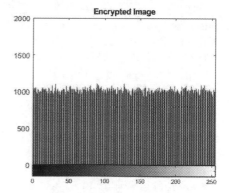

Fig. 4. Evaluation of the encryption method using histogram analysis

To subjectively verify the performance of the proposed work, a comparative histogram of the original cover image and marked images is presented in Fig. 3. This graphical comparison shows the high similarity between the visual quality of the two images shown in Fig. 4. An investigation of robustness measures how well a watermarking method can tolerate different assaults or distortions without losing the embedded watermark. It helps to guarantee that the embedded watermark endures various assaults that the watermarked content may encounter and still is legible.

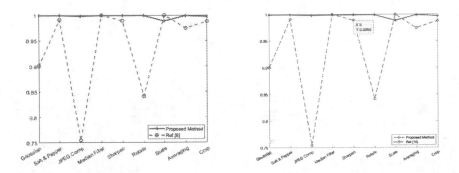

Fig. 5. Comparison results, in Ref. [8] and Ref. [15], using line graph analysis.

Table 3 provides a summary of the suggested watermarking method's robustness evaluation. Referring to the obtained results, an NC score ≥ 0.9887 clarifies high robustness for all the considered attacks. Using a fusion of NSST, BMEMD, and MSVD coupled with encryption of the final marked picture to increase security gives a comparative analysis of its excellence. Figure 5 compares the suggested approach [8] and [15], demonstrating the efficacy of the method's robustness and the imperceptibility of assaults made on the dual watermarks.

5   Conclusion

This study presents a dual watermarking method that first utilizes NSST and SVD domains for embedding 1st watermark into another and then for final watermark embedding. NSST-BMEMD-MSVD transforms are utilized for robust and imperceptible use in gray-scale images. Along with this FastMIE encryption technique is used to maintain the integrity and confidentiality of the data. The technique involves hiding the dual watermark inside the cover image and then encrypting the image to increase security. Results from the experiments demonstrate that the proposed approach is a robust, imperceptible, and secure watermarking method that can withstand various image attacks such as Salt and Pepper noise, Gaussian noise, histogram equalization, Median filtering, Laplacian sharpening, Blur filtering, and JPEG compression attacks. Furthermore, the watermarked image's quality is satisfactory for practical applications, particularly imperceptibility.

References

1. Tan, C.K., Ng, J.C., Xu, X., Poh, C.L., Guan, Y.L., Sheah, K.: Security protection of DICOM medical images using dual-layer reversible watermarking with tamper detection capability. J. Digit. Imaging **24**, 528–540 (2011)
2. Singh, A.K., Kumar, B., Singh, G., Mohan, A.: Medical Image Watermarking. Springer, Cham (2017). https://doi.org/10.1007/978-3-319-57699-2
3. Anand, A., Singh, A.K.: An improved DWT-SVD domain watermarking for medical information security. Comput. Commun. **152**, 72–80 (2020)
4. Wu, H.-T., Cheung, Y., Zhuang, Z., Tang, S.: Reversible data hiding in homomorphic encrypted images without preprocessing. In: You, I. (ed.) WISA 2019. LNCS, vol. 11897, pp. 141–154. Springer, Cham (2020). https://doi.org/10.1007/978-3-030-39303-8_11
5. Anand, A., Singh, A.K., Lv, Z., Bhatnagar, G.: Compression-then-encryption-based secure watermarking technique for smart healthcare system. IEEE Multimedia **27**(4), 133–143 (2020)
6. Singh, A.K., Anand, A., Lv, Z., Ko, H., Mohan, A.: A survey on healthcare data: a security perspective. ACM Trans. Multimed. Comput. Commun. Appl. **17**(2s), 1–26 (2021)
7. Zhao, J., et al.: Texture directionality-based digital watermarking in nonsubsample shearlet domain. Math. Probl. Eng. **2017** (2017)
8. Kumar, C., Singh, A.K., Kumar, P.: Dual watermarking: an approach for securing digital documents. Multimed. Tools Appl. **79**, 7339–7354 (2020)
9. Sharma, S., Zou, J.J., Fang, G.: A dual watermarking scheme for identity protection. Multimed. Tools Appl. **82**(2), 2207–2236 (2023)
10. Hussan, M., Gull, S., Parah, S.A., Qureshi, G.J.: An efficient encoding based watermarking technique for tamper detection and localization. Multimed. Tools Appl. 1–23 (2023)
11. Mahto, D.K., Singh, A.K.: Firefly optimization-based dual watermarking for colour images with improved capacity. Multimed. Tools Appl. 1–19 (2022)
12. Sivananthamaitrey, P., Kumar, P.R.: Optimal dual watermarking of color images with SWT and SVD through genetic algorithm. Circuits Syst. Signal Process. **41**, 224–248 (2022)
13. Islam, M.S., et al.: Robust dual domain twofold encrypted image-in-audio watermarking based on SVD. Circuits Syst. Signal Process. **40**, 4651–4685 (2021)
14. Mader, K.S.: Ct medical images. https://www.kaggle.com/datasets/kmader/siim-medical-images
15. Koley, S.: Visual attention model based dual watermarking for simultaneous image copyright protection and authentication. Multimed. Tools Appl. **80**(5), 6755–6783 (2021)

A Simplified 3D Ultrasound Freehand Imaging Framework Using 1D Linear Probe and Low-Cost Mechanical Track

Antony Jerald, A. N. Madhavanunni, Gayathri Malamal,
Pisharody Harikrishnan Gopalakrishnan,
and Mahesh Raveendranatha Panicker(✉)

Indian Institute of Technology Palakkad, Palakkad, India
mahesh@iitpkd.ac.in
https://www.iitpkd.ac.in

Abstract. Ultrasound imaging is the most popular medical imaging modality for point-of-care bedside imaging. However, 2D ultrasound imaging provides only limited views of the organ of interest, making diagnosis challenging. To overcome this, 3D ultrasound imaging was developed, which uses 2D ultrasound images and their orientation/position to reconstruct 3D volumes. The accurate position estimation of the ultrasound probe at low cost has always stood as a challenging task in 3D reconstruction. In this study, we propose a novel approach of using a mechanical track for ultrasound scanning, which restricts the probe motion to a linear plane, simplifying the acquisition and hence the reconstruction process. We also present an end-to-end pipeline for 3D ultrasound volume reconstruction and demonstrate its efficacy with an *in-vitro* tube phantom study and an *ex-vivo* bone experiment. The comparison between a sensorless freehand and the proposed mechanical track based acquisition is available online (shorturl.at/jqvX0).

Keywords: Mechanical track · 3D reconstruction · Volume visualisation · Freehand ultrasound imaging

1 Introduction

Ultrasound imaging is a popular point-of-care medical imaging modality due to its several advantages such as dynamic imaging, lack of ionizing radiations, comparatively low cost, and easy disinfection. However, conventional 2D ultrasound imaging suffers many disadvantages [1]. The most important is that the decision-making process in diagnosis and analysis is time-consuming and might lead to inaccurate judgments. This is because the physician needs to mentally transform a sequence of 2D ultrasound images to produce a 3D volume representation. Also, it is challenging to relocate the exact orientation of any previously captured image to record the progression and regression of pathology in response to therapy. Measurement of an organ volume, which is very important in some

H. Kaur et al. (Eds.): CVIP 2023, CCIS 2009, pp. 210–218, 2024.
https://doi.org/10.1007/978-3-031-58181-6_18

treatments and surgery, is highly inaccurate in 2D ultrasound imaging. Due to these limitations of 2D ultrasound imaging, there is a growing need for 3D ultrasound imaging, which provides more precise and integrated information about organs and is better suited for treatment and clinical diagnosis [2].

Various ultrasound data acquisition methods using 2D arrays and mechanical 3D probes have been developed over the years. Using a dedicated 2D array ultrasound probe is one of the fastest ways to view the 3D volume in real-time as it does not require precise orientation information for volume generation [3]. But a 2D array probe is costly and complex to design in terms of both hardware and software. Moreover the limited size of 2D array transducers, due to difficulties in fabrication, results in a smaller field of view in imaging [1]. In a mechanical 3D probe, a standard linear array transducer is motored to translate, rotate and tilt within the probe to acquire images, and the translation, rotation, and axis of rotation can be used as a reference for reconstruction. However, the mechanical 3D probes need to be held statically by the doctors while images are being taken, which introduces latent flaws in the data-collecting process [4]. Another method uses motorized mechanisms to tilt or translate the conventional linear array probe and rapidly acquire 2D ultrasound images [5]. Here the scanning position and orientation need to be predefined and are controlled by a stepper/servo motor, hence it acquires regularly spaced 2D ultrasound frames. However, these motorised probes are bulky, making them inconvenient for frequent scanning purposes [4].

In freehand ultrasound acquisition, orientation estimation sensors like electromagnetic (EM) tracking sensors are attached to the ultrasound probe to register the orientation/position of each frame along with the ultrasound frame. This method allows the user to move the probe freely, making it more flexible in terms of mobility [6]. However, EM trackers can be affected by interference from nearby magnetic sources, resulting in decreased tracking accuracy [1]. Deep learning-based sensor-less freehand ultrasound 3D reconstruction [7] techniques have gained popularity in the recent past. But the deep learning-based approach requires a lot of labelled training samples and high computational power for accurate results [8]. Also, in general, most of the approaches in literature have been proposed to enable 3D scanning on a moderately high-cost system not intended for point-of-care imaging.

In this work, a novel approach to overcome the challenge of orientation/position estimation in freehand-based scanning is attempted by using a low-cost mechanical track that simplifies position tracking using a predefined movement region. Interpolation techniques are utilized to reconstruct the acquired data into a 3D volume, which can then be visualized through volume rendering.

2 Proposed Approach

2.1 Proposed Mechanical Track

The use of a mechanical track for probe motion in 3D acquisition simplifies position tracking by confining the probe to linear motion in a plane. The mechanical

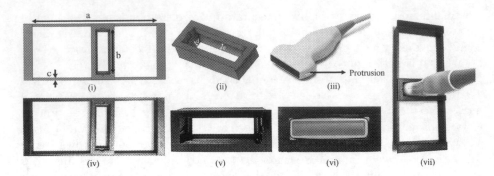

Fig. 1. (i) and (ii) Rectangular track and mask designed in Fusion 360, (iii) Verasonics L11-5v probe, (iv) and (v) 3D printed track and mask, (vi) and (vii) Probe on track

Table 1. Mechanical Track Dimensions

Symbol	Dimension (cm)	Use
a	12	Length for linear motion of probe
b	5.3	Width of the probe
c	0.2	Overlap which acts as a railing
d	Curve with radius of 7	For fitting the curved bottom part
e	Curve with radius of 14	For fitting the curved bottom part

track consists of two components: the probe mask, which reduces errors in linear scanning by preventing the probe from tilting, and the rectangular track, which serves as a guide rail for the smooth movement of the probe and prevents slipping from the operator's hands. The mechanical track, designed using Fusion 360 software (Fig. 1(i) & (ii)) to match the probe and scanning material, is 3D printed (Fig. 1(iv) & (v)) and is cost-effective. The Verasonics L11-5v probe (Fig. 1(iii)) is used in the proposed study. The track width is selected to guarantee seamless mask mobility. A curved bottom of the mask matching the probe shape is designed to ensure a snug fit (Fig. 1(vi) & (vii)) and prevents the vertical falling of the probe. Side cuts on the mask are provided to accommodate the probe protrusions. Table 1 summarizes the dimensions of the designed track and mask. The frames are acquired at high frame rates employing multi-angle plane-wave compounding which results in a high correlation among the acquired frames. This leads to low-complex 3D volume reconstruction using simple trilinear interpolation between frames, simplifying the volume reconstruction process and reducing computational complexity.

2.2 Proposed Image Processing Pipeline

Ultrasound images are typically characterized by speckles and hence the selection of image processing algorithms is a crucial stage in the reconstruction pipeline.

The various steps in the proposed image processing pipeline are shown in Fig. 2 and explained in detail in the subsequent sections.

Log Compression and Squaring. Log compression enhances the low-intensity values in images with strong reflections. Squaring the image increases contrast by intensifying the dark areas and brightening the bright regions. The improvement in the visibility of the acquired ultrasound images is illustrated in Fig. 2 (b).

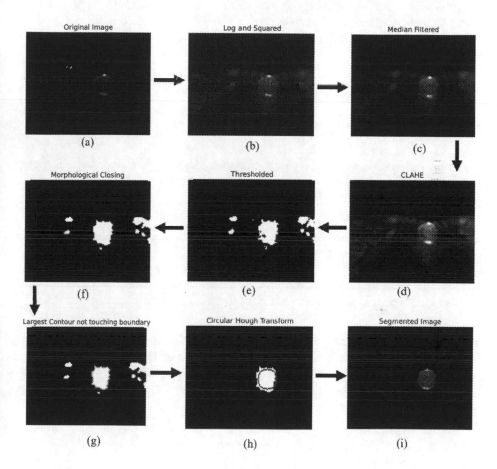

Fig. 2. Image Processing Steps: (a) Acquired ultrasound Image, (b) After log compression and squaring, (c) Median filtered image, (d) Contrast limited adaptive histogram equalized image, (e) Thresholded image, (f) Image after morphological closing, (g) Largest contour not touching boundary identified (green boundary), (h) Circle fitting using hough transform on the identified contour (blue circle), (i) Segmented region of interest. (The region of interest shown in the images is of size 2 cm × 3 cm). (Color figure online)

Median Filtering. Due to the log compression, the salt and pepper noise is increased and to suppress the same, a non-linear median filter was applied. A 3×3 overlapping window was employed for median filtering in this work, resulting in the filtered image shown in Fig. 2 (c).

Contrast Limited Adaptive Histogram Equalization. To further enhance the image quality, contrast limited adaptive histogram equalisation (CLAHE) [9], a variant of adaptive histogram equalisation is applied, that distributes the part of the histogram that exceeds the clip limit equally across all histograms to limit the contrast amplification to reduce amplified noise as demonstrated in Fig. 2 (d).

Thresholding. The next step is to segment the relevant region of interest. The initial step is to convert the image to binary using global thresholding (using a threshold value of 49 here), and the binary image is shown in Fig. 2 (e).

Morphological Operations. The morphological closing operation is performed on the thresholded image using a cross-shaped structuring element of size 3×3 and the result is shown in Fig. 2 (f).

Largest Contour Detection. The contours in an image are lines that outline objects or features with similar intensity levels. The Suzuki algorithm [10] is employed to detect all the contours present in the binary image. The detected contours are sorted based on the area, with the largest one not touching the image boundary chosen as the target contour, as shown in Fig. 2 (g).

Hough Transform. Since the objective of the tube phantom study is to extract objects which are cylindrical in nature, the Hough Transform [11] is employed to determine the best-fitting circle for the largest contour identified in each frame as shown in Fig. 2 (h).

Segmentation. The region enclosed by the identified circle is used as a binary mask and is then applied on the histogram equalised image to produce the final segmented image in Fig. 2 (i).

2.3   3D Reconstruction and Visualisation

After processing the data, the segmented ultrasound images of the cross-sectional view are obtained and will be employed for the volume reconstruction. The reconstruction was performed using the trilinear interpolation method. It increases the resolution of the dataset by estimating intensity values for voxels that were not present in the original data, resulting in improved quality and detail of the final volume, leading to more accurate diagnosis and reduced visual artefacts. Since the acquisition is done at high frame rates with subsequent frames having high correlation, trilinear interpolation is a suitable approach for effectively reconstructing the 3D volumes in the proposed work.

The reconstructed ultrasound volume dataset is visualized using the volume rendering approach available in the Volume Viewer tool in Matlab®, providing the three-dimensional structure of the tube. The algorithm traces rays from the viewpoint to each voxel in the volume and uses the intensity values of corresponding 2D images to determine the voxel's colour and opacity. This generates a realistic 3D representation of the ultrasound data, giving a more comprehensive understanding of the underlying structures.

3   Experiments and Results

3.1   *In-vitro* Tube Phantom Study

The proposed approach was evaluated by reconstructing the 3D volume of a circular tube from the 2D ultrasound images acquired using the proposed mechanical track. A single-tube phantom was designed as shown in Fig. 3 (a), and filled with a mixture of acoustic gel and chalk powder to act as a reflector. The tube was positioned in a cubic container filled with water to the top, ensuring that the tip of the probe touches water, thus ensuring impedance matching. The images were acquired using the 128-channel Verasonics Vantage research ultrasound platform with an L11-5v linear probe. Plane-wave transmission at a center frequency of 7.6 MHz is employed for insonification and the delay and sum beamformer on the Verasonics vantage system is adopted for receive beamforming and image reconstruction. A total of 150 beamformed grayscale images, each with dimensions of 100×192 pixels, were acquired with a single motion of the probe along the entire length of the mechanical track.

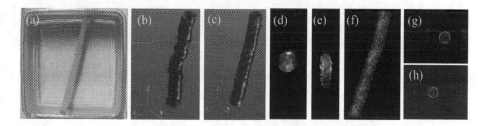

Fig. 3. (a) Top view of the tube phantom. Reconstructed volume visualized in MAT-LAB: (b) data acquired without mechanical track, (c) data acquired with the mechanical track. (d) XY Slice, (e) YZ Slice, (f) XZ Slice, (g), and (h) Comparison of the auto segmentation (blue) and manual segmentation (green) for a random two slices. (Color figure online)

3.2   3D Volume Visualisation and Evaluation

The reconstructed volume visualized in MATLAB is shown in Fig. 3 (c), with XY, YZ and XZ slices displayed in Fig. 3 (d), (e), and (f) respectively. The XY slice represents the cross-sectional view of the tube, the tube was kept at a slant of 45° so the YZ slice gave an oval shape and the XZ slice gives the top view of the phantom made.

The proposed auto segmentation is compared against the manual segmentation for 20 random samples from the image stack. The mean Intersection over Union (IoU) score between manual and automatic segmentation was determined to be 88.97%. As seen in Fig. 3 (g) and (h), the results demonstrate the high degree of similarity between manual and automatic segmentation.

3.3   *Ex-vivo* Validation

The proposed approach is validated with an *ex-vivo* experiment using a bone (tibia of a goat) placed in a water bath as shown in Fig. 4(a) and (b). A total of 300 beamformed grayscale images, each with dimensions of 128×128 pixels, were acquired with a single motion of the probe along the entire length of the mechanical track. The images are processed similarly to that of the *in-vitro* study and the results are shown in Fig. 4(d).

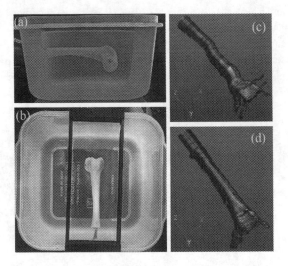

Fig. 4. *Ex-vivo* bone phantom setup: (a) side view (b) top view. Reconstructed volume visualized in MATLAB: (c) data acquired without the mechanical track (d) data acquired with the mechanical track.

4   Discussion and Conclusion

In this work, a novel framework for freehand scanning for 3D ultrasound imaging is proposed. The proposed approach consists of a 3D-printed mechanical track and a high frame rate acquisition. While the mechanical track ensured reduced errors caused by probe slippage or tilt while scanning, the high frame rate acquisition resulted in a high correlation among subsequent frames which helped in simpler approaches for volume reconstruction. The reconstructed volume of the *in-vitro* tube phantom and the *ex-vivo* bone phantom, shown in Fig. 3(b) and 4(c) respectively, were generated using ultrasound images obtained without the use of a mechanical track. Comparing these volumes with that obtained using the mechanical track (Fig. 3(c) and Fig. 4(d)) highlights the reduction in errors caused by probe slippage or tilt by incorporating the mechanical track in the imaging process. Detailed video results comparing 3D reconstruction with and without the use of the mechanical track are available online [12].

The proposed design is most effective for scanning on flat surfaces and can be improved by using a deformable material on the side that comes into contact with the scanning surface. To overcome errors due to variations in scanning velocity, a low-cost accelerometer can be employed for tracking probe motion and will be taken up as future work. While conventional segmentation techniques produced good results for the simple phantoms, neural network based segmentation techniques shall be employed for more complex structures as part of future work. Overall, the experimental results are encouraging and suggest that further research is warranted to address the current limitations to improve point-of-care ultrasound imaging.

References

1. Mohamed, F., Siang, C.V.: A survey on 3D ultrasound reconstruction techniques. Artif. Intell. Appl. Med. Biol. 73–92 (2019)
2. Wen, T., et al.: GPU-based volume reconstruction for freehand 3D ultrasound imaging. In: 39th Annual International Conference of the IEEE Engineering in Medicine and Biology Society. IEEE (2017)
3. Woo, J., Roh, Y.: Ultrasonic 2D matrix array transducer for volumetric imaging in real time. In: 2012 IEEE International Ultrasonics Symposium. IEEE (2012)
4. Huang, Q., Zeng, Z.: A review on real-time 3D ultrasound imaging technology. BioMed Res. Int. (2017)
5. Kaminski, J.T., Rafatzand, K., Zhang, H.K.: Feasibility of robot-assisted ultrasound imaging with force feedback for assessment of thyroid diseases. In: Medical Imaging 2020: Image-Guided Procedures, Robotic Interventions, and Modeling, vol. 11315. SPIE (2020)
6. Daoud, M.I., et al.: Freehand 3D ultrasound imaging system using electromagnetic tracking. In: 2015 International Conference on Open Source Software Computing (OSSCOM). IEEE (2015)
7. Prevost, R., et al.: 3D freehand ultrasound without external tracking using deep learning. Med. Image Anal. **48**, 187–202 (2018)

8. Liu, S., et al.: Deep learning in medical ultrasound analysis: a review. Engineering **5**(2), 261–275 (2019)
9. Zuiderveld, K.J.: Contrast Limited Adaptive Histogram Equalization. Graphics gems (1994)
10. Suzuki, S.: Topological structural analysis of digitized binary images by border following. Comput. Vis. Graph. Image Process. **30**(1), 32–46 (1985)
11. Kimme, C., Ballard, D., Sklansky, J.: Finding circles by an array of accumulators. Commun. ACM **18**(2), 120–122 (1975)
12. Center for Computational Imaging IIT Palakkad. Freehand 3D Ultrasound Using Low Cost Mechanical Track. https://www.youtube.com/playlist?list=PLiuuVhVNWBZS-Gr02aLdWSzz1iGOFr5zC. Accessed 12 Feb 2023

ExtSwap: Leveraging Extended Latent Mapper for Generating High Quality Face Swapping

P. N. Aravinda Reddy[1]([✉])[ID], K. Sreenivasa Rao[1][ID],
Raghavendra Ramachandra[2][ID], and Pabitra Mitra[1][ID]

[1] Indian Institute of Technology Kharagpur, Kharagpur, India
aravindareddy.27@iitkgp.ac.in
[2] Norwegian University of Science and Technology (NTNU), 2815 Gjøvik, Norway
raghavendra.ramachandra@ntnu.no

Abstract. We present a novel face swapping method using the progressively growing structure of a pre-trained StyleGAN. Previous methods use different encoder-decoder structures, embedding integration networks to produce high-quality results, but their quality suffers from entangled representation. We disentangle semantics by deriving identity and attribute features separately. By learning to map the concatenated features into the extended latent space, we leverage the state-of-the-art quality and its rich semantic extended latent space. Extensive experiments suggest that the proposed method successfully disentangles identity and attribute features and outperforms many state-of-the-art face swapping methods, both qualitatively and quantitatively.

Keywords: Disentanglement · Face swapping · Generative Adversarial Networks

1 Introduction

Nowadays there is obsolete rise in manipulated images, videos and audio because of the increasing elegance of camera technology and the accelerating reach of social media platforms have enabled the creation of images and videos more sophisticatedly. Before the advent of machine learning and computer vision techniques, many fake videos and their degree of resemblance to the original needed to be improved owing to a lack of domain expertise and sophisticated manual editing tools. However, with the dawn of machine learning, manual editing of videos and images has been drastically reduced.

The evolution of an Artificial Intelligence-based fake video generation method, called Deepfakes [1], has lured many masses. It takes input of a video/image of a source subject and a video/image of a target subject and outputs a swapped video/image consisting of identity features of the source subject and attributes of the target subject. The backbone for the creation of these

H. Kaur et al. (Eds.): CVIP 2023, CCIS 2009, pp. 219–230, 2024.
https://doi.org/10.1007/978-3-031-58181-6_19

deep fakes is Deep Neural Networks (DNNs). These DNNs are trained on facial images to map facial expressions from the source to the target images. Most of the aforementioned studies use generative adversarial networks (GANs), Autoencoders (AE), and generative normalization flows (Glows) to generate images and videos as deepfakes. Among the three networks, GANs are very popular for generating indistinguishable deepfakes.

In past years, generative adversarial networks (GANs) have been used for high-quality image synthesis, particularly for facial manifolds. In particular, StyleGAN [3,4] proposed a style-based generator architecture and synthesis of state-of-the-art face images. One of the core problem of machine learning is to learn the disentangled representation. Disentanglement is breaking down or disentangling each feature into narrowly defined variables and encoding them as separate dimensions. GANs assemble the latent codes of the source and target image to generate the swapped image. However, the latent codes are highly entangled, and directly assembling them may not guarantee the transfer of source and attribute features onto swapped face. We argue that identity and attribute features should be separately encoded and transferred onto the swapped face. So a proper disentanglement of identity and attributes are required.

With the expeditious evolution of GANs, numerous methods have demonstrated the capability of controlling the latent space of w [5], which has a disentanglement property that offers control and editing capabilities. These above mentioned works follow *"invert first, edit later"* approach (input image is invertible, i.e., there exists a latent code that can reconstruct the image, and with latent manipulations, the image can be edited), wherein the image is inverted into StyleGAN's latent space and then the latent code is edited in a conceptually meaningful form to obtain a new latent code and then this edited latent code is used by StyleGAN to generate the high-resolution image. However, inverting a real image into a 512-dimensional vector $w \in \mathbb{W}$ does not synthesize the image accurately. Inspired by this, many researchers [7] proposed an extended latent space $w \in \mathbb{W}^+$. The extended latent space is a concatenation of 18 different 512-dimensional w vectors, and each vector is fed as input to Adaptive Instance Normalisation (AdaIn) of StyleGAN. These studies map an image onto the extended latent space, which requires several minutes for an image to synthesize. To expedite this optimization process, they [7] proposed a domain-guided encoder and used it for further domain-regularized optimization. However, fast and precise inversion of real images in $\mathbb{W}^+$ remains challenging.

This paper proposes a new framework for face swapping called *ExtSwap*. We extend the work of [31] by passing the encoded features to the extended latent space of StyleGAN; we show that our method outperforms the current state-of-the-art methods both qualitatively and quantitatively. To accomplish this task, we use two encoders that encode the identity and attribute embeddings separately. The identity encoder E_{id} is the pre-trained face transformer [9] where modified tokens, and image patches, were made to overlap and projected onto the transformer encoder. For the attribute encoding, we use EfficientNetV2 [10]. EfficientNetV2 is well-known for faster training and improved parameter efficiency than EfficientV1 [11]. In the former, am automatic way of deriving architecture using Neural Architecture Search (NAS) and compound scaling of depth, width, and image size was performed with a fixed ratio. The features generated from these two encoders are concatenated and fed into four layer Multi-Layer Perceptron (MLP). The characteristic of MLP is that it can learn from nonlinear models. Because two different encoders encode the image and provide two other dimensional tensors to map them and feed into StyleGAN's generator, an MLP is used. The mapped style vectors generated from the MLP were inserted into a pre-trained StyleGAN generator. To generate a swapped face, the style vectors are encoded into extended space $\mathbb{W}^+$. The overall contribution of this paper is as follows:

1. A novel framework for high-resolution face swapping called ExtSwap. A novel method for disentangling identity and attribute features.
2. A new encoders for encoding and concatenating the identity and attribute features of facial images.
3. We compare our method with several other state-of-the-results and show that our method outperforms the current state-of-the-art methods.

2   Related Work:

2.1   Face Swapping

The first ever face swapping method was introduced by [12] by aligning both target and source images to a common coordinate system and then by replacing the six fiducial points of the source with the target. However, this method required the posture of the target face to be identical. Later [13] used CNNs to transfer a person's identity while keeping head, pose, identity, and lighting conditions intact. To pragmatically puppeteer and animate a face from a single RGB image, a 3D model is used to extract the textures and to transfer the textures onto target image GANs were used [14]. A parametric and data-driven model was proposed by [15] wherein a 3D mophing model (3DMM) model was used in the first stage, and in the later stage, GANs were used to synthesize the full image. In another work [16], two different encoders were used to extricate the identity and attribute of the face image, to generate a new image using GAN. A novel integrated editing system for face and hair was proposed by [17] wherein they used a separator network to separate the hair and face and a composer network that reconstructs the input face from two latent spaces and a discriminator that discriminates the real and fake sample. Face SwapGAN (FSGAN) [18] presented an RNN-based approach for face reenactment. They used a fully supervised method in three stages, reenactment, inpainting, and blending. This method yielded good results for face and hair occlusions but failed for glasses, veils, and so on. A high fidelity and occlusion aware face swapping technique was introduced by [19]. Recently, [20] proposes an encoder that swaps faces at high resolution, but their model needs to be subject-agnostic. MegaFS [30] designed an id-transfer block to combine their latent codes. However, the structure and appearance part of the latent codes are entangled in the latent space.

2.2   Latent Space of GAN

Many researchers in the past have attempted to understand and regulate the latent space of GAN since their origin. GAN inversion intends to invert the image back into the latent space of a pre-trained StyleGAN model. The image was faithfully reconstructed using the inverted code. Several methods, such as [21], thoughtfully train a variational autoencoder (VAE) to mimic that of conventional GAN, and parallel VAE is adversarially trained. Another work that mimics GAN was where they designed two latent encoders that are trained adversarially and can synthesize faces and bedroom images comparable to GAN [22]. Training encoders, such as GAN, often compromise the image quality and require a long training time. As a result, other methods use inversion as an alternate method, where the generator is pre-trained, and inversion is performed separately. The methods mentioned above either optimize the latent vectors to curtail the reconstruction error or train different encoders to improve the inversion efficiency [23]. Recently, several studies have proposed methods for latent-space manipulation. The images generated from StyleGAN are at high resolution, but there is no semantic control over the output, such as expression, pose, and illumination. Stylerig, proposed by [6], allows control over the pose, expression, and illumination parameters. In another study, [31] utilized a disentangled property to represent data with minimal supervision by a pre-trained StyleGAN.

3   Proposed Method

3.1   Overview

ExtSwap takes two inputs F_{id} and F_{attr}; we aim to construct the face image with identity features of source image F_{id} and the attributes of the target image F_{attr} such as pose, expression, and background. To do so, we first excerpt the identity features of source image F_{id} explained in Sect. 3.2 and the attribute features of target image F_{attr} are explained in Sect. 3.3. Identity and attribute features are concatenated and fed to the latent mapper, explained in Sect. 3.4. The latents are fed to the StyleGAN to synthesize the swapped image, which is explained in Sect. 3.6. The proposed architecture pipeline is shown in Fig. 1

3.2   Face Transformer

To excerpt the identity features of the source image, we utilize the Face transformer [9] we denote it as E_{id}. The face transformer architecture follows the exact structure of Vision Transformer [24], but the token generation method is modified compared to the standard ViT. The sliding patches are used to generate the tokens, where the image patches are made to overlap to preserve the interpatch information to generate 512-dimensional embeddings. Face transformer gives comparable results to the standard ArcFace embeddings and VGG2 based Face recognition [25].

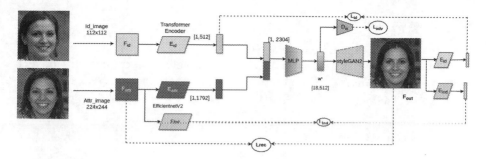

Fig. 1. ExtSwap framework uses two different encoders to generate the latent code z. The code is then mapped into the pre-trained generator's extended space $\mathbb{W}^+$. Losses are marked in the dashed lines, and data flow in the solid line.

3.3   EfficientNet-V2

To extract the attribute features of the target image F_{attr}, we use modified efficientnet [11]. The Efficientnet is a family of models optimized for floating point operations per second (FLOPS) and parameter efficiency. It clouts the NAS to search the baseline model B0 with better accuracy and trade-off and then applies compound scaling to obtain the B1–B7 family. This method proposes an upgraded method of progressive learning which adapt the image size and regularisation. This model has an 11x faster training speed when compared to the first version. We use this encoder to extract the attributes of a facial image. A total of 1792 features were extracted from a facial image, including pose, lightning, expression, and head posture, and this encoder is referred to as E_{attr}.

We concatenate the codes from two encoders E_{id} and E_{attr} as shown in the below Eq. 1

$$z_{space} = [E_{id}(F_{id}), E_{attr}(F_{attr})] \tag{1}$$

3.4   Latent Mapper

The identity features extracted from the Face Transformer and the attribute features extracted from EfficientNet-V2 are fed to a latent mapper that acts as a dimensionality-reduction network. The 512-dimensional identity and 1792 dimensional attribute features were concatenated to form a 2304 feature vector. This feature vector is fed to a 4-layer Multi-layer Perceptron with leaky ReLU activation layers. In this stage, 18 styles are injected in the training phase to form (18, 512)-dimensional vector that resembles $\mathbb{W}^+$ latent space. Eighteen style vectors were extracted for a batch of images using the following equation:

$$style_vectors = log_2(resolution) * 2 - 2 \tag{2}$$

where resolution = image resolution is 1024×1024.

3.5   Discriminator

Since the training the mapping between the extended latent space and $\mathbb{W}^+$ is cliche. Therefore, we add Discriminator $D_{\mathbb{W}+}$ to help predict the MLP predict the features lie within $\mathbb{W}^+$. So, in order to discriminate between real samples of $\mathbb{W}^+$ and MLPs predictions. we train the Discriminator in an adversarial manner.

3.6   StyleGAN2 Generator

ExtSwap is based on the synthesizing power of StyleGAN2 generator G and the extended space of $\mathbb{W}^+$. StyleGAN2 improves the perceptual quality by proposing improved weight demodulation, path length regularization, by altering the generator architecture, and shedding the progressive growth compared to the first version of StyleGAN. The concatenated vector $\mathbb{W}^+$ is fed into the extended space, usually employed in the AdaIn layers to obtain the swapped face given by Eq. 3.

$$F_{swap} = G(MLP([E_{attr}F_{attr}, E_{id}F_{id}])) \tag{3}$$

3.7   Training and Loss Functions:

We created 70,000 images by passing random Gaussian vectors into the pre-trained styleGAN2. The generated images were projected onto the extended space $\mathbb{W}^+$. We save the image and corresponding $\mathbb{W}^+$ vector. The StyleGAN generated images were used as the training dataset, and the latent $\mathbb{W}^+$ vectors were used as real samples for training the Discriminator. For training the Discriminator, we use a gradient regularization technique named R1 regularization that acts only on real data along with non-saturating loss

$$\mathbb{L}_{adv}^D = \frac{1}{2}(L_{D,1} + L_{D,2}) = -\frac{1}{2}[\underset{w \sim \mathbb{W}+}{\mathbb{E}}[log(D_{\mathbb{W}+}(\mathbb{W}^+))]] - \frac{1}{2}\underset{z \sim MLP}{\mathbb{E}} log[1 - D_{\mathbb{W}+}(MLP(z))] \tag{4}$$

$$\mathbb{L}_{adv}^G = \frac{1}{2}\underset{z \sim MLP}{\mathbb{E}} log[1 - D_{\mathbb{W}+}(MLP(z))] \tag{5}$$

To preserve the input identity we measure cosine similarity between source F_{id} and swapped image F_{out},

$$\mathbb{L}_{ID} = 1 - <R(x), R(E_{ID}(x))> \tag{6}$$

where R is the pre-trained ArcaFace [25] Model.

To model the motion of face, we use Facial landmarks. So we use L_2 loss to model attribute information F_{attr} to be consistent with F_{out}.

$$\mathbb{L}_{lnd} = \|E_{lnd}(F_{attr}) - E_{lnd}(F_{out})\|_2 \tag{7}$$

To perpetuate pixel-level information such as color and illumination, we adopt mix loss and use a weighted sum of L_1 loss and Multi scale Structural Similarity Index (MS-SSIM) loss:

$$\mathbb{L}_{mix} = \alpha(1 - MS - SSIM(F_{attr})) + (1 - \alpha||F_{attr} - F_{out}||_1) \qquad (8)$$

However, the F_{out} should not only contain the attribute information of F_{attr} and also the identity information F_{id} and both should be well confined. So we consider reconstruction loss only when $F_{id} = F_{attr}$, i,e.,

$$\mathbb{L}_{rec} = \begin{cases} \mathbb{L}_{mix} & \text{if } F_{id} = F_{attr} \\ 0 & \text{otherwise} \end{cases} \qquad (9)$$

The overall generator loss the weighted sum of above losses:

$$\mathbb{L}_{total} = \lambda_{id}\mathbb{L}_{id} + \lambda_{attr}\mathbb{L}_{attr} + \lambda_{rec}\mathbb{L}_{rec} \qquad (10)$$

4 Experiments

4.1 Implementation Details

We used StyleGAN pre-trained with 1024×1024 resolution for all our experiments. We trained the attribute encoder and latent mapper only during the training, and the remaining components, such as the identity encoder and Style-GAN, were frozen during training. The ratio of training of F_{id} and F_{attr} is a hyper parameter that controls the disentanglement. We optimize the adversarial loss L_{adv}^G and non-adversarial loss separately $L_{non-adv}^G$. We used the Adam optimizer with $\beta_1 = 0.9$ and $\beta_2 = 0.999$ and learning rate of $2e^{-5}$ when optimizing $L_{non-adv}^G$ and $6e^{-6}$ for adversarial loss L_{adv}^G and loss weights are set to $\lambda_1 = 1$, $\lambda_2 = 1$, $\lambda_3 = 0.0001$ and $\lambda_4 = 0.02$, $\alpha = 0.84$. To calculate the landmarks, we used the standard 68-point facial points. The model was implemented using a Pytorch and trained using paramshakti supercomputer which has 22 nodes, each has two GPUs of 16 GB named V100 Tesla and we used one node for training.[1].

4.2 Datasets

Datasets: We evalaute our model on 3 datasets:

1. Our test data: We split our 70,000 images into training and test sets in 80:20 manner and create random source and target pair and obtain the swapped images.
2. CelebA-HQ [32] contains 30,000 celebrities faces with high-resolution faces. We use this database for testing our model. First, we pass these images to get $\mathbb{W}^+$ vectors and create swapped faces by passing the source and target images.

---

[1] https://github.com/Aravinda27/ExtSwap.

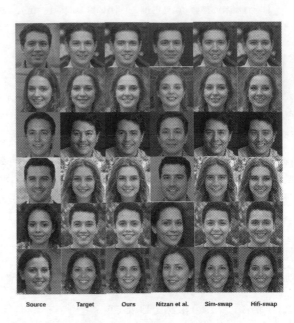

Fig. 2. ExtSwap results on our test data

Fig. 3. ExtSwap compared with state-of-the-art methods

3. FFHQ dataset [3] contains 70,000 high-resolution 1024 × 1024 face images. First, we pass these images to get $\mathbb{W}^+$ and record these vectors. We passed a batch of images by forming source and target image pair and obtained swapped images.

Evaluation Metrics: To evaluate the proposed method, we calculate cosine similarity by computing the Arcface embeddings between the source and swapped image so that the swapped image contains identity features. And also we calculated the pose and expression error, which is the l_2 distance between the target face and swapped face, using the pre-trained model [26,27], which shows the ability to transfer the attributes. The *Frechet Inception Distance* calculates the Wasserstein-2 distance between swapped faces and real faces, indicating the swapped faces' quality.

4.3   Experiments on Test Data

We conduct experiments to evaluate ExtSwap mainly on two aspects: how well the identity and attribute features appear on swapped faces and the quality of the synthesized image.

Qualitative Comparison: First, a qualitative inspection of ExtSwap is shown in Fig. 2. ExtSwap shows identity and attribute preservation in swapped images.

In addition, it can be used to generate the overall shape of the head and hair. Moreover, we observed a consistent transfer of attributes, such as smiles and glasses, in the swapped faces.

Source   Target   Swapped

Fig. 4. ExtSwap results on CelebA-HQ dataset

Fig. 5. ExtSwap compared with FFHQ dataset

Quantitative Comparison: We performed a quantitative comparison of the proposed methods. ExtSwap has an identity similarity of 0.5698, pose error of 3.477, expression error of 2.95, and FID score of 9.87. ExtSwap shows stronger identity preservation and attribute transfer while showing lower FID scores.

4.4   Comparison with Previous Methods

Qualitative Comparison: A qualitative comparison of the proposed method is shown in Fig. 3. We compared ExtSwap with Nitzan et al. [31], who projected the images into a latent space w rather than the extended latent space $\mathbb{W}^+$. They used VGGFace2 encoder for identity features extraction and Inception V2 network for excerpting the attribute features. VGGface uses 16 CNN layers in a sequential manner. The main disadvantage CNN networks are they do not cover long range dependencies of an image. But transformers uses self-attention thus making connection between distant image pixels. EfficientNet-V2 trains faster than inception since it uses NAS for training and thus extracting better attribute features. Also the our extended latent space has 18 styles each of 512-dimensional features which are encoded before feeding into the StyleGAN. Since it is evident from both qualitative (Fig. 3) and quantitative analysis ExtSwap achieves better result than [31]. We also compare ExtSwap with Simswap [28] where this framework has three parts: an encoder to extract the features of the target image, the Identity Injection Module (IIM), which transfers identity information from the source to the swapped, and the decoder part, which synthesizes the image. As shown in the figure, Simswap can transfer the identity features but fails to transfer the attribute features, leading to a blurred image. Next, we compare with another technique called HifiSwap [29], which uses four parts: the encoder part, where features of the target image are excerpted, and a decoder that fuses the encoder and 3D shape-aware identity and finally improves the face quality of the synthesized face. Again, this method preserves the identity features but fails to transfer the attribute parts of the target image, leading to a blurry image.

Quantitative Comparison: To compare ExtSwap quantitatively we use 3 different metrics mentioned in Table 1. ExtSwap shows stronger identity preservation and fewer errors for pose and expression. Furthermore, ExtSwap achieved lower FID scores than the other methods.

Table 1. Quantitative comparison of ExtSwap with other method with identity similarity, pose and expression error and FID scores

Method	ID similarity ↑	Pose error↓	Exp error ↓	FID ↓
HifiSwap [29]	0.5020	4.688	3.25	12.645
Simswap [28]	0.5174	4.856	3.10	11.98
Nitzan et al. [31]	0.5398	3.895	3.05	10.98
Ours	**0.5698**	**3.477**	**2.95**	**9.87**

4.5   Comparison with CelebA-HQ Dataset

Qualitative Comparison: We also test our model on high-quality 1024×1024 images. ExtSwap utilizes the disentangled identity and attribute features from the extended latent mapper to produce perfectly swapped faces, as shown in Fig. 4.

4.6   Comparison with FFHQ Dataset

Qualitative Comparison: We perform experiments on 1024×1024 high resolution FFHQ dataset. Our disentangled feature identity and attribute feature transfer led to perfect preservation of the identity and attribute features in the swapped image, as is evident in Fig. 5.

5   Conclusion

This paper presents an extended latent mapper as a novel disentangled representation. This disentangled representation acts as a key mapping technique fed into the StyleGAN to generate a quality image while requiring modest supervision. Extensive experiments demonstrate that ExtSwap can synthesize quality face images using the superiority of our disentangled identity and attribute transfer regarding hallucination, quality, and consistency of generated images.

References

1. Korshunov, P., Marcel, S.: DeepFakes: a new threat to face recognition? Assessment and detection. arXiv preprint arXiv:1812.08685 (2018)
2. Li, Y., Chang, M.-C., Lyu, S.: In ictu oculi: exposing AI created fake videos by detecting eye blinking. In: IEEE International Workshop on Information Forensics and Security (WIFS) (2018)
3. Karras, T., Laine, S., Aila, T.: A style-based generator architecture for generative adversarial networks. In: Proceedings of the IEEE/CVF Conference on Computer Vision and Pattern Recognition, pp. 4401–4410 (2019)
4. Karras, T., Laine, S., Aittala, M., Hellsten, J., Lehtinen, J., Aila, T.: Analyzing and improving the image quality of StyleGAN. In: Proceedings of the IEEE/CVF Conference on Computer Vision and Pattern Recognition, pp. 8110–8119 (2020)
5. Shen, Y., Gu, J., Tang, X., Zhou, B.: Interpreting the latent space of GANs for semantic face editing. In: Proceedings of the IEEE/CVF Conference on Computer Vision and Pattern Recognition, pp. 9243–9252 (2020)
6. Tewari, A., Elgharib, M., Bharaj, G., Bernard, F., Seidel, H.P.: StyleRig: rigging StyleGAN for 3D control over portrait images. In: Proceedings of the IEEE/CVF Conference on Computer Vision and Pattern Recognition, pp. 6142–6151 (2020)
7. Abdal, R., Qin, Y., Wonka, P.: Image2StyleGAN++: how to edit the embedded images? In: Proceedings of the IEEE/CVF Conference on Computer Vision and Pattern Recognition, pp. 8296–8305 (2020)
8. Zhu, J., Shen, Y., Zhao, D., Zhou, B.: In-domain GAN inversion for real image editing. In: Vedaldi, A., Bischof, H., Brox, T., Frahm, J.-M. (eds.) ECCV 2020. LNCS, vol. 12362, pp. 592–608. Springer, Cham (2020). https://doi.org/10.1007/978-3-030-58520-4_35
9. Zhong, Y., Deng, W.: Face transformer for recognition. arXiv preprint arXiv:2103.14803 (2021)
10. Tan, M., Le, Q.: EfficientNetV2: smaller models and faster training. In: International Conference on Machine Learning, pp. 10096–10106 (2021)
11. Tan, M., Le, Q.: EfficientNet: rethinking model scaling for convolutional neural networks. In: International Conference on Machine Learning, pp. 6105–6114 (2019)
12. Bitouk, D., Kumar, N., Dhillon, S., Belhumeur, P., Nayar, S.K.: Face swapping: automatically replacing faces in photographs. In: ACM SIGGRAPH 2008 Papers (2008)
13. Korshunova, I., Shi, W., Dambre, J., Theis, L.: Fast face-swap using convolutional neural networks. In: Proceedings of the IEEE International Conference on Computer Vision, pp. 3677–3685 (2017)
14. Olszewski, K., Li, Z., Yang, C., Zhou, Y., Yu, R., Huang, Z.: Realistic dynamic facial textures from a single image using GANs. In: Proceedings of the IEEE International Conference on Computer Vision, pp. 5429–5438 (2017)

15. Sun, Q., Tewari, A., Xu, W., Fritz, M., Theobalt, C., Schiele, B.: A hybrid model for identity obfuscation by face replacement. In: Proceedings of the European Conference on Computer Vision (ECCV), pp. 553–569 (2018)
16. Bao, J., Chen, D., Wen, F., Li, H., Hua, G.: Towards open-set identity preserving face synthesis. In: Proceedings of the IEEE Conference on Computer Vision and Pattern Recognition, pp. 6713–6722 (2018)
17. Natsume, R., Yatagawa, T., Morishima, S.: RSGAN: face swapping and editing using face and hair representation in latent spaces. arXiv preprint arXiv:1804.03447 (2018)
18. Nirkin, Y., Keller, Y., Hassner, T.: FSGAN: subject agnostic face swapping and reenactment. In: Proceedings of the IEEE/CVF International Conference on Computer Vision, pp. 7184–7193 (2019)
19. Li, L., Bao, J., Yang, H., Chen, D., Wen, F.: FaceShifter: towards high fidelity and occlusion aware face swapping. arXiv preprint arXiv:1912.13457 (2019)
20. Naruniec, J., Helminger, L., Schroers, C., Weber, R.M.: High-resolution neural face swapping for visual effects. In: Computer Graphics Forum, pp. 173–184 (2020)
21. Huang, H., He, R., Sun, Z., Tan, T.: IntroVAE: introspective variational autoencoders for photographic image synthesis. In: Advances in Neural Information Processing Systems, vol. 31 (2018)
22. Pidhorskyi, S., Adjeroh, D.A., Doretto, G.: Adversarial latent autoencoders. In: Proceedings of the IEEE/CVF Conference on Computer Vision and Pattern Recognition, pp. 14104–14113 (2020)
23. Richardson, E., et al.: Encoding in style: a StyleGAN encoder for image-to-image translation. In: Proceedings of the IEEE/CVF Conference on Computer Vision and Pattern Recognition, pp. 2287–2296 (2021)
24. Dosovitskiy, A., Beyer, L., Kolesnikov, A., Weissenborn, D., Zhai, X.: An image is worth 16×16 words: transformers for image recognition at scale. arXiv preprint arXiv:2010.11929 (2020)
25. Deng, J., Guo, J., Xue, N., Zafeiriou, S.: ArcFace: additive angular margin loss for deep face recognition. In: Proceedings of the IEEE Conference on Computer Vision and Pattern Recognition, pp. 4690–4699 (2019)
26. Chaudhuri, B., Vesdapunt, N., Wang, B.: Joint face detection and facial motion retargeting for multiple faces. In: Proceedings of the IEEE/CVF Conference on Computer Vision and Pattern Recognition, pp. 9719–9728 (2019)
27. Ruiz, N., Chong, E., Rehg, J.M.: Fine-grained head pose estimation without keypoints. In: Proceedings of the IEEE Conference on Computer Vision and Pattern Recognition Workshops, pp. 2074–2083 (2018)
28. Chen, R., Chen, X., Ni, B., Ge, Y.: SimSwap: an efficient framework for high fidelity face swapping. In: Proceedings of the 28th ACM International Conference on Multimedia, pp. 2003–2011 (2020)
29. Wang, Y., et al.: HifiFace: 3D shape and semantic prior guided high fidelity face swapping. arXiv preprint arXiv:2106.09965 (2021)
30. Zhu, Y., Li, Q., Wang, J., Xu, C.-Z., Sun, Z.: One shot face swapping on megapixels. In: Proceedings of the IEEE/CVF Conference on Computer Vision and Pattern Recognition, pp. 4834–4844 (2021)
31. Nitzan, Y., Bermano, A., Li, Y., Cohen-Or, D.: Face identity disentanglement via latent space mapping. arXiv preprint arXiv:2005.07728 (2020)
32. Liu, Z., Luo, P., Wang, X., Tang, X.: Deep learning face attributes in the wild. In: Proceedings of International Conference on Computer Vision (ICCV) (2015)

Dish Detection in Indian Food Platters: A Computational Framework for Diet Management

Mansi Goel[1,3], Shashank Dargar[1,2], Shounak Ghatak[1,2], Nidhi Verma[1,2], Pratik Chauhan[1,2], Anushka Gupta[1,2], Nikhila Vishnumolakala[1,2], Hareesh Amuru[1,2], Ekta Gambhir[1,2], Ronak Chhajed[1,2], Meenal Jain[1,2], Astha Jain[1,2], Samiksha Garg[1,2], and Ganesh Bagler[1,3(✉)]

[1] Infosys Center for Artificial Intelligence, Indraprastha Institute of Information Technology Delhi (IIIT-Delhi), New Delhi, India
bagler@iiitd.ac.in
[2] Department of Computer Science, Indraprastha Institute of Information Technology Delhi (IIIT-Delhi), New Delhi, India
[3] Department of Computational Biology, Indraprastha Institute of Information Technology Delhi (IIIT-Delhi), New Delhi, India

Abstract. Diet is central to the epidemic of lifestyle disorders. Accurate and effortless diet logging is one of the significant bottlenecks for effective diet management and calorie restriction. Dish detection is a challenging problem in Indian platters due to a visually complex traditional food layout. We present a comparative analysis of deep-learning-based object detection models for the 61 most popular Indian dishes. Rooted in a meticulous compilation of 68,005 platter images with 134,814 manual dish annotations, we first compare ten architectures for multi-label classification to identify ResNet152 (mAP = 84.51%) as the best model. YOLOv8x (mAP = 87.70%) emerged as the best model architecture for dish detection among the eight deep-learning models implemented after a thorough performance evaluation. By comparing with the state-of-the-art model for the IndianFood10 dataset, we demonstrate the superior object detection performance of YOLOv8x for this subset and establish Resnet152 as the best architecture for multi-label classification. The models trained on such a rich dataset have diverse applications for diet logging, food recommendation systems, nutritional interventions, and mitigation of lifestyle disorders. The proposed computational framework is extendable to include staple dishes from across global cuisines.

Keywords: Object Detection · Multi-label Classification · Indian Food Platter · Computer Vision · Deep Learning

Supplementary Information The online version contains supplementary material available at https://doi.org/10.1007/978-3-031-58181-6_20.

1   Introduction

Diet is central to the epidemic of lifestyle disorders such as obesity, type 2 diabetes, and cardiovascular conditions. Scientific evidence suggests that calorie restriction is among the most impactful preventive and remedial strategies. One of the significant challenges for effective dietary management is keeping track of diet and, therefore, calorie consumption. Given the penetration of smartphones and the internet, it would be helpful to have computational models that could accurately detect dishes from a food platter. This would facilitate the automation of the diet diary, thus enabling better diet management and other relevant applications.

Indian cuisine is known for its visually complex platters, making dish detection a challenging problem. Collecting platter images with manual dish annotations is a necessary precursor for building a computational pipeline for dish classification and detection. Building on the previous research to converge on the state-of-the-art model for the ten most popular dishes [25], we aimed to scale up labeled data compilation and identify the best model by comparing various architectures. The model thus identified will be a potent candidate for implementation in mobile devices and can help achieve public health goals through dietary interventions. Such a computational framework has diverse applications for food recommendation systems, diet logging, nutritional interventions, and mitigation of lifestyle disorders. Food detection systems can also be leveraged to locate foreign objects in meals and to empower visually impaired individuals. Herein, we present state-of-the-art deep-learning models for dish detection in Indian food platters by comparing diverse network architectures on a rich dataset of manually annotated images.

2   Literature Survey

Image classification has become a tractable problem with the development of deep convolutional neural networks [15] and the availability of large-scale, hand-labeled datasets such as ImageNet [9]. Implementing deep convolutional neural networks for multi-label classification has yielded promising results [8]. Pictures of food platters are complex owing to variations in perspective and patterns in dish arrangements. The application of food image classification has attracted much attention recently. Early applications of CNN architectures (AlexNet, GoogLeNet, and ResNet) for food image classification [26] yielded poor results. Amato et al. [1] used a pre-trained GoogLeNet [33] convolutional neural network model to analyze trends in food images from social media. ETHZ food-101 [5] dataset comprising 101,000 food images across 101 classes was used for fine-tuning the model before classifying images using KNN. With a similar spirit, Minija and Emmanuel [23] implemented a support vector machine model to classify food images from the FoodLog dataset (6,512 images) with an accuracy of 95%.

Kagaya et al. [12] trained a CNN model and outperformed other baseline models with an average accuracy of 73.7% for ten classes. In another experiment, a pre-trained AlexNet model was implemented on the UEC-FOOD-100 dataset [21] containing 100 Japanese food classes to achieve an accuracy of 72.26% [13]. In another AlexNet implementation, Yanai et al. [39] applied image classification for Japanese food datasets UEC-FOOD-100 and UEC-FOOD-256 [14] (each containing 100 images per class) to achieve the top-1 accuracy of 78.8% and 67.6%, respectively. Myers et al. [22] presented a protocol for food classification using a pre-trained GoogLeNet [33] model fine-tuned on Food101 to achieve the top-1 accuracy of 79%. In another oriental food classification implementation [34], a pre-trained Inception model fine-tuned on Thai food images (THFOOD-50) was used to achieve an accuracy of 80.34%.

Object detection is vital in computer vision tasks such as image segmentation, object tracking, and image classification. Among the earliest studies, object detection has been used for real-time human face detection [35,36]. Other applications have implemented SIFT [20], HOG [38], and SURF [2] techniques on ImageNet and COCO datasets. With the advances in deep learning, two-stage (SPPNet [10], Fast R-CNN [29], FPN [17]) and one-stage detectors (YOLO [28], SSD [19], RetinaNet [18], CornerNet [16], DETR [40]) were introduced for enhanced object detection.

Object detection has immense utility for industry and public health when applied in the context of food platters. Among the earliest applications of food detection, Matsuda et al. [21] used traditional computer vision techniques (SIFT, HOG) to achieve an accuracy of 55.8%. Another study proposed a food localization and recognition method with an activation map to detect food using bounding boxes [4].

With a dataset of 60 traditional Chinese food items (BTBUFood-60), Cai et al. [6] implemented a Faster R-CNN to achieve an accuracy of 67%. In the context of complex Indian food platters, the earliest study used Single Shot Detector and Inceptionv2 on a dataset with 60 classes (70 images per class) to achieve the mAP score of 73.8% [27]. This study had two significant flaws concerning the relevance and quantity of the data. Among the 60 classes, eight were not traditional Indian dishes (pizza, pasta, noodles, cake slice, ice cream, brownie, mayo, and ketchup) and included nine trivial or irrelevant food classes such as tomato, cucumber, water, lemon slice, onion sliced, boiled egg, milk, chilly, and juice.

Despite its rich and diverse culinary heritage, the shortage of labeled collections of Indian food images is a significant challenge in developing accurate and effective models for food classification, dish detection, and recipe recommendations. Among the recent efforts towards creating a rich dataset of labeled Indian food dishes, Pandey et al. [25] contributed a collection of around 10,000 manually annotated food images of ten traditional Indian dishes and implemented a YOLOv4 model with a mAP score of 91.8%. This study presents an enhanced dataset of 61 traditional Indian dishes (68,005 images with 134,814 manual dish annotations) to implement and compare state-of-the-art deep-learning models.

3   Materials and Methods

3.1   Data Compilation and Annotation

After making a list of the most popular traditional Indian dishes across its regional cuisines, we used Instagram to compile pictures with relevant hashtags. With over 1 billion users sharing more than 100 million posts daily, Instagram is one of the most prolific online sources of user-uploaded pictures along with their hashtag descriptors [24]. We scraped images potentially containing traditional Indian food platters from Instagram using Python selenium and requests library.

Thus compiled, our 'IndianFood61' dataset consists of 68,005 multi-class images with 61 food classes (~1000 images for each class). The average number of platter images for each dish class was 1115 ± 500. Among the outlier classes were *idli* (494) and *gulabjamun* (533), *plain rice* (4067), and *Indian bread* (3074). We manually annotated and labeled each image with a bounding box for every dish class using makesense.ai, an open-source software [31]. The number of annotations for each dish class reflects its occurrence across the platters. On average, a dish occurred in platters 2210 ± 1584 times. While dishes such as *dal* (853) and *rasam* (798) were found with low occurrence, *momos* (6496) and *barfi* (6375) were over-represented. The annotated images and corresponding text files were saved in YOLO format. The text file includes the food class ID and coordinates of the bounding boxes for each food item in the image.

3.2   Multi-label Classification

Image classification involves their categorization based on relevant features. Primitive classification strategies relied on traditional methods such as Bag-of-Words, PASCAL VOC, and SIFT. With advances in deep learning, CNN-based image classification techniques with end-to-end learning pipelines are increasingly used. These protocols overcome the bottleneck of manual extraction of image-specific features associated with traditional methods.

We implemented the below-mentioned CNN-based models that list the dishes appearing in an image without locating their coordinates. This task is computationally inexpensive than object detection.

AlexNet: AlexNet is a 60 million parameter model consisting of 8 layers with five convolutional layers, two fully connected hidden layers, and one fully connected output layer. Krizhevsky et al. [15] demonstrated that learned features could outperform manually designed features contrary to the known notion in computer vision.

SqueezeNet: SqueezeNet has fewer parameters than AlexNet, but implements fire modules, compression, and downsampling techniques to achieve enhanced accuracy. SqueezeNet1_1 combines 1×1 and 3×3 convolutional filters in the fire modules and has residual connections between fire modules that help reduce the network's computational complexity.

VGGNet: Visual Geometry Group or VGG [30] has a similar architecture to that of AlexNet with a large number of parameters and weight layers that enable improved performance. VGG-16 contains 16 weight levels with five convolutional blocks in series and two fully-connected layers with 4096 dimensions. VGG-19 has similar architecture to VGG-16 with 19 weight layers.

ResNet: Residual network [11] is a neural network with additional residual layers that enhance object classification performance. ResNet34 (with 34 weighted layers) contains 3*3 convolutional layers, a batch normalization layer, and ReLU activation function follows each convolutional layer. ResNet50 architecture is similar to ResNet34 with one significant difference–the building block is modified into a bottleneck design to handle training duration. With a 3-layer block, ResNet50 is more accurate than ResNet34. ResNet152 has an improved architecture with the addition of a 1×1 convolutional layer over and above the 3×3 layers.

DenseNet: DenseNet architecture is similar to ResNet, with one significant difference. DenseNet concatenates the previous layer's output with the future layer, whereas ResNet uses an additive method to merge layers.

3.3   Object Detection

Object detection is a critical problem in computer vision used to locate and identify all objects in an image by combining object localization and classification. Previously, handcrafted traditional methods such as Viola-Jones detectors, HOG detectors, and Deformable Part-based Models were used due to a lack of effective image representation techniques. We have implemented state-of-the-art object detection models to detect dishes from images of traditional Indian platters. Figure 1 shows the detailed methodology used for food detection.

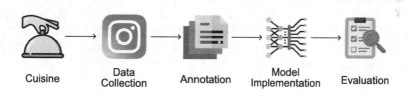

| Cuisine | Data Collection | Annotation | Model Implementation | Evaluation |

Fig. 1. Computational strategy implemented for dish detection in Indian platter.

DETR: DETR (DEtection TRansformer) is a transformer-based object detection algorithm that was introduced in 2020 by Facebook AI Research team [7]. DETR predicts the set of objects present in an image, along with their class labels and precise bounding boxes, as opposed to traditional object detection algorithms that use Region Proposal Networks or anchor boxes to predict object locations. It has achieved great performance on object detection benchmark (COCO) and is an end-to-end trainable architecture that eliminates the need for post-processing steps such as Non-Maximum Supervision.

Faster R-CNN: Faster R-CNN is a two-stage object detection model, where the first stage (Region Proposal Network) generates object proposals and the second stage (region-based CNN) classifies the proposed regions and generates bounding boxes [29].

RetinaNet: RetinaNet is a one-stage model that uses a Feature Pyramid Network to generate feature maps at different scales to make predictions. Each level produces a set of anchors (bounding boxes) of different sizes and aspect ratios to localize objects in the image. These anchors are then passed through a series of convolutional layers to predict each anchor's class probabilities and offsets. RetinaNet uses a standard CNN (ResNet-50/EfficientNet) as its backbone model [18].

YOLO: YOLO (You Only Look Once) is a one-stage object detection model with an architecture similar to a Fully Convolutional Neural Network. It consists of an input layer, a backbone network (CSPDarkNet53), a neck (Spatial Pyramid Pooling, Path Aggregation Network), and a head (locate bounding boxes and make the predictions). YOLOv4 [3] contributes mosaic data augmentation, which leads the model to find smaller objects and pay less attention to the environment. It uses the Spatial Attention module to improve the accuracy and speed compared to previous YOLO models. YOLOv5, developed by Ultralytics, is a faster model than YOLOv4. It introduces new backbone architecture CSP-Net, based on the PyTorch framework, which reduces the computations needed for detecting an object. YOLOv5 further improves object detection accuracy with three types of data enhancements: scaling, color space adjustment, and mosaic enhancement. YOLOv7 [37] has a faster and more robust network architecture with an optimized feature integration method, more accurate object detection performance, a better loss function, and increased model training efficiency. YOLOv8 is the latest version of YOLO which introduces new features and improvements to enhance performance, flexibility, and efficiency. YOLOv8x is a variant of YOLOv8 consisting of 68.2M parameters. YOLO are state-of-the-art object detection models with impressive speed and performance. The main difference between them lies in the details of architecture and the techniques used for performance optimization.

3.4   A Computational Framework for Dish Detection

We implemented pre-trained state-of-the-art models on the ImageNet dataset and fine-tuned them on the IndianFood61 dataset for the multi-label classification. All images were resized to 512*512 pixels. The class labels and targets were represented as one-hot vectors. For fine-tuning the model, we modified the last layer by converting it into a linear layer with an output dimension equal to the number of classes (61), adding a sigmoid layer to obtain probabilities between 0 and 1 for each class, and using the pre-trained weights for the training of models. The output is a vector of dimension 61 (number of classes), with each entry representing the probability of each class.

We used a two-stage process for fine-tuning the models. First, we froze the weights for the backward layers and trained the weights for the last layer with a higher learning rate. Next, we unfroze the model and trained all the layers with a lower learning rate. For finding the learning rate, we used the learning rate finder proposed by Leslie Smith in 2015 [32]. The basic idea here is to start with a small learning rate and gradually increase it in small batches. We used BCELoss (Binary Cross Entropy Loss) with Adam optimizer for the loss function.

To detect each item from an Indian food platter, we split the IndianFood61 dataset containing 61 food classes with a 90:10 ratio for training and testing. We implemented Faster R-CNN, DETR, RetinaNet, YOLOv4, YOLOv5, YOLOv7, and YOLOv8 object detection algorithms. The YOLO models were trained for 100 epochs using ReLU and sigmoid activation functions.

3.5   Evaluation Metrics

Precision (Eq. 1), Recall (Eq. 2), F1 score (Eq. 3), and mAP score (Eq. 4) were used for evaluating the performance of the models. mAP score represents the mean of average precision across the classes. The mAP score of multi-label classification differs from the evaluation of object detection models because we use Intersection over Union (IoU) as the threshold for detection. IoU is a metric measuring the overlap between the predicted and ground truth boxes. We set the IoU threshold to 0.5 for calculating the precision and mAP score for object detection.

$$Precision = \frac{TP}{TP + FP} \tag{1}$$

$$Recall = \frac{TP}{TP + FN} \tag{2}$$

$$F1 = \frac{2 * P * R}{P + R} \tag{3}$$

$$mAP = \frac{1}{N} \sum_{i=1}^{N} AP_i \tag{4}$$

4   Results

4.1   Multi-label Classification on IndianFood61 Dataset

To begin with, we compared the performance of ten deep-learning models for multi-label classification. Table 1 presents the performance of models on the IndianFood61 dataset. Resnet152 presented a state-of-the-art performance with mAP score, F1 score, and precision of 84.51%, 88.01%, and 90.56%, respectively. Dishes such as *dal*, *papad*, *mutton*, *kabab*, and *chicken tikka* were towards the lower end of the performance spectrum with lesser than 70% F1 score which could be attributed to a relatively low number of annotations corresponding to these dishes.

Table 1. Comparison of multi-label classification models on IndianFood61 dataset.

Classification Model	mAP (%)	F1 (%)	P (%)	R (%)
AlexNet	47.20	59.55	81.49	46.91
SqueezeNet1_0	56.04	67.39	80.97	57.71
SqueezeNet1_1	57.19	68.01	81.47	58.36
DenseNet 121	72.93	79.22	83.99	74.96
VGG16	75.69	81.68	86.04	77.74
DenseNet 201	77.16	82.38	86.34	78.76
VGG19	77.98	83.36	88.01	79.17
ResNet50	82.30	86.72	89.56	84.05
DenseNet169	83.75	87.21	89.78	84.78
ResNet152	**84.51**	**88.01**	**90.56**	**85.59**

Table 2. Comparison of object detection models on IndianFood61 dataset.

Object Detection Model	mAP (%)	F1 (%)	P (%)	R (%)
DETR	52.02	60.97	52.00	73.70
RetinaNet	71.80	72.30	71.80	72.80
Faster R-CNN	75.45	70.14	75.50	65.49
YOLOv5	78.80	74.00	60.60	95.00
YOLOv7	83.50	78.92	76.60	81.40
YOLOv8	83.40	78.94	78.70	79.20
YOLOv8x	**87.70**	**83.94**	**83.90**	**84.00**

4.2 Object Detection on IndianFood61 Dataset

Beyond the classification ability of the models for the correct identification of dishes in the picture of a platter, marking the pixels of each dish is of practical importance for diet logging. Table 2 presents the comparison of eight object detection models on the IndianFood61 dataset. YOLOv8x outperformed all other models with state-of-the-art performance on mAP (87.70%), F1 (83.94%), and precision (83.90%) metric. The model detects most dishes with high accuracy (greater than 95%) except for *mutton, kabab, chicken tikka*, and *aloo gobi*, which had mAP scores lesser than 60%.

Figure 2 shows the Precision, Recall, PR, and F1 curves for the IndianFood61 dataset using the YOLOv8x model. Figure 3 depicts the mAP score and loss (training and validation) at each epoch.

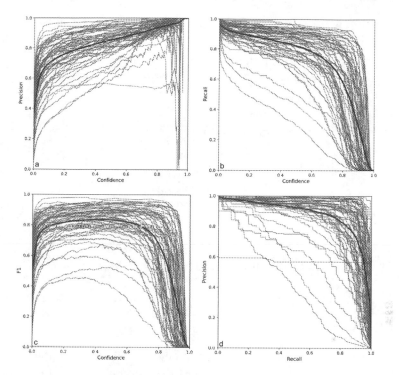

Fig. 2. Performance of YOLOv8x model on IndianFood61 dataset. **a.** Precision curve, **b.** Recall curve, **c.** F1 curve, and **d.** PR curve.

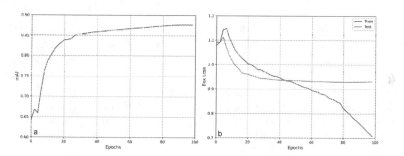

Fig. 3. a. mAP scores, and **b.** box loss over 100 epochs for IndianFood61 dataset using YOLOv8x model.

4.3   Comparison on 10-Class Dataset

Given that the previous state-of-the-art result for the Indian dishes was implemented on ten dish classes [25], it is imperative to compare the model performance with those data. To that end, we evaluated the performance of our models for image classification and object detection on IndianFood10, a dataset of ten Indian dishes that are a subset of the IndianFood61 (see Table 3). The state-of-the-art YOLOv8x model returns an impressive performance with a mAP score of

Table 3. A. Comparison of multi-label classification models on IndianFood10 dataset. **B.** Comparison of object detection models on IndianFood10 dataset.

Classification	mAP (%)	F1 (%)
SqueezeNet1_0	84.22	95.39
SqueezeNet1_1	83.85	95.79
DenseNet 121	95.02	95.71
VGG16	93.68	95.43
DenseNet 201	95.19	81.62
VGG19	94.27	86.04
ResNet50	95.12	94.68
DenseNet169	95.13	94.22
ResNet152	**95.14**	**95.14**

Object Detection	mAP (%)	F1 (%)
RetinaNet	83.91	76.74
DETR	86.00	83.70
Faster R-CNN	86.32	78.50
YOLOv4 [25]	**91.80**	**90.00**
YOLOv5	93.52	89.00
YOLOv7	94.41	90.00
YOLOv8	94.60	91.40
YOLOv8x	**95.55**	**92.00**

95.55% in contrast to the 91.80% returned by YOLOv4; the best model reported earlier [25].

5   Conclusions

Effortless diet logging is crucial to mitigating lifestyle disorders through nutrition management and calorie restriction. Object detection applied to identify dishes in food platters can be of value in this objective. We created IndianFood61, an extensive compilation of 68,005 images of food platters with 134,814 manual dish annotations for 61 popular Indian traditional dishes. We further built a range of deep-learning models for multi-label classification and object detection to achieve state-of-the-art performance. ResNet152 and YOLOv8x were identified as the best architecture for image classification and dish detection, respectively.

Acknowledgements. GB thanks Indraprastha Institute of Information Technology Delhi (IIIT-Delhi) for the computational support. GB thanks Technology Innovation Hub (TiH) Anubhuti for the research grant. MG is a research scholar in Prof. Bagler's lab and is thankful to IIIT-Delhi for the support. This study was supported by the Infosys Center for Artificial Intelligence, IIIT-Delhi.

References

1. Amato, G., Bolettieri, P., Monteiro de Lira, V., Muntean, C.I., Perego, R., Renso, C.: Social media image recognition for food trend analysis. In: Proceedings of the 40th International ACM SIGIR Conference on Research and Development in Information Retrieval, pp. 1333–1336 (2017)
2. Bay, H., Tuytelaars, T., Van Gool, L.: SURF: speeded up robust features. In: Leonardis, A., Bischof, H., Pinz, A. (eds.) ECCV 2006. LNCS, vol. 3951, pp. 404–417. Springer, Heidelberg (2006). https://doi.org/10.1007/11744023_32
3. Bochkovskiy, A., Wang, C.Y., Liao, H.Y.M.: Yolov4: optimal speed and accuracy of object detection. arXiv:2004.10934 (2020)

4. Bolaños, M., Radeva, P.: Simultaneous food localization and recognition. In: 2016 23rd International Conference on Pattern Recognition (ICPR), pp. 3140–3145 (2016)

5. Bossard, L., Guillaumin, M., Van Gool, L.: Food-101 – mining discriminative components with random forests. In: Fleet, D., Pajdla, T., Schiele, B., Tuytelaars, T. (eds.) ECCV 2014 Part VI. LNCS, vol. 8694, pp. 446–461. Springer, Cham (2014). https://doi.org/10.1007/978-3-319-10599-4_29

6. Cai, Q., Li, J., Li, H., Weng, Y.: Btbufood-60: dataset for object detection in food field. In: 2019 IEEE International Conference on Big Data and Smart Computing (BigComp), pp. 1–4. IEEE (2019)

7. Carion, N., Massa, F., Synnaeve, G., Usunier, N., Kirillov, A., Zagoruyko, S.: End-to-end object detection with transformers. In: Vedaldi, A., Bischof, H., Brox, T., Frahm, J.-M. (eds.) ECCV 2020 Part I. LNCS, vol. 12346, pp. 213–229. Springer, Cham (2020). https://doi.org/10.1007/978-3-030-58452-8_13

8. Coulibaly, S., Kamsu-Foguem, B., Kamissoko, D., Traore, D.: Deep convolution neural network sharing for the multi-label images classification. Mach. Learn. Appl. **10**, 100422 (2022)

9. Deng, J., Dong, W., Socher, R., Li, L.J., Li, K., Fei-Fei, L.: Imagenet: a large-scale hierarchical image database. In: 2009 IEEE Conference on Computer Vision and Pattern Recognition, pp. 248–255. IEEE (2009)

10. He, K., Zhang, X., Ren, S., Sun, J.: Spatial pyramid pooling in deep convolutional networks for visual recognition. IEEE Trans. Pattern Anal. Mach. Intell. **37**(9), 1904–1916 (2015)

11. He, K., Zhang, X., Ren, S., Sun, J.: Deep residual learning for image recognition. In: Proceedings of the IEEE Conference on Computer Vision and Pattern Recognition, pp. 770–778 (2016)

12. Kagaya, H., Aizawa, K., Ogawa, M.: Food detection and recognition using convolutional neural network. In: Proceedings of the 22nd ACM International Conference on Multimedia. pp. 1085–1088 (2014)

13. Kawano, Y., Yanai, K.: Food image recognition with deep convolutional features. In: Proceedings of the 2014 ACM International Joint Conference on Pervasive and Ubiquitous Computing: Adjunct Publication, pp. 589–593 (2014)

14. Kawano, Y., Yanai, K.: Automatic expansion of a food image dataset leveraging existing categories with domain adaptation. In: Agapito, L., Bronstein, M.M., Rother, C. (eds.) ECCV 2014 Part III. LNCS, vol. 8927, pp. 3–17. Springer, Cham (2015). https://doi.org/10.1007/978-3-319-16199-0_1

15. Krizhevsky, A., Sutskever, I., Hinton, G.E.: Imagenet classification with deep convolutional neural networks. Commun. ACM **60**(6), 84–90 (2017)

16. Law, H., Deng, J.: Cornernet: Detecting objects as paired keypoints. In: Proceedings of the European Conference on Computer Vision (ECCV), pp. 734–750 (2018)

17. Lin, T.Y., Dollár, P., Girshick, R., He, K., Hariharan, B., Belongie, S.: Feature pyramid networks for object detection. In: Proceedings of the IEEE Conference on Computer Vision and Pattern Recognition, pp. 2117–2125 (2017)

18. Lin, T.Y., Goyal, P., Girshick, R., He, K., Dollár, P.: Focal loss for dense object detection. In: Proceedings of the IEEE International Conference on Computer Vision, pp. 2980–2988 (2017)

19. Liu, W., et al.: SSD: single shot multibox detector. In: Leibe, B., Matas, J., Sebe, N., Welling, M. (eds.) ECCV 2016 Part I. LNCS, vol. 9905, pp. 21–37. Springer, Cham (2016). https://doi.org/10.1007/978-3-319-46448-0_2

20. Lowe, D.G.: Object recognition from local scale-invariant features. In: Proceedings of the seventh IEEE International Conference on Computer Vision, vol. 2, pp. 1150–1157. IEEE (1999)

21. Matsuda, Y., Hoashi, H., Yanai, K.: Recognition of multiple-food images by detecting candidate regions. In: 2012 IEEE International Conference on Multimedia and Expo, pp. 25–30. IEEE (2012)

22. Meyers, A., et al.: Im2calories: towards an automated mobile vision food diary. In: Proceedings of the IEEE International Conference on Computer Vision, pp. 1233–1241 (2015)

23. Minija, S.J., Emmanuel, W.S.: Food image classification using sphere shaped-support vector machine. In: 2017 International Conference on Inventive Computing and Informatics (ICICI), pp. 109–113. IEEE (2017)

24. Nobles, A.L.: Automated image analysis of Instagram posts: implications for risk perception and communication in public health using a case study of# HIV. PLoS ONE **15**(5), e0231155 (2020)

25. Pandey, D., et al.: Object detection in Indian food platters using transfer learning with yolov4. In: 2022 IEEE 38th International Conference on Data Engineering Workshops (ICDEW), pp. 101–106 (2022)

26. Pandey, P., Deepthi, A., Mandal, B., Puhan, N.B.: FoodNet: recognizing foods using ensemble of deep networks. IEEE Signal Process. Lett. **24**(12), 1758–1762 (2017)

27. Ramesh, A., Sivakumar, A., Angel, S.S.: Real-time food-object detection and localization for Indian cuisines using deep neural networks. In: 2020 IEEE International Conference on Machine Learning and Applied Network Technologies (ICMLANT), pp. 1–6. IEEE (2020)

28. Redmon, J., Divvala, S., Girshick, R., Farhadi, A.: You only look once: unified, real-time object detection. In: Proceedings of the IEEE Conference on Computer Vision and Pattern Recognition, pp. 779–788 (2016)

29. Ren, S., He, K., Girshick, R., Sun, J.: Faster R-CNN: towards real-time object detection with region proposal networks. IEEE Trans. Pattern Anal. Mach. Intell. **39**(6), 1137–1149 (2017)

30. Simonyan, K., Zisserman, A.: Very deep convolutional networks for large-scale image recognition. arXiv:1409.1556 (2014)

31. Skalski, P.: Make Sense (2019). https://github.com/SkalskiP/make-sense/

32. Smith, L.N.: Cyclical learning rates for training neural networks. In: 2017 IEEE Winter Conference on Applications of Computer Vision (WACV), pp. 464–472. IEEE (2017)

33. Szegedy, C., et al.: Going deeper with convolutions. In: Proceedings of the IEEE Conference on Computer Vision and Pattern Recognition, pp. 1–9 (2015)

34. Termritthikun, C., Kanprachar, S.: Accuracy improvement of Thai food image recognition using deep convolutional neural networks. In: 2017 International Electrical Engineering Congress (IEECON), pp. 1–4. IEEE (2017)

35. Viola, P., Jones, M.: Rapid object detection using a boosted cascade of simple features. In: Proceedings of the 2001 IEEE Computer Society Conference on Computer Vision and Pattern Recognition. CVPR 2001, vol. 1, pp. 511–518. IEEE (2001)

36. Viola, P., Jones, M.J.: Robust real-time face detection. Int. J. Comput. Vis. **57**, 137–154 (2004)

37. Wang, C.Y., Bochkovskiy, A., Liao, H.Y.M.: YOLOv7: trainable bag-of-freebies sets new state-of-the-art for real-time object detectors. arXiv:2207.02696 (2022)

38. Wang, H., Ullah, M.M., Klaser, A., Laptev, I., Schmid, C.: Evaluation of local spatio-temporal features for action recognition. In: British Machine Vision Conference, pp. 1–11. BMVA Press (2009)
39. Yanai, K., Kawano, Y.: Food image recognition using deep convolutional network with pre-training and fine-tuning. In: 2015 IEEE International Conference on Multimedia & Expo Workshops (ICMEW), pp. 1–6. IEEE (2015)
40. Zhu, X., Su, W., Lu, L., Li, B., Wang, X., Dai, J.: Deformable DETR: deformable transformers for end-to-end object detection. arXiv:2010.04159 (2020)

A Deep Learning Approach to Enhance Semantic Segmentation of Bacteria and Pus Cells from Microscopic Urine Smear Images Using Synthetic Data

Vidyashree R. Kanabur[1]([✉]), Deepu Vijayasenan[1], Sumam David S[1], and Sreejith Govindan[2]

[1] National Institute of Technology Karnataka, Surathkal, Karnataka, India
vidyashreekanabur.207ec010@nitk.edu.in
[2] Department of Basic Medical Sciences, MAHE, Manipal, Karnataka, India

Abstract. Urine smear analysis aids in preliminary diagnosis of Urinary Tract Infection. But it is time-consuming and requires a lot of medical expertise. Automating the process using machine learning can save time and effort. However obtaining a large medical dataset is difficult due to data privacy concerns and medical expertise requirements. In this study, we propose a method to synthesize a large dataset of gram-stained microscopic images containing pus cells and bacteria. We train a machine learning model to achieve semantic segmentation of bacteria and pus cells using this dataset. Later we use it to perform transfer learning on a relatively small dataset of gram stained urine microscopic images. Our approach improved the F1-score from 50% to 63% for bacteria segmentation and from 77% to 83% for pus cell segmentation. This method has the potential to improve the turn-around time and the quality of preliminary diagnosis of Urinary Tract Infection.

Keywords: Synthetic data · Machine learning · Transfer learning

1 Introduction

Urine culture is the most reliable tool to diagnose Urinary Tract Infection(UTI). But it can yield negative results in about 60% of the cases [1]. It is also costly, labour-intensive and time-consuming. The preliminary diagnosis of UTI can be performed using microscopic examination of urine specimen. Subsequently, depending on the concentration of pus cells and bacteria, a culture examination can be suggested. However, manual microscopic examination by expert microbiologists is time-consuming, costly, and requires quality time of medical professional. Therefore, automating the process of microscopic urine smear image analysis is necessary.To diagnose UTI using microscopic images of urine samples, we need to detect and count both pus cells and bacteria from each image. Many researchers have tried to classify bacteria from microscopic images, for example,

H. Kaur et al. (Eds.): CVIP 2023, CCIS 2009, pp. 244–255, 2024.
https://doi.org/10.1007/978-3-031-58181-6_21

Goswami et al. [2] tried to detect and classify pus cells, red blood cells and other urine sediments using YOLOv3 and RetinaNet models, Yan et al. [3] performed detection of red blood cells, casts and white blood cells from urine specimen using ResNet50 and Hiremath et al. [4] tried to classify pus cells from microscopic images using color segmentation approach, Tasnim et al. [5], Jessica et al. [6] and Li et al. [7] classified bacteria and other sediments from urine microscopic images using deep learning approach. Iida et al. [8] proposed a detection system of gram types for bacteria from gram stained smear images using Support Vector Machine (SVM) and Deep Neural Networks (DNN). Costa et al. [9] proposed a method to segment and identify bacteria type using CNN and image mosaicing techniques. Abdul et al. [10] proposed an unsupervised model and UNet based supervised learning model to extract objects such as RBC, yeast, bacteria, etc from the urine microscopy images. Most of them have performed classification of sediments but not semantic segmentation and counting of bacteria and pus cells together from the same urine microscopic image which is necessary to diagnose and grade the UTI.

In this paper, we propose automatic urine smear analysis using deep neural networks to segment bacteria and pus cells from microscopic images. Deep neural networks require large datasets to perform semantic segmentation. However, obtaining a large number of microscopic urine samples from patients is challenging due to data security issues and the time needed to generate the dataset. Furthermore, annotating a large dataset is not always feasible. Microscopic images have objects with varying size and stain artifacts. For example, medically important bacteria are small in size (generally they are 2–5 μm in diameter) whereas pus cells are generally ten times bigger than bacteria in size (5–15 μm in diameter). Hence detecting and quantifying them from a microscopic image is challenging. To address these challenges, we develop an algorithm to generate synthetic microscopic urine smear images using various image processing tools and algorithms. Deep learning model gets trained on this synthetic dataset and then the trained model will be fine-tuned in the relatively smaller real dataset. To summarize, our major contributions include the following:

- A simple image processing algorithm is proposed to synthesize images.
- A deep learning approach is presented to achieve semantic segmentation of bacteria and pus cells from microscopic urine smear images.

This paper is organized into six sections. Section 2 gives the details of the dataset used in training our model. Synthetic data generation is explained in Sect. 3. Section 4 and 5 describe the implementation details along with the results. Finally, the conclusion is drawn in Sect. 6.

2   Dataset

Around 100 gram-stained microscopic urine smear images are collected from microbiological laboratory of a tertiary care center after Institute Ethical Clearance bearing Project No. 732/2021. All the images are of 100x magnification with size 1200×1600. 40 images among them have only pus cells, 12 images contain only bacteria and 55 images contain bacteria and pus cells both. These images are annotated using image editing tool and are validated by an expert microbiologist. It is observed that the concentration of bacteria in this dataset is less. These images are not sufficient to perform semantic segmentation of bacteria and pus cells from microscopic urine smear images. Therefore another publicly available dataset, that is, Digital Images of Bacterial Species (DIBaS) dataset is used [11]. It contains 33 genera and species of bacteria. Each species has 20 images and so there are 660 images in this dataset each image of size 2048×1532. It is available for public access at https://github.com/gallardorafael/DIBaS-Dataset. Chethan et al. [12] published the annotated label of DIBaS dataset using semiautomatic labelling approach such as k-means clustering, otsu thresholding and morphological closing operations. The annotated groundtruth images are validated by the expert microbiologists.

3   Synthetic Data Generation

Our dataset has just 55 images and the number of bacteria in each image is less. Bacteria are tiny and detection of such tiny particles is challenging. The dataset collected from the microbiological laboratory does not cover different classes of bacteria such as single, pairs, chains and clusters. So we propose a method to perform data synthesis.

Synthetic data generation is the process of artificially generating data which resembles the real world data. The synthetically generated data does not have a one-to-one mapping with real data which will preserve patients' data privacy and hence it can be adopted in medical data generation [13]. Synthetic data is believed to give enhanced results in many real world applications of machine learning such as microscopic image analysis [14], pedestrian detection [15], histopathological applications [16] and so on. Generative Adversarial Networks (GAN) is most widely used approach to generate synthetic data and it is introduced by Goodfellow et al. [17]. GAN networks need lot of training samples to get high quality images and also it takes a lot of time to train such networks. As we have limited number of images in our real dataset and most of the images have only single arrangement of bacteria, the GAN networks may overfit. So we chose a simple cut and paste method of synthetic data generation. Data synthesis is performed by pasting the bacteria from DIBaS dataset on the real dataset containing only pus cells. Synthetic image generation is carried out by first selecting an appropriate patch of bacteria. Figure 1 explains the procedure involved in choosing appropriate patch of image. Images containing bacteria and their corresponding groundtruth label are referred as foreground image and foreground mask respectively. Similarly, images containing just the pus cells are labelled as background image and mask. The patch size is selected by manually examining the size of bacteria across different classes and choosing an area slightly larger than the bacteria area. From the large image containing bacteria, patches of fixed size is extracted and the patches with single bacteria at the center or very close to the center are saved. This ensures proper blending of the bacteria with the background image.

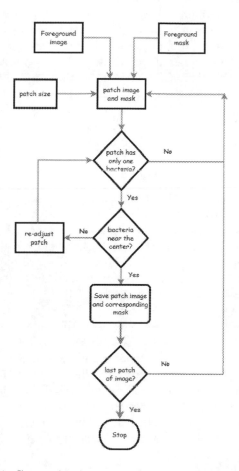

Fig. 1. Generating image patches containing bacteria

The next step in generating synthetic image is choosing appropriate background image and then pasting the patch of bacteria on it. For this purpose, we employed the cut and paste instance segmentation approach as described in [18]. Next step is to paste this patch of bacteria on the background image and mask. This involves two steps, namely image blending and blurring operations. Image blending is performed at the time of synthesis while image blurring is included as a data augmentation process while training the network. These operations are explained in the following sections.

3.1   Image Blending

If the foreground patch is cut and pasted into the background patch, there will be prominent discontinuity along the edges. The deep learning models will learn to identify such discontinuities rather than the actual bacteria [18]. We choose a blending operation to reduce such discontinuities. First stain matching using Reinhard [19] and histogram equalization is carried out then blending is involved. Image blending is transforming the source pixels' RGB values to those of the target image. This involves simple arithmetic operations like addition and multiplication of pixel intensities. In this work, two type of blending operations, namely, linear blending and gaussian blending, are used. This will ensure that the model does not learn the artifacts of any one blending operation.

$$bl\_img = bg\_img * dist + fg\_img + dist\_inv \tag{1}$$

Linear blending is defined as Eq. 1. fg_img and bg_img represent foreground patch and background patch respectively. dist and dist_inv represent the distance transformed foreground mask and its inverse distance transformed mask. bl_img is the blended image patch. From the background image containing pus cells, a small patch, of same size as that of the foreground bacteria patch, is extracted. The binary mask of foreground mask is determined. Euclidean distance on this mask is computed as the distance between each bacteria pixel with value 0 and the nearest non-bacteria pixel with value 1 . We then normalize the distance transform image and apply a thresholding on this image to set all the pixels outside this threshold to a value of 1. This image is inverted to get the inverted distance patch. Both the transformed image and its inverse transform are bought to 0 to 255 range before further operations. The background patch is multiplied with the distance transformed patch of bacteria. Similarly, the foreground patch of bacteria is multiplied with the inverted distance transformed bacteria patch. The resultant images are combined to get the linearly blended background patch. This blended patch is replaced back in the background region. An example of linear blending is illustrated in Fig. 2.

3.2   Image Blurring

The blended images are close to the natural images except for the edge details being retained in the synthesized image. So image blurring is performed to smooth out the edges of the pasted bacteria patch. Gaussian blurring and a number of motion blurring operations such as horizontal blurring, vertical blurring and diagonal blurring are carried out to increase the number of images used for training the deep learning model. The blurred images are shown in Fig. 3. Motion blur(a) is blurring in vertical direction, motion blur(b) is in horizontal direction, motion blur (c) and (d) are blurring in diagonal directions. All these blurring are performed using a 9×9 kernel. Gaussian blurring is performed using sigma of 2.

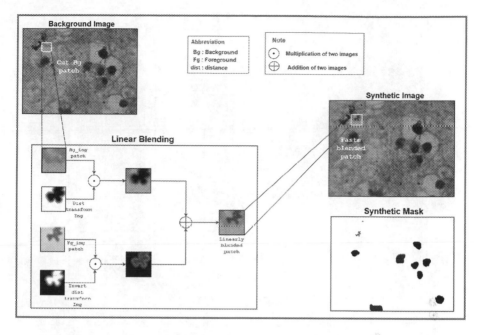

Fig. 2. Bacteria patches pasted on background image containing pus cells using distance transformation and linear blending

Around 2000 synthetic images are generated by random combination of above mentioned image blending and stain normalization. The blurring operation is performed on these samples during network training.

4   Training

There exists a lot of semantic segmentation models in the literature. Abhinaav et al. [20] proposed semantic segmentation of nucleus and cytoplasm from Papanicolaou smear images using ResNet to detect the presence of cervical cancer and the authors have claimed that the segmented labels outperformed those obtained from manual labeling. Hoorali F et al. [21] proposed a novel method to automatically detect and segment anthracis bacteria. They performed their experiment using UNet and UNet++ and compared their performances. They obtained good results for both the models. However, the overall performance in terms of precision, recall, F1 score and accuracy were good for UNet++ models. Therefore, we choose ResUNet++ model as a baseline model to perform semantic segmentation of bacteria and pus cells from microscopic urine smear images. Since our dataset has just 55 images, a 5-fold cross validation approach is employed to evaluate the performance of semantic segmentation of bacteria and pus cells from microscopic images. The 55 images are divided into 5 sets with each set having 11 images in test set and 44 images in train set. The images of size 1200×1600 are

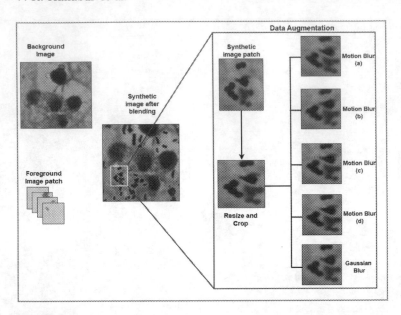

Fig. 3. Various blurring and resizing operations performed on synthetic data as part of data augmentation

split into patches of size 512×512 and the patches with less than 5% foreground pixels are eliminated. Various image augmentation techniques such as rotation, flipping, shifting, crop and resize are employed to increase the variability in the data. We trained our model using TensorFlow framework. Each set is trained for 200 epochs. The network is trained using RMS prop optimizer, weighted dice-loss function and the learning rate of 0.0001 is chosen. The images are processed using a batch size of 4. The performance of the model is evaluated using precision, recall and F1 score. It is seen that the F1 score of bacteria segmentation is 50.11% and the F1 score of pus cells segmentation is 77.62%.

To enhance the segmentation scores of bacteria, we used a pre-trained ResUNet++ network which is trained on synthetic dataset for fine tuning. This synthetic dataset consisted of 2000 images split into 1200 train images, 400 images each in validation and test set. The images are of size 1200×1600 which are split into overlapping patches in train set and non-overlapping patches in validation set having the size 512×512. Some of the patches containing more than 95% of background or less than 5% of foreground pixels are discarded from training. So, 6989 images are available in train set and 1298 images in validation set. The images are trained using RMS prop optimizer, weighted dice-loss function and the learning rate of 0.0001. The images are processed using a batch size of 4. Various blurring operations such as Gaussian blur and motion blur, rotation, shifting, flipping, crop and resize operations are incorporated for data augmentation. The trained weight and model parameters are used to fine-tune the 5-fold cross validation dataset.

5   Results and Discussion

The 5-fold cross-validation dataset contains bacteria having single arrangement. When we tested its performance with bacteria having chained arrangement, it segmented these bacteria pixels as background pixels. This is because the dataset does not have bacteria in pairs, chains and clusters. So, synthetic data is generated and care is taken that the synthetic images have many bacteria in them covering all the classes. Now, the ResUNet++ model is first trained on synthetic data and the trained weights are used to fine-tune the real dataset . This is known as transfer learning approach. The average performance metrics are tabulated in Table 1. An example of the predictions is shown in Fig. 4. As seen in the figure, the predicted label is close to the groundtruth label when transfer learning approach is employed. The transfer learning network has predicted almost all the pus cells and bacteria. Another example of predictions is shown

Table 1. Performance of the model with and without transfer learning approach

Performance measure	Without transfer learning		With Transfer Learning	
	pus cells	bacteria	pus cells	bacteria
precision	0.8076	0.7208	0.7755	0.6909
recall	0.7543	0.3912	0.9002	0.5871
F1 score	0.7762	0.5011	0.8322	0.6326
rmse of count	3.07	13.96	3.75	5.62

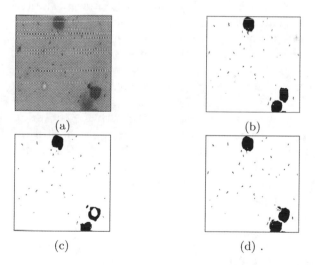

(a)   (b)

(c)   (d) .

Fig. 4. Predicted labels of the model with and without transfer learning, here (a)image, (b) groundtruth mask where bacteria is labelled red, pus cell is labelled black and background as white, (c)predicted label after 5-fold cross validation, (d)predicted label with transfer learning approach (Color figure online)

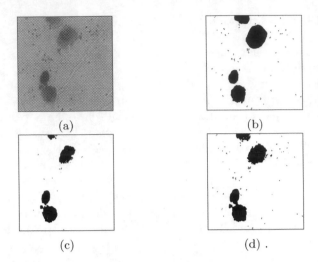

(a)   (b)

(c)   (d) .

Fig. 5. Transfer learning approach has detected most of the bacteria which were missed when no transfer learning is involved. (a)image, (b) groundtruth mask where bacteria is labelled red, pus cell is labelled black and background as white, (c)predicted label after 5-fold cross validation, (d)predicted label with transfer learning approach (Color figure online)

in Fig. 5. Without transfer learning approach, this is the worst label predicted without chains in them. The precision score of this image is 29% and recall is 10%. The predicted label has shown significant improvement after transfer learning with the precision score increased to 80% and recall to 68%. This is because we included many patches of bacteria in the synthetic images. Since, there are lot of bacteria included in each synthetic image, the root mean squared error in count of bacteria improved from 13.96 to 5.62 using transfer learning approach. Also the F1 score of bacteria segmentation improved from 50% to 63% and pus cell segmentation increased from 77% to 83%. The model has detected some of the bacteria chains which is otherwise missed with the network trained without transfer learning. An example of this is shown in Fig. 6. Still, we are unable to segment all the chains of bacteria because our dataset does not contain many chains of bacteria and therefore, we could not synthesize and train the network with many images containing chains of bacteria in them. Some of the background artifacts got classified as bacteria and pus cells after transfer learning. So the precision degraded by nearly 3% in both the cases. We also tried to evaluate the patch level accuracy of bacteria class. We generated 385 patches of size 299×299 from 55 groundtruth labels and their corresponding predicted labels. These patches are analysed to check for the presence of bacteria in them and then a confusion matrix is obtained and patch accuracy is calculated. Accuracy increased from 83% to 85% using transfer learning approach. The accuracy can be further enhanced by synthesizing images with multiple bacteria patches in them.

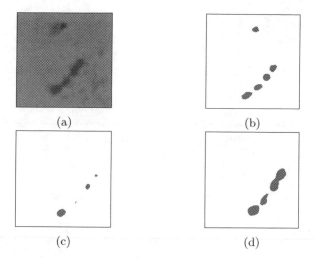

Fig. 6. The transfer learning approach aids in segmenting few bacteria chains. (a)image, (b) groundtruth mask where bacteria is labelled red, pus cell is labelled black and background as white, (c)predicted label after 5-fold cross validation, (d)predicted label with transfer learning approach (Color figure online)

6   Conclusion

A deep learning system is proposed to perform automatic segmentation of bacteria and pus cells from urine smear images. It reduces the need for expert medical personnel significantly and increases the efficiency of the diagnosis process. The study demonstrates the effectiveness of synthetic data generation and transfer learning in enhancing the accuracy of automated microscopic urine smear analysis. The proposed method can be used to segment tiny particles from the images. With this approach we are able to segment most of the single bacteria and few chains of bacteria. We aim to further improve the performance by generating more patches of bacteria having chains and cluster arrangements. This approach can also be extended to other medical image analysis tasks where obtaining large annotated datasets is a challenge. We believe that our work can pave the way for more efficient and accurate diagnosis of urinary tract infections, leading to better patient outcomes.

References

1. Oyaert, M., Delanghe, J.: Progress in automated urinalysis. Ann. Lab. Med. **39**(1), 15–22 (2019)
2. Goswami, D., Aggrawal, H., Agarwal, V.: Cell Detection and Classification from Urine Sediment Microscopic Images (2020)
3. Yan, M., Liu, Q., Yin, Z., Wang, D. Liang, Y.: A bidirectional context propagation network for urine sediment particle detection in microscopic images. In: IEEE

International Conference on Acoustics, Speech and Signal Processing (ICASSP), pp. 981–985 (2020). https://doi.org/10.1109/ICASSP40776.2020.9054367

4. Hiremath P.S., Parashuram, B., Geeta, S.: Automated identification and classification of white blood cells (leukocytes) in digital microscopic images. Int. J. Comput. Appl. (2010)

5. Ahmed, T., Wahid, M.F., Hasan, M.J.: Combining deep convolutional neural network with support vector machine to classify microscopic bacteria images. In: 2019 International Conference on Electrical, Computer and Communication Engineering(ECCE), pp. 1-5 (2019). https://doi.org/10.1109/ECACE.2019.8679397

6. Velasco, J.S., Cabatuan, M.K., Dadios, E.P.: Urine sediment classification using deep learning. Lect. Notes Adv. Res. Electr. Electron. Eng. Technol. 180–185 (2019)

7. Ji, Q., Li, X., Qu, Z., Dai, C.: Research on urine sediment images recognition based on deep learning. IEEE Access **7**, 166711–166720 (2019). https://doi.org/10.1109/ACCESS.2019.2953775

8. Iida, R., Hashimoto, K., Hirata, K., Matsuoka, K., Yokoyama, S.: Detection system of gram types for bacteria from gram stained smears images. In: 9th International Conference on Pattern Recognition Applications and Methods, vol. 1, pp. 477–484 (2020). https://doi.org/10.5220/0008964404770484

9. Serrão, M.K.M., Costa, M.G.F., Fujimoto, L.B., Ogusku, M.M., Filho, C.F.F.C.: Automatic bacillus detection in light field microscopy images using convolutional neural networks and mosaic imaging approach. In: 42nd Annual International Conference of the IEEE Engineering in Medicine & Biology Society (EMBC), pp. 1903–1906 (2020). https://doi.org/10.1109/EMBC44109.2020.9176105

10. Aziz, A., Pande, H., Cheluvaraju, B., Rai Dastidar, T.: Improved extraction of objects from urine microscopy images with unsupervised thresholding and supervised u-net techniques. In: 2018 IEEE/CVF Conference on Computer Vision and Pattern Recognition Workshops (CVPRW), pp. 2311–23118 (2018). https://doi.org/10.1109/CVPRW.2018.00299

11. Zieliński, B., Plichta, B., Misztal, K., Spurek, P., Brzychczy-Włoch, M., Ochońska, D.: Deep learning approach to bacterial colony classification. In: 27th International Conference on Artificial Neural Networks, Rhodes, Greece, 2018 Proceedings (2018)

12. Reddy, P.A., Kanabur, V.R., Vijayasenan, D., David, S.S., Govindan, S.: Semi-automatic labeling and semantic segmentation of gram-stained microscopic images from DIBaS dataset. in: 2023 2nd International Conference on Computational Systems and Communication (ICCSC), Thiruvananthapuram, India, pp. 1–6 (2023). https://doi.org/10.1109/ICCSC56913.2023.10142976

13. Jean-Francois, R., Bergen, R., Buckeridge, D.L., Khaled, E., Ng, R., Strome, E.: Synthetic data as an enabler for machine learning applications in medicine. iScience, **25**(11), 2589-0042 (2022)

14. P, T., et al.: Deep neural networks for analysis of microscopy images-synthetic data generation and adaptive sampling. Crystals **11**(3), 258 (2021). https://doi.org/10.3390/cryst11030258

15. Poibrenski, A., Sprenger, J., Müller, C.: Toward a methodology for training with synthetic data on the example of pedestrian detection in a frame-by-frame semantic segmentation task. In: Proceedings of the 2018 IEEE/ACM 1st International Workshop on Software Engineering for AI in Autonomous Systems (SEFAIAS), Gothenburg, Sweden, pp. 31–34 (2018)

16. Moghadam, P.A., et al.: A morphology focused diffusion probabilistic model for synthesis of histopathology images. arXiv preprint arXiv:2209.13167 (2022)

17. Goodfellow, I.J., et al.: Generative adversarial networks. arXiv preprint arXiv:1406.2661 (2014)

18. Dwibedi, D., Misra, I., Hebert, M.: Cut, Paste and learn: surprisingly easy synthesis for instance detection. In: IEEE International Conference on Computer Vision 2017, ICCV, pp. 1310–1319 (2017). https://doi.org/10.1109/ICCV.2017.146
19. Reinhard, E., Ashikhmin, M., Gooch, B., Shirley, P.: Color transfer between images. IEEE Comput. Graphics Appl. **21**, 34–41 (2001). https://doi.org/10.1109/38.946629
20. Abhinaav, R., Akshaya Sapthasri, M., Anusha, V., Nivetha, S., Pujithagiri, G., Padmapriya, B.: Segmentation of nucleus and cytoplasm from unit papanicolaou smear images using deep semantic networks. Int. Res. J. Eng. Technol. (IRJET) **6**(10), 56–63 (2019)
21. Hoorali, F., Khosravi, H., Moradi, B.: Automatic Bacillus anthracis bacteria detection and segmentation in microscopic images using UNet+D. J. Microbiol. Methods **177**, 106056 (2020). https://doi.org/10.1016/j.mimet.2020.106056

Bit Plane Segmentation and LBP-Based Coverless Video Steganography for Secure Data Transmission

Sourabh Debnath$^{(\boxtimes)}$ ⓘ, Ramesh Kumar Mohapatra ⓘ,
and Tejas Shirish Kulkarni ⓘ

National Institute of Technology Rourkela, Rourkela 769008, Odisha, India
{sourabh_debnath,mohapatrark,221cs2295}@nitrkl.ac.in

Abstract. Traditional information hiding techniques alter carriers to embed secret information, which steganalysis algorithms can find. In the area of covert communication, coverless information concealment has been suggested as a way of preventing steganalysis. A new methodology for sharing secret data through coverless video steganography using Local Binary Pattern (LBP) before bit-plane segmentation has been proposed. In this technique, a single frame is converted into multiple bit-planes, and various hash sequences are generated from these bit-planes. After extracting frames from the video, each frame is converted into grayscale using LBP and then split into multiple bit-planes using Bit-plane Complexity Segmentation (BPCS). The hash sequences are obtained by calculating the average median values of corresponding bit-plane sub-blocks. A retrieval database is created to relate the obtained hash sequences with the bit-plane features. And for the first time security analysis is done in this proposed technique. The experimental results demonstrate that this approach achieves better robustness against various attacks, has a larger capacity, requires less time to extract hash sequences, and has a higher success rate of concealing information than existing coverless video steganography techniques.

Keywords: Steganography · Bit-plane Complexity Segmentation (BPCS) · Local Binary Pattern (LBP) · Coverless Video Steganography · Cover Object

1 Introduction

The digitalization of information has led to a significant shift of business to the internet due to its efficiency in terms of time, effort, and cost savings. However, the internet is often perceived as a vulnerable platform for digital data transmission, as it can be exposed to various security and privacy risks such as unauthorized manipulation, dissemination, and duplication [1, 2]. However, because it can be subject to a number of security and privacy threats, including unauthorised manipulation, dissemination, and duplication, the internet is frequently seen as

H. Kaur et al. (Eds.): CVIP 2023, CCIS 2009, pp. 256–268, 2024.
https://doi.org/10.1007/978-3-031-58181-6_22

a weak platform for the transmission of digital data. Compared to conventional techniques [3], coverless information concealment has a number of benefits. First off, it doesn't call for any carrier modifications, therefore the existing carrier is left alone. The second characteristic is anti-steganalysis, which makes it challenging for attackers to find secret information by analysing the modifications made to the carrier. Contrarily, conventional approaches call for the carrier to be changed in order to incorporate the sensitive information, which can make it simpler for attackers to find the concealed information. Utilising the carrier's existing characteristics, coverless information concealing increases the information's robustness and security. The contribution of this proposed approach is outlined as follows:

1. A coverless video steganography method based on LBP on Bit Plane Segmentation is proposed to enhance capacity and robustness in the corresponding frame for secret data sharing.
2. In this approach, a single frame is converted into bit-planes for multiple uses, and several mapping hash sequences are generated from various bit-planes of the single frame.
3. The hash bit sequences are created by comparing the average median coefficient of consecutive subblocks within a block in a bit-plane frame image.
4. The experimental results demonstrate that the proposed method surpasses currently used coverless video steganography techniques.

The paper is structured as follows: Sect. 2 provides literature study, Sect. 3 presents the suggested coverless method, Sect. 4 presents the experimental findings and analysis, and Sect. 5 concludes the paper.

2 Literature Study

Coverless video steganography is a technique that hides confidential information in the video without leaving any traces of modification on the carrier. Traditional video steganography [3] involves altering the video frames to hide sensitive information, which steganalysis algorithms can spot. On the other hand, coverless video steganography [4–8] does not embed any data in the video and can successfully withstand steganalysis tools.

The first coverless steganography technique that uses photographs as carriers was created by Zhou et al. [9]. Hash sequences are created by dividing the image into non-overlapping chunks and comparing the average intensities of each block. Zhou et al. [10] used a library of partially exact duplicates of the given secret image as a cover image in their work. In contrast to Zhou et al.'s method [10], Luo et al. [11] suggested a novel coverless steganography method based on dense convolutional networks and image block matching. A reliable coverless image steganography technique based on discrete cosine transform (DCT) [12] and latent dirichlet allocation (LDA) subject categorization was recently developed by Zhang et al. [13]. Some other features are also employed to extract features from respective images such as BOF [14] as in [15]. Video sequences, as opposed to still images, contain both temporal and spatial information. The first coverless video steganography method was put forth by Pan et al. [4] and used a neural network to construct a statistical histogram for semantic segmentation.

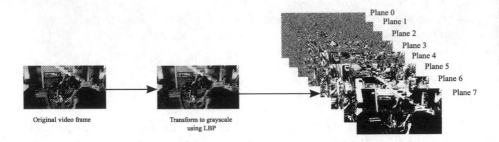

Fig. 1. Bit Plane Complexity Segmentation on a video frame

3   Proposed Coverless Scheme

Linear Binary Patterns (LBP) is a feature extraction method commonly used in computer vision and image analysis [16]. The LBP operator creates a binary pattern based on the comparison of a central pixel's gray-level intensity values to those of its surrounding pixels. It has been discovered that LBP is resistant to variations in illumination, noise, and other types of image deterioration. A grayscale image frame is converted into eight bit planes using BPCS, with each pixel value denoting the intensity at a specific location. Figure 1 shows how the grayscale image frame is transformed into eight distinct planes using BPCS.

The recommended method involves four essential elements: hash sequence creation, video index structuring, secret information concealment, and secret information extraction. To begin, hash sequences are produced from the video utilizing the proposed technique. The color channel of each video frame is converted to grayscale using LBP, and then each frame is partitioned into N × N blocks. By comparing the median intensity values of successive subblocks of an image block, the hash sequence is generated. This comparison is carried out in a raster scan order. Subsequently, the produced hash sequences, along with their corresponding frame location and video path, are indexed into the established video index structure in the database. At the sender's end, the secret information is preprocessed and divided into P segments, each with a fixed length of S. During the preprocessing stage, the secret data is transformed into a binary bit stream.

Next, the mapping indexes corresponding to each segment are searched for in the constructed video index structure database. The receiver obtains all videos and auxiliary information, which is then used to extract the segmented secret information by following the suggested hash sequence extraction process. The original secret information is restored by combining all the segmented hash

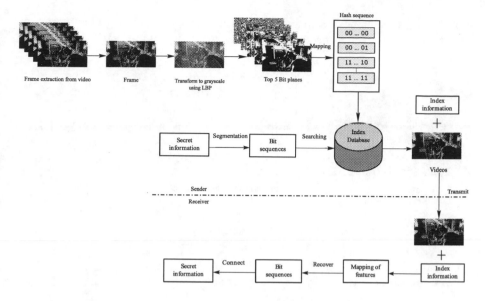

Fig. 2. Proposed coverless video steganography framework

sequences. The proposed framework is depicted in Fig. 2. The length of the secret information after segmentation may or may not be a multiple of S. To achieve a length of S, the final segment is padded with additional '0' numbers, and the number of '0' is recorded. The original video remains unaltered throughout the entire procedure, making it undetectable to steganalysis.

3.1 Hash Sequences Mapping

The mapping of hash sequences plays a crucial role in achieving both robustness and accuracy in the mapping algorithm. To achieve this, frames are initially extracted from a video using an extraction algorithm, which are then converted to gray-scale using LBP. Bit planes are then extracted from the gray-scale frames, which are subsequently divided into non-overlapping sub-blocks of 3×3. The process of hash sequence generation is illustrated in Fig. 3.

After the image frame is divided into sub-blocks of $M \times M$, the hash sequence can be generated by comparing the average median value of a sub-block with its neighbouring sub-block average median value. The comparison of the sub-block's median values can be expressed using the following equation.

$$H_i = \begin{cases} 1, if \ median_i \geq median_{i+1}, \\ 0, if \ median_i < median_{i+1} \end{cases} \quad 1 \leq i \leq M^2 - 1 \quad (1)$$

The hash sequence resulting from comparing the median values of two sub-blocks is 1 if the median value of the first sub-block is greater than or equal to the second sub-block's median value; otherwise, it is 0. After comparing all the sub-blocks, an 8-bit hash sequence is obtained from one plane. This process is repeated to calculate hash sequences for other bit planes.

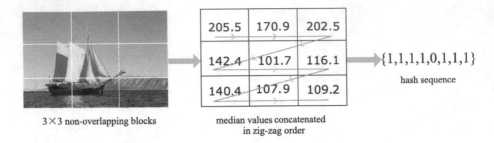

Fig. 3. The process of hash sequence generation

3.2   Construction of Retrieval Database

Locating the cover video smoothly and accurately is crucial. The sender can quickly find the desired frame by using a retrieval database, which is similar to confidential information. Figure 4 shows a two-level index database that has been efficiently constructed. The first index level is represented by hash sequences, and the second index level is represented by corresponding index information, such as video path location, frame location, and corresponding plane location of the cover video frame. The hash sequences are binary and sorted in order, while the second index level information is sorted according to the hash sequences. The decimal value of the hash sequence, which ranges from 0 to 255, is used to order

Hash sequence	Index ID	Video ID	Frame ID	Plane ID
00000000 →	1	\Video\walking.avi	120	7
00000001 →	2	\Video\running.avi	10	5
	⋮	⋮	⋮	⋮
	6	\Video\basketball.avi	1 5	6
00000010 →	7	\Video\walking.avi	24	4
	10	\Video\walking.avi	167	6
	⋮	⋮	⋮	⋮
⋮	13	\Video\crawling.avi	40	4
11111111 →	702	\Video\walking.avi	220	5
	703	\Video\boxing.avi	30	7
	⋮	⋮	⋮	⋮
	1000	\Video\crawling.avi	78	4

Fig. 4. Retrieval database structure

the index IDs. Up until all distinct byte sequences from 00000000 to 11111111 are mapped, this entire process is repeated. These procedures are designed to make it easier to organise and retrieve data from the retrieval database.

For instance, let us consider the hash sequence generated by the 4th plane of the 24th frame of the video *"walking.avi"* to be "00000010". It is stored in the 7th index ID of the retrieval video database. The same process is carried out until all videos are included in the video index database. Figure 4 illustrates the structure of the retrieval video database.

3.3   Transmitting Secret Information

The critical process in transmitting secret information is mapping it with a cover video. The private data is divided into segments of 1 byte length and, if necessary, padded with extra '0' bits. The database is then queried for the data related to each byte. Until all bytes in the secret information match those in the information that was retrieved, this process is repeated. Finally, the receiver receives the carrier video and the retrieval data.

$$L_p = \begin{cases} \lfloor \frac{L_s}{8} \rfloor + 1, \ if \ mod(L_s, 8) = 0, \\ \\ \lfloor \frac{L_s}{8} \rfloor + 2, \quad\quad Otherwise \end{cases} \tag{2}$$

If $mod(L_s, 8) \neq 0$, append extra '0' bits to the end of SI to form a complete byte. To represent the number of '0' bits added, add one byte to the sequence. If $mod(L_s, 8) = 0$, append one byte of extra '0's to indicate no padding was done to the original secret information.

3.4   Recovering the Secret Information

Using the mapping rule, the receiver separates the desired information from the retrieval data. The index ID is used to access information about other IDs. The relevant plane is located using the frame ID and plane ID, and the corresponding frame is found using the video ID and frame ID. The median is determined for each sub-block once the plane is divided into smaller blocks. Based on the information that was found, the secret data was recovered. If padding is present, the padded bits of '0' are removed, and the secret information's length is changed appropriately.

To illustrate the process, let's consider an example. A video is selected from the database with the path location ".../video/bike-packing.avi" and frames are extracted from it. After frame extraction, the frame path location is ".../video/bike-packing/00003.jpg" and it is converted to grayscale. The top 5 bit-planes from the given frame are extracted, and the hash sequence of the selected frame is "01110101". The sequences of the top 5 bit-planes, namely $plane_7$, $plane_6$, $plane_5$, $plane_4$ and $plane_3$, are "01110101", "00111001", "00011001", "00011000" and "01101010", respectively. Thus, from a single frame, five unique hash sequences can be obtained, which increases the per-frame capacity.

4   Results and Analysis

The experiments were conducted using the following configurations: Intel(R) Core(TM) i7 - 7700K@4.20 GHz, NVIDIA Quadro K420, and 64 GB RAM. MATLAB 2022a and Python 3.10.4 were used to conduct the experiments. The proposed experiment and analysis were performed on the DAVIS 2017 [17] and UCF101 datasets [18]. Figure 5 displays a screenshot of the DAVIS-2017 dataset.

Fig. 5. DAVIS 2017 Dataset

From the video, frames are extracted, and the color image frames are converted to grayscale using LBP. The corresponding bit-planes are then extracted by BPCS. For the experiment, a video frame is randomly selected from the database, and the upper bit planes are chosen for mapping relationships and storing corresponding retrieval information into the retrieval database. The outputs of the experiment are evaluated and analyzed with existing schemes [4–8]. The evaluation mainly considers three performance metrics, namely capacity, robustness, efficiency analysis and security.

4.1   Capacity

The capacity of each bit plane is 8 bits, resulting in the requirement for the retrieval database to contain at least 256 different hash sequences. Capacity is quantified by the number of bits hidden per video frame. H_j, represented by $H_j = \{h_1, h_2, ..., h_8\}$, is the hash sequence formed by the j-th frame, and DC, the decimal conversion of the j-th frame, is obtained using Eq. 3.

$$DC_{H_i} = \sum_{j=1}^{8} h_j \times 2^{8-j} \qquad (3)$$

In this context, DC_{H_i} represents the decimal value of various hash sequences generated by mapping, with DC_{H_1} being the decimal value of the first frame.

$$E_C = \sum_{i=0}^{255} f(i), f(i) = \begin{cases} 1, \text{ if } i \text{ in } DC \\ 0, otherwise \end{cases} \qquad (4)$$

The effective capacity of the proposed approach, E_C, is the total number of unique hash sequences generated from a single video using Eq. 4. If the total number of frames in a video is M, the capacity of the video using this approach will be $40 \times M$ bits per video. The capacity of the proposed scheme is five times that of Pan et al. [4] and more than three times that of Zou et al. [6], as shown in Table 1.

Table 1. Comparison of capacity with other techniques

Method	Capacity (bits per frame)	Capacity (bits per video)
Tan *et al.* [7]	32	$32 \times M$
Zou *et al.* [6]	16	$16 \times M$
Pan *et al.* [4]	8	$8 \times M$
Proposed	**40**	$\mathbf{40 \times M}$

4.2 Robustness

The proposed work's robustness is evaluated by comparing the bit sequence B_1, which is recovered using the retrieval information with B_0, the bit sequence extracted from the secret information.

Assume that $B_i = \{b_1, b_2, ..., b_8\}$ represents the bit-stream calculated for each frame, m is 8, and L_c represents the sum of the bit numbers. The accuracy rate formula is as follows:

$$ACC = \frac{\sum_{j=1}^{m} f(j)}{L_c}, f(j) = \begin{cases} 1, if \ B_0 = B_1 \\ 0, otherwise \end{cases} \qquad (5)$$

The robustness of the proposed method on bit planes along with Meng's approach is shown in Table 2 and with other approaches is shown in Table 3, and is found to be more robust than other techniques, although it is less robust to centered cropping and rotation. The detailed comparison with existing coverless approaches using the UCF101 dataset is described in Table 4.

The proposed approach is more robust than existing techniques such as Pan et al. [4], Meng et al. [5], Zou et al. [6] and Tan et al. [7]. Pan's method has weak anti-interference ability against certain noise attacks and its robustness is also weak due to the extraction of deep features. On the other hand, Tan's approach takes more time to extract deep features because of its higher complexity in finding hierarchical optical flow. In contrast, the proposed method extracts features from bit planes by taking into account the median values of corresponding bit-plane sub-blocks, making it more robust than the aforementioned schemes.

4.3   Efficiency Analysis

To evaluate the efficiency of the proposed approach, the time required to hide one byte of secret information was measured in seconds per byte 's/B.' Table 5 presents a comparison of the time costs of different methods, demonstrating that the proposed approach takes less time compared to existing coverless approaches .

4.4   Security

When transmitting secret information through an untrusted channel like the internet, the security of the information is crucial. For the first time, the security

Table 2. Accuracy at different planes in DAVIS2017 Dataset

Attacks	Parameter	Plane 7	Plane 6	Plane 5	Plane 4	Plane 3	Average of 5 planes	Meng *et al.* [5]
Gaussian noise	$\sigma = 0.001$	1.0000	0.8750	1.0000	0.7500	0.7500	0.8750	0.9524
	$\sigma = 0.005$	1.0000	0.7500	0.8750	0.7500	0.6250	0.8000	0.9013
	$\sigma = 0.01$	1.0000	0.7500	1.0000	0.7500	0.7500	0.8500	0.7358
Speckle noise	$\sigma = 0.01$	1.0000	0.8750	0.8750	0.7500	0.5000	0.8000	0.9337
	$\sigma = 0.05$	1.0000	0.7500	0.7500	0.7500	0.7500	0.8000	0.8589
	$\sigma = 0.1$	1.0000	0.7500	0.8750	0.7500	0.7500	0.8250	0.8034
Salt & Pepper noise	$\sigma = 0.001$	1.0000	0.8750	0.8750	1.0000	0.7500	0.9000	0.9798
	$\sigma = 0.005$	1.0000	0.8750	1.0000	1.0000	0.5000	0.8750	0.9448
	$\sigma = 0.01$	1.0000	0.8750	0.8750	0.7500	0.7500	0.8500	0.8448
JPEG compression	$Q = 10$	1.0000	0.8750	1.0000	0.7500	0.8750	0.8750	0.9745
	$Q = 70$	1.0000	0.8750	1.0000	1.0000	0.7500	0.9250	0.9874
	$Q = 90$	1.0000	1.0000	1.0000	1.0000	0.7500	0.9500	0.9918
Centered Cropping	Ratio = 10%	1.0000	0.8750	1.0000	1.0000	0.7500	0.9250	0.9047
	Ratio = 20%	1.0000	0.8750	1.0000	1.0000	0.7500	0.9250	0.7538
	Ratio = 50%	1.0000	0.7500	0.8750	0.6250	0.7500	0.8000	0.4238
Edge Cropping	Ratio = 10%	1.0000	0.8750	0.8750	1.0000	1.0000	0.9500	0.7584
	Ratio = 20%	1.0000	0.8750	0.8750	0.8750	0.7500	0.8750	0.6528
	Ratio = 50%	1.0000	0.6250	0.7500	0.3750	0.6250	0.6750	0.4073
Rotation	Angle = 10°	1.0000	0.8750	1.0000	0.7500	0.6250	0.8500	0.2158
	Angle = 15°	1.0000	0.8750	1.0000	0.7500	0.6250	0.8500	0.1947
	Angle = 30°	1.0000	0.6250	0.8750	0.7500	0.6250	0.7750	0.1248
	Angle = 50°	1.0000	0.7500	0.8750	0.8750	0.6250	0.8250	0.1084
Translation	(16,10)	1.0000	1.0000	0.6250	0.6250	0.8750	0.8250	0.4528
	(40,25)	1.0000	0.8750	0.8750	0.7500	0.8750	0.8750	0.3985
	(80,50)	1.0000	0.8750	0.7500	0.7500	0.7500	0.8250	0.1547
	(160,100)	1.0000	0.7500	0.7500	0.6250	0.6250	0.7500	0.1218
	(320,200)	1.0000	0.7500	0.7500	0.7500	0.7500	0.8000	0.1426
Mean filtering	Kernel = 3 × 3	1.0000	1.0000	1.0000	0.8750	0.8750	0.9500	0.9508
Mean filtering	Kernel = 5 × 5	1.0000	1.0000	1.0000	1.0000	0.8750	0.9750	0.9078
Median filtering	Kernel = 3 × 3	1.0000	1.0000	0.8750	1.0000	0.8750	0.9500	0.9688
Median filtering	Kernel = 5 × 5	1.0000	1.0000	1.0000	1.0000	0.8750	0.9750	0.9286
Gauss filtering	Kernel = 3 × 3	1.0000	1.0000	0.7500	0.5000	0.6250	0.7750	0.8978
	Kernel = 5 × 5	1.0000	1.0000	0.7500	0.7500	0.6250	0.8250	0.8075
	Kernel = 7 × 7	1.0000	1.0000	0.7500	0.7500	0.6250	0.8250	0.7228
Gamma Correction	Factor = 0.8	1.0000	0.6250	1.0000	0.7500	0.5000	0.7750	0.6984
CHE	None	0.8750	0.7500	0.7500	0.6250	0.7500	0.7500	0.5039

is conducted by applying AES encryption method to auxiliary information. And the key exchange illustration is depicted in Fig. 6.

In this key exchange method, the Generator (G) is known to both the Sender and Receiver. The Sender generates a random number x and calculates G^x, which is then sent to the Receiver. The Receiver generates a random number y and calculates $G^{(xy)}$, sending G^y back to the Sender. The Sender then calculates $G^{(xy)}$, which is the common key that is shared between the Sender and Receiver. Since x is only known to the Sender and y is only known to the Receiver, any unintended user who tries to read the intermediate packet will not be able to generate $G^{(xy)}$. This method uses AES to encrypt data, and part of $G^{(xy)}$ is used as the initialization vector. The data regarding the Frame number and Block number is encrypted using AES using the shared key. Along with that, the bit sequence which was XORed with the Hash sequence is sent to the Receiver with a cover image. Upon receiving this data, the Receiver decrypts the auxiliary information using the shared key. With the use of auxiliary information and cover image, the hash sequence is calculated. Then, the Receiver performs an XOR operation between the hash sequence and bit sequence to get back the original message.

Table 3. Bit success rates of different techniques in DAVIS 2017 dataset

Attacks	Parameter	Pan's *et al.* [4]	Zou's *et al.* [6]	Tan's *et al.* [7]	Proposed
S&P noise	$\sigma = 0.001$	0.8332	0.7323	0.9986	1.000
	$\sigma = 0.005$	0.6169	0.4252	0.9923	1.000
	$\sigma = 0.01$	0.3413	0.3672	0.9877	1.000
Gaussian noise	$\sigma = 0.001$	0.3055	0.5739	0.7005	1.000
	$\sigma = 0.005$	0.2075	0.5171	0.6485	1.000
	$\sigma = 0.01$	0.2250	0.1330	0.6198	1.000
Speckle noise	$\sigma = 0.01$	0.4959	0.5250	0.8000	1.000
Speckle noise	$\sigma = 0.05$	0.3002	0.5152	0.7877	1.000
JPEG compression	Q = 70	0.7717	0.8030	0.9698	1.000
JPEG compression	Q = 90	0.8833	0.8897	0.8667	1.000
Centered Cropping	Ratio = 10%	0.2267	0.0467	0.3571	1.000
Centered Cropping	Ratio = 20%	0.0853	0.0213	0.1524	1.000
Rotation	Angle = 10°	0.0333	0.0131	0.2476	1.000
Rotation	Angle = 15°	0.0333	0.0067	0.1753	1.000
Mean filtering	Window size = 3 × 3	0.5958	0.5822	0.6197	1.000
Mean filtering	Window size = 5 × 5	0.3542	0.2788	0.4429	1.000
Median filtering	Window size = 3 × 3	0.7542	0.6978	0.6992	1.000
Median filtering	Window size = 5 × 5	0.5214	0.4517	0.5479	1.000

Table 4. Accuracy at different methods on UCF101 dataset

Attacks	Variance (σ)	Tan *et al.* [7]	Pan *et al.* [4]	Zhang *et al.* [8]	Proposed
Gaussian noise	0.001	0.7005	0.7889	0.9139	**1.0000**
	0.005	0.6485	0.7889	0.8292	**1.0000**
	0.01	0.6198	0.7821	0.7473	**1.0000**
Salt and pepper noise	0.001	0.9986	0.9559	0.9763	**1.0000**
	0.005	0.9923	0.9063	0.9504	**1.0000**
	0.01	0.9877	0.8731	0.9186	**1.0000**
Speckle noise	0.001	0.8235	0.9150	0.9466	**1.0000**
	0.005	0.8098	0.8698	0.8829	**1.0000**
	0.01	0.8000	0.8431	0.7952	**1.0000**
H.264-encoded compressed MPEG-4 file (.mp4 file)	None	0.9589	0.9172	0.9594	**0.9824**
Motion-compressed JPEG 2000 file (.mj2 file)	None	0.8476	0.9676	0.9790	**0.9786**

Table 5. Time cost comparison

Methods	Pan *et al.* [4]	Zou *et al.* [6]	Tan *et al.* [7]	Zhang *et al.* [8]	Proposed
Time cost (s/B)	1.3769	1.2994	0.7416	0.1755	**0.1607**

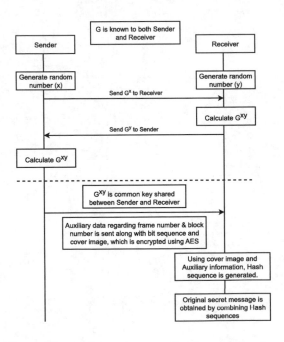

Fig. 6. Key exchange between Sender and Receiver

5 Conclusion

This paper introduces a novel technique of secret data sharing through coverless steganography using Local Binary Pattern (LBP) before bit-plane segmentation. The proposed approach utilizes multiple mappings of a single frame by dividing it into bit-planes, and mapping hash sequences are generated from each bit-plane. The mapping relation is established by comparing corresponding sub-block average median intensity values. The results demonstrate that the proposed scheme outperforms existing techniques with five times higher capacity per frame than Pan's method, stronger robustness, low time cost for mapping, and better extraction accuracy against most noises and attacks. The future direction will focus on enhancing the effective capacity per frame and robustness against various video attacks such as trans-coding and frame rate changes.

References

1. Qin, J., Luo, Y., Xiang, X., Tan, Y., Huang, H.: Coverless image steganography: a survey. IEEE Access **7**, 171372–171394 (2019)
2. Debnath, S., Mohapatra, R.K.: A study on secret data sharing through coverless steganography. In: 2022 2nd International Conference on Artificial Intelligence and Signal Processing (AISP), pp. 1–6. IEEE (2022)
3. Dalal, M., Juneja, M.: A secure and robust video steganography scheme for covert communication in h. 264/avc. Multimedia Tools Appl. 80(9), 14383–14407 (2021)
4. Pan, N., Qin, J., Tan, Y., Xiang, X., Hou, G.: A video coverless information hiding algorithm based on semantic segmentation. EURASIP J. Image Video Process. **2020**(1), 1–18 (2020)
5. Meng, L., Jiang, X., Zhang, Z., Li, Z., Sun, T.: Coverless video steganography based on maximum dc coefficients arXiv preprint arXiv:2012.06809 (2020)
6. Zou, L., Wan, W., Wei, B., Sun, J.: Coverless video steganography based on inter frame combination. Geom. Vis. **1386**, 134–141 (2021)
7. Tan, Y., Qin, J., Xiang, X., Zhang, C., Wang, Z.: Coverless steganography based on motion analysis of video. Secur. Commun. Netw. **2021** (2021)
8. Zhang, C., Tan, Y., Qin, J., Xiang, X.: Coverless video steganography based on audio and frame features. Secur. Commun. Netw. **2022** (2022)
9. Zhou, Z., Sun, H., Harit, R., Chen, X., Sun, X.: Coverless image steganography without embedding. In: Huang, Z., Sun, X., Luo, J., Wang, J. (eds.) ICCCS 2015. LNCS, vol. 9483, pp. 123–132. Springer, Cham (2015). https://doi.org/10.1007/978-3-319-27051-7_11
10. Zhou, Z., Mu, Y., Wu, Q.J.: Coverless image steganography using partial-duplicate image retrieval. Soft. Comput. 23(13), 4927–4938 (2019)
11. Luo, Y., Qin, J., Xiang, X., Tan, Y., Liu, Q., Xiang, L.: Coverless real-time image information hiding based on image block matching and dense convolutional network. J. Real-Time Image Proc. 17(1), 125–135 (2020)
12. Kulkarni, T., Debnath, S., Kumar, J., Mohapatra, R.K.: DCT based robust coverless information hiding scheme with high capacity. In: 2023 7th International Conference on Trends in Electronics and Informatics (ICOEI), pp. 358–364. IEEE (2023)

13. Zhang, X., Peng, F., Long, M.: Robust coverless image steganography based on DCT and LDA topic classification. IEEE Trans. Multimedia **20**(12), 3223–3238 (2018)
14. Panda, S.K., Panda, C.S.: A review on image classification using bag of features approach. Int. J. Comput. Sci. Eng. **7**(6), 538–542 (2019)
15. Yuan, C., Xia, Z., Sun, X.: Coverless image steganography based on sift and BOF. J. Internet Technol. **18**(2), 435–442 (2017)
16. Huang, D., Shan, C., Ardabilian, M., Wang, Y., Chen, L.: Local binary patterns and its application to facial image analysis: a survey. IEEE Trans. Syst. Man, Cybern. Part C (Appl. Rev.) **41**(6), 765–781 (2011)
17. Pont-Tuset, J., Perazzi, F., Caelles, S., Arbeláez, P., Sorkine-Hornung, A., Van Gool, L.: The 2017 Davis challenge on video object segmentation, arXiv preprint arXiv:1704.00675 (2017)
18. Soomro, K., Zamir, A.R., Shah, M.: Ucf101: a dataset of 101 human actions classes from videos in the wild, arXiv preprint arXiv:1212.0402 (2012)

A Deep Face Antispoofing System with Hardware Implementation for Real-Time Applications

Saiyed Umer[1], Shubham Sarvadeo Singh[2], Vikram Kangotra[2], and Ranjeet Kumar Rout[2(✉)]

[1] Computer Science and Engineering, Aliah University, Kolkata, India
[2] Computer Science and Engineering, National Institute of Technology, Srinagar, Jammu and Kashmir, India
ranjeetkumarrout@nitsri.ac.in

Abstract. A deep learning-based face anti-spoofing system has been proposed here. This work has been implemented in four segments. Firstly, an image preprocessing task is performed to extract the facial region. Then, the texture analysis of the facial region is performed to compute discriminant features. For this, a robust approach to deep learning techniques is needed, starting with defining some convolutional neural network (CNN) architectures for feature computation, followed by the classification of genuine vs. imposter face liveliness. The motivation of this work is to find both software- and hardware-based solutions to access biometric-based real-time systems through robust and vigorous face-liveliness detection techniques. The recognition system's performances are further improved by image acquisition-challenging issues, image augmentation, fine-tuning, transfer learning, and the fusion of various trained CNN models. Finally, the above steps have been embedded in Raspberry Pi devices to build the system for real-time applications. The experimentation with two benchmark databases, NUAA and CASIA Replay-Attack, and comparing the performance with some well-known methods relating to the proposed system area show the proposed system's superiority.

Keywords: Face-liveliness · Anti-spoofing · CNN · Fusion · Raspberry-Pi

1 Introduction

In recent times, the reliance on technology has been increasing very rapidly. Advanced computers and computations are helping to fulfill diverse requirements. The rapid demand for technology was made apparent recently during the COVID pandemic. The need for virtualization roared into the market as every educational institute resorted to online mode and companies brought work home. Thanks to some of the existing advanced technologies, like passwords, pattern locks, fingerprints, biometric authentication, and biometric securities, which

H. Kaur et al. (Eds.): CVIP 2023, CCIS 2009, pp. 269–282, 2024.
https://doi.org/10.1007/978-3-031-58181-6_23

boost security and confidentiality. Imposters these days use various techniques to bypass biometric security [10]. Presentation and Indirect attacks are two types of spoofing techniques in practice nowadays. Various efforts have been made to tackle these vulnerabilities and are in progress using AI and deep learning. A robust biometric anti-spoofing model is the need of the hour for enhancing security [17].

The biometric anti-spoofing system is a technology that uses biometric data to prevent fraudulent attempts to access secure systems or information. This is typically done by comparing the biometric data of the person attempting to access the system, such as their fingerprints or facial features, to a reference sample to verify their identity [8]. One standard biometric anti-spoofing system is a liveness detection system, which uses various methods to determine whether the biometric data presented is from a live person or a fake copy. Another method of biometric anti-spoofing is to use behavioural biometric data, such as the way a person types on a keyboard or the way they move their mouse. Overall, biometric anti-spoofing systems are important for ensuring the security and integrity of sensitive information, and systems protect against fraud and other cyber threats. There are a few ways to address the challenges and issues associated with biometric antispoofing systems. One approach is to use multiple sensors and algorithms to capture and analyze different aspects of biometric data to improve the system's accuracy and reliability. Another solution is to use liveness detection algorithms to identify fake copies of biometric data. These algorithms can analyze biometric data for signs of authenticity, such as the movements of a person's facial features or the way they press their fingerprint onto a scanner. Overall, addressing the challenges of biometric antispoofing systems requires a combination of technical and non-technical solutions to ensure their effectiveness and success of the systems. The objectives of this paper are: (i) To propose a deep learning-based convolutional neural network (CNN) architecture to extract discriminant facial features and for face liveliness detection during online authentication; (ii) To provide a unified hardware/software framework for person liveliness Devices and Applications. The remaining content of this paper is represented as follows: The work relating to biometric anti-spoofing has been demonstrated in the second Section. The ways of implementing the proposed methodology are discussed in detail in the third Section. The system proposed in this study has been experimented with to validate the system proposed in this study, and the results are reported in the fourth section. The outcomes of this work are well concluded in the last Section.

2 Related Work

A Generative Adversarial network-based speaker Antispoofing system has been proposed in [23]. There exist several hand-crafted features like LBP [7], HoG [16], SIFT [9], and SURF [2] are used for facial features extraction for face antispoofing systems. The different color spaces such as HSV and YCbCr [2] and the Fourier spectrum [5] are utilized for the face antispoofing system. A patchNet deep learning model with patch-wise detection for face antispoofing systems has been proposed in [14]. A face antispoofing system to handle video replay attacks with tracking eye-blinking and lip movement is performed in [3]. The introduction of handling physical domain attacks with the adversarial spoof image for face antispoofing systems has been developed in [19]. As we know, any biometric antispoofing and recognition system truly depends on the feature representation of that biometric trait. So, some good methods for analyzing the texture patterns in the biometric trait have been demonstrated in [11,12], and citehossain2021unified. A well-known method of Generative adversarial networks for biometric anti-spoofing has been proposed in [23] for text-to-speech and voice conversion-based spoofing attacks for automatic speaker verification systems. A biometric authentication smart card system-on-a-chip with the integration of an analog front-end for fingerprint sensors has been proposed in [24]. A MultiModal Mobile-based fusion of visual and auditory modalities for a Face Anti-Spoofing System is implemented in [25]. Xu et al. implemented a JPEG Codec Hardware IP core for CE security systems for Retinal Biometric traits in [26]. A detailed discussion about implementing the proposed methodology has been demonstrated in the below sections.

3   Proposed Methodology

One of the main challenges is ensuring that the system is accurate and reliable. Biometric data can vary from person to person, and there can be differences in the quality of the data captured by different sensors. This can make it difficult to verify the identity of individuals using the system consistently. Another challenge is dealing with fake copies of biometric data. Technology advancements have made it increasingly easy to create fake copies of biometric data, such as fingerprints or facial scans. Biometric anti-spoofing systems must be able to accurately distinguish between real and fake biometric data to be effective. There can be challenges with user acceptance and adoption of biometric anti-spoofing systems. Some people may be uncomfortable using biometric data for security purposes or may find the systems inconvenient. This can make it challenging to implement the systems effectively. Implementing biometric anti-spoofing systems requires careful planning and consideration of these and other challenges. For better understanding and clarity, a working-flow diagram about the proposed face anti-spoofing system has been designed in Fig. 1, where all four segments such as 'image-preprocessing', 'feature computation followed by classification', 'real-time spoofing detection to preserve from attack', and 'embedding with hardware implementation', are shown. From this figure, it has been shown that face liveliness detection is being performed by the trained CNN model, which is trained by the detected facial regions. As the end product, the hardware implementation is done of the derived face liveliness detection system.

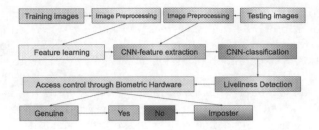

Fig. 1. Overview of working-flow for the proposed methodology.

3.1 Image Preprocessing

The first step in the implementation of the proposed system is image preprocessing. Here, the input data is a sequence of images in the form of a video. Each image is preprocessed to extract the facial texture as a region of interest. A tree-structured part model [22] is employed to detect the facial region from the given image. The detected facial region undergoes some image alignments and is then cropped and resized to a pre-defined image $\mathcal{F}$ of the size of $n \times n \times 3$ (Fig. 2). The noise is deliberately added to an image wherein the pixels are randomly converted to black or completely white. This is done to avoid overfitting the dataset on the wrong element and ensure that the model's performance remains stable despite the disturbances. The pixel values of the extracted facial region are rescaled within a confined range of [0,1], which helps regarding the issue of propagating gradients. This way, the model learns more efficiently by generalizing various situations through several image challenges. The detected facial region $\mathcal{F}$ undergoes feature computations.

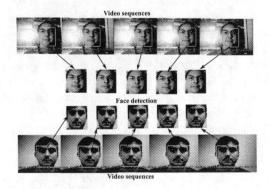

Fig. 2. Face region of interest extraction for the proposed system.

3.2   Feature Computation for Prediction

The extraction of features from processed biometric traits is a crucial task. Since each biometric trait is rich in texture information, extracting valuable and distinctive texture information takes time and effort. During recognition, each preprocessed biometric trait undergoes the feature representation task. Then, features in the form of a feature vector corresponding to each input image arc computed. Several handcrafting methods exist; transformed, structural, and statistical-based features are commonly used in practices [1]. In the current state-of-the-art computer vision and pattern recognition methods, CNN based on deep learning (DL) features have succeeded wildly. The modern generic CNN features have improved capabilities to articulate and handle situations in unconstrained imaging environments with outstanding performance. Here, using the concept of deep learning, the Convolutional Neural Networks (CNN) architecture is proposed using some blocks. Each block comprises mainly three layers: convolution, pooling, and fully connected. The convolutional and pooling layers perform feature extraction, whereas a fully connected layer transforms the extracted features into the final output. Optimizable feature extractors and kernels are crossed with the input images (tensors) to obtain the feature map. This process is repeated, applying multiple kernels to represent different features of the input tensor effectively. The convolution output is passed through an activation function (here, a Rectified linear unit (ReLU) is used). Max-pooling is then applied over the feature map, which extracts the fragments from it and outputs the maximum value from each fragment, discarding all other values. The final output feature maps are flattened, converted to a 1-D array, and passed to the dense, fully connected neural network with the same number of output nodes as the number of classes. In this training process, parameters like kernels in the convolution layer and weights in the dense layer are optimized through the backpropagation method, where the loss function and gradient descent optimization techniques play an important role. The examples of these layers with the flow of functionalities have been demonstrated in Fig. 3.

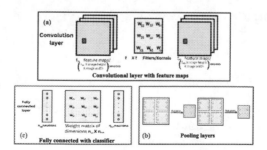

Fig. 3. (a) Convolution layer, (b) Average pooling operation and Max pooling operation, (c) Fully connected layer.

Hence, with these layers, the proposed CNN architecture is built using six main and two-dense blocks, shown in Fig. 4. Here, each main block is composed of a sequence of Convolution ($\mathcal{F}_{n \times n \times r}$ is convolved with kernels of size (3 × 3)) → Activation (Rectified Linear Unit (ReLU)) → Batch-normalization → Maxpooling layers. Each dense block is performed based on the sequence of Batch-normalization → Activation → Dropout → Softmax classifier. The total number of parameters is 1,274,167, among which 1,270,327 is Trainable and 3,840 is Non-trainable. The purposes of the arrangement of these blocks are: (i) to extract the discriminant features from the input facial pattern, (ii) to enhance the classification performance to distinguish well between genuine and imposter facial patterns, (iii) to reduce the overfitting problems during training the classification problem. A list of parameters has been demonstrated in Fig. 5 corresponds to each layer of the proposed CNN_1 architecture.

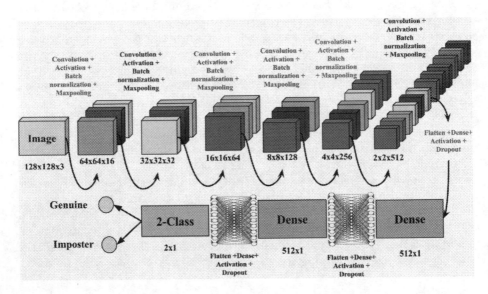

Fig. 4. A CNN architecture proposed for feature representation and classification purposes.

3.3   Qualitative Implementation into Hardware Specification

The above deep learning-based CNN model is deployed to use its responses for the hardware-based implementation. The obtained deep learning model has been deployed on a palm-sized, low cost and lightweight hardware - Raspberry Pi 4. It consists of an ARM Cortex-A72 64-bit CPU working at a frequency of 1.5 GHZ with a RAM of 2 GB. It has a Micro-SD card slot for loading the operating system, Raspberry Pi OS (previously called Raspbian), and data storage. VNC Server, which runs on the Raspberry Pi, and VNC Viewer, which runs on the local computer, display the Raspberry Pi on the computer. A camera is connected directly to its port to capture real-time images. A Python program

Layer (type)	Output Shape	Param #
conv2d_6 (Conv2D)	(None, 128, 128, 16)	448
batch_normalization_10 (Batc	(None, 128, 128, 16)	64
max_pooling2d_6 (MaxPooling2	(None, 64, 64, 16)	0
dropout_10 (Dropout)	(None, 64, 64, 16)	0
conv2d_7 (Conv2D)	(None, 64, 64, 32)	4640
batch_normalization_11 (Batc	(None, 64, 64, 32)	128
max_pooling2d_7 (MaxPooling2	(None, 32, 32, 32)	0
dropout_11 (Dropout)	(None, 32, 32, 32)	0
conv2d_8 (Conv2D)	(None, 32, 32, 64)	18496
batch_normalization_12 (Batc	(None, 32, 32, 64)	256
max_pooling2d_8 (MaxPooling2	(None, 16, 16, 64)	0
dropout_12 (Dropout)	(None, 16, 16, 64)	0
conv2d_9 (Conv2D)	(None, 16, 16, 128)	73856
batch_normalization_13 (Batc	(None, 16, 16, 128)	512
max_pooling2d_9 (MaxPooling2	(None, 8, 8, 128)	0
dropout_13 (Dropout)	(None, 8, 8, 128)	0
conv2d_10 (Conv2D)	(None, 8, 8, 256)	295168

batch_normalization_14 (Batc	(None, 8, 8, 256)	1024
max_pooling2d_10 (MaxPooling	(None, 4, 4, 256)	0
dropout_14 (Dropout)	(None, 4, 4, 256)	0
conv2d_11 (Conv2D)	(None, 4, 4, 512)	1180160
batch_normalization_15 (Batc	(None, 4, 4, 512)	2048
max_pooling2d_11 (MaxPooling	(None, 2, 2, 512)	0
dropout_15 (Dropout)	(None, 2, 2, 512)	0
flatten_2 (Flatten)	(None, 2048)	0
dense_6 (Dense)	(None, 512)	1049088
batch_normalization_16 (Batc	(None, 512)	2048
activation_4 (Activation)	(None, 512)	0
dropout_16 (Dropout)	(None, 512)	0
dense_7 (Dense)	(None, 512)	262656
batch_normalization_17 (Batc	(None, 512)	2048
activation_5 (Activation)	(None, 512)	0
dropout_17 (Dropout)	(None, 512)	0
dense_8 (Dense)	(None, 2)	1026

Total params: 2,893,888
Trainable params: 2,889,682
Non-trainable params: 4,064

Fig. 5. List of parameters employed at each layer of proposed CNN architecture.

is incorporated to process and feed the captured image into the model as input. The output is reflected on the corresponding LEDs, green LED for a real face and Red LED for an imposter. Depending on the needs, such hardware implementation can prevent unauthorized access to face-detecting machines or other security devices. The architectural diagram describing each point of the employed Raspberry Pi has been demonstrated in Fig. 6(a). In contrast, the working flow of the proposed system in the employed Raspberry Pi has been demonstrated in Fig. 6(b).

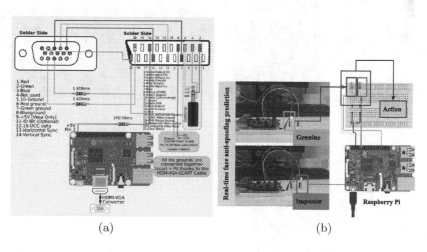

(a)   (b)

Fig. 6. Demonstration of (a) employed Raspberry Pi with (b) its working flow for real-time face liveliness detection.

4   Experiments

Here, the experimental results and the hyperparameter settings are described, and performing model comparisons are made with other existing liveness detection methods. For experimental purposes, two standard benchmark databases, such as NUAA database [21], and Replay-Attack database [20], have been employed. The first database, NUAA, comprises genuine and imposter photographs of 15 people (subject). Initially, this database is prepared by capturing images with a frame rate of 20 frames per second of both live subjects and the frames of their images. The captured images are frontal with neutral expressions. Some actions like blinking eyes and movements of heads are prohibited during image capturing for this database. So, after extracting frames into images, there are 3491 training and 9123 testing images. Among 3491 training, 1743 genuine and 1748 imposter images are obtained. Our second experimentation database, Replay-Attack, comprises 50 subjects in 1300 video clips. Each video is captured under different lighting conditions through a webcam camera. The videos are composed of real and attack clips. So, 7200 images for training and 4485 for testing are employed for this experiment. Among the training images, 1200 are genuine, and 6000 are imposter. Among the testing images, 1600 are genuine, and 2885 are imposters. The description of the NUAA and Relay-Attack databases are demonstrated in Table 1 and database image samples are shown in Fig. 7(a), and 7(b) respectively.

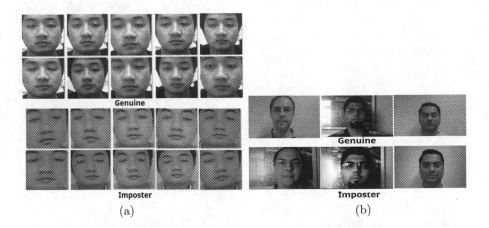

Fig. 7. Some image samples from the (a) NUAA, (b) Replay-Attack database.

4.1   Results with Discussion

The proposed system uses an NVIDIA 4 GB GPU with 512 GB RAM and an Intel Core i7 processor. The proposed system is based on face biometric

Table 1. Description of employed databases.

NUAA database			Relay-Attack Database		
Class	Train	Test	Class	Train	Test
Genuine	1743	3362	Genuine	1200	1600
Imposter	1748	5761	Imposter	6000	2885
Total	3491	9123	Total	7200	4485

traits. This work is coded in Python using the following libraries: TensorFlow: for implementing, training, and deploying machine learning models; Keras: to implement neural network architectures that run on both CPUs and GPUs. Matplotlib: illustrating interactive charts and images. The proposed model is trained with an Adam optimizer and a 0.001 learning rate. The below factors affect the proposed system's performance.

(a) **Epoch vs. Batch effect:** Learning weight depends on batches and epochs. These two factors influence the CNN model's learning capabilities. The performance evaluation with the adjustment of epoch and batch is shown in Fig. 8, where it is observed that the performance is better for 32 batch-size and 1000 epochs, so there are employed for further experiments.

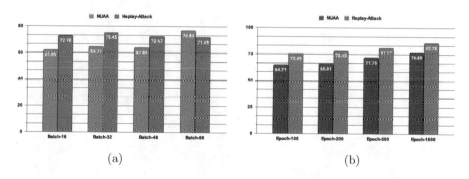

(a)   (b)

Fig. 8. Effect of (a) Batch-sizes vs. (b) # of epochs during CNN parameter learning.

(b) **Image-augmentation Effect:** The methods employed in [13] are used here for image augmentation, where seventeen augmented images are obtained for each image, where Affine transformations, flipping, and image filtering processes are utilized for image augmentation. The effect of data augmentation techniques is demonstrated in Fig. 9, which shows the performance increases of the proposed system.

(c) **Fine-tuning with transfer learning effect:** The first approach uses the CNN architecture CNN_1 with the corresponding image sizes (128×128 3), i.e., refreshed models (fine-tuning). While in the second approach, the CNN architecture is retrained (transfer-learning) with progressive image resizing such

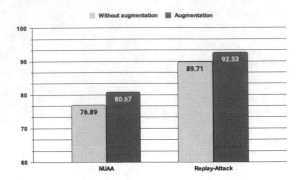

Fig. 9. Effect of data augmentation techniques.

as $96 \times 96 \times 3$ that derives CNN_2 model, and $144 \times 144 \times 3$, which derives CNN_3 model such that during CNN_3 learning, an upper layer is added to CNN_1. During CNN_2, the upper layer of CNN_1 is removed. The usability of CNN_2 and CNN_3 are that (i) the CNN architecture is trained with progressive image resizing with lower to upper abstraction of images, and (ii) the discriminant feature analysis is being performed to reduce the overfitting problems. The performance of the proposed system due to CNN_1, CNN_2, and CNN_3 are shown in Table 2.

Table 2. Fine-tuning with and transfer learning effects on the proposed systems' performance.

Database	Refreshed model		
	CNN-1	CNN-2	CNN-3
NUAA	80.67	81.32	85.89
Relay-Attack	92.53	92.71	93.78
	Re-trained model		
	CNN-1	CNN-2	CNN-3
NUAA	83.33	82.05	89.61
Relay-Attack	95.67	95.19	98.61

(d) **Fusion:** The classifier's decision obtained due to CNN_1, CNN_2, and CNN_3 are fused using the decision-level fusion technique to enhance the performance of the proposed system (Fig. 10). Let's assume that $\alpha = (\alpha_1, \alpha_2)$, $\beta = (\beta_1, \beta_2)$, and $\gamma = (\gamma_1, \gamma_2)$ be the binary decisions during each subject's liveliness detection due to CNN_1, CNN_2, and CNN_3 respectively. Here, the decision level fusion is defined as (δ_1, δ_2), where $\delta_1 = \alpha_1 \bigoplus \beta_1 \bigoplus \gamma_1$, and $\delta_2 = \alpha_2 \bigoplus \beta_2 \bigoplus \gamma_2$. Here $\bigoplus$ denotes the OR-ing operator and with the majority voting analysis, the subject's genuineness is decided.

The performance of the proposed face antispoofing system has been compared with Yu [18], Hasan [4], Liu [6], and Yang [15] methods corresponds to

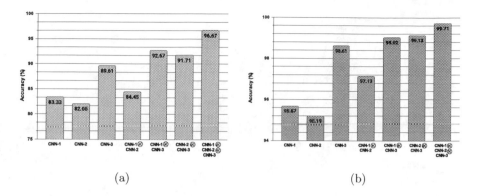

(a)   (b)

Fig. 10. Effect of decision level fusions.

NUAA and Relay-Attack databases. These competing methods have been implemented corresponding to their papers, and the features are extracted accordingly. The performance of these competing methods has been tested under the same training-testing protocols employed by the proposed system, which are reported in Table 3; it has been observed that the proposed system overcomes other competing methods employed for this work. Finally, the implemented system has been embedded in Raspberry Pi. The execution starts from the data acquisition through the A/D board to all the components, such as image preprocessing, feature extraction, and classification. Each step of face liveliness detection has been embedded in the Raspberry Pi 4 Model B. The Raspberry model, configuration, and the proposed face antispoofing system's performance in the Raspberry Pi have been demonstrated in Table 4.

Table 3. Performance comparison with some existing methods.

Method	NUAA	Relay-Attack
	Acc.(%)	Acc.(%)
Yu [18]	93.34	96.14
Hasan [4]	91.71	98.05
Liu [6]	95.52	99.31
Yang [15]	94.41	98.16
Proposed	96.67	99.71

Table 4. Proposed system's performance in the employed Raspberry Pi model.

Model	Raspberry pi 4 Model B			
Configuration	**CPU**-Broadcom, BCM2711, quad-core, Cortex-A72, 64-bit, 1.5 GHz			
	RAM-4 GB, **GPIO**-40-pins, **Power sources**-USB-C			
	USB - 2 x USB3.0 + 2 x USB2.0 + USB-C OTG			
Performance in millisecond (ms)				
Database	Image size	Face detection	Feature extraction	Liveliness detection	Total
NUAA	$200 \times 200 \times 3$	641.21	64.13	22.15	727.49
Relay-Attack	$200 \times 200 \times 3$	710.23			796.51

5 Conclusions

This paper proposes a biometric antispoofing system by performing face liveliness detection. The proposed system has been implemented using four steps. The first step is image preprocessing, where the facial region of interest is segmented from the input image. The technique employed for face detection accepts several challenging issues that occurred during image acquisition, both by the camera device and human-created noises. Then some core building blocks of convolutional neural network (CNN) architecture have been proposed to extract discriminant features from the facial region followed by their classification to distinguish the genuine and imposter facial patterns for liveliness detection of a person. The proposed systems' performance has been improved utilizing several factors, such as batch vs. epoch variations, image-augmentation, fine-tuning, transfer-learning, and fusion of binary decisions of different CNN models due to progressive-image resizing. Finally, all these steps are integrated and embedded into a Raspberry-pi device for real-time applications. The proposed systems' performance has been tested using NUAA and CASIA-Replay attack databases and compared with existing state-of-the-art methods that show the proposed system outperforms other competing methods.

References

1. Bisogni, C., Castiglione, A., Hossain, S., Narducci, F., Umer, S.: Impact of deep learning approaches on facial expression recognition in healthcare industries. IEEE Trans. Industr. Inf. **18**(8), 5619–5627 (2022)
2. Boulkenafet, Z., Komulainen, J., Hadid, A.: Face antispoofing using speeded-up robust features and fisher vector encoding. IEEE Signal Process. Lett. **24**(2), 141–145 (2016)
3. Hadiprakoso, R.B., Setiawan, H., et al.: Face anti-spoofing using CNN classifier & face liveness detection. In: 2020 3rd International Conference on Information and Communications Technology (ICOIACT), pp. 143–147. IEEE (2020)
4. Hasan, M.R., Mahmud, S.H., Li, X.Y.: Face anti-spoofing using texture-based techniques and filtering methods. In: Journal of Physics: Conference Series, vol. 1229, p. 012044. IOP Publishing (2019)

5. Li, J., Wang, Y., Tan, T., Jain, A.K.: Live face detection based on the+ analysis of fourier spectra. In: Biometric Technology for Human Identification, vol. 5404, pp. 296–303. SPIE (2004)
6. Liu, Y., Jourabloo, A., Liu, X.: Learning deep models for face anti-spoofing: binary or auxiliary supervision. In: Proceedings of the IEEE Conference on Computer Vision and Pattern Recognition, pp. 389–398 (2018)
7. Määttä, J., Hadid, A., Pietikäinen, M.: Face spoofing detection from single images using micro-texture analysis. In: 2011 International Joint Conference on Biometrics (IJCB), pp. 1–7. IEEE (2011)
8. Marcel, S., Nixon, M.S., Li, S.Z.: Handbook of Biometric Anti-Spoofing, vol. 1. Springer, Singapore (2014). https://doi.org/10.1007/978-981-19-5288-3
9. Patel, K., Han, H., Jain, A.K.: Secure face unlock: spoof detection on smartphones. IEEE Trans. Inf. Forensics Secur. **11**(10), 2268–2283 (2016)
10. Sardar, A., Umer, S., Rout, R.K., Wang, S.H., Tanveer, M.: A secure face recognition for IoT-enabled healthcare system. ACM Trans. Sens. Netw. (TOSN) (2022)
11. Umer, S., Dhara, B.C., Chanda, B.: Face recognition using fusion of feature learning techniques. Measurement **146**, 43–54 (2019)
12. Umer, S., Dhara, B.C., Chanda, B.: NIR and VW iris image recognition using ensemble of patch statistics features. Vis. Comput. **35**, 1327–1344 (2019)
13. Umer, S., Sardar, A., Dhara, B.C., Rout, R.K., Pandey, H.M.: Person identification using fusion of iris and periocular deep features. Neural Netw. **122**, 407–419 (2020)
14. Wang, C.Y., Lu, Y.D., Yang, S.T., Lai, S.H.: Patchnet: a simple face anti-spoofing framework via fine-grained patch recognition. In: Proceedings of the IEEE/CVF Conference on Computer Vision and Pattern Recognition, pp. 20281–20290 (2022)
15. Yang, J., Lei, Z., Li, S.Z.: Learn convolutional neural network for face anti-spoofing. arXiv preprint arXiv:1408.5601 (2014)
16. Yang, J., Lei, Z., Liao, S., Li, S.Z.: Face liveness detection with component dependent descriptor. In: 2013 International Conference on Biometrics (ICB), pp. 1–6. IEEE (2013)
17. Yang, X., et al.: Face anti-spoofing: model matters, so does data. In: Proceedings of the IEEE/CVF Conference on Computer Vision and Pattern Recognition, pp. 3507–3516 (2019)
18. Yu, Z., Li, X., Niu, X., Shi, J., Zhao, G.: Face anti-spoofing with human material perception. In: Vedaldi, A., Bischof, H., Brox, T., Frahm, J.-M. (eds.) ECCV 2020 Part VII. LNCS, vol. 12352, pp. 557–575. Springer, Cham (2020). https://doi.org/10.1007/978-3-030-58571-6_33
19. Zhang, B., Tondi, B., Barni, M.: Attacking CNN-based anti-spoofing face authentication in the physical domain. arXiv preprint arXiv:1910.00327 (2019)
20. Zhang, S., et al.: A dataset and benchmark for large-scale multi-modal face anti-spoofing. In: Proceedings of the IEEE/CVF Conference on Computer Vision and Pattern Recognition, pp. 919–928 (2019)
21. Zhang, Z., Yan, J., Liu, S., Lei, Z., Yi, D., Li, S.Z.: A face antispoofing database with diverse attacks. In: 2012 5th IAPR International Conference on Biometrics (ICB), pp. 26–31. IEEE (2012)
22. Zhu, X., Ramanan, D.: Face detection, pose estimation, and landmark localization in the wild. In: 2012 IEEE Conference on Computer Vision and Pattern Recognition, pp. 2879–2886. IEEE (2012)
23. Gomez-Alanis, A., Gonzalez-Lopez, J., Peinado, A.: GANBA: generative adversarial network for biometric anti-spoofing. Appl. Sci. **12**, 1454 (2022)

24. Chang, J., et al.: A 1.05-A/m minimum magnetic field strength single-chip, fully integrated biometric smart card SoC achieving 792.5-ms transaction time with anti-spoofing fingerprint authentication. IEEE J. Solid-State Circ. **58**, 155–166 (2022)
25. Kong, C., Zheng, K., Liu, Y., Wang, S., Rocha, A., Li, H.: M3fas: an accurate and robust multimodal mobile face anti-spoofing system. ArXiv Preprint ArXiv:2301.12831 (2023)
26. Xu, W., et al.: Anti-spoofing facial authentication based on COTS RFID. IEEE Trans. Mob. Comput. (2023)

Experimental Evaluation of Needle Tip Prediction Using Kalman Filtering Approach

Surender Hans[1(✉)], Payal Bansal[2], Geetika Mathur[2], Karan Nathwani[3], and M. Felix Orlando[4]

[1] Department of Electrical Engineering, Malaviya National Institute of Technology, Jaipur, India
surender.ee@mnit.ac.in
[2] Department of Electronics and Communication Engineering, Poornima College of Engineering, Jaipur, India
[3] Department of Electrical Engineering, IIT Jammu, Jagti, India
karan.nathwani@iitjammu.ac.in
[4] Department of Electrical Engineering, Indian Institute of Technology Roorkee, Roorkee, Uttarakhand, India
felixfee@iitr.ac.in

Abstract. In both manual and autonomous needle steering procedures involved in percutaneous interventions, target reaching accuracy depends on feedback of the actual needle tip position through imaging feedback modalities such as CT, MRI, and US. For online analysis, US imaging modality is preferred compared to others. In this article, we propose a linear Kalman filtering based online prediction of a brachytherapy needle using US imaging modality. Extensive experimental studies were performed to confirm the accuracy of the needle prediction in both artificial and biological tissues. From the results, we show that the proposed methodology gives clinically acceptable outcomes as we compare with the standard electromagnetic (EM) sensory feedback values of the needle tip position.

Keywords: Needle Steering · Robust Control · Nonholonomic System · Minimal Invasive Surgery

1 Introduction

IN general, minimal invasive therapeutic procedures such as biopsy, brachytherapy, chemotherapy, radiofrequency thermal ablation, anesthesia and cryoablation involve insertion of several needles into the target region of patients [1]. The primary focus of these percutaneous interventional procedures is the accurate placement of the needle tip in the target region thereby leading to functional radioactive drug/dose delivery, targeted ablation and definitive diagnostic samples acquisition. Currently, needle interventions are executed in either manual or

H. Kaur et al. (Eds.): CVIP 2023, CCIS 2009, pp. 283–292, 2024.
https://doi.org/10.1007/978-3-031-58181-6_24

autonomous fashion with the guidance of imaging modalities such as computed tomography (CT), magnetic resonance imaging (MRI) and ultrasound (US). The needle placement accuracy in the target region depends on this feedback which provides the actual tip position of the needle. Nearly one third of the minimal invasive surgical procedures are inadequate due to the erroneous tumor locations and improper needle placement, for instance in liver cryoablation cases [2]. Thus, we have planned to develop a real-time needle tip localization technique based on simple linear Kalman filtering approach as a solution to address the challenge towards the significant cases of inadequate therapeutic procedures.

Several researchers have extensively worked on the prediction of needle tip during percutaneous interventions in tissue environments [1–20]. For the localization of needle tip position in US medical imaging modality, Ding and Fenster [3] proposed an Hough transform based detection of biopsy needle with less computational effect using coarse-fine search and optimal imaging resolution detection. Later, Qiu et al. [4] have proposed a new real time needle segmentation procedure using real time grey scale Hough transform especially for biopsy application. Then, Zhao et al. [5,6] have used random sample consensus (RANSAC) and speckle tracking methods with Kalman filtering using 3D US for the estimation of needle position and its direction. Renfrew et al. [7] have presented a probabilistic approach for active localization of needle and specific targets in the tissue through extensive simulation study. However, an hardware implementation has not been done by them.

In the same year, Mathiassen et al. [8] have proposed a novel real-time needle tip estimation (with B-mode US images) using a unique set of features to find the needle tip location using both position and orientation information of the needle tip from an optical tracking system. They claim that this method avoids the need of human interference in segmentation process. Likewise, Vrooijink et al. [9] have presented a novel work on the three dimensional tracking of passive flexible needles while insertion in tissue environment using two dimensional US images. In the tracking experiments, they have accomplished an error in both position and orientation that makes the tracking feasible for clinical scenario. Nevertheless, they have not implemented on the biological tissue environment. Using Electromagnetic (EM) trackers, Sadjadi et al. [10] have presented a simulation study involving the needle deflection estimation method with both Kalman and Extended Kalman filters. Their sensitivity analyses show promising outcomes suitable for clinical implementation. Next, to improve the robustness in needle tracking inside tissue, Geraldes and Rocha [11] have presented a neural network approach using Kalman filter. Focusing on real-time application, Zhao et al. [12] have proposed a biopsy needle estimation based on region of interest (ROI) and RANSAC and Kalman (RK) filtering approach. Next, Adebar and Okamura [13] have presented a recursive estimation of position and orientation of a neele within biological tissue through unscented Kalman filter (UKF). In the same year, Zou et al. [14] have compared the estimations of extended Kalman filter (EKF), UKF and particle filter (PF) and found that the estimation accuracy of EKF is worse than PF and UKF. To increase the robustness in needle localization, Kaya and Bebek [15,16] have proposed Gabor filtering based localization technique and have performed experiments in three different tissue phantoms. Then, in 2015, Joseph et al. [17–22] have performed the real-time experiments on closed loop control of an active needle using three different sensory feedbacks. Mathiassen et al. [23] have performed a robust real-time tracking of a needle in 2D US images using Kalman filtering and compared the tracking with a physicians manual observation within the US images. Later in 2018, Mwikirize et al. [24] have proposed a needle tracking method using convolution neural networks (CNN) as a first researcher. In the same year, as a first researcher, Lapouge et al. [25] have executed a multi-rate unscented Kalman filtering for pose and curvature estimation for 3D needle steering. In the last year, Nisha et al. [26] have performed a real-time needle tip localization using KF and compared its performance with that of Canny edge detection. In order to perform a real-time needle tip detection for closed loop control of a robot guided needling system with imaging modality feedback, through this study we are proposing a simple, less computation based KF approach through solid experimental validation.

The rest of the paper is organized as follows: Sect. 2 describes the linear Kalman filtering algorithm employed in our study. In Sect. 3, experimental results of both artificial tissue phantom and biological tissue are discussed elaborately. Finally, concluding remarks are drawn in Sect. 4.

2   Methodology

2.1   Kalman Filtering Algorithm

Kalman filter is an optimal iterative method which contains a set of mathematical model used for estimating the state of the process. In order to optimally estimate an unknown state of a dynamic system with random disturbances [27] and fusing multi sensory measurement data [28], Kalman filter proves to be a promising approach [29]. The filter computes the estimated state by minimizing the mean of the squared error. As it predicts the future state, it can be used to predict and correctly estimate the needle's position.

The actual system is defined as

$$\dot{\psi} = A\psi + Bu \tag{1}$$

$$w = C\psi + E \tag{2}$$

where A and B is the system and control matrices, respectively, w is the system output and E matrix containing noise. Then the estimated system state can be defined as

$$\dot{\hat{\psi}} = A\hat{\psi} + Bu \tag{3}$$

$$\hat{w} = C\hat{\psi} \tag{4}$$

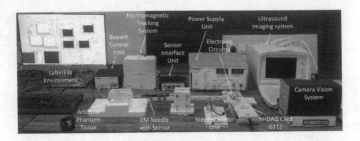

Fig. 1. Experimental setup with artificial tissue phantom.

Fig. 2. Experimental setup with biological tissue.

From Eqs. (1) and (3), we get,

$$\dot{\psi} - \dot{\hat{\psi}} = A\psi - A\hat{\psi} + Z(w - \hat{w})$$

where Z is the kalman gain.

From Eqs. (2) and (4),

$$w - \hat{w} = C(\psi - \hat{\psi})$$

$$\dot{\rho} = A\rho - Z(C\rho)$$

$$\dot{\rho} = (A - ZC)\rho$$

The Z should be chosen such that

$$A - ZC < 0$$

Now, the prediction equation is given by,

$$\hat{\psi}_k = A\hat{\psi}_{k-1} + Bu_k + z_k(w_k - C(\hat{x}_k))$$

where ψ_k is the prediction term given by,

$$\psi_k = A\hat{\psi}_{k-1} + Bu_k$$

and

$$\eta_k = A\eta_{k-1}A^T + Q$$

where η is the covariance matrix which contain disturbance and Q is the matrix which contain noise. To update the prediction state

$$Z_k = \frac{\eta_k C^T}{C \eta_k C^T + E}$$

$$\hat{\psi} = \hat{\psi}_k + z_k(w_k - C\hat{\psi}_k)$$

$$\eta_k = (I - Z_k C)\eta_{k-1}$$

This prediction state of the needle tip represents the real value in terms of noise, which suppresses the view of the needle in the imaging modality.

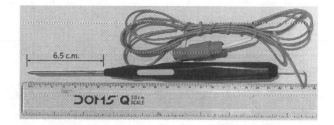

Fig. 3. NDI-Aurora electromagnetic sensing based needle.

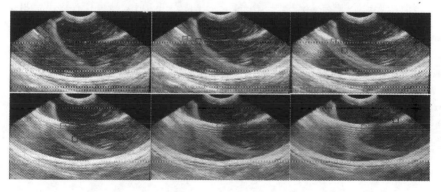

☐ Kalman. ☐ Needle. ☐ Image.

Fig. 4. Experimental setup with biological tissue.

3   Results and Discussion

In general clinical scenario, during percutaneous needing insertion, the needle tip is missing due to the noise in the imaging feedback modality. While performing autonomous or manual needle steering, due to this mis-representative data of the needle tip, agitation happens in the overall system leading to erroneous target reaching with severe tissue trauma. Thus the objective of this research work is to update the needle tip in the tissue environment through linear Kalman filtering algorithm which gives the continuous true position of the needle within the tissue environment.

To observe the efficacy of the Kalman filtering based online needle prediction of the needle tip using US imaging feedback, we have performed real-time experiments involving artificial tissue phantoms and biological tissues. Figures 1 and 2, shows the experimental setups of the NDI-Aurora needle based system for percutaneous interventions in artificial and biological tissues, respectively. The EM sensor integrated brachytherapy NDI-Aurora needle employed in our study is shown in Fig. 3. The components included in the experimental set up are: NDI-Aurora Electromagnetic sensor based needle, stepper motor, NI-DAQ card 6212, motor driver(experimental circuitry), ultrasound imaging system and camera vision system. An insertion depth of up to 6.5 cm is considered in our study with the needle. Due to the linear actuation of the stepper motor unit, the EM sensor-integrated conical tip needle mounted on the gear-train arrangement, moves forward inside the tissue phantom. Ultrasound imaging system tracks the position of a conical needle tip inside the tissue. Based on the initial and present position of the needle tip in the ultrasound image, the Kalman filtering algorithm gives us the estimated position of the needle tip even though the needle is missing inside the tissue due to noise. This estimated conical needle tip trajectory is feedback to the actuation unit of the system. The working demo snap shots of the online needle prediction in comparison to the real value of the needle tip (through EM sensory feedback) and the vision system imaging data is shown in Fig. 4. From the left till the right images of the first and second row, we observe that the Kalman filtering based needle prediction is close enough to the actual needle tip, whereas, the vision system based Canny Edge prediction gives erroneous actual positions of the needle tip. We have considered two cases of needle visibility indicating more noisy (where the needle is invisible inside the tissue environment after a few cm depth way before reaching the target) and less noisy indicating continuous needle tip positioning till the target depth. As shown in Fig. 5(a), the needle trajectory is going upto 4 cm depth inside the artificial tissue phantom. After this distance, the actual needle is missing in the imaging feedback modality. But, based on the past and present values of the

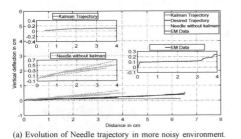
(a) Evolution of Needle trajectory in more noisy environment.

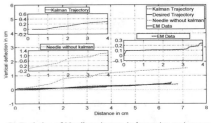
(b) Evolution of Needle trajectory in less noisy environment.

Fig. 5. Comparison of Needle trajectory and EM data in artificial tissue phantom.

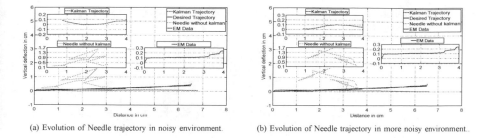

(a) Evolution of Needle trajectory in noisy environment.   (b) Evolution of Needle trajectory in more noisy environment..

Fig. 6. Comparison of Needle trajectory and EM data in biological tissue.

needle tip, Kalman filtering method gives the estimation of needle position till
the depth of desired target point. Through the standard feedback modality by
EM data (giving the accurate measurement of the needle tip), we justify the
true prediction of the needle-tip trajectory given by the Kalman filtering approach (Fig. 5). Then in Fig. 5(b), we have performed the same experiment with
less noisy imaging feedback positioning of the needle. However, the deviation
towards the target depth with respect to the actual needle position is larger by
the vision system based feedback due to noise. As observed here, our approach
based on Kalman filtering predicts the needle tip position more accurately than
the previous case. The same experiment has been done in biological tissue environment (chicken breast) as shown in Fig. 6 (a) and (b). As the biological tissue
is heterogeneous in nature, the vision system data indicating the actual needle
tip position is invisible more as compared to that of the needle steering in arti
ficial tissue phantom (Fig. 5). However, the Kalman filter's needle tip prediction
is as accurate as the EM sensor's data in both the less noisy and more noisy
environments. The experimental summary of performance criteria of the needle
prediction under the respective feedback modalities are given in Table 1. In general, the vision system based needle tip position feedback gives more error as
compared to Kalman filtering based needle tip prediction and the standard EM
sensory feedback. Being the standard sensory feedback in percutaneous needling
interventions, the EM feedback gives a unperturbed performance criteria values
irrespective of the tissue environment [26]. Finally, it is observed from the Table
that Kalman filtering based needle prediction is having the accuracy close to
that of the EM standard feedback, is greater than that of the vision feedback
and is continuously providing the needle tip position (due to which the control
input to the needling system actuator is uniform).

Table 1. Experimental summary of performance criteria[1] with EM needle in artificial and biological tissue.

Tissue Environment	Types of Noisy Environment	Trajectories	RMSE	MAE	SD	Standard Error
Artificial tissue phantom	Less Noisy	Needle trajectory by vision system	0.7894	0.7322	0.4287	0.0347
		Predicted Needle Trajectory by Kalman Filtering	0.0335	0.0023	0.1506	0.0122
		EM sensor based needle trajectory	0.0906	0.0817	0.1477	0.0119
	More Noisy	Needle trajectory by vision system	0.2713	0.0084	0.2216	0.0179
		Predicted Needle Trajectory by Kalman Filtering	0.1512	0.1103	0.0281	0.0023
		EM sensor based needle trajectory	0.0906	0.0817	0.1477	0.0119
Biological tissue	Less Noisy	Needle trajectory by vision system	0.5466	0.3892	0.4132	0.0334
		Predicted Needle Trajectory by Kalman Filtering	0.1885	0.1488	0.0354	0.0029
		EM sensor based needle trajectory	0.0906	0.0817	0.1477	0.0119
	More Noisy	Needle trajectory by vision system	0.8397	0.6574	0.4540	0.0367
		Predicted Needle Trajectory by Kalman Filtering	0.2110	0.1586	0.0369	0.0030
		EM sensor based needle trajectory	0.0906	0.0817	0.1477	0.0119

[1] Unit: cm

3.1 Future Work

Our immediate future work is to implement a robust control strategy to track a given 3D desired trajectory. Currently, the study involves a rigid needle whereas in the near future, we will include active flexible needle so as to predict its complete shape during insertion into the tissue environment.

4 Conclusion

In this research article, we have proposed a linear Kalman filtering based needle tip position prediction during online percutaneous interventions in both artificial and biological tissues. The results obtained through this study are accurate enough in comparison to the standard EM sensory feedback of the needle tip position. Thus, both autonomous and manual needle steering approaches will be benefited by our proposed simple approach which will be helpful in real-time percutaneous clinical tests.

Acknowledgments. The authors would like to thank and acknowledge the full financial funding support from Science and Engineering Research Board (SERB) India (Project No. ECR/2017/001035).

References

1. Abolhassani, N., Patel, R., Moallem, M.: Needle insertion into soft tissue: a survey. Med. Eng. Phys. **29**(4), 413–431 (2007)
2. Mala, T., et al.: Cryoablation of colorectal liver metastases: minimally invasive tumour control. Scand. J. Gastroenterol. **39**(6), 571–578 (2004)
3. Ding, M., Fenster, A.: A real-time biopsy needle segmentation technique using hough transform. Med. Phys. **30**(8), 2222–2233 (2003)
4. Qiu, W., Zhou, H., Ding, M., Zhang, S.: New real time needle segmentation technique using gray-scale Hough transformation. In: Proceedings of SPIE 6789, MIPPR 2007 Medical Imaging, Parallel Processing of Images, and Optimization Techniques (2007)
5. Zhao, Y., Liebgott, H., Cachard, C.: Tracking biopsy needle using Kalman filter and RANSAC algorithm with 3D ultrasound. In: Proceedings of Acoustics, Nantes, France, pp. 231–236 (2012)
6. Zhao, Y., Cachard, C., Liebgott, H.: Automatic needle detection and tracking in 3D ultrasound using an ROI-based RANSAC and kalman method. Ultrason. Imaging **35**(4), 283–306 (2013)
7. Renfrew, M., Bai, Z., Cavusoglu, M.C.: Particle filter based active localization of target and needle in robotic image-guided intervention systems. In: IEEE International Conference on Automation Science and Engineering (CASE), pp. 448–454 (2013)
8. Mathiassen, K., Dall'Alba, D., Muradore, R., Fiorini, P., Elle, O.J.: Real-time biopsy needle tip estimation in 2D ultrasound images. In: IEEE International Conference on Robotics and Automation (ICRA), pp. 4363–4369 (2013)
9. Vrooijink, G.J., Abayazid, M., Misra, S.: Real-time three-dimensional flexible needle tracking using two-dimensional ultrasound. In: IEEE International Conference on Robotics and Automation (ICRA), pp. 1688–1693 (2013)
10. Sadjadi, H., Hashtrudi-Zaad, K., Fichtinger, G.: Fusion of electromagnetic trackers to improve needle deflection estimation: simulation study. IEEE Trans. BioMed. Eng. **60**(10), 2706–2715 (2013)
11. Geraldes, A.A., Rocha, T.S.: A neural network approach for flexible needle tracking in ultrasound images using kalman filter. In: 5th IEEE RAS EMBS International Conference on Biomedical Robotics and Biomechatronics (BioRobs), pp. 70–75 (2014)
12. Zhao, Y., Bernard, A., Cachard, C., Liebgott, H.: Biopsy needle localization and tracking using ROI-RK method. In: Abstract and Applied Analysis, vol. 2014 (2014)
13. Adebar, T.K., Okamura, A.M.: Recursive estimation of needle pose for control of 3D-ultrasound-guided robotic needle steering. In: IEEE/RSJ International Conference on Intelligent Robots and Systems, Chicago, IL, pp. 4303–4308 (2014)
14. Zou, Y.J., Zhao, X.G., Han, J.D.: Estimation methods of flexible tip-steerable needles: a comparative study. In: Proceeding of the 11th World Congress on Intelligent Control and Automation, Shenyang, pp. 5051–5056 (2014)

15. Kaya, M., Bebek, O.: Needle localization using Gabor filtering in 2D ultrasound images. In: IEEE International Conference on Robotics and Automation (ICRA), Hong Kong, pp. 4881–4886 (2014)
16. Kaya, M., Bebek, O.: Gabor filter based localization of needles in ultrasound guided robotic interventions. In: IEEE International Conference on Imaging Systems and Techniques (IST) Proceedings, Santorini, pp. 112–117 (2014)
17. Orlando, M.F., et al.: Control of shape memory alloy actuated flexible needle using multimodal sensory feedbacks. J. Autom. Control Eng. **3**(5), 428–434 (2015)
18. Surender, H., Orlando, M.F.: Continuous higher order sliding mode control of bevel-tip needle for percutaneous interventions. In: 2019 28th IEEE International Conference on Robot and Human Interactive Communication (RO-MAN). IEEE (2019)
19. Hans, S., Joseph, F.O.M.: Robust control of a bevel-tip needle for medical interventional procedures. IEEE/CAA J. Automatica Sinica **7**(1), 244–256 (2020)
20. Hans, S., Joseph, F.O.M.: Control of a flexible bevel-tipped needle using super twisting controller based sliding mode observer. ISA Trans. **109**, 186–198 (2021)
21. Hans, S., Goyal, J.K., Sachan, A., Bansal, P., Soni, S., Djemai, M.: Control of a smart active flexible needle for therapeutic procedures. In:: SICE International Symposium on Control Systems (SICE ISCS), Kusatsu, Japan 2023, pp. 41–46 (2023)
22. Orlando, F., et al.: Inverse kinematic control of a shape memory alloy actuated smart active needle for percutaneous intervention. In: IEEE TENCON Annual Conference, pp. 1159–1164 (2017)
23. Mathiassen, K., Dall'Alba, D., Muradore, R., Fiorini, P., Elle, O.J.: Robust real-time needle tracking in 2-D ultrasound images using statistical filtering. IEEE Trans. Control Syst. Technol. **25**(3), 966–978 (2017)
24. Mwikirize, C., Nosher, J.L., Hacihaliloglu, I.: Convolution neural networks for real-time needle detection and localization in 2D ultrasound. Int. J. Comput. Assist. Radiol. Surg. **13**(5), 647–657 (2018)
25. Lapouge, G., Troccaz, J., Poignet, P.: Multi-rate unscented Kalman filtering for pose and curvature estimation in 3D ultrasound-guided needle steering. Control. Eng. Pract. **80**, 116–124 (2018)
26. Agarwal, N., Yadav, A.K., Gupta, A., Orlando, M.F.: Real-time needle tip localization in 2D ultrasound images using kalman filter. In: 2019 IEEE/ASME International Conference on Advanced Intelligent Mechatronics (AIM), Hong Kong, China, pp. 1008–1012 (2019)
27. Chui, C.K., Chen, G.: Kalman Filtering: With Real-Time Applications. Springer, Berlin (2008). https://doi.org/10.1007/978-3-319-47612-4
28. Hall, D.L., Llinas, J.: An introduction to multisensor data fusion. Proc. IEEE **85**(1), 6–23 (1997)
29. Jiang, B., et al.: Kalman filter-based EM-optical sensor fusion for needle deflection estimation. Int. J. Comput. Assist. Radiol. Surg. **13**(4), 573–583 (2018)

Coping with Increased Levels of Label Noise in Facial Expression Recognition

Badveeti Naveen Siva Kumar$^{(\boxtimes)}$ ⓘ, Bobbili Veerendra Raj Kumar ⓘ,
Darshan Gera ⓘ, and S. Balasubramanian ⓘ

Sri Sathya Sai Institute of Higher Learning, Puttaparthi, India
bnaveensivakumar@gmail.com , darshangera@sssihl.edu.in,
sbalasubramanian@sssihl.edu.in

Abstract. An important problem in facial expression recognition
(FER) is the presence of inaccurate annotations referred to as noisy
annotations in the datasets. These noisy annotations are present in the
datasets due to the subjectivity of annotators, poor quality of images, etc.
In our work, we use a sample selection method based on a dynamic adaptive threshold to separate confident samples from non-confident ones. We
impose consistency in the negative classes of the non-confident samples to
effectively use all the samples. Unlike other methods which consider low
label noise (10–30%), we have considered synthetic label noisy datasets
with a higher rate of label noise (up to 80%) and demonstrated the
proposed framework's effectiveness using quantitative as well as qualitative results. Our method performs better than the SOTA model at higher
rates of label noise in the range of 0.1–3.36% on RAFDB and 0.19–5.84%
improvement in FERPlus.

Keywords: Negative class · Facial Expression Recognition · dynamic
adaptive threshold · noisy annotations

1 Introduction

In recent years, significant progress has been made towards developing deep
learning (DL) based robust facial expression recognition (FER) systems
[7,18,27]. Making machines understand human emotions and intentions through
the use of facial features is the goal of automatic FER. Numerous real-world
applications of FER exist, including the detection of driver weariness [12], mental health analysis [3], increasing student-teacher interaction in distance learning environments [13], virtual assistants [22], social robots [20], and others. In
a supervised setting, learning the positive class is quite faster but if there are
noisy labeled samples (i.e. samples with inaccurate labels) in the dataset, then
the model starts learning incorrect features leading to poor generalization [1].

Several methods have been proposed to tackle the noisy label problem. They
can be broadly categorized as methods that use sample selection [7,9,15,21,23],
robust loss functions [27], re-weighting [17,18], feature-mixup [26]. These

H. Kaur et al. (Eds.): CVIP 2023, CCIS 2009, pp. 293–304, 2024.
https://doi.org/10.1007/978-3-031-58181-6_25

works suffer from some limitations such as being computationally heavy in [9,15,17,21,23] due to the usage of multiple networks or multiple branches, having a self-confirmation bias in [18] due to relabeling. Moreover in [26,27] cross entropy (CE) loss is used on all the samples but CE loss is not robust to noisy labels.

None of the above-mentioned models cater to inter-class size imbalance problems and intra-class difficulty present in FER datasets. To address this issue, we use a dynamic adaptive threshold which we calculate at every mini-batch. So, we don't need to have prior knowledge of noise rate and we use only a single network unlike some of the earlier methods [9,21,23]. Going by general intuition that if we are not confident about something, we don't force ourselves to do that. Similarly, on non-confident samples, we are not sure about the prediction of the model. So instead of enforcing consistency in all the classes where we have classes whose prediction is not sure, we enforce consistency only in negative classes. In our case, other than the ground-truth label, we can treat all the other classes as negative classes. The extent of how many negative classes should we consider for consistency is treated as a hyper-parameter.

We call the proposed framework NCCTFER that utilizes learning from Negative Classes and Class wise adaptive Threshold to mitigate the effect of noisy labels in Facial Expression Recognition. We show the effectiveness of NCCTFER in Sect. 4. Overall our contributions can be summarized as follows:

- We deal with inter-class similarities and intra-class difficulties by using a dynamic adaptive threshold.
- We utilize all the samples in learning the expression features. We make use of the model's confidence on some samples and learn "which class it belongs to" from the positive class classifier. For other samples, since the model is not sure of its prediction, we impose consistency on the negative classes based on the softmax output of the negative class classifier.
- We use a single network model, unlike previous works, ensuring that our model is not computationally expensive.
- Our method is an end-to-end framework that is architecture independent and achieves superior performance on FER datasets in the presence of synthetic label noise (10–80%) as well as on real-world noisy annotated datasets.

The remainder of this paper is organized in the following manner: Sect. 2 gives an overview of other related methods in this field. Section 3 describes the proposed method, and provides the architecture and algorithm for training our framework. Section 4 shows the effectiveness of the framework using quantitative and qualitative results. We conclude the paper in Sect. 5.

2   Related Work

2.1   General Noisy Label Problem

If we train a deep learning(DL) model in the presence of noisy labels, its performance hampers due to the strong memorizing capacity [1]. Several ways are explored in order to solve the noisy label problem. These works can be grouped into a few categories such as sample re-weighting, label cleansing, robust loss functions, and selecting clean samples based on small loss. Works [9,15,23] use small loss samples to train but they need the prior knowledge of noise rate in the dataset except for [15] but getting to know the noise rate beforehand is not always possible in real-world scenarios. They also use multiple networks using peer/joint training either with agreement [9] on the samples selected or by disagreement [23]. Our method also works based on sample selection but we don't need to know the noise rate beforehand like the aforementioned methods. We use a dynamic adaptive threshold [6] generated from posterior prediction probabilities.

2.2 Noisy Label Problem in FER

Due to the availability of real-world FER datasets like RAFDB [11], FERPlus [2], AffectNet [14], etc. FER has become a well-explored field of research. In spite of this, obtaining good performance when trained on the noisy annotated FER dataset is not a trivial task. Recent works like SCN [18], DMUE [17], IPA2LT [24], and RUL [26] have attempted to handle the noisy labels in FER datasets. In IPA2LT, the real label is learned by maximizing the log-likelihood of multiple inconsistent human-made annotations and machine-predicted annotations. But for this model, we need to have multiple annotations from different annotators. SCN uses weighted CE loss and does relabeling, which leads to self-confirmation bias. RUL performs a mix-up of feature vectors based on the learned uncertainty values and uses CE loss on the mixed feature vector. EAC [27] uses attention consistency on class activation maps for consistency loss and CE loss on all samples. CE loss is not robust to noisy labels. DMUE uses multiple branches to mine the latent distribution but this is computationally heavy.

Unlike DMUE, our proposed NCCTFER is independent of the number of classes and not expensive in computations. Compared to other methods, our model differs in utilizing only confident samples to be fed to CE loss for positive class prediction, where we obtain confident samples from the dynamic adaptive threshold. None of the above-mentioned methods deal with the intra-class sample size imbalances and inter-class difficulties, we address them by using dynamic adaptive threshold, and instead of discarding the non-confident samples, we learn from them as well by imposing consistency on the negative classes. All the above-mentioned methods try to use loss functions that try to make even the non-confident samples learn the positive class (which can be wrong due to noisy annotations). Here we don't do that instead, we impose consistency only on negative classes.

3   Proposed Method

In this section, we first provide the motivation for the proposed method. Then we list out the details of our method. Following it, we provide a training algorithm. The architecture for our model is shown in Fig. 1.

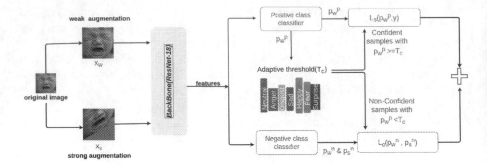

Fig. 1. Architecture of NCCTFER. Here a batch of x_w and x_s (weak and strong augmentations) are sent through the backbone(ResNet-18). Extracted features are sent to the positive class classifier (pcc) as well as the negative class classifier(ncc). On the predictions of weak augmentation from pcc, we calculate the adaptive threshold and get confident and non-confident indices for the given batch of samples. Only the confident samples are used for supervision loss (L_s) and the non-confident ones are sent to consistency loss (L_c).

3.1   Motivation and Overview

Our method is based on the idea of sample selection. We use a dynamic class-wise adaptive threshold [6] for the selection process, which is based on posterior probabilities in order to tackle the issue of inter-class sample imbalance problems and intra-class difficulties. Usually, consistency loss or supervision loss is imposed on all the samples. Since we are not sure about the prediction of the model on non-confident samples, imposing consistency on different views or supervision with the provided label distribution may not help the model as the label noise rate increases. Thus we impose consistency in different views of the same image only on negative classes predicted by the negative class classifier.

3.2   Problem Formulation

Given a batch of N samples $S = \{(x_i, y_i)\}_{i=1}^{N}$ where each face image x_i has an expression label $y_i \in \{1, 2, ..., C\}$ here C denotes the number of expression classes. The shared backbone network is ResNet-18. It is parameterized by θ. Features from the backbone are classified using two fully connected layers (FC) followed by softmax to obtain prediction probabilities. The first FC layer is to predict the positive class and the other FC layer predicts the negative class. We use two different augmentations one weak-augmented image and another strongly-augmented image which are denoted by x_w and x_s respectively. Prediction probabilities obtained by passing x_w and x_s through the positive class classifier are denoted as p_w^p and p_s^p respectively and through the negative class classifier are denoted as p_w^n and p_s^n respectively. Standard cropping along with horizontal flipping with a probability of 50% is used for weak augmentations. And for strong augmentation, Randaugment [4] is used. During training, for each mini-batch S_n, dynamic adaptive threshold T_c is calculated from the predictions of positive class classifier p_w^n as per Eq. 1, where X_c is a set of samples in the current mini-batch with label c.

$$T_c = \frac{1}{X_c} \sum_{x \in S_c} p^c(x; \theta) \tag{1}$$

After finding the dynamic adaptive threshold T_c, we choose those images whose ground truth prediction probabilities are greater than T_c. This can be represented by Eq. 2 as follows:.

$$X_c^{clean} = \{x \in X_c \ni p^c \geq T_c\} \tag{2}$$

We learn better from the positive class by propagating the losses only from these confident samples. Instead of discarding the other samples from the mini-batch, we use them for feature learning using consistency loss. For this, we take the prediction probabilities from negative class classifier p_w^n and p_s^n and use masked CE loss defined in Sect. 3.3. We say it is masked because we choose only bottom K classes from the negative class classifier predictions and impose consistency loss only on those classes. K is a hyper-parameter obtained based on ablation study in Sect. 4.4.

3.3   Loss Functions

We use Cross-Entropy loss on a positive class classifier represented by L_s(supervision loss). Inspired from [5], we define consistency loss L_c on negative class classifier predictions in Eq. 3, where M_k represents the mask: M_k becomes zero if the prediction probability for a given class is not among bottom k otherwise it is one.

$$L_c = -\frac{1}{N} \sum_{i=1}^{N} M_k p_w^n log(p_s^n) \tag{3}$$

The overall loss is denoted as $L_{overall}$ is a linear combination of supervision loss and consistency loss.

4   Experiments

4.1   Datasets

We evaluate our model on three popular real-world benchmarks FER datasets RAFDB [11], FERPlus [2], AffectNet [14], and synthetic noisy annotated datasets. In the latter datasets, the noise distribution introduced in the labeled space of the ground truth is random. The performance of our model is reported on the corresponding clean test/validation sets.

Algorithm 1: Training algorithm

Input: Given a model f with parameters θ, dataset $S = \{(x_i, y_i)\}_{i=1}^{N}$,
      mini-batch size (b), learning rate(η), number of expression classes (C),
      total epochs E_{max}, warm-up epochs (E_{warm})

Output: Updated model parameters θ

1 Initialize θ randomly.

2 **for** $e = 1, 2, .., E_{max}$ **do**

3   Shuffle training samples $\{(x_i, y_i)\}_{i=1}^{N}$

4   Sample mini-batch S_n from S

5   **for** *each class* $c \in \{1, 2, .., C\}$ **do**

6   **if** $e < E_{warm}$ **then**

7   Compute loss L_s on all samples using CE loss;

8   **else**

9   Compute dynamic adaptive threshold T_c using Eq. 1

10   Select confident samples S_c^{clean} from current mini-batch using Eq. 2

11   Compute supervision loss L_s on above selected confident samples

12   On non-confident samples, based on negative class classifier
           prediction probabilities, compute consistency loss L_c using Eq. 3

13   Compute total loss $L_{overall}$

14   Update model parameters $\theta = \theta - \eta \nabla L_\theta$ as per gradient descent rule

15 return θ

4.2   Implementation Details

In the experiments below, we used MTCNN [25] to recognize and resize the images of facial expressions to 224×224. The PyTorch DL toolbox is used to build our technique, and a single Tesla K40C GPU with 11.4 GB RAM is used to run our experiments. The backbone network utilized is ResNet-18, which was previously trained on the MS-Celeb-1M [8] face recognition dataset. In addition to random cropping with 4 pixels and resizing to 224×224, random horizontal flipping with a chance of 0.5 is employed for weak augmentation. RandAugment [4] is used for strong augmentation. From a selection of transformations including contrast adjustment, rotation, color inversion, translation, etc. RandAugment chooses two augmentations at random. Similar to [18], oversampling is used for AffectNet. The batch size used for training is 128. The model is optimized using the Adam optimizer, with a learning rate of 0.0001 for the backbone and 0.001 for the positive class classifier and negative class classifier (FC layers). We trained the model for 40 epochs.

4.3   Experiment Results on Synthetic Noisy Annotated Datasets

Synthetic symmetric noise is manually added on RAFDB, and FERPlus datasets by randomly shuffling different percentages of labels for each expression class. The percentages considered in our study are 10, 20, 30, 50, 60, 70, 80. We compare NCCTFER with SCN [18], RUL [26], and EAC [27] which are SOTA

Table 1. Performance evaluation comparison on synthetic symmetric label noise on FERPlus

FERPlus	10%noise	20%noise	30%noise	50%noise	60%noise	70%noise	80%noise
SCN [18]	84.28	84.99	82.47	75.33	68.06	39.43	37.62
RUL [26]	85.94	84.99	82.75	77.18	73.54	64.07	43.39
EAC [27]	**87.03**	**86.07**	**85.44**	81.48	79.82	74.98	62.19
NCCTFER	86.29	85.66	84.79	**81.73**	**80.20**	**75.17**	**68.03**

Table 2. Performance evaluation comparison on synthetic symmetric label noise on RAFDB

RAFDB	10%noise	20%noise	30%noise	50%noise	60%noise	70%noise	80%noise
SCN [18]	82.18	79.79	77.46	73.5	59.55	41.98	38.82
RUL [26]	86.22	83.35	82.06	73.5	69.62	57.66	36.34
EAC [27]	**88.02**	86.05	84.42	80.54	76.37	68.9	47.46
NCCTFER	86.7	**86.147**	**85.169**	**81.486**	**79.73**	**71.9**	**48.89**

models and showed the efficacy of NCCTFER on higher levels of noise in Table 1 and Table 2 on FERPlus and RAFDB respectively.

Automatically annotated subset of AffectNct-7 is a challenging noisy dataset because of heavy class imbalance as well as intra-class difficulty and the annotations are generated automatically without human intervention. No method is able to achieve good performance. Our method gave 56.67% accuracy when tested on the validation set of the AffectNet dataset. The confusion plot for this model is shown in Fig. 2

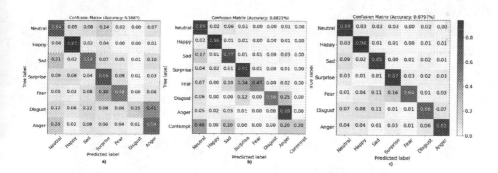

Fig. 2. Confusion Matrix of model performance when trained on a) real noisy datasubset of AffectNet, b) FERPlus, and c) RAFDB respectively.

Performance on Asymmetric Noise: Apart from symmetric noise, the effectiveness of the model is shown on synthetic asymmetric noise on the RAFDB dataset. For every expression, the noise is introduced by replacing the label with its most confused pair. The most confused pairs in RAFDB, based on confusion plots of some SOTA methods are Surprise-Anger, Fear-Surprise, Disgust-Anger, Happy-Neutral, Sad-Neutral, Anger-Happy, and Neutral-Sad. From these confusion pairs, if the former is the ground truth label, we replaced it with the latter for the required amount of noise rate. We have conducted experiments with 10% to 50% of asymmetric noise rates generated as per the above-mentioned method. Our method improves from 1.66–9.59% over the baseline. The results are shown in Table 3.

Table 3. Performance evaluation in the presence of synthetic asymmetric label noise on RAFDB

RAFDB	10%noise	20%noise	30%noise	40%noise	50%noise
Baseline	84.81	80.73	77.28	68.87	48.10
NCCTFER	86.47	85.4	83.34	78.46	56.71
improvement	**1.66**	**4.67**	**6.06**	**9.59**	**8.61**

Visualizations: We have visualized our model's performance as a confusion matrix as shown in Fig. 2. It can be observed that Happy, Surprise, and Neutral are easy classes to predict mainly because of the availability of more samples with these labels. Whereas Disgust and Fear are most confused among all three datasets. Fear is most confused with Surprise and Disgust is confused with neutral in FERPlus and RAFDB but Disgust is most confused with Anger in the automatically annotated subset of the AffectNet dataset. Contempt in the FERPlus dataset is most confused with Neutral, Anger, and Sad in the mentioned order.

Performance on Benchmark Datasets: The performance of NCCTFER on benchmark datasets like FERPlus and RAFDB is shown in Table 5.

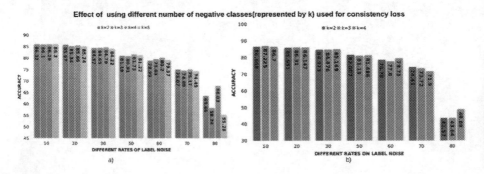

Fig. 3. Effect of k shown on synthetic symmetric label noise of a)FERPlus and b)RAFDB

Table 4. Ablation study on the importance of learning from positive class and negative class on synthetic symmetric noise on RAFDB (Here Baseline+pc refers to model learning from only confident samples and Baseline+nl refers to baseline with loss functions defined in [10])

RAFDB	10%noise	30%noise	50%noise	60%noise	70%noise	80%noise
Baseline	84.7	81.2	77.1	69.2	60.26	41.59
Baseline+nl	84.2	80.54	75.488	71.35	62.9	39
Baseline+pc	86.7	83.3	78.94	75.4	61.3	33.1
NCCTFER	**86.7**	**85.169**	**81.486**	**79.73**	**71.9**	**48.89**

4.4   Ablation Study

We demonstrate the effectiveness of masking different numbers of negative classes among the non-confident samples. The hyper-parameter k is used to determine how many classes we are going to use for consistency loss. Results are shown in Fig. 3. We have adjusted the value for k as 4 because when we mask the top 4 negative classes, we achieve good performance over various levels of noisy labels.

Apart from this, we have verified the importance of each component in learning by removing the other components from the model and checking for their performance. Table 4 shows that the baseline is far from below compared to the NCCTFER. The effectiveness of learning from negative classes on the non-confident samples is also shown by the increase in performance compared to the model that learns only from confident samples(Baseline+pc).

Table 5. Performance on real-world datasets RAFDB and FERPlus (* represents trained on AffectNet and RAFDB combined.)

Models\Datasets	RAFDB	FERPlus
IPA2LT [24]	86.77*	-
RAN [19]	86.90	88.55
SCN [18]	88.14*	88.01
DMUE [17]	88.76	88.64
RUL [26]	88.98	88.75
NCCTFER	87.97	88.21

Attention Maps: In order to investigate the salient regions focused by NCCT-FER, the attention-weighted activation maps are visualized using Grad-CAM [16]. The baseline trained on RAFDB and NCCTFER trained on 30% and 60% synthetic label noise on RAFDB are compared. Darker color indicates high attention while lighter color indicates negligible attention. The baseline sometimes focuses on irrelevant parts or misses out on relevant parts. In comparison to the baseline, the NCCTFER attends to non-occluded and relevant parts for expression recognition. These visualizations validate the effectiveness of our framework in the prediction of the correct label instead of over-fitting to the noisy label. In Fig. 4, the emotion given below each image is the label that is predicted by the model and green represents correct whereas red represents incorrect prediction. On top of every image, we have given the prediction probability with which, the model predicted the label. Clearly, our method is able to learn robust features in the presence of noisy labels.

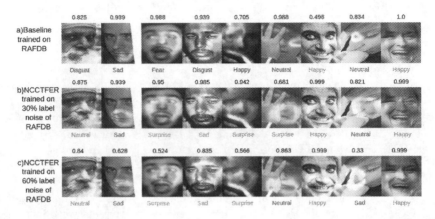

Fig. 4. The attention maps of a)the baseline trained on RAFDB, b)NCCTFER trained on 30%, and c)60% synthetic label noise of RAFDB. on test images from RAFDB using Grad-CAM are compared in this figure.

5   Conclusions

In this paper, we have proposed a new method NCCTFER to handle the problem of noisy annotations in FER datasets. Our model uses posterior prediction probabilities from a positive class classifier and uses a dynamic adaptive threshold to get confident and non-confident samples. On the confident samples, we use CE loss, and on the non-confident samples using the prediction probabilities from the negative class classifier, we use consistency loss. In contrast to previous works, our model NCCTFER neither needs to know the noise rates nor needs to learn using multiple networks, nor needs a separate supplement of clean data. NCCTFER uses all the samples either for consistency loss on the predictions of the negative class classifier or supervision loss on the predictions of the positive class classifier. By using the dynamic adaptive threshold, it also handles the class imbalance problem as well as caters to intra-class difficulties. Instead of imposing the non-confident samples to learn the positive class which might be wrong in our case due to noisy labels, we impose consistency only on the negative classes of these non-confident samples but not on the positive class. A limitation of NCCFER is it doesn't outperform the SOTA models on lower rates of label noise even though it outperforms other models at higher rates of label noise. Our future work will involve improving this framework to perform well at all levels of label noise.

Acknowledgments. We dedicate this work to Bhagawan Sri Sathya Sai Baba, Divine Founder Chancellor of Sri Sathya Sai Institute of Higher Learning, Prasanthi Nilayam, A.P., India.

References

1. Arpit, D., et al.: A closer look at memorization in deep networks. In: International Conference on Machine Learning, pp. 233–242. PMLR (2017)
2. Barsoum, E., Zhang, C., Ferrer, C.C., Zhang, Z.: Training deep networks for facial expression recognition with crowdsourced label distribution. In Proceedings of the 18th ACM International Conference on Multimodal Interaction, pp. 279–283 (2016)
3. Bisogni, C., Castiglione, A., Hossain, S., Narducci, F., Umer, S.: Impact of deep learning approaches on facial expression recognition in healthcare industries. IEEE Trans. Industr. Inf. **18**(8), 5619–5627 (2022). https://doi.org/10.1109/TII.2022.3141400
4. Cubuk, E.D., Zoph, B., Shlens, J., Le, Q.V.: Randaugment: practical automated data augmentation with a reduced search space. In: Proceedings of the IEEE/CVF Conference on Computer Vision and Pattern Recognition Workshops, pp. 702–703 (2020)
5. Duan, Y., et al.: Mutexmatch: semi-supervised learning with mutex-based consistency regularization. IEEE Trans. Neural Netw. Learn. Syst. (2022)
6. Gera, D., Badveeti, N.S.K., Kumar, B.V.R., Balasubramanian, S.: Dynamic adaptive threshold based learning for noisy annotations robust facial expression recognition. arXiv preprint arXiv:2208.10221 (2022)
7. Gera, D., Vikas, G., Balasubramanian, S.: Handling ambiguous annotations for facial expression recognition in the wild. In: Proceedings of the Twelfth Indian Conference on Computer Vision, Graphics and Image Processing, pp. 1–9 (2021)
8. Guo, Y., Zhang, L., Hu, Y., He, X., Gao, J.: MS-Celeb-1M: a dataset and benchmark for large-scale face recognition. In: Leibe, B., Matas, J., Sebe, N., Welling, M. (eds.) ECCV 2016. LNCS, vol. 9907, pp. 87–102. Springer, Cham (2016). https://doi.org/10.1007/978-3-319-46487-9_6
9. Han, B., et al.: Co-teaching: robust training of deep neural networks with extremely noisy labels. In: Proceedings of the 32nd International Conference on Neural Information Processing Systems, pp. 8536–8546 (2018)
10. Kim, Y., Yim, J., Yun, J., Kim, J.: Nlnl: negative learning for noisy labels. In: Proceedings of the IEEE/CVF International Conference on Computer Vision, pp. 101–110 (2019)
11. Li, S., Deng, W.: Reliable crowdsourcing and deep locality-preserving learning for unconstrained facial expression recognition. IEEE Trans. Image Process. **28**(1), 356–370 (2019)
12. Liu, Z., Peng, Y., Hu, W.: Driver fatigue detection based on deeply-learned facial expression representation. J. Vis. Commun. Image Represent. **71**, 102723 (2020)
13. Maqableh, W., Alzyoud, F.Y., Zraqou, J.: The use of facial expressions in measuring students' interaction with distance learning environments during the covid-19 crisis. Visual Inform. **7**(1), 1–17 (2023)

14. Mollahosseini, A., Hasani, B., Mahoor, M.H.: Affectnet: a database for facial expression, valence, and arousal computing in the wild. IEEE Trans. Affect. Comput. (2017)
15. Sarfraz, F., Arani, E., Zonooz, B.: Noisy concurrent training for efficient learning under label noise. In: Proceedings of the IEEE/CVF Winter Conference on Applications of Computer Vision, pp. 3159–3168 (2021)
16. Selvaraju, R.R., Cogswell, M., Das, A., Vedantam, R., Parikh, D., Batra, D.: Gradcam: visual explanations from deep networks via gradient-based localization. In: Proceedings of the IEEE International Conference on Computer Vision, pp. 618–626 (2017)
17. She, J., Hu, Y., Shi, H., Wang, J., Shen, Q., Mei, T.: Dive into ambiguity: latent distribution mining and pairwise uncertainty estimation for facial expression recognition. In: Proceedings of the IEEE/CVF Conference on Computer Vision and Pattern Recognition, pp. 6248–6257 (2021)
18. Wang, K., Peng, X., Yang, J., Lu, S., Qiao, Y.: Suppressing uncertainties for large-scale facial expression recognition. In: CVPR, pp. 6897–6906 (2020)
19. Wang, K., Peng, X., Yang, J., Meng, D., Qiao, Y.: Region attention networks for pose and occlusion robust facial expression recognition. IEEE Trans. Image Process. **29**, 4057–4069 (2020)
20. Webb, N., Ruiz-Garcia, A., Elshaw, M., Palade, V.: Emotion recognition from face images in an unconstrained environment for usage on social robots. In: 2020 International Joint Conference on Neural Networks (IJCNN), pp. 1–8. IEEE (2020)
21. Wei, H., Feng, L., Chen, X., An, B.: Combating noisy labels by agreement: a joint training method with co-regularization. In: Proceedings of the IEEE/CVF Conference on Computer Vision and Pattern Recognition, pp. 13726–13735 (2020)
22. Yan, L., Sheng, M., Wang, C., Gao, R., Yu, H.: Hybrid neural networks based facial expression recognition for smart city. Multimedia Tools Appl. 1–24 (2022)
23. Yu, X., Han, B., Yao, J., Niu, G., Tsang, I., Sugiyama, M.: How does disagreement help generalization against label corruption? In: International Conference on Machine Learning, pp. 7164–7173. PMLR (2019)
24. Zeng, J., Shan, S., Chen, X.: Facial expression recognition with inconsistently annotated datasets. In: Proceedings of the European Conference on Computer Vision (ECCV), pp. 222–237 (2018)
25. Zhang, K., Zhang, Z., Li, Z., Qiao, Y.: Joint face detection and alignment using multitask cascaded convolutional networks. IEEE Signal Process. Lett. **23**(10), 1499–1503 (2016). https://doi.org/10.1109/LSP.2016.2603342
26. Zhang, Y., Wang, C., Deng, W.: Relative uncertainty learning for facial expression recognition. Adv. Neural. Inf. Process. Syst. **34**, 17616–17627 (2021)
27. Zhang, Y., Wang, C., Ling, X., Deng, W.: Learn from all: erasing attention consistency for noisy label facial expression recognition. In: Avidan, S., Brostow, G., Cissé, M., Farinella, G.M., Hassner, T. (eds.) ECCV 2022 Part XXVI. LNCS, vol. 13686, pp. 418–434. Springer, Cham (2022). https://doi.org/10.1007/978-3-031-19809-0_24

Efficient Seizure Prediction from Images of EEG Signals Using Convolutional Neural Network

Ranjan Jana[1,2]([envelope]) [iD] and Imon Mukherjee[1] [iD]

[1] Indian Institute of Information Technology, Kalyani, India
ranjan.rcciit@gmail.com, imon@iiitkalyani.ac.in
[2] RCC Institute of Information Technology, Kolkata, India

Abstract. Epileptic seizures are abnormal electrical activities in the brains of epilepsy patients. Seizure causes life threats due to sudden unconsciousness. An efficient seizure prediction technique can improve the lifestyle of epilepsy patients. In this article, raw EEG data are converted into images of EEG signals. The Convolutional neural network (CNN) is the most commonly used deep learning technique for efficient feature extraction from images. Hence, CNN is applied here for automatic feature extraction from images of EEG signals. CNN is also used to classify different states of epilepsy patients to predict seizures in advance. The achieved classification accuracy, sensitivity, and specificity are 0.9994, 0.9783, and 0.9083, respectively. The proposed method uses only six channels of EEG signals, which will be applicable for designing lightweight devices with less power consumption to run long periods in every recharge. The results indicate that the proposed method is one of the best among the state-of-the-art works.

Keywords: Convolutional neural network · EEG signal · Epileptic seizure · Majority voting · Seizure prediction

1 Introduction

An epileptic seizure causes a sudden loss of consciousness due to excessive electrical impulses in the brain [1]. Seizures cause several injuries like burning, drowning, and road accidents, which affect the lifestyle of epilepsy patients. The anti-epileptic drug can be applied to control seizures to avoid unwanted life-threat. It works effectively for only 70% of epilepsy patients though it has some side effects [1]. Hence, seizure prediction is highly desirable in advance for epilepsy patients to avoid unwanted life risks. The recording of electrical activities of the brain is called Electroencephalogram (EEG). The EEG signals are captured by placing metal electrodes on the scalp. Medical practitioners predict seizures by analyzing EEG signals, which is the most commonly used method [2]. The four states of epilepsy patients are ictal (during seizure), preictal (before seizure), postictal (after seizure), and interictal (normal situations) [2]. EEG signal patterns of the four states are different, as shown in Fig. 1. Seizures can be predicted in advance by identifying the preictal states [3]. The main task of seizure prediction is the classification of preictal and interictal states. The most important feature of EEG signals provide more

© The Author(s), under exclusive license to Springer Nature Switzerland AG 2024
H. Kaur et al. (Eds.): CVIP 2023, CCIS 2009, pp. 305–317, 2024.
https://doi.org/10.1007/978-3-031-58181-6_26

accurate classification, which leads to the design of efficient prediction models. Although it is very difficult to implement an efficient seizure prediction model for several reasons, as follows [2]:

1. EEG recordings have noise.
2. EEG signal pattern is unique for each individual.
3. EEG signal pattern is time-variant for each individual.

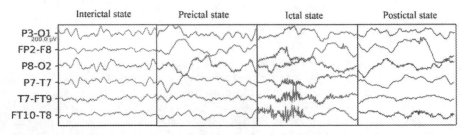

Fig. 1. EEG signals pattern of patient CHB01 (6 channels).

In this article, we propose an image-based seizure prediction model. The raw EEG data are used to construct the images of EEG signals. A Convolutional neural network (CNN) is used for automatic feature extraction from these images. Subsequently, these features are also classified using the same CNN. Only six EEG channels are used, which will be beneficial for designing low-cost and low-powered seizure prediction devices. The subsequent sections of this article are represented as follows. Section 2 mentioned several state-of-art-the works. Section 3 informs about the database used for this research work. This section also describes the proposed methodology. The experimental results are presented in Sect. 4. The conclusion of the research work and future research directions are mentioned in Sect. 5.

2 Related Works

Researchers have proposed many seizure prediction methods in the last 20 years. The primary objective of seizure prediction is to classify the preictal and interictal states [3]. Hence, it is necessary to identify the important features of these states for efficient classification. Researchers applied different feature extraction techniques to EEG signals for seizure prediction. The commonly used features are spectral entropy features [4], spatial features [3], fuzzy entropy features [5], and wavelet packet decomposition [6]. Researchers have used several machine-learning techniques for efficient feature classification. The commonly used machine-learning techniques are support vector machine [5], k-nearest neighbor [7], multi-layer perceptron [8], linear discriminant analysis [9], and random forest [7]. The classification performances of these machine-learning techniques were remarkable. Most researchers extracted different handcrafted features for seizure prediction [3–6]. Hence, automatic feature extraction techniques are required, which will be generalizable.

Deep Learning (DL) comes into existence to extract relevant features automatically from the data and classify the features efficiently. The commonly used DL techniques to predict seizure are recurrent neural networks [10], CNN [11, 12], long short-term memory (LSTM) [13, 14], and DenseNet [15, 16]. Although DL can extract relevant features from raw EEG data. Researchers have applied several transformations of EEG signals to feed the EEG data into the DL network. The most frequently used transformations are continuous-wavelet-transform (CWT) [11], short-term-Fourier-transform (STFT) [17], and discrete-wavelet-transform (DWT) [16, 18]. In this article, the raw EEG data are converted into EEG images. Then, a CNN network is applied to extract relevant features from images of the EEG signal. Most researchers have proposed their seizure prediction methods using all EEG channels. All EEG channels are irrelevant for seizure prediction [2]. Hence, a channel reduction technique is required to implement portable and less power consumable devices with less number of channels. In this article, we have proposed an efficient seizure prediction method, which uses only six EEG channels.

3   Material and Methodology

In this work, the CHB-MIT EEG database is used, which is the frequently used standard database for seizure prediction [19]. This database consists of 129 seizure and 535 non-seizure recordings. These are collected from 23 epilepsy patients admitted at Children's Hospital, Boston. The sampling frequency of all recordings was 256 Hz. Most recordings have unique 22 channels though some recordings have more channels. All channels are not relevant for predicting seizure events; therefore, Jana et al. proposed a channel reduction technique to reduce channels for designing portable and power-efficient seizure prediction devices [2]. They suggested that only six EEG channels (P3-O1, FP2-F8, P8-O2, P7-T7, T7-FT9, and FT10-T8) are sufficient for efficient seizure prediction. Hence, we have considered only these six channels for this research work. The proposed methodology is divided into three parts: pre-processing of EEG signals, CNN for features extraction and classification, and training and testing procedure. The graphical representation of our proposed model is shown in Fig. 2.

3.1   Pre-processing of EEG Signals

Physicians predict seizures by analyzing EEG signals. They extract relevant features unknowingly from the images of EEG signals. Hatipoglu et al. proposed an approach of signal-to-image transformation of EEG and MEG signals for pattern classification [20]. Their approach provided excellent accuracy for biomedical signal classification. Hence, we have converted the Time-domain EEG data into 2-D images of EEG signals. These images are used for feature extraction for the classification of preictal and interictal states.

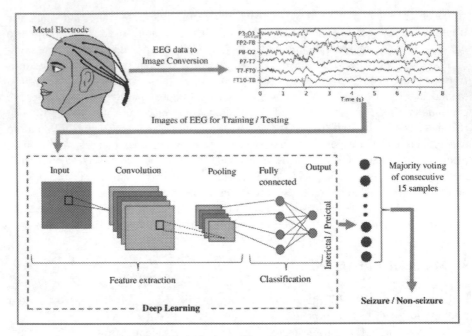

Fig. 2. Graphical representation of our proposed model.

Jana *et al.* proposed a seizure prediction method using the sample duration of 8-s EEG signals [2]. Hence, we have transformed an 8-s EEG signal into an image for each training sample. An 8-s EEG signal with a sampling rate of 256 Hz has 2048 discrete intensity values. Only 512 discrete values are considered in the horizontal direction with a gap of 4 to construct the image for each EEG channel due to limited CPU time and memory requirements. A total of 384 (6 × 64) values for six channels are considered in vertical directions, where 64 values are reserved for each EEG channel. Hence, each image sample is represented by 384 × 512. All discrete intensity values are projected into the transformed row numbers for plotting, as shown in Fig. 3. The plotted EEG signal is not continuous. Hence, the most efficient Bresenham line drawing algorithm is applied to get the continuous plot, as shown in Fig. 4.

3.2 CNN for Features Extraction and Classification

DL is a powerful machine-learning tool that extracts features automatically. CNN is an important DL technique for image classification [21]. CNNs are capable of relevant features extraction automatically from the EEG signals for pattern classification [20]. Hence, we have applied a CNN on images of EEG signals for feature extraction. We have also applied the same CNN for feature classification to predict seizure efficiently. In this proposed method, the input image size is 384 × 512. The architecture of our proposed CNN model is shown in Fig. 5.

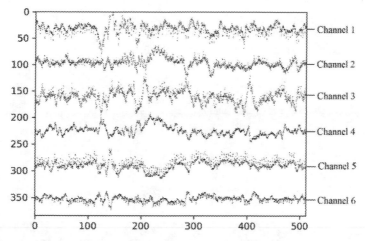

Fig. 3. A sample image plot of 8-s EEG data.

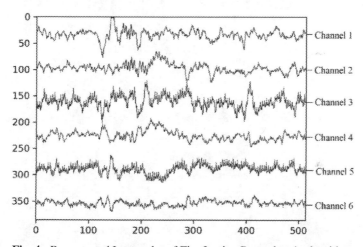

Fig. 4. Regenerated Image plot of Fig. 3 using Bresenham's algorithm.

In this CNN model, only eight convolution layers are applied to extract features using several kernels. The 2-D kernel size is $(2N + 1) \times (2N + 1)$, where N is a positive integer. The image I is convolved with the kernel $W(p, q)$ using Eq. 1, where $O(m, n)$ is the convolved output at location (m, n). The ReLU activation function is used after each convolution layer to introduce non-linearity. ReLU produces the same output value for each positive input value and 0 for each negative input value, as shown in Eq. 2. The max-pool function is used in eight pooling layers to reduce the dimension of features. Finally, two fully connected layers are used for feature classification. A total of 128 neurons are used in the 1st fully connected layer with the ReLU activation function. Only two neurons are used in the 2nd fully connected layer, one for the preictal state and another for the interictal state. The Softmax activation function is applied in this layer to generate the probabilities of preictal and interictal classes, as mentioned in Eq. 3. Here, x_i is the ith input, and n is the number of target classes. We have used the binary cross entropy loss and the Adam optimizer in our CNN model.

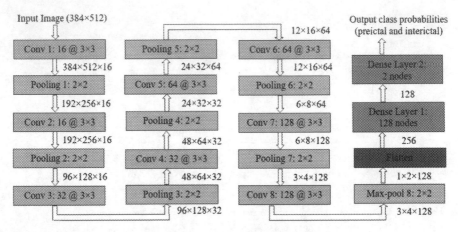

Fig. 5. Proposed CNN architecture.

$$O(m, n) = \sum_{p=-N}^{N} \sum_{q=-N}^{N} W(p, q) \times I(m - p, n - q) \tag{1}$$

$$ReLU(z) = Max(0, z) \tag{2}$$

$$Softmax(x_i) = \frac{e^{x_i}}{\sum_{j=1}^{n} e^{x_j}} \tag{3}$$

3.3 Training and Testing Procedure

The proposed CNN model is trained patient-wise using the images of EEG signals. Only two seizure and two non-seizure recordings are considered from each patient. Only 10 min of EEG data (600-s) are taken from each non-seizure recording as interictal states. Ten minutes of EEG data (600-s) before 10 min of the seizure event from each seizure recording are considered as preictal states. A 600-s EEG data can generate 593 image samples by taking the 8-s data with a gap of 1 s. Hence, a total of 1186 interictal samples and 1186 preictal samples from each patient are considered for training and validation checking. A total of 25 epochs is considered due to stability after 20 epochs at most times, as depicted in Fig. 6. The performance is measured using classification accuracy (ACC), sensitivity (SEN), specificity (SPEC), and false-positive rate (FPR), those are evaluated using Eqs. (4), (5), (6), and (7), respectively. Here, TP stands for true prediction and FP stands for false prediction.

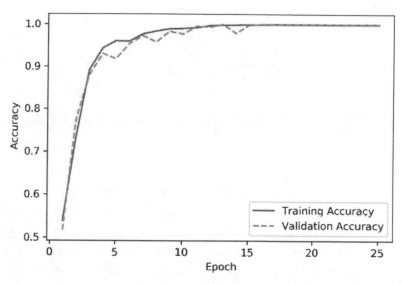

Fig. 6. Epoch vs. classification accuracy.

$$ACC = \frac{TP\ of\ preictal\ and\ interictal\ states}{Total\ number\ of\ samples} \tag{4}$$

$$SEN = \frac{TP\ of\ preictal\ states}{TP\ of\ preictal\ states + FP\ of\ interictal\ states} \tag{5}$$

$$SPEC = \frac{TP\ of\ interictal\ states}{TP\ of\ interictal\ states + FP\ of\ preictal\ states} \tag{6}$$

$$FPR = \frac{FP\ of\ preictal\ states}{TP\ of\ interictal\ states + FP\ of\ preictal\ states} \tag{7}$$

4 Experimental Results

The 5-fold cross-validation technique is used to calculate patient-wise classification accuracy, as shown in Table 1. The average accuracy is 0.9994, which is remarkable. A new EEG data set from 23 patients is applied to calculate sensitivity, specificity, FPR, and area-under-curve (AUC). The sensitivity of our proposed method is measured by testing 96 seizure recordings. The specificity and FPR are calculated based on 106 h of EEG data collected from 74 non-seizure recordings. The performance of our model is measured using two approaches. The 1st approach is using one sample of an 8-s EEG signal. The 2nd approach is using majority voting of a sequence of 8-s EEG samples.

Table 1. Patient-wise classification accuracy using 5-fold cross-validation.

Patient ID	Fold1	Fold2	Fold3	Fold4	Fold5	Avg.	Std.
01	1.0000	1.0000	1.0000	1.0000	1.0000	1.0000	0.0000
02	0.9958	1.0000	1.0000	0.9979	0.9979	0.9983	0.0016
03	1.0000	1.0000	1.0000	1.0000	1.0000	1.0000	0.0000
04	1.0000	1.0000	1.0000	1.0000	1.0000	1.0000	0.0000
05	1.0000	1.0000	1.0000	1.0000	0.9979	0.9996	0.0008
06	1.0000	1.0000	1.0000	1.0000	1.0000	1.0000	0.0000
07	1.0000	1.0000	1.0000	1.0000	1.0000	1.0000	0.0000
08	1.0000	1.0000	1.0000	1.0000	1.0000	1.0000	0.0000
09	1.0000	1.0000	1.0000	0.9979	1.0000	0.9996	0.0008
10	1.0000	0.9979	1.0000	1.0000	0.9979	0.9992	0.0010
11	1.0000	1.0000	1.0000	1.0000	1.0000	1.0000	0.0000
12	1.0000	1.0000	1.0000	1.0000	1.0000	1.0000	0.0000
13	1.0000	0.9937	1.0000	1.0000	1.0000	0.9987	0.0025
14	1.0000	0.9937	1.0000	1.0000	1.0000	0.9987	0.0025
15	1.0000	1.0000	1.0000	0.9937	1.0000	0.9987	0.0025
16	1.0000	1.0000	1.0000	0.9958	1.0000	0.9992	0.0017
17	1.0000	1.0000	0.9979	1.0000	1.0000	0.9996	0.0008
18	1.0000	1.0000	1.0000	1.0000	1.0000	1.0000	0.0000
19	1.0000	1.0000	1.0000	1.0000	1.0000	1.0000	0.0000
20	1.0000	1.0000	1.0000	1.0000	1.0000	1.0000	0.0000
21	0.9937	0.9979	0.9979	0.9958	1.0000	0.9970	0.0022
22	1.0000	1.0000	0.9958	0.9958	1.0000	0.9983	0.0021
23	1.0000	1.0000	1.0000	0.9979	0.9958	0.9987	0.0017
Avg.	0.9995	0.9993	0.9996	0.9989	0.9995	0.9994	0.0009

4.1   Performance Measure Using One Sample

Initially, the performance is measured using one sample image of an EEG signal with a duration of 8 s. The patient-wise sensitivity, specificity, and FPR are shown in Table 2. The achieved average sensitivity, specificity, and FPR are 0.9217, 0.8558, and 0.1442, respectively. The achieved AUC is 0.9542, which is excellent, as shown in Fig. 7.

4.2 Performance Measure Using the Majority Voting Technique

The achieved performance is acceptable using one sample of 8-s EEG signals; however, 8-s EEG signals are inadequate for efficient seizure prediction [2]. Physicians use long-duration EEG signals to predict seizures in advance. Hence, a majority voting from a sequence of 8-s signals is considered in our proposed method. The performance is better using the majority voting technique. Although, we have taken only 15 samples for voting due to more early prediction of seizure. It is found that the majority voting improves the performance of our proposed method. The achieved average sensitivity, specificity, and FPR are 0.9783, 0.9083, and 0.0917, respectively, which is remarkable, as indicated in Table 2.

In this article, a proficient seizure prediction method is proposed, which uses images of EEG signals. The most effective deep learning technique is CNN, which is used to mimic physicians for seizure prediction. A comparison of the proposed method with some state-of-the-art works is mentioned in Table 3. All the works mentioned in the table have applied the CHB-MIT database, though the number of patients and channels are different, as mentioned in Table 3. Our proposed method provides excellent classification accuracy. The achieved sensitivity is one of the best among others. The achieved specificity is not best compared with other works. The sensitivity is more important than the specificity for epilepsy patients to take necessary precautions. Our proposed method uses only six channels of EEG signals, which will be applicable for designing small-sized and less-power consumable seizure prediction devices.

Table 2. Performance measure using one sample and majority voting.

Patient Id	Using one sample			Using majority voting		
	SPEC	FPR	SEN	SPEC	FPR	SEN
01	0.8867	0.1133	1.0000	0.9083	0.0917	1.0000
02	0.8556	0.1444	1.0000	0.9333	0.0667	1.0000
03	0.8028	0.1972	0.9200	0.9000	0.1000	1.0000
04	0.6048	0.3952	0.9667	0.6387	0.3613	1.0000
05	0.8640	0.1360	0.9500	0.9250	0.0750	1.0000
06	0.8813	0.1188	0.9667	0.8917	0.1083	1.0000
07	0.8830	0.1170	1.0000	0.9250	0.0750	1.0000
08	0.9917	0.0083	1.0000	1.0000	0.0000	1.0000
09	0.7215	0.2785	0.9667	0.7815	0.2185	1.0000
10	0.7547	0.2453	0.8778	0.8333	0.1667	1.0000
11	0.8449	0.1551	0.9667	0.9333	0.0667	1.0000
12	0.9644	0.0356	1.0000	1.0000	0.0000	1.0000

(*continued*)

Table 2. (*continued*)

Patient Id	Using one sample			Using majority voting		
	SPEC	FPR	SEN	SPEC	FPR	SEN
13	0.9856	0.0144	0.8333	1.0000	0.0000	1.0000
14	0.7267	0.2733	0.7000	0.8833	0.1167	0.8333
15	0.9030	0.0970	0.9000	0.9778	0.0222	1.0000
16	0.7617	0.2383	0.7111	0.8583	0.1417	0.6667
17	0.8322	0.1678	0.9333	0.8500	0.1500	1.0000
18	0.8844	0.1156	0.9111	0.9467	0.0533	1.0000
19	0.9811	0.0189	1.0000	0.9917	0.0083	1.0000
20	1.0000	0.0000	1.0000	1.0000	0.0000	1.0000
21	0.8274	0.1726	0.7333	0.9556	0.0444	1.0000
22	0.8000	0.2000	0.9556	0.8000	0.2000	1.0000
23	0.9264	0.0736	0.9067	0.9574	0.0426	1.0000
Avg.	0.8558	0.1442	0.9217	0.9083	0.0917	0.9783

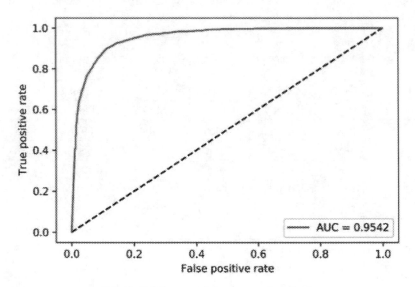

Fig. 7. ROC curve of our proposed method.

Table 3. Comparison study of our proposed method with few existing State-of-the-art works.

Research Work	Preprocessing / Feature extraction	Learning Technique	No. of channels	ACC	SEN	SPEC
Yao et al. [14]	EEG data	Bi-LSTM	17	0.8780	0.8730	0.8830
Jana et al. [2]	EEG data	CNN	06	0.9947	0.9783	0.9236
Ryu et al. [16]	DWT	DenseNet and LSTM	22	0.9328	0.9292	0.9365
Usman et al. [17]	EMD, CNN	SVM, CNN, LSTM	23	---	0.9628	0.9565
Guo et al. [18]	DWT	Easy-Ensemble	18	0.9262	0.9555	0.9257
Zhao et al. [22]	Raw EEG data	AddNet-SCL	23	---	0.9490	0.9230
Shen et al. [23]	Tunable-Q wavelet transform	CNN	08	0.9757	0.9890	0.9790
Kapoor et al. [24]	Statistical features	Ensemble classifier	22	0.9661	0.9467	0.9136
Proposed method	EEG data to image	CNN	06	0.9994	0.9783	0.9083

5 Conclusion and Future Research Directions

This article presents an efficient image-based seizure prediction model. The images of EEG signals are constructed from raw EEG data. The features are extracted from these images of the EEG signal. The proposed model predicts seizures before ten minutes of any seizure event. It will help patients or their well-wishers to avoid unwanted life risks. The important features are extracted from only six EEG channels using a CNN. The same CNN is also used to classify the preictal and interictal states. Our method provides an average accuracy and sensitivity of 0.9994 and 0.9783, respectively. It is one of the best methods among state-of-the-art works. The proposed seizure prediction model is patient-specific. One future research direction is the implementation of a patient-independent prediction model that will work efficiently for all epilepsy patients. The other research direction is the channel minimization. Our method uses only six EEG channels. It will be better to use fewer channels to implement small-sized devices, which will also consume less power to run for a longer time in each recharge.

References

1. World Health Organization, https://www.who.int/news-room/fact-sheets/detail/epilepsy, Accessed 15 June 2022
2. Jana, R., Mukherjee, I.: Deep learning based efficient epileptic seizure prediction with EEG channel optimization. Biomed. Signal Process. Control **68**, 102767 (2021)
3. Williamson, J.R., et al.: Seizure prediction using EEG spatiotemporal correlation structure. Epilepsy Behav. **25**(2), 230–238 (2012)
4. Zhang, Z., Parhi, K.K.: Low-complexity seizure prediction from IEEG/SEEG using spectral power and ratios of spectral power. IEEE Trans. Biomed. Circuits Syst. **10**(3), 693–706 (2016)
5. Xiang, J., et al.: The detection of epileptic seizure signals based on fuzzy entropy. J. Neurosci. Methods **243**, 18–25 (2015)
6. Dash, D.P., Kolekar, M.H., Jha, K.: Surface EEG based epileptic seizure detection using wavelet based features and dynamic mode decomposition power along with KNN classifier. Multimedia Tools Appl. **81**, 42057–42077 (2022)
7. Alickovic, E., Kevric, J., Subasi, A.: Performance evaluation of empirical mode decomposition, discrete wavelet transform, and wavelet packed decomposition for automated epieptic seizure detection and prediction. Biomed. Signal Process. Control **39**, 94–102 (2018)
8. Kumar, Y., Dewal, M.L., Anand, R.S.: Epileptic seizures detection in EEG using dwt-based apen and artificial neural network. SIViP **8**, 1323–1334 (2014)
9. Alotaiby, T.N., et al.: Epileptic seizure prediction using CSP and LDA for scalp EEG signals. Comput. Intell. Neurosci. **2017**, 1–11 (2017)
10. Chen, X., et al.: Cost-sensitive deep active learning for epileptic seizure detection. In: Proceedings of the 2018 ACM International Conference on Bioinformatics, Computational Biology, and Health Informatics, New York, USA, pp. 226–235 (2018)
11. Khan, H., et al.: Focal onset seizure prediction using convolutional networks. IEEE Trans. Biomed. Eng. **65**(9), 2109–2118 (2018)
12. Jana, R., Mukherjee, I.: Epileptic seizure prediction from raw EEG signal using convolutional neural network. In: Machine Vision and Augmented Intelligence—Theory and Applications, Lecture Notes in Electrical Engineering, Springer, Singapore, vol. 796, pp. 235–244 (2021) https://doi.org/10.1007/978-981-16-5078-9_20
13. Hu, X., Yuan, S., Xu, F., Leng, Y., Yuan, K., Yuan, Q.: Scalp EEG classification using deep Bi-LSTM network for seizure detection. Comput. Biol. Med. **124**, 103919 (2020)
14. Yao, X., et al.: A robust deep learning approach for automatic classification of seizures against non-seizures. Biomed. Signal Process. Control **64**, 102215 (2021)
15. Jana, R., Bhattacharyya, S., Das, S.: Epileptic seizure prediction from EEG signals using densenet. In: 2019 IEEE Symposium Series on Computational Intelligence, pp. 604–609 (2019)
16. Ryu, S., Joe, I.: A hybrid densenet-LSTM model for epileptic seizure prediction. Appl. Sci. **11**(11), 7661 (2021)
17. Usman, S.M., Khalid, S., Aslam, M.H.: Epileptic seizures prediction using deep learning techniques. IEEE Access **8**, 39998–40007 (2020)
18. Guo, Y., et al.: Epileptic seizure detection by cascading isolation forest-based anomaly screening and easyensemble. IEEE Trans. Neural Syst. Rehabil. Eng. **30**, 915–924 (2022)
19. Goldberger, A.L., et al.: PhysioBank, PhysioToolkit, and PhysioNet: Components of a New Research Resource for Complex Physiologic Signals, vol. **101**(23), pp. 215–220. Circulation Electronic Pages, (1998)
20. Hatipoglu, B., Yilmaz, C.L., Kose, C.: A signal-to-image transformation approach for EEG and MEG signal classification. SIViP **13**, 483–490 (2019)
21. LeCun, Y., Bengio, Y., Hinton, G.: Deep learning. Nature **521**, 436–444 (2015)

22. Zhao, Y., et al.: Patient-specific seizure prediction via adder network and supervised contrastive learning. IEEE Trans. Neural Syst. Rehabil. Eng. **30**, 1536–1547 (2022)
23. Shen, M., et al.: Real-time epilepsy seizure detection based on EEG using tunable-q wavelet transform and convolutional neural network. Biomed. Signal Process. Control **82**, 104566 (2023)
24. Kapoor, B., Nagpal, B., Jain, P.K., Abraham, A., Gabralla, L.A.: Epileptic seizure prediction based on hybrid seek optimization tuned ensemble classifier using EEG signals. Sensors **23**(1), 423 (2022). https://doi.org/10.3390/s23010423

Adjust Your Focus: Defocus Deblurring from Dual-Pixel Images Using Explicit Multi-Scale Cross-Correlation

Kunal Swami[1,2(✉)]

[1] Samsung Research, Bangalore, India
kunal.swami@samsung.com
[2] Indian Institute of Science, Bengaluru, India
kunalswami@iisc.ac.in

Abstract. Defocus blur is a common problem in photography. It arises when an image is captured with a wide aperture, resulting in a shallow depth of field. Sometimes it is desired, e.g., in portrait effect. Otherwise, it is a problem from both an aesthetic point of view and downstream computer vision tasks, such as segmentation and depth estimation. Defocusing an out-of-focus image to obtain an all-in-focus image is a highly challenging and often ill-posed problem. A recent work exploited dual-pixel (DP) image information, widely available in consumer DSLRs and high-end smartphones, to solve the problem of defocus deblurring. DP sensors result in two sub-aperture views containing defocus disparity cues. A given pixel's disparity is directly proportional to the distance from the focal plane. However, the existing methods adopt a naïve approach of a channel-wise concatenation of the two DP views without explicitly utilizing the disparity cues within the network. In this work, we propose to perform an explicit cross-correlation between the two DP views to guide the network for appropriate deblurring in different image regions. We adopt multi-scale cross-correlation to handle blur and disparities at different scales. Quantitative and qualitative evaluation of our multi-scale cross-correlation network (MCCNet) reveals that it achieves better defocus deblurring than existing state-of-the-art methods despite having lesser computational complexity.

Keywords: Dual-Pixel Sensors · Defocus Deblurring · Cross-Correlation · All-in-focus Image

1 Introduction

In photography, defocus blur is a common problem. When the aperture size is large, the depth of field becomes shallow, resulting in defocus blur. Sometimes defocus blur is desired, e.g., portrait effect. In other cases, it results from a trade-off between aperture size and shutter speed. To obtain a well-lit sharp image, the photographer can decrease the shutter speed while keeping the aperture fixed or increase the aperture while keeping the shutter speed fixed. The first option can lead to motion blur if the scene is dynamic, whereas the second

H. Kaur et al. (Eds.): CVIP 2023, CCIS 2009, pp. 318–330, 2024.
https://doi.org/10.1007/978-3-031-58181-6_27

option decreases the depth of field, leading to defocus blur. Apart from being an aesthetic problem, defocus blur also affects downstream computer vision tasks, such as depth estimation and semantic segmentation. As a result, it is essential to address this problem.

The task of defocus deblurring is ill-posed. If the blur is high, the original scene information is lost. The blur is also spatially varying because it depends on scene depth, the distance of the point from the focal plane, aperture size, and the optical properties of the camera.

Recently, Abuolaim et al. [2] exploited Dual-Pixel (DP) image information to solve the problem of defocus deblurring. DP sensors provide two sub-aperture views, which contain the defocus disparity cues. Specifically, in DP images, a given pixel's disparity is proportional to its distance from the focal plane. This disparity information can serve as a valuable cue to guide the network about the amount of deblurring required for a pixel or image region.

However, the authors in [2] use a naïve approach of a channel-wise concatenation of the two DP views without explicitly utilizing the disparity cues within the network. This approach leads to partial deblurring and artifacts in the output. Therefore, we are motivated to explore correspondence matching or cross-correlation between the dual pixel images within the network architecture to assist the network in accurate deblurring.

Therefore, in this work, we propose a new architecture to perform explicit cross-correlation between the DP images. More specifically, we adopt multi-scale cross-correlation within the network architecture to guide the network to perform appropriate deblurring in a given image region. The proposed multi-scale cross-correlation mechanism significantly improves network performance at the defocus deblurring task. We also show that the proposed model requires fewer parameters and FLOPS than DPDNet [2] and other state-of-the-art methods in literature to achieve better defocus deblurring with higher PSNR and SSIM.

To summarize, following are the important contributions of this work:

1. We propose a new network architecture for DP defocus image deblurring called MCCNet that utilizes an explicit multi-scale cross-correlation between the DP left and right images.
2. The proposed model achieves state-of-the-art quantitative and qualitative results on the standard DPDD [2] dataset and demands lesser computational complexity. We also report the results of several ablation studies to demonstrate the effectiveness of different modules in MCCNet.

2   Related Work

2.1   Dual-Pixel Sensors

Figure 1 shows the image formation in a traditional camera sensor and a DP sensor. A DP sensor contains two photodiodes at each pixel, allowing the pixel reading to split into two halves. As a result, any points which do not lie on the focal plane get distributed across multiple pixels, and exhibit disparity in

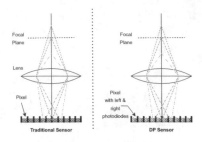

Fig. 1. DP sensor image formation.

DP left and right images. Considering the DP left image as a reference, the disparity direction of a point depends on whether the point lies in front (yellow in Fig. 1) or behind (green in Fig. 1) the focal plane. The amount of disparity of a point depends on the number of sensor pixels it gets spread. This point spread function (PSF) depends on the aperture size and the distance of the point from the focal plane. The defocus disparity information in DP images is a valuable cue to determine the deblurring required for a given pixel or image region. The reader is encouraged to refer to [2,3] for a detailed technical discussion on DP image formation.

2.2   Defocus Deblurring

The defocus deblurring methods can be classified into two categories in the literature. The methods in the first category adopt a two-stage approach. The first stage estimates a defocus map, and the second uses the defocus map to perform non-blind deconvolution to restore the all-in-focus image. The methods in the second category adopt an end-to-end learning-based approach to generate deblurred output images directly. Representative methods from the first category include [6,8,12]. [6] used image gradients to compute the blur difference between the original and re-blurred images. [8] proposed a deep learning based approach for defocus map estimation.

Recently, Abuolaim *et al.* [2] proposed and performed DP based defocused deblurring for the first time. They adopt a UNet [11] style encoder-decoder network, which takes the concatenated DP left and right images as input. Abuolaim *et al.* [3] recently also proposed a method to generate a realistic synthetic DP dataset to solve misalignment issues in real-world DP dataset in [2]. Apart from these methods, a recent method [1] adopts a multi-task learning approach using three decoders. The three decoders learn to estimate the left, right, and all-in-focus images, respectively. Lee *et al.* [9] incorporate an auxiliary DP view supervision based disparity estimation task for improving the performance of the main defocus deblurring task.

In contrast to the existing methods, we focus on incorporating an explicit cross-correlation within the network architecture to guide the network about the amount of deblurring required for a given image region.

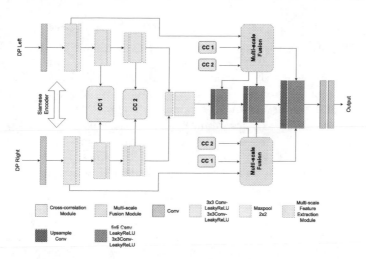

Fig. 2. The architecture of the proposed MCCNet architecture. Note that the Cross-correlation module outputs both left and right features. The two Multi-scale Fusion modules (one each for left and right features) share parameters.

3 Proposed Method

The proposed method exploits the disparity information from the two DP images using cross-correlation within the network architecture. In this section, we first describe the proposed network architecture MCCNet, followed by a detailed explanation of different modules in the MCCNet.

3.1 MCCNet Architecture

Figure 2 shows the detailed architecture of MCCNet. MCCNet adopts a siamese encoder to extract the DP left and right image features. More specifically, the parameters of the left and right encoder branches are shared. There are four encoder blocks, each composed of Conv-LeakyReLU-Conv-LeakyReLU layers. A MaxPool layer for downsampling follows the first, second and third encoder blocks. In the third and fourth encoder blocks, we adopt a Multi-scale Feature Extraction module (see Sect. 3.3) to achieve a higher receptive field crucial to restoring severely blurred image regions. The fourth encoder block fuses the DP left and right features, which the decoder uses to output a single deblurred image. The first convolution layer in the encoder outputs 16 channel feature map, whereas each encoder block outputs 32, 64, 64, and 128, channel feature maps, respectively.

The decoder blocks gradually upsample the feature maps while using the skip connections from the Multi-scale Fusion module (see Sect. 3.4). Each decoder block comprises an upsample layer and a 1x1 convolution layer to merge the skip connections. Lastly, the decoder block consists of Conv-LeakyReLU-Conv-LeakyReLU layers, where, unlike encoder blocks, the first convolution layer kernel size is 5x5. Three decoder blocks in MCCNet finally output full resolution deblurred output image.

The skip connections to the decoder blocks consist of multi-scale cross-correlation feature maps. Two Cross-correlation blocks (CC1 and CC2 in Fig. 2) are employed to perform cross-correlation at the second and third encoder blocks. Due to the high resolution of the input images (1680x1120), cross-correlation at the first encoder block becomes prohibitively memory expensive. A Multi-scale Fusion module fuses the cross-correlation information from multiple scales, which are then used by the decoder blocks as skip connections. Finally, the last two convolution layers output the full-resolution deblurred output image.

3.2   Cross-Correlation Module

Similar to the case of stereo images, where the correspondence matching needs to be performed only along the epipolar line, in the case of DP images, we need to perform the cross-correlation along the disparity direction. Figure 3 shows that because of the DP disparity constraint, a given pixel in DP left only needs to be matched with pixels along the same row in the DP right image. Recently, [14] proposed a modified self-attention mechanism by applying the stereo constraint. Motivated from [14], we also use the modified self-attention to compute the cross-correlation between a given pixel in the DP left image with all the pixels along the disparity direction in the DP right image. The detailed structure of the cross-correlation module is shown in Fig. 4.

As shown in Fig. 4, the Cross-correlation module used in this work takes the DP left and right feature maps and performs cross-correlation across the disparity direction. The computed attention maps are used to scale the input left and right feature maps. Mathematically, given two the DP left and right feature maps $\mathbf{A}, \mathbf{B} \in \mathbb{R}^{H \times W \times C}$, they are first passed through a residual block with shared parameters, followed by a 1x1 convolution to obtain the query $\mathbf{Q} \in \mathbb{R}^{H \times W \times C}$ and key $\mathbf{K} \in \mathbb{R}^{H \times W \times C}$ feature maps respectively. Then batch matrix multiplication (considering H as batch size) is performed between $\mathbf{Q}$ and $\mathbf{K}$ to obtain the matrix $\mathbf{S} \in \mathbb{R}^{H \times W \times W}$. Now, to compute the attention map of right feature maps w.r.t. the left feature maps, we take batch transpose (considering H as batch size) of $\mathbf{S}$, which is equivalent to obtaining $\mathbf{Q}$ from right feature maps and $\mathbf{K}$ form left feature maps and computing $\mathbf{S}$. $\mathbf{S}$ and $\mathbf{S}^T$ are passed through the softmax function to obtain the attention scores. The attention scores are multiplied with the input left and right feature maps.

Compared to the mechanism in [14], we simplify the Cross-correlation module by excluding the occlusion mask computation since it is not required in the case of DP images. DP images only have a few pixel disparities and thus do not contain significant occlusions.

3.3   Multi-scale Feature Extraction Module

Figure 5 shows the structure of the Multi-scale Feature Extraction module. This module is used to achieve a larger receptive field crucial to restoring severely

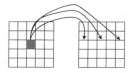

Fig. 3. This figure shows how a given pixel in the left DP image is cross-correlated with pixels in the right DP image.

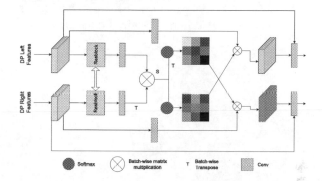

Fig. 4. This figure describes the Cross-correlation module used in this work for explicit cross-correlation between the left and right DP images.

blurred image regions. It also performs multi-scale feature fusion, which helps to detect features of different scales and makes the network robust to different blur sizes [7,10]. The incoming features are processed by 3x3 and 5x5 convolution layers, respectively. The outputs of previous convolution layers are concatenated and fed to the next 3x3 and 5x5 convolution layers, respectively. Finally, the outputs of previous convolutions layers are merged using a 1x1 convolution layer, which forms the output of this module. This module is inspired by the multi-scale residual block used for image super-resolution task [10].

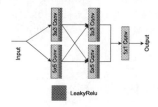

Fig. 5. This figure describes the Multi-scale Feature Extraction module.

3.4 Multi-scale Fusion Module

The Multi-scale Fusion module aims to perform interaction across cross-correlation features of different scales. Figure 6 shows the detailed structure of this module. Given three feature maps at different scales, the Multi-scale Fusion module fuses these feature maps at different scales. It outputs three modified feature maps, each corresponding to one of the input feature maps. More specifically, a scaler module is used to scale all the feature maps to the feature map's scale under consideration (e.g., the smallest one in Fig. 6). The scaled feature maps are then concatenated and processed by a 1×1 convolution layer, followed by a Multi-scale Feature Extraction module. A 1×1 convolution layer finally outputs the modified feature map corresponding to the one under consideration. The other input feature maps at different scales undergo the same process.

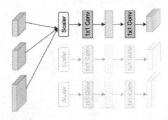

Fig. 6. This figure describes the Multi-scale Fusion module, which is used to fuse the encoder and cross-correlation features at different scales.

3.5   Loss Functions

We consider the Charbonnier [4] and MS-SSIM [15,16] loss functions for training our model MCCNet. Charbonnier loss function is a fully differentiable formulation of the L_1-norm loss function, which has a discontinuity at the origin. The Charbonnier loss function is formulated as follows:

$$\sqrt{x^2 + \epsilon^2} \tag{1}$$

The ϵ is set to a lower value, such as $1e-3$. This formulation of the L_1-norm smoothes the curve at the origin, thus, making it fully differentiable.

As advocated in [16], we adopt a mix [16] loss function combining the Charbonnier loss and the MS-SSIM loss functions with equal weightage, leading to superior results.

4   Experimental Setup

This section describes the dataset details, implementation details, and evaluation criteria used in this work.

4.1   Dataset

We use the DPDD dataset from the seminal work by Abuolaim *et al.* [2]. The DPDD dataset was captured using a Canon DSLR camera. It contains 500 samples, each containing three images, viz., left and right DP views, and all in-focus

Table 1. Quantitative comparison against state-of-the-art methods. Compared to other methods, MCCNet removes defocus deblurring more effectively and efficiently. Note: DPDNet+ and RDPD+ were additionally trained with synthetic DP data in [3].

Method	Year	PSNR ↑	SSIM ↑	MAE ↓	Params ↓	FLOPS ↓
JNB [12]	CVPR 2020	23.84	0.715	0.048	-	-
EBDB [6]	CVPR 2020	23.45	0.683	0.049	-	-
DMENet [8]	CVPR 2020	23.55	0.720	0.049	26.94M	-
IFAN [9]	CVPR 2021	25.37	0.789	0.039	10.48M	725.8G
KPAC [13]	ICCV 2021	25.22	0.774	0.040	1.58M	730.91G
MDP [1]	WACV 2022	25.35	0.763	0.040	46.8M	7751.27G
DPDNet [2]	ECCV 2020	25.13	0.786	0.041	34.52M	1883.74G
DPDNet+ [3]	ECCV 2020	25.12	0.784	0.042	34.52M	1883.74G
RDPD+ [3]	ICCV 2021	25.39	0.772	0.040	27.51M	612.05G
MCCNet	-	25.85	0.802	0.037	5.52M	978.79G

images captured using a narrow aperture. Following [2], 350 samples are used for training, 74 for validation and 76 samples are used for testing. For training and validation, the images are cropped into patches with size 512x512. In contrast, the evaluation is performed on original 1680x1120 size images.

4.2 Implementation Details

The implementation of our work is done using the PyTorch deep learning framework. During training, the parameters of all models were initialized using the strategy proposed by He *et al.* [5]. Adam optimization is used with an initial learning rate of $1e - 4$, $\beta_1 - 0.9$, and $\beta_2 = 0.999$. The learning rate is halved after every 60 epoch. The total number of training epochs is set to 200.

4.3 Evaluation Criteria

For quantitative evaluation purposes, we adopt Peak Signal-to-Noise Ratio (PSNR) [16], Structural Similarity Index Measurement (SSIM) [15] and Mean Absolute Error (MAE) [16] metrics. The number of model parameters and FLOPS are also considered for the quantitative evaluation. Additionally, qualitative evaluation and comparison of results are also performed. We used publicly available source codes provided by authors to generate the quantitative and qualitative results for comparison.

5   Results and Discussion

Table 1 show the quantitative results of MCCNet against the state-of-the-art defocus deblurring methods in the literature. Similar to DPDNet [2] and other methods in the literature, we include JNB [12], and EBDB [6], which use traditional hand-crafted features to estimate a defocus map which is used to perform non-blind deconvolution. DMENet [8] uses a deep neural network to only estimate a defocus map. Also, DPDNet+ and RDPD+ [3] were trained on an additional synthetic DP dataset.

It can be seen that MCCNet obtains the highest PSNR, SSIM values and lowest MAE value compared to the other state-of-the-art methods. MCCNet obtains a 1.81% increase (0.46 dB increase) in PSNR value compared to the second best PSNR value obtained by RDPD+ [3], whereas 1.65% increase in SSIM value compared to the second best SSIM value obtained by IFAN [9]. Regarding MAE, MCCNet obtains a 5.13% decrease compared to the second best MAE value obtained by IFAN [9].

Furthermore, the number of parameters of MCCNet is the second lowest after IFAN [9]. Compared to DPDNet [2] and RDPD+ [3], MCCNet parameters are lesser by at least 80%. The FLOPS of MCCNet are $25-30\%$ higher than $[3,9,13]$ methods, whereas it is 2x lesser than DPDNet [2] and almost 8x lesser than [1].

The quantitative results and comparison reveals that MCCNet generates defocus deblurring more effectively and efficiently than the state-of-the-art.

The qualitative results and comparison of MCCNet are shown in two parts in Fig. 7 and 8 due to the space limitation. In Fig. 7, the improvements of MCCNet are visible in the zoomed section of test images. In the first image, MCCNet can remove the defocus blur on words much better than the other methods, making it possible to read them. In the second image, it is visible that the other methods fail to recover the lines on the wall and floor fully. MCC recovers the text details in the third, fourth, and fifth images much better than other methods.

In Fig. 8, it can be seen that MCC can recover the lamp post details much better than other methods in the first image. Similarly, in the second and third images, the details of the thin net and lines in the wall are recovered by MCCNet, while other methods fail to do so.

The qualitative results and comparison of MCCNet against the state-of-the-art methods reveal the superiority of MCCNet in removing the defocus blur.

6   Ablation Study

In this section, we present the ablation study results to understand the impact of various modules in MCCNet. The ablation study was designed to understand the impact following modules: Multi-scale Fusion module, Cross-correlation module and Multi-scale Feature Extraction module. We remove these modules individually and train MCCNet to observe the resulting PSNR and SSIM values. Table 2 shows the results of this ablation study.

It can be seen in Tab. 2 that removing the Multi-scale Fusion module decreases the PSNR and SSIM values slightly, whereas removing the Cross-correlation module decreases the PSNR and SSIM values considerably. The model does not use a siamese encoder in the *no Cross-correlation module* setting, the DP left and right images are concatenated and fed to the network. Finally,

Table 2. Results of ablation study to understand the effect of different modules in MCCNet.

Setting	PSNR	SSIM
MCCNet	**25.85**	**0.802**
No Multi-scale Fusion	25.61	0.791
No Cross-correlation	25.12	0.784
No Muti-scale Feature Extraction	24.82	0.776

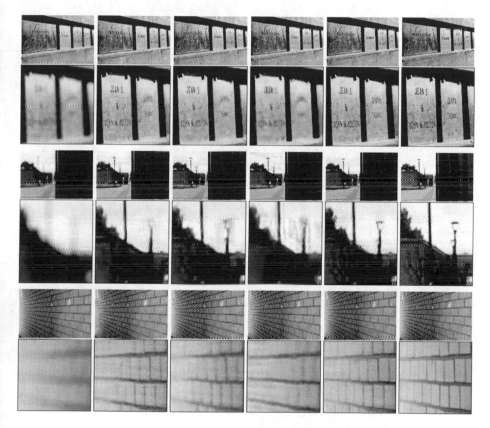

Fig. 7. Qualitative comparisons (part 1) of MCCNet against state-of-the-art methods. We include some zoomed and cropped regions for each test image to demonstrate the clear advantages of MCCNet. From left to right: Input, DPDNet [2], RDPD+ [3], MDP [1], MCCNet, Ground-truth.

when the Multi-scale Feature Extraction module is also removed, the performance drops even more. Interestingly, adding the Cross-correlation module (*No Multi-scale Fusion* setting) leads to state-of-the-art PSNR and SSIM results.

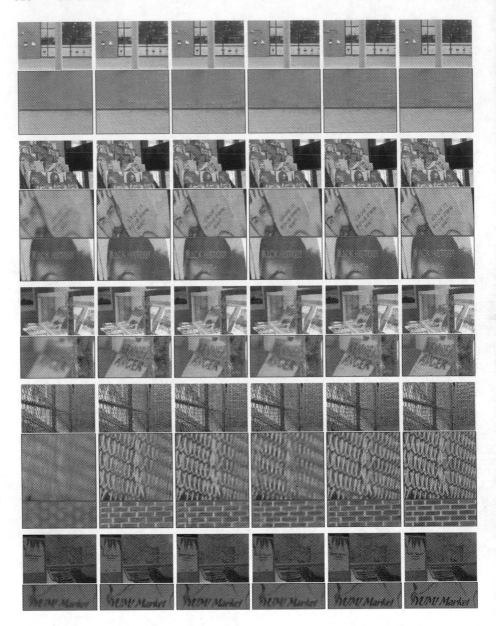

Fig. 8. Qualitative comparisons (part 2) of MCCNet against state-of-the-art methods. We include some zoomed and cropped regions for each test image to demonstrate the clear advantages of MCCNet. From left to right: Input, DPDNet [2], RDPD+ [3], MDP [1], MCCNet, Ground-truth.

7 Conclusion

In this work, we proposed a new defocused image deblurring method from dual-pixel images using an explicit cross-correlation between the dual-pixel image pair. More specifically, we adopted multi-scale cross-correlation to handle blur and disparities at different scales. Qualitative and quantitative evaluation of the proposed method established its superior performance compared to the state-of-the-art methods in the literature. The proposed method achieves state-of-the-art results with significantly less computational complexity than most defocus deblurring methods. Additionally, an ablation study was conducted to demonstrate the efficacy of various modules in the proposed network architecture.

References

1. Abuolaim, A., Afifi, M., Brown, M.S.: Improving single-image defocus deblurring: How dual-pixel images help through multi-task learning. In: WACV, pp. 82–90 (2022)
2. Abuolaim, A., Brown, M.S.: Defocus deblurring using dual-pixel data. In: ECCV, pp. 111–126 (2020)
3. Abuolaim, A., Delbracio, M., Kelly, D., Brown, M.S., Milanfar, P.: Learning to reduce defocus blur by realistically modeling dual-pixel data. In: ICCV, pp. 2289–2298 (2021)
4. Barron, J.T.: A general and adaptive robust loss function. In: CVPR, pp. 4331–4339 (2019)
5. He, K., Zhang, X., Ren, S., Sun, J.: Delving deep into rectifiers: surpassing human-level performance on imagenet classification. In: ICCV, pp. 1026–1034 (2015)
6. Karaali, A., Jung, C.R.: Edge-based defocus blur estimation with adaptive scale selection. IEEE Trans. Image Process. $27(3)$, 1126–1137 (2017)
7. Lee, D., Lee, C., Kim, T.: Wide receptive field and channel attention network for JPEG compressed image deblurring. In: CVPR, pp. 304–313 (2021)
8. Lee, J., Lee, S., Cho, S., Lee, S.: Deep defocus map estimation using domain adaptation. In: CVPR, pp. 12222–12230 (2019)
9. Lee, J., Son, H., Rim, J., Cho, S., Lee, S.: Iterative filter adaptive network for single image defocus deblurring. In: CVPR, pp. 2034–2042 (2021)
10. Li, J., Fang, F., Mei, K., Zhang, G.: Multi-scale residual network for image super-resolution. In: Ferrari, V., Hebert, M., Sminchisescu, C., Weiss, Y. (eds.) ECCV 2018. LNCS, vol. 11212, pp. 527–542. Springer, Cham (2018). https://doi.org/10.1007/978-3-030-01237-3_32
11. Ronneberger, O., Fischer, P., Brox, T.: U-net: convolutional networks for biomedical image segmentation. In: Navab, N., Hornegger, J., Wells, W.M., Frangi, A.F. (eds.) MICCAI 2015. LNCS, vol. 9351, pp. 234–241. Springer, Cham (2015). https://doi.org/10.1007/978-3-319-24574-4_28
12. Shi, J., Xu, L., Jia, J.: Just noticeable defocus blur detection and estimation. In: CVPR, pp. 657–665 (2015)
13. Son, H., Lee, J., Cho, S., Lee, S.: Single image defocus deblurring using kernel-sharing parallel atrous convolutions. In: ICCV, pp. 2642–2650 (2021)
14. Wang, L., et al.: Parallax attention for unsupervised stereo correspondence learning. IEEE Trans. Pattern Anal. Mach. Intell. $44(4)$, 2108–2125 (2022)

15. Wang, Z., Bovik, A.C., Sheikh, H.R., Simoncelli, E.P.: Image quality assessment: from error visibility to structural similarity. IEEE Trans. Image Process. **13**(4), 600–612 (2004)
16. Zhao, H., Gallo, O., Frosio, I., Kautz, J.: Loss functions for image restoration with neural networks. IEEE Trans. Comput. Imaging **3**(1), 47–57 (2017)

A Gradient-Based Approach
to Interpreting Visual Encoding Models

Subhrasankar Chatterjee$^{(\boxtimes)}$ and Debasis Samanta

Indian Institute of Technology, Kharagpur 721302, West Bengal, India
subhrasankarphd@iitkgp.ac.in

Abstract. The field of Computational Neuroscience has boomed over the past few decades. Research has been focused on devising neuroscientific models with state-of-the-art performance in replicating neural responses. A significant role is played by Deep Neural Networks (DNNs) in this pursuit. However, DNNs have a drawback in terms of interpretability. DNNs are infamous for their 'black box' nature that diminishes their usefulness in neuroscientific interpretability. In this article, we have proposed a gradient-based approach to address this issue. The proposed Voxelwise Stimulus Optimization Algorithm optimizes the stimulus image by backpropagating the loss calculated from the neural responses. The optimization algorithm generates an activated image map that determines the areas responsible for the predicted neural response. In other words, it develops a more generalized stimulus-response relationship. The study uses an AlexNet model and generates an activation map for all stimulus images from the Kay 2008 dataset based on the responses from the Lateral Occipital Lobe. The result obtained suggests that the shape-based features are responsible for activating the Lateral Occipital Lobe. The observation is consistent with previous literature, acting as a validation for our proposed algorithm.

Keywords: Optimization · Interpretablity · Neuroscience

1 Introduction

In recent years, technological advancements have allowed scientists to use computational models to understand better how the brain works. This level of understanding has dramatically impacted the field of neuroscience, as these models have helped researchers better understand the human brain's visual perception. Modeling techniques have evolved over the decade from early retinotopic models to handcrafted voxelwise encoding models (ENMs) [10], and more recently, deep neural networks (DNNs) based encoding models [1]. DNNs have gained popularity in object detection and classification due to their property as universal approximators [5]. The popularity has also spread in the field of neuroscience, causing researchers to model visual system components with various DNN models [1,6–8,18,21,26]. However, one of the significant challenges with deep neural networks is that they are often considered a "black box" - the internal workings of these systems are not fully understood. The processing of DNNs happens in multiple hidden layers with non-linear activation functions, which makes it harder to understand and interpret. This lack of interpretability is a significant obstacle that must be addressed to utilize these models' potential in neuroscientific research fully.

Models in DNNs often make correct predictions, but for the "wrong reasons," i.e., there might not be any medical or neuroscientific reasoning to their predicted output [2]. Due to this unexplainable nature of their behavior, understanding and interpreting a model is highly significant. Interpretability in DNNs has been under constant study since 2009. In 2009, it was identified that there is a need to analyze the representation of features in DNNs beyond the first layer [4]. Since then, various visualization techniques have been proposed, including the use of Deconvolutional Networks (convents) [27] and numerical optimization to project the feature activations back to the input pixel space [13,15,20,24,25]. In 2015, a technique called Class Activation Map was introduced that highlights the critical regions in the image for predicting a class [28]. This method was later improved by introducing DeepLIFT (Learning Important Features), which compares each neuron's activation to its 'reference activation' to assign contribution scores [22,23]. In 2019, Gradient-weighted Class Activation Mapping (Grad-CAM) was proposed as a widely applicable approach to generate visual explanations for decisions from a large class of CNN-based models [19]. As discussed, most of the literature is focused on classification-based models. However, models in neuroscience predict the response pattern, which is not a classification problem. Therefore, the nature of interpretation is not directly applicable to neuroscience.

Models in neuroscience are more complex than conventional classification-based models because they must apply to novel images irrespective of the training data [10]. Classification-based models are unfit for the task as any stimuli from a class outside the training data are beyond comprehension, and hence, the models are not generalized. Visual Encoding models try to predict the neural responses instead of which class the stimuli belong to, forming a more generalized learning paradigm [11,16]. Earlier visual encoding models like the Gabor Wavelet Pyramid [10] or Semantic Labelling-based models [17] were transparent in terms of interpretability. Traditional Encoding models are trained in the stimulus-to-feature transformation phase and the feature-to-response transformation phase [11,16]. The transparency can be attributed to the feature-to-response transformation phase due to its regression-based modeling, where one can quickly identify the features used to make the prediction. However, as we move towards end-to-end trainable neural network models, the transparency gets lost [1,6–8,18,21,26]. A need for post hoc explanation arises as we go deeper to understand the workings of the human brain. The scope of post hoc explanation can be narrowed down to understanding the relationship between the stimulus and the response instead of directly aiming to understand the active neuronal circuitry. The literature shows that as the representation changes deeper down

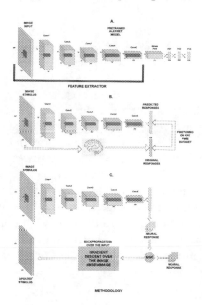

Fig. 1. Methodology. A. General Framework of AlexNet Model. It has five Convolutional Layers, a Global Average Pooling, and three Fully Connected Layers. We have used a pre-trained AlexNet Model, trained on the ImageNet Dataset. The features from each layer are extracted, and their performance is verified against the voxel responses of LatOcc. Based on the outcome, the first five layers are considered the 'Feature Extractor.' B. General Framework of Encoding Model. The Feature Extractor of AlexNet is concatenated with an untrained, Fully Connected Layer. The Fully Connected Layer is fine tuned on the voxel responses of Kay 2008 fMRI Dataset, while the other parameters of the Model are kept fixed. This newly trained Model acts as our Encoding Model. C. Optimization Over Image. The Validation Stimulus is passed on to the Model to generate predicted responses. Mean Squared Error (MSE) is calculated to calculate the dissimilarity between predicted and original responses. The Mean Squared Error is differentiated for the Input Stimuli to generate the modified Image.

the layers of DNN, specific areas of an image contribute higher to the predicted class [4]. We are interested in observing whether the same happens for the human brain. Therefore, the research question can be formulated as "Which part of the input stimulus (image) is responsible for generating the targeted neural responses (voxelwise fMRI response)?

With the availability of varied literature on explainable AI, it is comparatively harder to choose which algorithm fits our requirement the best. The selection of the algorithm is based on domain adaptability. Interpretability is a domain-dependent concept, i.e., the perspective of interpretability changes as we shift domains such as DNN-based Computer Vision to DNN-based Visual Encoding. We are interested in a mathematical construct that would keep the interpretation consistent, even when shifted from Computer Vision to Visual Neuroscience [9]. In this article, we have adapted the Gradient Descent Optimization Algorithm and extended it to voxelwise interpretability for Deep Neural Networks. Traditionally, methods such as Grad-CAM [19] and Guided Backpropagation [25] aim to determine what the model sees based on its classification results. On the other hand, our Voxelwise Stimulus Optimization (VSO) algorithm determines what the model is seeing based on the predicted voxel information. Initially, we assumed a pre-trained deep neural network model trained on the ImageNet Dataset [3], namely, AlexNet [12]. Secondly, we verified the prediction performance of generated feature sets against the neural responses of Lateral Occipital Voxels. The layer with the highest prediction performance was then used as a "Feature Extractor" and was appended with a fully connected layer to act as the neural response predictor. The fully connected layer was then fine-tuned on the Kay 2008 fMRI dataset [10]. The generated voxel-wise prediction was then backpropagated to the input image for any given image. This optimization resulted in a modified version of the input image with noisy grains at the model focus points. The resulting image was subtracted from the original to generate the saliency map. The produced map highlights parts of the image responsible for the targeted voxel response.

2   Hypothesis

2.1   Conceptual Structure

The question of understanding how the functions of the physical brain correspond to visual processing and perception has always been the center of research in the field of Visual Neuroscience. Various Modelling techniques have been applied over the years to try and understand the internal mechanisms of the brain. One such technique is Voxelwise Visual Encoding, where the neuron's (voxels) activity is described as a function of the input stimulus or task. Encoding models can typically be divided into two constituent phases: non-linear feature extraction and linear regression. The feature extraction phase uses a non-linear transformation function to transform the input stimulus to an N-dimensional feature space [10,11,16]. The linear regression phase projects the feature space onto the generated responses. The generated responses are compared with the original neural responses to measure the model's goodness. Theoretically, a model with high prediction performance is regarded as a functional equivalent of the human brain for that particular task.

For performance verification and validating our proposed method, we have used the Kay 2008 dataset [10]. The Kay 2008 dataset contains 1750 training and 120 validation images and their respective fMRI responses. The images do not have class labels-the images and the fMRI voxel data act as the stimulus and the responses, respectively. The training and validation set images are mutually exclusive, i.e., the model receives novel images for validation irrespective of the training dataset. The fMRI voxel responses are segregated according to different brain regions involved in visual processing, such as V1, V2, V3a, V3b, V4, Lateral Occipital Lobe. In this article, we will only consider the responses of the lateral occipital lobe.

2.2   Transparency of a Model

In this context, a model can be considered transparent if an intuitive explanation can be attributed to each part of the model, i.e., the stimulus, features, and the relationship. A nave example would be a linear regression model where the parameters could be interpreted as strength representing the association between the features and the generated response. On this note, Encoding models can be initially thought of as transparent. Let us consider an encoding model, shown in 2, that replicates the behavior of the primary visual cortex for orientation detection. The input stimulus (oriented bar) is presented as a 3 × 3 matrix. The output is the neural response generated from the cells in V1. The diagram shows that the presented stimulus is received by the Lateral Geniculate Nucleus (LGN). The information is processed by the LGN and passed on to the simple cells. The simple cells extract local orientation information, and the complex cells sum up the total activation to determine the final orientation of the object [14]. The mathematical basis of simple and complex cells is well understood from previous literature, so this model can be considered transparent.

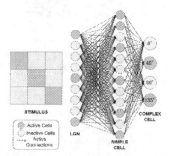

Fig. 2. An interpretable model of the primary visual cortex. A 3 × 3 strobe of light is presented as input. The Lateral Geniculate nucleus initially receives the input. The information from the LGN activates some of the simple cells. The simple cells detect orientation information and pass it on to the complex cells, which sums up the activation of the simple cells. The complex cells represent the orientation of the strobe. This framework is easy to explain and hence, is termed "transparent."

However, this only applies when we have an intrinsic understanding of the feature space. In the case of Deep DNNs, neither the learning mechanism nor the generated feature space is fully understood, making DNNs infamous as the 'Black Box' Models.

2.3   Interpretablity in Neuroscience

Interpretability in AI tries to understand the contribution of model components toward its targeted prediction-however, the perspective of interpretability changes based on its application domain [9]. Interpretability in Neuroscience is more concerned with understanding how the human brain achieves a given processing task and the neural circuitry involved. A similar explanation is expected out of models engaged in Computational Neuroscience. Neuroscientific interpretability has no common ground truth and is a relative term. It largely depends on the scientific question under study. This factual basis gives us the liberty to define interpretability in our terms for the sake of this study. We proposed a simple question that will shed some light on the internal mechanism of processing involved in visual perception. Research Question: "Which part of the input stimulus (image) is responsible for the evoked neural responses (voxelwise fMRI response)?". As discussed previously, DNNs do not exhibit a transparent nature. Therefore, this kind of question requires additional mathematical processing. We tried to generate a saliency map based on and provide an ad hoc explanation concerning the generated map.

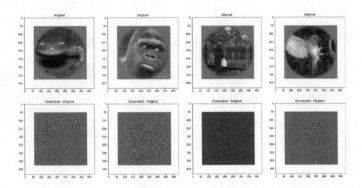

Fig. 3. Activation Images. The top row presents the images of some stimuli shown to the model during validation. The bottom row illustrates the activated areas in the image stimulus (Original Image - Modified Image). It can be observed that the activated regions correspond to the areas containing some distinctive shape in the original stimulus. In other words, the image's background does not activate as much as the object in focus. This observation can be interpreted as the model is focused on detecting shape information more than what is in the background.

2.4 Voxelwise Stimulus Optimization

For simplicity and understanding, let us consider a vanilla neural network with three layers, an input layer, a hidden layer, and an output layer. Let the prediction of the output layer be $a^{(L)}$, then

$$z^{(L)} = W^{(L-1)} . a^{(L-1)} + b^{(L-1)} \tag{1}$$

$$a^{(L)} = f(z^{(L)}) \tag{2}$$

where, $W^{(L-1)}$ and $b^{(L-1)}$ are the weight matrix and bais vector for $(L-1)th$ layer respectively, and $f(.)$ is the activation function.

From Eq. 1 and 2, the same can be extended for the $(L-2)th$ layer. Then,

$$z^{(L-1)} = W^{(L-2)}.a^{(L-2)} + b^{(L-2)} \tag{3}$$

$$a^{(L-1)} = f(z^{(L-1)}) \tag{4}$$

where, $a^{(L-2)}$ is my input vector to the neural network.

The Mean Squared Error (MSE) loss can be calculated as,

$$E = \frac{1}{n}\sum_{i=1}^{n}(Y - a^{(L)})^2 \tag{5}$$

where Y is the Original Neural Response, and n is the number of instances.

Now, we are interested in updating the input for the Error term,

$$\frac{\delta E}{\delta a^{(L-2)}} = \frac{\delta E}{\delta a^{(L)}}.\frac{\delta a^{(L)}}{\delta z^{(L)}}.\frac{\delta z^{(L)}}{\delta a^{(L-1)}}.\frac{\delta a^{(L-1)}}{\delta z^{(L-1)}}.\frac{\delta z^{(L-1)}}{\delta a^{(L-2)}} \tag{6}$$

$$\frac{\delta E}{\delta a^{(L-2)}} = \frac{1}{n}\sum(Y - a^{(L)}).f'(z^{(L)}).W^{(L-1)}.f'(z^{(L-1)}).W^{(L-2)} \tag{7}$$

Therefore, the input can be modified for the loss as,

$$a^{(\hat{L}-2)} = a^{(L-2)} - \frac{\delta E}{\delta a^{(L-2)}} \tag{8}$$

The features move towards minimizing the error as the input is modified over iterations. Hence, the features with higher contributions to the predicted output will have higher gradients and, therefore, will be highlighted. Extending the same concept to Convolutional Neural Networks(CNN), it can be intuitively inferred that the features responsible for predicting a target will be highlighted. This optimization mechanism is called 'Voxelwise Stimulus Optimization.'

3   Result

3.1   Experimental Setup

We have adopted the encoding model approach to investigate the relationship between stimulus and response. We have chosen a pre-trained AlexNet model with five convolutional layers and three fully connected layers. The general structure of the proposed framework is given in Fig. 1. Firstly, we want to verify the model's performance for the neural responses. Each layer of the pre-trained AlexNet model acts as an individual feature descriptor. Seven different feature sets can be obtained by passing the image stimulus through the model. To determine which feature set is best suited for the responses of LatOcc, we train an individual regressor model for each feature set. Each regressor model generates a set of predicted neural responses that correlate with the initial neural response. The layer with the highest prediction performance is considered for further analysis (refer to Fig. 4). The training part of the model was trained for 100 epochs

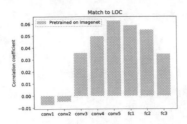

Fig. 4. Prediction performance of features generated from each layer of the AlexNet Model. It can be observed from the bar graph that the correlation of response predicted from Conv5 for the original neural responses of LatOcc is the highest. Hence, the pretrained AlexNet model up to layer Conv5 is considered for feature extraction in our framework.

on the LatOcc part of the fMRI dataset, with SGD as the optimizer and a 0.01 Learning rate. The training data was partitioned into 32, 64, and 128 batch sizes. The best results were yielded by Batch size 32.

Finally, we want to optimize the image for the predicted response from the nth layer of the Alexnet model. So, all layers after the nth layer are removed. The nth layer is connected to a fully connected layer, initialized with random weights. The fully connected layer is regarded as the output layer and is finetuned on the image-response pair from the training set. The modified AlexNet model is now ready to optimize the original input image. However, the generated image is a distorted version of the original image and is uninterpretable. So, a couple of post-processing steps are also included to generate a more precise image. For the testing part of the model, Activation Maps were generated for different no of iterations, i.e., 1, 3, 5, 10, and 20. It has been observed that the best results are obtained for ten iterations. The learning rate was set to 0.01, and an SGD optimizer was used.

The generated activation image is first smoothened with a 13×13 blur filter. The smoothened image is subtracted from the original image. This image generated the regions of interest for each input image. Following this, the ROI image is thresholded globally with a cutoff of 127. This process binarizes the image and only keeps the necessary parts. Then, a heat map is generated by forming contours from the dispersed patches of pixels. A better understanding can be gained from the images Fig. 5 and 6.

3.2   Analysis

The first experiment was designed to determine which layer from the model adequately represents the behavior of LatOcc responses. Responses generated from features of each layer were correlated with the original responses, as shown in Fig. 4. The features from the last convolutional layer (Conv 5) were observed to present the highest degree of correlation among all the feature sets. As we go from the initial convolutional layer (Conv 1) towards the deeper layers (Conv 4 and Conv 5), the similarity with responses for LatOcc increases. Therefore, the initial layers of a CNN are more suited to represent primary features like edges, similar to the human visual processing system. The higher visual areas capture complex information, such as shapes or objects, which the deeper layers of a CNN can represent (refer to Fig. 3 and Fig. 5).

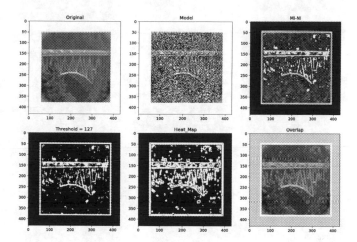

Fig. 5. Generated Mask from Backpropagation. Input Stimulus (Top Left), Activation Image (Top Middle), Activation Image - Original Input (Top Right), Thresholded Image (Bottom Left), Heat Map (Bottom Middle), and Generated Mask. The generated mask covers almost all areas of the object in the foreground. In this case, the area under focus is the bridge.

The second part of the experiment is designed to answer the question, "Which part of the input stimulus (image) is responsible for the evoked neural responses (voxelwise fMRI response)?". The input stimulus was modified by backpropagating the loss through each model layer. The obtained results are presented in 3. From the activated image, it can be inferred that the areas with distinctive shapes are highlighted. The activation areas are not focused on the background of the image. This observation can be interpreted as the model focusing more on objects or shapes than scenery or background areas. The model was trained with neural responses from the Lateral Occipital Lobe. So, it could be interpreted as the Lateral Occipital Lobe is more focused on the shapes and objects in the presented stimulus. This explanation is consistent with the literature where we know that the higher visual areas, such as LatOcc and IT, are involved in processing more complex visual information, such as shapes and objects.

Further processing of the activated image is done to generate understandable saliency maps. However, a major issue still pertains. As from Fig. 5 and 6, it can be observed that the saliency map contains a lot of small patches and blobs. This lack of precision is caused by the fact that the model does not produce a perfect prediction. Since the correlation between the model prediction and the actual neural response is mathematically low, this amount of error is observable.

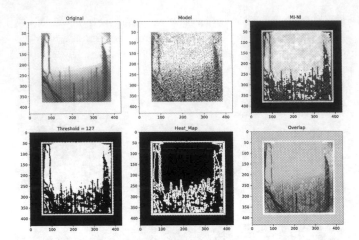

Fig. 6. Generated Mask from Backpropagation. Input Stimulus (Top Left), Activation Image (Top Middle), Activation Image - Original Input (Top Right), Thresholded Image (Bottom Left), Heat Map (Bottom Middle), and Generated Mask. The generated mask covers almost all areas of the object in the foreground. In this case, the area under focus is the trees.

With improvement in model prediction performance, this issue can also be mitigated. It is to be noted that a mathematically low correlation is not necessarily scientifically low, as neural responses have a very low explainable variance.

4   Discussion

The present work investigated the relationship between the stimulus and the response by adopting the encoding model approach. The study utilized a pre-trained AlexNet model, which has five convolutional layers and three fully connected layers, to determine the best-suited feature set for the responses of LatOcc. The findings showed that the features from the last convolutional layer (Conv 5) presented the highest degree of correlation with the original neural responses.

The results of this work provide valuable insights into the neural representation of visual stimuli in higher visual areas such as LatOcc. The fact that the deeper layers of a CNN are more suited to represent complex information, such as shapes or objects, is consistent with the literature, where higher visual areas are involved in processing more complex visual information.

However, the results also indicated room for improvement in the model's prediction performance, as the generated saliency maps contained a lot of small patches and blobs due to the low correlation between the model prediction and the actual neural response. Further research can be conducted to enhance the model's performance and better understand the neural representation of visual stimuli in different brain regions.

In conclusion, the present study represents a step toward understanding the relationship between visual stimuli and neural responses in higher visual areas. The results can be used to guide future studies in the field of cognitive neuroscience. The findings also highlight the potential of encoding models in investigating the neural basis of perception and cognition.

References

1. Agrawal, P., Stansbury, D., Malik, J., Gallant, J.: Pixels to voxels: modeling visual representation in the human brain (2014)
2. DeGrave, A., Janizek, J., Lee, S.I.: AI for radiographic COVID-19 detection selects shortcuts over signal. Nat. Mach. Intell. **3** (2021). https://doi.org/10.1038/s42256-021-00338-7
3. Deng, J., Dong, W., Socher, R., Li, L.J., Li, K., Li, F.F.: Imagenet: a large-scale hierarchical image database, pp. 248–255 (2009). https://doi.org/10.1109/CVPR.2009.5206848
4. Erhan, D., Bengio, Y., Courville, A., Vincent, P.: Visualizing higher-layer features of a deep network. Technical report, Univeristé de Montréal (01 2009)
5. Girshick, R., Donahue, J., Darrell, T., Malik, J.: Rich feature hierarchies for accurate object detection and semantic segmentation (2014)
6. Güçlü, U., van Gerven, M.: Deep neural networks reveal a gradient in the complexity of neural representations across the ventral stream. J. Neurosci. Official J. Soc. Neurosci. **35**, 10005–10014 (2015). https://doi.org/10.1523/JNEUROSCI.5023-14.2015
7. Güçlü, U., van Gerven, M.: Increasingly complex representations of natural movies across the dorsal stream are shared between subjects. NeuroImage **145** (2015). https://doi.org/10.1016/j.neuroimage.2015.12.036
8. Han, K., Wen, H., Shi, J., Lu, K.H., Zhang, Y., Liu, Z.: Variational autoencoder: An unsupervised model for modeling and decoding FMRI activity in visual cortex (2017). https://doi.org/10.1101/214247
9. Kar, K., Kornblith, S., Fedorenko, E.: Interpretability of artificial neural network models in artificial intelligence vs. neuroscience (2022). https://doi.org/10.48550/arXiv.2206.03951
10. Kay, K., Naselaris, T., Prenger, R., Gallant, J.: Identifying natural images from human brain activity. Nature **452**, 352–5 (2008). https://doi.org/10.1038/nature06713
11. Kay, K.N.: Principles for models of neural information processing. NeuroImage **180**, 101–109 (2018). https://doi.org/10.1016/j.neuroimage.2017.08.016
12. Krizhevsky, A., Sutskever, I., Hinton, G.: Imagenet classification with deep convolutional neural networks. In: Neural Information Processing Systems, vol. 25 (2012). https://doi.org/10.1145/3065386
13. Lapuschkin, S., Binder, A., Montavon, G., Klauschen, F., Müller, K.R., Samek, W.: On pixel-wise explanations for non-linear classifier decisions by layer-wise relevance propagation. PLoS ONE **10**, e0130140 (2015). https://doi.org/10.1371/journal.pone.0130140
14. Li, B., Todo, Y., Zheng, T.: Artificial visual system for orientation detection based on Hubel-Wiesel model. Brain Sci. **12**, 470 (2022). https://doi.org/10.3390/brainsci12040470

15. Montavon, G., Lapuschkin, S., Binder, A., Samek, W., Müller, K.R.: Explaining nonlinear classification decisions with deep taylor decomposition. Pattern Recogn. **65**, 211–222 (2017). https://doi.org/10.1016/j.patcog.2016.11.008

16. Naselaris, T., Kay, K.N., Nishimoto, S., Gallant, J.L.: Encoding and decoding in fMRI. NeuroImage **56**, 400–410 (2011). https://doi.org/10.1016/j.neuroimage.2010.07.073

17. Naselaris, T., Prenger, R.J., Kay, K.N., Oliver, M., Gallant, J.L.: Bayesian reconstruction of natural images from human brain activity. Neuron **63**, 902–915 (2009). https://doi.org/10.1016/j.neuron.2009.09.006

18. Oquab, M., Bottou, L., Laptev, I., Sivic, J.: Learning and transferring mid-level image representations using convolutional neural networks. In: Proceedings of the IEEE Computer Society Conference on Computer Vision and Pattern Recognition (2014). https://doi.org/10.1109/CVPR.2014.222

19. Rs, R., Cogswell, M., Das, A., Vedantam, R., Parikh, D., Batra, D.: Grad-cam: visual explanations from deep networks via gradient-based localization. Int. J. Comput. Vis. **128** (2020). https://doi.org/10.1007/s11263-019-01228-7

20. Samek, W., Binder, A., Montavon, G., Lapuschkin, S., Müller, K.R.: Evaluating the visualization of what a deep neural network has learned. IEEE Trans. Neural Netw. Learn. Syst. **28**, 2660–2673 (2017). https://doi.org/10.1109/TNNLS.2016.2599820

21. Shi, J., Wen, H., Zhang, Y., Han, K., Liu, Z.: Deep recurrent neural network reveals a hierarchy of process memory during dynamic natural vision. Hum. Brain Mapp. **39** (2018). https://doi.org/10.1002/hbm.24006

22. Shrikumar, A., Greenside, P., Kundaje, A.: Learning important features through propagating activation differences (2017)

23. Shrikumar, A., Greenside, P., Shcherbina, A., Kundaje, A.: Not just a black box: learning important features through propagating activation differences (2016)

24. Simonyan, K., Vedaldi, A., Zisserman, A.: Deep inside convolutional networks: visualising image classification models and saliency maps. preprint (2013)

25. Springenberg, J., Dosovitskiy, A., Brox, T., Riedmiller, M.: Striving for simplicity: the all convolutional net (2014)

26. Wen, H., Shi, J., Chen, W., Liu, Z.: Deep residual network predicts cortical representation and organization of visual features for rapid categorization. Sci. Rep. **8** (2018). https://doi.org/10.1038/s41598-018-22160-9

27. Zeiler, M.D., Fergus, R.: Visualizing and understanding convolutional networks. In: Fleet, D., Pajdla, T., Schiele, B., Tuytelaars, T. (eds.) ECCV 2014. LNCS, vol. 8689, pp. 818–833. Springer, Cham (2014). https://doi.org/10.1007/978-3-319-10590-1_53

28. Zhou, B., Khosla, A., Lapedriza, A., Oliva, A., Torralba, A.: Learning deep features for discriminative localization (2016). https://doi.org/10.1109/CVPR.2016.319

Isolated Sign Language Recognition Using Deep Learning

Sukanya Das$^{(\boxtimes)}$ ⓘ, Sumit Kumar Yadav ⓘ, and Debasis Samanta ⓘ

Department of Computer Science and Engineering, Indian Institute of Technology
Kharagpur, Kharagpur 721302, West Bengal, India
emailtosukanyadas@gmail.com

Abstract. Communicating with individuals who have hearing disabilities presents a significant challenge. Deaf and mute individuals rely on sign language to communicate, making it difficult for hearing individuals to understand. To bridge this communication gap and promote social inclusion, we focus on developing a system to recognize sign language gestures and convey information to hearing individuals. We conducted extensive research in this field by reviewing relevant research papers. Throughout the project, we explored various models and datasets, explicitly detecting word-level sign language using Long-term Recurrent Convolutional Networks (LRCN), Convolutional Neural Networks (CNN), and Convolutional Long Short-Term Memory (ConvLSTM) models on the WLASL dataset. Our approach involved multiple steps, starting with extracting frames from video data. We then applied preprocessing techniques to enhance the quality of input images, leading to improved model performance. Additionally, we utilized image segmentation methods to isolate the hand from the background, enabling our models to focus on relevant regions and enhance detection accuracy. In the future, we aim to incorporate word-level annotations to facilitate sentence-level and real-time sign language detection.

Keywords: Sign Language · Sign Language Recognition · Isolated sign · Deep Learning · Gesture Classification · CNN · LRCN · ConvLSTM

1 Introduction

Sign language plays a vital role in facilitating communication within the community of individuals who have difficulties with speech and hearing (deaf and mute). They interact with one another through hand gestures, facial expressions, and body actions. However, there is a significant communication barrier when deaf and hard-of-hearing individuals want to interact with individuals who do not understand sign language. This challenge is a pressing issue in society. Interpreters are often relied upon to bridge this communication gap by translating between sign language and spoken language. However, this solution is

H. Kaur et al. (Eds.): CVIP 2023, CCIS 2009, pp. 343–356, 2024.
https://doi.org/10.1007/978-3-031-58181-6_29

expensive and may not be accessible throughout a deaf person's lifetime. Therefore, advancements in automatic recognition of sign language gestures hold great promise for the deaf and mute community, as they have the potential to break down the existing communication barrier [15].

Developing accurate Sign Language Recognition (SLR) tools is a complex task, and achieving 100% accuracy for a large vocabulary is not feasible. Therefore, it is crucial to continue researching and developing new methods to gradually improve the reliability of SLR solutions. Deep learning models are widely recognized as the most suitable approach, but there is an ongoing debate about the optimal network architecture. Different designs have shown promising results, and thorough experimental evaluations are necessary to identify the best-performing algorithms. Collaboration and knowledge-sharing among research teams are valuable in refining SLR techniques. Given the regional variations in sign language, research efforts often focus on specific local contexts and involve individuals proficient in regional signs. Consequently, a substantial amount of scientific literature is addressing SLR problems, and the performance of proposed solutions is steadily improving each year [2].

The main objective of this research paper is to evaluate the effectiveness of deep learning techniques in recognizing and categorizing words from video frames in American Sign Language. The research aims to determine the suitability of the deep learning approach in improving the accuracy of sign language detection and classification for enhanced communication and accessibility for individuals with hearing impairments.

After extracting frames from the video, we applied preprocessing techniques to the image frames and segmented the data. The resultant dataset was classified by three deep learning techniques: CNN, ConvLSTM, and LRCN.

The subsequent sections of the document are structured in the following manner: We examine existing works on isolated SLR in Sect. 2. We then give the details of our baseline models in Sect. 3. Next, we present our practical assessments in Sect. 4, and we finalize the paper in Sect. 5.

2   Literature Survey

Al-Hammadi et al. [1] carried out Sign Language Recognition (SLR) using three datasets involving both sign-dependent and sign-independent recognition. They employed single and fusion parallel 3D Convolutional Neural Network (3DCNN) structures for their research. Sincan and Keles [14] developed an SLR model for Turkish Sign Language based on CNN and Long Short-Term Memory (LSTM). Using an attention model, they enhanced feature extraction with the Feature Pooling Module (FPM) and improved convergence speed. Yuan et al. [17] proposed a model for hand gesture recognition combining Deep Convolutional Neural Networks (DCNN) and LSTM. They handled challenges like gradient vanishing and overfitting by incorporating a residual module and addressed the complexity of hand gesture long-distance dependencies through an enhanced deep feature fusion network. Compared to Bayes, KNN, SVM, CNN, LSTM, and CNN-LSTM models, the Deep Feature Fusion Network (DFFN) has demonstrated strong performance on ASL and CSL datasets. Aly and Aly [3] developed an Arabic Sign Language Recognition (SLR) model utilizing a deep Bidirectional Long Short-Term Memory (BiLSTM) recurrent neural network. Hand shape features were extracted using Convolutional Self-Organizing Map, and hand regions were extracted using DeepLabv3+. The effectiveness of the suggested model was evident in signer-independent real-time Arabic SLR. It proves particularly suitable for recognizing isolated signs, and potential future research could emphasize continuous sign-based analysis. Rastgoo et al. [13] investigated a multi-modal, multi-view SLR model based on hand skeletons. They conducted feature fusion and assessed the effectiveness of both single-view and multi-view projections of hand skeleton data. They introduced deep pipeline architectures, which encompassed the Single Shot Detector (SSD), 2D Convolutional Neural Network (2DCNN), 3D Convolutional Neural Network (3DCNN), and Long Short-Term Memory (LSTM) for the automatic recognition of hand sign language. Lee et al. [10] devised an American Sign Language Recognition (SLR) model by integrating the k-Nearest Neighbors (KNN) approach with LSTM. Sign data was acquired using the Leap Motion controller. The proposed model (LSTM with KNN) achieved a superior performance of 99.44% to SVM, RNN, and LSTM models. Wei et al. [16] applied a code-matching technique and the Fuzzy K-mean algorithm to a CSL dataset that contained 2750 sign word samples for each subject. Botros et al. [4] performed Linear Discriminant analysis as a classification method and used Principal Component Analysis (PCA) to reduce dimensionality. And, several papers helped the understanding of this research area [4–9, 12] (Fig. 1).

Fig. 1. Samples from the dataset

3 Proposed Methodology

3.1 Problem to Be Addressed

In this paper, We have proposed deep learning techniques such as LRCN, CNN, and ConvLSTM to detect word-level sign language on the WLASL dataset. We first extract frames from the video data and preprocess them to improve the quality of the input images. We then apply image segmentation techniques to separate the hand from the background, which helps focus on the images' relevant regions. Finally, we will evaluate the performance of our model on a test set of videos from the WLASL dataset, using metrics such as accuracy, precision, and recall. The proposed approach for sign language recognition involves the following steps (Fig. 2):

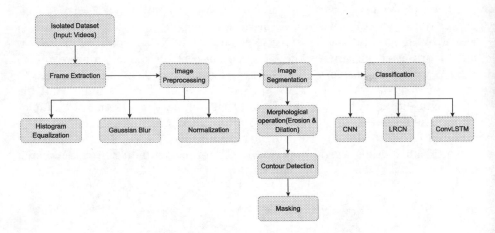

Fig. 2. Overview of the work

Data Preprocessing. In Sign language recognition for word-level datasets, frame extraction was performed to obtain individual images from sign language videos. Python's OpenCV library was used to load the videos, and frames were extracted at a chosen frame rate. The selected frame rate ensured an adequate representation of sign language gestures while minimizing redundancy. The extracted frames were saved in separate folders corresponding to each sign gesture. These frames underwent different techniques like image preprocessing and segmentation, which helped to separate the hand from the background and focus on the relevant regions of the images. For our recognition task, 40 frames were extracted from each video, with a frame rate of 25 frames per second. The frames were resized to a fixed size of 224×224 pixels, ensuring consistent dimensions for all frames.

Image Preprocessing. Histogram Equalization enhances the contrast in an image by redistributing pixel intensity values evenly across a broader range. Which ensures visual quality, distinguishes between features better, and enhances the visibility of details by making darker areas more visible and brighter areas less saturated.

Gaussian Blur reduces noise and smooths an image by applying a filter that removes high-frequency noise while preserving edges and essential features. The Gaussian kernel convolves the image, giving more weight to the centre and less to the surrounding pixels. It improves subsequent image processing steps and preserves edges.

Normalization scales pixel intensity values between 0 and 1, improving deep learning model performance by standardizing the data's scale and distribution. It facilitates more accessible learning and processing by the model.

Image Segmentation separates the foreground object (hand) from the background. It involves thresholding using Otsu's method to automatically determine a threshold separating foreground and background based on pixel intensity histogram. Morphological operations (erosion and dilation) refine the segmentation. Contour detection identifies hand boundaries, creating a binary mask. Then, to produce a segmented image, the original image is masked, focusing on the hand for further analysis or recognition.

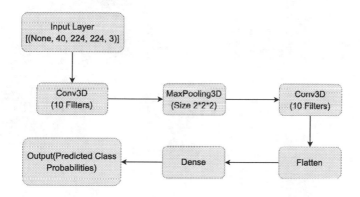

Fig. 3. Flowchart for CNN model architecture

CNN. The model consists of two 3D convolutional layers, each with 10 filters, followed by a 3D max pooling layer. The output of the max pooling layer is flattened to a 1D array. A fully connected dense layer with a softmax activation function produces a probability distribution over the classes. The first convolutional layer of a CNN extracts basic spatio-temporal features, such as edges, corners, and simple motion patterns. The second convolutional layer builds on these features to extract more complex spatio-temporal patterns and relationships, such as hand shapes, facial expressions, and body postures. However, some information can be lost while extracting spatio-temporal features, such as long-range temporal information, fine-grained temporal information, global spatial information, individual frame context, noise and artifacts, etc. The max pooling layer reduces spatial dimensions while retaining important features. The flatten layer converts the previous layer's output into a 1D array for the dense layer. The dense layer with softmax activation function provides the predicted class probabilities. The number of filters, filter sizes, activation functions, and pool size can be adjusted based on the specific requirements of the classification problem (Fig. 3).

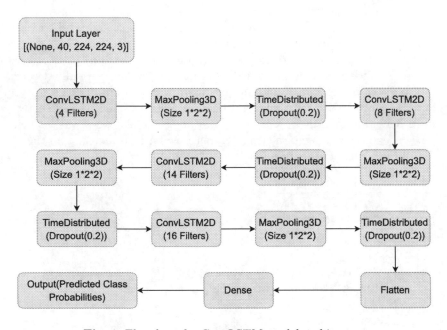

Fig. 4. Flowchart for ConvLSTM model architecture

ConvLSTM. A ConvLSTM is an LSTM network incorporating convolutional operations in its architecture, allowing it to capture spatial features while considering the temporal relation. ConvLSTM cells are LSTM cells with convolution embedded, making them suitable for spatio-temporal data modelling. For video classification, ConvLSTM effectively captures spatial and temporal relations in frames. The model uses ConvLSTM2D recurrent layers from Keras, with a specified number of filters and kernel size for convolutional operations. MaxPooling3D layers reduce frame dimensions and avoid unnecessary computations, while Dropout layers prevent overfitting. The architecture is simple, with a small number of trainable parameters. ConvLSTM2D layers extract spatio-temporal features from each frame, while MaxPooling3D and Dropout layers help with overfitting. The Flatten layer converts the output of ConvLSTM2D layers into a

1D array, and the Dense layer with softmax activation produces the final classification probabilities. The input shape is (Sequence length, Image height, Image width, 3) where 3 represents the RGB colour channels. The model consists of multiple ConvLSTM2D layers with increasing filter sizes, followed by MaxPooling3D and Dropout layers. TimeDistributed layers are used to apply Dropout to each frame independently. The Flatten layer flattens the output of the ConvLSTM2D layers, and the Dense layer outputs the classification probabilities with the number of units equal to the number of output classes (Fig. 4).

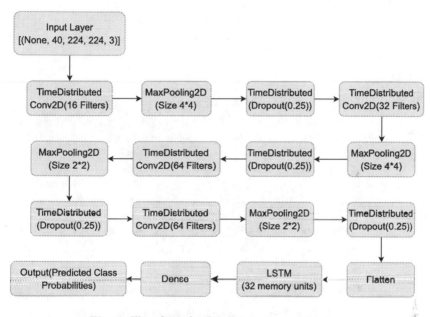

Fig. 5. Flowchart for LRCN model architecture

LRCN. LRCN approach combines Convolutional and LSTM layers in a single model for robust spatio-temporal feature learning. Convolutional layers extract spatial features from frames, which are then passed to LSTM layer(s) for temporal modelling. The timeDistributed wrapper layer allows applying the same layer to each frame independently, enabling the entire video sequence input. The LRCN architecture consists of time-distributed Conv2D layers, followed by MaxPooling2D and Dropout layers. The extracted features are flattened using the Flatten layer and fed into an LSTM layer. The Dense layer with softmax activation predicts the action category based on the output from the LSTM layer. The model is designed to classify sign language gestures from video sequences. CNN layers extract frame-level features, while the LSTM layer learns temporal dependencies. The input shape is (Sequence length, Image height, Image width, 3) where 3 represents the RGB colour channels. TimeDistributed Conv2D layers have increasing filter sizes, followed by TimeDistributed MaxPooling2D layers. Dropout layers are applied after each TimeDistributed MaxPooling2D layer. The output of the last Conv2D layer is flattened using the TimeDistributed Flatten layer. An LSTM layer with 32 memory units is used for temporal modeling. The Dense layer with softmax activation produces the final classification probabilities with the number of units equal to the number of output classes (Fig. 5).

4   Experiments and Experimental Results

Our research aims to assess the suitability of the deep learning approach in recognizing and classifying words from video frames in American Sign Language.

4.1   Dataset

The WLASL (Word-level American Sign Language) dataset [11] is a large-scale dataset of American Sign Language (ASL) videos contain over 1,000 signs from the ASL lexicon. The dataset contains over 20,000 annotated videos, each showing a single sign, with an average duration of about 5 s. The videos were collected from the internet and span a wide variety of signing styles and camera viewpoints. The signs are categorized into 2,000 unique glosses, which are English glosses representing the sign's meaning. Glosses are sorted in descending order in terms of the sample number of videos for that gloss, i.e., Top-K glosses with K = 100, 300, 1000, 2000, named WLASL100, WLASL300, WLASL1000 and WLASL2000, respectively (Fig. 1).

4.2   Implementation Setup

The experiment is implemented using the following software and hardware setup.

- Operating system: Windows
- Programming Language: Python 3.9.1
- Python Libraries: OpenCV, Matplotlib, Numpy
- A system with the following hardware specification: Ryzen 9 7950X CPU, RTX3090Ti GPU, 64 GB DDR4 RAM, 1000W PSU, X570-A Pro Motherboard, M.2 NVME SSD GEN4

4.3   Implementation of the Proposed Approach

After collecting the WLASL dataset, preprocessing by resizing and normalization has been done, and conversion of the videos to sequences of frames is done. Thresholding using Otsu's method is also done for segmenting the image. And then, we employ CNN, LRCN, and ConvLSTM on the resultant dataset.

Table 1. CNN model

Activation Function	Accuracy	Macro-average		
		Precision	Recall	F1-Score
ReLU (Rectified Linear Unit)	36.84%	0.38	0.42	0.39
Tanh (hyperbolic tangent)	43.54%	0.44	0.47	0.44

Table 2. CNN model

Activation Function	Accuracy	Weighted-average		
		Precision	Recall	F1-Score
ReLU (Rectified Linear Unit)	36.84%	0.35	0.37	0.35
Tanh (hyperbolic tangent)	43.54%	0.39	0.42	0 39

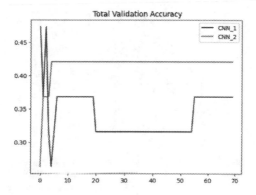

Fig. 6. [CNN] Accuracy wrt to epoch(Red: Tanh, Blue: ReLU) (Color figure online)

4.4 Analysis of Results

CNN. In this experiment, we trained a Convolutional Neural Network (CNN) on our dataset using two different activation functions: Rectified Linear Unit (ReLU) and hyperbolic tangent (tanh) (Fig. 6, Table 1 and Table 2).

ConvLSTM. The ConvLSTM2D layers extract spatio-temporal features from each frame of the video sequence, while the MaxPooling3D and Dropout layers help to reduce overfitting. The Flatten layer flattens the output of the ConvL-STM2D layers, and the Dense layer produces the final classification result with NB CLASSES representing the number of output classes (Fig. 7, Table 3 and Table 4).

Table 3. ConvLSTM model

Activation Function	Accuracy	Macro-average		
		Precision	Recall	F1-Score
ReLU (Rectified Linear Unit)	42.11%	0.56	0.45	0.46
Tanh (hyperbolic tangent)	49.21%	0.47	0.51	0.46

Table 4. ConvLSTM model

Activation Function	Accuracy	Weighted-average		
		Precision	Recall	F1-Score
ReLU (Rectified Linear Unit)	42.11%	0.54	0.42	0.43
Tanh (hyperbolic tangent)	49.21%	0.46	0.47	0.44

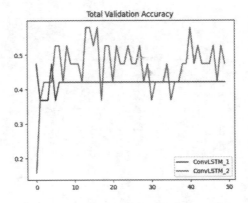

Fig. 7. [ConvLSTM] Accuracy wrt to epoch(Red: Tanh, Blue: ReLU) (Color figure online)

LRCN. LRCN(Long-term Recurrent Convolutional Network) model is a Sequential model with time-distributed Conv2D layers, which will be followed by MaxPooling2D and Dropout layers. The purpose of this model is to classify sign language gestures from video sequences. The CNN layers extract features from each frame of the video sequence, and the LSTM layer learns the temporal dependencies between frames. The Dense layer produces the final classification result (Fig. 8, Table 5 and Table 6).

Table 5. LRCN model

Activation Function	Accuracy	Macro-average		
		Precision	Recall	F1-Score
ReLU (Rectified Linear Unit)	47.37%	0.42	0.53	0.46
Tanh (hyperbolic tangent)	52.63%	0.45	0.58	0.5

Table 6. LRCN model

Activation Function	Accuracy	Weighted-average		
		Precision	Recall	F1-Score
ReLU (Rectified Linear Unit)	47.37%	0.38	0.47	0.42
Tanh (hyperbolic tangent)	52.63%	0.42	0.53	0.46

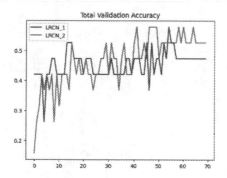

Fig. 8. [LRCN] Accuracy wrt to epoch(Red: Tanh, Blue: ReLU) (Color figure online)

Example outputs of the LRCN model

1. Example 1
   (a) Actual class: candy
   (b) Predicted class: candy
   (c) Top-5 probability distribution over the classes:
       i. candy: 0.32076123
       ii. drink: 0.30855024
       iii. computer: 0.1521432
       iv. book: 0.12326215
       v. who: 0.058250185
2. Example 2
   (a) Actual class: go
   (b) Predicted class: go
   (c) Top-5 probability distribution over the classes:
       i. go: 0.46057162
       ii. computer: 0.39901358

iii. who: 0.0555924
iv. before: 0.03168453
v. chair: 0.027591107

Accuracy Comparison with the Existing Methods. The proposed method achieved an accuracy of 52.63%, which outperformed the Pose-GRU and VGG-GRU methods with accuracies of 46.51% and 25.97%, respectively. These results demonstrate that the proposed method, which combines 3D convolutional and LSTM layers with appropriate preprocessing techniques, effectively detects word-level sign language on the WLASL dataset. The high accuracy achieved by the I3D method indicates the importance of incorporating temporal information in the model. The success of the Pose-TGCN method highlights the relevance of graph-based models for sign language recognition (Table 7).

Table 7. Accuracy Comparison with previously used methods

Method	Top-1 (WLASL 100)
Pose-GRU	46.51%
Pose-TGCN	55.43%
VGG-GRU	25.97%
I3D	65.89%
Proposed Method	**52.63%**

5   Conclusion and Future Scope

In conclusion, our project demonstrates the feasibility of using deep learning models for word-level sign language detection on the WLASL dataset. Our experiments showed that all three models achieved promising results on the test set. The LRCN model achieved the highest accuracy of 52.63%, followed by the ConvLSTM model with 49.21% accuracy and the CNN model with 43.54% accuracy. The results showed that the LRCN model outperformed the other two models.

Further research can explore the use of more advanced architectures, such as attention-based models, and transfer learning techniques. There is a need for real-time sign language recognition.

References

1. Al-Hammadi, M., Muhammad, G., Abdul, W., Alsulaiman, M., Bencherif, M.A., Mekhtiche, M.A.: Hand gesture recognition for sign language using 3DCNN. IEEE Access **8**, 79491–79509 (2020). https://doi.org/10.1109/ACCESS.2020.2990434
2. Al-Qurishi, M., Khalid, T., Souissi, R.: Deep learning for sign language recognition: current techniques, benchmarks, and open issues. IEEE Access **9**, 126917–126951 (2021). https://doi.org/10.1109/ACCESS.2021.3110912
3. Aly, S.K.H., Aly, W.: DeepArSLR: a novel signer-independent deep learning framework for isolated Arabic sign language gestures recognition. IEEE Access **8**, 83199–83212 (2020)
4. Botros, F.S., Phinyomark, A., Scheme, E.J.: Electromyography-based gesture recognition: is it time to change focus from the forearm to the wrist? IEEE Trans. Industr. Inf. **18**(1), 174–184 (2020)
5. Dawod, A.Y., Chakpitak, N.: Novel technique for isolated sign language based on fingerspelling recognition. In: 2019 13th International Conference on Software, Knowledge, Information Management and Applications (SKIMA), pp. 1–8. IEEE (2019)
6. Fatmi, R., Rashad, S., Integlia, R.: Comparing ANN, SVM, and HMM based machine learning methods for American sign language recognition using wearable motion sensors. In: 2019 IEEE 9th Annual Computing and Communication Workshop and Conference (CCWC), pp. 0290–0297. IEEE (2019)
7. Gupta, R., Kumar, A.: Indian sign language recognition using wearable sensors and multi-label classification. Comput. Electr. Eng. **90**, 106898 (2021)
8. Hoang, V.T.: HGM-4: a new multi-cameras dataset for hand gesture recognition. Data Brief **30**, 105676 (2020)
9. Jiang, S., et al.: Feasibility of wrist-worn, real-time hand, and surface gesture recognition via sEMG and IMU sensing. IEEE Trans. Industr. Inf. **14**(8), 3376–3385 (2017)
10. Lee, C., Ng, K.K., Chen, C.H., Lau, H., Chung, S., Tsoi, T.: American sign language recognition and training method with recurrent neural network. Expert Syst. Appl. **167**, 114403 (2021). https://doi.org/10.1016/j.eswa.2020.114403, https://www.sciencedirect.com/science/article/pii/S0957417420310745
11. Li, D., Rodriguez, C., Yu, X., Li, H.: Word-level deep sign language recognition from video: a new large-scale dataset and methods comparison. In: Proceedings of the IEEE/CVF Winter Conference on Applications of Computer Vision, pp. 1459–1469 (2020)
12. Mummadi, C.K., et al.: Real-time and embedded detection of hand gestures with an imu-based glove. In: Informatics, vol. 5, p. 28. MDPI (2018)
13. Rastgoo, R., Kiani, K., Escalera, S.: Hand sign language recognition using multi-view hand skeleton. Expert Syst. Appl. **150**, 113336 (2020). https://doi.org/10.1016/j.eswa.2020.113336, https://www.sciencedirect.com/science/article/pii/S0957417420301615
14. Sincan, O.M., Keles, H.Y.: AUTSL: a large scale multi-modal Turkish sign language dataset and baseline methods. IEEE Access **8**, 181340–181355 (2020). https://doi.org/10.1109/access.2020.3028072
15. V., A., R., R.: A deep convolutional neural network approach for static hand gesture recognition. Procedia Comput. Sci. **171**, 2353–2361 (2020). https://doi.org/10.1016/j.procs.2020.04.255, https://www.sciencedirect.com/science/article/pii/S1877050920312473. third International Conference on Computing and Network Communications (CoCoNet'19)

16. Wei, S., Chen, X., Yang, X., Cao, S., Zhang, X.: A component-based vocabulary-extensible sign language gesture recognition framework. Sensors **16**(4) (2016). https://doi.org/10.3390/s16040556, https://www.mdpi.com/1424-8220/16/4/556
17. Yuan, G., Liu, X., Yan, Q., Qiao, S., Wang, Z., Yuan, L.: Hand gesture recognition using deep feature fusion network based on wearable sensors. IEEE Sens. J. **21**, 539–547 (2021)

Identity Preserved Expressive Talking Faces with Synchrony

Karumuri Meher Abhijeet[(✉)] [iD], Arshad Ali[iD], and Prithwijit Guha[iD]

Department of Electronics and Electrical Engineering, Indian Institute of Technology Guwahati, Guwahati, India
meherabhijeet@gmail.com, pguha@iitg.ac.in

Abstract. This work proposes a novel approach to talking face generation using driving audio. The driving audio and a single image of the target person are provided as input to the proposed model. The model generates a realistic video of the target person uttering the driving audio. Recent works in this domain have focused on either one of expressions or lip-sync or identity preservation. This model provides supervision over photo realism, expression fulfilment, identity preservation and audio-visual synchrony which are crucial factors in synthesizing a realistic video. The proposed system is end-to-end trainable and the learning is performed with six losses. This method can generate photo realistic, expressive and audio-synced talking faces while preserving the identity of the target person. This work proposes a discriminator network to impose audio-visual synchrony in the generated video. The proposed model is trained on RAVDESS dataset containing 24 professional actors (12 female and 12 male), uttering two statements in a neutral North American accent with disgust, sad, angry, happy, surprise, fearful and calm emotions. This work is benchmarked on the VID-TIMIT dataset against three baseline models.

Keywords: Talking Faces · GANs · Face Animation · Action-Unit

1 Introduction

Facial reenactment plays a major role in computer graphics. The issue of producing photo-realistic talking faces is multifaceted. It requires realistic faces, face movements synchronized with the audio, and conceivable facial expressions. It is particularly challenging as human beings are proficient at identifying unnatural facial movements and lack of audio-visual synchronization.

Facial motion capture methods make use of motion sensors placed on the subject's face. This makes the process invasive, expensive and time-consuming. As an alternative, facial transformations were captured using cameras. This process achieves good results at the cost of some accuracy. Such vision based methods are also challenged by occlusions (person is wearing glasses). In such cases, other input modalities like audio and text can be explored to infer facial actions. Facial

H. Kaur et al. (Eds.): CVIP 2023, CCIS 2009, pp. 357–368, 2024.
https://doi.org/10.1007/978-3-031-58181-6_30

reenactment techniques can be broadly categorized based on the driving input. They are either video driven or audio driven.

In *Video driven Facial Reenactment* techniques, the task is to mimic or reenact the movements of the source video. Various methods have been developed to serve as means to transfer these movements from the source video to a single target image or from the source video to a target video. The main idea behind this line of work is to identify a few facial key points on each video frame after which the task is reduced to making these key points in the target frame mimic the movement of their corresponding points in the source frame (Fig. 1).

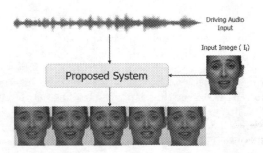

Fig. 1. The proposed model takes a driving audio and a single image (I_i) of the target person as input. The model generates a photo realistic video of the person speaking the (input) audio.

Audio driven Face Reenactment extracts the face parameters from the input audio. Unlike video driven methods, ground truth frames are not available here. Thus, the identity, background and color information of the target person are learned from a single image.

Existing audio driven methods (Sect. 2) which use 2D landmark points as visual features [10,20] have a limited range of expressions because landmark points provide very little information about the facial expression. To address this shortcoming, the proposed work (Sect. 3) uses Action Units (AUs, Henceforth) as visual features. This work takes as input an audio sequence and a single image of the target person. Sequence of spectrograms are first extracted by windowing the audio sequence. Each of these spectrograms is passed to an AU regressor network (*AUNet*) to predict an AU probability vector. For each AU vector, an output image is generated by passing the predicted AU vector along with the input image of the target person to a generator network. We form the output video by joining the images generated for each of the AU vectors. Hence, each audio window has a corresponding spectrogram and each spectrogram has a corresponding AU vector which in turn has a corresponding output image. The major contributions of this work are as follows.

- Introduction of a novel, end-to-end trainable audio driven talking face generation model. This model provides supervision over photo realism, expression fulfilment, audio-visual synchronization and identity preservation.

– Proposal of a novel discriminator network to impose audio-visual synchronization.

2   Related Works

The classical approaches to facial reenactment have primarily used Hidden
Markov Models (HMM) with limited success. The methods involving HMMs
were trained to learn the change of emotional intensities as a pattern and would
predict the next emotional intensity conditioned on the current one. These methods often generated animations with jerky transitions between frames.

The recent deep learning based approaches can be broadly divided into two
groups based on the modality of input. These methods are based on audio and
video driven facial reenactment. Video driven reenactment methods aim at generating talking faces by taking a set of video frames as input. Here, the task is to
transfer parameters (pose, expression and gaze) of the source face to the target
face.

This proposal falls under the audio-driven reenactment setup, wherein the
task is to generate talking faces by taking only an audio segment and a single
image of the target person as input. The present work is audio-driven. Accordingly, the next sub-sections focuses on reviewing the relevant literature on audio-
driven facial reenactment techniques.

The task of audio driven facial reenactment can be broadly divided into
two sub-tasks. First, visual feature extraction from driving audio input. Second,
generation of a photo realistic video using the visual features obtained from the
first task.

Visual Features of Face – Visual features are used to provide intermediate
representation of the required target face. The most commonly used visual features are 2D landmark points, Action Units (AUs), 3D landmark points and 3D
Morphable Models (3DMMs). Facial landmark points describe principal regions
of the face like eyebrows, eyes, nose, mouth and jawline. Each landmark point is
represented using its (x, y) coordinate. Most face datasets [15,16] are annotated
with 68 landmark points for each face image.

Another widely used visual feature is the Action units (AUs). Any facial
expression can be broken down into individual components of muscle movement,
called Action Units (AUs) [4]. The Face Action Coding System (FACS) [11]
uses these AUs to accurately annotate facial expressions. Each AU defines the
emotional intensity level of a specific region of the face. They range between
$[0, 1]$ with 0 indicating no emotional intensity and 1 indicating high emotional
intensity. Popular datasets [15,16] annotate each face image with 40 AUs.

Extracting Visual Features from Audio – Visual features like 2D facial
landmark points, Action Units (AUs) and 3D Morphable Model (3DMM) parameters are often extracted from the input. Existing works have used facial landmark points as visual features for photo-realistic image generation. Approaches
presented in [17,22] propose networks to regress AUs from the driving audio.

While the AUs efficiently describe facial expressions, they provide no information about head pose and gaze [11].

Most recent works [12,21] have made use of 3D morphable face models to overcome the quality related constraints caused by using 2D facial landmarks and AUs. Recent works [12,21] have estimated 3DMM parameters from the source face to extract identity, expression, pose, texture and illumination information. The required 3DMM parameters i.e. expression and pose of the target face are extracted from the driving audio and transferred to the source face model. This animates the source face by preserving its identity, illumination and texture. Although the 3DMM parameter estimation provides good control over the target face parameters, it requires significantly higher compute resources than the models based on 2D facial landmarks and AUs [22].

Visual Parameters to Realistic Video – After obtaining the visual features in terms of landmark points or AUs, the next task is to generate a photorealistic video of the target person conditioned on the obtained features. Recent approaches like [9,23] that propose to generate the entire face. These methods first compute different embeddings from various encoders. These embeddings are then concatenated and up-sampled to obtain the output face image.

Researchers [18,20] have proposed the application of deep networks to generate color and attention maps from input visual features like 2D facial landmark points or AUs. The color map contains information of fine scale details like self-shadows, creases and hallucinated pixels of hidden areas. On the other hand, the attention mask indicates the extent to which each pixel of the color mask contributes to the output image. The output face image is constructed by linearly combining the color and attention masks.

For identity preservation in the generated video, several works like Cycle-GAN [25], DiscoGAN [14] and StarGAN [7] have exploited cycle consistency to preserve key attributes between the input and the mapped image. However these approaches have taken video as input and have not provided supervision for other aspects like identity and expression fulfilment.

3   Proposed Work

The proposed audio driven facial animation network is end-to-end trainable. This work is an extension of [18], making it audio driven with supervision on audio synchronization. This model takes an audio sequence and a still image of the target person as input and animates the input image as output. This model (Fig. 2) consists of three components namely, Audio to AU network ($AUNet$), Generator (G) and Discriminator (D). In this work, subscripts i and o are used to indicate input and output respectively.

3.1   Audio to AU

Audio windows of duration t_{aw} are first extracted from the input audio sequence which are sampled at f_s. A spectrogram S_i is computed by applying FFT with a window size of $2n_f$ samples and a stride length of n_{st} on each audio window. For each audio window, the task is to generate a fake image (I_o) conditioned on the AUs (β_o) extracted from S_i. During inference, S_i is passed through $AUNet$ to obtain β_o. The input I_i and predicted β_o are then passed through generator G to obtain I_o. This section describes the networks of $AUNet$, G and D in further details.

The function of $AUNet$ is to predict AUs ($\beta_o \in \mathbb{R}^{n_{au}} \times 1$) from the driving spectrogram ($S_i \in \mathbb{R}^{n_f \times n_t}$). The $AUNet$ is adopted from [17], with a change in the final dense layer dimension.

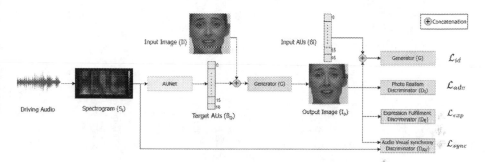

Fig. 2. Block diagram of the proposed model. The model takes a driving audio sequence and still image of target person (I_i) as input and generates the animated image sequence (I_o) uttering the driving input audio. After windowing the audio sequence, a spectrogram is extracted for each audio window. AUs predicted from this spectrogram are then passed along with I_i to a generator to obtain I_o.

3.2 Generator (G)

The architecture of G is motivated by the one proposed in [18]. First, β_o and I_i are concatenated along the channel dimension by representing β_o as n_{au} arrays of size $n_h \times n_w$ where, each array is filled with its corresponding AU value to obtain the concatenated input $C_i \in \mathbb{R}^{(n_{au}+3) \times n_h \times n_w}$ [18]. Given C_i as input, G generates an Attention map $A \in [0,1]^{n_h \times n_w}$ and a Color Regression map $C \in \mathbb{R}^{3 \times n_h \times n_w}$. The target image $I_o \in \mathbb{R}^{3 \times n_h \times n_w}$ can be obtained using A and C as

$$I_o = (\mathbf{1}_{n_h \times n_w} - A) \times C + A \times I_i \tag{1}$$

where, $\mathbf{1}_{n_h \times n_w}$ is a $n_h \times n_w$ matrix of all ones.

3.3 Discriminator Networks (D)

This model has the following three discriminator networks. The first discriminator $D(I)$ classifies the images into real or fake based on their photo-realism.

The architecture of $D(I)$ resembles the discriminator proposed in PatchGan [13] network. The second discriminator $D(E)$ is trained to check if I_o satisfies the target expression β_o. It takes $I_o \in \mathbb{R}^{3 \times n_h \times n_w}$ as input and outputs $\hat{\beta}_o \in \mathbb{R}^{n_{au} \times 1}$ which is the expression of the generated face (I_o). The loss between β_o and $\hat{\beta}_o$ is then minimized for ensuring expression fulfilment. The architecture of $D(E)$ is motivated by a similar discriminator proposed in [18].

This work proposes the third discriminator $D(AV)$ to impose audio-visual synchrony between S_i and I_o. $D(AV)$ has two networks. First, audio network $(ANet)$ which takes $S_i \in \mathbb{R}^{n_f \times n_t}$ as input and outputs an audio embedding $\mathbf{emb_a} \in \mathbb{R}^{n_{ae} \times 1}$. Second, a video network $(VNet)$ which extracts a visual embedding $\mathbf{emb_v} \in \mathbb{R}^{n_{ve} \times 1}$ from an input image $\in \mathbb{R}^{3 \times n_h \times n_w}$. $D(AV)$ imposes audio visual synchrony by minimizing the distance between $\mathbf{emb_a}$ and $\mathbf{emb_v}$. Here, $\mathbf{emb_a}$ and $\mathbf{emb_v}$ are of same size i.e. $n_{ae} = n_{ve}$.

3.4 Loss Function

The above mentioned networks are trained using the following six losses. These are **(a)** Image adversarial loss; **(b)** Attention loss; **(c)** Expression loss; **(d)** Identity loss; **(e)** Synchrony loss and **(f)** AU loss. This section provides a brief description of the losses mentioned above.

The *Image adversarial loss* $(\mathcal{L}_{adv})$ is adopted from WGAN-GP [2]. Formally, $\mathcal{L}_{adv}$ can be written as

$$\mathcal{L}_{adv} = \mathbb{E}\left(D(I)\left(G\left(I_i|\beta_o\right)\right)\right) - \mathbb{E}\left(D(I)\left(I_i\right)\right) + GP \qquad (2)$$

where, $\mathbb{E}(\bullet)$ refers to the mathematical expectation operator, I_i is the input image, β_o is the target expression and GP is the gradient penalty term [2]. The networks of generator G and discriminator $D(I)$ networks are adversarially trained using $\mathcal{L}_{adv}$.

The *Attention loss* $(\mathcal{L}_{att})$ is used to train G and has two terms. First, a Total Variation regularization on A, to impose smooth color transformation when combining I_i and C. Second, a l_2 regularization on A, to keep the mask from saturating to $\mathbf{1}_{n_h \times n_w}$.

$$\mathcal{L}_{att} = \lambda.\mathbb{E}\left[\sum_{i,j}^{n_h,n_w}\left[\left(A_{i+1,j} - A_{i,j}\right)^2 + \left(A_{i,j+1} - A_{i,j}\right)^2\right]\right] \qquad (3)$$

The *Expression loss* $(\mathcal{L}_{exp})$ provides supervision for I_o to satisfy the target expression (β_o). It is defined as

$$\begin{aligned}\mathcal{L}_{exp} = &\mathbb{E}\left(\parallel D(E)\left(G\left(I_i \mid \beta_o\right)\right) - \beta_o \parallel_2^2\right) \\ &+ \mathbb{E}\left(\parallel D(E)\left(I_i\right) - \beta_i \parallel_2^2\right)\end{aligned} \qquad (4)$$

where, $\beta_i \in \mathbb{R}^{n_{au}}$ is the expression of I_i. G and $D(E)$ are trained using $\mathcal{L}_{exp}$.

The *Identity loss* ($\mathcal{L}_{id}$) is a cycle consistency loss [25] and is used to train G for retaining the identity of the individual in I_i (target identity preservation).

$$\mathcal{L}_{id} = \mathbb{E}\left(\ \| \ G\left(\ G\left(I_i \mid \beta_{\mathbf{o}}\right) \mid \beta_{\mathbf{i}}\ \right) - I_i \ \|_1\ \right) \tag{5}$$

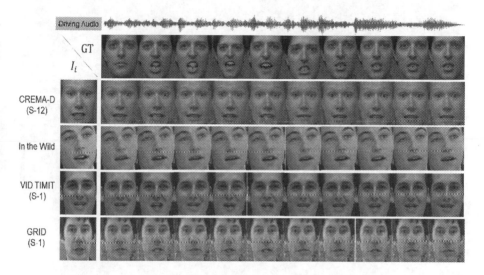

Fig. 3. Generated images with out of domain audio input taken from [19]. The target faces include image of speaker–12 from CREMA database [5], in the wild image, image of speaker–1 from VidTIMIT dataset [19] and image of speaker–1 from the GRID corpus [1].

Chung et al. [8] used contrastive loss between the audio and visual embeddings for the task of lip reading. This motivated the present proposal to use the *Synchrony loss* ($\mathcal{L}_{sync}$) in a similar setup to impose audio-visual synchronization in the output. The Synchrony loss can be written as

$$\mathcal{L}_{sync} = \frac{1}{2N}\sum_{n=1}^{N}(y_n)d_n^2 \ + \ (1 - y_n)\left\{max\left(m - d_n, 0\right)\right\}^2 \tag{6}$$

where, $d_n = \|\mathbf{emb_a} - \mathbf{emb_v}\|_2$, y_n is the training label for the nth training pair, N is the total number of training pairs and m is the margin which is set to 15. This proposal uses $\{I_{gt}, S_i\}_n$ with $y_n = 1$ and $\{I_o, S_i\}_n$ with $y_n = 0$ as positive and negative training pairs respectively while training $D(AV)$. Here, I_{gt} is the ground truth frame corresponding to S_i in the training data. According to Eq. 6, when $y_n = 1$, $\mathcal{L}_{sync}$ tries to minimize d_n^2, which is the square of the distance between the audio and visual embeddings of the positive training pair. For a negative training pair ($y_n = 0$), $\mathcal{L}_{sync}$ minimizes $max\left(m - d_n, 0\right)$. This term is non-zero only when $m > d_n$. Hence, $\mathcal{L}_{sync}$ is effective for a negative training

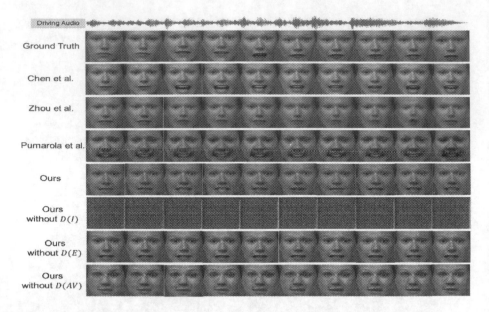

Fig. 4. Comparison of our results with Chen et al. [6], Zhou et al. [24] and Pumarola et al. [18]. Ablation study results are also presented to show the effect of each discriminator in our model. All the models were driven with the same inputs.

pair only if the distance between the audio and visual embeddings for that pair is lesser than the margin m.

In this work, G and $D(AV)$ are trained adversarially using $\mathcal{L}_{sync}$. Thus, this loss tries to introduce audio-visual synchronization by reducing the distance between the embeddings of the generated image (I_o) and the spectrogram (S_i) of the driving audio.

The AU loss ($\mathcal{L}_{au}$) is used for training the $AUNet$ and is defined as the normalized l_2 norm between ground truth AU (β_{gt}) and the predicted AU (β_o).

$$\mathcal{L}_{au} = \mathbb{E}\left[\frac{1}{N} \left(\sum_{n=1}^{N} \left(\frac{\beta_{gt}{}^n - \beta_o{}^n}{\sigma_n} \right)^2 \right) \right] \qquad (7)$$

where, σ_j ($j = 1, \ldots n_{au}$) is the standard deviation of the jth AU component which is found from the training data. Here, L_{au} is normalized by variance to reduce the bias towards specific AUs [17].

The proposed model is end-to-end trainable. It is trained using the total loss ($\mathcal{L}_T$) given by

$$\mathcal{L}_T = \lambda_{adv}\mathcal{L}_{adv} + \lambda_{att}\mathcal{L}_{att} + \lambda_{exp}\mathcal{L}_{exp} + \lambda_{id}\mathcal{L}_{id} + \lambda_{sync}\mathcal{L}_{sync} + \lambda_{au}\mathcal{L}_{au} \qquad (8)$$

where λ_{adv}, λ_{att}, λ_{exp}, λ_{id}, λ_{sync} and λ_{au} are hyper parameters which decide the weights associated with corresponding loss terms.

4 Experiments

4.1 Dataset

The proposed model is trained on the Ryerson Audio-Visual Database of Emotional Speech and Song (RAVDESS) [16]. It contains 24 professional actors (12 female, 12 male), speaking two statements in a neutral North American accent. The face region in every video frame available in the database is cropped. The ground-truth AUs for these cropped frames are obtained using [3]. In addition to the AUs regressed from the input spectrogram, randomly generated AUs are used to train G, $D(I)$ and $D(E)$ networks following the proposal in [18].

4.2 Results

A good talking face model must be able to seamlessly animate target face images with unique skin colors, head poses, background conditions and expressions. In addition to this, the model must also predict accurate AUs from driving audio input. This is a challenging task because the driving audio can have varying accents, voices and emotions.

This proposal can generalize to target face images with different skin color, head pose and background color (Fig. 3). This model is tested with out-of-domain target faces taken from some commonly used datasets like CREMA [5], VidTIMIT [19], GRID [1] and an In-The-Wild image with a tilted head pose (Fig. 3). These target faces were driven with an out-of-domain audio taken from [19]. It is observed that in the images generated by this proposal, the opening and closing of the mouth region closely follows the trend in the ground truth (GT) images. The model is also capable to address fine scale details like teeth generation when the mouth is open and modification of eyebrow(s), forehead and the cheek region(s) according to the predicted expression.

The performance of the proposed model is compared with the state-of-the art methods proposed in [6, 24] and an open source implementation of the proposal of Pumarola et al.[1] [18]. All the models were driven with the same out-of-domain input taken from [19]. All the models preserved identity and background information in the generated images (Fig. 4). From Fig. 4, it can be inferred that [6] generates highly expressive images. However these expressions do not correspond to the ground truth (GT) image expressions. Further it can be noted that [6] does not preserve the skin color and generates brighter skin colors when compared to the ground truth (GT). The output of [24] has blurred lip and eye brows and [18] generates images with distorted colors (Fig. 5).

On the other hand, this proposal generates expressive images with clear lip and teeth regions (Fig. 5). When compared to other methods, this proposal produces facial expressions which are consistent with the ground truth (GT) expressions (Fig. 4). This improvement can be attributed to the proposed audio-visual synchrony based discriminator which ensures that the generated image expressions are always in sync with the audio.

---

[1] https://github.com/vipermu/ganimation.

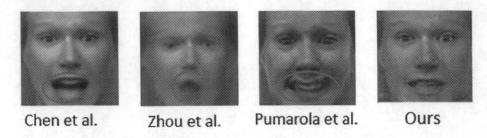

Chen et al.   Zhou et al.   Pumarola et al.   Ours

Fig. 5. Analysis of images generated using the proposed work and the state-of-art methods [6,18,24]. Artifacts present in the images are marked in red. Models in [6, 18,24] fail to generate fine scale face details and output a blurry mouth region. This proposal generates a comparatively sharper image with clear teeth and lip regions. (Color figure online)

4.3   Ablation Analysis

Ablation analysis is performed to understand the contributions of each of the three discriminators, namely $D(I)$, $D(E)$ and $D(AV)$ (Subsect. 3.3). The role of $D(I)$ is to preserve the identity of the target person and to classify the images into real or fake based on their photo-realism. This proposal, when trained without $D(I)$ generates noisy images with no facial information (sixth row, Fig. 4). Discriminator $D(E)$ was used in the model to ensure that the target image satisfies the underlying expression requirements. Without $D(E)$, the model provides no supervision for generating expressive faces and hence, generates faces with no change in expression (seventh row, Fig. 4). The discriminator $D(AV)$ was introduced in the model to enforce audio-visual synchrony. To ensure audio-visual synchrony, the generator updates the attention and color map such that the generated facial expression matches the audio. Without $D(AV)$, the model generates inaccurate color and attention maps thereby resulting in images with distorted colors (eighth row, Fig. 4).

4.4   Implementation Details

The values of sampling rate, audio window size, spectrogram dimensions, AU numbers etc. are set as $n_{au} = 17, n_f = 128, n_t = 32, t_{aw} = 96\,\text{ms}, \text{f}_\text{s} = 44.1\,\text{kHz}, \text{n}_\text{st} = 128, \text{n}_\text{h} = 128, \text{n}_\text{w} = 128, \text{n}_\text{ve} = 256$ and $n_{ae} = 256$. It was observed that a pretrained $AUNet$ provided better results. Hence, $AUNet$ is first trained for 300 epochs. The full model is then trained for 30 epochs. The learning rate is linearly decayed to zero over the last 10 epochs. The generator network is updated once for every 2 optimization steps of the discriminator networks. The Adam optimizer is used with a learning rate of 0.0001, $\beta_1 = 0.5$, $\beta_2 = 0.999$ and batch size 16. The weight coefficients for the loss terms in Eq. 8 are empirically set to $\lambda_{adv} = 10$, $\lambda_{att} = 0.1$, $\lambda_{sync} = 0.5$, $\lambda_{au} = 2$, $\lambda_{exp} = 160$ and $\lambda_{id} = 10$. The model took two days to train on a single Tesla V100 GPU. The source code for this proposal is available at https://github.com/meherabhi/IETaFS.

5   Conclusion

This paper proposes a novel audio driven talking face generation method. This model takes an audio sequence and a still image of the target person as input and provides the animated image as output. This proposal consists of three components namely, Audio to AU network ($AUNet$), Generator (G) and Discriminator (D). In addition to identity preservation and expression fulfilment, this proposal also imposes audio-visual synchrony using a novel discriminator network. Qualitative analysis shows that the proposed model performs better on out-of-domain inputs.

This work can be extended in the following directions. First, the present model cannot change the head pose of the target person. Thus, head pose changes can be incorporated in the present work. Second, this work can also be extended to develop an input text driven talking face model with intermediate speech synthesis.

References

1. Alghamdi, N., Maddock, S., Marxer, R., Barker, J., Brown, G.J.: A corpus of audio-visual Lombard speech with frontal and profile views. J. Acoust. Soc. Am. **143**(6), 523–529 (2018)
2. Arjovsky, M., Chintala, S., Bottou, L.: Wasserstein generative adversarial networks. In: Proceedings of the 34th International Conference on Machine Learning, vol. 70, pp. 214–223 (2017)
3. Baltrusaitis, T., Zadeh, A., Lim, Y.C., Morency, L.: Openface 2.0: facial behavior analysis toolkit. In: 13th IEEE International Conference on Automatic Face and Gesture Recogniton, pp. 59–66 (2018)
4. Breuer, R., Kimmel, R.: A deep learning perspective on the origin of facial expressions, arXiv:1705.01842 (2017)
5. Cao, H., Cooper, D.G., Keutmann, M.K., Gur, R.C., Nenkova, A., Verma, R.: Crema-d: crowd-sourced emotional multimodal actors dataset. IEEE Trans. on Affective Comput. **5**(4), 377–390 (2014)
6. Chen, L., Zheng, H., Maddox, R., Duan, Z., Xu, C.: Sound to visual: hierarchical cross-modal talking face generation. In: Proceedings of the IEEE/CVF Conferenc on Computer Vision and Pattern Recognition (CVPR) Workshops, pp. 1–4 (2019)
7. Choi, Y., Choi, M., Kim, M., Ha, J.W., Kim, S., Choo, J.: Stargan: unified generative adversarial networks for multi-domain image-to-image translation. In: Proceedings of the IEEE Conference on Computer Vision and Pattern Recognition, pp. 8789–8797 (2018)
8. Chung, J.S., Zisserman, A.: Out of time: automated lip sync in the wild. In: Chen, C.-S., Lu, J., Ma, K.-K. (eds.) ACCV 2016. LNCS, vol. 10117, pp. 251–263. Springer, Cham (2017). https://doi.org/10.1007/978-3-319-54427-4_19
9. Emre Eskimez, S., Zhang, Y., Duan, Z.: Speech driven talking face generation from a single image and an emotion condition, arXiv:2008.03592, (2020)
10. Eskimez, S.E., Maddox, R.K., Xu, C., Duan, Z.: Generating talking face landmarks from speech. In: Deville, Y., Gannot, S., Mason, R., Plumbley, M.D., Ward, D. (eds.) LVA/ICA 2018. LNCS, vol. 10891, pp. 372–381. Springer, Cham (2018). https://doi.org/10.1007/978-3-319-93764-9_35

11. Freitas-Magalhães, A.: Facial action coding system 3.0-manual of scientific codification of the human face. Leya (2020)
12. Han, Y., Li, Y., Gao, Y., Xue, J., Wang, S., Yang, L.: A keypoint based enhancement method for audio driven free view talking head synthesis. In: IEEE 24th International Workshop on Multimedia Signal Processing (MMSP), pp. 1–6 (2022)
13. Isola, P., Zhu, J., Zhou, T., Efros, A.A.: Image-to-image translation with conditional adversarial networks. In: 2017 IEEE Conference on Computer Vision and Pattern Recognit. (CVPR), pp. 5967–5976 (2017)
14. Kim, T., Cha, M., Kim, H., Lee, J.K., Kim, J.: Learning to discover cross-domain relations with generative adversarial networks. Proc. of Mach. Learn. Res. **70**, 1857–1865 (2017)
15. Liu, Z., Luo, P., Wang, X., Tang, X.: Deep learning face attributes in the wild. In: Proceedings of the IEEE International Conference on Computer Vision (ICCV), pp. 3730–3738 (2015)
16. Livingstone, S.R., Russo, F.A.: The ryerson audio-visual database of emotional speech and song (RAVDESS): a dynamic, multimodal set of facial and vocal expressions in north American English **13**(5) (2018)
17. Pham, H.X., Wang, Y., Pavlovic, V.: End-to-end learning for 3d facial animation from speech. In: 20th ACM International Conference on Multimodal Interaction, pp. 361–365 (2018)
18. Pumarola, A., Agudo, A., Martinez, A.M., Sanfeliu, A., Moreno-Noguer, F.: Ganimation: one-shot anatomically consistent facial animation. Int. J. Comput. Vision **128**(3), 698–713 (2020)
19. Sanderson, C., Lovell, B.C.: Multi-region probabilistic histograms for robust and scalable identity inference. In: Tistarelli, M., Nixon, M.S. (eds.) ICB 2009. LNCS, vol. 5558, pp. 199–208. Springer, Heidelberg (2009). https://doi.org/10.1007/978-3-642-01793-3_21
20. Sinha, S., Biswas, S., Bhowmick, B.: Identity-preserving realistic talking face generation. In: 2020 International Joint Conference on Neural Networks (IJCNN), pp. 1–10 (2020)
21. Song, L., Wu, W., Qian, C., He, R., Loy, C.C.: Everybody's talkin': let me talk as you want. IEEE Trans. Inf. Forensics Secur. **17**, 585–598 (2022)
22. Thies, J., Elgharib, M., Tewari, A., Theobalt, C., Nießner, M.: Neural voice puppetry: audio-driven facial reenactment. In: Vedaldi, A., Bischof, H., Brox, T., Frahm, J.-M. (eds.) ECCV 2020. LNCS, vol. 12361, pp. 716–731. Springer, Cham (2020). https://doi.org/10.1007/978-3-030-58517-4_42
23. Zhao, Z., Zhang, Y., Wu, T., Guo, H., Li, Y.: Emotionally controllable talking face generation from an arbitrary emotional portrait. Appl. Sci. **12**(24), 12852 (2022)
24. Zhou, H., Liu, Y., Liu, Z., Luo, P., Wang, X.: Talking face generation by adversarially disentangled audio-visual representation. In: Proceedings of the AAAI Conference on Artificial Intelligence, vol. 33, pp. 9299–9306 (2019)
25. Zhu, J., Park, T., Isola, P., Efros, A.A.: Unpaired image-to-image translation using cycle-consistent adversarial networks. In: 2017 IEEE International Conference on Computer Vision (ICCV), pp. 2242–2251 (2017)

An Integrated Approach: Combining GrabCut and Contour-Matching for Hand Gesture Segmentation in Indian Sign Language

B. V. Poornima$^{(\boxtimes)}$, S. Srinath, S. Rashmi, and R. Rakshitha

JSS Science and Technology University, Mysuru, India
Poornimabv.85@gmail.com

Abstract. Hand Segmentation plays a vital role in human-computer interaction using computer vision. It serves as an initial step in hand gesture recognition systems or to recognize various sign languages and is considered essential pre-processing. The region of interest (ROI) in an image requires filtering or modification, which can be represented as a bounding box or a binary mask picture. Accurate hand segmentation is the critical first phase in sign language recognition (SLR) systems. Segmenting the ROI reduces processing time and enhances the precision of sign recognition. This study proposes two methods: a contour-matching technique applied to a simple black background dataset, and a novel hybrid algorithm that combines the GrabCut method with the contour-matching method to extract the ROI from images with complex backgrounds. This work's purpose is to use the segmented images for the Indian sign language (ISL) recognition system. The results show that the contour-based segmentation technique achieves excellent results for the dataset with a black background. The number of iterations the GrabCut algorithm needs to separate the foreground varies depending on the complexity of the background. The algorithms are evaluated on datasets of ISL consisting of images with a black background and images with a complex background.

Keywords: Indian sign language (ISL) · Hand gesture recognition (HGR) · SLR · Simple background · Complex background · Contour matching · Graphcut

1 Introduction

Sign language recognition (SLR) [1] is a computational task that involves recognizing actions from sign languages used by speech and hearing-impaired people. People who are deaf or mute communicate with hand gestures, therefore normal people have difficulty understanding their sign language. A system that can recognize signs and transmit information is thus necessary. The hand tracking and segmentation algorithm (HTS) has been shown to be the most efficient technique for overcoming vision-based systems' challenges with skin color detection [2] and challenging background removal. The segmentation method is the initial step in the recognition of visual gestures. A crucial step in

© The Author(s), under exclusive license to Springer Nature Switzerland AG 2024
H. Kaur et al. (Eds.): CVIP 2023, CCIS 2009, pp. 369–381, 2024.
https://doi.org/10.1007/978-3-031-58181-6_31

the image recognition process is segmentation [3], which extracts the subject of our interest for later processing, such as description or recognition. Since signers use their hands prominently to perform the gestures, the challenge is to segment the hand portion of a signer which is considered as the ROI. There are several image segmentation techniques [4] like thresholding, edge detection, clustering, and artificial neural network-based.

Image segmentation refers to the partitioning of a digital image into multiple segments or regions, aiming to simplify or transform the image into a more meaningful and interpretable representation. The primary objective of segmentation is to identify objects and delineate boundaries within the image, such as lines, curves, and other distinct entities. This process involves assigning a label to each pixel in the image, and grouping pixels with similar properties under the same label. It is utilized in a wide variety of real-world situations, such as medical image analysis, autonomous vehicles, computer vision, face recognition and detection, video surveillance, satellite image analysis, object detection, and many more. Segmenting the hand region in SLR is one of the important pre-processing steps that reduces the computation time in recognizing the sign. The ROI is extracted from the images using this procedure. If facial indications are used in addition to hand signs, the ROI might either be hands or face. Figure 1 shows the basic block diagram of the SLR system. Segmentation is the crucial step before feature extraction and it reduces the complexity of recognizing the gestures.

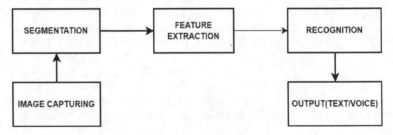

Fig. 1. Basic block diagram of the SLR system.

The main challenge involved in the SLR system is segmenting the hand region from the complex background which could be a signer with different colored costumes, a cluttered background with many objects present in the background, varied lighting conditions, indoor/outdoor location, and background color similar to the skin color. Thus to recognize the signs efficiently and accurately, extracting the hand region is very important. This paper addresses the problem of segmenting the hand region from the simple black background as well as the complex background datasets to accurately recognize the ISL gestures. Two efficient algorithms are presented in this paper that segment the hand region precisely: a) Contour matching b) Hybrid GrabCut algorithm. Hand segmentation is a crucial step in SLR system, enabling communication for the hearing-impaired, and in gesture recognition. Additionally, hand segmentation is vital for tracking and interaction in virtual and augmented reality, controlling smart homes, and assisting in medical imaging. It plays a role in human pose estimation, biometric security, robotics, art, and entertainment, as well as educational software. Precisely isolating the hand region from backgrounds contributes to improved accuracy and functionality in these applications, making it a foundational technology in numerous fields.

2   Literature Review

In [5], the RGB image is initially converted to YCbCr shading space to identify skin shading in the image and then it is divided into portions for brightness-Y and chrominance, Cb and Cr. As a result, a binary image is obtained. YCbCr is the most widely used technique when extracting the skin component of a picture using chrominance values. Work done is on ISL numerals (0–9) with a uniform simple background. The authors of [6] have developed a novel framework, the main goal of which is to extract human hands and palms from both simple, uniform backgrounds and complicated, non-uniform backgrounds under numerous contrasting lighting situations in both indoor and outdoor settings. The Viola-Jones algorithm and skin region identification technique are used to identify upper body regions and the face in input gestures in order to segment them and extract the human hand and palm. American sign language alphabets were taken into account for segmentation, and the results were 97.62% accurate. In [7], the input images are transformed into binary images, leaving the final image with just two distinct segments: the foreground (hand region) and the background. The work done is under strong, dark, and normal illumination. The overall accuracy achieved for ISL is 81.66%. The authors in [8] have used an adaptive probabilistic model for skin detection. In this model, 32 * 32 * 32 RGB color histograms are created for the look of the skin and the background using manually annotated skin and background images, and these histograms were standardized and utilized to create probabilistic models of the skin and background. The skin value is calculated and normalized, and the skin area is identified. In the second stage, filtering and noise removal are done. The input image is subjected to filtering and numerous morphological processes, which will reduce the noise. In [9], the SIFT's key-point generation stage is hybridized with adaptive thresholding and Gaussian blurring. The image is reduced in size to 200 × 200 pixels. The original image that has been resized must be turned into a grayscale version in the second stage. In the third phase, a Gaussian blur filter is used to smooth out the grayscale image. Adaptive thresholding is then used to binarize the smoothened grayscale image. Following that, the binarized image is subjected to the SIFT method's key-point formation step. In [10], the video frames are transformed into the HSV color space for images captured against a simple background. This is because the hue color of the skin differs significantly from that of the background, allowing for straightforward extraction. A thresholding technique is then applied experimentally to compute the hue and eliminate pixels with skin tones from the image. The resulting image is converted into a binary format, followed by noise removal through blurring. The largest contour, assumed to represent the hands due to its area, is extracted from the output. To further eliminate errors, a median filter and morphological techniques are employed. In [11], the authors employed a multi-step image processing strategy. They began by equalizing luminance using the LAB color scheme and CLACHE, followed by Gaussian blurring for noise reduction. Skin regions were identified through thresholding in the HSV color space, with adaptable thresholds accounting for varying lighting conditions. The final step involved detecting the largest contours and enclosing them within 637-square boxes, displaying the output classification results as text. This comprehensive approach enhances feature visibility and aids in effective image analysis. In [12], to identify edges, the Sobel edge detector method was initially employed, which calculates the gradient using the discrete differences between neighboring pixels in a 3×3 kernel. By approximating the derivative using the Sobel technique, this method effectively detects edges in the image. Hand gestures are formed as silhouette images in [13]. Each frame is converted into the HSV (Hue, Saturation, Value) color space. To identify the skin region, only the Hue (H) and Saturation (S) values that meet specific criteria are considered. Specifically, pixels are classified as non-skin if they satisfy any of the following conditions: $H > 0.55$, $S \leq 0.20$, or $S > 0.95$. This area is then designated as zero for skin extraction. The outer boundary (edges) of the segmented region is preserved by using a median filter. Binary representation is applied to the images after median filtering. Preprocessing is completed by removing the face, which is the most linked region. The input images are converted to monochrome images in the paper [14] and then shrunk to a size of 20 * 30 pixels. By removing rows and columns from the matrix containing background information, unnecessary data is also eliminated from the feature vector, enhancing its relevance and effectiveness in subsequent analysis. The raw image has been transformed into a binary mask and the hand shape has been obtained using canny edge detection [15]. Although the hand's outline is noticeable and can be utilized to extract features, the computation cost goes up because only the necessary section of the image is not extracted and the unnecessary black area in the image can be noticed.

3   Materials and Methods

The successful completion of HGR [16] heavily relies on accurately segmenting the hand region from the image. In this section, two efficient methods are described that achieve precise segmentation of the hand region from both a simple black background and a non-uniform complex background.

3.1   Dataset Details

The proposed method is evaluated on three datasets. Dataset I & II are standard datasets and Dataset III is a self-created data named "ISL 2022: A novel dataset creation on Indian sign language" [17]. The images considered are the ISL gestures which include alphabets and numbers. The description of the datasets is given in Table 1.

Table 1. Details of the Dataset

Dataset Source	Gesture	Volume	Background Type	Description
Kaggle (Dataset I) [18]	ISL Alphabets, Digits	42000	Uniform-Simple	Images are captured on a plain black background
Github (Dataset II) [19]	ISL Alphabets, Digits	16000	Non-uniform, complex	Images are taken indoors against a complicated scene with varying lighting and background colors
Self-created data (Dataset III)	ISL Alphabets, Digits	10000	Non-uniform, complex, cluttered	Images are captured on a non-uniform, cluttered background in varied lighting conditions, indoors with real speech & hearing-impaired students trained by a professional interpreter

3.2 Contour Matching Segmentation Algorithm

The foreground in an image with a dark background is segmented using this technique, which is based on contours [20]. Contours can be described as curves that connect contiguous points along a boundary with uniform color or intensity. These contours serve a crucial role in tasks such as shape analysis and object detection by providing a clear representation of an object's outline and structure. This approach works well with binary images because edge clarity will be good as it has only 0 or 255-pixel values. In other words, finding contours is like finding a white object from a black background. The foreground and background histograms do not overlap when using a contour-based image segmentation technique, therefore gestures captured against a plain dark background can be correctly identified. In such circumstances, classifying the image pixels as either background or foreground would be simple.

Algorithm:
Input: RGB image with black background
Output: Extracted hand region

- Step 1: Convert the image into a grayscale format
- Step 2: Apply binary thresholding
- Step 3: Find the contours
- Step 4: Draw contours on the image
- Step 5: Obtain the ROI

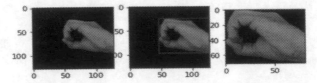

Fig. 2. Extracted ROI by applying the contour-based method.

Figure 2 shows the output obtained by using the contour-matching algorithm. The experiment is done on Dataset-I which consists of 35 gestures (26 ISL alphabets and 1–9 digits). However, there might not always be a plain, dark background in the input images for a gesture recognition system. Certain circumstances can arise where the background of the image is complicated and contrasts with the signer's skin tone. The proposed contour-based image segmentation method might not be successful in such situations. In this paper, an interactive foreground extraction method based on iterated graph cuts called the GrabCut algorithm [21–23], explained in Sect. 3.3, is used to solve the issue present with complex background images.

3.3 Hybrid GrabCut Segmentation Algorithm

In certain images, it's difficult to find the hand's portion from the complex background. The contour-based segmentation technique does not produce an appropriate foreground boundary for those images. As a result, this paper proposes a hybrid approach where the GrabCut algorithm is combined with contour matching for segmenting the foreground from images with complex backgrounds. It is a technique for segmenting images using graph cuts. The graph is generated using the Gaussian mixture model (GMM) [24] with pixels as nodes and is repeatedly sliced. The algorithm determines the color distribution [25] of the target object and the background by starting with a bounding box that the user has defined around the object to be segmented. This technique links all the pixels based on how closely the colors of each pixel match the labels, one label for the background and the other for the foreground. Foreground and background pixels are modeled by GMM. The bounding box parameters [26] can exhibit variations across different images, contingent upon the specific region intended for extraction. To attain the ultimate segmentation of the target area, a recurring process of iterative adjustments to these parameters is necessary. This procedure continues until the ideal configuration is reached for accurately delineating the desired region within each unique image. The working of the graph cut algorithm is represented in Fig. 3.

- The process begins with the user applying the bounding box on the desired foreground. While the areas outside the bounding box are designated as background objects.
- To model the foreground and background, a GMM is employed. The GMM learns to identify the unknown pixels based on the user's input, clustering each pixel according to color statistics.
- Next, a graph is constructed based on the pixel distribution. Additional nodes, namely the source node and sink node, are added along with the pixels, which serve as nodes in the network. The source node links to all foreground pixels, while the sink

node connects to all background pixels, forming the basis for graph-based image segmentation.

- The edge weights between pixels and source/sink nodes are based on the probability of a pixel being part of the foreground or background, essential for graph-based segmentation. Edges with a significant difference in pixel color are assigned low weights.
- Using a cost function that considers the total weights of the segmented edges, the algorithm separates the graph into two parts by splitting the source and sink nodes.
- The repetition of this process ultimately leads to pixel labeling, designating those connected to the source as foreground and those connected to the sink as background following segmentation. As a result, the foreground is extracted.

Once the foreground object is distinguished from the background object, the foreground object has to be extracted which is the actual output. In order to obtain this, contour-matching is applied to the foreground object obtained by the GrabCut algorithm. Hence fusion of GrabCut and contour matching approaches gives an accurate desired result as shown in Fig. 4. This method is mainly used for complex background datasets. The experiment is done on Dataset II & III where the images have a complex backdrop that includes a cluttered background, a multi-colored costume worn by a signer, and a non-uniform background.

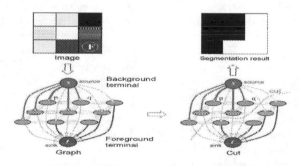

Fig. 3. Representation of Graph cut method [31].

Algorithm:
Input: RGB image with non-uniform, complex background
Output: Extracted hand region
Step 1: Estimating the color distribution of the foreground and background via a GMM
Step 2: Constructing a Markov random field over the pixel's labels
Step 3: Apply the GrabCut method to make the background black and get the foreground object
Step 4: Apply the contour matching algorithm on the output obtained in step 3 to extract the ROI.

Input RGB image	Output obtained by GrabCut method	Output obtained by hybrid method
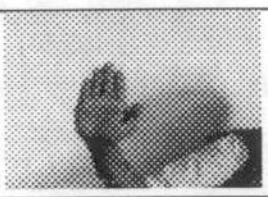	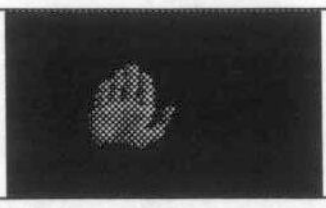	

Fig. 4. Fusion of GrabCut and contour matching approaches.

4   Results and Discussion

This section discusses the results obtained using the proposed algorithms on all three datasets mentioned. Figure 5 gives the details of the images and the corresponding output obtained using the hybrid GrabCut approach which is applied on Dataset II & III. Figure 6 represents the output obtained using the contour matching algorithm which is applied on Dataset I. The accuracies obtained using the proposed methods are illustrated in Fig. 7 and 8.

The contour matching algorithm requires the images to be converted into binary masked images by setting the pixel values to lower and upper boundary values which distinguishes the black and white pixels that fall in a certain range of the defined lower and upper boundary. Next, contours are drawn around the highlighted edge once the image is converted to a binary mask. That is, it draws a boundary by connecting all the white pixels. Next, a rectangular box is drawn over the images which helps to crop the exact region of interest.

In our experiment, the hybrid GrabCut algorithm had to undergo several iterations for a few images to get the foreground object accurately. The important parameter to be considered here is the bounding box values around the ROI. The four values that are passed as the arguments are the starting values of the x and y coordinates and the height & width of the required portion of the image. Few images with a more complex background required a maximum of 5 iterations to get the exact foreground wherein we had to adjust the bounding box values and check for the proper segmentation. Few images gave the best results with only one set of bounding box values.

Segmentation Accuracy (SA) [6] for both algorithms is calculated using the Eq. (1) as follows:

$$SA = (\sum n \% \sum N) * 100 \tag{1}$$

where, n = No. of gestures with successful segmentation & N = No. of gestures considered for segmentation.

From Fig. 7 it is noticed that contour matching for Dataset I gives 100% accuracy and Fig. 8 represents the accuracy obtained by the hybrid GrabCut algorithm, which gives around 97% accuracy for Dataset II and 91% for Dataset III. For Dataset III, accuracy decreased as it involves a cluttered and more complicated background compared to Dataset I & II.

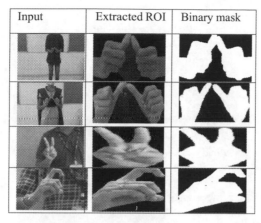

Fig. 5. Output obtained by using the hybrid GrabCut method.

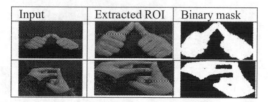

Fig. 6. Output obtained by using the Contour-matching method.

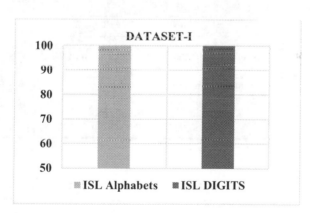

Fig. 7. Accuracy obtained by using the contour-matching approach.

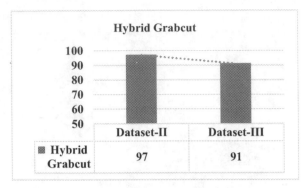

Fig. 8. Accuracy obtained using a novel hybrid approach.

4.1 State-of-the-Art Result Comparison

Table 2. Comparison of proposed methods with existing work.

Year	Methodology	Dataset description	Outcome
2020, [27]	Skin mask, Canny edge detection	Plain black background	
2021, [28]	Context subtracting, Skin color detection, Edge detection	Plain black background	
2020, [29]	Gaussian Blur, Converted to HSV.	Simple black background	
2020, [30]	Histogram depth thresholding	Complex background	
Proposed	**Combined Grabcut & Contour matching**	**Simple black background, Complex, Cluttered background**	

The segmentation techniques explained in the literature survey and the state of the art work which is represented in Table 2, exhibit several common limitations. Canny edge detection may oversimplify hand shapes, potentially missing finer details. Context subtracting methods may struggle in complex backgrounds and require careful parameter setting. Skin color detection's accuracy can be hindered by variations in lighting. Gaussian blur, although useful for noise reduction, may inadvertently smooth out important features. Converting to the HSV color space for segmentation may fail when backgrounds share hues with skin tones. Histogram depth thresholding may be sensitive to small variations, necessitating frequent adjustments. These limitations highlight the need for adaptable and context-aware segmentation strategies that can robustly handle diverse real-world scenarios. In contrast, the hybrid GrabCut and contour matching algorithms offer a promising solution for segmenting foreground objects from both simple and complex backgrounds. These algorithms excel in adapting to diverse scenarios, leveraging user-provided input to iteratively refine the segmentation boundary. By combining the strengths of region-based segmentation (GrabCut) with contour-based precision (contour matching), they provide a versatile and robust means of accurately separating foreground objects from challenging backgrounds, making them a valuable choice for various image segmentation tasks.

5 Conclusion

This paper introduces two effective segmentation algorithms tailored to the extraction of the hand region from image datasets featuring simple and diverse backgrounds which is later used in sign language or gesture recognition tasks. The proposed algorithm employs a contour-based segmentation approach, precisely separating the foreground object from a simple black background. To address the challenges of backgrounds in complex scenarios, a hybrid approach is introduced, integrating the GrabCut algorithm with a contour-matching technique. Our findings reveal that the GrabCut algorithm may require more iterations to accurately segment intricate backgrounds compared to simpler ones. The proposed method showcases remarkable results, achieving an overall segmentation accuracy of 97% for datasets with complex backgrounds and a flawless 100% accuracy for datasets with black backgrounds. This segmentation process contributes to the recognition of Indian Sign Language gestures.

References

1. Aparna, A., D'Souza, D.J.: Sign language recognition. In: 2021 IEEE International Conference on Distributed Computing VLSI, Electrical Circuits and Robotics Discover 2021 - Proceedings, no. August, pp. 104–106 (2021). https://doi.org/10.1109/DISCOVER52564. 2021.9663629
2. Shaik, K.B., Ganesan, P., Kalist, V., Sathish, B.S., Jenitha, J.M.M.: Comparative study of skin color detection and segmentation in HSV and YCbCr color space. Procedia Comput. Sci. **57**, 41–48 (2015). https://doi.org/10.1016/J.PROCS.2015.07.362
3. Behera, J., Pradhan, S.: Segmentation techniques of image processing : a review 63–66 (2017)
4. Jaglan, P., Dass, R., Duhan, M.: A comparative analysis of various image segmentation techniques. In: Krishna, C.R., Dutta, M., Kumar, R. (eds.) Proceedings of 2nd International Conference on Communication, Computing and Networking. LNNS, vol. 46, pp. 359–374. Springer, Singapore (2019). https://doi.org/10.1007/978-981-13-1217-5_36
5. Ekbote, J., Joshi, M.: Indian sign language recognition using ANN and SVM classifiers. In: Proceedings of 2017 International Conference on Innovations Information, Embedded Communication Systems ICIIECS 2017, vol. 2018- January, pp. 1–5 (2018). https://doi.org/ 10.1109/ICIIECS.2017.8276111
6. Shivashankara, S., Srinath, S.: Palm extraction in american sign language gestures using segmentation and skin region detection. Int. J. Innov. Technol. Explor. Eng. **8**(7), 2409–2418 (2019)
7. Itkarkar, R.R., Nandi, A., Mane, B.: Contour-based real-time hand gesture recognition for Indian sign language. Adv. Intell. Syst. Comput. **556**, 683–691 (2017). https://doi.org/10. 1007/978-981-10-3874-7_65

8. Rokade, Y.I., Jadav, P.M.: Indian sign language recognition system. Int. J. Eng. Technol. **9**(3S), 189–196 (2017). https://doi.org/10.21817/ijet/2017/v9i3/170903s030

9. Dudhal, A., Mathkar, H., Jain, A., Kadam, O., Shirole, M.: Hybrid SIFT feature extraction approach for Indian sign language recognition system based on CNN. In: Pandian, D., Fernando, X., Baig, Z., Shi, F. (eds.) ISMAC 2018. LNCVB, vol. 30, pp. 727–738. Springer, Cham (2019). https://doi.org/10.1007/978-3-030-00665-5_72

10. Katoch, S., Singh, V., Tiwary, U.S.: Indian sign language recognition system using SURF with SVM and CNN. Array **14**, 100141 (2022). 10.16/J.ARRAY.2022.100141

11. Tolentino, L.K.S., Juan, R.S., Thio-ac, A.C., Pamahoy, M.A.B., Forteza, J.R.R., Garcia, X.J.O.: Static sign language recognition using deep learning. Int. J. Mach. Learn. Comput. **9**(6), 821–827 (2019). https://doi.org/10.18178/ijmlc.2019.9.6.879

12. Sharma, M., Pal, R., Sahoo, A.K.: Indian sign language recognition using neural networks and KNN classifiers. ARPN J. Eng. Appl. Sci. **9**(8), 1255–1259 (2014). www.arpnjournals. com. Accessed 25 Feb 25 2022

13. Tripathi, K., Nandi, N.B.G.: Continuous Indian sign language gesture recognition and sentence formation. Procedia Comput. Sci. **54**, 523–531 (2015). https://doi.org/10.1016/j.procs. 2015.06.060

14. Sahoo, A.K.: Indian sign language recognition using machine learning techniques. In: Macromolecular Symposia, vol. 397, no. 1, pp. 1–7 (2021).https://doi.org/10.1002/masy.202 000241

15. Priyanka Parvathy, D., Subramaniam, K.: Performance comparison of segmentation algorithms for hand gesture recognition. Int. J. Eng. Technol. **7**(3), 1227–1232 (2018). https://doi. org/10.14419/ijet.v7i3.12842

16. Bhushan, S., Alshehri, M., Keshta, I., Chakraverti, A.K., Rajpurohit, J., Abugabah, A.: An experimental analysis of various machine learning algorithms for hand gesture recognition. Electronics (Switzerland) **11**(6), 968 (2022). https://doi.org/10.3390/electronics11060968

17. Poornima, B.V., Rakshitha, R., Srinath, S., Rashmi, S.: ISL2022: a novel dataset creation on Indian sign language. In: 2023 10th International Conference on Signal Processing and Integrated Networks (SPIN), pp. 363-366. IEEE (2023)

18. https://www.kaggle.com/datasets/kshitij192/isl-dataset

19. https://github.com/sajanraj/Indian-Sign-Language-Recognition

20. Pramada, S.: Intelligent sign language recognition using image processing. IOSR J. Eng. **03**(02), 45–51 (2013). https://doi.org/10.9790/3021-03224551

21. Sangüesa, A.A., Jørgensen, N.K., Larsen, C.A., Nasrollahi, K., Moeslund, T.B.: Initiating GrabCut by color difference for automatic foreground extraction of passport imagery. In: 2016 6th International Conference on Image Processing Theory, Tools Appl. IPTA 2016 (2017). https://doi.org/10.1109/IPTA.2016.7820964

22. Belim, S.V., Belim, S.Y.: Images segmentation based on cutting the graph into communities. Algorithms **15**(9), 312 (2022). https://doi.org/10.3390/a15090312

23. Mira, B.S., Ravichandran, T., Yamuna, G., Durga, R.: A review on Grabcut algorithm, October, pp. 194–200 (2018)

24. Drygala, C., Rottmann, M., Gottschalk, H., Friedrichs, K., Kurbiel, T.: Background- foreground segmentation for interior sensing in automotive industry, pp. 1–19 (2021). http:// arxiv.org/abs/2109.09410

25. Meghana, R.K., Chitkara, Y., Apoorva, S., Mohana: Background-modelling techniques for foreground detection and tracking using Gaussian mixture model. In: Proceedings of the 3rd International Conference on Computing Methodologies and Communication, ICCMC2019, pp. 1129–1134 (2019). https://doi.org/10.1109/ICCMC.2019.8819825

26. Meng, F., Guo, L., Wu, Q., Li, H.: A new deep segmentation quality assessment network for refining bounding box based segmentation. IEEE Access **7**, 59514–59523 (2019). https://doi. org/10.1109/ACCESS.2019.2915121

27. Shravani, K., Lakshmi, A.S., Geethika, M.S., Sapna, B.K.: Indian sign language character recognition. IOSR J. Comput. Eng. **22**(3), 14–19 (2020). https://doi.org/10.9790/0661-220 3011419

28. Patil, R., Patil, V., Bahuguna, A., Datkhile, G.: Indian sign language recognition using convolutional neural network. In: ITM Web Conference, vol. 40, no. July, p. 03004 (2021). https://doi.org/10.1051/itmconf/20214003004

29. Prajapati, M., Makawana, M., Hada, S.: Indian sign language recognitio for static anddynamic hand gestures (2020). https://doi.org/10.26438/ijcse/v8i9.5458

30. Paul, S., Bhattacharyya, A., Mollah, A.F., Basu, S., Nasipuri, M.: Hand segmentation from complex background for gesture recognition. Adv. Intell. Syst. Comput. **937**, 775–782 (2020). https://doi.org/10.1007/978-981-13-7403-6_68

31. https://julie-jiang.github.io/image-segmentation/

Improved Metric Space for Shape Correspondence

Manika Bindal[1]($\boxtimes$) and Venkatesh Kamat[2]

[1] Goa University, Goa, India
`manika.bindal@gmail.com`
[2] Indian Institute of Technology (IIT) Goa, Goa, India
`vvkamat@iitgoa.ac.in`

Abstract. Shape correspondence is a fundamental task of finding a map among the elements of a pair of shapes. Particularly, non-rigid shapes add to the challenge of computing correspondences as they have their respective metric structures. In order to establish a mapping between non-rigid shapes, it is necessary to bring them into a common metric space. The idea is to identify shape forms that are invariant to isometric deformations and are embedded in a Euclidean space. These pose-invariant features are then aligned to identify point-to-point correspondences. Geodesic distances have been utilized to compute these shape-invariant forms. However, these distances are quite sensitive to topological noise present in the shape. This work proposes to overcome these challenges by utilizing shape-aware distances to identify invariant forms that are unaffected by topological variations of the shape and are smoother than geodesic distance. These distances along with the non-rigid alignment of shape forms in the Euclidean domain led to an improved point-to-point correspondence, enabling it to work effectively, even when dealing with different triangulations of the shape.

Keywords: Shape correspondence · Surface distance · Invariant forms

1 Introduction

In computational context, shapes refer to digital representations of real-world objects such as chairs, humans, and more. With the increasing technological capability to capture high-resolution data with detailed information, the shape analysis community has been actively addressing challenges in this field, such as shape compression [1], shape segmentation [2], etc. The field of shape matching has garnered significant interest from researchers in various domains, including computer graphics, image processing, geometry processing, and computer vision. A specific sub-area within shape matching involves the computation of shape correspondences. In this case, the goal is not only to determine if two shapes are similar or match, rather also to establish a mapping between the

Supported by Visvesvaraya PhD Scheme, MeitY, Government of India.

different elements of the given shapes. The computation of correspondences is a fundamental task, as it enables the efficient transfer of attributes such as texture and deformation from one shape to another. This is necessary for various critical tasks, including the statistical modeling of shape collections, as well as shape interpolation, morphing, and more.

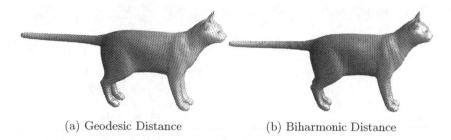

(a) Geodesic Distance   (b) Biharmonic Distance

Fig. 1. Surface distances computed on cat shape from a point near tail to every other point

The task of shape correspondence involves the computation of a mapping $T : \mathcal{M} \to \mathcal{N}$ between the elements of two shapes, $\mathcal{M}$ and $\mathcal{N}$. There are various approaches to computing shape correspondences that have been suggested, depending on factors such as the deformations that the shapes can undergo and whether partial or full correspondences are being computed. A survey by Van Kaick et al. [3] provides an overview of these different approaches. Rigid shapes undergo transformations that preserves euclidean distances i.e. extrinsic features remain intact while non-rigid shapes deform anyhow [4]. Finding correspondences for rigid shapes has numerous efficient solutions available. Recently, learning based techniques based on neural networks [5,6] are also attracting a lot of interest in dense shape correspondence. However, due to the vast space of possible deformations for non-rigid shapes, along with added challenges such as noise, occlusion, and missing information, it remains an interesting and challenging area of research.

In this work, the analysis is restricted to identify point-to-point correspondence between shapes that are susceptible to isometric deformations, wherein the distances along the surface do not change if the surface of the shape undergoes deformation without any stretching or tearing in the process. To digitally represent the surfaces, triangulated meshes are utilized. In this context, shape correspondence refers to the task of finding a vertex-to-vertex mapping between given shape meshes.

The paper is organized as Sect. 2 discussing the related work regarding rigid and non-rigid shape matching. Section 3 & 4 provides a short background regarding the concepts utilized and motivates the work while detailing the contribution. Section 5 discusses the implementation methodology whereas Sect. 6 talks about the future scope of the work.

2   Related Work

Shape matching can be viewed as the process of finding the geometric transformation between shapes that aligns them with each other, and subsequently identifying correspondences based on proximity [7]. Alternatively, correspondences can be computed directly based on feature descriptors, without the need to align the shapes at all [8]. Another approach is a hybrid method, in which alignment and computation of correspondence are performed iteratively, leading to improved results over certain iterations. Iterative Closest Point (ICP) algorithm [9] is a widely used technique for finding correspondences between rigid shapes. The algorithm iteratively aligns the shapes by first finding the optimal geometric transformation consisting of rotations and translations, and then utilizing a Nearest Neighbour approach to identify the closest points for the computed alignment. Over time, various efficient versions of the ICP algorithm have been proposed [10], which have contributed to its strength and effectiveness. Other methods for rigid shapes are surveyed in [11]. Matching shapes that can deform in arbitrary ways, such that different points on the shape undergo different transformations, can be quite challenging since no global transformation exists for all points on the shape. Hence, for non-rigid shapes, to allow any kind of mathematical analysis is to restrict the deformation to an isometry, wherein the distances along the surface are preserved, while the shape is undergoing isometric deformation.

Given that rigid shape matching is mostly a solved problem, one way to approach the correspondence problem for non-rigid, isometrically deformed shapes is to consider the shapes in terms of their metric spaces, i.e., as $(\mathcal{M}, d_\mathcal{M})$ and $(\mathcal{N}, d_\mathcal{N})$. For extrinsic shape similarity, both the shapes belong to an ambient euclidean space with respect to euclidean metric. Intrinsic similarity, on the other hand, is characterized by different metric spaces for the respective shapes $(\mathcal{M}, d_\mathcal{M})$ and $(\mathcal{N}, d_\mathcal{N})$, which cannot be compared directly. To address the challenge of comparing the respective metric spaces $d_\mathcal{M}$ and $d_\mathcal{N}$ for intrinsic similarity, [12] proposed the concept of a pose-invariant shape form that belongs to a common metric space and can describe the original shape. The common space is referred to as an embedding space. This embedding space can be euclidean, non-euclidean or can be one of the shapes itself [13]. Identifying such a metric space amounts to finding an invariant representation of shape with respect to the space of isometric deformations.

Spectral embedding, a similar concept involving eigenfunctions and eigenvalues of a linear operator which is defined on the surface of the shape is proposed [14] to embed the shape in a different domain. This common space is then utilized for further analysis of the shape. The use of spectral embedding has spawned numerous techniques in the field of shape analysis, including compression, parameterization, clustering, segmentation, remeshing, and more. Refer [15] for a detailed survey of spectral mesh processing techniques. Functional maps, as proposed by [16], represent another promising avenue that involves defining a space of functions for each shape and then seeking to match shapes by finding a map between these functional spaces.

Fig. 2. Isometric embedding computed via multidimensional scaling method with original shape (left) and its computed canonical form (right)

In this work, the main objective is to explore techniques for embedding isometric shapes into the Euclidean domain using pairwise relationship information between the shape elements. This embedding allows for establishing point-to-point correspondences between shapes by means of alignment and closest-point approaches.

3   Background

Consider isometrically deformable non-rigid shapes with respect to their metric spaces i.e. $(\mathcal{M}, d_\mathcal{M})$ and $(\mathcal{N}, d_\mathcal{N})$. As these shapes exist in different metric spaces, a direct comparison between them with respect to their metric structure is not possible. Therefore, a common space is required where they can be compared. Rigid shapes are typically considered as subsets of a common metric space, often the Euclidean domain $\mathbb{R}^3$. In contrast, embedding various non-rigid shapes into a common metric space is required to tackle the problem of establishing correspondences between them.

3.1   Isometric Embedding

The goal is to embed a shape's surface into a Euclidean domain in a way that preserves the distance between any two points along the surface. In other words, the distance between the same pair of points in the embedded domain should be equal to the distance between those points along the surface. Formally, the process of embedding a shape $(\mathcal{M}, d_\mathcal{M})$ into an *m-dimensional* Euclidean domain $\mathbb{R}^m$ involves determining a mapping:

$$f : (\mathcal{M}, d_\mathcal{M}) \to (\mathbb{R}^m, d_{\mathbb{R}^m}) \tag{1}$$

such that $d_{\mathcal{M}}(p, q) = d_{\mathbb{R}^m}(f(p), f(q))$ for all $p, q \in \mathcal{M}$, where $d_{\mathcal{M}}$ and $d_{\mathbb{R}^m}$ denote the distance metrics in the original and the embedded Euclidean space, respectively. The function f represents the desired isometric embedding, and $f(\mathcal{M})$ is known as the canonical form of the embedded shape [13].

To begin the process, the shape mesh $\mathcal{M}$ undergoes the establishment of a discrete linear operator. This operator takes the form of a matrix and is constructed using intrinsic features of the shape that are derived from its geometry and topology. The matrix may take the form of a pairwise relationship matrix, such as an affinity matrix, which indicates the proximity between any two points on the shape. Alternatively, it could indicate the immediate neighbouring points for all elements. Then an isometric embedding is desired which involves identifying a shape that satisfies the constraint specified in Eq. 1. It is not feasible to obtain a completely accurate isometric embedding for a shape in the Euclidean domain, especially for complex shapes. The idea is to minimize the level of distortion as much as possible. To accomplish this, powerful multidimensional scaling (MDS) techniques are employed, as outlined in [17]. These techniques seek to identify an embedding f into $\mathbb{R}^m$ that minimizes distortion, subject to the condition that:

$$f = \operatorname*{argmin}_{f:\mathcal{M} \to \mathcal{R}^m} \sum_{p,q \in \mathcal{M}} | d_{\mathbb{R}^m}(f(p), f(q)) - d_{\mathcal{M}}(p, q) |^2$$

For details on the various versions of multidimensional scaling techniques proposed, please refer to [13]. An isometric embedding for a human triangular mesh, computed using the MDS algorithm, is illustrated in Fig. 2. These canonical forms are basically a bending invariant signature which are typically free from various poses (isometric deformations) of shapes.

3.2 Geodesic Distances

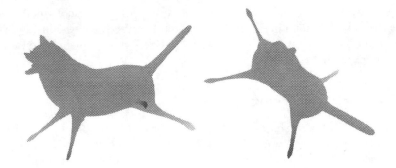

Fig. 3. Canonical forms via geodesic distances for both wolf meshes

In mathematical terms, distance functions are typically known as metrics. Specifically, the geodesic distance refers to the shortest path that can be calculated along the surface between any two points for a given shape. In the early stages of developing methods for computing distances on shapes, Dijkstra's algorithm from graph theory was employed. This involved selecting a fixed source point and then determining the distances to every other vertex on the shape. While utilizing Dijkstra's algorithm to compute distances on shapes was a useful starting point, it had its limitations. Specifically, because this approach was based on the edges of the mesh, it did not accurately capture the true geodesic distances that were necessary. To obtain the more precise geodesic distances that were needed, [18] introduced a widely-used method known as the "Fast Marching" algorithm. This method involves solving an Eikonal equation in a computationally efficient way, thereby allowing pairwise geodesic distances to be computed on triangulated domains. The Eikonal equation is a partial differential equation that describes the propagation of wavefronts and specified as $\|\nabla(u)\| = 1$, where $\nabla(u)$ is the gradient of the distance function, which describes the fact that the distance function should increase at a constant rate as one moves away from the source point in the direction of the geodesic path. For a mesh of n vertices, the computational complexity of fast marching algorithm is $\mathcal{O}(n^2 \log n)$. Recently [19] introduced a faster approach to compute such distances via heat method. See Fig. 1(a) for visualizing geodesic distances from a point to all other points on a cat mesh computed by fast marching method.

3.3   Biharmonic Distances

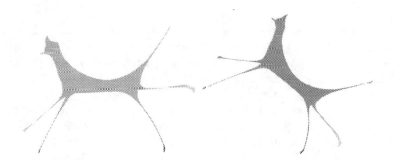

Fig. 4. Canonical forms via biharmonic distances for both wolf meshes

Biharmonic distances [20] are based on the eigenvalues and eigenfunctions of discrete Laplace-Beltrami operator (LBO) [21,22]. On shape $\mathcal{M}$, the biharmonic distance between any two points $p, q \in \mathcal{M}$ is defined as,

$$d_B\,(p,q)^2 = \sum_{k=1}^{\infty} \frac{(\phi_k\,(p) - \phi_k\,(q))^2}{\lambda_k^2}$$

where squared distances between two points p, q is given in terms of Laplace-Beltrami eigenfunctions computed at respective points as $\phi_k(p)$ and $\phi_k(q)$ and λ_k

denotes the respective eigenvalues. The computational complexity of computing biharmonic distances on a mesh with n vertices and k Laplace-beltrami eigenvectors is $\mathcal{O}(kn + k)$. See Fig. 1(b) for visualizing Biharmonic distances computed from a single source to all other points on cat mesh.

Fig. 5. Canonical forms aligned in a non-rigid manner for forms compute via geodesic distances (left), via biharmonic distances (right)

4   Motivation and Contribution

Since geodesic distances between any two points are only affected by the infinitely small neighbourhood around the shortest path, they are shape-oblivious i.e. have local flavour. Also these distances are highly sensitive to changes in the topology of the shape, such as the missing region, presence of noise, or short-circuit among edges. In the presence of such defects, the shortest path will be significantly altered, resulting in a different outcome. In contrast to geodesic distances, biharmonic distances take into account the overall shape of an object, particularly when considering points that are far apart, hence, are shape-aware. They are also topologically insensitive, owing to their dependence on the Laplace-Beltrami operator. This gives them an advantage over geodesic distances. While geodesic distances represent the shortest distances on a shape's surface and exhibit local isotropy, they do not capture the global geometry of the shape and are sensitive to topology. Biharmonic distances address these shortcomings by taking into account the shape of the object and being insensitive to topological noise. Due to these unique characteristics, biharmonic distances are employed as an affinity matrix that describes the pairwise relationships among all points on a shape's surface. When this matrix is embedded in a low-dimensional Euclidean domain, it led to improved point-to-point matching.

   In this work, the authors propose to utilize biharmonic distances instead of geodesic distances for describing the shape geometry better. It's worth noting that when dealing with embedded shapes, a usual approach is to perform rigid alignment in order to establish point-to-point correspondences. Apart from using Biharmonic distances as pairwise relationship between elements of shapes, authors also propose to utilize non-rigid alignment of canonical forms in the euclidean domain which ultimately led to improved shape correspondences. In a nutshell, the contribution is to utilize biharmonic distances to determine canonical forms in the Euclidean domain along with non-rigid alignment of respective forms, a combination that yields better results than other similar approaches.

Fig. 6. Geodesic error visualized in terms of heat map on the shape itself; via geodesic distances (left), via biharmonic distances (right) (Color figure online)

5   Implementation

Dataset. To evaluate the method, the TOSCA dataset [13] was employed, which comprises of high-resolution non-rigid shapes in multiple poses. The dataset consists of 80 objects, including 11 cats, 9 dogs, 3 wolves, 8 horses, 6 centaurs, 4 gorillas, 12 female figures, and two different male figures, each with 7 and 20 poses respectively. Ground truth point-to-point correspondences are also provided, which are utilized to evaluate methods.

Methodology. The implementation details discussed in this work will focus on two wolf meshes extracted from the TOSCA dataset, specifically wolf0 and wolf1. In order to compute point-to-point correspondences between two shapes, the approach taken is to establish canonical forms for each shape. This transforms the problem of matching non-rigid shapes into the easier task of matching rigid shapes. It is necessary to establish canonical forms for the shapes in order to align them within a shared metric space. Since biharmonic distances being shape-aware and smooth are utilized to compute canonical forms by generating pairwise affinity matrices for both the shapes. Hence, the initial step in the process is to calculate biharmonic distances among all pair of vertices in both meshes separately. After computing the biharmonic distance matrix, the next step involves utilizing multi-dimensional scaling algorithms to identify canonical forms that are embedded in a Euclidean domain. Particularly, SMACOF (Scaling by MAjorizing a COmplicated Function) multidimensional scaling algorithm [23] with Reduced Rank Extrapolation (RRE) technique is utilized to compute the canonical forms for each shape. Refer Fig. 4 for the canonical forms of wolf meshes computed via biharmonic distances as pairwise relationship matrices and Fig. 3 respectively for geodesic distances for comparison purposes. The usual approach for aligning canonical forms involves utilizing rigid alignment algorithms such as iterative closest point (ICP). In this work, the alignment process is enhanced by utilizing a non-rigid version of ICP [24] that employs thin-plate splines. This approach is preferable as it more accurately captures the deformations present in non-rigid shapes. Once shapes are embedded in the euclidean domain then non-rigid version of ICP is utilized to bring them in alignment.

The third step of the process involves deforming the canonical form of wolf1 mesh while the canonical form of the wolf0 mesh is kept intact. Please refer to Fig. 5 for a visualization of the aligned canonical forms for both meshes, which were computed using pairwise relationship matrices based on biharmonic and geodesic distances, respectively. Computing correspondences for aligned shapes is based on the "closest-point" approach where an energy function based on distance measure between shape elements is minimized. After the alignment of the shapes, a point-to-point correspondence is established by identifying the nearest point on one shape for each point on the other shape. Hence, the next step is to determine desired correspondence map by standard nearest-neighbour algorithm.

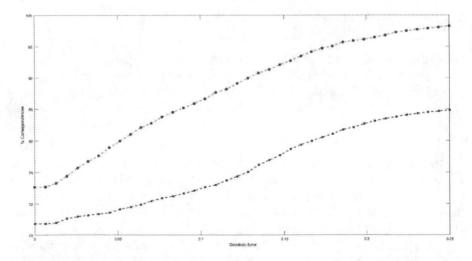

Fig. 7. Accuracy of point-to-point correspondences obtained via Biharmonic distances (green line with circles) and Geodesic distances (red line with squares) with respect to the increasing geodesic error on the x-axis for wolf shape (Color figure online)

In order to evaluate the effectiveness of the chosen approach, it is necessary to assess the accuracy of the resulting point-to-point correspondence map. To do so, the geodesic error is calculated by summing all the geodesic distances between the computed mapping of points and the ground-truth mapping. Suppose there is a vertex p in the wolf0 mesh and the corresponding vertex in the wolf1 mesh is obtained via proposed method as q. However, the ground-truth establishes vertex r in wolf1 mesh as the corresponding vertex for vertex p in wolf0 mesh. The geodesic error at vertex p is then calculated as the geodesic distance between vertices q and r on the wolf1 mesh. The geodesic error for the obtained mapping is determined by summing up the geodesic error at each vertex on the wolf0 mesh. Please refer to Fig. 7 to visualize the accuracy of the point-to-point correspondence map, as determined by the geodesic error. On the x-axis is the increasing geodesic error plotted against on y-axis the percentage of correct matches. Both the biharmonic and geodesic distances were used as pairwise relationship distance matrices to compute canonical forms. Also refer to Fig. 6 for a visual representation of the geodesic error that arises when computing the point-to-point correspondence map. The heat map shows the distribution of the error, with red indicating the highest error and black indicating zero error. The computational complexity of the proposed approach depends mainly on the computation of distances. Since it is faster to compute biharmonic distances, the proposed approach is faster as compared to the one with geodesic distances. Note that for wolf meshes via geodesic distances along with non-rigid alignment only 72.68% vertices mapped with geodesic error less than 0.1 whereas via biharmonic distances the accuracy jumped up to 86.65%. For human meshes utilizing biharmonic distances enhanced the accuracy of point-to-point correspondences by 2% as compared to that of geodesic distances.

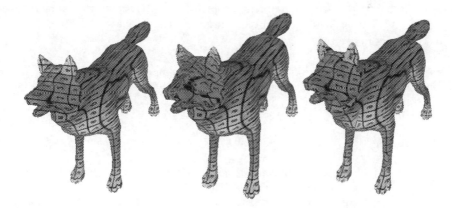

Fig. 8. Texture transfer from wolf0 to wolf1; via groundtruth map (left), map via geodesic distances (middle), map via biharmonic distances (right)

Application. Consider an application of texture transfer for obtained point-to-point correspondence map via proposed approach. By examining the degree of smoothness in the texture transfer process, we can assess the efficacy of using the obtained correspondence map to transfer a texture from wolf0 mesh to wolf1 mesh in a visual manner. To observe the quality of the texture transfer process, please refer Fig. 8 where the texture is transferred via ground-truth (left), via correspondence map obtained by geodesic distance matrices to compute canonical forms (middle) and via biharmonic distances (right). Notice particularly the face texture has been transferred well in case of biharmonic distances as compared to geodesic distances.

6   Discussions and Future Scope

In this work, the impact of using shape-aware biharmonic distances in order to more accurately capture shape geometry, specifically for addressing the challenge of shape correspondence is discussed. In particular, incorporating the non-rigid version of the ICP algorithm to align the canonical forms using biharmonic distances resulted in more effective point-to-point correspondences, as it was better able to capture the deformation information of the shape. It is worth noting that, as demonstrated in the texture transfer application shown in Fig. 8, the canonical forms generated using biharmonic distances are more successful in capturing the facial features of the wolf mesh when compared to those generated using geodesic distances. This observation supports the idea that biharmonic distances are more effective than geodesic distances in terms of shape matching. Although biharmonic distances are advantageous in shape matching, they have a tendency to smooth out high frequency details in shapes due to their reliance on Laplace-Beltrami operators. To address this limitation, an intriguing area for future exploration would be to incorporate Hamiltonian operators with intrinsic potentials that capture high frequency features in their spectra to determine biharmonic distances which can further improve the accuracy of the point-to-point correspondence map.

Acknowledgement. This work was financially supported by Visvesvaraya PhD Scheme, Ministry of Electronics and Information Technology, Government of India under Grant MEITY-PHD-1090.

References

1. Alliez, P.: Recent advances in compression of 3D meshes. In: 2005 13th European Signal Processing Conference, pp. 1–4. IEEE (2005)
2. Shamir, A.: A survey on mesh segmentation techniques. In: Computer Graphics Forum, vol. 27, no. 6, pp. 1539–1556. Wiley Online Library (2008)
3. Van Kaick, O., Zhang, H., Hamarneh, G., Cohen-Or, D.: A survey on shape correspondence. In: Computer Graphics Forum, vol. 30, no. 6, pp. 1681–1707. Wiley Online Library (2011)
4. Bronstein, A.M., Bronstein, M.M., Kimmel, R.: Rock, paper, and scissors: extrinsic vs. intrinsic similarity of non-rigid shapes. In: 2007 IEEE 11th International Conference on Computer Vision, pp. 1–6. IEEE (2007)

5. Marin, R., Rakotosaona, M.-J., Melzi, S., Ovsjanikov, M.: Correspondence learning via linearly-invariant embedding. In: Advances in Neural Information Processing Systems, vol. 33, pp. 1608–1620 (2020)
6. Abdelreheem, A., Eldesokey, A., Ovsjanikov, M., Wonka, P.: Zero-shot 3D shape correspondence. arXiv preprint arXiv:2306.03253 (2023)
7. Gelfand, N., Mitra, N.J., Guibas, L.J., Pottmann, H.: Robust global registration. In: Symposium on Geometry Processing, Vienna, Austria, vol. 2, no. 3, p. 5 (2005)
8. Castellani, U., Cristani, M., Fantoni, S., Murino, V.: Sparse points matching by combining 3D mesh saliency with statistical descriptors. In: Computer Graphics Forum, vol. 27, no. 2, pp. 643–652. Wiley Online Library (2008)
9. Besl, P.J., McKay, N.D.: Method for registration of 3-D shapes. In: Sensor Fusion IV: Control Paradigms and Data Structures, vol. 1611, pp. 586–607. International Society for Optics and Photonics (1992)
10. Rusinkiewicz, S., Levoy, M.: Efficient variants of the ICP algorithm. In: 2001 Proceedings Third International Conference on 3-D Digital Imaging and Modeling, pp. 145–152. IEEE (2001)
11. Bellekens, B., Spruyt, V., Berkvens, R., Weyn, M.: A survey of rigid 3D pointcloud registration algorithms. In: AMBIENT 2014: The Fourth International Conference on Ambient Computing, Applications, Services and Technologies, Rome, Italy, 24–28 August 2014, pp. 8–13 (2014)
12. Elad, A., Kimmel, R.: On bending invariant signatures for surfaces. IEEE Trans. Pattern Anal. Mach. Intell. **25**(10), 1285–1295 (2003)
13. Bronstein, A.M., Bronstein, M.M., Kimmel, R.: Numerical Geometry of Non-Rigid Shapes. Springer, New York (2008). https://doi.org/10.1007/978-0-387-73301-2
14. Taubin, G.: A signal processing approach to fair surface design. In: Proceedings of the 22nd Annual Conference on Computer Graphics and Interactive Techniques, pp. 351–358 (1995)
15. Zhang, H., Van Kaick, O., Dyer, R.: Spectral mesh processing. In: Computer Graphics Forum, vol. 29, no. 6, pp. 1865–1894. Wiley Online Library (2010)
16. Ovsjanikov, M., Ben-Chen, M., Solomon, J., Butscher, A., Guibas, L.: Functional maps: a flexible representation of maps between shapes. ACM Trans. Graph. (TOG) **31**(4), 1–11 (2012)
17. Borg, I., Groenen, P.J.: Modern Multidimensional Scaling: Theory and Applications. Springer, New York (2005). https://doi.org/10.1007/0-387-28981-X
18. Kimmel, R., Sethian, J.A.: Computing geodesic paths on manifolds. Proc. Natl. Acad. Sci. **95**(15), 8431–8435 (1998)
19. Crane, K., Weischedel, C., Wardetzky, M.: Geodesics in heat: a new approach to computing distance based on heat flow. ACM Trans. Graph. (TOG) **32**(5), 1–11 (2013)
20. Lipman, Y., Rustamov, R., Funkhouser, T.: Biharmonic distance. ACM Trans. Graph. **29**(3), 1–11 (2010)
21. Reuter, M., Biasotti, S., Giorgi, D., Patanè, G., Spagnuolo, M.: Discrete Laplace-Beltrami operators for shape analysis and segmentation. Comput. Graph. **33**(3), 381–390 (2009)
22. Reuter, M., Wolter, F.-E., Peinecke, N.: Laplace-Beltrami spectra as 'Shape-DNA' of surfaces and solids. Comput. Aided Des. **38**(4), 342–366 (2006)
23. Groenen, P., van de Velden, M.: Multidimensional scaling. Technical report (2004)
24. Jain, V., Zhang, H., Van Kaick, O.: Non-rigid spectral correspondence of triangle meshes. Int. J. Shape Model. **13**(01), 101–124 (2007)

Reinforcement Algorithm-Guided ROI Extraction of Fingerprint Biometric Data

Santhoshkumar Peddi[(✉)], Alka Ranjan, Mahajan Rohan Raj, Nishkal Prakash, Monalisa Sharma, and Debasis Samanta

Indian Institute of Technology, Kharagpur, Kharagpur, West Bengal, India
santhoshpps11@gmail.com

Abstract. Fingerprint recognition is a widely used biometric technique for personal identification. A crucial step in the fingerprint recognition process is feature extraction, where the unique characteristics of the fingerprint are identified and used for recognition. One of the challenges in fingerprint feature extraction is to select a region of interest (ROI) that can provide stable and reliable features for recognition. The existing techniques select an ROI around the core point for feature extraction. However, it is tough to detect the core point in noisy or low-quality images accurately. This paper proposes a novel deep learning-based method for fingerprint ROI selection that enables stable feature extraction. Furthermore, this method does not require cumbersome pre-processing steps such as fingerprint alignment or segmentation. The proposed fingerprint ROI selection method consists of two steps. In the first step, novel deep learning estimates the fingerprint region, including the core point. Next, reinforcement learning is used to optimize the region obtained from the previous step to get the required ROI. The approach's effectiveness has been tested with standard fingerprint databases such as SPD2010, FVC2002 DB2, and synthetic fingerprints. Experimental results show that our proposed method effectively identifies a stable ROI for feature extraction. The proposed method can be applied to various fingerprint recognition applications.

Keywords: Fingerprint Biometric · Region of Interest · Deep Learning · Reinforcement Learning · Fingerprint recognition

1 Introduction

In today's age, fingerprint biometrics have gained significant popularity for identifying individuals based on their unique physical characteristics. Fingerprint recognition is preferred due to its permanent and distinctive nature, offering non-repudiation [14]. Furthermore, fingerprint biometrics provides high security and convenience, eliminating the need for easily forgotten, stolen, or hacked passwords or other authentication methods. Moreover, fingerprint recognition is the most widely used and has been highly successful, owing to its ease of capture,

H. Kaur et al. (Eds.): CVIP 2023, CCIS 2009, pp. 394–405, 2024.
https://doi.org/10.1007/978-3-031-58181-6_33

cost-effectiveness, and convenience. Despite great success over the years in fingerprint recognition, extracting discriminative features from fingerprint data is challenging due to fingerprint variation, low quality, partial capture etc.

Many researchers have focused on identifying ROI in fingerprints to overcome the above-mentioned challenges. In fingerprint recognition, an ROI refers to a specific area or region of the fingerprint selected for feature extraction and is consistent or stable across multiple scans of the same fingerprint of the same individual. The selected ROI is overcome the challenges posed by the variability of fingerprint patterns, noise and distortion, and finger position. A stable and reliable ROI can mitigate the effects of these challenges and ensure accurate feature extraction. Different methods have been proposed for ROI selection in fingerprint biometrics, such as applying Monte Carlo dropout for ROI segmentation [9]. Thai et al. have used morphological operation (convex hull following binarization and two-scale opening and closing) [17]. Using Gaussian filtering, dilation and erosion, and thresholding, Joshua et al. [7] cropped the area in the centre of fingerprint images with a resolution of 448 * 448 to 128 * 128 that increased the processing speed of learning discriminative features from fingerprint images. However, relying solely on cropping a specific region may not ensure the required accuracy and reliability for fingerprint authentication. Moreover, the existing methods depend on the threshold value and use morphological operations for ROI selection which is not optimal. However, accurately detecting ROI can be challenging, particularly in noisy or low-quality images. Addressing these challenges is crucial for developing robust and accurate fingerprint ROI selection.

The objectives of the proposed method are mentioned below:

- The consistent selection of the ROI is essential to ensure the stability and reliability of the extracted features.
- It should be consistent across multiple scans of the same fingerprint of an individual.
  It should be quick and efficient.

This paper aims to review the existing techniques for ROI selection in fingerprint recognition and to propose a novel deep learning-based method that enables stable and reliable feature extraction without the need for cumbersome pre-processing steps such as fingerprint alignment or segmentation. The proposed method consists of two steps: deep learning-based region estimation and reinforcement learning-based ROI optimization. In the deep learning-based region estimation step, a bounding region, which includes the core point, is determined. Next, the bounding region obtained in the previous step is optimized using reinforcement learning to get the desired ROI of the fingerprint. Furthermore, keypoint-based feature vectors are derived from the ROIs to check the efficacy of the proposed method.

The proposed method has the following contributions:

- The proposed reinforcement-guided ROI selection can automate the process, improving the overall efficiency and accuracy of the system while reducing the need for manual intervention.

- It enables more efficient and faster processing by reducing the need for cumbersome pre-processing steps such as fingerprint alignment or segmentation.
- The selected ROI consistency ensures robustness to noise, distortion, and finger position variations, ensuring accurate recognition under different conditions.
- It ensures stable and reliable feature extraction, which is critical for accurate fingerprint recognition.

The rest of the paper is organized as follows: Sect. 2 reviews existing methods for ROI extraction. Section 3 describes the proposed methodology. Experiments and results have been presented in Sect. 4. Finally, the conclusions are drawn in Sect. 5.

2   Related Work

The ROI is one of the essential components of the preprocessing pipeline that plays a vital role in accurate matching, authentication, and security. Several techniques for ROI selection in fingerprint recognition have been proposed, including traditional image processing techniques and deep learning-based methods. Some of these techniques are depicted in the following paragraphs.

Cao et al. used different ridge orientations and spacings to build dictionary elements. The latent image is split into 32 * 32 patches with 16 * 16 pixel overlapping sizes to determine the flow and spacing of ridges. The similarity between each dictionary entry and each patch P is calculated. Ridge-quality patches greater than a threshold value are taken into account as appropriate fingerprint patches. Morphological procedures, like open and close operations, are utilized to achieve smooth cropping that is considered the ROI of the latent image [2]. In terms of image quality, there is little room for flexibility. As this method relies on a convex hull and learned dictionary terms for a smooth mask. The method is more generally applicable to image representation and, to a lesser extent in the segmentation of latent fingerprints.

Instead of patches, Nguyen et al. [13] used attention mechanisms to explore significant regions from entire images. Furthermore, a voting scheme technique was applied to choose the pertinent ROIs from all of the ROIs. Later, FCN combined object detection methods to divide the regions that received the most votes to recognize better areas of the entire image. The FCN focuses on patch-size dependency issues and the associated issues. Overall, the strategy was difficult to understand, too complex and cumbersome to put into action.

One of the essential parts of the pre-processing pipeline is choosing a stable area of interest. It separates the foreground part from the background region so that feature extraction is performed only on the ROI instead of the entire image. The fingerprint area (the foreground) is divided so that features from regions of the fingerprint that are noisy or in the background can not be considered [8]. In most of the existing work, the accuracy of finding ROI has not been mentioned [5], especially for individual datasets. Only a specific region of defined dimension is cropped, and it is considered as ROI.

The proposed work first finds the region around the core point using a YOLO concept, and that region is optimized using reinforcement learning which identifies the fingerprint accurately.

3   Proposed Method

This study aims to find a region consistent across multiple scans of the same fingerprint of an individual. To that end, the proposed method (Fig. 1), assumes the area of interest as a rectangular object and performs dimensionality increment or decrement operations to achieve the task.

Using an object detection algorithm (Fig. 2), the first operation extracts a partial region from a fingerprint image (including a core point) to estimate the ROI. The second operation modifies the extracted partial region using Double Deep Q-Network (DDQN) (Fig. 3) agent into the ROI. The DDQN agent performs the necessary actions to modify the dimensions of the partial region along each of the sides and validates the predicted region.

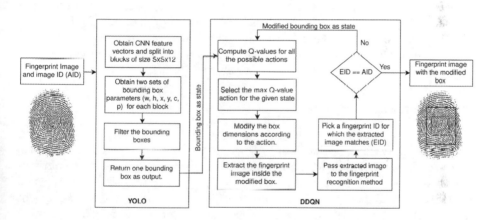

Fig. 1. Overview of the method.

3.1   Extraction of ROI

This step uses YOLO to extract the ROI from the fingerprint image. As this necessitates the definition of the object and its centre, they are assumed to be the ROI and the core point, respectively. Unlike standard object detection methods, the object's dimensions are fixed for the proposed method. The objects' dimensions are to be selected such that it fully encloses the core point and is as small as possible.

Extraction of the ROI involves dividing the image into equal-sized grids, which YOLO uses to predict bounding boxes for each grid. The prediction of the bounding box involves computing values like the confidence of the core point (c), probability of the class (p), width (w), height (h) and centre of the object

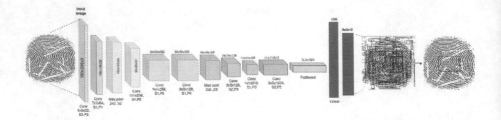

Fig. 2. CNN architecture

coordinates (x, y). Suppose the centre of the object coordinates can be assumed to be the core point. In that case, the class probability can be defined as the probability that the core point is in the bounding box. The confidence value signifies the likeliness of the core point being in the bounding box. This results in two bounding boxes for each grid, and the best bounding box must be selected.

Using non-max suppression (NMS), the bounding box with the highest confidence is selected and compared with other bounding boxes. The intersection of union (IoU) metric is used for comparison, and a threshold for the IoU value is set. When the initial bounding box is compared to neighbouring boxes, the neighbour is ignored if the IoU value exceeds the set threshold. After the process, the remaining bounding boxes will constitute the ROI.

3.2   Optimisation of ROI

In the previous step, the bounding box parameters, like the dimensions, are manually set by the user and could result in a bounding box of non-ideal dimensions. However, the study requires a bounding box of minimum dimensions to authenticate the fingerprint image with high accuracy; hence, this step is performed to modify and minimise the bounding box dimensions using a reinforcement learning (RL) agent, DDQN. The agent has the advantage of being a model-free RL agent that works in continuous state space and performs discrete actions on the environment. In this study, the environment is the fingerprint image with a bounding box from the previous step; the state itself is the bounding box, and the reward is calculated based on fingerprint recognition accuracy (FRA). The agent has an action set with eight actions, increasing or decreasing the bounding box dimensions along each side.

The main agenda of DDQN is to build the optimal policy to modify the current bounding box into the ROI for any given fingerprint image. The optimal policy is the agent's behaviour to select the best action for each state which can be determined from the state-action value function (Q-value). The best action A of a state S is an action with the maximum Q-value among all the actions for that particular state S. Q-value for the actions are computed by the DDQN using a function approximation that takes the state as input and produces Q-values for the actions as an output. Thus, if a neural network with the best parameters is available, it can be used for the optimal policy.

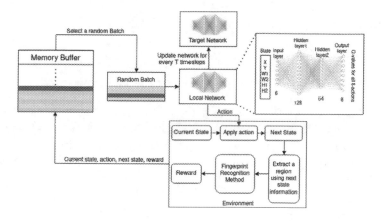

Fig. 3. DDQN Agent

An iterative approach has been used to obtain the network with the best parameters. The process starts with initialising two networks (Q-network and Target network) with random weights. The bounding box from the estimation step is passed as input to the Q-network, and Q-values for all actions are computed. Epsilon-greedy approach [16] is used to explore all the actions at a state and select one that could be random or the best. The chosen action is passed to the environment, which modifies the bounding box according to the action in consideration. The modified bounding box extracts a part of the fingerprint image, which is passed to the fingerprint recognition method.

This study uses the Harris corner [6] fingerprint recognition method to identify the corner points in the extracted fingerprint image, which are used to localise the ORB (Oriented FAST and Rotated BRIEF) [15] key points. A similarity score is computed for the extracted image by calculating the Euclidean distance between its ORB key points and all of the fingerprint images in the database. The index of the extracted image is compared to that of the original image if the similarity score is maximum. If the indices match, the similarity score is passed to the agent as the reward, and if they don't match, the reward will be set to the negative of the similarity score.

Reward, action, current state (initial bounding box) and next state (modified bounding box) information are obtained as responses from the environment and stored in the memory buffer as experience. Once the buffer size exceeds the batch size, a random batch is selected from the buffer to update the parameters of the Q-network. This is done by training the Q-network with the MSE loss function, and for every T timestep, the Target network is updated with the Q-network parameters. This process is repeated for N episodes, each consisting of one image and a bounding box. An episode is considered to have ended when a positive reward is passed to the agent. A random image and its bounding box will be selected for each episode and passed to the DDQN. After N episodes, the Q-network, which has been fully trained, is considered the optimal policy.

4   Experiment and Results

The objectives of this experiment are:

- To evaluate the performance of YOLO in providing a partial region containing the core point.
- To evaluate the performance of DDQN in optimizing the partial region obtained from YOLO.
- To compare the fingerprint recognition accuracy with and without ROI.
- To compare the time taken for fingerprint identification with and without ROI.

4.1   Experimental Setup

The proposed method employs YOLO with 8 convolutional layers and 2 max-pooling layers (Fig. 2) along with a DDQN network having 2 hidden layers of sizes 128 and 64, an input layer, and an output layer with 6 and 8 neurons, respectively. The input layer has 6 values representing state information, including w_1, h_1, w_2, h_2, and core point coordinates (x, y). w_1 is the edge of the bounding box on the left side, and h_1 is the edge of the bounding box on the top side, with w_2 and h_2 being the other edges. The output layer represents the eight actions that can be performed on the edges, i.e., to increment or decrement the dimension along the direction perpendicular to the edge.

The YOLO is trained using the MSE loss function and Adam [10] optimizer with a learning rate of 0.00001 and a weight decay of 0.0001. The training is performed for 100 epochs with a grid size of 11×11. For the DDQN, the following hyperparameters are used: a batch size of 64, 400 epochs, discount factor (γ) of 0.99, τ of 0.001, ϵ of 1, ϵ_{min} of 0.01, replace count of 100, ϵ_{decay} of 0.0001, and a memory size of 10^6. The DDQN weight parameters are optimized using RMSProp with a learning rate of 0.001.

4.2   Dataset

This study uses three different datasets to validate the proposed method. The details of the datasets are shown in Table 1

The datasets SPD and Synthetic provide the core points for fingerprint images, and for all three datasets, the dimensions of w1, h1, w2, and h2 in pixels are set to match 10% of the image size. The training and testing data for SPD and Synthetic datasets are split in an 80–20 ratio. To evaluate the proposed model on different impressions, the FVC dataset is used.

Table 1. List of datasets used for this experiment

Dataset	Total	format, size	Used for
SPD2010 [11]	500	BMP, 355×390	Training, Testing
FVC2002 DB2 [12]	80	TIF, 296×560	Testing
Synthetic [1,3]	5000	TIFF, 275×400	Training, Testing

4.3   Results Obtained

Performance Evaluation of YOLO: The YOLO performance against the datasets SPD2010 and Synthetic is demonstrated using the Average Precision (AP) metric (Eq. 1). The training details are presented in Fig. 4.

$$AP = \sum_{k=1}^{n} (R_k - R_{k-1}) \cdot P_k \tag{1}$$

where n denotes the number of detections, R_k is the recall at the k-th precision value P_k, and R_{k-1} is the recall at the previous precision value P_{k-1}.

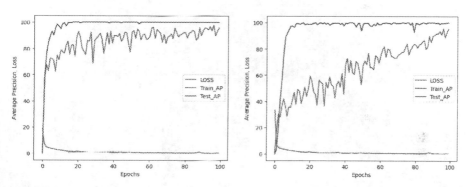

(a) YOLO training with Synthetic dataset   (b) YOLO training with SPD2010 dataset

Fig. 4. Training results of YOLO

Figure 5 illustrates the effectiveness of YOLO in identifying partial regions containing core points in fingerprints. Figure 5 displays the bounding box outputs of YOLO on selected fingerprints from the SPD and Synthetic datasets. Notably, the selected fingerprint from Synthetic belongs to a single individual, thereby demonstrating the ability of YOLO to localize partial regions in a specific fingerprint.

Performance of YOLO-DDQN: The DDQN agent was trained for 5000 episodes, and the average reward score for the last 50 iterations was computed

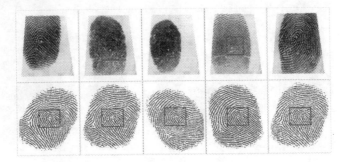

Fig. 5. Selected fingerprints from the SPD and synthetic datasets with their corresponding bounding box outputs from YOLO to identify partial regions with core points.

for each episode. It was observed that the average reward went positive after half of the episodes. To further evaluate the performance of DDQN, fingerprints from the FVC and Synthetic datasets were selected for one individual, and the ROI of those impressions are shown in Fig. 6.

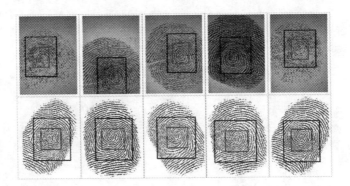

Fig. 6. Optimised and YOLO ROIs for different impressions of a fingerprint in the FVC2002 DB2 and Synthetic datasets. Red and blue boxes indicate the optimised ROI and the ROI obtained from YOLO, respectively. (Color figure online)

Fingerprint Recognition: To evaluate fingerprint recognition accuracy, the datasets are divided into two groups, with each group considered to be either genuine or imposter. A randomly selected fingerprint from one group is compared with all fingerprints in the genuine group. If the matching score exceeds the set threshold, the corresponding ID is compared with the fingerprint that gave the maximum score; otherwise, it is classified as an imposter. If the IDs match, a match is found; otherwise, a non-match is found. A confusion matrix is constructed for each dataset based on whether the random fingerprint is identified as genuine or imposter and whether it results in a match or a non-match, as shown in Fig. 7. Alongside the confusion matrix, the metrics of precision, accuracy, recall, and F1 score have been computed and presented in Fig. 8.

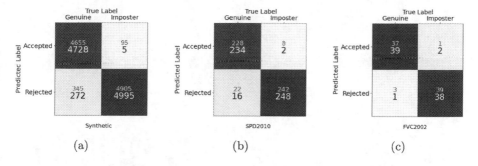

(a) (b) (c)

Fig. 7. Confusion matrix for fingerprint recognition with and without ROI. The top values correspond to results obtained without ROI, while the bottom values correspond to results obtained with ROI

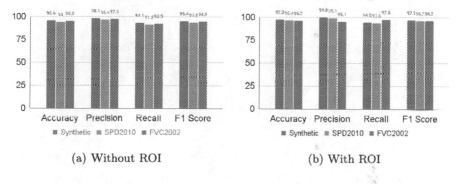

(a) Without ROI (b) With ROI

Fig. 8. Performance of the model based on the confusion matrix

It can be seen from Fig. 8 that the set of fingerprints with ROI has better results as compared to the set without ROI. Additionally, Table 2 presents the computation of FAR, FRR, GAR, and GRR for the set of images with and without ROI, along with the confusion matrix shown in Fig. 8. The results demonstrate that the set with ROI outperforms the set without ROI, as it has lower FAR and FRR values.

Comparison of Identification Time: The average identification time for each fingerprint in the dataset is computed by comparing it with all the fingerprints in the dataset, and the results are shown in Fig. 9. It is observed that the average identification time for the full fingerprint is higher than that for the ROI.

Table 2. Fingerprint Recognition Performance with ROI and Full Fingerprint

Type	Dataset	Accuracy	FAR	FRR	GAR	GRR
Without ROI	SPD2010	94.05%	3.20%	8.70%	91.3%	96.8%
	FVC2002 DB2	95.87%	2.86%	5.40%	94.6%	97.14%
	Synthetic	95.61%	1.88%	6.90%	93.10%	98.12%
With ROI	SPD2010	96.44%	0.82%	6.30%	93.7%	99.18%
	FVC2002 DB2	97.51%	0.75%	4.22%	95.78%	99.25%
	Synthetic	97.22%	0.10%	5.45%	94.55%	99.9%

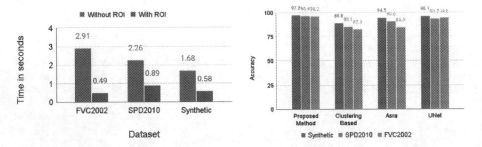

Fig. 9. Comparison of the performance with respect to time and ROI and, recognition accuracy with respect to existing methods

Comparison with Existing Methods: The proposed method's accuracy is compared with the existing Cluster-based [4] and others [9,14] methods as shown in Fig. 9.

5   Conclusion

The proposed approach employs a combination of YOLO and DDQN for extracting an ROI from fingerprint images. The experimental findings indicate that this method achieves promising results on three datasets, namely FVC2002, SPD2010, and Synthetic. The extracted ROI is consistent and can be utilized for fingerprint authentication and verification. Moreover, the ROI extraction process significantly reduces the identification time by 83.16%, 60.16%, and 65.47% for the three datasets, while also enhancing the identification accuracy by 1.64%, 2.39%, and 1.61%, respectively. In future, the step process can be converted to a one-step approach, which could further reduce the training time and lead to even better results.

References

1. Ansari, A.H.: Generation and storage of large synthetic fingerprint database. ME thesis (2011)
2. Cao, K., Nguyen, D.L., Tymoszek, C., Jain, A.K.: End-to-end latent fingerprint search. IEEE Trans. Inf. Forensics Secur. **15**, 880–894 (2019)
3. Cappelli, R., Erol, A., Maio, D., Maltoni, D.: Synthetic fingerprint-image generation. In: Proceedings 15th International Conference on Pattern Recognition, ICPR-2000, vol. 3, pp. 471–474 (2000)
4. Mehdi Cherrat, E., Alaoui, R., Bouzahir, H.: Improving of fingerprint segmentation images based on K-means and DBSCAN clustering. Int. J. Electr. Comput. Eng. (IJECE) **9**(4), 2425–2432 (2019)
5. Dargan, S., Kumar, M.: A comprehensive survey on the biometric recognition systems based on physiological and behavioral modalities. Expert Syst. Appl. **143**, 113114 (2020)
6. Derpanis, K.G.: The Harris corner detector. York University **2**, 1–2 (2004)
7. Engelsma, J.J., Cao, K., Jain, A.K.: Learning a fixed-length fingerprint representation. IEEE Trans. Pattern Anal. Mach. Intell. **43**(6), 1981–1997 (2019)
8. Gupta, R., Khari, M., Gupta, D., Crespo, R.G.: Fingerprint image enhancement and reconstruction using the orientation and phase reconstruction. Inf. Sci. **530**, 201–218 (2020)
9. Joshi, I., et al.: Explainable fingerprint ROI segmentation using Monte Carlo dropout. In: Proceedings of the IEEE/CVF Winter Conference on Applications of Computer Vision, pp. 60–69 (2021)
10. Kingma, D.P., Ba, J.: Adam: a method for stochastic optimization. arXiv preprint arXiv:1412.6980 (2014)
11. Magalhães, F., Oliveira, H.P., Campilho, A.: SPD2010 - fingerprint singular points detection competition database. http://paginas.fe.up.pt/~spd2010/
12. Maltoni, D., Maio, D., Jain, A.K., Prabhakar, S., et al.: Handbook of Fingerprint Recognition, vol. 3, 3rd edn. Springer, Cham (2022)
13. Nguyen, D.L., Cao, K., Jain, A.K.: Automatic latent fingerprint segmentation. In: 2018 IEEE 9th International Conference on Biometrics Theory, Applications and Systems (BTAS), pp. 1–9. IEEE (2018)
14. Pandey, F., Dash, P., Samanta, D., Sarma, M.: ASRA: automatic singular value decomposition-based robust fingerprint image alignment. Multimedia Tools Appl. **80**, 15647–15675 (2021)
15. Rublee, E., Rabaud, V., Konolige, K., Bradski, G.: ORB: an efficient alternative to SIFT or SURF. In: 2011 International Conference on Computer Vision, pp. 2564–2571 (2011)
16. Sutton, R.S., Barto, A.G.: Reinforcement Learning: An Introduction. MIT Press, Cambridge (2018)
17. Thai, D.H., Huckemann, S., Gottschlich, C.: Filter design and performance evaluation for fingerprint image segmentation. PLoS ONE **11**(5), e0154160 (2016)

Cartilage Segmentation from MRI Images Towards Prediction of Osteoarthritis

Puja Das[1], Rabin Bhaumik[1], Sourav Dey Roy[1], Satyabrata Nath[2],
and Mrinal Kanti Bhowmik[1(✉)]

[1] Tripura University (A Central University), Suryamaninagar 799022, India
mrinalkantibhowmik@tripurauniv.ac.in
[2] Agartala Government Medical College (AGMC) and Gobind Ballav Pant (GBP) Hospital,
Government of Tripura, Agartala 799006, India

Abstract. Mostly occurred arthritis in world-wide as well as in India is Osteoarthritis. Knee cartilage loss is the most preliminary and significant symptom for Osteoarthritis diagnosis. The automatic segmentation of knee cartilage from Magnetic Resonance Images (MRI) has a tremendous impact on research for diagnosis related to osteoarthritis. Even though deep learning approaches achieve success in this field, but effectively and accurately segmenting knee cartilage is challenging due to the complex and overlapping structure of the soft tissues in the MRI images. Thus it is necessary to study the performance of the existing conventional methods implementation in knee cartilage segmentation from MRI. This can infer the challenges of the existing segmentation methods which can be solved by the recent deep learning based segmentation concept towards building a new generalized segmentation model. Depending upon this phenomenon, we have investigated the state-of-the-art conventional and deep learning based segmentation methods for knee cartilage segmentation using MRI images. After that, we have also introduced an encoder-decoder framework inspired from U-Net segmentation architecture for solving the knee cartilage segmentation challenges. Experimental results reveal that the proposed encoder-decoder framework inspired from U-Net architecture is well-performed as compared to the state-of-the-art segmentation methods for cartilage segmentation with dice similarity index value of 0.905 using publicly available OAI dataset.

Keywords: Osteoarthritis · Articular Cartilage · Magnetic Resonance Imaging · Soft Tissue · Segmentation · Encoder-Decoder Framework · Performance Evaluation

1 Introduction

Inflammation related to radiation from the skin surface, synovitis, and irregular blood flow pattern provides valuable diagnostic information and understanding of disease abnormalities which will predict early abnormality and severity inside the human body. Among various diseases, arthritis is a chronic disease that is the leading cause of functional dependency in the activities of daily living. The pain from arthritis is due to

© The Author(s), under exclusive license to Springer Nature Switzerland AG 2024
H. Kaur et al. (Eds.): CVIP 2023, CCIS 2009, pp. 406–418, 2024.
https://doi.org/10.1007/978-3-031-58181-6_34

inflammation that occurs around the joint and performs damage to the joint along with restriction of movement. Towards diagnosis of joint disease related to knee joint, it is very tedious to analyse the anatomical structure with manual segmentation. Knee cartilages are the protective cushion between bones and absorb shock produced when the knee is in movement [1]. When the cartilage breaks down or is damaged, the person suffers from normal movability. Daily work life of a human gets suffer because of the inability of their movement [3]. Among various types of arthritis, the most common disease of the knee joint is Osteoarthritis (OA) which affects millions of people worldwide. As stated by WHO 18.0% of women and 9.6% of men with age over 60 years have symptomatic osteoarthritis worldwide. In India, Osteoarthritis is the second frequently observed joint disease with a prevalence of 22% to 39% [4].The diagnosis criteria provided by the American College of Rheumatology for osteoarthritis include clinical, radiological, or clinic-radiological assessments. However, these criteria primarily identify the advanced stages of osteoarthritis. Advancements in medical imaging technology have introduced various modalities such as X-Ray, ultrasound, magnetic resonance imaging (MRI), infrared thermography, CT scans, and more for diagnosing joint diseases like osteoarthritis [5]. MRI is a significant diagnostic imaging technique for complex and heterogeneous structure analysis. Among these imaging modalities, MRI is considered as a more suitable modality for the early detection of knee joint disease as this modality can demonstrate cartilage and soft tissue changes, as well as inflammation features. Cartilage loss can result from injury or osteoarthritis, and therefore, segmentation of the cartilage is required to analyze the cartilage loss pattern for precise diagnosis of the disease. To build a computerized automated system which can segment the significant part that is an early feature of the knee joint disease (i.e., Osteoarthritis disease) researchers are focusing on the technique by which that particular feature (like cartilage) can be segmented optimally. However, the segmentation of knee cartilage is a significant challenge for the medical imaging research community due to the complex and heterogeneous structure of the knee joint. Cartilage, being a thin and soft tissue, exhibits intensity inhomogeneity, low tissue contrast, and shape irregularity in MR images, making it difficult to segment automatically. Acquisition challenges can cause MRI scan variations, and hence making it difficult to differentiate between femoral and tibia cartilage boundaries and surrounding tissues. Signal intensities and contrasts vary in knee MRIs due to different pulse sequences. Chemical shift artifacts create dark and bright rims on tissue edges. Additionally, limited availability of large knee MRI datasets hinders research, often resulting in studies with a small number of MRI scans. In existing literature, there are many automated methods for medical image segmentation. But till date there is no availability of the comparative study of cartilage segmentation based on different state-of-the-art segmentation methods using the Osteoarthritis Initiative (OAI) dataset which is publicly available. Moreover, development of an automated system that can optimally segment cartilage from knee joint MRI images is crucial for the early detection and diagnosis of knee joint diseases such as osteoarthritis.

Depending upon this phenomenon, the main goal of the proposed work is to extract meaningful information about cartilage morphology for Osteoarthritis diagnosis in the early stage non-invasively. To meet up the specific necessities of this research work, in this paper, we have investigated the performance of the state-of-the-art conventional and deep learning based medical image segmentation methods for Femoral and Tibial cartilage segmentation altogether from the musculoskeletal MRI images towards Osteoarthritis detection. Also, based on the observation, we proposed an encode-decoder based framework inspired from U-net architecture by O. Ronneberger et al. [26] for Femoral (Femur) and Tibial (Tibia) joint cartilage segments together from MRI images thereby reducing the over and under segmentation challenges (Fig. 1).

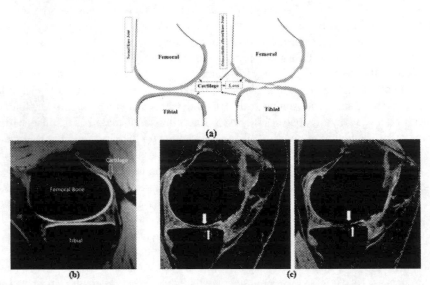

Fig. 1. Knee Joint Cartilage structure (a)Cartilage appearance in normal and Osteoarthritis Condition, (b) Healthy Knee Joint MRI Scan (Cartilage is marked by blue and yellow shade color) [2], (c). Osteoarthritis affected Knee Joint MRI Sample with Cartilage loss (Cartilage is indicating by the arrow) [6].

2   Related Work

According to a recent survey, there has been significant progress in the field of cartilage segmentation for MRI images of patients with osteoarthritis. Jianfei Pang et al. [7] utilized the Canny detector to extract cartilage initially. Then, they used Bayesian classifiers, SVM to segment the cartilage with minimal error, and finally improved the primary segmentation by using morphological operations on the Southwest Hospital's Department of Radiology provided dataset. The average dice similarity coefficient (DSC) value was 0.761. In [8], Satyananda Kashyap et al. applied LOGISMOS segmentation on 53 knees from the OAI dataset. Level set-based segmentation was used by Chunsoo Ahn et al. [9] on 20 regular patients from the OAI dataset. They got Dice similarity coefficients (DSC) from 10 participants for the patellar, femoral, and tibia cartilage which were 84.8%, 87.1%, and 81.7%, respectively. A KNN classifier was used by P.S. Satapure et al. [10] to categorize voxels in a dataset taken from Mumbai's Nanavati Hospital. The Dice Similarity Coefficient (DSC) ranges from 0.730 to 0.820. Yaodong Du et al. [11] evaluated artificial neural networks (ANN), support vector machines (SVM), random forests, and naive Bayes on 100 pairs of knees from the OAI dataset. Their receiver operating characteristic of 0.761 and F-measure of 0.714. A 3D Fully Convolution Neural Network called μ-Net was applied by Archit Raj et al. [12] to 176 knee MRI images from 88 patients from the OAI dataset. They received Dice similarity coefficient (DSC) scores for the femoral, patellar, and tibia cartilages of 0.849, 0.785, and 0.832, respectively. U-Net was used on the Osteoarthritis Initiate Dataset (OAI) by Berk Norman et al. [13] and they achieved Dice similarity coefficients (DSCs) for the lateral and medial meniscus of 0.800 and 0.730, respectively, and 0.770 and 0.878 for the cartilage compartments. With 1378 subjects from the Imorphics dataset, Alexander Tack et al. [14] used 3D CNNs to achieve a segmentation accuracy of 88.02 ± 4.62. The segmentation accuracy was assessed using the same dataset, and it marginally dropped to 82.85 ± 5.53. In 176 patients from the OAI dataset, knee cartilage was segmented using CGAN by Sibaji Gaj et al. [15] the patellar cartilage has a Dice coefficient (DSC) ranging from 0.840 to 0.910, with an average DSC of 0.880. To segment knee cartilage in 1000 images, Wen Jet Nyee et al. [16] coupled U-net with adversarial training using CNNs. They used 900 images for training, 50 for validation, and 50 for testing, and when tested on the 50 images, they had an accuracy of 96.80%. In order to compare manual and automatic segmentation of cartilage volumes in 62 people with knee OA and 29 healthy control participants, Wenjing Hou et al. [17] employed ANOVA, ICC, and Pearson correlation coefficient. The patella, femur, tibia, and knee joint respective ICC values were 0.7840, 0.8150, 0.7400, and 0.7970. Femoral and tibia bone and cartilage were divided using the OAI ZIB Dataset by Yang Deng et al. [18] using the U-Net++ network. Femoral bone, tibia bone, tibia cartilage, and femoral cartilage each had mean DSCs of 99.1%, 98.2%, 85.8%, and 90.9%. 65 individuals' cartilage was divided using a transfer learning based U-Net CNN model by Yan-Ping Xue et al. [19] their average VOE and DSC were also 29.86% and 0.82, respectively. The cartilage in the femur, lateral tibia, medial tibia, and patella was segmented using two stages of CNNs using the OAI dataset by Anthony A. Gatti et al. [20] and they reported respective DSCs of 0.907, 0.913, 0.876, and 0.840. The multimodal co-registration approach was employed by Vladimir Juras et al. [21] a mean Dice coefficient of 0.848 ± 0.025 and a mean Jaccard coefficient of 0.709 ± 0.010 were discovered using the data of thirteen patients. Neubert et al. [22] analyzed 821 knee examinations from 214 participants in the Osteoarthritis Initiative using a 3D U-Net design with a target contrast of slice thickness and 0.37 x 0.37mm in plane resolution. Their results showed improved cartilage volume segmentation compared to TSE, with the tibia showing the greatest improvement (+0.17, $p < 0.001$), followed by the patella (+0.09, $p < 0.05$) and femur (+0.07, $p < 0.001$). To create enhanced simulated MR images for automatic knee cartilage segmentation, Neubert, Aleš, et al. [23] used a U-Net convolutional neural network. Sagittal acquired 3D DESS with water excitation pictures to provide the goal contrast, and the model is trained on a dataset of 578 MR examinations from the OAI. However, because each patch was inferred independently, there might be gaps between patch regions in the final image. OAI1, OAI2, and a few MR pictures are included in the Revathi, S. A. et al. [24] collection. For the 1-year follow-up, 88 DESS pictures are acquired at baseline in OAI2 and ground truth segmentation is performed using the Atlas-based approach. Femoral segmented cartilage thickness and volume had an average DICS of 0.86 of 0.96 for femur cartilage thickness and 0.98 for cartilage volume. Li, Zezhong, et al. [25] employ nnU-Net for segmenting hard tissues and articular cartilage. A different nnU-Net enhances the segmentation. The proposed method achieves an average DSC of 92.1 ± 0.99% for combined hip cartilage, 89.8 ± 2.5% for femoral cartilage, and 86.4 ± 4.13% for tibia cartilage using a dataset of 507 3D MR volumes from the OAI database.

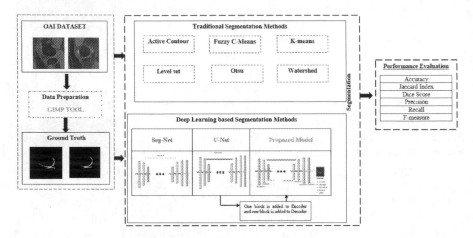

Fig. 2. Flow Diagram of the Proposed Work

3   Materials and Methods

In our study, we developed an encoder-decoder based framework inspired by U-Net architecture [26] for segmentation of the cartilage using publicly available Osteoarthritis Initiative (OAI) [27] dataset. The overall flow diagram of the paper is shown in Fig. 2.

3.1   Dataset Collection and Preparation

In our work, we have used the only available benchmark Osteoarthritis Initiative (OAI) dataset [27]. Men and women participated in a multi-center observational study called the Osteoarthritis Initiative (OAI). The OAI seeks to educate the public about knee osteoarthritis in order to improve prevention and treatment. It is one of the most prevalent causes of adult disability. This resource provides a dataset of patients with osteoarthritis. The Osteoarthritis Initiative (OAI) provided 700 T2 MRI images at a resolution of 384 × 384 and are used for this study. Moreover, we also annotated the ground truths of MRI images using open-source software called GNU Image Manipulation Programming, or GIMP [28]. Using GIMP, the area of interest (i.e., Femur and Tibia cartilage) pixels are annotated with white pixels (i.e., pixel values of 1) and the remaining background (i.e., other than Femur and Tibia cartilage of MRI images) are annotated with black pixels (i.e., pixel values of 1). To reduce the ambiguity in annotating the ground truths of MRI images as mentioned above, a maximum voting policy scheme is adopted so that the final ground truth images (i.e., resultant ground truths) is the outcome of the broadest consensus among all annotators as a consequence.

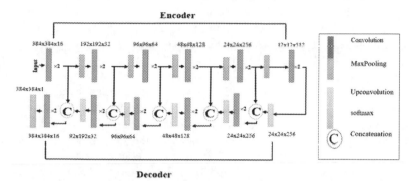

Fig. 3. Proposed Encoder-Decoder Framework for Femur and Tibia Cartilage Segmentation

3.2 Segmentation of Femur and Tibia Cartilage Using Conventional State-of-the-Art Segmentation Methods and Their Parameters Settings

Segmentation of Femur and Tibia cartilage from the MRI images and their morphological and structural analysis can predict the abnormality related to osteoarthritis. In our present work, from literature we have adopted six conventional state-of-the art segmentation methods for Femur and Tibia cartilage extraction from the holistic MRI images. We have used 700 MRI images from OAI dataset [27] for measuring the performance of the segmentation methods. These methods are: (a) the Active Contour Model [35] with elastic constant; curvature constant, and image energy constant values of 1, 1, and 2 respectively and total 250 iterations; (b) Level-Set method [32] with desired cluster value of 12, exponential threshold value of 2, and tune parameter value of 20 with maximum iteration of 100; (c) The Watershed segmentation method [33] with kernel size of 2 × 2; (d) K-Means clustering method [30] with cluster number of 2; (e) Fuzzy C Means clustering method [31] with cluster number of 9 and membership value of 1.2; and (f) Otsu Thresholding method [34] with threshold value of 130. Each of these parameters are adjusted based on the best results obtained from the selected parameters. The performance of each of these segmentation methods against the best parameters selection as stated above is reported in Table 2.

3.3 Segmentation of Femur and Tibia Cartilage Using Deep Learning Based Segmentation Methods and Their Parameters Settings

With the advancement of deep learning technologies in various computer vision problems, semantic segmentation methods based on convolutional neural network (CNN) framework are adopted by the research communities for medical image segmentation.

In our work, we have used two most popular deep learning based segmentation methods i.e., SegNet [29] and U-Net [26] for Femur and Tibia cartilage segmentation from MRI images. These two architectures are employed on OAI dataset [27]. The performance of these two segmentation methods and their comparison are also reported in Table 2. For effective comparison, 700 MRI images from the OAI dataset are divided into 4:1 ratio with approximately 500 images for training and validation purposes and 200 images for testing purposes. We implemented the deep learning models on a workstation with an NVIDIA TITAN XP graphics card, Pascal GPU architecture, 12 GB G5X frame buffer, 11.4 Gbps memory speed, and 1582 MHz boost clock. Moreover, we have conducted the experiment from 50 epoch to 300 epoch with 50 epoch interval, where we can observe at 200 epoch these models achieved almost the highest training and validation accuracy. Based on the performance of these comparisons, it has been observed that U-Net [26] has performed well. Therefore, based on this observation, to improve the performance of segmentation of cartilage from OAI dataset, we have proposed a new encoder-decoder framework inspired from U-Net architecture [26] and the details of the model are provided in the next subsection.

Table 1. Training and Validation Accuracy and Loss of the Proposed Encoder Decoder Framework with Varying Epochs

Dataset	Epoch	Training Accuracy	Training Loss	Validation Accuracy	Validation Loss
Osteoarthritis Initiative (OAI) [27]	50	0.995	0.181	0.982	0.191
	100	0.997	0.062	0.984	0.086
	150	0.998	0.033	0.982	0.079
	200	**0.998**	**0.017**	**0.985**	**0.067**
	250	0.999	0.011	0.982	0.078
	300	0.998	0.018	0.982	0.068

Table 2. Comparison of training performance of state-of-the-art deep method with proposed model.

Dataset	Architecture	Epoch	Training Accuracy	Training Loss
Osteoarthritis Initiative (OAI) [27]	Seg-Net [29]	200	0.998	0.059
	U-Net [26]	200	0.998	0.046
	Our Method	**200**	**0.998**	**0.017**

3.4 Proposed Encoder Decoder Framework for Segmentation of Femur and Tibia Cartilage

In the proposed framework, we have extended the traditional U-Net [26] segmentation architecture with one extra encoder block i.e., six block layers made up the proposed encoder design whereas in U-Net [26] there are five block layers in encoder design. To design the model operationally correct we add one block layer in decoder design. Two convolution layers are present in each layer, followed by batch normalization and the RELU activation function in each layer. A softmax activation function was applied to the output of the final decoder layer, producing an output probability map for each output label. At each depth of the encoder, there were 16, 32, 64, 128, 256, and 512 convolutional filters, respectively. The decoder network's up-sampling route was made up of 512, 256, 128, 64, 32 and 16 filters at each depth, respectively. The proposed framework is employed in images with size 384 × 384. During training, the binary cross-entropy loss function is fine-tuned. This function quantifies the disparity between

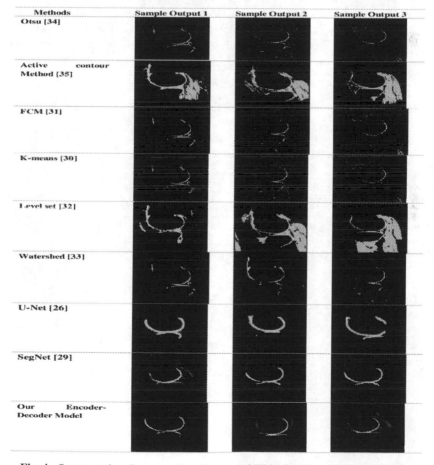

Fig. 4. Segmentation Outputs of the Femur and Tibia Cartilage from MRI Images

the predicted binary masks and the true binary masks. The Adam optimizer continuously refines the model's parameters to reduce this loss, bringing the model's predictions into better alignment with the real binary masks. Figure 3 provides a jagged representation of the proposed encoder-decoder framework for segmentation of Femur and Tibia Cartilage from holistic MRI images. Table 1 reports the performance of the proposed encoder-decoder framework in terms of training and validation accuracy cum loss with varying epochs (i.e., ranging from 50 to 300 number of epochs with studying intervals of 50). Here also, 700 MRI images from the OAI dataset are divided into 4:1 ratio with approximately 500 images for training and validation purposes and 200 images for testing purposes. It has been observed that our proposed model performed well for segmentation of Femur and Tibia Cartilage on 200 epochs with training accuracy (0.998), training loss (0.017), validation accuracy (0.985), and validation loss (0.067). Therefore, in Sect. 4, we have reported the testing performance of the proposed framework for the model obtained after 200 epochs. Table 2 infer deep segmentation model's learning accuracy in training period with corresponding loss. The incorporation of this additional component leads to improved performance. If we eliminate a layer from both the encoder and decoder, the model's performance significantly deteriorates. Conversely, introducing more than one additional layer to the encoder-decoder stack yields only marginal enhancements in comparison to the current model, while also substantially increasing the model's complexity.

Table 3. Performance Comparison of Our Proposed Model with the State-of-the-Art Segmentation Methods

Method	Accuracy	Jaccard Index	DSC	Precision	Recall	F-measure
ACM [35]	0.877 ± 0.152	0.113 ± 0.052	0.204 ± 0.056	0.115 ± 0.103	0.997 ± 0.132	0.206 ± 0.066
FCM [31]	0.988 ± 0.202	0.405 ± 0.065	0.577 ± 0.066	0.672 ± 0.041	0.584 ± 0.082	0.624 ± 0.183
K-means [30]	0.991 ± 0.032	0.382 ± 0.058	0.553 ± 0.142	0.561 ± 0.034	0.545 ± 0.058	0.552 ± 0.096
Level set [32]	0.952 ± 0.110	0.233 ± 0.034	0.379 ± 0.049	0.244 ± 0.089	0.999 ± 0.076	0.392 ± 0.074
Otsu [34]	0.991 ± 0.301	0.384 ± 0.048	0.555 ± 0.048	0.551 ± 0.107	0.566 ± 0.019	0.558 ± 0.044
Watershed [33]	0.990 ± 0.087	0.304 ± 0.018	0.467 ± 0.071	0.488 ± 0.022	0.467 ± 0.087	0.477 ± 0.031
SegNet [29]	0.982 ± 0.091	0.395 ± 0.032	0.566 ± 0.053	0.287 ± 0.018	0.804 ± 0.108	0.423 ± 0.011
U-Net [26]	0.986 ± 0.067	0.661 ± 0.070	0.695 ± 0.219	0.434 ± 0.094	0.689 ± 0.092	0.532 ± 0.092
Our Method	$\mathbf{0.997 \pm 0.072}$	$\mathbf{0.827 \pm 0.016}$	$\mathbf{0.905 \pm 0.101}$	$\mathbf{0.976 \pm 0.152}$	$\mathbf{0.969 \pm 0.044}$	$\mathbf{0.972 \pm 0.012}$

ACM- Active Contour Model; FCM- Fuzzy C-Means Method; DSC- Dice Similarity Coefficient

Table 4. Comparison of Our Proposed Method with Methods Reported by Other Authors using OAI dataset

Method	Cartilage Part	DSC
Level set with adaptive force function [9]	Patellar	84.80%
	Femoral	87.10%
	Tibia	81.70%
μ-Net [12]	Femoral	84.90%
	Patellar	78.50%
	Tibia	83.20%
Conditional generative adversarial networks [15]	Patellar	88.00%
Multi-stage convolutional neural networks [20]	Femur	90.70%
	Lateral tibia	91.30%
	Medial Tibia	87.60%
	Patella	84.00%
2D-3D ensemble U-Net [36]	Femoral	90.3 ± 2.89%
	Tibial	86.7 ± 4.07%
3D Statistical Shape Models, 2D and 3D CNNs [37]	Femoral	89.1 ± 2.41
	Medial Tibia	85.8 ± 5.00
	Lateral tibia	90.0 ± 2.57
Our Method	Combined Femoral and Tibial	**90.5 ± 1.01%**

4 Results and Discussions

This section evaluates and compares the effectiveness of our proposed encoder-decoder model with the state-of-the-art conventional and deep learning based segmentation techniques on OAI dataset [27]. Six conventional segmentation methods, including Active Contour Model (ACM) [35], Fuzzy c-means (FCM) [31], K-means [30], Level set [32], Otsu [34], and Watershed algorithm [33] as described in Subsect. 3.2, were assessed. Moreover, two deep learning based segmentation methods including SegNet [29] and U-Net [26] are compared with our proposed model. Figure 4 displays the segmentation outputs of the Femur and Tibia Cartilage from MRI images. Fore effective and fair comparison, six pixel oriented evaluation metrics i.e., Accuracy, Jaccard Index, Dice Score, Precision, Recall, and F-measure are measured from each of the considered segmentation methods and are reported in Table 3. Each of these evaluation metrics ranges from the values of 0 to 1 (i.e., in point scale) with value of 1 as observed to be the accurate segmentation method. From Table 3, it has been observed that among the conventional segmentation methods, Fuzzy c-means (FCM) method [31] has performed well for segmentation of femur and tibia cartilage from MRI images with average accuracy (0.988 ± 0.202), Jaccard index (0.405 ± 0.065), DSC (0.577 ± 0.066), recall (0.584 ± 0.082), precision (0.672 ± 0.041), and F-Measure (0.624 ± 0.183). Moreover, in comparison of all the state-of-the-art segmentation (including conventional and deep learning segmentation methods), it has been observed that U-Net segmentation is observed to be well performed method with an average accuracy (0.986 ± 0.067), Jaccard index (0.661 ± 0.070), DSC (0.695 ± 0.219), recall (0.689 ± 0.092), precision (0.434 ± 0.094), and F-Measure (0.532 ± 0.092). In comparison of all the methods (including our proposed model), it has been observed that our proposed encoder-decoder model best performed with an average accuracy (0.997 ± 0.072), Jaccard index (0.827 ± 0.016), DSC (0.905 ± 0.101), recall (0.969 ± 0.044), precision (0.976 ± 0.152), and F-Measure (0.972 ± 0.012). Moreover, Table 4 reports the performance comparison of our proposed model with other existing models reported by other authors. From Table 3, we can infer that the dice similarity coefficient of [20] seems better for segmentation as they have done the segmentation separately for different bones. Considering Femoral and Tibial bone cartilage together, there is no work present for segmentation which is very significant for early diagnosis with faster speed. Comparing and contrasting all scenarios, we can conclude that our proposed approach is more suitable for segmentation of knee cartilage with Femoral and Tibial together. Our proposed approach gives 0.905 DSC for Femoral and Tibial cartilage segmentation at the same time.

5   Conclusion

The diagnosis of joint diseases related to the knee joint is crucial in preventing long-term disability and discomfort for patients. Manual segmentation of the anatomical structure can be tedious and time-consuming, making it challenging to identify cartilage damage. Osteoarthritis is a prevalent knee joint disease that affects millions of people worldwide, making accurate diagnosis methods essential. In this study, we proposed encoder-decoder model inspired by the U-Net model for segmentation of Femur and Tibia Cartilage from holistic MRI images. Experimental results suggest that our proposed deep-learning model can be a powerful tool for accurate cartilage segmentation, which can aid in the diagnosis and treatment of knee joint diseases.

Acknowledgement. The work presented herein was being conducted at the Bio-Medical Infrared Image Processing Laboratory (BMIRD) of the Computer Science and Engineering Department, Tripura University (A Central University), Suryamaninagar-799022, Tripura (W).This work was supported by the Department of Biotechnology, (DBT) Government of India, under Grant No. BT/PR33087/BID/7/889/2019, Dated: 23/03/2022. The first author is grateful to Department of Science and Technology (DST), Government of India, for the DST INSPIRE Fellowship, under Grant No. IF200476.

References

1. Carballo, C.B., Nakagawa, Y., Sekiya, I., Rodeo, S.A.: Basic science of articular cartilage. Clin. Sports Med. **36**(3), 413–425 (2017)
2. Shapiro, L.M., McWalter, E.J., Son, M.S., Levenston, M., Hargreaves, B.A., Gold, G.E.: Mechanisms of Osteoarthritis in the knee: MR imaging appearance. J. Magn. Reson. Imaging **39**(6), 1346–1356 (2014)

3. Stoneclinic Homepage. https://www.stoneclinic.com/articular-cartilage. Accessed 11 May 2023
4. Pal, C.P., Singh, P., Chaturvedi, S., Pruthi, K.K., Vij, A.: Epidemiology of knee Osteoarthritis in India and related factors. Indian J. Orthop. **50**, 518–522 (2016)
5. Hayashi, D., Roemer, F.W., Guermazi, A.: Imaging of osteoarthritis—recent research developments and future perspective. Br. J. Radiol. **91**(1085), 20170349 (2018)
6. Davies-Tuck, M.L., et al.: The natural history of cartilage defects in people with knee Osteoarthritis. Osteoarthritis Cartilage **16**(3), 337–342 (2008)
7. Pang, J., Li, P., Qiu, M., Chen, W., Qiao, L.: Automatic articular cartilage segmentation based on pattern recognition from knee MRI images. J. Digit. Imaging **28**(6), 695–703 (2015)
8. Kashyap, S., Oguz, I., Zhang, H., Sonka, M.: Automated segmentation of knee MRI using hierarchical classifiers and just enough interaction based learning: data from Osteoarthritis Initiative. In: Ourselin, S., Joskowicz, L., Sabuncu, M.R., Unal, G., Wells, W. (eds.) MICCAI 2016. LNCS, vol. 9901, pp. 344–351. Springer, Cham (2016). https://doi.org/10.1007/978-3-319-46723-8_40
9. Ahn, C., Bui, T.D., Lee, Y.W., Shin, J., Park, H.: Fully automated, level set-based segmentation for knee MRIs using an adaptive force function and template: data from the Osteoarthritis Initiative. Biomed. Eng. Online **15**(1), 1–14 (2016)
10. Satapure, P.S., Rajurkar, A.M., Kottawar, V.G.: Automatic articular cartilage segmentation with multiple models. In: Proceedings of the 2017 1st International Conference on Intelligent Systems and Information Management (ICISIM), pp. 30–37. IEEE, October 2017
11. Du, Y., Shan, J., Zhang, M.: Knee Osteoarthritis prediction on MR images using cartilage damage index and machine learning methods. In: Proceedings of the 2017 IEEE International Conference on Bioinformatics and Biomedicine (BIBM), pp. 671–677. IEEE, November 2017
12. Raj, A., Vishwanathan, S., Ajani, B., Krishnan, K., Agarwal, H.: Automatic knee cartilage segmentation using fully volumetric convolutional neural networks for evaluation of osteoarthritis. In: Proceedings of the 2018 IEEE 15th International Symposium on Biomedical Imaging (ISBI 2018), pp. 851–854. IEEE, April 2018
13. Norman, B., Pedoia, V., Majumdar, S.: Use of 2D U-Net convolutional neural networks for automated cartilage and meniscus segmentation of knee MR imaging data to determine relaxometry and morphometry. Radiology **288**(1), 177 (2018)
14. Tack, A., Zachow, S.: Accurate automated volumetry of cartilage of the knee using convolutional neural networks: data from the Osteoarthritis Initiative. In: Proceedings of the 2019 IEEE 16th International Symposium on Biomedical Imaging (ISBI 2019), pp. 40–43. IEEE, April 2019
15. Gaj, S., Yang, M., Nakamura, K., Li, X.: Automated cartilage and meniscus segmentation of knee MRI with conditional generative adversarial networks. Magn. Reson. Med. **84**(1), 437–449 (2020)
16. Nyee, W.J., Hum, Y.C., Chai, T.Y., Tee, Y.K.: The design and development of automated knee cartilage segmentation framework. In: Proceedings of the 2019 IEEE International Conference on Signal and Image Processing Applications (ICSIPA), pp. 84–88. IEEE, September 2019
17. Hou, W., et al.: Quantitative measurement of cartilage volume with automatic cartilage segmentation in knee Osteoarthritis. Clin. Rheumatol. **40**(5), 1997–2006 (2021)
18. Deng, Y., You, L., Wang, Y., Zhou, X.: A coarse-to-fine framework for automated knee bone and cartilage segmentation data from the Osteoarthritis Initiative. J. Digit. Imaging **34**(4), 833–840 (2021)
19. Xue, Y.P., et al.: Automated cartilage segmentation and quantification using 3D ultrashort echo time (UTE) cones MR imaging with deep convolutional neural networks. Eur. Radiol. **31**(10), 7653–7663 (2021)

20. Gatti, A.A., Maly, M.R.: Automatic knee cartilage and bone segmentation using multi-stage convolutional neural networks: data from the Osteoarthritis Initiative. Magn. Reson. Mater. Phys., Biol. Med. **34**(6), 859–875 (2021)

21. Juras, V., Szomolanyi, P., Janáčová, V., Trattnig, S.: Initial experience with automatic knee cartilage segmentation using MR chondral health, musculoskeletal imaging clinical (2021)

22. Neubert, A., et al.: Applying simultaneous super-resolution and contrast synthesis to routine clinical magnetic resonance images for automated segmentation of knee joint cartilage. In: International Conference on Medical Imaging with Deep Learning--Extended Abstract Track, April 2019

23. Neubert, A., et al.: Simultaneous super-resolution and contrast synthesis of routine clinical magnetic resonance images of the knee for improving automatic segmentation of joint cartilage: data from the Osteoarthritis Initiative. Med. Phys. **47**(10), 4939–4948 (2020)

24. Revathi, S.A., Holi, G.: Segmentation and analysis of knee femoral cartilage for Osteoarthritis using MR images. IOP Conf. Ser. Earth Environ. Sci. **704**(1), 012047 (2021)

25. Li, Z., Chen, K., Liu, P., Chen, X., Zheng, G.: Entropy and distance maps-guided segmentation of articular cartilage: data from the Osteoarthritis Initiative. Int. J. Comput. Assist. Radiol. Surg. **17**(3), 553–560 (2022)

26. Ronneberger, O., Fischer, P., Brox, T.: U-net: Convolutional networks for biomedical image segmentation. In: Navab, N., Hornegger, J., Wells, W.M., Frangi, A.F. (eds.) MICCAI 2015. LNCS, vol. 9351, pp. 234–241. Springer, Cham (2015). https://doi.org/10.1007/978-3-319-24574-4_28

27. OAI Homepage. https://nda.nih.gov/oai/. Accessed 11 May 2023

28. GIMP Homepage. https://www.gimp.org/. Accessed 11 May 2023

29. Badrinarayanan, V., Kendall, A., Cipolla, R.: SegNet: a deep convolutional encoder-decoder architecture for image segmentation. IEEE Trans. Pattern Anal. Mach. Intell. **39**(12), 2481–2495 (2017)

30. Mucha, H.J., Späth, H.: Cluster Dissection and Analysis: Theory, FORTRAN Programs, Examples. (Translator: Johannes Goldschmidt), vol. 1985, 226 pp. Ellis Horwood Ltd Wiley, Chichester (1986)

31. Peizhuang, W.: Pattern recognition with fuzzy objective function algorithms (James C. Bezdek). SIAM Rev. **25**(3), 442 (1983)

32. Gray, A., Abbena, E., Salamon, S.: Modern Differential Geometry of Curves and Surfaces with Mathematica. CINECA IRIS Institutional Research Information System (2006)

33. Meyer, F.: Topographic distance and watershed lines. Signal Process. **38**(1), 113–125 (1994)

34. Otsu, N.: A threshold selection method from gray-level histograms. IEEE Trans. Syst. Man Cybern. **9**(1), 62–66 (1979)

35. Menet, S., Saint-Marc, P., Medioni, G.: Active contour models: overview, implementation and applications. In: Proceedings of the 1990 IEEE International Conference on Systems, Man, and Cybernetics Conference Proceedings, pp. 194–199. IEEE, November 1990

36. Abd Latif, M.H., Faye, I.: Automated tibiofemoral joint segmentation based on deeply supervised 2D–3D ensemble U-Net: data from the Osteoarthritis Initiative. Artif. Intell. Med. **122**, 102213 (2021)

37. Ambellan, F., Tack, A., Ehlke, M., Zachow, S.: Automated segmentation of knee bone and cartilage combining statistical shape knowledge and convolutional neural networks: data from the Osteoarthritis Initiative. Med. Image Anal. **52**, 109–118 (2019)

Image Captioning with Visual Positional Embedding and Bi-linear Pooling

Sidharth Nair[1,2]([✉]) [iD] and Prithwijit Guha[2] [iD]

[1] HCLTech, Chennai, India
sidharth.nair@hcl.com
[2] Department of Electronics and Electrical Engineering,
Indian Insitute of Technology Guwahati, Guwahati, India
pguha@iitg.ac.in

Abstract. Recent approaches to image captioning typically follow an encoder-decoder architecture. The feature vectors extracted from the region proposals obtained from an object detector network serve as input to encoder. Without any explicit spatial information about the visual regions, the caption synthesis model is limited to learn relationship from captions only. However, the structure between the semantic units in images and sentences is different. This work introduces a grid based spatial position encoding scheme to learn relationship from both domains. Furthermore, bi-linear pooling is used with attention for exploiting spatial and channel-wise attention distribution to capture second order interaction between multi-modal inputs. These are integrated within the Transformer architecture achieving a competitive CIDEr score.

Keywords: Transformer · Positional Embedding · Image Captioning · Bi-linear Pooling

1 Introduction

Image captioning is a challenging task that involves the generation of accurate natural language descriptions for visual content, which may include objects and their attributes, scene features, object interactions, or even objects that are not present. Advanced natural language generation is required to select, organize, and articulate the content. Most conventional image captioning models follow the encoder-decoder framework, where the input image is encoded into an intermediate representation like a feature vector [24], feature map [25], or set of features [1], and subsequently decoded into a caption using RNNs [1, 24, 25] or attention networks [9, 21]. However, the spatial relationship among the regions is not explicitly considered in most of the current methods, which limits the expressibility of the model (see Fig. 1). Some recent works [9] have utilized spatial information in attention computation, but this work encodes spatial information in the form of positional embeddings.

© The Author(s), under exclusive license to Springer Nature Switzerland AG 2024
H. Kaur et al. (Eds.): CVIP 2023, CCIS 2009, pp. 419–431, 2024.
https://doi.org/10.1007/978-3-031-58181-6_35

Two elephants standing next to   A small airplane sitting on top
each other in a field.   of a metal fence.
A baby elephant standing next   A small airplane parked next to
to an adult elephant.   a fence.

Fig. 1. Comparison of captions generated with and without explicit spatial information of the salient regions. (Color figure online)

This work proposes to model the spatial relationships of salient regions and the second-order interaction of multi-modal features for image captioning. The method includes grid-based spatial positional embedding and bi-linear pooling with attention for multi-modal inputs. The spatial positional embedding considers the relative spatial position of image regions, and the bi-linear pooling captures complex interactions between different modalities. These can generate more accurate and descriptive captions of the visual content. This overcomes the limitations of several previous methods that did not explicitly consider spatial relationships [24,25] or second-order interactions of multi-modal features [1,9].

The remaining part of this paper is organized in the following manner. A brief literature review of related works is presented in Sect. 2. The proposed model is described in Sect. 3. Experiments and results are presented in Sect. 4. Section 5 summarizes the present work and discusses the possible future extensions.

2   Related Works

Image Captioning – Most approaches to factual image captioning are based on the encoder-decoder architecture. Input images were encoded as feature vectors in [24] which were replaced with top-down attention on feature maps [25] and later with bottom-up attention using object proposals from a region proposal network [1]. The RNN based decoding methods used in [1,24,25] were replaced with a more powerful and parallelizable architecture based on transformers [23]. Models relying on such an architecture were modified to suit multi-modal needs of image captioning. This includes reweighing attention using geometric information [9], use of higher order interaction in attention [21], multiple masked layers in parallel [8], perturbing learnable masks [3] among others. Learning models only on cross-entropy loss using teacher forcing makes the model mimic captions

seen during training. Also, the models are evaluated on non-differentiable metrics [20], which are very different from cross-entropy loss. These limitations were
overcome through a proposal of a REINFORCE algorithm [22] that allowed the
model to be trained directly on non-differentiable metrics. A detailed review of
works in image captioning can be found in [20].

Visual Relation – Attention-based models, such as transformer [23], are
agnostic to the ordering of input sequences. However, this shortcoming can be
addressed by incorporating positional embeddings or by adjusting the attention weights to consider geometric relationships among the inputs. To further
improve the visual relationships among objects, the model can also consider
explicit semantic relationships [15]. Positional embeddings can be generated
using learnable networks [18] or fixed functions [6,23] based on the bounding
boxes corresponding to objects or salient regions. On the other hand, attention
weights can be modified by adding a learned bias component that considers
appearance and geometric features [7] or by reweighing the appearance-based
attention weights using geometric information [9]. Alternatively, the proposal of
[8] employed multiple attention layers in parallel, each with a fixed mask encoding a pre-defined spatial relationship. This work proposes a positional embedding
approach that divides the image into grids and learns an embedding based on
the overlap areas of each input.

Bi-linear Pooling – This process computes the outer product of two vectors
enabling multiplicative interaction between all elements of both vectors. In the
multi-modal case, this has led to improved phrase localization accuracy and
better interaction among the inputs [4,21]. For fine-grained visual recognition,
pooled outer-product of features from two CNNs were used in [17]. On the other
hand, hierarchical bi-linear pooling was used to aggregate multiple cross-layer
pooling features in [28]. In Visual Question Answering, Compact Bi-linear Pooling [5] to the multi-modal case in [4], and bi-linear attention networks were used
to learn bi-linear attention distributions in [13]. Recently, bi-linear pooling with
attention was introduced in image captioning to exploit higher-order intra- and
inter-modal interactions [21]. This work uses bi-linear pooling as proposed in
[21] with a few modifications detailed in Sect. 3.2.

3   Proposed Model

An Image Captioning system outputs a caption $\hat{y}$ for an input image $I \in \mathcal{I}$.
Figure 2 shows an overview of the proposed image captioning model. Following recent works [1,7,9,21], we utilize adaptive bottom-up features [1] as visual
features $A = [a_1, a_2, \ldots]$ ($a \in \mathbb{R}^d$) and geometric information $B = [b_1, b_2, \ldots]$
($b \in \mathbb{R}^4$) of the salient regions in the image. These are further processed by
a spatial position encoding block for injecting spatial information in the visual
features. This positional encoding scheme is elaborated in Subsect. 3.1. The position encoded features are fed to a Transformer [23] based encoder wherein they
are refined using self-attention. The transformer based decoder uses the refined

visual features and previously decoded tokens to predict the next token. Inner product based cross attention layer in the decoder is replaced with bi-linear pooled attention which is detailed in Subsect. 3.2.

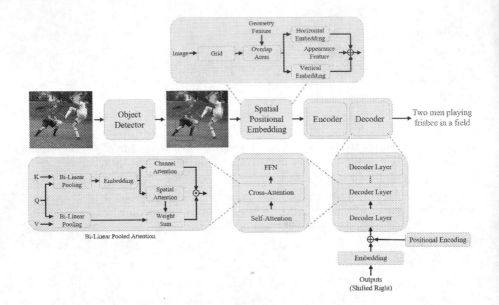

Fig. 2. Overview of the proposed model. Faster R-CNN is used to detect a variably sized set of objects and other salient regions. These regions are passed through a grid-based spatial positional embedding block encoding spatial information of the detected regions. Bi-Linear Pooling with Attention is used in the decoder layer's cross-attention module, allowing higher-order multi-modal feature interaction.

3.1   Spatial Positional Embedding

Consider the appearance feature $\mathbf{a} \in \mathbb{R}^d$ extracted from the bounding box $\mathbf{b}^1$ $\in \mathbb{R}^4$ of a salient region of the input image I. The image I is divided into $n_g \times n_g$ number of grids $\mathbf{g}_{ij}$ where $1 \leq i, j \leq n_g$. The overlap area between each grid and $\mathbf{b}$ is computed resulting in the overlap matrix $\tilde{O} \in \mathbb{R}^{n_g \times n_g}$ such that $\tilde{O}_{ij}$, the $(i, j)^{\text{th}}$ entry of $\tilde{O}$ is given by

$$\tilde{O}_{ij} = area\left(\mathbf{b} \cap \mathbf{g}_{ij}\right) \tag{1}$$

The overlap matrix $\tilde{O}$ is summed along its rows and columns giving weights along horizontal and vertical directions respectively.

$$\tilde{\mathbf{o}}_x = \tilde{O}^T \mathbf{1}_{n_g} \qquad\qquad \tilde{\mathbf{o}}_y = \tilde{O}\mathbf{1}_{n_g} \tag{2}$$

---

[1] Bounding box and grid are represented as $[x_1, y_1, x_2, y_2]^T$ where (x_1, y_1) and (x_2, y_2) are normalized top left and bottom right coordinates.

Here, $\mathbf{1}_{n_g} \in \mathbb{R}^{n_g \times 1}$ represents a $n_g \times 1$ vector of all ones.

These horizontal and vertical spatial weights are used to compute a weighted sum of learned embeddings associated with each column and row respectively.

$$\mathbf{p}_x = W_x \tilde{\mathbf{o}}_x \qquad\qquad \mathbf{p}_y = W_y \tilde{\mathbf{o}}_y \qquad (3)$$

Here, $W_x \in \mathbb{R}^{d \times n_g}$ represents the learned embeddings corresponding to the columns of the grid. Similarly, W_y corresponds to the rows of the grid. The resulting horizontal and vertical embeddings are combined with the input as given below.

$$\tilde{\mathbf{a}} = \mathbf{a} + \mathbf{p}_x + \mathbf{p}_y \qquad (4)$$

3.2   Bi-linear Pooled Attention

Bi-linear pooling as introduced in [21] is employed in the decoder to exploit second-order interaction among the multi-modal features. It takes as input, queries $Q = \left[\mathbf{q}_1 \ldots \mathbf{q}_{n_q}\right]$, keys $K = \left[\mathbf{k}_1 \ldots \mathbf{k}_{n_k}\right]$ and values $V = \left[\mathbf{v}_1 \ldots \mathbf{v}_{n_k}\right]$, where $\mathbf{q}_i \in \mathbb{R}^{d_q}$, $\mathbf{k}_i \in \mathbb{R}^{d_k}$, $\mathbf{v}_i \in \mathbb{R}^{d_v}$, n_q is the number of tokens and n_k is the number of detected salient regions.

Low-rank bi-linear pooling is performed between each query-key pair to achieve a joint bi-linear query-key representation $\mathbf{f}_{ij}^k \in \mathbb{R}^{d_f}$ ($1 \leq i \leq n_q$, $1 \leq j \leq n_k$). Similarly, enhanced query-key representation $\mathbf{f}_{ij}^v \subset \mathbb{R}^{d_f}$ is computed between each query-value pair.

$$\mathbf{f}_{ij}^k = \mathrm{CELU}(W_q^k \mathbf{q}_i) \odot \mathrm{CELU}\left(W_k \mathbf{k}_j\right) \qquad (5)$$
$$\mathbf{f}_{ij}^v = \mathrm{CELU}(W_q^v \mathbf{q}_i) \odot \mathrm{CELU}\left(W_v \mathbf{v}_j\right) \qquad (6)$$

Here, $W_q^k \in \mathbb{R}^{d_f \times d_q}$, $W_k \in \mathbb{R}^{d_f \times d_k}$, $W_q^v \in \mathbb{R}^{d_f \times d_q}$, $W_v \in \mathbb{R}^{d_f \times d_v}$ are linear transformations, and $\odot$ is element-wise multiplication. The joint bi-linear query-key representation $\mathbf{f}_{ij}^k$ is further transformed to $\tilde{\mathbf{f}}_{ij}^k$. The transformed representation is used to compute spatial and channel-wise attention.

$$\tilde{\mathbf{f}}_{ij}^k = \mathrm{ReLU}\left(W_f \mathbf{f}_{ij}^k\right) \qquad (7)$$

Here, $W_f \in \mathbb{R}^{c \times d_f}$ is a linear transformation. The joint bi-linear query-key representation is used to obtain spatial attention $\boldsymbol{\alpha}_i^s \in \mathbb{R}^{n_k}$ as follows

$$a_{ij}^s = \mathbf{w}_s^T \tilde{\mathbf{f}}_{ij}^k \qquad (8)$$
$$\boldsymbol{\alpha}_i^s = \mathrm{softmax}\left(\mathbf{a}_i\right) \qquad (9)$$

where, $\mathbf{w}_s \in \mathbb{R}^c$ is a linear transformation. Channel-wise attention $\boldsymbol{\alpha}_i^c \in \mathbb{R}^b$ is computed from the joint bi-linear query-key representation by performing a squeeze-excitation operation [11] in the following manner.

$$\bar{\mathbf{f}}_i = \frac{1}{n_k} \sum_{j=1}^{n_k} \tilde{\mathbf{f}}_{ij}^k \tag{10}$$

$$\boldsymbol{\alpha}_i^c = \text{sigmoid}\left(W_c \bar{\mathbf{f}}_i\right) \tag{11}$$

Here, $W_c \in \mathbb{R}^{f \times c}$. The enhanced query-key value is accumulated using spatial and channel-wise attention values.

$$\mathbf{z}_i = \boldsymbol{\alpha}_i^c \odot \sum_{j=1}^{n_k} \alpha_{ij}^s \mathbf{f}_{ij}^v \tag{12}$$

While this work uses bi-linear pooling as proposed in [21], there are a few differences in the implementation. First, the above steps are performed on each query instead of taking the mean query as the input in the first layer. Second, the attended feature vector $\mathbf{z}$ is not used to update the keys and values to be used in the next layer. Instead, learned linear projections are used at every layer following [23]. Third, the output from the last layer is used for further processing instead of using output from all the layers.

3.3   Loss Function

Formally, the goal is to maximize the likelihood of the ground truth caption y given image I.

$$\hat{\boldsymbol{\Theta}} = \arg \max_{\boldsymbol{\Theta}} \sum_{(I,y)} \log p\left(y|I; \boldsymbol{\Theta}\right) \tag{13}$$

Here, $\boldsymbol{\Theta}$ represents the set of parameters of the model.

During training, the model is provided with image-caption pair (I, y). Furthermore, the decoder uses previous tokens from ground truth caption y to predict the next token. Each token is represented using a one-hot vector $\mathbf{y}_t \in \{0,1\}^{|\Sigma|}$ where $1 \leq t \leq |y|$, $|\Sigma|$ is the size of vocabulary and $|y|$ is the length of ground truth caption. The model is trained using cross entropy loss $\mathcal{L}$ which can be formulated as

$$\mathcal{L} = -\sum_{t=1}^{|y|} \sum_{j=1}^{|\Sigma|} \mathbf{y}_t[j] \log p_t[j] \tag{14}$$

where p_t is the probability distribution generated by the model for the token at decoding step t.

4   Experiment

Dataset and Metrics – The proposed models were trained and evaluated on the MS-COCO dataset [16]. This work used the commonly followed Karpathy split[2] comprising of 113k images in the training set and 5k images each in the validation and test set. Each image is associated with five ground truth captions. All the sentences are lower-cased and non-alphanumeric characters were discarded. All words occurring not more than five times were mapped to a special token, resulting in a vocabulary size of 9487. The models were evaluated with BLEU, METEOR, ROUGE, CIDER-D and SPICE metrics [20] using publicly available code[3]. Additionally, the generalization performance of the models was evaluated on the Flickr30k [27] dataset.

Implementation Details – All the models were trained for 30 epochs optimizing cross-entropy loss using Adam optimizer [14]. This work used a learning rate scheduling (following [23]) with an initial learning rate of 1×10^{-3} for 10,000 steps. Adaptive Bottom-up features extracted using a Faster R-CNN pre-trained on Visual Genome dataset [1] were used, where $10 \leq n_k \leq 100$. The transformer architecture used $h = 8$ attention heads, $N = 6$ layers and $d = 512$ embedding size. For spatial positional embedding, 6×6 number of grids were used. Beam search with a beam size of 3 was used during inference. All the models were implemented in PyTorch and trained on a NVIDIA Tesla V100 GPU. The code is available at https://github.com/sidharth5n/Spatial-Image-Captioning.

Table 1. Performance summary of various models on the Karpathy test split of MS-COCO and Flickr30k dataset. The performances are reported in terms of BLEU@N (BN), METEOR (M), ROUGE (R), CIDEr-D (C) and SPICE (S). † indicates our implementation and * indicates non-autoregressive approach.

Model	MS-COCO						Flickr30k					
	B1	B4	M	R	C	S	B1	B4	M	R	C	S
NIC† [24]	68.6	27.1	23.1	50.5	82.2	15.9	55.3	13.3	14.1	37.2	20.4	8.0
Attention† [25]	73.7	32.6	25.9	54.3	102.3	19.0	58.9	16.2	16.2	40.2	31.4	9.8
BUTD† [1]	75.9	35.8	27.3	56.2	110.3	20.2	61.5	17.8	17.1	41.8	34.5	10.9
Transformer† [23]	76.4	36.1	27.9	56.7	116.3	21.0	62.1	18.6	17.9	42.5	39.4	11.7
AoA [12]	77.0	37.1	28.4	57.2	117.4	21.4	62.9	19.2	18.3	43.0	39.8	11.8
ORT [9]	76.5	35.9	28.0	56.6	115.4	21.1	62.7	**20.1**	**18.3**	**43.2**	41.0	**12.0**
SGAE [26]	77.6	36.9	27.7	57.2	116.7	20.9	–	–	–	–	–	–
IT [8]	77.6	37.8	28.5	57.5	119.1	21.5	**64.0**	19.7	**18.3**	**43.2**	41.0	11.8
X-Transformer [21]	77.0	37.0	28.6	57.3	119.0	21.6	63.9	19.2	**18.3**	42.7	**41.9**	**12.0**
ER-SAN [15]	78.2	**38.8**	**29.2**	**58.5**	122.9	**22.2**	–	–	–	–	–	–
AttentionAligned [3]	78.6	38.2	**29.2**	58.3	**125.0**	22.1	–	–	–	–	–	–
SCD-Net* [19]	**79.0**	37.3	28.1	58.0	118.0	21.6	–	–	–	–	–	–
Spatial	76.3	36.6	27.5	56.5	116.9	20.5	61.6	19.3	18.0	42.6	39.8	11.9
Bi-Linear	75.4	34.6	27.4	56.0	115.4	20.6	61.9	19.0	17.8	42.5	40.2	11.9
Spatial + Bi-Linear	76.4	36.9	27.6	57.3	118.2	21.4	**64.0**	19.9	**18.3**	42.7	41.2	11.9

---

[2] https://github.com/karpathy/neuraltalk.
[3] https://github.com/tylin/coco-caption.

Comparative Analysis – The proposed model is compared against the following three baselines – (a) the Bottom-Up and Top-Down Attention Network (BUTD) [1]; (b) Attention on Attention (AoA) Network [12], and (c) Object Relation Transformer (ORT) [9]. Table 1 summarizes the performance comparison on the Karpathy test split. The proposed model with spatial positional embedding is denoted as *Spatial*. *Bi-Linear* refers to our model with scaled inner-product attention replaced with bi-linear pooled attention in the cross-attention layer of the decoder. The complete model, which combines both spatial and bi-linear approaches, is referred to as *Spatial + Bi-Linear* and is illustrated in Fig. 2. The proposed model outperforms the BUTD model and Transformer model by 7.2% and 1.6% respectively in terms of CIDEr score. The spatial positional encoding scheme of the proposed model surpasses ORT. However, it falls short of IT [8] and X-Transformer [21]. This can be attributed to our proposed model not utilizing relative positional information in computing positional embeddings or higher-order interaction in non-multi-modal layers (Fig. 3).

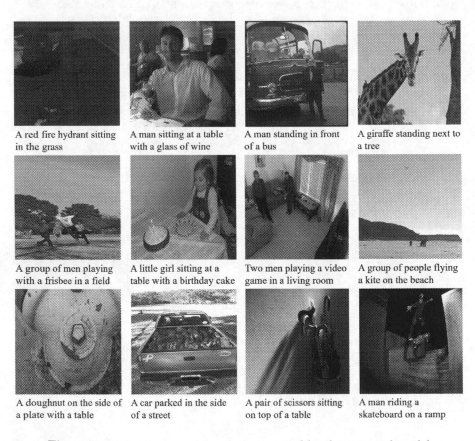

A red fire hydrant sitting in the grass

A man sitting at a table with a glass of wine

A man standing in front of a bus

A giraffe standing next to a tree

A group of men playing with a frisbee in a field

A little girl sitting at a table with a birthday cake

Two men playing a video game in a living room

A group of people flying a kite on the beach

A doughnut on the side of a plate with a table

A car parked in the side of a street

A pair of scissors sitting on top of a table

A man riding a skateboard on a ramp

Fig. 3. Example images and captions generated by the proposed model.

4.1 Ablation Studies

Higher Order Interaction – Table 2 demonstrates the efficacy of incorporating higher-order interactions in multi-modal layers. This leads to the natural inquiry of whether this approach is equally effective in uni-modal layers. To explore this question, we applied bi-linear pooling to the encoder and summarized the results in Table 3. Although extending bi-linear pooling to the encoder yielded a modest improvement in performance, it also led to a significant increase in inference time. Therefore, we concluded that bi-linear pooling should be restricted to multi-modal layers exclusively.

Table 2. Performance comparison of our proposed models with Standard Transformer on the validation split of MS-COCO dataset. The p values marked in (.) come from two-tailed t-tests using paired samples. Values marked in bold were considered significant at $\alpha = 0.05$.

Model	B1	B4	M	R	C	S
Transformer [23]	75.9	34.0	27.6	56.1	111.9	20.6
Spatial	77.7	34.7	27.0	56.4	116.3	20.2
	(0.21)	(0.52)	**(0.03)**	(0.17)	**(0.001)**	**(<0.001)**
Bi-Linear	75.9	32.8	27.4	56.1	115.8	20.6
	(<0.001)	(0.98)	(0.64)	(0.07)	**(<0.001)**	**(0.003)**
Spatial + Bi-Linear	77.8	34.9	27.6	57.3	118.2	21.4
	(0.25)	(0.59)	(0.65)	(0.07)	**(<0.001)**	**(0.003)**

Table 3. Effect of higher order interaction on captioning performance on the Karpathy validation split of MS-COCO dataset. Inference time (Time) is reported with respect to a model without higher-order interaction.

Location	B1	B4	M	R	C	S	Time
None	75.9	**34.0**	**27.6**	56.1	111.9	20.6	1
Encoder	76.0	**34.0**	27.4	56.1	113.2	20.6	1.12
Decoder	75.9	32.8	27.4	56.1	115.8	20.6	1.37
Encoder + Decoder	**76.1**	33.0	27.5	56.1	**115.9**	20.6	1.47

Spatial Relation Encoding – The proposed approach for encoding spatial information is compared with both attention modification-based methods [7,9,10] and positional embedding-based techniques [2,23] discussed in Sect. 2. Moreover, the performances of two variations of the proposed method (namely, $Grid_{Vector}$ and $Grid_{Fixed}$) are evaluated. In $Grid_{Vector}$, the overlap matrix $\tilde{O}$ is flattened and linearly projected to the model dimension and used as positional embedding. The method $Grid_{Fixed}$ uses fixed trigonometric embeddings (as in

[23]) in W_x and W_y instead of learned embeddings. Table 4 provides a summary of the performances of various spatial relation encoding techniques on the validation split of MS-COCO dataset. As argued in previous works, simple positional embedding like [2,23] are unable to capture the complex spatial relationship of the objects resulting in performances that are significantly worse than the baseline models without any positional encoding. However, the performance of the proposed grid based spatial encoding shows that carefully designed positional embeddings can capture the complex spatial relationship of regions.

Table 4. Performance analysis of different methods of spatial positional encoding on the Karpathy validation split of MS-COCO dataset.

Positional Encoding	B1	B4	M	R	C	S
None	75.9	34.0	27.6	56.1	111.9	20.6
Reweighing [9]	76.2	34.3	**27.7**	**56.4**	112.5	20.6
Positional Bias [10]	76.5	34.3	27.5	56.3	112.5	20.7
Geometric Bias [7]	76.6	34.6	27.6	**56.4**	112.6	**20.8**
Trigonometric [23]	75.7	33.4	27.2	55.6	109.1	20.2
MLP [2]	74.1	31.7	26.2	54.7	103.1	19.4
Grid$_{Fixed}$	77.0	33.5	26.6	55.9	113.8	20.2
Grid$_{Vector}$	76.8	33.9	26.6	56.0	113.4	20.1
Ours	**77.7**	**34.7**	27.0	**56.4**	**116.3**	20.2

Number of Grids – We evaluate the effect of number of grids (n_g) used in spatial positional embedding on the captioning performance. Table 5 shows that the best performance in terms of CIDEr is achieved when $n_g = 6$. This corresponds to having at the minimum two grids with complete overlap for at least half of the detections in the train split (refer Table 6). Any increase in n_g beyond 6 results in numerous grids with max overlap for more than half of the detections. This leads to equal spatial weightage for the corresponding embeddings

Table 5. Effect of the number of grids used in proposed spatial positional embedding on captioning performance.

No. of grids	B1	B4	M	R	C	S
5×5	77.2	34.7	26.9	56.2	115.6	20.2
6×6	**77.7**	34.7	**27.0**	56.4	**116.3**	20.2
7×7	77.3	34.7	26.9	56.4	115.6	20.2
8×8	77.2	**35.0**	26.9	**56.5**	115.3	20.2
9×9	77.0	34.5	26.9	56.4	115.5	**20.3**
10×10	77.4	34.4	26.6	56.1	113.3	19.8

Table 6. Statistics computed on salient regions obtained on Train split of MS-COCO dataset.

Statistic	Width	Height	Area
Min	0.023	0.023	0.001
Max	0.999	0.999	0.997
Mean	0.308	0.288	0.117
Median	0.216	0.218	0.043

resulting in performance degradation. On the other hand, when n_g is less than 6, very few grids have non-zero overlap for small-sized detections. This results in poor training of the embeddings.

5   Conclusion

This work introduces a novel grid-based spatial positional embedding scheme and integrates bi-linear pooled attention within the transformer architecture. The results of our experiments indicate that the model is effective in encoding the spatial relationship of objects, and we observed performance improvements due to the higher-order interaction of features. In the future, we could modify the positional embedding scheme to leverage relative spatial information. Furthermore, we suggest that the model could be further enhanced through fine-tuning using Self Critical Sequence Training [22].

References

1. Anderson, P., et al.: Bottom up and top-down attention for image captioning and visual question answering. In: 2018 IEEE/CVF Conference on Computer Vision and Pattern Recognition, pp. 6077–6086 (2018)
2. Chen, Y.-C., et al.: UNITER: UNiversal Image-TExt Representation learning. In: Vedaldi, A., Bischof, H., Brox, T., Frahm, J.-M. (eds.) ECCV 2020. LNCS, vol. 12375, pp. 104–120. Springer, Cham (2020). https://doi.org/10.1007/978-3-030-58577-8_7
3. Fei, Z.: Attention-aligned transformer for image captioning. In: Proceedings of the AAAI Conference on Artificial Intelligence, vol. 36, no. 1, pp. 607–615 (2022)
4. Fukui, A., Park, D.H., Yang, D., Rohrbach, A., Darrell, T., Rohrbach, M.: Multimodal compact bilinear pooling for visual question answering and visual grounding. In: Proceedings of the 2016 Conference on Empirical Methods in Natural Language Processing, pp. 457–468. ACL (2016)
5. Gao, Y., Beijbom, O., Zhang, N., Darrell, T.: Compact bilinear pooling. In: 2016 IEEE Conference on Computer Vision and Pattern Recognition (CVPR), pp. 317–326 (2016)
6. Garncarek, Ł., Powalski, R., Stanisławek, T., Topolski, B., Halama, P., Graliński, F.: LAMBERT: layout-aware (language) modeling using BERT for information extraction (2020). arXiv:cs.CL/2002.08087

7. Guo, L., Liu, J., Zhu, X., Yao, P., Lu, S., Lu, H.: Normalized and geometry-aware self-attention network for image captioning. In: 2020 IEEE/CVF Conference on Computer Vision and Pattern Recognition, pp. 10324–10333 (2020)
8. He, S., Liao, W., Tavakoli, H.R., Yang, M., Rosenhahn, B., Pugeault, N.: Image captioning through image transformer. In: Proceedings of the Asian Conference on Computer Vision (2020)
9. Herdade, S., Kappeler, A., Boakye, K., Soares, J.: Image captioning: transforming objects into words. In: Advances in Neural Information Processing Systems, vol. 32, pp. 11137–11147 (2019)
10. Hong, T., Kim, D., Ji, M., Hwang, W., Nam, D., Park, S.: BROS: a pre-trained language model focusing on text and layout for better key information extraction from documents (2021). arXiv:cs.CL/2108.04539
11. Hu, J., Shen, L., Sun, G.: Squeeze-and-excitation networks. In: 2018 IEEE/CVF Conference on Computer Vision and Pattern Recognition, pp. 7132–7141 (2018)
12. Huang, L., Wang, W., Chen, J., Wei, X.Y.: Attention on attention for image captioning. In: Proceedings of the IEEE/CVF International Conference on Computer Vision (ICCV) (2019)
13. Kim, J.H., Jun, J., Zhang, B.T.: Bilinear attention networks. In: Advances in Neural Information Processing Systems, vol. 31 (2018)
14. Kingma, D.P., Ba, L.J.: Adam: a method for stochastic optimization. In: Proceedings of the Third International Conference on Learning Representations (2015)
15. Li, J., Mao, Z., Fang, S., Li, H.: ER-SAN: enhanced-adaptive relation self-attention network for image captioning. In: Proceedings of the Thirty-First International Joint Conference on Artificial Intelligence, pp. 1081–1087 (2022)
16. Lin, T.-Y., et al.: Microsoft COCO: common objects in context. In: Fleet, D., Pajdla, T., Schiele, B., Tuytelaars, T. (eds.) ECCV 2014. LNCS, vol. 8693, pp. 740–755. Springer, Cham (2014). https://doi.org/10.1007/978-3-319-10602-1_48
17. Lin, T.Y., RoyChowdhury, A., Maji, S.: Bilinear CNN models for fine-grained visual recognition. In: 2015 IEEE International Conference on Computer Vision (ICCV), pp. 1449–1457 (2015)
18. Lu, J., Batra, D., Parikh, D., Lee, S.: ViLBERT: pretraining task-agnostic visiolinguistic representations for vision-and-language tasks. In: Advances in Neural Information Processing Systems, vol. 32 (2019)
19. Luo, J., et al.: Semantic-conditional diffusion networks for image captioning. In: Proceedings of the IEEE/CVF Conference on Computer Vision and Pattern Recognition (CVPR), pp. 23359–23368 (2023)
20. Ming, Y., Hu, N., Fan, C., Feng, F., Zhou, J., Yu, H.: Visuals to text: a comprehensive review on automatic image captioning. IEEE/CAA J. Autom. Sin. 9(8), 1339–1365 (2022)
21. Pan, Y., Yao, T., Li, Y., Mei, T.: X-linear attention networks for image captioning. In: 2020 IEEE/CVF Conference on Computer Vision and Pattern Recognition, pp. 10968–10977 (2020)
22. Rennie, S.J., Marcheret, E., Mroueh, Y., Ross, J., Goel, V.: Self-critical sequence training for image captioning. In: 2017 IEEE Conference on Computer Vision and Pattern Recognition, pp. 1179–1195 (2017)
23. Vaswani, A., et al.: Attention is all you need. In: Advances in Neural Information Processing Systems, vol. 30, pp. 5998–6008 (2017)
24. Vinyals, O., Toshev, A., Bengio, S., Erhan, D.: Show and tell: a neural image caption generator. In: 2015 IEEE Conference on Computer Vision and Pattern Recognition (CVPR), pp. 3156–3164 (2015)

25. Xu, K., et al.: Show, attend and tell: neural image caption generation with visual attention. In: Proceedings of the 32nd International Conference on Machine Learning, vol. 37, pp. 2048–2057 (2015)
26. Yang, X., Tang, K., Zhang, H., Cai, J.: Auto-encoding scene graphs for image captioning. In: 2019 IEEE/CVF Conference on Computer Vision and Pattern Recognition, pp. 10677–10686 (2019)
27. Young, P., Lai, A., Hodosh, M., Hockenmaier, J.: From image descriptions to visual denotations: new similarity metrics for semantic inference over event descriptions. Trans. Assoc. Comput. Linguist. **2**, 67–78 (2014)
28. Yu, C., Zhao, X., Zheng, Q., Zhang, P., You, X.: Hierarchical bilinear pooling for fine-grained visual recognition. In: Ferrari, V., Hebert, M., Sminchisescu, C., Weiss, Y. (eds.) ECCV 2018. LNCS, vol. 11220, pp. 595–610. Springer, Cham (2018). https://doi.org/10.1007/978-3-030-01270-0_35

Automated Cricket Commentary Generation for Videos

K. Shashank Yadav, V. Lohith[(✉)], M. S. Sachin, Madan V. Patil, and Surabhi Narayan

Department Of Computer Science and Engineering, PES University, Bengaluru, India
lohith.5292@gmail.com

Abstract. Cricket is one of the most popular sports in the world, and its fan base is growing rapidly. However, the quality of the commentary during cricket matches can vary widely, and it often relies on the subjective opinions of the commentators. In this paper, we present a groundbreaking approach to auto-generate cricket commentary using state-of-the-art computer vision and machine learning techniques. Our framework can automatically identify different events happening in a cricket video and produce insightful and engaging commentary based on the state of the game. We focus on the six essential cricket shots played by the batsman, including the Straight Drive, Cover Drive, Lofted shot, Sweep shot, and Cut Shot, and use a machine learning model to recognize each of these shots based on visual signals within the video. Along with that the length and line for the type of ball bowled has been analysed which facilitates a overall complete commentary. We also incorporate relevant data, such as the score, stage of the game, and players involved, to create contextually appropriate commentary. Our approach has the potential to revolutionize the field of sports commentary, providing a new and immersive experience for cricket fans worldwide. With our innovative approach, we believe that auto-generated commentary can become an integral part of the live sports viewing experience, enhancing fan engagement and providing new opportunities for sports broadcasters and content creators.

Keywords: computer vision · machine learning · auto-generation

1 Introduction

Cricket is the most highly followed game in India, the excitement for this game is a bit higher. The popularity of this game has mainly evolved because of the quality players playing the game and heart touching commentary that feels the game. From a business point of view, this game also creates a lot of opportunities to make money. There are certain areas in this domain that can be automated, such as the umpiring or the commentary, but this needs a deep understanding of the game by the machine.

The machine generated commentary can overcome the as- pects such as emotional interpretations of the target audience. One may say that "the commentator ruined my game" or "his commentary was biased towards some player or a team". Since the machine works only on data, the commentary generated by it would be unbiased and won't favor

H. Kaur et al. (Eds.): CVIP 2023, CCIS 2009, pp. 432–444, 2024.
https://doi.org/10.1007/978-3-031-58181-6_36

any side. Also, the cost of commentary from the machine would be cheaper than the cost of hiring a commentator, irrespective of the quality of it.

The main objective of the commentary lies in classifying the type of shot played by the batsman. Helping to Classify Shots played by the batsman would really mean having a batting coach at an affordable price. Since we know that the balance or outcome of a shot is heavily dependent on the posture in which the players play the shot. So hence we can say that if the posture of a particular shot is proper then we can expect good results for that shot. So, this would not only help in generating the commentary, but also could help a player to adjust his posture for particular shot.

The foundation of generating commentary lies in identifying the objects, the activities happening in the game and converting them then and there into textual commentary, many components of a cricket match are visible, such as batting strokes, type of ball bowled, whether it's a boundary or not, whether it's a wicket or not, or is it a good ball or not and so on. The scope of the model is mainly focused on determining six uniquely identifiable shots played by the batsman. These shots include square cut, straight drive, pull shot, loft, sweep and cover drive.

The outbreak of Covid-19 pandemic has created unprecedented challenges for various industries, and the sports industry is no exception. With travel restrictions and safety measures in place, sports commentators have encountered obstacles in reaching their studios to deliver their commentary. Even when they have the opportunity to stay within a bio-bubble, which is a controlled environment created to minimize the risk of Covid-19 transmission, the experience can become mentally exhausting. The constant presence of the same people, in the same place, and being confined to the same rooms can lead to a feeling of monotony and isolation, which can adversely impact their mental well-being. It is crucial to acknowledge and address these challenges to ensure the mental health and well-being of sports commentators, who play an essential role in the sports industry.

In addition, leveraging Computer Vision and Machine Learning algorithms for automated commentary generation can also prove to be immensely useful in generating multilingual commentary, catering to both international and regional languages in India. This approach would significantly reduce costs associated with hiring commentators proficient in multiple languages, making the commentary accessible to a wider audience and enhancing the overall viewer experience.

In such situations, we can make the best out of Computer Vision and Machine Learning algorithms by building a model that gains the knowledge from previous instances and combines the power of image processing to generate the commentary in the form of text and audio. The aim of this project is to make the process of commentary generation easier and in an automated way that can help us to solve the prior mentioned problems easily.

2   Related Work

Many works are reported in literature to classify cricket shot but not much works were found in literature to analyse and classify the length and the type of the ball bowled.

In Deoker et al. (2015) work on possible blear segmenting and classification of videos. Frame attributes like color and motion features have been used to achieve results which are stable for illumination change. Hegde et al. (2022) uses dynamic web scraping to scrape live scores and associated parameters like run rate, outcome of each ball, etc. which are then fed to a supervised learning algorithm that uses all these parameters and generates a commentary for the current ball event by selecting an appropriate commentary template from a pool of predefined commentary templates. Prathibha et al. (2015) proposes a solution which is an AI based approach that will assist the commentators in effective storytelling that is interesting to the audience, and related to what is actually happening in the game being broadcast. Lee et al. (Lee 2014) present a system called the sports commentary recommendation system (SCoReS) that can automatically suggest stories for commentators to tell during games. Devanandan et al. (2021) develop a Random Forest model to classify the cricket shot images using human body keypoints extracted with MediaPipe. Experiment results show the proposed model achieves an F1-score of 87 percent.

Jayanth et al. (Jayanth and Gowri 2014) propose visualcontent based algorithms to automate the extraction of video frames with the cricket pitch in focus. Kolekar et al. (2008) proposed video event detection and classification model using hierarchical tree which avoids shot detection and clustering. U. Arora et al (2017) devised a classification method using convolutional neural network (CNN) with Inception v3 to automatically analyze the decisions made by the third umpire and scoring systems such as umpire signal decisions. They also employed the Deep CNN technique to improve the CNN's performance. Although they have been successful in the identification of the ball and tracing its path, they haven't determined line and length of the ball which is a distinctive feature our work. Md. Ferdouse Ahmed Foysal et al (2018) proposed a 13-layered Convolutional Neural Network known as "Shot-Net" for classifying six categories of cricket shots, namely Cut Shot, Cover Drive, Straight Drive, Pull Shot, Scoop Shot, and Leg Glance Shot. This model achieved high accuracy with a low cross-entropy rate. This model only focused on the classification of the static images of the shot played upon which our work has be built to extend the work for the sequence of images treated as a video.

3   Proposed Methodology

3.1   Dataset

In the proposed method, we used a comprehensive dataset comprising of short cricket video clips for training machine learning models. The data was collected from various online platforms such as Hotstar and YouTube. The dataset contains around 800 video clips, with each shot having a duration of one to five seconds. The videos were collected for the below six shots shown in Fig. 1. Approximately 120 videos pertaining to each shot were collected.

Fig. 1. Cricket shots for which the data is collected

To classify pitch and non-pitch views, an image dataset of approximately 5000 images was collected for each. In order to reduce computational complexity the non-pitch frames were removed using the Inception V3 model. In addition, for bowling classification, 49 videos from Cricket-07 Game were obtained which had 60 balls bowled in each video among which approximately 45% were full length delivery, 35% were short pitched deliveries and remaining were full tosses or yorker length deliveries. For testing the proposed method videos of IPL 2015 matches of duration 2–3 min. were used.

The dataset was processed using MediaPipe [19] to detect the key points, with 33 keypoints being detected and trained using random forest model. Approximately 30–50 keypoints in each video clip was collected and the dataset augmentation was used to increase its size. This resulted in a total of 22000 keypoints (Fig. 2).

Fig. 2. Differentiating between non-pitch view and pitch view

Our proposed approach focuses on identifying and classifying relevant frames that contain actual gameplay, while filtering out non-pitch frames. This enables us to improve the accuracy of our classification models and generate automated cricket commentary based solely on the actual gameplay footage. By eliminating irrelevant footage, we increase the efficiency and accuracy of our approach, enhancing the overall quality of the generated commentary.

3.2 Workflow

The system comprises various modules that are organized to achieve its overall goal. These modules include Video- to-Frame conversion, Key Features extraction from frames, Classification of frames into two classes, Shot Classification, Ball Classification and Generation of video with commentary (Fig. 3).

Fig. 3. Architecture for Shot Classification Module

3.3 Shot Classification Using Pose Estimation

Pose estimation of players can be achieved through the use of the Mediapipe framework. Mediapipe is a powerful tool that can build multimodal audio, video, or time series data, and can be used for media processing and inference models like TensorFlow and TFLite.

Mediapipe being an open source framework also provides capabilities for real-time data processing, making it ideal for applications that require low-latency performance (Fig. 4).

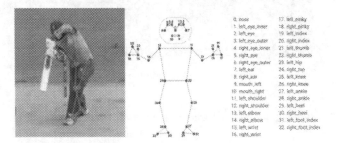

Fig. 4. Pose Estimation Points

By marking the points on the pose where the batsman is playing the shot, the coordinates can be sent to the model for training and testing, which can help determine the type of shot played by the batsman. The 33 key points collected by Mediapipe are used by the shot classification model for training and validation. Four different models were tried, but the Random Forest model performed the best, with an impressive accuracy of 98 percent.

The Ridge Classifier, Gradient Boost Classifier and the Logistic Regression model were discarded due to low metric scores. Overall, the Random Forest model was used for shot classification in this work, and proved to be the most effective in accurately classifying the type of shot played by the batsman (Fig. 5).

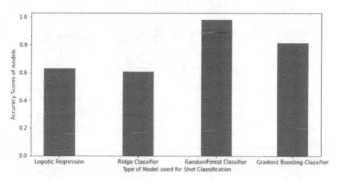

Fig. 5. Comparing the Accuracy Scores of different models that can be used for shot classification

3.4 Ball Classification

Ball classification is crucial for identifying the type of delivery being bowled, such as line and length of the delivery. This information is used to generate commentary that provides insights into the bowler's tactics, the batsman's response, and the overall match situation. Accurate ball classification helps ensure that the generated commentary is relevant and insightful, enhancing the viewer's experience and understanding of the game. By automating the process of ball classification and commentary generation, we can provide real-time analysis and insights that were previously only available to expert commentators and analysts (Fig. 6).

The automated process of ball classification begins with the identification of the ball using color segmentation, followed by contouring to determine the coordinates of the ball. These coordinates are then utilized to derive the line and length of the ball. The length of a cricket ball is determined by where it hits the pitch, and it can be classified into different categories such as short length, good length, full length, yorker, and full toss. However, for simplicity, we focus on three classifications: short-pitched bouncer, over-pitched full length delivery, and non-pitching full toss. And for the line of the ball, each ball has been classified as either of the three of outside off stump delivery, on the stump delivery and down the leg delivery.

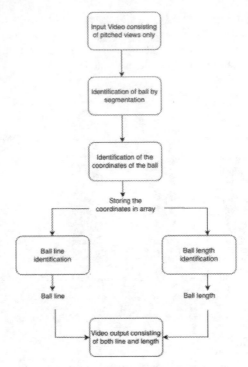

Fig. 6. Architecture for Ball Classification Module

3.5 Commentary Generation

Commentary generation is the process of automatically generating audio commentary for sports events using machine learning algorithms. By analyzing various aspects of the game such as ball identification, shot classification, and player statistics, the generated commentary can provide insightful and engaging analysis for viewers.

Shot classification and ball identification provide vital in- formation about the type of delivery bowled and the corresponding shot played. By writing this information into a file, we can then extract the necessary data to aid in generating commentary. The gathered data is formatted into readable English that is semantically correct and ready to be converted into audio. Using the built-in Python module, the data is then converted into audio and overlaid onto the video to provide a more immersive viewing experience. This process is repeated for all shot videos, and the resulting videos are then combined into a single video that represents the entire match. It is essential to ensure that the generated commentary is accurate and engaging to enhance the viewer's experience. Therefore, the quality of the data and the accuracy of the models used in shot classification and ball identification are crucial in creating an engaging commentary (Fig. 7).

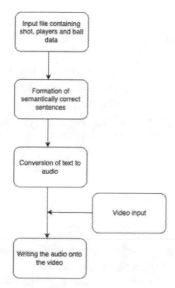

Fig. 7. Architecture for Commentary Generation Module

4   Implementation

The implementation can be broken down into four different components which are needed to be integrated together to achieve the final result.

4.1   Pitch Classification

For the task of classifying whether a frame is a pitched view or non-pitched view, the pre-existing Inception V3 was chosen as the primary model. The subsisting base model of the Inception V3 was imported and utilized for the classification. The input video was considered as a sequence of frames, and the model was applied to each frame to determine if it was a pitched view or not. The training data consisted of 5000 images of both pitched and non-pitched views. This data was obtained through physical validation and augmentation, which included flipping, rescaling, rotating, shearing, and zooming, all by a minuscule factor. The model was trained utilizing this data, and the resulting model was saved locally in the .h5 format. When a video needed to be classified, the saved model was accessed, and the video was classified. To obviate overfitting of the data and to maintain high accuracy, early stopping was utilized.

4.2   Shot Classification

A short video clip of 2–3 min. is given as input to the model, which is decomposed into frames that are used as input for the model. The first classification task is to identify whether each frame represents a pitch view or a non-pitch view. Once a pitch view is identified, the model predicts the type of shot played by the batsman in that particular frame. It is important to note that the accuracy of the model's predictions depends heavily on the quality of the input frames and the training data used to train the model. Therefore, it is essential to ensure that the video clip is of good quality and that the model is trained on a diverse set of data to improve its performance.

Subsequently, the shot classification model is applied to the frames that have been classified as pitch view frames. It is important to note that frames preceding the contact of the ball with the bat are given lesser weightage compared to frames after the contact as the latter frames are more critical for shot classification. Once the weights are assigned to the frames, the results are aggregated to determine the sequence of shots played in the pitch view frames. Overall, this process involves a step-by-step approach that efficiently categorizes the frames and assigns the necessary weights to determine the shots played during the game.

4.3   Ball Line Length Classification

The ball classification is further divided into four different phases which are ball detection, ball tracking, ball line identification and ball length identification. The first of the four phases, ball detection, is done to detect and track the ball in a cricket game video by identifying the line and length of the ball bowled. To achieve this, the processed video is converted to frames and the center pitch area is extracted utilizing ROI and thresholding. The frames with the designated

ROI are converted to grayscale and then subjected to Gaussian blur with a size of 15*15 to negate color effects. These grayscale frames are then converted to binary frames and used to engender contours that avail identify the ball. The contours are relegated as ball and non-ball classes utilizing a Random Forest Classifier. Around 500 manually validated and augmented images are utilized for both the ball and non-ball classes.

After classifying the contours as the ball, the next step is to identify the coordinates of the ball and map them into a data frame utilizing the pandas Python library. The coordinates in the data frame are then mapped to the corresponding frame, which avails in identifying the balls in that particular frame. Executing the ball identification code sanctions all the coordinates of the ball to be stored in an array, which is further utilized for determining the ball length and ball line. The stored coordinates in the array are then utilized for ball path tracing. This is achieved by joining the ball coordinates in each frame and carrying them forward to all the remaining frames. By memorizing the ball coordinates from each frame onto the further last frames, the path of the ball can be traced. For determining the length of the ball, the coordinates of the ball are plotted on a graph and the valley point is used to determine the ball length. If no valley is found, it indicates a full toss. The identified valley is then used to classify the ball into its respective length class, such as a short-pitched bouncer, an over-pitched full length delivery, or a non-pitching full toss. The ball bowled is analysed with respect to the stumps in the frame to accurately classify the line of the ball (Fig. 8).

Fig. 8. Identification of valley point to determine ball length

It is important to note that the accuracy of the ball classification process is highly dependent on the quality of the video and the effectiveness of the segmentation algorithm employed. As such, it is crucial to ensure that the input video is of high quality and that the segmentation algorithm is optimized to improve the overall accuracy of ball classification. By achieving accurate ball classification, we are able to generate insightful commentary that enhances the viewer's understanding and engagement with the game.

4.4 Audio Commentary Generation

The process of generating audio commentary for a cricket match involves formatting data on players and shots, randomly choosing adjectives to describe the shots, converting text to audio using gTTS, and using moviePy to write the audio onto the video. The audio is mapped to the corresponding frames of the video and the resulting videos are concatenated to create the final commentary.

5   Results

We evaluated our automated commentary generation system for cricket on a dataset of 2015 IPL highlight videos spanning a duration of around 2–3 min. each, a total 60 such videos consisting around 25 balls in each to total of around 1500 balls. The system successfully generated commentary for each ball, with an average overall accuracy rate of 89.06%. The following results highlight the key findings of our study.

The results obtained were through combination of the various models used three individual components namely pitch classifier, shot identifier and the ball classifier. The first of the three pitch classifier was used to classify the frames of the video into pitch and non-pitched views this was done with a dataset of 5000 pitch images and 5000 non-pitch images. The inception V3 model used here promised an accuracy of 91% (Fig. 9).

The shot identifier was used to classify the shot played by the batsman into one of the six shots previously chosen. There were four different models used for the classification which was done on the basis of the 22000 key points collected by 800 shot videos and random forest classifier was prominent among them with an accuracy of 98%. The ball classification comprised of two parts with line identification and length identification. This was brought about by classifying the patches identified as ball and non-balls this was trained using 500 ball image data and 500 non-ball image data. The former gave an accuracy of 99.6% while the latter gave an accuracy of 99%. Hence the combined total accuracy came to be 89.06% (Fig. 10 and Table 1).

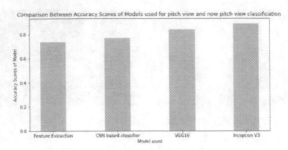

Fig. 9. Variation in accuracy with increase in dataset size for shot classification

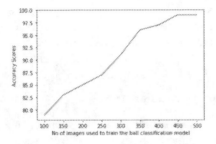

Fig. 10. Variation in accuracy with increase in dataset size for ball classification

Table 1. Metrics for Different Shot-classes

	Precision	Recall	F1-Score	Support
Cover Drive	0.98	0.96	0.97	857
Cut Shot	0.98	0.97	0.97	958
Lofted Shot	0.99	0.99	0.99	1457
Pull Drive	0.98	1.00	0.99	1441
Straight Drive	0.99	0.98	0.99	790
Sweep Shot	0.97	0.97	0.97	877

During the training process of the ball classification model, a dataset consisting of both ball and non-ball images was used. As the number of images in this dataset increased, the accuracy of the model also improved. It was observed that the accuracy of the model increased gradually with an increase in the number of both ball and non-ball images in the dataset.

The accuracy of the model eventually reached a plateau point at 500 training images for both the ball and non-ball data, meaning that further increasing the number of training images did not significantly improve the model's accuracy.

The accuracy of the random forest classifier seemed pretty low when the number of training videos were less and this number kept increasing with number of videos indicating a strong positive correlation between the two. The final accuracy came to be 98% for 800 training videos (Fig. 11).

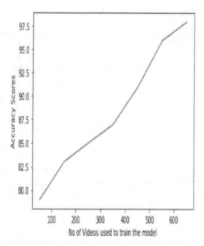

Fig. 11. Variation in accuracy with increase in dataset size for shot classification

6   Conclusion

In this work, we have developed a model for automated cricket commentary generation, recognizing the intellectual demands of the task. The model uses Inception V3 for pitch and non-pitch view classification, along with the MediaPipe library for key point extraction. Random Forest Classifier is used for shot classification based on pose. A novel method is proposed to determine ball length and line. Limitations were encountered with the Mediapipe architecture, which sometimes misidentified the wicket-keeper instead of the bats- man and had reduced accuracy for unorthodox shots. Future research aims to expand the model by exploring more cricket shots and determining shot outcomes, such as boundaries, wickets, or dot balls. Ball length can be classified based on the shot played, and swing type (inswing, outswing, or straight) can be identified.

References

1. Deokar, M.: Video shot detection & classification in cricket videos (2015)
2. Hegde, A.S., Jha, K., Suganthi, S., Honnavalli, P.B.: Automating live cricket commentary using supervised learning. In: Gupta, D., Polkowski, Z., Khanna, A., Bhattacharyya, S., Castillo, O. (eds.) Proceedings of Data Analytics and Management. LNDECT, vol. 91, pp. 37–48. Springer, Singapore (2022). https://doi.org/10.1007/978-981-16-6285-0_4
3. Prathibha and SheenaAnees. Video-based automated generation of commentary in cricket (2015)
4. Lee, G., et al.: Automated story selection for color commentary in sports. IEEE Trans. Comput. Intell. AI Games **6**, 144–155 (2014)

5. Devanandan, M., et al.: Cricket shot image classification using random forest. In: 2021 3rd International Conference on Advancements in Computing (ICAC), pp. 425–430 (2021)
6. Jayanth, S., Gowri, S.: Automated classification of cricket pitch frames in cricket video. Electron. Lett. Comput. Vis. Image Anal. **13**, 33–49 (2014)
7. Kolekar, M.H., et al.: Semantic event detection and classification in cricket video sequence. In: 2008 Sixth Indian Conference on Computer Vision, Graphics & Image Processing, pp. 382–389 (2008)
8. Soomro, K., Zamir, A.R.: Action recognition in realistic sports videos. In: Moeslund, T., Thomas, G., Hilton, A. (eds.) Computer Vision in Sports. Advances in Computer Vision and Pattern Recognition, pp. 181–208. Springer, Cham (2014). https://doi.org/10.1007/978-3-319-09396-3_9
9. Arora, U., Verma, S., Sahni, S., Sharma, T.: Cricket umpire assistance and ball tracking system using a single smartphone camera. PeerJ Preprints **5**, e3402v1 (2017)
10. Mora, S.V., Knottenbelt, W.J.: Deep learning for domain-specific action recognition in tennis. In: Proceedings of IEEE Conference on Computer Vision and Pattern Recognition Workshops (CVPRW), p. 170178 (2017)
11. Foysal, M.F.A., Islam, M.S., Karim, A., Neehal, N.: Shot-Net: a convolutional neural network for classifying different cricket shots. In: Santosh, K., Hegadi, R. (eds.) Recent Trends in Image Processing and Pattern Recognition, RTIP2R 2018, CCIS, vol. 1035, pp. 111–120. Springer, Singapore (2019). https://doi.org/10.1007/978-981-13-9181-1_10
12. Kumar, R., Santhadevi, D., Janet, B., Dr.: Outcome classification in cricket using deep learning (2019)
13. Khan, M.Z., Hassan, M.A., Farooq, A., Khan, M.U.G.: DeepCNN based data-driven recognition of cricket batting shots (2018)
14. Li, F.-F., Andrej, K., Justin, J.: Cs231n-stanford- winter1516-lecture11-slide34 (2016). Accessed 12 Mar 2016
15. Simonyan, K., Zisserman, A.: Very deep convolutional networks for large-scale image recognition (2014)
16. Wikipedia. Cross entropy — Wikipedia, the free encyclopedia (2016). Accessed 12 Mar 2016
17. Russakovsky, O., et al.: ImageNet large scale visual recognition challenge. Int. J. Comput. Vis. (IJCV) **115**(3), 211–252 (2015)
18. Wikipedia. Depth map — Wikipedia, the free encyclopedia (2014). Accessed 12 Mar 2016
19. Mediapipe Documentation - https://developers.google.com/mediapipe
20. Tensorflow Documentation. https://www.tensorflow.org/apidocs/python/tf
21. Python Documentation. https://docs.python.org/3/whatsnew/3.10.html
22. Pandas Documentation. https://developers.google.com/mediapipe

Driver Drowsiness Detection Using Vision Transformer

Shaheen Usmani, Bharat Chandwani, and Debanjan Sadhya[✉]

ABV-Indian Institute of Information Technology and Management Gwalior,
Gwalior, India
{shaheen,bcs_2019012,debanjan}@iiitm.ac.in

Abstract. The issue of driver drowsiness poses a considerable safety risk, which can result in accidents and loss of life. To confront this issue, reliable and user-friendly systems that can detect early signs of drowsiness are needed. Vision-based drowsiness detection (DDD) systems have emerged as a promising approach to achieve this goal. DDD systems combine image processing methods with artificial intelligence to monitor the driver's eyes and facial expressions and identify signs of drowsiness. In this work, we present a DDD approach using vision transformers (ViT). The attention mechanism in our proposed method focuses on the specific patches of the input image which contribute to the drowsiness phenomenon. Empirical results on the UTA-RLDD dataset show that our proposed model achieves a high level of test accuracy of **98.10** and an average prediction time of **17 ms** per frame. Hence, our approach offers a solution for detecting early signs of drowsiness, providing drivers with enough time to take corrective action and reduce accident risks.

Keywords: Driver Drowsiness Detection(DDD) · Image Processing · Vison Transformers(ViT)

1 Introduction

Driver drowsiness is a serious concern for road safety, as it can cause symptoms such as slowed response time, absence of consciousness, or micro-sleeps, all of which significantly increase the probability of accidents. In fact, continuous fatigue can impair performance levels also. The consequences of drowsy driving are alarming. According to WHO statistics, every 24 s, people die on the road. Road accidents are predicted to rank as the seventh most common cause of fatalities by the year 2030[1]. Driver drowsiness can be caused by many reasons, including lack of sleep, more workloads, uninteresting driving conditions, and environmental influences. Therefore, there is a lot of interest in the development of intelligent in-vehicle systems that monitor driver behavior to reduce accidents and improve road safety. A major area of study in this domain is Driver Drowsiness Detection (DDD) systems, which are designed to notify drivers before they fall asleep.

---

[1] https://www.who.int/news-room/fact-sheets/detail/road-traffic-injuries.

H. Kaur et al. (Eds.): CVIP 2023, CCIS 2009, pp. 445–454, 2024.
https://doi.org/10.1007/978-3-031-58181-6_37

The measures used to detect drowsiness can be broadly classified into three categories: vehicle-based, physiological, and behavioral [10]. Vehicle-based measures include monitoring lane deviation, steering wheel movements, and speed changes, which may indicate drowsiness or inattention. Physiological measures focus on changes in the driver's body that may indicate drowsiness, such as electroencephalography (EEG), heart rate variability (HRV), and pupil diameter. Behavioral measures analyze changes in the driver's behavior that may indicate drowsiness, such as eye movements, head movements, and vocalizations. In general, a combination of these measures may be used to detect drowsiness with greater accuracy. Therefore, many researchers have turned to behavioral-based signs, which are non-invasive and rely on cameras, utilizing deep learning and computer vision methodologies to extract attributes like eye blinking, facial expressions, head orientation, and instances of yawning.

The usage of deep learning techniques to detect driver drowsiness is a promising solution to prevent accidents. This can be achieved by analyzing frontal images of the driver captured by a camera mounted on the vehicle. In this regard, vision-based DDD models have significantly increased in popularity. However, identifying and classifying drowsy behaviors might be difficult, particularly in situations when there are multiple factors that can degrade video quality. Some of the more prominent factors include occlusion, illumination, weather, and bumpy roads. Therefore, a reliable DDD system should work efficiently across these conditions to be useful in real-life scenarios. The objective of this work is to present an approach to driver drowsiness detection using vision transformers and to compare its performance with existing methods. We aim to demonstrate the potential of vision-based drowsiness detection systems in improving road safety and minimizing accidents resulting from driver fatigue.

2   Related Work

Driver drowsiness detection is a significant field of research in intelligent transportation systems. Xiao et al., [10] proposed a fatigue-driving recognition system that utilizes a combination of CNN and LSTM. The system extracts the region of interest using MTCNN to extract image sequences of eyes from each video clip. The authors evaluated their system on the TJPU FDD dataset with an accuracy of 95.83% on the test set with an average test time of 132.34 ms. However, the authors note that the reflective spot affects eye clarity when the driver wears glasses. Magan et al., [6] proposed two approaches for driver drowsiness detection. The RNN and CNN are used to analyze the driver images. The second approach utilizes Dlib to extract important features from the image, such as the number of times eyes blink, average blinking duration, and the total number of micro-sleeps. The authors evaluated their system on the UTA-RLDD dataset and provides an accuracy of 55% for the first approach and 63% for the second approach.

Kang et al., [4] proposed a DDD system that employs a 3D convolutional neural network (3DCNN). The system extracts five landmarks using RetinaFace from the given input image and directly detects the mouth and right eye. The authors evaluated their system on the NTHU-DDD dataset and achieved a test accuracy of 94.74% at a sampling of 10 frames with 5 overlap frames [4]. Sara et al., [8] proposed a lightweight DDD system that utilizes a 3D-CNN and LSTM. The 3D-CNN-LSTM method processes long sequences by utilizing 3D-CNN to extract features from frames The video is normalized and resized to 60×60, and the last 50 frames are fed to 3D CNN, then LSTM. The authors evaluated their system on the 3-MDAD dataset and YawDD dataset and with an accuracy of 96% on YawDD, 90% on front 3MDAD and 93% on side 3MDAD.

3   Proposed Methodology

3.1   Face Detection and Extraction

To extract the face from an image, the DLIB library is used. This process involves four essential steps: preprocessing, face detection, face alignment, and cropping. Firstly, the original image is preprocessed by applying a Gaussian blur, which helps to smooth edges and remove noise from the image while preserving most of the image's information. Next, DLIB's face detector is utilized to identify the region of the image containing the face. The face detection step is using histograms of oriented gradients (HOG) and a support vector machine (SVM) classifier. HOG is a feature descriptor that extracts facial features from an image, and SVM is a classification algorithm that distinguishes facial from non-facial regions [5]. After the face is detected, DLIB's facial landmark detector is used to align the face by identifying the key points such as the eyes, nose, and mouth. Finally, the aligned face region is cropped and saved separately.

3.2   Model Architecture

After face detection and image augmentation, Vision Transformer (ViT) [2] is used for driver drowsiness classification. The overall architecture of ViT for driver drowsiness detection is illustrated in Fig. 1. The model basically comprises three parts: patch and positional embedding, transformer encoder and classification head.

Patch Creation. To convert the input image I into a sequence of patches IP, the image is first resized and then divided into N patches. The resolution of each patch is represented by a tuple (P, P) that is determined by the user. We represent this conversion as:

$$I \in \mathbb{R}^{H \times W \times C} \rightarrow IP \in \mathbb{R}^{N \times (P \times P \times C)} \tag{1}$$

where H, W, and C represent the height, width, and channels of the original image. Noticeably,

$$N = \frac{H \times W}{P^2} \tag{2}$$

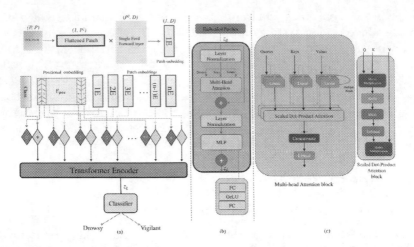

Fig. 1. (a) ViT model (b) Transformer Encoder module (c) Multi-Head Attention Block

Patch and Class Embedding. After splitting the image into patches of size $P \times P$, each patch is flattened into a matrix of size $1 \times P^2$. To obtain a linear projection of the patch, the flattened patch matrix is multiplied with an embedding matrix $F \in \mathbb{R}^{P^2 \times D}$ using a single feed-forward layer. This results in a linear projection of the patch of size $1 \times D$. This projection is then transformed into a fixed-size latent vector of dimension D, called the patch embedding $E \in \mathbb{R}^{1 \times D}$. A trainable class embedding $I_{class} \in \mathbb{R}^{1 \times D}$ is introduced and combined with the linear patch projections to support the classification head. The concatenated matrix consisting of the patch embeddings E and the class embedding I_{class} is then augmented with positional encodings to take into account the spatial relationship between patches.

Positional Encoding. In a typical transformer, the input is a sequence of tokens, each with its own positional information. In the ViT framework, the patches are treated as tokens, and positional information is added to capture the spatial relationship between the patches. To add positional encoding, a learnable positional embedding matrix $E_{pos} \in \mathbb{R}^{(N+1) \times D}$ is used. The positional encoding for each patch embedding is generated by adding the corresponding row of E_{pos} to the patch embedding, along with the class embedding. The resulting embedded sequence of patch embeddings with the class token z_0 is given by:

$$z_0 = [I_{class}; x_1 E; x_2 E; \ldots; x_n E] + E_{pos} \tag{3}$$

where x_i denotes the ith patch and E denotes the corresponding patch embedding.

Transformer Encoder. The embedded sequence of patch embeddings with the class token z_0 is input into a transformer encoder. The transformer encoder is composed of a stack of L uniform layers, each containing Multi-Headed Self-Attention (MSA) blocks and Multi-Layer Perceptron (MLP) blocks. The MSA block calculates the scaled dot-product attention for each head and concatenates the results before passing them through a feed-forward layer with learnable weights W_0. The MLP block comprises two hidden layers. The transformer encoder also comprises of a normalization layer (LN) and residual connections defined as:

$$z'l = MSA(LN(zl - 1)) + z_{l-1} \qquad (4)$$

$$z_l = MLP(LN(z'_l)) + z'_l \qquad (5)$$

where, z_{l-1} denotes the input to the lth layer, z'_l denotes the output of the MSA block in the lth layer, and z_l denotes the output of the MLP block in the lth layer.

Multi-Head Self-Attention. The Multi-Head Self-Attention (MSA) block is a key component of the transformer encoder. It operates on the input sequence in parallel, using multiple attention heads to learn different relationships between tokens. Each head has its own set of learnable query, key, and value weight matrices, which allows it to attend to different aspects of the input. The outputs from each head are concatenated and passed through a linear projection to obtain the final attention output.

3.3 Data Preparation

The input vectors are first stacked and multiplied by three weight matrices to produce three individual matrices of queries Q, keys K, and values V. Specifically, the weight matrices are $W_q \in \mathbb{R}^{d_{model} \times d_k}$, $W_k \in \mathbb{R}^{d_{model} \times d_k}$, and $W_v \in \mathbb{R}^{d_{model} \times d_v}$, where d_{model} is the dimension of the model, d_k is the dimension of the keys, and d_v is the dimension of the values. The queries, keys, and values are calculated as follows:

$$Q = XW_q, \quad K = XW_k, \quad V = XW_v \qquad (6)$$

where $X \in \mathbb{R}^{n \times d_{model}}$ is the input matrix.

$$\text{Attention}(Q, K, V) = \text{softmax}\left(\frac{QK^T}{\sqrt{d_k}}\right) V, \qquad (7)$$

where the scaling factor $\frac{1}{\sqrt{d_k}}$ is introduced to stabilize the gradients. The attention weights are calculated by feeding the dot product results to the softmax function. These weights determine how much each value in V contributes to the final output for the corresponding query. Once the attention weights are computed, the output of the MSA block is obtained by multiplying the attention weights by the value matrix V:

$$\text{MultiHead}(X) = \text{concat}\left(\text{head}_1, \ldots, \text{head}_h\right) W^O, \tag{8}$$

where h is the number of attention heads, $\text{head}_i = \text{Attention}\left(QW_i^Q, KW_i^K, VW_i^V\right)$ is the output of the i-th attention head, and W^O is a weight matrix that maps the concatenated output of all heads back to the original dimension of the input.

Multi-layer Perceptron. After the MSA block, the output is passed through a Multi-Layer Perceptron (MLP) block, which consists of two fully connected dense layers with the GeLU activation function and a skip connection with layer normalization. The output of the MSA block is first passed through a dense layer with learnable weights W_1 and bias b_1:

$$\text{MLP}_1(Q) = \text{GELU}(\text{LN}(Q)W_1 + b_1), \tag{9}$$

where LN denotes layer normalization. The output of the first dense layer is then passed through a second dense layer with learnable weights W_2 and bias b_2:

$$\text{MLP}_2(Q) = \text{LN}(\text{MLP}_1(Q)W_2 + b_2). \tag{10}$$

The output of the MLP block is computed by summing the input with the output of the second dense layer.

$$\text{MLP}(Q) = Q + \text{MLP}_2(Q). \tag{11}$$

Classification Head. After passing through the transformer encoder, the output sequence of patch embeddings is passed to the classification head for final classification. The first token of the sequence, which represents the learnable class embedding, is passed to a linear layer with weights W_{class} to obtain the class prediction probabilities, given by:

$$y = \text{softmax}(W_{class} z_0) \tag{12}$$

where y is a vector of probabilities for each class, and z_0 is the first token of the output sequence from the transformer encoder.

4   Experiments and Results Analysis

4.1   Description of the Dataset

In this work, the UTA-RLDD dataset was employed for driver drowsiness detection [3]. The dataset consists of 120 videos recorded from 60 volunteers. Each volunteer participated in two video sessions, one when they were drowsy and one when they were vigilant, resulting in a total of 120 video sessions. The duration of each video session was about 10 min, during which the volunteer was monitored with a camera. To prepare the dataset, we extracted one image per second from each video, resulting in a total of 66,521 images. The images were divided into two classes: drowsy and vigilant sessions. There were 33,211 images in the drowsy class and 33,310 images in the vigilant class.

4.2 Face Detection and Extraction

In our work, we used DLIB's face detection and extraction process to obtain a high-quality dataset for our ViT model. Once the face is detected, DLIB's facial landmark detector is used to align the face by identifying key points. The aligned face is then cropped and saved as a separate image. The resulting dataset was split into 72% training, 8% validation and 20% testing sets. The training dataset was utilized to train the deep learning models, while the validation dataset played a role in fine-tuning the hyperparameters and preventing overfitting. Lastly, the test dataset was employed to assess the models' performance on data they hadn't seen during training. The dataset consisted of 47,894 training images, 5,322 validation images, and 13,305 testing images. Figure 2 illustrates the face extraction process.

Original frame   Gaussian blur   Detected face   Cropped face

Fig. 2. Face Extraction using the DLIB library. The image sample is taken from the UTA-RLDD dataset.

4.3 ViT Parameter Tuning

The utilized ViT model was implemented using PyTorch and trained on our preprocessed dataset using the following hyper-parameters: learning rate of 0.0002, train batch size of 16, eval batch size of 8, and the seed of 42. The Adam optimizer with β of (0.9,0.999) and ϵ of 1e-08 was used, and a linear learning rate scheduler was employed. The model was trained on an input image size of 224×224 with a patch size of 16×16, resulting in 196 patches per image with 768 elements per patch. All the tuned parameter values are presented in Table 1.

Table 1. Tuning of hyper-parameters for the proposed VIT-based DDD model.

Hyperparameter	Value
Learning-Rate	0.0002
Training Batch Size	16
Evaluation Batch Size	8
Seed value	42
Optimizer	Adam
β	(0.9,0.999)
ϵ	1e-08
Numbert of Epochs	5
Image size	224×224
Patch size	16×16
Number of transformer layers	12
Number of heads	12

4.4   Simulation Results

The model's performance was evaluated using a range of metrics, such as test loss, test accuracy, test runtime and test samples per second. Figure 3 illustrates the test loss of the model, which was found to be 0.021, indicating that the model performed well in terms of minimizing the loss function. The test accuracy of the model was 0.981, which indicates that the model was able to classify the drowsy and vigilant states of the drivers with a high degree of accuracy. The corresponding confusion matrix graph is shown in Fig. 4. The test runtime of the model was 231 s, and the test samples per second were 58, which indicates that the model was efficient in processing the input data.

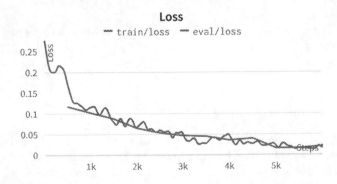

Fig. 3. Variation of the training and evaluation loss with the number of steps.

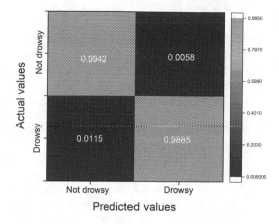

Fig. 4. The confusion matrix obtained from the proposed model.

4.5 Comparative Analysis

Table 2 demonstrates a comparison of different existing methods for driver drowsiness detection over the UTA-RLDD dataset. As observable, the proposed model comprehensively outperforms other models over the dataset. The vision transformer architecture uses a multi-head attention mechanism that highlights the important parts of an image. The proposed model is able to detect driver drowsiness efficiently due to the incorporation of the attention mechanism.

Table 2. Comparison with existing SOTA methods for DDD.

Method	Accuracy (%)
Tamanani et al. [9]	91.80
Adhinata et al. [1]	94.68
Xiao et al. [10]	94.74
Anh-Cang et al. [7]	97.00
Proposed	98.10

5 Conclusion

In this work, we propose a model for driver drowsiness detection using vision transformers. Our experimental results describe that our proposed model achieves high accuracy, with a test accuracy of 98.10% and a test loss of 0.021. Furthermore, the model was capable of processing 58 samples per second with an average test runtime of 17 ms per frame. The success of this study highlights the potential of ViTs in addressing the issue of DDD. By utilizing deep learning and computer vision techniques, we can develop more reliable and accurate systems that can help prevent accidents caused by drowsy driving, ultimately saving lives on the road. However, there is still much work to be done to further enhance the performance in this domain of study. One future direction could be the application of generative adversarial networks to augment the training data. Additionally, incorporating sensors such as heart rate monitors or eye trackers could also boost the accuracy of driver drowsiness detection.

References

1. Adhinata, F.D., Rakhmadani, D.P., Wijayanto, D.: Fatigue detection on face image using facenet algorithm and k-nearest neighbor classifier. J. Inf. Syst. Eng. Bus. Intell. **7**(1), 22–30 (2021). https://doi.org/10.20473/jisebi.7.1.22-30, https://e-journal.unair.ac.id/JISEBI/article/view/24144

2. Dosovitskiy, A., et al.: An image is worth 16 *times* 16 words: transformers for image recognition at scale (2020). https://doi.org/10.48550/ARXIV.2010.11929

3. Ghoddoosian, R., Galib, M., Athitsos, V.: A realistic dataset and baseline temporal model for early drowsiness detection. In: Proceedings of the IEEE Conference on Computer Vision and Pattern Recognition Workshops (2019)

4. Kang, N., et al.: Driver drowsiness detection based on 3d convolution neural network with optimized window size. In: 2022 13th International Conference on Information and Communication Technology Convergence (ICTC), pp. 425–428 (2022). https://doi.org/10.1109/ICTC55196.2022.9952988

5. King, D.E.: Dlib-ml: a machine learning toolkit. J. Mach. Learn. Res. **10**, 1755–1758 (2009)

6. Magán, E., Sesmero, M.P., Alonso-Weber, J.M., Sanchis, A.: Driver drowsiness detection by applying deep learning techniques to sequences of images. Appl. Sci. **12**(3) (2022). https://doi.org/10.3390/app12031145, https://www.mdpi.com/2076-3417/12/3/1145

7. Phan, A.C., Nguyen, N.H.Q., Trieu, T.N., Phan, T.C.: An efficient approach for detecting driver drowsiness based on deep learning. Appl. Sci. **11**(18) (2021). https://doi.org/10.3390/app11188441, https://www.mdpi.com/2076-3417/11/18/8441

8. Sara A. Alameen, A.M.A.: A lightweight driver drowsiness detection system using 3dcnn with LSTM. Comput. Syst. Sci. Eng. **44**(1), 895–912 (2023). https://doi.org/10.32604/csse.2023.024643, http://www.techscience.com/csse/v44n1/48052

9. Tamanani, R., Muresan, R., Al-Dweik, A.: Estimation of driver vigilance status using real-time facial expression and deep learning. IEEE Sens. Lett. **PP**, 1 (2021). https://doi.org/10.1109/LSENS.2021.3070419

10. Xiao, Z., Hu, Z., Geng, L., Zhang, F., Wu, J., Li, Y.: Fatigue driving recognition network: fatigue driving recognition via convolutional neural network and long short-term memory units. IET Intell. Transp. Syst. **13**, 1410–1416(6) (2019). https://digital-library.theiet.org/content/journals/10.1049/iet-its.2018.5392

ConvMTL: Multi-task Learning via Self-supervised Learning for Simultaneous Dense Predictions

Vijayasri Iyer[1] , Senthil Kumar Thangavel[1]([✉]) ,
Madhusudana Rao Nalluri[2] , and Maiga Chang[3]

[1] Department of Computer Science and Engineering, Amrita School of Computing,
Amrita Vishwa Vidyapeetham, Coimbatore 641112, India
t_senthilkumar@cb.amrita.edu
[2] Department of Computer Science and Engineering, Amrita School of Computing,
Amrita Vishwa Vidyapeetham, Amaravati 522503, India
n_madhusudanarao@av.amrita.edu
[3] School of Computing Information and Systems, Athabasca University,
Alberta, Canada
maigac@athabascau.ca

Abstract. Perception systems in autonomous vehicles are required to perform multiple scene-understanding tasks under tight constraints of latency and power. Single-task neural networks can become unscalable when the number of tasks increases in the perception stack. Multi-task learning has been shown to improve parameter efficiency and enable models to learn more generalizable task representations compared to single-task neural networks. This work explores a novel convolutional multi-task neural network architecture that simultaneously performs two dense prediction tasks, semantic segmentation and depth estimation. A self-supervised ResNet-50 backbone is used as the basis of the proposed network, along with a multi-scale feature fusion module and a dense decoder. The model uses a simple weighted loss function with an informed search algorithm identifying the optimal parameters. The performance of the proposed model on the segmentation task is assessed using the mean Intersection of Union (mIoU) and pixel accuracy. In contrast, absolute and relative errors assess the depth estimation task. The obtained results for segmentation and depth estimation are mIoU of 73.81%, pixel accuracy of 93.52%, an absolute error of 0.130, and a relative error of 29.05. The model's performance is comparable to existing multitask algorithms on the Cityscapes dataset, using only 2975 training samples.

Keywords: Multi-task Learning · Transfer Learning · Deep Learning · Computer Vision · Autonomous Driving

1 Introduction

The increased demand for intelligent transport systems has spurred the development of autonomous vehicles. Such a vehicle depends on its software system

H. Kaur et al. (Eds.): CVIP 2023, CCIS 2009, pp. 455–466, 2024.
https://doi.org/10.1007/978-3-031-58181-6_38

to make efficient, quick, and safe decisions on the road. The perception stack of an autonomous vehicle leverages recent advances in deep learning to make sense of the surroundings using sensors like Cameras, RADAR, and LiDAR. This safety-critical application must operate within the deployed hardware platform's stringent cost and power limitations. The perception system performs hundreds of downstream tasks, which can make the single neural network per task setup unscalable. As a consequence, companies are slowly transitioning towards multi-task learning. Multi-task learning involves using a single neural network that simultaneously learns to solve multiple tasks. The Multi-task learning paradigm is considered a good fit for autonomous vehicle software systems for several reasons, including parameter efficiency, implicit data augmentation, and better generalisation of learned representations by a neural network [1]. Apart from the latency reduction at inference time, multiple works have also demonstrated that specific tasks learned by a neural network could benefit from sharing the model parameters and representations and learning from richer loss functions [2].

This work proposes a novel convolutional neural network architecture to perform two dense prediction tasks: semantic segmentation and depth estimation via transfer learning. Semantic segmentation and depth estimation allow for precise localization and navigation of an autonomous vehicle by enabling many downstream tasks, such as obstacle distance estimation, scene understanding, and reconstruction. In the domain of autonomous vehicles, the primary challenge lies not in the scarcity of data, but from the lack of labelled data, especially for multi-task learning. To address this limitation, we enhanced our multi-task learning framework by incorporating a backbone that is pre-trained using self-supervised learning [3]. Self-supervised learning is a methodology employed to train models in a supervised manner, using unannotated raw data, with the objective of learning intricate and informative representations. Lastly, in a multi-task learning setup, combining tasks and loss functions in a naive manner can be detrimental, leading to negative transfer, a form of destructive interference. This reduces accuracy across all tasks over the single neural network per task setup. We discuss how to deal with this issue using an informed search method to find the optimal weight parameters for each loss for smooth training. Our contributions are as follows :

1. A self-supervised approach to pre-training the multi-task model's encoder network (ResNet-50) using 19,998 raw unlabelled images.
2. A novel decoder architecture using multi-scale feature fusion that can perform semantic segmentation and depth estimation via transfer learning with a limited number of labelled samples.

The structure of our paper is as follows: Sect. 2 will cover previous works done in multi-task learning and self-supervised learning. Section 3 will cover the model architecture and the dataset in detail. Section 4 discusses our results and the details for training and hyperparameter tuning. Section 5 is the conclusion, followed by references.

2   Related Work

2.1   Datasets

Ideally, a multi-task learning dataset should be annotated using the same input data for multiple tasks. The popular datasets that exist for multi-task learning on joint semantic segmentation and depth prediction are the Cityscapes dataset [4], the KITTI benchmark suite [5], Virtual KITTI [6], NYUD dataset [7] and the SUN RGBD Dataset [8]. Since Cityscapes [4] has balanced and synchronous annotations for real road scenes, we train and evaluate our proposed model using this dataset for both the semantic segmentation and depth estimation tasks. Due to the challenging nature of the dataset, most of the proposed multi-task models employ relatively complex task-weighting strategies and have a large number of parameters.

2.2   Multi-task Learning

Multi-task learning architectures can be categorized as hard-parameter sharing and soft-parameter methods. The hard-parameter sharing methods are generally more parameter-efficient than their soft counterparts. Some of the popular soft parameter sharing methods include the MTAN network [9] with an attention-augmented SegNet, the GradNorm [10], PCGrad [11], CrossStitch [12] and Sluice Networks [13], AdaMT-Net [14]. The main challenge with these methods is that they either require meticulous tuning of hyperparameters, are hard to inter- pret or are computationally expensive. Simple approaches that primarily focus on the loss weighting, are the uncertainty weighting method [15], which dynami- cally balances the importance of different tasks based on via a homoskedastic loss function, MultiNet++ [16] that uses a geometric mean of the loss function to cal- culate weights. The XTasc-Net [17] and methods introduce attention structures between the decoders and MT-UNet [18] introduces an adaptive weight learn- ing mechanism along with decoder cross-talk. Previous approaches following a similar network architecture to ours have been successful, including Quadronet [19], which proposes a state-of-the-art, RetinaNet-based [20] architecture, deliv- ering real-time results on four tasks of the Cityscapes dataset; however, the train their approach with a large annotated private dataset (1.2 million images), requiring significant labour and resources. Some noteworthy references such as the ParetoMTL [21] and NashMTL [22], consider the multi-task loss function as a multi-objective optimization problem. The uniqueness of our work is that we employ a simple loss weighting approach coupled with the use of Bayesian optimization search to find weight parameters, which we use for optimal weight tuning.

2.3   Self-supervised Multi-task Learning

The combination of self-supervised and multi-task learning has gained attention recently as it offers a potential solution to acquiring labelled data for various tasks. The model can benefit from both the learned representations and the shared knowledge across tasks by pre-training a model on a self-supervised task and then fine-tuning it for multiple downstream tasks. The seminal approach to self-supervised learning is the SimCLR [23]. Other approaches, such as the SimSiam [24], BYOL [25], and Masked Autoencoders [26], are used in conjunction with datasets of different sizes and different architectures. While traditional multi-task methods well explore the Cityscapes dataset, there has been limited exploration into efforts that leverage unlabelled data. The most popular work on multi-task self-supervised learning is [27], where the authors propose a ResNet101-based network. The work that is the most similar to ours is [28], where the authors propose a framework that uses self-supervised learning to improve performance on semantic segmentation and learning depth and colourization in a multi-task fashion using the ResNet18 model. Instead of using the Imagenet data for self-supervised pre-training, we propose a simple pre-training of the encoder using the extra training data from the same dataset for learning raw representations.

Multitask Learning models require a large number of simultaneous labelled samples for training. Self-supervised models also require very large amounts of unlabelled data for self-supervised training. However, this requires a lot of data annotation and computational training resources. This work primarily focuses on an approach that performs comparably to the top-performing multi-task models on the Cityscapes dataset with limited labelled data. Furthermore, the self-supervised training scheme is also resource-efficient, making it suitable for scenarios with low computing resources and training time constraints.

3   Methodology

The two most important components of a multi-task learning problem are the network architecture and the choice of the loss function. In this section, we discuss the preliminaries of the architecture and the architecture in detail. We also provide details of the loss function and the task weighting strategy used for our model.

3.1   Architecture

Our multi-task network architecture consists of the following components: an encoder, a multi-scale feature fusion module, two task-specific decoders and task heads (Fig. 1).

Encoder. We choose a ResNet-50 backbone having 23 M parameters as our encoder network due to its superior performance on the ImageNet benchmark. The encoder model is trained in a self-supervised manner with extra training data provided in the Cityscapes dataset. The ResNet architecture was chosen for its training stability and ease of use in the self-supervised setting.

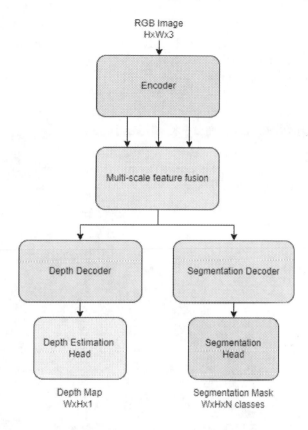

Fig. 1. ConvMTL Architecture

Multi-scale Feature Fusion. The multi-scale feature fusion module consists of a BiFPN (Bidirectional Feature Pyramid Network) [29] that takes in features from various levels of the encoder as an input and aggregates them using repeating pyramidal structures of neurons. The BiFPN model uses a series of bottom-up and top-down pathways to generate a rich set of features at multiple scales, merged through the bidirectional connections to produce a set of features that can be used for downstream perception tasks. The BiFPN also possesses a channel-wise attention mechanism, making it helpful in learning task-specific features.

Decoder. The model has two task-specific decoders. The inputs from the BiFPN are sent to the decoder to learn task-specific features. The structure of the dense decoder is identical for both tasks. It consists of 5 upsampling blocks, each consisting of a convolution, a batch normalization layer and the Mish [30] activation function. The output from the decoder is then sent to the task-specific heads.

Task Heads. The semantic segmentation head consists of a single convolutional layer followed by a bilinear upsampling layer and an output layer. The depth estimation head is identical in structure with the main difference being in the number of output feature maps (N,C,H,W) where N is the number of classes, C is the number of channels and H,W is the height and width of the output map.

3.2   Self-supervised Pre-training

The encoder model is trained using the SimSiam [24] algorithm. In SimSiam, a Siamese neural network architecture is employed, consisting of two identical branches that share weights. The network is trained to predict the representations of augmented versions of the same input data while maximizing the similarity between the representations produced by the two branches. Like SimCLR, SimSiam also uses a contrastive loss. However, the latter does not require negative samples and works well in situations with limited data. Figure 2 illustrates the SimSiam method.

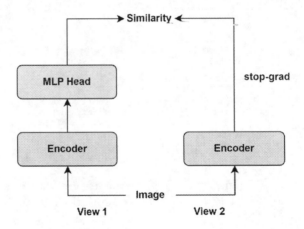

Fig. 2. SimSiam Architecture

3.3   Loss Function

Multi-task learning is considered to be a multi-objective optimization problem. Since a network is learning multiple tasks simultaneously, the resulting loss function required to be optimized has a complex search space compared to the individual task losses involved. As mentioned in the introduction, many methods have been proposed to find the optimal weights for a multi-objective weighted loss and optimal solutions for the loss search space. We experiment with a simple linear weighted loss function with α and β as the corresponding weight coefficients for each task loss. We use a simple pixel-wise cross-entropy loss shown in

Eq. 1 function for the semantic segmentation task. The depth estimation task is performed with an L1 Norm loss shown in Eq. 2

$$L_{Seg} = -\sum_{c=1}^{M} y_{o,c} \log(p_{o,c}) \tag{1}$$

where c is the number of classes, o is the observation and

$$L_{Depth} = \sum_{i=1}^{M} \|y_{true} - y_{pred}\| \tag{2}$$

and

$$L_{Total} = \alpha \cdot L_{Seg} + \beta \cdot L_{Depth} \tag{3}$$

The deep learning model's convergence depends on the scales, convergence rates and complexities of the individual loss function. We use a Bayesian search optimisation method to find the weighted parameters α and β.

4 Experimental Results

This section discusses the dataset, evaluation metrics, implementation details, and the qualitative results for each task.

4.1 Dataset Description

The Cityscapes dataset [3] consists of high-resolution images of urban street scenes for a wide range of object and semantic classes collected across many European cities. The semantic segmentation annotations consist 2975 images, with 19 semantic class-level labels and 7 category-level labels. To avoid any issues of class imbalance, we choose the 7 category-level labels for our segmentation task. For depth estimation, a disparity map is provided, which is the inverse depth map, computed from stereo images using the SGM algorithm. For this task, we use the raw disparity map to avoid any artifacts created when converting the disparity to a depth map for the ground truth labels. The dataset also contains an extra training set consists of 19998 images with coarse annotations which we use as raw images for our self-supervised backbone.

4.2 Experimental Setup

The proposed network architecture was implemented in PyTorch. During training, we used the AdamW optimizer with an initial learning rate of 1e–3 and a weight decay of up to 1e–6. For the learning rate scheduler, we use cosine annealing with warm restarts to boost gradient updates in the network and prevent optimizing to a local minimum. The model was trained for 100 epochs with a batch size of 4. The training was performed on an A100 GPU, taking approximately 5 min per epoch. The data were downsampled to an input size of 128

× 256 and augmented using the scales of 1.0, 1.2, 1.5 and random flips. All the parameters were initialized with a seed of 54321. The BiFPN, decoder and heads were initialized with 'Xavier Normal' weights.

SimSiam Training: We use a ResNet50 backbone with the initialized Imagenet weights for our contrastive pre-training. The network was trained using the 19998 extra training images provided in the dataset. The network was trained for 20 epochs with a batch size of 32 along with a scaled learning rate. An embedding dimension of 1000 is used along with a bottleneck dimension of 128.

Encoder: During the multi-task training phase, we use the pre-trained ResNet50 backbone. To provide more learning capacity to the model, we unfreeze the last block of the backbone network so that the network can learn a high-level generalized feature space.

BiFPN Parameters: The BiFPN consists of 128 pyramid channels, 3 cell repeats, and convolutional channels of 512, 1024, and 204 for each repeat. The attention mode of the BiFPN was set to true, and the value of the epsilon parameter was set to 1e-5. The epsilon value of 1e-5 is suited for low-resolution images and objects of large sizes.

Decoder Parameters: The dense decoder also had 128 pyramid channels and 128 segmentation channels with a dropout of 0.4 in the last layer of the decoder.

Loss Weights: Through a parameter sweep via Bayesian Optimization, the optimal alpha and beta values are found to be 0.1 and 0.5.

The total size of our network amounts to 30M parameters. The evaluation metrics used for the segmentation task are mean-intersection over union (mIoU) and pixel-wise accuracy. At the same time, the depth estimation task uses mean absolute error and relative error to measure the accuracy of the depth map. For the Bayesian search optimization to find alpha and beta, we use the Bayesian sweep method in the Weights and Biases SDK to perform our search with the total loss as the objective. The Lightly library was used to perform the contrastive pre-training.

4.3   Discussion

The ResNet50 model is trained in a self-supervised manner with the SimSiam algorithm before it is used in the multi-task learning setup. A plot of the image embeddings encoded by the backbone model is shown in Fig. 3. The images sent to the self-supervised backbone are converted to embeddings and then plotted as clusters. Hence, images with similar surroundings and scene representations appear close to each other (semantically similar).

The proposed model is compared against the other multi-task learning methods mentioned in the introduction section that performs 7-class semantic segmentation and depth estimation on the Cityscapes dataset. The results are provided in Table 1. We also provide the results for the 19-class segmentation task with depth estimation in Table 2.

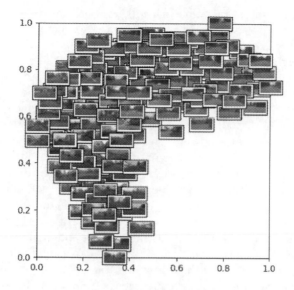

Fig. 3. Self-supervised Embeddings Scatterplot

Table 1. Results: 7-class segmentation and depth estimation on the Cityscapes validation dataset.

Method Name	Segmentation		Depth Estimation	
	$mIoU\uparrow$	$Pix.\ Acc\uparrow$	$Abs.\ Err\downarrow$	$Rel.\ Err\downarrow$
STAN	51.90	90.87	0.0145	27.46
Dense	51.89	91.22	0.0134	25.36
CrossStitch	50.31	90.43	0.0152	31.26
MTAN	53.04	91.11	0.0144	33.63
PCGrad	53.59	91.45	0.0171	31.34
AdaMT-Net	62.53	94.16	0.0125	22.23
XTasc-Net	66.51	93.56	0.0122	19.40
MT-Unet	73.19	96.86	0.0137	27.50
Ours	**73.81**	**93.52**	**0.0130**	**29.05**

Table 2. Results: 19-class segmentation and depth estimation on the Cityscapes validation dataset.

Method Name	Segmentation		Depth Estimation	
	$mIoU\uparrow$	$Pix.\ Acc\uparrow$	$Abs.\ Err\downarrow$	$Rel.\ Err\downarrow$
MT-Unet	34.53	94.42	0.0142	28.75
Ours	51.31	90.56	0.0135	30.34

With the Bayesian optimization method, we were able to examine the early impact of the choice of α and β on L_{total} as the main objective. The weight choice of α has a more significant impact on performance. Moreover, lower values of α along with higher values of β lead to the better overall performance of the model. This can be attributed to the difference in the scales of the cross-entropy and L1 norm losses. Since the segmentation loss is of a higher scale, the value of the objective function tends to depend more on the segmentation task for convergence, leading to poor convergence on the depth estimation task.

We employ smaller batch sizes for the training and validation set. The training process of the network results in minor but constant oscillations during the process of loss convergence. Our model reported a training mIoU of 78.89% and 95.56% segmentation pixel accuracy along with 0.0078 absolute error and 20.33 relative error. The convergence rates of different tasks in multi-task learning can vary depending on various factors, such as the similarity of the tasks, the complexity of the network architecture, and the amount and quality of training data available for each task. In general, tasks that are more similar and share common features tend to converge faster than dissimilar tasks. Depth estimation is a more complex task that requires a longer convergence time but whereas segmentation which is a task that requires lower-level feature representations converges faster than tasks that require higher-level abstractions, such as scene-understanding or reasoning. Secondly, convergence also depends upon the bounds of the loss function. The segmentation loss and depth estimation loss have output values which are orders of magnitude apart from each other.

5   Conclusion

In this work, we have presented a self-supervised convolutional model capable of performing semantic segmentation and depth estimation simultaneously. We demonstrated how the encoder-decoder architecture is ideal for feature extraction and learning of task-specific features even with a very limited set of parameters. Our results indicate that the method achieves competitive performance concerning the baseline multi-task algorithms on the Cityscapes dataset. Our approach offers a training framework that learns from labelled and unlabeled data and can be easily extended to other tasks, such as instance segmentation and optical flow estimation, by adding additional output heads to the network and extracting features at multiple levels of the multi-scale feature extraction module. The limitations of our approach are that it has undergone testing on a very limited diversity of data, and the parameter tuning is done specifically for the Cityscapes dataset. To evaluate the robustness of this model, we aim to test it on various large and small multi-task datasets. Exhaustive search trials need to be conducted to compare multiple optimization techniques and other loss weighting methods. Further research can also be conducted to devise larger datasets and task-weighting schemes to achieve state-of-the-art and real-time performance.

References

1. Ruder, S.: An overview of multi-task learning in deep neural networks. arXiv preprint arXiv:1706.05098 (2017)
2. Standley, T., Zamir, A., Chen, D., Guibas, L., Malik, J., Savarese, S.: Which tasks should be learned together in multi-task learning?. In: International Conference on Machine Learning, pp. 9120-9132. PMLR (2020)
3. Balestriero, R., et al.: A cookbook of self-supervised learning. arXiv preprint arXiv:2304.12210 (2023)
4. Cordts, M., et al.: The cityscapes dataset for semantic urban scene understanding. In: Proceedings of the IEEE Conference on Computer Vision and Pattern Recognition, pp. 3213–3223 (2016)
5. Liao, Y., Xie, J., Geiger, A.: KITTI-360: A novel dataset and benchmarks for urban scene understanding in 2D and 3D. IEEE Trans. Pattern Anal. Mach. Intell. **45**(3), 3292–3310 (2022)
6. Gaidon, A., Wang, Q., Cabon, Y. and Vig, E.: Virtual worlds as proxy for multi-object tracking analysis. In: Proceedings of the IEEE Conference on Computer Vision and Pattern Recognition, pp. 4340–4349 (2016)
7. Couprie, C., Farabet, C., Najman, L., LeCun, Y.: Indoor semantic segmentation using depth information. arXiv preprint arXiv:1301.3572 (2013)
8. Song, S., Lichtenberg, S., Xiao, J.: SUN RGB-D: A RGB-D scene understanding benchmark suite. In: Proceedings of the 28th IEEE Conference on Computer Vision and Pattern Recognition (CVPR 2015) (2015)
9. Liu, S., Johns, E., Davison, A.J.: End-to-end multi-task learning with attention. In: Proceedings of the IEEE/CVF Conference on Computer Vision and Pattern Recognition, pp. 1871–1880 (2019)
10. Chen, Z., Badrinarayanan, V., Lee, C.Y., Rabinovich, A.: Gradnorm: Gradient normalization for adaptive loss balancing in deep multitask networks. In: International Conference on Machine Learning, pp. 794–803. PMLR (2018)
11. Yu, T., Kumar, S., Gupta, A., Levine, S., Hausman, K., Finn, C.: Gradient surgery for multi-task learning. In: Advances in Neural Information Processing Systems, vol. 33, pp. 5824–5836 (2020)
12. Misra, I., Shrivastava, A., Gupta, A., Hebert, M.: Cross-stitch networks for multi-task learning. In: Proceedings of the IEEE Conference on Computer Vision and Pattern Recognition, pp. 3994–4003 (2016)
13. Ruder, S., Bingel, J., Augenstein, I., Søgaard, A.: Latent multi-task architecture learning. In: Proceedings of the AAAI Conference on Artificial Intelligence, vol. 33, no. 01, pp. 4822–4829 (2019)
14. Jha, A., Kumar, A., Banerjee, B., Chaudhuri, S.: AdaMT-Net: an adaptive weight learning based multi-task learning model for scene understanding. In: 2020 IEEE/CVF Conference on Computer Vision and Pattern Recognition Workshops (CVPRW), Seattle, WA, USA, pp. 3027–3035 (2020). https://doi.org/10.1109/CVPRW50498.2020.00361.
15. Kendall, A., Gal, Y., Cipolla, R.: Multi-task learning using uncertainty to weigh losses for scene geometry and semantics. In: Proceedings of the IEEE Conference on Computer Vision and Pattern Recognition, pp. 7482–7491 (2018)
16. Chennupati, S., Sistu, G., Yogamani, S., Rawashdeh, S.A.: Multinet++: Multi-stream feature aggregation and geometric loss strategy for multi-task learning. In: Proceedings of the IEEE/CVF Conference on Computer Vision and Pattern Recognition Workshops (2019)

17. Nakano, A., Chen, S., Demachi, K.: Cross-task consistency learning framework for multi-task learning. arXiv preprint arXiv:2111.14122 (2021)
18. Jha, A., Kumar, A., Banerjee, B., Chaudhuri, S.: AdaMT-net: an adaptive weight learning based multi-task learning model for scene understanding. In: 2020 IEEE/CVF Conference on Computer Vision and Pattern Recognition Workshops (CVPRW), Seattle, WA, USA, pp. 3027–3035 (2020). https://doi.org/10.1109/CVPRW50498.2020.00361
19. Goel, K., Srinivasan, P., Tariq, S., Philbin, J.: Proceedings of the IEEE/CVF Winter Conference on Applications of Computer Vision (WACV), pp. 315–324 (2021)
20. Lin, T.Y., Goyal, P., Girshick, R., He, K., Dollár, P.: Focal loss for dense object detection. In: Proceedings of the IEEE International Conference on Computer Vision, pp. 2980–2988 (2017)
21. Lin, X., Zhen, H.L., Li, Z., Zhang, Q.F., Kwong, S.: Pareto multi-task learning. In: Advances in Neural Information Processing Systems, vol. 32 (2019)
22. Navon, A., et al.: Multi-task learning as a bargaining game. arXiv preprint arXiv:2202.01017 (2022)
23. Chen, T., Kornblith, S., Norouzi, M., Hinton, G.: A simple framework for contrastive learning of visual representations. In: International Conference on Machine Learning, pp. 1597–1607. PMLR (2020)
24. Chen, X., He, K.: Exploring simple siamese representation learning. In: Proceedings of the IEEE/CVF Conference on Computer Vision and Pattern Recognition, pp. 15750–15758 (2021)
25. Grill, J.B., et al.: Bootstrap your own latent-a new approach to self-supervised learning. Adv. Neural. Inf. Process. Syst. **33**, 21271–21284 (2020)
26. He, K., Chen, X., Xie, S., Li, Y., Dollár, P., Girshick, R.: Masked autoencoders are scalable vision learners. In: Proceedings of the IEEE/CVF Conference on Computer Vision and Pattern Recognition, pp. 16000–16009 (2022)
27. Zhang, J., Zhang, H., Wang, Y., Sun, Q., Gao, J., Li, J.: Boosting semantic segmentation with multi-task self-supervised learning for autonomous driving applications. arXiv preprint arXiv:2204.08412 (2022)
28. Doersch, C., Zisserman, A.: Multi-task self-supervised visual learning. In: IEEE International Conference on Computer Vision (ICCV), pp. 2051–2060 (2017)
29. Tan, M., Pang, R., Le, Q.V.: Efficientdet: scalable and efficient object detection. In: Proceedings of the IEEE/CVF Conference on Computer Vision and Pattern Recognition, pp. 10781–10790 (2020)
30. Misra, D.: Mish: a self regularized non-monotonic activation function. arXiv preprint arXiv:1908.08681 (2019)

Payload Length and Location Identification Using a Novel CNN and Re-embedding Strategy in Stego Images Created by Content Adaptive Steganographic Algorithms

E. Amrutha$^{(\boxtimes)}$ ⓘ, S. Arivazhagan ⓘ, W. Sylvia Lilly Jebarani ⓘ, and S. T. Veena ⓘ

Mepco Schlenk Engineering College, Sivakasi 626005, Tamil Nadu, India
amrutha@mepcoeng.ac.in

Abstract. With the rapid development of technology in the modern digital world, covert communication of secret information as a payload without instigating visible attention by using steganography emerged as a possible threat. Steganalysis is the counter attack to steganography. Research is being carried out vastly to differentiate an innocent cover image from stego image and identifying steganographic method while very few attempts have been made to identify payload length and location information. In this work, a novel convolutional neural network regressor is proposed to identify the embedding change rate which gives the length of payload. In addition to identifying the suspicious content length, location of the payload bits is identified using a re-embedding algorithm from the flipped locations of stego images. Then this information is used to provide an estimate of the hidden secret. Experiments are carried out using spatial content-adaptive algorithms namely Highly Undetectable SteGO with Bounding Distortion (HUGO-BD), Wavelet Obtained Weights (WOW) and Spatial Universal Wavelet Distortion (S-UNIWARD) on BOSSBase database with five payload bins such as 0.1, 0.2, 0.3, 0.4 and 0.5 bpp. From the experimental results it is shown that the proposed model outperforms state-of-the-art steganalysis features and regressors.

Keywords: Steganography · Steganalysis · Convolutional neural network regressor · Re-embedding

1 Introduction

Steganography is an art of information hiding to hide secret data i.e., payload within any media. The counter process which unearths the hidden payload is referred as steganalysis [1]. With the abundant availability of steganographic tools in the Internet some unlawful agencies use this technique to convey illicit information in the form of web images and other media files such as audio, text, image, etc. Due to the popular usage of digital images in social media they prevail to be common choice for any illicit steganographer to communicate secrets. Steganalysis can be passively done to just identify whether or not an image is cover (image before data is hidden) or stego (image after data is hidden).

© The Author(s), under exclusive license to Springer Nature Switzerland AG 2024
H. Kaur et al. (Eds.): CVIP 2023, CCIS 2009, pp. 467–478, 2024.
https://doi.org/10.1007/978-3-031-58181-6_39

Active steganalysis focusses on identifying the specific embedding method. Quantitative steganalysis estimates some important parameters for further analysis, such as message length, embedded locations, secret keys used in embedding, etc. Steganographic algorithms are generally of two types namely, content-adaptive and non content adaptive. Content-adaptive algorithms embed payload in difficult image content regions. This makes steganalysis of such algorithms a tougher task. Hence this research focusses on quantitative steganalysis of content-adaptive steganographic algorithms. The remainder of the paper is organized as follows: Sect. 2 provides related works, Sect. 3 details the proposed work followed by experimental results and discussions in Sect. 4. Finally, conclusion is given in Sect. 5.

2   Related Works

Many researchers have developed high dimensional feature sets and powerful classifiers to attack steganography. Both machine learning [2, 3] and deep learning [4–10] approaches are crafted to achieve passive and active steganalysis. But the estimation of payload hidden using content-adaptive algorithms is very meagre. A preliminary search for the stego key using a distributed computing framework was done by [11]. In [12] and [13], methods for estimating secret message hidden using least significant bit (LSB) embedding at random pixel positions was developed. A weighted stego filter approach to determine the locations of payload for LSB Replacement steganographic algorithm was developed [14]. An improved method of universally identifying stego payload locations in the LSB steganography is proposed in [15]. They estimated the cover from the stego image by a locally weighted bivariate shrinkage function using wavelet transforms. In regression based quantitative steganalysis as proposed by [16], stego images created with multiple payloads by a steganographic method are used for training a regressor which is fed with the embedding change rate between corresponding stego and cover as train label. The regressor tries to fit a curve for the estimated change rate values for the train samples and while testing, new sample's embedding change rate can be obtained from regressor's prediction. From the embedding change rate, payload length can be estimated as $M = n \times q$, where n is the number of pixels in the stego image after embedding q bits [12]. Liu et al. proposed an attempt to locate flipped pixel locations in stego images created by content-adaptive algorithms [17]. In [18], a CNN model is proposed to estimate the hidden message length. By analyzing the syndrome-trellis encoding process, embedded messages under known cover images are extracted in [19].

From the careful study of literature in different aspects of steganalysis of content-adaptive steganographic algorithms it is observed that, research in quantitative steganalysis of spatial content-adaptive algorithms is hardly attempted due to the high correlation of interclass and also intraclass variation in the embedding pattern among those stego images. This served as a main motivation for the proposed work. The contributions of the proposed research work are given below:

a) Quantitative steganalysis is accomplished using a novel convolutional neural network as a regressor with reduced errors in estimating the payload length for spatial content-adaptive steganographic algorithms.

b) Location of the flipped pixel locations is identified by a re-embedding strategy with the end result of extracting the hidden secrets from stego images.

3   Proposed Methodology

3.1   Quantitative Steganalysis for Payload Length Estimation in Content-Adaptive Stego Images

Quantitative steganalysis estimates the number of embedding changes or the secret message length in stego images. In this work, a novel CNN model is proposed to estimate the length of hidden payload for the steganographic algorithm identified from the previous process. It is accomplished by regression using hand-crafted features proposed by authors in [9]. Figure 1 depicts the block diagram of the convolutional neural network architecture proposed for quantitative steganalysis of content-adaptive steganographic algorithms.

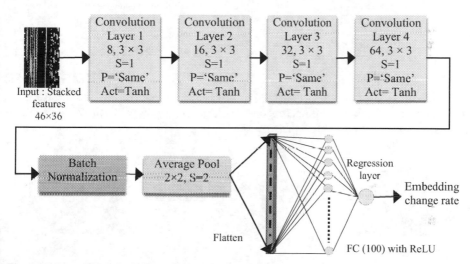

Fig. 1. Schematic of the CNN architecture proposed for Quantitative steganalysis of content-adaptive steganographic algorithms

The CNN architecture displayed in Fig. 1 consists of four convolution layers with Tanh activation to learn the embedding change rate. This proposed CNN architecture with four layers is a result of the experimentation with different number of layers and activation functions. The regression layer with only one neuron and loss function as 'mean-squared-error' acts as quantitative regressor. This neuron predicts the embedding change rate of a given test sample, since the training is done with the embedding change rates of training samples as labels. The network is trained by Momentum based Stochastic Gradient Descent (MSGD) optimization algorithm for 1000 epochs, momentum value of 0.9 and constant learning rate of 0.001 to learn the stego images with varying payloads of individual algorithms.

3.2 Re-embedding Strategy for Payload Location Estimation in Content-Adaptive Stego Images

Inspired from [17], in this work re-embedding strategy is used by modifying the locations of stego pixels considered. The pseudocode to locate suspicious regions modified by content-adaptive steganography is provided below.

Algorithm	Location of flipped pixels by Re-embedding method

Input   : S – Stego Image   α bpp – relative payload
Output: Extended Modification Map
1: Generate a random bit stream at relative payload α bpp.
2: Use the same algorithm (used to generate S) and generate a new stego image S' by embedding the bit stream into S. This is termed as re-embedding process.
3: Form a modification map from the original and modified images as follows:

$$Mod_{map}(i,j) = \begin{cases} 255, & \text{if pixel at } (i,j) \text{ is modified} \\ 0, & \text{otherwise} \end{cases} \tag{1}$$

4: Since it is not always guaranteed for a pixel to be modified twice, an attempt is made by additionally marking a modified pixel's neighbour also as modified within a margin $K \in [1, 3]$. This is now called as extended modification map and expressed as follows.

$$Mod^e_{map}(i \pm K, j \pm K) = \begin{cases} 255, & \text{if pixel at } (i,j) \text{ is modified} \\ 0, & \text{otherwise} \end{cases} \tag{2}$$

The dimension of the adjacent pixel regions is $(2K + 1) \times (2K + 1)$ and the non zero locations correspond to the flipped pixels. An example to illustrate the re-embedding process by using WOW at 0.1 bpp is depicted in Fig. 2.

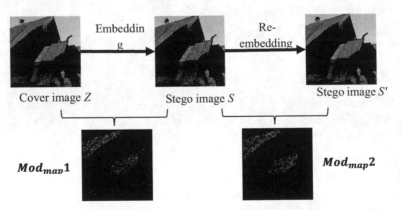

Fig. 2. Illustration of Re-embedding steps using WOW algorithm at 0.1 bpp payload

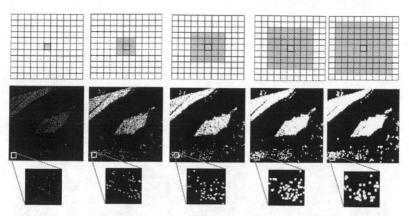

Fig. 3. Illustration of adjacent 'Full pattern' regions of a pixel in several different margin values $K = 0, 1, 2, 3, 4$

From Fig. 3 it can be observed that, with increasing margin, a greater number of innocent cover pixels might also be considered as stego pixels. For a K value of 1, 2, 3 and 4, the number of neighbour pixels selected are 8, 24, 49 and 81 respectively. Thus, in the place of just one pixel, large numbers of pixels are chosen. In order to overcome this drawback, in the proposed work there are few changes made in selecting the adjacent pixels for $K \in [1, 4]$. First method is done by only considering the adjacent next pixel in row and column. It is referred as 'Fourth quadrant pattern' because it looks like fourth quadrant of a 2-D graph. Second and third methods are done by interleaving one pixel in different positions and thereby referred as 'Checkerboard pattern' and 'Plus pattern'

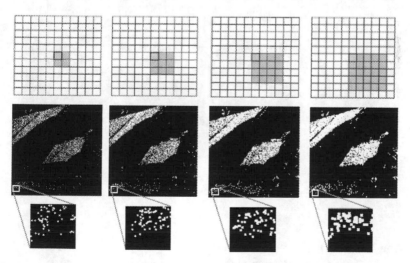

Fig. 4. Illustration of adjacent 'Fourth quadrant pattern regions of a pixel in several different margin values $K = 1, 2, 3, 4$

respectively. Figure 4, 5 and 6 depict the adjacent regions of a modified pixel using the proposed three methods.

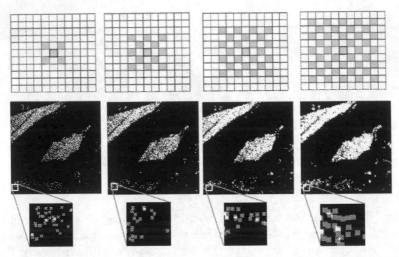

Fig. 5. Illustration of adjacent 'Checkerboard pattern' regions of a pixel in several different margin values $K = 1, 2, 3, 4$

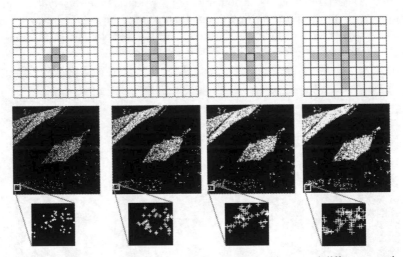

Fig. 6. Illustration of adjacent 'Plus pattern' regions of a pixel in several different margin values $K = 1, 2, 3, 4$

The number of neighbour pixels of a single modified pixel (i,j) selected by the four patterns for $K = 1, 2, 3$ and 4 inferred from Fig. 4, 5 and 6 are given as follows:

- Full pattern - 8, 24, 48 and 80
- Fourth quadrant pattern - 3, 8, 15 and 24
- Checkerboard pattern - 4, 12, 24 and 41

– Plus pattern - 4, 8, 12 and 16

Thus, compared to the existing Full pattern method, the count of neighbourhood pixels is remarkably reduced by the proposed three methods which leads to lesser innocent pixels to be mistaken for stego pixels.

4 Experimental Results and Discussions

4.1 Steganographic Algorithms and Dataset

The spatial domain content-adaptive steganographic algorithms namely HUGO-BD [20], S-UNIWARD [21] and WOW [22] are used to generate stego images with relative low volume payloads of 0.1 bpp, 0.2 bpp, 0.3 bpp, 0.4 bpp and 0.5 bpp. The payload is a random binary bit stream generated according to the relative payload size. MATLAB codes for these algorithms are downloaded and used from Binghamton web site [23]. The cover images are taken from the standard dataset Break Our Steganographic System database (BOSSbase v1.01) [24] which consists of 10,000 Gy scale images in raw, uncompressed format. They have been converted to BMP format. There are totally 15,000 stego images generated from 1,000 cover images using 3 algorithms in 5 payload bins.

4.2 Quantitative Steganalysis of Content-Adaptive Steganographic Algorithms

The main aim of this experiment is to get an approximate estimate of the length of the payload hidden. The performance metrics used for analyzing the quantitative steganalysis task are given as follows: Mean Squared Error, Root Mean Square Error and Interquartile range.

$$MSE(y, \hat{y}) = \frac{1}{N} \sum_{i=1}^{N} (y - \hat{y})^2 \tag{3}$$

$$RMSE(y, \hat{y}) = \sqrt{\frac{1}{N} \sum_{i=1}^{N} (y - \hat{y})^2} \tag{4}$$

$$IQR = Q_3 - Q_1 \tag{5}$$

where, y is the target and $\hat{y}$ is the predicted value of a given sample. Lower the MSE, better is the performance of the regressor. A similar measure to evaluate the regressor is the RMSE, which tells how concentrated the data points are around the best fit line. IQR is a variability measure obtained by dividing the given data samples into quartiles. $Q1$ is the first quartile which calculates the median of the smallest n samples. $Q2$ is simply the median of the entire samples and the median of the n largest samples is the third quartile $Q3$. The performance of the CNN regressor is compared with two traditional regressors such as Least-squares boosting regressor [25] and Support Vector Regressor [26]. The regressors are trained and tested with the combination of MoR features. Table 1

Table 1. Quantitative steganalysis results for stego images created using content-adaptive algorithms

Algorithm	Regressor type	RMSE	MSE	IQR
HUGO-BD	SVR [25]	4.627×10^{-2}	3.581×10^{-3}	7.458×10^{-2}
	LSBoost [26]	3.315×10^{-2}	1.416×10^{-3}	2.882×10^{-2}
	Proposed CNN	$\mathbf{1.528 \times 10^{-2}}$	$\mathbf{3.257 \times 10^{-4}}$	$\mathbf{2.827 \times 10^{-2}}$
WOW	SVR [25]	4.677×10^{-2}	4.251×10^{-3}	7.122×10^{-2}
	LSBoost [26]	3.430×10^{-2}	1.655×10^{-3}	2.999×10^{-2}
	Proposed CNN	$\mathbf{1.559 \times 10^{-2}}$	$\mathbf{3.319 \times 10^{-4}}$	$\mathbf{2.950 \times 10^{-2}}$
S-UNIWARD	SVR [25]	3.025×10^{-2}	1.529×10^{-3}	5.010×10^{-2}
	LSBoost [26]	2.758×10^{-2}	9.889×10^{-4}	2.433×10^{-2}
	Proposed CNN	$\mathbf{1.309 \times 10^{-2}}$	$\mathbf{2.374 \times 10^{-4}}$	$\mathbf{2.366 \times 10^{-2}}$

provides the quantitative steganalysis results for the proposed CNN regressor along with the traditional regressors.

From Table 1 it is inferred that, compared to the traditional regressors the proposed CNN architecture achieved reduced errors in estimating the embedding change rate. Among the three content-adaptive algorithms, MSE is minimum for S-UNIWARD algorithm due to the difference observed among stego images created with varying payloads. Since WOW algorithm produces the lowest embedding change rate, it is difficult to identify the change rate among WOW stego images of multiple payloads.

Comparison with Existing Steganalyzers

For comparing the developed quantitative steganalyzer with existing works, state-of-the-art (SOTA) features namely SRMQ1 [2] and maxSRMd2 [3] are used with support vector regressor for HUGO-BD, WOW and S-UNIWARD. Table 2 provides the comparison of MSE obtained by the proposed and existing steganalytic regressors for content-adaptive steganographic algorithms. It can be inferred that MSE of the proposed method is much lower than the SOTA regressors.

Table 2. MSE Comparison of Proposed Quantitative steganalyzer with existing steganalytic regressors for content-adaptive algorithms

Algorithm	SRMQ1 regressor [2]	maxSRMd2 regressor [3]	Proposed CNN regressor
HUGO-BD	1.857×10^{-3}	7.358×10^{-3}	$\mathbf{3.257 \times 10^{-4}}$
WOW	1.938×10^{-3}	7.754×10^{-3}	$\mathbf{3.319 \times 10^{-4}}$
S-UNIWARD	1.362×10^{-3}	5.371×10^{-3}	$\mathbf{2.374 \times 10^{-4}}$

4.3 Locating Payload in Content-Adaptive Steganographic Algorithms

The metric to analyze the performance of the proposed method is: F1-score, $F1 = (2 \times P \times R)/(P + R)$, where Precision rate, $P = m/n$, Recall rate, $R = m/q$, m is the number of pixels correctly predicted by re-embedding, n is the number of pixels modified by the first embedding and q is the number of pixels modified by the re-embedding.

The location of stego pixels using $K = 0$ is depicted in Fig. 7 for WOW algorithm at payloads 0.1 bpp, 0.3 bpp and 0.5 bpp payload bins.

(a) 0.1 bpp   (b) 0.2 bpp   (b) 0.5 bpp

Fig. 7. Payload Locations for a sample stego image created by WOW using 'Full Pattern'

From Fig. 7 it is seen that, for 0.1 bpp payload, the number of original flipped locations is 4,395 and the number of identified locations through re-embedding is 4,334. Among the 4,334 locations only 551 locations correspond to the original flipped locations of the stego image. When the payload in increased to 0.5 bpp, the flipped locations are also increased to 3,623. Now, the re-embedding process locates 31,449 flipped pixels with 9,273 correct locations. Thus, when the neighbourhood margin is 0, the probability of acquiring flipped pixel locations is very low. Hence in the proposed method different neighbourhood margins are proposed to extract correct flipped pixel locations. Comparison of F1-scores is given in Table 3.

From Table 3, it is observed that, as the margin is increased, F1-score begins to drop. It is mainly due to the inclusion of innocent cover as modified pixels. For each of the three algorithms, the Plus pattern neighbourhood alone yields improved F1-score. The F1-score is somewhat better for HUGO-BD and WOW algorithms but low for S-UNIWARD. Thus, it is concluded that, payload location identification is difficult for S-UNIWARD stego images compared to WOW and HUGO-BD.

Table 3. F1-score comparison for the Neighbourhood methods for different algorithms

Pattern	Algorithm	HUGO-BD		WOW		S-UNIWARD	
	Margin	*K = 1*	*K = 3*	*K = 1*	*K = 3*	*K = 1*	*K = 3*
Full	**0.1 bpp**	0.1823	0.1066	0.197	0.1269	0.1054	0.0764
	0.3 bpp	0.286	0.2115	0.3088	0.2421	0.2005	0.1587
	0.5 bpp	0.3774	0.3105	0.4189	0.3564	0.2737	0.2229
Fourth Quadrant	**0.1 bpp**	0.2014	0.1428	0.2052	0.1634	0.1033	0.0939
	0.3 bpp	0.3024	0.2518	0.3202	0.2832	0.2025	0.187
	0.5 bpp	0.3882	0.3498	0.4236	0.3952	0.2774	0.2584
Checker board	**0.1 bpp**	0.1898	0.1299	0.2033	0.1538	0.1089	0.0909
	0.3 bpp	0.2958	0.2387	0.3185	0.2743	**0.2014**	0.1852
	0.5 bpp	0.3844	0.3372	0.4232	0.3848	0.2746	0.2548
Plus	**0.1 bpp**	**0.2025**	**0.1546**	**0.207**	**0.1784**	**0.1105**	**0.0998**
	0.3 bpp	**0.3041**	**0.2623**	**0.3217**	**0.2927**	0.2012	**0.1931**
	0.5 bpp	**0.3896**	**0.3568**	**0.4269**	**0.401**	0.2774	**0.2659**

4.4 Extraction of Secret Hidden Using Content-Adaptive Steganographic Algorithms

By obtaining an approximate estimate of the stego pixel locations from the proposed neighbourhood patterns, secret can be extracted approximately. For visual interpretation, once the locations are extracted, bits are ordered as per the original payload location with zeros filling up unidentified locations for this experimentation, a standard test image – Mandrill [27] is considered as secret. The results are given in Table 4.

Table 4. Extracted Secrets from Content Adaptive stego images for $K = 4$

Algorithm	0.1 bpp	0.2 bpp	0.3 bpp	0.4 bpp	0.5 bpp
HUGO-BD					
WOW					
S - UNIWARD					

5 Conclusion

This paper presented the quantitative steganalysis to estimate payload length and payload location identification which is a very important step in active steganalysis leading to extraction of secret. For estimating the embedding payload length of stego images created using content-adaptive steganographic algorithms, the proposed CNN regressor gave reduced MSE of 3.257×10^{-4}, 3.319×10^{-4} and 2.374×10^{-4} for HUGO-BD, WOW and S-UNIWARD respectively compared to the other regressors. From the experiments carried out for payload location estimation, re-embedding method using the same algorithm with proposed Plus pattern neighbourhood is the best than other patterns and provided better F1-score for the three algorithms considered. As a future work, the proposed work shall be employed for non-content adaptive steganographic algorithms.

References

1. Fridrich, J.: Steganography in Digital Media: Principles, Algorithms, and Applications. Cambridge University Press, New York (2010)
2. Kodovský, J., Fridrich, J.: Rich models for steganalysis of digital images. IEEE Trans. Inf. Forensics Secur. **7**(3), 868–882 (2012)
3. Denemark, T., Sedighi, V., Holub, V., Cogranne, R., Fridrich, J.: Selection-Channel-Aware rich model for steganalysis of digital images. In: IEEE International Workshop on Information Forensics and Security (2014)
4. Pibre, L., et al.: Deep learning is a good steganalysis tool when embedding key is reused for different images, even if there is a cover source-mismatch. In: Proceedings of Media Watermarking, Security, Forensics, San Francisco, pp. 14–18 (2016)
5. Xu, G., et al.: Structural design of convolutional neural networks for steganalysis. IEEE Signal Process. Lett. **23**(5), 708–712 (2016)
6. Xu, G., et al.: Ensemble of CNNs for steganalysis: an empirical study. In: Proceedings of the of 4th ACM Workshop Information Hiding and Multimedia Security, Vigo, Spain, pp. 103–107 (2016)
7. Liu, K., et al.: Ensemble of CNN and rich model for steganalysis. In: Proceedings of the International Conference on Systems, Signals and Image Processing (IWSSIP), Poznan, Poland, May 2017

8. Arivazhagan, S., Amrutha, E., Sylvia Lilly Jebarani, W., Ananthi Roy, S.: Digital image steganalysis: a survey on paradigm shift from machine learning to deep learning based techniques. IET Image Process. **15**(2), 504–522 (2021)

9. Arivazhagan, S., Amrutha, E., Sylvia Lilly Jebarani, W., Veena, S.T.: Hybrid convolutional neural network architecture driven by residual features for steganalysis of spatial steganographic algorithms. Neural Comput. Appl. **33**(17), 11465–11485 (2021)

10. Amrutha, E., Arivazhagan, S., Sylvia Lilly Jebarani, W.: MixNet: a robust mixture of convolutional neural networks as feature extractors to detect stego images created by content-adaptive steganography. Neural Process. Lett. (2022)

11. Provos, N., Honeyman, P.: Detecting Steganographic Content on the Internet. Michigan, USA (2001)

12. Fridrich, J., Goljan, M., Du, R.: Reliable detection of LSB steganography in color and grayscale images. In: Proceedings of the ACM Workshop on Multimedia and Security (2001)

13. Fridrich, J., Goljan, M.: On estimation of secret message length in LSB steganography in spatial domain. In: Proceedings of the SPIE 5306, Security, Steganography, and Watermarking of Multimedia Contents VI (2004). https://doi.org/10.1117/12.521350

14. Ker, A.D.: Locating steganographic payload via WS residuals. In: Proceedings of the 10th workshop on Multimedia & Security (MM&Sec 2008), pp. 27–32 (2008)

15. Veena, S.T., Arivazhagan, S.: Universal secret payload location identification in spatial LSB stego images. Ann. Telecommun. **74**, 273–286 (2018)

16. Chen, M., Boroumand, M., Fridrich, J.: Deep learning regressors for quantitative steganalysis. IS&T Proc. Electron. Imaging Media Watermarking Secur. Forensics **30**, 160-1–160-7 (2018)

17. Liu, Q., Qiao, T., Xu, M., Zheng, N.: Fuzzy localization of steganographic flipped bits via modification map. IEEE Access **7**, 74157–74167 (2019)

18. Gomis, F.K., Bouwmans, T., Camara, M.S., Diop, I.: Estimation of the hidden message length in steganography: a deep learning approach. In: Boumerdassi, S., Renault, É., Mühlethaler, P. (eds.) MLN 2019. LNCS, vol. 12081, pp. 333–341. Springer, Cham (2020). https://doi.org/10.1007/978-3-030-45778-5_22

19. Li, J., Luo, X., Zhang, Y., Zhang, P., Yang, C., Liu, F.: Extracting embedded messages using adaptive steganography based on optimal syndrome-trellis decoding paths. Digit. Commun. Netw. **8**(4), 455–465 (2022)

20. Filler, T., Fridrich, J.: Gibbs construction in steganography. IEEE Trans. Inf. Forensic Secur. **5**(4), 705–720 (2010)

21. Holub, V., Fridrich, J.: Designing steganographic distortion using directional filters. In: Proceedings of the IEEE International Workshop on Information Forensics and Security (WIFS 2012), Costa Adeje, Spain, pp. 234–239 (2012). https://doi.org/10.1109/WIFS.2012.6412655

22. Holub, V., Fridrich, J.: Digital image steganography using universal distortion. In: Proceedings of the ACM Workshop on Information Hiding and Multimedia Security, IH&MMSec, vol. 13, p. 59 (2013)

23. Holub, V., Sedighi, V., Denemark, T., Fridrich, J.: Steganographic algorithms (2015). http://dde.binghamton.edu/download/stego_algorithms/

24. Bas, P., Filler, T., Pevný, T.: Break our steganographic system: the ins and outs of organizing BOSS. In: Filler, T., Pevný, T., Craver, S., Ker, A. (eds.) IH 2011. LNCS, vol. 6958, pp. 59–70. Springer, Heidelberg (2011). https://doi.org/10.1007/978-3-642-24178-9_5

25. Hastie, T., Tibshirani, R., Friedman, J.: The Elements of Statistical Learning. Springer Series in Statistics. Springer, New York (2009). https://doi.org/10.1007/978-0-387-84858-7

26. Awad, M., Khanna, R.: Support vector regression. In: Efficient Learning Machines, pp. 67–80. Apress, Berkeley (2015). https://doi.org/10.1007/978-1-4302-5990-9_4

27. USC-SIPI image database. https://sipi.usc.edu/database/

Feature Fusion and Multi-head Attention Based Hindi Captioner

Virendra Kumar Meghwal[✉], Namita Mittal, and Girdhari Singh

Malaviya National Institute of Technology, Jaipur, Rajasthan, India
2018rcp9061@mnit.ac.in
http://www.mnit.ac.in

Abstract. Deep learning-based methods are extensively used in image captioning, but most of these methods depend on features from a single encoder for generating captions. Different encoders capture different features of an image, and thus, using features from multiple encoders may help improve the models' performance. Moreover, there needs to be more research on Hindi caption generation on large datasets such as MSCOCO. Recently, transformers have performed well on tasks such as image classification and object detection. One such transformer is the Swin Transformer. It captures both local as well as global information present in the image. A Faster RCNN, on the other hand, captures only local (object-level) information but does not capture global details. Using a single image feature generation method might sometimes result in incorrect feature generation, or some important objects may be missed while generating the feature vector. This problem can be mitigated by combining features from different methods. Furthermore, as local features-based models have produced better results in different domains, utilizing both Swin Transformer and Faster RCNN may result in better captioning models. This work proposes to use Swin Transformer-based image features along with Faster RCNN-based image features to generate Hindi captions for images. A decoder with two GRUs and Multi-head Attention uses these image features to build Hindi captions. Experiments demonstrate that the proposed method can generate high-quality captions while improving the performance of automatic evaluation metrics, establishing the method's efficacy.

Keywords: Image Captioning · Feature Fusion · Computer Vision · Natural Language Processing

1 Introduction

Automatic image captioning is a task that involves training deep neural networks to enable them to generate captions for a given image in any natural language. For this, the machines first need to learn to identify different types of information about the image, such as different objects, their relationship, context, and scene. As this task is computationally intensive, performing it along with the image

H. Kaur et al. (Eds.): CVIP 2023, CCIS 2009, pp. 479–487, 2024.
https://doi.org/10.1007/978-3-031-58181-6_40

captioning task is difficult. Transfer Learning (TL) helps us in this regard. The encoder models are trained separately on large datasets to learn different features from the image. Then, using TL, these pre-trained models are used to extract image features, and these features are input to our downstream task of image captioning. Thus, the work is reduced to training a decoder for the task of image captioning. Such networks using an encoder and a decoder are called encoder-decoder networks.

Different image feature generation models have been proposed by researchers from time to time. Swin Transformer (ST) [1] has shown promising results in various computer vision tasks, such as image classification and object detection. Its hierarchical structure and shifting windows allow it to efficiently capture long-range dependencies and fine-grained details. Faster R-CNN, on the other, is used for detecting objects in an image. It first generates object proposals using a region proposal network and then uses a region-based Convolutional Neural Network (CNN) to detect and classify objects in an image. Both these encoder networks are state-of-the-art (SOTA) models in Computer Vision related tasks. Existing models use a single encoder, which might sometimes generate incorrect features or may miss some important objects while generating the features. This problem can be mitigated by combining features from multiple encoders. This work proposes to utilize two encoders ST and Faster RCNN for feature generation. Moreover, local features-based models have produced better results in different domains, so combining local features from different encoders may help improve model performance. Furthermore, a decoder is also proposed that utilizes two Gated Recurrent Units (GRU) as it can remember long-term dependencies and a Multi-head Attention (MHA) network to attend to multiple features simultaneously and select the salient features among them during caption generation.

This work has following contributions:

- Extracting and employing multiple image features from Swin Transformer and a Faster RCNN.
- Experimenting with different decoder networks to utilize these image features for Hindi caption generation.
    - a decoder with two GRUs and a MHA network to generate Hindi captions is proposed.
    - Training and testing these models using MSCOCO dataset and compare the results show our model's performance.

2   Related Work

Image captioning has been gaining popularity among researchers. Most methods use the Encoder-Decoder-based framework [2–5]. Following are some of the key approaches for image captioning.

Xu et al. [3] proposed visual attention for generating the captions. They used a CNN to encode image features and an Long Short-Term Memory (LSTM) as a decoder, along with soft attention or hard attention to generate captions.

Anderson et al. [5] presented a bottom-up attention network for caption generation. They used a Faster RCNN for extracting image features followed by a two LSTM-based decoder with bottom-up attention. Cornia et al. [6] proposed a Transformer with meshed memory. The encoder of the model consists of a stack of memory-augmented encoding layers, and the decoder consists of a stack of meshed decoding layers. The encoder, with the help of memory-augmented attention, encodes multi-level visual relationships exploiting a priori knowledge. The meshed decoding layers use meshed cross attention, and each layer takes advantage of all the encoding layers while generating the sentence words. Pan et al. [7] X-Linear Attention Network (X-LAN) that utilizes a bilinear pooling mechanism and squeeze-excitation to help the model to capture higher-order inter-modal and intra-modal features. The encoder uses a Faster R-CNN to identify image regions, which are then used by a stack of X-LAN to generate enhanced region and image-level features. The decoder employs a combination of LSTM, X-LAN, and gated linear unit to build the caption.

However, most of these methods are based on the English language. Recently, researchers have started using developing image captioning methods for other languages. Following is some of the work that has been done in this domain for the Hindi language. In [8], the author performed automatic translation followed by a manual correction to generate Hindi annotations for the Visual Genome dataset [9]. Using this dataset, authors in [10,11] presented a VGG16 and LSTM-based network for caption generation in Hindi. Another paper [12] proposed a VGG19-based encoder and a stacked LSTM decoder for caption generation.

MSCOCO dataset [13] was translated and manually annotated by authors of [14,15]. They proposed an attention-based GRU decoder and a transformer-based decoder for generating captions. EfficientNet(B5)-based encoder followed a decoder with attention, and GRU is proposed in [19]. In another work [20], the authors used a dynamic convolution-based ResNet101 followed by X-LAN and LSTM. Dense image captioning models are proposed in [21,22].

Most approaches discussed above use image features extracted from a single pre-trained encoder. Some of the work that employs features from multiple models are: In [23], the authors use features from a ResNet101 and a Faster R-CNN along with spatial information and apply spatial attention and an adaptive LSTM to generate captions. Meghwal et al. [24] proposed a decoder with two LSTM with self-attention and MHA in between them to attend to features from ResNet101 and a Faster R-CNN. However, both of these methods generate captions in the English language and are based on combining global features with local features. Thus, research and experimentation are required to investigate the use of multiple features. Moreover, with the development of newer deep learning architectures, better feature encoders are available, and their usage and fusion with other encoder features need further work.

3 The Proposed Work

In this section, first, overview of our architecture is discussed briefly, and then the decoder's architecture is covered in detail.

3.1   Overview of Architecture

The overview of the proposed model is presented in Fig. 1. Image feature vectors are extracted using a pre-trained ST and a pre-trained Faster R-CNN [5] for the MSCOCO dataset denoted by S and L, respectively. These features are then passed to the proposed decoder for further processing and generation of the caption. The proposed decoder consists of two GRUs and an MHA [25] between them. The first GRU takes the ST features (S) as input, and its output is passed to the MHA along with feature vector L to select the attended features. The second GRU then uses these attended features to select the caption words.

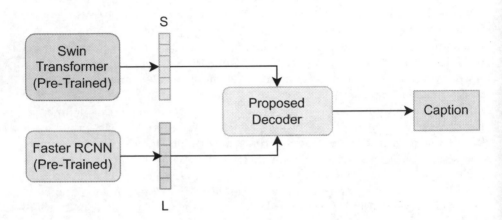

Fig. 1. Architectural overview of the presented model. (L, S denotes object features from Faster RCNN and ST features respectively.)

3.2   Decoder Architecture

The proposed decoder consists of 2 GRUs and a MHA network, as shown in Fig. 2. The image feature vector S generated by the ST is passed to GRU-1 with the context embedding vector X_t. The X_t represents the embedding vector of the currently formed sentence at time t-1 generated by an embedding layer. The task for GRU-1 is to understand the current context from X_t and, based on that, select important information from S, represented by hidden vector h_1.

$$h_1 = GRU_1(x_t \oplus S) \tag{1}$$

This hidden vector, along with features L, is then passed to the MHA network, which uses multiple heads to apply attention over them and selects the attended features A_t. These features are then concatenated with the hidden vector h_1.

$$A_t = MHA(h_1, L) \tag{2}$$

$$C_t = A_t \oplus h_1 \tag{3}$$

The concatenated vector C_t is then passed to the second GRU (GRU-2), which processes the vector to generate hidden vector h_2 containing information that helps to select next word.

$$h_2 = GRU_2(C_t) \tag{4}$$

$$W_t = Softmax(h_2 \tag{5}$$

Softmax is finally applied on the hidden vector h_2 to generate a probability vector for different words. The word with the highest probability is selected and appended to the current sentence. This process is repeated till the caption is complete.

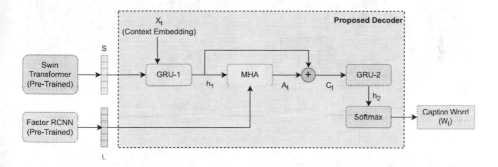

Fig. 2. Detailed diagram of the proposed decoder. (h_1, x_t, A_t, C_t, h_2 and W_t represents hidden state vector from GRU-1, context vector, attended features from MHA, concatenated feature vector, hidden state vector from GRU-2 and caption word generated at time stamp t respectively.)

4   Experiments and Results

This section, briefly describes the dataset, experimental configurations, and evaluation metrics used for performing the experiments. Then, various SOTA methods for Hindi captioning are contrasted using metrics for automatic evaluation. Further, sample images are presented along with captions generated by our proposed model and different experimented models in Fig. 3.

Our model(s) use the openly available and widely used MSCOCO [13] dataset for training. The images and their respective captions (five each) are divided into training, validation, and testing sets according to the Karpathy split [26]. For experimentation, a minibatch size of 12 and a starting learning rate of $2e^{-4}$, which is updated periodically is used. The model is trained for around 40 epochs,

Model-1: एक बिल्ली बिस्तर पर लेटी हुई है ।
Model-5: एक बिल्ली बिस्तर के ऊपर लेटी हुई है ।
Proposed: एक बिल्ली कंबल के नीचे से झाँक रही है ।

Model-1: एक इमारत के पास एक ट्रेन ट्रैक पर एक ट्रेन ।
Model-5: एक यात्री ट्रेन जो एक पुल के ऊपर से जा रही है ।
Proposed: एक नीली ट्रेन एक पुल के ऊपर से जा रही है ।

Model-1: एक डेस्क पर एक डेस्कटॉप कंप्यूटर और एक कीबोर्ड ।
Model-5: एक डेस्क पर एक कंप्यूटर , कीबोर्ड और माउस ।
Proposed: एक डेस्क पर एक कंप्यूटर , कीबोर्ड , माउस और अन्य सामान ।

Model-1: एक रेस्तरां में कई अलग-अलग प्रकार के पिज्जा ।
Model-5: एक काउंटर के ऊपर बैठे पिज्जा का एक गुच्छा ।
Proposed: एक काउंटर पर कई अलग-अलग प्रकार के पिज्जा ।

Model-1: एक कड़ाही में एक कड़ाही में सब्जियों का एक गुच्छा ।
Model-5: एक कड़ाही में मांस और सब्जियों का मिश्रण ।
Proposed: एक कड़ाही में सब्जियों के साथ भोजन का मिश्रण ।

Model-1: सड़क के किनारे एक बड़ी घड़ी ।
Model-5: शहर की सड़क पर एक पोल पर एक घड़ी ।
Proposed: शहर की सड़क पर एक पोल पर एक घड़ी ।

Fig. 3. Some sample images with captions generated by different models.

and during check-pointing, the model state with the lowest loss is saved as the best model. Label smoothing is applied, and KL Divergence loss is used for training the models.

The BLEU [27] automatic evaluation metrics is used to compare the proposed work with existing SOTA methods. It uses n-gram precision to evaluate generated captions based on the ground truth captions. Different decoder architectures are explored and the results are presented in Table 1.

Table 1. Comparing the proposed method with existing SOTA methods based on encoder, decoder and n-gram BLEU evaluation scores. Existing SOTA methods for hindi image captioning use a split of 82K, 800, 800 for training, validation and testing purpose. As, this split is currently unavailable, Karpathy split [26] of 113k, 5k, 5k is used in our experiments.

Method	Encoder	Decoder	B1	B2	B3	B4
Dhir et al. [14]	ResNet101	Attention + GRU + FC	57.0	39.1	26.4	17.3
Mishra et al. [15]	ResNet101	Transformer	62.9	43.3	29.1	19.0
Mishra et al. [16]	MUXNet	X-Linear Attention + Bi-LSTM	67	47.9	32.1	20.8
Mishra et al. [17]	ResNet101	Attention + GRU	67	47.8	31.9	21.2
Mishra et al. [18]	ECA-Net	Attention + GRU	**67.4**	49	33.3	21.9
Model-1	ST	LSTM + FC	63.3	46.5	33.2	23.4
Model-2	ST + F-RCNN	LSTM + FC	63.0	46.6	33.5	23.9
Model-3	ST + F-RCNN	LSTM + Attention + LSTM	63.6	47.2	34.1	24.2
Model-4	ST + F-RCNN	GRU + Attention + GRU	63.2	46.5	33.3	23.6
Model-5	ST + F-RCNN	LSTM + MHA + LSTM	63.5	46.7	33.4	23.7
Proposed	ST + F-RCNN	GRU + MHA + GRU	63.9	47.4	**34.2**	**24.3**

As evident from Table 1, the proposed work outperforms existing works on B3 and B4 metrics. Higher B3 and B4 scores are more desirable compared to B1 and B2, as it means that more consecutive words generated by our approach match those in the ground truth caption. Most existing architectures use image features from a single pre-trained model; in contrast, our model uses features from two different pre-trained models and is thus able to outperform existing works. Moreover, when comparing the proposed model with Model-5, the MHA network performed comparatively better with the GRU-based decoder than it did with the LSTM-based decoder. The performance improvement thus can be attributed to the use of multiple features and the combination of GRU and MHA networks.

One limitation of this work is that it is computationally and memory-wise more expensive compared to approaches based on a single encoder. Another limitation is that it always uses both types of features; instead, a mechanism can be developed to identify when to use a single feature and when to use both.

5   Conclusion

This paper presents a method that employs image features extracted from a pre-trained Swin Transformer and a Faster R-CNN. It also presents different variations of decoder designs to utilize both these features for caption generation. The proposed decoder makes use of two GRUs and an MHA network for caption generation. The experiments conducted show that the presented method exceeds the performance of existing works on BLEU-3 and BLEU-4 automatic evaluation metrics indicating the superiority of our approach. In future work, we aim to conduct experiments combining other pre-trained SOTA methods for extracting better features and developing a mechanism to decide when to use and when not to use multiple features.

References

1. Liu, Z., et al.: Swin transformer: Hierarchical vision transformer using shifted windows. In: Proceedings of the IEEE/CVF International Conference on Computer Vision, pp. 10012–10022 (2021)
2. Vinyals, O., Toshev, A., Bengio, S., Erhan, D.: Show and tell: a neural image caption generator. In Proceedings of the IEEE Conference on Computer Vision and Pattern Recognition, pp. 3156-3164 (2015)
3. Xu, K., et al.: June. Show, attend and tell: Neural image caption generation with visual attention. In International Conference on Machine Learning, pp. 2048–2057. PMLR (2015)
4. Lu, J., Xiong, C., Parikh, D., Socher, R.: Knowing when to look: adaptive attention via a visual sentinel for image captioning. In: Proceedings of the IEEE Conference on Computer Vision and Pattern Recognition, pp. 375–383 (2017)
5. Anderson, P., et al.: Bottom-up and top-down attention for image captioning and visual question answering. In: Proceedings of the IEEE Conference on Computer Vision and Pattern Recognition, pp. 6077–6086 (2018)
6. Cornia, M., Stefanini, M., Baraldi, L., Cucchiara, R.: Meshed-memory transformer for image captioning. In: Proceedings of the IEEE/CVF Conference on Computer Vision and Pattern Recognition, pp. 10578–10587 (2020)
7. Pan, Y., Yao, T., Li, Y., Mei, T.: X-linear attention networks for image captioning. In: Proceedings of the IEEE/CVF Conference on Computer Vision and Pattern Recognition, pp. 10971–10980 (2020)
8. Parida, S., Bojar, O., Dash, S.R.: Hindi visual genome: a dataset for multi-modal English to Hindi machine translation. Computación y Sistemas **23**(4), 1499–1505 (2019)
9. Krishna, R., et al.: Visual genome: connecting language and vision using crowd-sourced dense image annotations. Int. J. Comput. Vision **123**, 32–73 (2017)
10. Laskar, S.R., Singh, R.P., Pakray, P., Bandyopadhyay, S.: English to Hindi multi-modal neural machine translation and Hindi image captioning. In: Proceedings of the 6th Workshop on Asian Translation, pp. 62–67, November 2019
11. Singh, A., Meetei, L.S., Singh, T.D., Bandyopadhyay, S.: Generation and evaluation of hindi image captions of visual genome. In: Maji, A.K., Saha, G., Das, S., Basu, S., Tavares, J.M.R.S. (eds.) Proceedings of the International Conference on Computing and Communication Systems. LNNS, vol. 170, pp. 65–73. Springer, Singapore (2021). https://doi.org/10.1007/978-981-33-4084-8_7
12. Singh, A., Singh, T.D., Bandyopadhyay, S.: An encoder-decoder based framework for Hindi image caption generation. Multimedia Tools Appl. **80**(28–29), 35721–35740 (2021)
13. Lin, T.Y., et al.: Microsoft coco: Common objects in context. In: European Conference on Computer Vision, pp. 740–755, September 2014
14. Dhir, R., Mishra, S.K., Saha, S., Bhattacharyya, P.: A deep attention based framework for image caption generation in Hindi language. Computación y Sistemas **23**(3), 693–701 (2019)

15. Mishra, S.K., Dhir, R., Saha, S., Bhattacharyya, P., Singh, A.K.: Image captioning in Hindi language using transformer networks. Comput. Electr. Eng. **92**, 107114 (2021)
16. Mishra, S.K., Peethala, M.B., Saha, S., Bhattacharyya, P.: An information multiplexed encoder-decoder network for image captioning in Hindi. In: 2021 IEEE International Conference on Systems, Man, and Cybernetics (SMC), pp. 3019–3024. IEEE, October 2021
17. Mishra, S.K., Dhir, R., Saha, S., Bhattacharyya, P.: A hindi image caption generation framework using deep learning. Trans. Asian Low-Resour. Lang. Inf. Process. **20**(2), 1–19 (2021)
18. Mishra, S.K., Rai, G., Saha, S., Bhattacharyya, P.: Efficient channel attention based encoder-decoder approach for image captioning in Hindi. Trans. Asian Low-Resour. Lang. Inf. Process. **21**(3), 1–17 (2021)
19. Mishra, S.K., Saha, S., Bhattacharyya, P.: A scaled encoder decoder network for image captioning in Hindi. In: Proceedings of the 18th International Conference on Natural Language Processing (ICON), pp. 251–260, December 2021
20. Mishra, S.K., Sinha, S., Saha, S., Bhattacharyya, P.: Dynamic convolution-based encoder-decoder framework for image captioning in Hindi. ACM Trans. Asian Low-Resour. Lang. Inf. Process. **22**(4), 1–18 (2023)
21. Gill, K., Saha, S., Mishra, S.K.: Dense image captioning in Hindi. In: 2021 IEEE International Conference on Systems, Man, and Cybernetics (SMC), pp. 2894–2899. IEEE, October 2021
22. Mishra, S.K., Saha, S., Bhattacharyya, P.: An object localization based dense image captioning framework in Hindi. Trans. Asian Low-Resour. Lang. Inf. Process. **22**(2), 1–15 (2022)
23. Zhong, X., Nie, G., Huang, W., Liu, W., Ma, B., Lin, C.W.: Attention-guided image captioning with adaptive global and local feature fusion. J. Vis. Commun. Image Represent. **78**, 103138 (2021)
24. Meghwal, V.K., Mittal, N., Singh, G.: Attending local and global features for image caption generation. In: Gupta, D., Bhurchandi, K., Murala, S., Raman, B., Kumar, S. (eds.) Computer Vision and Image Processing. CVIP 2022. CCIS, vol. 1776, pp. 627–636. Springer, Cham (2023). https://doi.org/10.1007/978-3-031-31407-0_47
25. Vaswani, A., et al.: Attention is all you need. In: Advances in Neural Information Processing Systems, vol. 30, pp. 5998–6008 (2017)
26. Karpathy, A., Fei-Fei, L.: Deep visual-semantic alignments for generating image descriptions. In: Proceedings of the IEEE Conference on Computer Vision and Pattern Recognition, pp. 3128–3137 (2015)
27. Papineni, K., Roukos, S., Ward, T., Zhu, W.J.: Bleu: a method for automatic evaluation of machine translation. In: Proceedings of the 40th annual meeting of the Association for Computational Linguistics, pp. 311–318, July 2002

MCCNet: A Multi-scale Cross Connection Network for Low-Light Image Enhancement

Santosh Kumar Panda[ID], Devidutta Nayak[ID], and Pankaj Kumar Sa[✉][ID]

National Institute of Technology Rourkela, Rourkela, Odisha, India
{SantoshKumar_Panda,119cs0144,PankajKSa}@nitrkl.ac.in

Abstract. Low-light images are captured either during nighttime or in environments with limited illumination. These images typically suffer from reduced visibility and increased noise levels, making it challenging to extract relevant information. Enhancing such images is a decisive task in many fields, like medical imaging and night surveillance, where the clarity and detailing of the image are required for better image processing. This article introduces a novel deep-learning-based approach for enhancing low-light images. Our technique utilizes a multi-scale cross-connection network (MCCNet) that employs region-specific analysis to improve feature extraction. Moreover, our method also includes a calibrated network to fine-tune the features to get improved results. The critical section of the model is the region selection of the images, where some overlapping regions help provide contextual information between the extracted features. The cross-connection network helps to share the distinct features extracted and concatenate them to a single feature block, further improving the model's performance. Substantial simulations show our model's haughty performance compared with the state-of-the-art benchmark methods. The GitHub code is available at https://github.com/santoshpanda1995/Multiscale-cross-connection-network

Keywords: Low-light image enhancement (LLIE) · Multi-scale Regions · Cross-connection · Calibrated-CNN

1 Introduction

Images captured under poor lighting conditions are considered to be visually unappealing. These images are more towards the darker shades due to under-exposed illumination, leading to poor visibility, low contrast, and high noise. Due to these characteristics, the features from the images get blurry and noisy. Enhancing these images will include conserving the images' details and adjusting

The authors acknowledge the assistance under Grant# IF190566, from the scheme "Innovation in Science Pursuit of Inspired Research (INSPIRE)" by the Department of Science & Technology, Government of India.

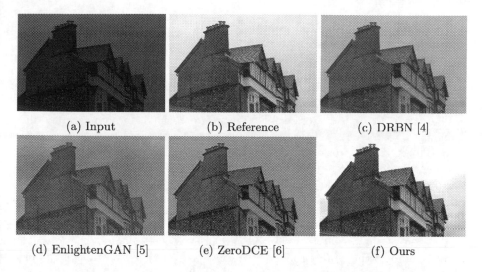

Fig. 1. Subjective comparison of our method with other state-of-the-art methods like DRBN [4], EnlightenGAN [5] and ZeroDCE [6] (Zoom in for better view).

the brightness with proper color correction. Traditional methods like histogram equalization [1], gamma transform [1], and retinex model [2] use many linear or non-linear stretching of the intensity values to enhance those images. Considering a dark environment where pixel intensities are not evenly distributed, some areas may be underexposed, and others may be overexposed. Extracting features directly by stretching the pixels globally may give poor results. In such cases, local feature extraction methods can be considered, which extract the features from the image in different scales. Such a method will focus on a single local region of the image without considering the whole image at a time.

Based on the above condition, a multi-scale cross-connection network (MCCNet) is suggested for the low-light image enhancement problem. It not only helps to enhance the dark images but also can deal with the problem of global contrast stretching problem. The whole network consists of three sub-networks or modules. The first module is responsible for extracting the images in multiple scales from the image. Then, in the second module, the cross-connection network is used, which helps to share the features of different regions of the image and correlate with the original image. Then, finally, inspired by the self-calibrated network [3], a calibrated convolution neural network is used that can eliminate or reduce the need for some post-processing steps. Instead, the network learns to produce well-calibrated probabilities during the training process. As depicted in Fig. 1, our research outcomes exhibit an outstanding improvement compared to several state-of-the-art methods.

The overall contribution of this article is as follows:

– The bright light images from the LOL [7] and SICE [8] datasets are used to generate our own synthetic paired dataset.
– We propose a multi-scale cross-connection network (MCCNet) consists of three sub-networks to solve the problem of Low-light image enhancement.
– The first block of the model is used to extract features in multiple scales from the input image.
– The second block is a cross-connection network that can share the features among different image scales.
– A calibrated convolution neural network is used as the third block of the model that helps to adjust its prediction features to be better aligned with the true features of the image.
– Finally, our model is evaluated by subjective and objective evaluation metrics to showcase its efficiency among various state-of-the-art methods.

The rest of the article is organized as follows: Sect. 2 depicts the literature survey related to the LLIE problem. Section 3 presents the overview of the proposed model. In Sect. 4, the simulations and results are discussed. Finally, Sect. 5 provides the concluding remarks.

2   Related Works

Extensive research has been conducted in low-light image enhancement, as researchers worldwide have delved into this area. In our article, we have simplified the discussion by categorizing the approaches into two primary domains: traditional methods and learning-based methods.

2.1   Traditional Methods

Some of the few traditional LLIE methods are histogram equalization, contrast stretching, and standard image processing techniques that may include image sharpening, color correction, noise reduction, deblurring, or combinations of these operations. Among those, the most famous method for image enhancement is histogram equalization [1], which seeks to increase the contrast and brightness of an image by redistributing its intensities. The technique involves changing the image's histogram to distribute equally among the distribution of pixel intensities over the complete range of potential values. The result is an image with higher contrast and brightness, making it easier to interpret and analyze. Some of the modified versions of this approach are adaptive histogram equalization (AHE) [9], contrast-limited adaptive histogram equalization (CLAHE) [10], dualistic sub-image histogram equalization (DSIHE) [11], etc.

The Retinex family of image enhancement techniques imitates the capacity of the human visual system to adjust to changing lighting conditions to enhance an image's apparent brightness and contrast. An image's illumination and reflectance components are separated to create an image using this algorithm. While the reflectance component represents the actual colors and textures of the objects in the image, the illumination component describes the overall lighting conditions of the scene. The Retinex algorithm can improve the contrast and brightness of the image while maintaining the color and texture details. The abstract formula for this method where $R(x, y)$ is the reflection component, which represents the reflective characteristics of the object surface, and $L(x, y)$ is the illumination component, which depends on the environmental light characteristics.

$$I(x, y) = R(x, y)L(x, y) \tag{1}$$

Another method is gamma correction, used in image processing to modify an image's contrast and brightness. It entails applying a non-linear adjustment to the image's pixel values to account for how the human eye and a digital camera or display device perceive brightness differently. Gamma correction is applying a non-linear transformation to an image's pixel values to counterbalance this difference in brightness perception.

$$f(x, y) = g(x, y)^{(1/\gamma)} \tag{2}$$

Here, $g(x, y)$ is the pixel intensity value, and γ is some tuned constant based on the image for enhancement. The authors in [12,13] have used gamma and log transform as pre-processing tasks for multi-feature and multi-illumination-based backlit image enhancement.

2.2 Learning-Based Method

Convolutional neural network (CNN) based image enhancement techniques are widely used in deep learning approaches. CNNs employ convolutional filters to learn spatial features from image data automatically. By stacking multiple convolutional layers, CNNs learn complex and abstract representations of the input image. These networks can be trained using a loss function to map degraded images to their enhanced versions. LLNet was the first deep-learning approach for the LLIE problem, proposed by Lore et al. [14] in 2017. After that, it made a benchmark among the other models. After that, numerous researchers suggested many more techniques worldwide, where some directly use a CNN approach, and some use a fusion of CNN with other methods. Before the deep learning steps, some authors focused on the feature extraction step using machine learning techniques like scale-invariant feature transform (SIFT) [15], speed up robust feature (SURF) [16], bag-of-features [17] etc. These techniques are key for many image processing tasks like image classification, image steganography [18], object detection, scene classification, etc.

In [19], the authors use a spatially variant recurrent neural network (RNN) to extract edge details and an auto-encoder model to extract vital features. Some authors [20,21] used a fusion of multiple images or exposures for low-light image enhancement. Jia et al. [22] proposed a novel visible infrared fusion dataset and technique that can be extended to enhance nighttime images. Generative adversarial networks [23] are also used for LLIE. GANs can create augmented images that are incredibly realistic and visually appealing by training the generator

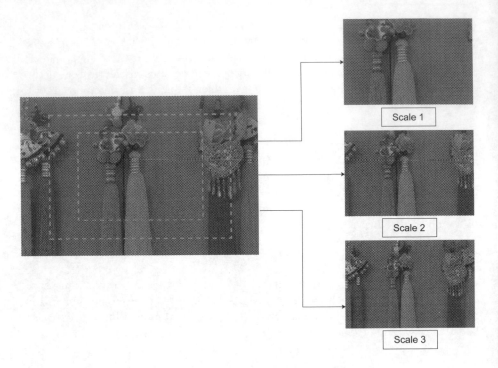

Fig. 2. Multi-scale selection of the image

and discriminator networks in an adversarial manner. One example is EnlightenGAN [5], where the authors have used unpaired learning. It can overcome the drawbacks of conventional image-enhancing methods like gamma correction and histogram equalization, which frequently yield unrealistic or unnatural-looking images. Some other deep learning based methods include RUAS [24], RetinexNet [7], UretinexNet [25], DRBN [4], DSLR [26], EnlightenGAN [5], SGM [27], ZeroDCE [6], ZeroDCE++ [28] and many more.

3 Proposed Method

In this section, first, the synthetic dataset generation process used by us is described, followed by a detailed description of MCCNet.

3.1 Dataset Generation

The dataset is a crucial aspect of any deep-learning approach. Most of the supervised learning approaches will require a dataset. LLIE problems require a paired dataset that contains a dark image and the subsequent bright image pair of the same scene. However it is challenging to capture an image of the same scene both day and night, as many objects may move from their place or some new objects may appear in one of the pair of images. Considering all these challenges, researchers make their synthetic images using image processing methods like reducing the brightness component, contrast stretching, adding noise, gamma transform, and changing the ISO values. We have chosen 1000 random images

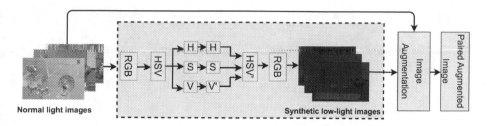

Fig. 3. Our approach for paired dataset generation.

from LOL [7] and SICE [8] datasets in our approach. Then, the images are converted from RGB to HSV format, as we can directly manipulate the intensity value (V). Then, the intensity value is reduced by 80 percent, producing (V'); after that, it is changed back to RGB, representing a nighttime image. It is followed by image augmentation techniques like upside down, left-right, and many more to obtain 4000 paired images. Of these images, 3200 paired images were used for training and the rest for validation. The detailed process is shown in Fig. 3.

After the paired dataset generation, the images undergo rescaling as shown in Fig. 2. Our model requires three input images: the original and two cropped and rescaled images. These additional images are adjusted to match the size of the original image, ensuring uniformity across different channels. The regions of the images that are cropped are the regions of interest. The images are captured so that the main focus is kept at the center. Thus, the other two images are considered as the more magnified version of the original image, with the focus being kept at the center.

3.2 Overview

The overall architecture of the model has three parts, as shown in Fig. 4. First, the input image generates two scaled images where the focus needs to be kept by doing appropriate cropping and rescaling. Secondly, the cross-connection module, where the encoded data of the input images are exchanged and concatenated so that the image channels can share the information extracted from the image of each channel. Lastly, after exchanging the feature maps, the encoded data is passed through a calibrated network, which acts as a final improvement in the network. The convolution operations are done separately and merged to get the final output of the given sample image. The rest of the sub-modules are described in the following sections.

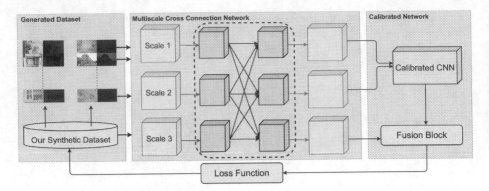

Fig. 4. Overall architecture of the proposed model divided into submodules. The first module shows the generated dataset, and after that, the multiscale cross-connection module divides the image into multiple scales and then the cross-connections between the layers. Finally, the calibrated network is followed by a fusion layer.

3.3   Multi-scale Cross Connection

The input image is first cropped to multiple scales, namely scale 1, scale 2, and scale 3, respectively; each scaled image is passed through a convolution layer. These scaled feature maps are then passed to a cross-connection network, which is shown as a dotted rectangle in Fig. 4. The feature maps inside the cross-connection are shown as blue-coded convolution layers to denote the downsampled version of the original scaled feature maps. The cross-connection part helps share features of each scaled feature map with others so that every feature map should have the complete information extracted from each image. Each channel will have the features extracted to that region of the image only. Applying this cross-connection enables to make the network to be more information-rich across all the channels. The cross-connection layer works by concatenating the encoded features from other layers and the convolution-operated encoded feature of the corresponding layer. Finally, after the cross-connection feature sharing, the layers are again upsampled to the original scaled feature maps.

$$g_i = \Lambda\left(f_0, \cdots, f_{i-1}, conv(f_i), f_{i+1}, \cdots, f_n\right) \tag{3}$$

Here, g_i is the new encoded data after applying cross-connection operations. The f_i represents the encoded data just previous to the cross-connection layer. The Λ function does the concatenation operation, and the *conv* function does the convolution operations. The final output size of the three feature maps from this block is $200 \times 300 \times 128$.

3.4   Calibrated CNN

The output of the multi-scale cross-connection is then passed to a calibrated network, where the feature maps are used as input for the calibrated CNN network. This module enables the network to adjust its parameters based on the

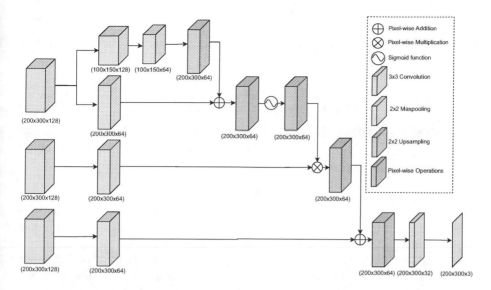

Fig. 5. Calibrated CNN architecture

input feature maps dynamically. The cropped branches of the encoded features are decoded and merged in the calibrated network to get a single output by up-sampling. The sigmoid activation function is then applied, which gives the probabilistic value of each pixel within the range of 0 to 1. It is followed by a pixel-wise multiplying, which is then used and concatenated with the original input image to return the pixel intensities according to the probability values obtained from the sigmoid function. Finally, the original scaled feature map, which was not rescaled, is added to get the final enhanced image as the output. The detailed structure is shown in Fig. 5

4 Simulation and Results

4.1 Training Parameters

The model is created with the TensorFlow framework and trained on the NVIDIA Tesla T4 GPU system. Adam optimizer is used for optimization with an initial learning rate of 0.0001, $\epsilon = 10^{-7}$, $\beta_1 = 0.9$, and $\beta_2 = 0.999$. The images are shuffled during the training process to maintain consistency. The model is trained with a batch size of 32 for 600 epochs. We have used the $L1$ loss function, also called mean absolute error denoted by-.

$$MAE = \frac{1}{n} \sum_{i=1}^{n} |y_{true} - y_{pred}| \qquad (4)$$

We have used the structural similarity index measure (SSIM) [29] to evaluate the accuracy during the model's training.

$$SSIM(x,y) = \frac{(2\mu_x\mu_y + c_1)(2\sigma_{xy} + c_2)}{(\mu_x^2 + \mu_y^2 + c_1)(\sigma_x^2 + \sigma_y^2 + c2)} \qquad (5)$$

where, μ_x is the mean of the image x, μ_y is the mean of the image y, σ_x^2 is the variance of x, σ_y^2 is the variance of y, σ_{xy} is the covariance of x and y, $c_1 = (K_1 L)^2, c_2 = (K_2 L)^2$, L is the dynamic range of image, $K_1 = 0.01$ and $K_2 = 0.03$ by default.

4.2 Evaluation Metrics

We have used subjective and objective evaluation metrics to evaluate the performance of our model compared to the state-of-the-art benchmark methods. The subjective evaluation depends upon human perception. One result can be marked best for some audiences but can be viewed as bad for others. The objective assessment is dependent on mathematical and statistical models and results. The result obtained from such evaluation can be considered for evaluating the performance. For some metrics, the higher number is the better result, but for some, it is the opposite. Our experiment used standard metrics like PSNR, PSNR-B, MSE, RMSE, SSIM, MS-SSIM, UQI, SAM, and SCC.

4.3 Results

This section shows our simulation results, which evaluate our method in both subjective and objective evaluation metrics. We have compared our method with many state-of-the-art methods like RUAS [24], RetinexNet [7], SGM [27], DRBN [4], DSLR [26], EnlightenGAN [5], UretinexNet [25], ZeroDCE [6] and ZeroDCE++ [28]. For the subjective evaluation, we have shown the original low-light image, the ground-truth image, our enhanced image, and the output of all the above methods. It is shown in Fig. 6. For the objective evaluation,

Table 1. Objective evaluation of image used in Fig. 6 (**Bold**: Best) and ↑ means higher the value is better; ↓ means lower the value is better.

	PSNR↑	PSNR-B↑	MSE↓	RMSE↓	SSIM↑	MS-SSIM↑	UQI↑	SAM↓	SCC↑
RUAS [24]	20.62	21.52	563.24	23.73	0.89	0.95	0.95	0.11	0.36
RetinexNet [7]	14.45	15.74	2330.59	48.27	0.70	0.81	0.84	0.32	0.37
SGM [27]	16.50	16.32	1455.05	38.14	0.82	0.90	0.89	0.25	0.36
DRBN [4]	16.74	17.46	1375.32	37.08	0.84	0.92	0.93	0.19	0.44
DSLR [26]	14.37	15.38	2375.48	48.73	0.73	0.86	0.81	0.11	0.44
EnlightenGAN [5]	18.77	19.23	862.21	29.36	0.87	0.91	0.93	0.15	0.47
UretinexNet [25]	20.39	21.01	594.05	24.37	0.85	0.91	0.94	0.15	0.46
ZeroDCE [6]	15.11	17.19	2000.97	44.73	0.85	0.91	0.93	0.16	0.46
ZeroDCE++ [28]	16.71	20.08	1385.58	37.22	0.87	0.94	0.94	0.13	0.46
Ours	**27.51**	**26.85**	**115.34**	**10.73**	**0.93**	**0.98**	**0.98**	**0.06**	**0.50**

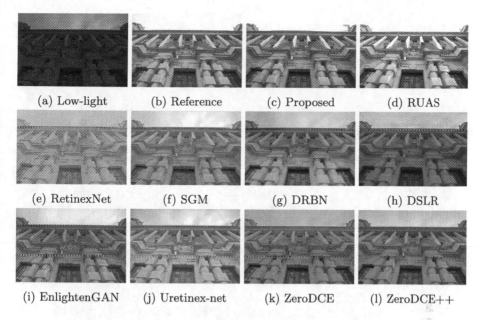

Fig. 6. Subjective evaluation of our proposed method on an image having groundtruth for comparison with many state-of-the-art methods like RUAS [24], RetinexNet [7], SGM [27], DRBN [4], DSLR [26], EnlightenGAN [5], UretinexNet [25], ZeroDCE [6] and ZeroDCE++ [28] (Zoom in for better view).

the compared output is shown in Table 1. Some metrics have higher values as best, and some have lower values as best. The table shows that the values in bold show the best result. From Fig. 6, we can see that our method is most efficient in enhancing the low-light image compared to other methods. As we can see, RUAS, RetinexNet, and UretinexNet are blurred when seen from a zoom-in view. The other methods, like DSLR, ZeroDCE, *etc*, look dark and dull compared to the ground truth image from the Table 1, we can see that our method performs superior to all the state-of-the-art methods.

5 Conclusion

This article proposes a multi-scale cross-connection network for the LLIE problem. We generated our dataset from two benchmark datasets, LOL and SICE. Then, we extracted multiple scales from a single input image. Our primary focus was extracting features from multiple scales of the image to build a more robust feature map that can mitigate most of the challenges an LLIE problem faces. We also used cross cross-connection network, which helps share features of each scaled feature map with others so that our network will not lose any details while convolutions. We compared our model with many state-of-the-art methods, both subjectively and objectively. The simulations and results confirmed that our method performs superior to the compared methods. In the future, this work can be extended by using attention mechanisms to both underexposed and overexposed areas of the image to limit the enhancement of some patchy bright areas present in low-light images.

References

1. Gonzalez, R.C.: Digital Image Processing. Prentice Hall, Hoboken (1992)
2. Land, E.H., McCann, J.J.: Lightness and retinex theory. J. Opt. Soc. Am. **61**(1), 1–11 (1971)
3. Liu, J.-J., Hou, Q., Cheng, M.-M., Wang, C., Feng, J.: Improving convolutional networks with self-calibrated convolutions. In: Proceedings of the IEEE/CVF Conference on Computer Vision and Pattern Recognition, pp. 10 096–10 105 (2020)
4. Yang, W., Wang, S., Fang, Y., Wang, Y., Liu, J.: Band representation-based semi-supervised low-light image enhancement: bridging the gap between signal fidelity and perceptual quality. IEEE Trans. Image Process. **30**, 3461–3473 (2021)
5. Jiang, Y.: EnlightenGAN: deep light enhancement without paired supervision. IEEE Trans. Image Process. **30**, 2340–2349 (2021)
6. Guo, C., et al.: Zero-reference deep curve estimation for low-light image enhancement. In: Computer Vision and Pattern Recognition (CVPR), pp. 1780–1789 (2020)
7. Wei, C., Wang, W., Yang, W., Liu, J.: Deep retinex decomposition for low-light enhancement. In: British Machine Vision Conference (2018)
8. Cai, J., Gu, S., Zhang, L.: Learning a deep single image contrast enhancer from multi-exposure images. IEEE Trans. Image Process. **27**(4), 2049–2062 (2018)
9. Pizer, S.M., et al.: Adaptive histogram equalization and its variations. Comput. Vis. Graph. Image Process. **39**(3), 355–368 (1987)
10. Pizer, S.M.: Contrast-limited adaptive histogram equalization: speed and effectiveness. In: Visualization in Biomedical Computing, Atlanta, Georgia, vol. 337, p. 1 (1990)
11. Wang, Y., Chen, Q., Zhang, B.: Image enhancement based on equal area dualistic sub-image histogram equalization method. IEEE Trans. Consum. Electron. **45**(1), 68–75 (1999)
12. Yadav, G., Yadav, D.K.: Multiple feature-based contrast enhancement of ROI of backlit images. Mach. Vis. Appl. **33**(1), 14 (2022)
13. Yadav, G., Yadav, D.K.: Contrast enhancement of region of interest of backlit image for surveillance systems based on multi-illumination fusion. Image Vis. Comput. **135**, 104693 (2023)
14. Lore, K.G., Akintayo, A., Sarkar, S.: LLNet: a deep autoencoder approach to natural low-light image enhancement. Pattern Recogn. **61**, 650–662 (2017)
15. Cruz-Mota, J., Bogdanova, I., Paquier, B., Bierlaire, M., Thiran, J.-P.: Scale invariant feature transform on the sphere: theory and applications. Int. J. Comput. Vision **98**, 217–241 (2012)
16. Bay, H., Ess, A., Tuytelaars, T., Van Gool, L.: Speeded-up robust features (SURF). Comput. Vis. Image Underst. **110**(3), 346–359 (2008)
17. Panda, S.K., Panda, C.S.: A review on image classification using bag of features approach. Int. J. Comput. Sci. Eng. **7**(6), 538–542 (2019)
18. Debnath, S., Mohapatra, R.K.: A study on secret data sharing through coverless steganography. In: 2022 2nd International Conference on Artificial Intelligence and Signal Processing (AISP), pp. 1–6. IEEE (2022)

19. Ren, W., et al.: Low-light image enhancement via a deep hybrid network. IEEE Trans. Image Process. **28**(9), 4364–4375 (2019)
20. Wang, W., Chen, Z., Yuan, X., Wu, X.: Adaptive image enhancement method for correcting low-illumination images. Inf. Sci. **496**, 25–41 (2019)
21. Tang, L., Xiang, X., Zhang, H., Gong, M., Ma, J.: Divfusion: darkness-free infrared and visible image fusion. Inf. Fusion **91**, 477–493 (2023)
22. Jia, X., Zhu, C., Li, M., Tang, W., Zhou, W.: LLVIP: a visible-infrared paired dataset for low-light vision. In: International Conference on Computer Vision, pp. 3496–3504 (2021)
23. Goodfellow, I., et al.: Generative adversarial networks. Commun. ACM **63**(11), 139–144 (2020)
24. Liu, R., Ma, L., Zhang, J., Fan, X., Luo, Z.: Retinex-inspired unrolling with cooperative prior architecture search for low-light image enhancement. In: Proceedings of the IEEE/CVF Conference on Computer Vision and Pattern Recognition (CVPR), pp. 10 561–10 570 (2021)
25. Wu, W., Weng, J., Zhang, P., Wang, X., Yang, W., Jiang, J.: Uretinex-net: Retinex-based deep unfolding network for low-light image enhancement. In: Computer Vision and Pattern Recognition (CVPR), p. 5901–5910 (2022)
26. Lim, S., Kim, W.: DSLR: Deep stacked laplacian restorer for low-light image enhancement. IEEE Trans. Multimedia **23**, 4272–4284 (2020)
27. Yang, W., Wang, W., Huang, H., Wang, S., Liu, J.: Sparse gradient regularized deep retinex network for robust low-light image enhancement. IEEE Trans. Image Process. **30**, 2072–2086 (2021)
28. Li, C., Guo, C.G., Loy, C.C.: Learning to enhance low-light image via zero-reference deep curve estimation. In: IEEE Transactions on Pattern Analysis and Machine Intelligence (2021)
29. Wang, Z., Bovik, A.C., Sheikh, H.R., Simoncelli, E.P.: Image quality assessment: from error visibility to structural similarity. IEEE Trans. Image Process. **13**(4), 600–612 (2004)

A Novel Framework for Cognitive Load Estimation from Electroencephalogram Signals Utilizing Sparse Representation of Brain Connectivity

Subrata Pain[1(✉)], Aritra Shome[2], Tutan Nama[2], Debasis Samanta[2], and Monalisa Sarma[3]

[1] Advanced Technology Development Center, IIT Kharagpur,
Kharagpur 721302, India
subrataatdc@iitkgp.ac.in
[2] Department of Computer Science, IIT Kharagpur, Kharagpur 721302, India
[3] Subir Chowdhury School of Quality and Reliability,
IIT Kharagpur, Kharagpur 721302, India

Abstract. Cognitive load is the quantity of mental activity imposed on a user's working memory while performing any cognitive task. As the performance of a human depends on the imposed mental workload, estimating cognitive load is critical for maintaining human efficiency through cognitive monitoring. Recently, cognitive load estimation utilizing the brain signals recorded by Electroencephalogram (EEG) has gained popularity. Traditional EEG signal-based cognitive load detection methods generally focus on extracting temporal and frequency-based features from individual EEG electrodes, thus neglecting dynamic functional relationships between the brain regions. This study proposes a cognitive load estimation framework utilizing the sparse representation of the brain network data. From the multichannel EEG data, brain networks are obtained using functional connectivity measures, and the sparse codes of the same are computed using the Orthogonal Matching Pursuit algorithm. Then a sparse representation-based classifier is developed that utilizes the sparse codes. The proposed framework is implemented on a 3-class cognitive load dataset recorded at IIT Kharagpur, and the model's efficacy is measured through sparse reconstruction error and classification performances.

Keywords: Sparse Modelling · Brain Network Topology · Cognitive Load · Electroencephalogram Signal Processing · Sparsity-based Classification

1 Introduction

For many real-time applications, assessing the cognitive workload of a human being is crucial. Traditional subjective assessments, performance-based, and

H. Kaur et al. (Eds.): CVIP 2023, CCIS 2009, pp. 500–511, 2024.
https://doi.org/10.1007/978-3-031-58181-6_42

physiological methods of estimating cognitive load often fail due to participant dependency. In this context, Electroencephalogram (EEG) recordings are frequently used to estimate cognitive load because they provide accurate indicators of cognitive activity by monitoring changes in neural activation in the brain.

The power spectral density (PSD) and event-related potential (ERP) components of EEG signals have been established in the literature as the two most important biomarkers for cognitive load assessment. In [1,2], the power spectral density (PSD) features for five EEG frequency bands have been extracted from individual channels using Fast Fourier Transform (FFT), and the classification was performed using Support Vector Machine (SVM) and Linear Discriminant Analysis (LDA) classifiers. Further, in [3], multiple event-related potential components (ERP) were utilized as features, and compared to the PSD features, high classification accuracy was achieved. In contrast to the above-mentioned ML-based approaches, deep learning-based classification models have been proposed in [4,5]. Specifically in [4], a Bidirectional Long Short-Term Memory (BiLSTM) and Long Short-Term Memory (LSTM)-based hybrid DL model was utilized, considering approximate entropy, Hurst Exponent, and statistical features, along with PSD features. Moreover in [5], a convolutional neural network (CNN)-based DL model was developed for automated feature extraction and classification of the mental workload of simultaneous EEG and functional near-infrared spectroscopy (fNIRS) recordings.

All the ML and DL-based models mentioned above mainly focus on the local features extracted from individual EEG electrodes while ignoring the dynamic functional connectivity between the interacting brain regions at different levels of mental workload. Unlike the traditional methods, the Brain Connectivity Analysis (BCA) methods [6] attempt to investigate the nature of global interaction and the information flow between multiple brain regions that work synchronously to achieve a particular brain function, forming a functional brain network. Thus, the invention of BCA methods has been a paradigm shift in neuro-imaging research, successfully discovering multiple task-dependent and inhibitory brain networks. In [7], the alterations of Phase Lag Index (PLI)-based brain connectivity of the Beta band during simulated flight conditions have been investigated, and significant alterations of the PLI-based brain network's efficiency have been observed. So, to develop a precise framework for automated mental workload estimation, brain connectivity features should be given importance.

The sparse representation and dictionary learning methods attempt to obtain a sparse representation of the input signals by using some convenient basis dictionary and then utilize those sparse codes for signal denoising [8], compression, or classification purposes [9]. Though widely used in real-world images and signals, sparse code computation of the connectivity network data has not been much investigated. This work proposes a novel framework for computing the sparse codes of the brain network. Further, utilizing the sparse codes, a 3-class classification of cognitive load is developed. The main contributions of this study are as follows:

- To develop a framework for generating accurate sparse codes for connectivity network data with minimum reconstruction error.
- To develop an efficient sparsity-based classification framework for different levels of cognitive load

2   Methodology

Figure 1 depicts the proposed methodology. From each preprocessed EEG epoch belonging to three levels (classes) of cognitive loads, the pairwise connectivity between all the electrode's signals is computed, resulting in a symmetric connectivity matrix. The upper triangular part of the obtained connectivity matrix is then flattened to obtain the 1-D feature vectors. After that, resulting feature vectors are fed to the sparsity-based classification model, where the sparse codes of the connectivity features are obtained, and a 3-class classification is performed.

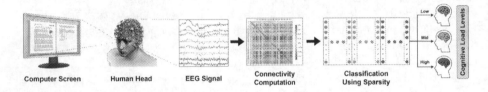

Fig. 1. The overview of the proposed methodology

2.1   Connectivity Feature Extraction from Multi-channel EEG Data

To estimate connectivity, a set of time, frequency, and phase domain estimators are utilized that compute the pairwise connectivity relationships between a pair of electrodes' signals, as described next.

Pearson's Correlation Coefficient (PCC): Pearson's correlation coefficient measures the strength of linear association between two variables. Correlation functional connectivity (CFC) has been extensively used for BCA analysis for EEG and time-converted fMRI recordings. Given two EEG signals x_t and y_t, Pearson Correlation coefficient r_{xy} is defined [10] as given in Eq. 1.

$$r_{xy} = \frac{\Sigma_{i=1}^{n}(x_t(i) - \bar{x}_t)(y_t(i) - \bar{y}_t)}{\sqrt{\Sigma_{i=1}^{n}(x_t(i) - \bar{x}_t)^2}\sqrt{\Sigma_{i=1}^{n}(y_t(i) - \bar{y}_t)^2}} \tag{1}$$

where n is the length of a signal, $x_t(i)$, $y_t(i)$ are the signal values at ith time instance, $\bar{x}_t =$ the sample mean; and analogously for $\bar{y}_t$. r_{xy} can take values between -1 and 1, where 1 indicates perfectly related, -1 indicates a strong negative relationship and 0 indicates no relation. We consider the absolute value of r_{xy} to consider both strong positive and strong negative relationships.

Coherence (COH) or Magnitude-Squared Coherence (MSC): Coherency or complex coherence measure represents the linear correlation in the frequency domain between two signals originating from two brain regions [6]. For any two signals x_t and y_t, coherence is computed by obtaining the Fourier Transform x_v and y_v of the said signals, which is given by Eq. 2.

$$C_{xy}(v) = \frac{x_v y_v^*}{|x_v||y_v|} \tag{2}$$

where, $*$ represents the complex conjugate. MSC is defined as the squared magnitude of the coherency, which stays in the $0 - 1$. Although MSC provides the relationship of two signals in the frequency domain, care must be taken for spurious connections originating from common source effects.

Phase Locking Value(PLV): The application of phase synchronization methods [11] in connectivity analysis is based upon the idea that if two neural masses are functionally coupled, then the phase difference of the generated electrical signals from those regions will be more or less constant. Phase Locking Value (PLV) [12] and Phase Lag Index (PLI) [13] are two such phase connectivity estimators. For any two signals x_t and y_t, originating from two different brain regions, the PLV is computed by obtaining the instantaneous phases $\phi(x)$ and $\phi(y)$ using the Hilbert Transform, as shown in Eq. 3.

$$PLV(x_t, y_t) = \frac{1}{n}|\sum_{k=1}^{n} \exp(i(\phi_k(x) - \phi_k(y)))| \tag{3}$$

Phase Lag Index(PLI): PLI is significantly less affected by volume conduction effects [13] than PLV. For two sensor signals, the PLI is given by Eq. 4 -

$$PLI(x_t, y_t) = \frac{1}{n}|\sum_{k=1}^{n} sgn(Im[\exp(i(\phi_k(x) - \phi_k(y)))])| \tag{4}$$

where sgn is the *signum* function, Im represents the imaginary part.

For each EEG epoch belonging to the three classes, a connectivity matrix of size $W \in \mathbb{R}^{N \times N}$, (where N is the total number of EEG channels or electrodes) is thus obtained.

2.2 Feature Vector from Connectivity Matrices

As the connectivity parameters utilized in the study are non-directional in nature, the obtained W is symmetric. We consider only the upper triangular part of this symmetric W to build the feature vector for that epoch, as it reduces the algorithm's unnecessary calculations and time complexity. Further, the diagonal entries of W are also excluded. The upper triangular matrix is then flattened to get the desired 1-D feature representation (See Fig. 2) of shape $K = N \times (N - 1)/2$.

2.3   Sparsity-Based Classification Model

Sparse Representation of Signals: According to the compressed sensing (CS) theory [14], most of the naturally occurring signals (and images) can be sparsely represented by using some convenient basis [15]. Given an over-complete dictionary matrix $D \in \mathbb{R}^{K \times T}$ (K is the length of the individual feature vector, and T is the number of trials that are used to build the dictionary), and a test feature x, the objective of the sparse representation is to compute the sparse coefficient vector $s \in \mathbb{R}^T$, such that $\tilde{x} \approx Ds$ and the coefficient vector is sparse, i.e., s contains a limited number of non-zero coefficients. Here, the test feature x is sparsely represented as a linear combination of atoms of the dictionary D [16]. Obtaining the sparse coefficient vector alpha or the sparse codes can be done by solving the following optimization problem

$$min||s||_0, \text{ subject to } ||x - Ds||_2 < \epsilon, \text{ where } \epsilon \text{ is positive and } \epsilon \to 0. \quad (5)$$

Many approximation algorithms are available in the literature to achieve sparse codes, the most famous are the matching pursuit (MP) and orthogonal MP (OMP) algorithms.

Construction of a Tailored Dictionary for Sparse Representation: A dictionary is a set of prototype signals containing all possible input information. The feature vectors obtained from all epochs previously are combined class-wise, i.e., the feature vectors of class, say C_i, form a sub-matrix d_i of the dictionary D, where,

$$d_i = [d_{i,1}, d_{i,2}, d_{i,3}, ..., d_{i,n}] \quad (6)$$

where $d_{i,j}$ is a column vector also called an atom of dictionary matrix with all $d_{i,j} \in \mathbb{R}^{K \times 1}$, where K is the length of the feature vectors, i.e., no of features considered. Considering c number of classes in a data, the dictionary $D = [d_1; d_2; ...; d_c]$. The construction of the dictionary is shown in Fig. 2.

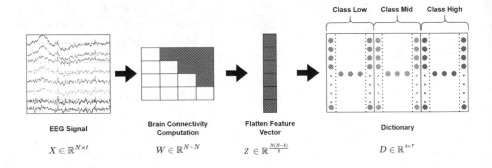

Fig. 2. Construction of a three-class tailored dictionary for sparse representation of the feature vectors

Classification Using the Sparse Coefficient Vector: Given basis dictionary D, for a test feature vector x, the corresponding sparse codes s are computed by the OMP algorithm as shown in Eq. 5. Ideally, the test signal x is similar in nature to the dictionary atoms belonging to the same class as x. For example, if x belongs to class C_2, the sparse code s should have its non-zero entries in the locations corresponding to the sub-dictionary atoms of class C_2. However, due to the non-stationarity of EEG features, a few non-zero entries might also lie in locations corresponding to other classes. This work develops a simple classifier where the sum of the non-zero coefficients belonging to individual classes is considered. Then the class with the maximum sum is assigned to the test signal, shown as Eq. 7.

$$s = \{s_0, s_1, s_2, ...s_{(T-1)}\} \in \mathbb{R}^T$$
$$= \{s^1; s^2; s^3\}, s^i \in \mathbb{R}^{T/3} \text{considering three classes} \qquad (7)$$

So, class label of x = Class label of s^i, for which $\sum s^i$ is maximum

3   Experiment and Dataset

The cognitive load experiment was performed in the HCI-BCI laboratory at IIT Kharagpur by the authors of [17]. A 64-channel EEG device from RMS India following the international 10-20 system and a sampling frequency of 256 Hz was used to capture the EEG signals. For three levels of cognitive loads, three English text paragraphs were selected with increasing levels of reading difficulties. Six (three male and three female) subjects participated in the experiments. Each subject was presented with three consecutive paragraphs on a computer screen for one minute. All subjects were proficient in formal English, had normal vision, and received adequate training. An extended version of the dataset published in [17] is utilized here.

Preprocessing: Firstly, a band-pass filter (0.1–50 Hz) is applied to the acquired EEG data to obtain the clinical EEG. Then a notch filter centered around 50 Hz removes electrical interference. Further, a common average reference (CAR) spatial filter is applied to reduce the effects of volume conduction. Further, a few noisy channels are removed, and the remaining 56-channel data is utilized for the study. Lastly, to generate a sizeable amount of data for the classification models, each sixty-second trial data is subdivided into 120 segments (each of size 56×128 = number of channels $\times$ number of time points), each of 0.5-second duration. So, a total of 2160 (Number of subjects $\times$ number of experiments per subject $\times$ number of segments per experiment = $6 \times 3 \times 120 = 2160$) samples, belonging to three different classes, are generated. In the mixed-subject classification models, a 10-fold cross-validation scheme is utilized, where, in each fold, 90% of these samples are randomly chosen as training data, and the remaining 10% are chosen as test data.

4   Results and Discussion

Feature Space Exploration: After obtaining the feature vectors of segmented individual trials, the T-Distributed Stochastic Neighbor Embedding (TSNE) plots (perplexity = 30) are obtained using *sci-kit learn* library, *Python 3.6.* Figure 3 shows the resulting plots for all connectivity estimators. From Fig. 3, it is observed that TSNE plots for PCC, COH, and PLI estimators reveal that three different data clusters corresponding to three different cognitive load levels are isolated and visible in the plots. It indicates that these features can provide enough discriminative knowledge for cognitive load analysis. TSNE plots for all subjects with low perplexity values also suggest that there exists proper discrimination between the three cognitive load levels, indicating that these features may be used for classification purposes.

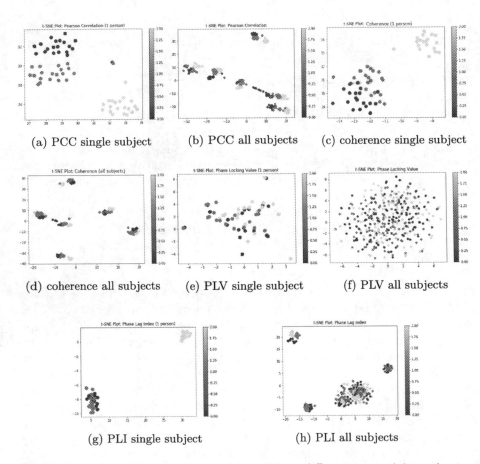

(a) PCC single subject   (b) PCC all subjects   (c) coherence single subject

(d) coherence all subjects   (e) PLV single subject   (f) PLV all subjects

(g) PLI single subject   (h) PLI all subjects

Fig. 3. TSNE plots of feature spaces originated from different connectivity estimators for a single subject and all subjects

Sparse Representation of Connectivity Network Features: Using the flattened connectivity features of all the available trials (2160) from all six subjects (i.e., mixed-subject classification approach), a 10-fold cross-validation split is performed where connectivity features of 90% of the trials connectivity are used to create the dictionary, and the remaining 10% is used as test samples (Please check the 'Preprocessing' paragraph, Sect. 3, for a detailed description of the dataset dimensions and segmentation scheme). Using this dictionary, the sparse codes of the test signals are obtained through the OMP algorithm, with varying maximally allowed numbers of non-zero coefficients in that sparse code. Figure 4a, 4b and 4c show the sparse codes (No of non-zero coeff. = 5) for three test samples belonging to three cognitive load classes, namely, low, medium, and high, respectively. From 4a, 4b and 4c, it is evident that the test signals are represented as a combination of a few (Only 5 in this case) dictionary atoms belonging to the same class only. Further, the quality and information-preserving capability of the sparse codes are computed by measuring the root mean square error (RMSE) between the original (x) and the reconstructed connectivity graph ($x_{reconstructed} = D \times s$), as shown in Fig. 4c. It is seen from Fig. 4c the RMSE is pretty low, indicating less amount of connectivity information is lost while sparse representation and reconstruction. Moreover, the RMSE gradually decreases with the increasing number of non-zero coefficients, as a combination of more atoms can represent the original vector more efficiently.

Classification Performance. After obtaining the sparse codes, utilizing the sparse classifier defined in Eq. 7, a 10-Fold cross-validated, 3-class classification is performed for the PCC, COH, PLV, and PLI feature vectors, and considering the 20 non-zero coefficients. The measured classification matrices are accuracy, precision, recall, and f-1 score; the 10-fold average of the same, along with the standard error, are reported in Table 1. A quick inspection of Table 1 reveals that the highest classification is obtained using the PCC (96.49%) feature, followed by coherence (93.30%). It is also observed that the performance of the PLV features is quite low compared to others, which is in line with the TSNE plots shown in Fig. 3, where a mixed and non-separable data-cluster is obtained (see Fig. 3f) for the PLV features. This result further highlights the lack of consensus between different connectivity measures while investigating the same neurological fact (i.e., the cognitive load), as each computes the brain network differently, and caution should be taken while neurologically interpreting the originating brain connectivity network.

Figure 5a and 5b depict the averaged confusion matrix (averaged across 10 folds) and the variation of the classification performance with the varying number of non-zero coefficients of the sparse codes. The confusion matrix shows the efficiency of the proposed model in classifying the individual classes. It is observed from 5b that the accuracy is significantly increased (from 91.30% to 96.49%) with the increase of the non-zero coefficients' number (from 5 to 20) in the sparse codes. The drawback of the increased accuracy is the execution time (or test time, i.e., time taken by the model to classify a single test instance, in

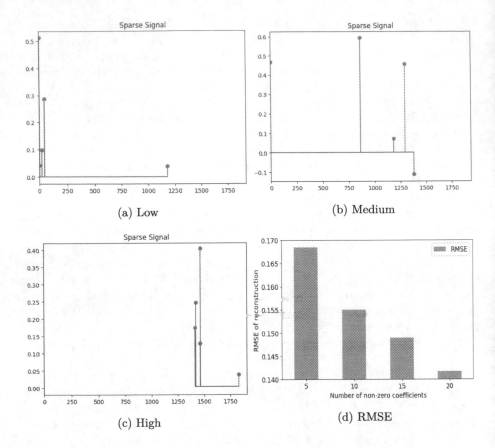

Fig. 4. Sparse representation of connectivity network features

milliseconds) also increases slightly, which might have a negative impact while using the proposed model in real-time applications.

As the proposed connectivity feature-based sparse classifier is first utilized for EEG analysis, there is a need to compare the efficiency of the same with the state-of-the-art and baseline models. Unfortunately, not much published work is available that utilizes the same dataset, except in [17]. So, a few self-defined baseline models are developed utilizing traditional ML models and the PCC feature set. The ML models are Support Vector Machine (SVM) with Radial Basis Function as kernel, Decision Tree (D-Tree), Random Forrest (RF), Linear Discriminant Analysis (LDA), Extra Tree Classifier (ETC), Gaussian Naive Bayes (GNB), and Adaptive Boosting classifier. The optimum hyper-parameters of the ML models are obtained through a grid search.

Figure 6 depicts the comparison with the baseline ML models. Among the ML models, the ETC, RF, and SVM perform significantly better than others, but the proposed model significantly outperforms these models. The proposed model also outperforms the DL-based models proposed in [17], where a complex

Table 1. 10-fold cross-validated average classification performance along with standard error for 20 non-zero sparse coefficients

	Accuracy	Precision	Recall	F1-score
Correlation	96.49 ± 0.42	96.50 ± 0.43	96.40 ± 0.45	96.38 ± 0.44
Coherence	93.30 ± 0.59	93.21 ± 0.60	93.27 ± 0.60	93.13 ± 0.61
Phase Locking Value	76.88 ± 1.24	75.82 ± 1.51	76.21 ± 1.94	76.73 ± 1.67
Phase Lag Index	86.34 ± 0.57	86.30 ± 0.56	86.44 ± 0.57	86.22 ± 0.56

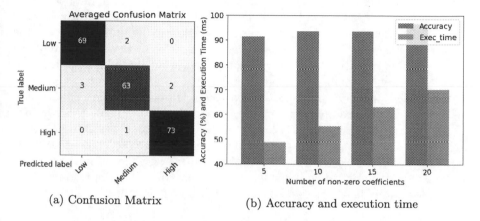

(a) Confusion Matrix   (b) Accuracy and execution time

Fig. 5. a) Confusion matrix with PCC feature b) Variation of performance and execution time with changing number of non-zero coefficients

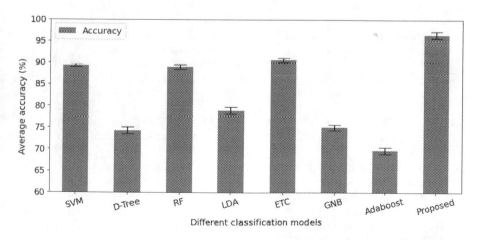

Fig. 6. Comparison with traditional Machine Learning models

SDAE-MLP model (Stacked Denoising Autoencoder (SDAE) followed by Multilayer Perceptron (MLP)) has been proposed, and the highest accuracy of 89.51% is achieved. The primary reason behind the superior performance of the proposed model lies in its capability of handling high-dimensional, noisy training data, as while computing the approximate sparse codes, some noise that may be present in the original signal gets removed. The high signal-to-noise (SNR) of EEG data and the low variance present in individual features of the connectivity data reduces the efficiency of the traditional models.

5   Conclusion

This work proposes a novel classification framework for the automated detection of human cognitive load from EEG signals. Unlike traditional approaches to cognitive load detection using local features extracted from individual channels, the proposed framework instead utilizes the global functional connectivity information of different cognitive loads. A sparse representation of the high-dimensional brain connectivity graph is proposed, and utilizing the sparse codes, a novel sparsity-based 3-class cognitive load classifier is developed. The experimental analysis reveals that a sparse representation of the brain connectivity graphs can be obtained with significantly low reconstruction error (RMSE). Finally, the high classification performance compared to the baseline models, along with the low testing time the superiority of the proposed model. The proposed method can be further utilized to obtain a sparse representation of human connectivity graphs, for graph de-noising, and also for EEG-based classification purposes.

References

1. Lim, W.L., Sourina, O., Wang, L.P.: Stew: simultaneous task EEG workload data set. IEEE Trans. Neural Syst. Rehabil. Eng. **26**(11), 2106–2114 (2018)
2. Fernandez Rojas, R., et al.: Electroencephalographic workload indicators during teleoperation of an unmanned aerial vehicle shepherding a swarm of unmanned ground vehicles in contested environments. Front. Neurosci. **14**, 40 (2020)
3. Roy, R.N., Charbonnier, S., Campagne, A., Bonnet, S.: Efficient mental workload estimation using task-independent EEG features. J. Neural Eng. **13**(2), 026019 (2016)
4. Chakladar, D.D., Dey, S., Roy, P.P., Dogra, D.P.: EEG-based mental workload estimation using deep BLSTM-LSTM network and evolutionary algorithm. Biomed. Sig. Process. Control **60**, 101989 (2020)
5. Saadati, M., Nelson, J., Ayaz, H.: Convolutional neural network for hybrid fNIRS-EEG mental workload classification. In: Ayaz, H. (ed.) AHFE 2019. AISC, vol. 953, pp. 221–232. Springer, Cham (2020). https://doi.org/10.1007/978-3-030-20473-0_22
6. He, B., et al.: Electrophysiological brain connectivity: theory and implementation. IEEE Trans. Biomed. Eng. **66**(7), 2115–2137 (2019)
7. Kakkos, I., et al.: Mental workload drives different reorganizations of functional cortical connectivity between 2d and 3d simulated flight experiments. IEEE Trans. Neural Syst. Rehabil. Eng. **27**(9), 1704–1713 (2019)
8. Sreeja, S.R., Sahay, R.R., Samanta, D., Mitra, P.: Removal of eye blink artifacts from EEG signals using sparsity. IEEE J. Biomed. Health Inf. **22**(5), 1362–1372 (2017)

9. Wu, Z., Xu, Y., Liu, J.: Sparsity-based methods for classification. In: Prasad, S., Chanussot, J. (eds.) Hyperspectral Image Analysis. ACVPR, pp. 233–257. Springer, Cham (2020). https://doi.org/10.1007/978-3-030-38617-7_8

10. Pearson, K.: On the theory of contingency and its relation to association and normal correlation (1904)

11. Rosenblum, M.G., Pikovsky, A.S., Kurths, J.: Phase synchronization of chaotic oscillators. Phys. Rev. Lett. **76**(11), 1804 (1996)

12. Wu, Z., Xu, Y., Liu, J.: Sparsity-based methods for classification. In: Prasad, S., Chanussot, J. (eds.) Hyperspectral Image Analysis. ACVPR, pp. 233–257. Springer, Cham (2020). https://doi.org/10.1007/978-3-030-38617-7_8

13. Stam, C.J., Nolte, G., Daffertshofer, A.: Phase lag index: assessment of functional connectivity from multi channel EEG and meg with diminished bias from common sources. Hum. Brain Mapp. **28**(11), 1178–1193 (2007)

14. Donoho, D.L.: Compressed sensing. IEEE Trans. Inf. Theor. **52**(4), 1289–1306 (2006)

15. Candes, E.J., Romberg, J.K., Tao, T.: Stable signal recovery from incomplete and inaccurate measurements. Commun. Pure Appl. Math. J. Issued Courant Inst. Math. Sci. **59**(8), 1207–1223 (2006)

16. Rubinstein, R., Bruckstein, A.M., Elad, M.: Dictionaries for sparse representation modeling. Proc. IEEE **98**(6), 1045–1057 (2010)

17. Saha, A., Minz, V., Bonela, S., Sreeja, S.R., Chowdhury, R., Samanta, D.: Classification of EEG signals for cognitive load estimation using deep learning architectures. In: Tiwary, U.S. (ed.) IHCI 2018. LNCS, vol. 11278, pp. 59–68. Springer, Cham (2018). https://doi.org/10.1007/978-3-030-04021-5_6

Automatic *Bharatanatyam* Dance Video Annotation Tool Using CNN

Himadri Bhuyan[1]([✉])(iD), Partha Pratim Das[2](iD), and Vishal Tewari[2]

[1] GITAM (Deemed to be University), Visakhapatnam 530045, AP, India
himadribhuyan@gmail.com
[2] Indian Institute of Technology Kharagpur, Kharagpur 721302, West Bengal, India
ppd@cse.iitkgp.ac.in

Abstract. Dance video analysis and interpretation have been challenging tasks in computer vision due to the lack of availability of annotated data. We may get several videos available in the public domain but hardly annotated because it incurs much time, cost, and expert knowledge. This paper addresses a solution to this problem in the field of *Bharatanatyam*, an Indian Classical Dance (ICD) form. The video annotation itself has a broad area of coverage. It may include the annotation of objects, activities, hand gestures, facial expressions, the semantics of a video, and many more. However, the paper annotates the elementary postures of the *Bharatanatyam* dance videos. The proposed tool takes a video as an input and segments it into motion and stationary/non-motion frames. The non-motion frames are part of the elementary postures and our point of interest. After segmentation, the tool recognizes the postures and labels the postures' duration of occurrence inform of frame number. The data set on which it is applied covers most basic dance variations in the *Bharatanatyam*, which was not addressed earlier on this large scale. The basic dance variations used to learn *Bharatanatyam* are called *Adavus*. The paper includes 13 *Adavus* and its 52 variations, which three dancers have performed. We use this as our data set. This annotation tool may significantly contribute to the state of the arts, saving the time and cost involved in manual annotation. The tool uses the deep learning technique for dance video annotation and gets an accuracy above 75%.

Keywords: *Bharatanatyam* · *Adavu* · Elementary Posture · CNN

1 Introduction

The computer interpretation and analysis of dance videos are necessary for applications such as building tutoring systems, dance transcription, preserving cultural heritage digitally, motion & posture recognition, dance simulation, and many more. However, we require a massive annotated data set for all these applications. The unavailability of an annotated data set sometimes becomes an obstacle for the ICD researchers. Let us take an example to understand this problem clearly. If a researcher wants to recognize the postures or motions in an ICD video using machine learning, then it requires a set of pre-labeled data (annotated data). Even though several videos are available on public platforms, a researcher can not work on those. This paper takes a step to solve this annotation problem, starting with *Bharatantyam* dance videos.

Bharatanatyam is one of the antediluvian ICD forms, around 2,000 years old. Among all the ICDs, we chose this dance form because of its discrete geometric pattern. Since it follows a pattern, it is implementable in machine learning. In *Bharatanatyam*, teachers use *Adavu* as an elementary unit for teaching. Listening to the audio beat, the dancer moves its limbs, head, and hands in different directions during the *Adavu* performance. The associated audios are *Sollukattus*. The dancer's performance goes hand in hand with the audio. This paper only concentrates on visual information.

By analyzing the dance video, we find all the frames are not in motion. There exists a set of non-motion frames. We call them Posture Frames (PFs), part of the key/elementary postures (P or KP). The following Fig. 1 gives an abstract view of the occurrence of the motion and elementary postures (P or KP), which occur alternately. During the dance, the dancer changes one posture to another by performing some movements. The associated frames with this motion are called motion frames (MF). The paper aims to annotate the elementary postures only. It is a complicated task considering the involvement of the complex motions and dance poses.

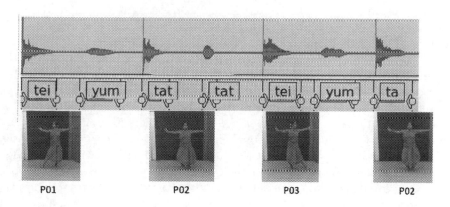

Fig. 1. Pictorial view of an *Adavu* showing the occurrence of postures

The paper covers works related to annotation (dance and non-dance) in Sect. 2, to realize the necessity of the proposed annotation tool. It highlights the research gap from this survey. Section 3 provides the information regarding the data set involved in this work. The system architecture is described in Sect. 4. The result analysis, and evaluation of the tool are done in Sect. 4.1, 4.2, and 4.3. Finally, the paper concludes in Sect. 5 with the future work and authors' view.

2   Related Work

The researchers [15, 25, 30] work on gesture and posture recognition. The semantics of ICDs are defined based on the body and hand gestures using CNN by [25]. In this, they report that CNN works better than SVM. Different ICDs are classified by [30] using pose descriptors. 3D dance postures are recognised by [15]. Mallick et al. [4, 23] recognize the posture and *Adavus* in *Bharatanatyam* dance form. In [8, 16, 27, 37]. Pose recognition and estimation are done.

Mallick [21] uses Gaussian Mixture Model, CNN, and SVM to recognize postures in *Bharatanatyam*. Sharma [33] reports the *Adavu* recognition by recognizing the sequence of postures in a particular order. Whereas, [33] uses (HMM) [28] for the same. The authors in [2, 17] report similar work. Himadri et al. [5] classifies the dance motions in *Bharatanatyam* dance videos.

In all the above works, authors consider the manually annotated data sets. In the thesis, Mallick [21] precisely pointed out the manual annotation's overhead in the given dance data. The proposed tool can make this work easy.

Several video annotation tools exist that annotate the objects (living or non-living) available in a video. Bianco et al. [6] proposed a video annotation tool to track the horse-jockey, African elephants, pedestrians, and other objects. Bruna et al. [7] design a mobile-based application that supports temporal video annotations. The authors [38] developed a video annotation tool to evaluate the learners' engagement with a MOOCs video. It fosters learners to self-organize themselves during the MOOCs. The similar annotation tools [14, 20, 34, 36] also help to improve the teaching-learning. The software [10] allows the video, audio, and image annotation. Like [7], it is also a manual annotation tool.

Santos et al. [31] develop a dance-based manual video annotation tool that can help the teacher to evaluate the learners' dance performance. The application provides several parameters for the teacher to provide feedback in a given dance video. The dance type *Forró* is used in this case. The paper [19] proposes a web-based system to annotate the dance videos based on the ontology concepts. In this, frame-wise annotation is possible. Users select a frame or a set of it, then choose a predefined ontology for the annotation or build its own. The intended work in [12] was manually used for the dance video annotation. It is web-based and supports search, brows, personalizing visualization, and textual annotation functionalities. The article [35] offers a manual tool that annotates and distinguishes between time-coded textual and graphical annotations. The article [11] provides the procedure and context of the dance to create the annotator using the web movement library. The paper [9] inspects the implementation of an annotation tool to store and search the dance media content. It also studies the tools' usability aspects. Shailesh et al. [32] annotate dance videos based on the six-foot postures of an ICD. The CNN model recognizes the foot postures within the given videos. In [26], the author uses the Motion Bank System *PieceMaker* manual annotator to explore the necessity of dance annotation in the choreography. For cultural heritage material or choreographs, other such tools [13, 29] also have been developed.

The following observations are made from this survey.

- Most of the ICD works are done on posture, gesture, or motion recognition with the available manual annotated data. Here, annotations imply the duration of a posture, motion, or gesture. This type of work needs an automatic annotation tool to minimize the cost overhead for manual annotation.
- Several works exist on non-dance video annotations, but none addresses the problem we are looking at.
- We get some of the dance annotation tools, but none of them address the duration of occurrence of the events. Most of them are manual and used for teaching and learning purposes.

Finally, we conclude that the duration of occurrence of the motion or non-motion (posture) frames' annotation is yet to be done. This is the research gap which we address in this paper.

3   Data Set

We use Kinect Xbox 360 [24] sensor to record the dance videos. It captures three streams of data, which are synchronized at 30 fps. These are the skeleton, depth, and RGB. We choose to work on RGB videos where each frame is of size 480×640 over the depth and skeleton. Since the skeleton is derived from the kinect depth information and the depth data has certain limitations [18]. The papers [1] and [21] reveal the details of the tools, sensors, and studio set-up. A piece of data set is published at [22]. The paper includes 13 *Adavus* and its 52 variations that three dancers have performed. The only exception is in *Nattal*. Only two dancers perform this dance. Table 1(a) shows variations of the *Adavus* and the data set in each (number of recordings) which we use in this work. Here, we have 53 variations of *Adavu* and 151 videos in total.

Table 1. Data Set

(a) *Adavu* Video Data

(b) Sample Annotation

Adavus' Name	Variations	Number of Recordings	*Adavus'* Name	Variations	Number of Recordings	Posture ID	Start frame	End frame
Joining	3	9	Paikal	3	9	U1D1B1P179	148	160
Kartari	1	3	Sarika	4	12	U1D1B2P180	173	183
Nattal	8	16	Tatta	8	24	U1D1B3P181	247	257
Tattal	5	15	Tei-TeiDhatta	3	9	U1D1B4P182	271	287
Mandi	2	6	Tirmana	3	9	...	...	...
Mettu	4	12	Uttsanga	1	3	...	...	...
Natta	8	24	Total	53	151	U1D1B4P182	468	475

Since this work is based on machine learning, we require a pre-labeled data set. So, we annotate all the videos with the help of the experts. The elementary postures are annotated in each video. Table 1(b) shows an annotation sample for *Uttsanga Adavu*. In this annotation, Posture ID provides information about the *Adavu* variation, dancer, and the audio beat on which a particular posture occurs. For example, in U1D1B1P179, U1 = *Uttasanga Adavu* of variation 1, D1 = Dancer-1 has performed this variation, B1 = the beat number one on which the posture = P179 occurs. There are 182 unique postures in these 151 videos and 50,390 samples in total. This paper treats the nomenclature of posture and elementary posture as the same. The elementary postures are the set of frames that remain stationary during an *Adavu* performance. It may also be referred to as keyframes. In between two postures, there exists a motion. The frames associated with it are called motion frames.

4   System Architecture

It is a system of three-layered architecture, including an extra layer for validating the annotation. Figure 2 shows the workflow.

- **First:** Segments the video to mark or identify the KP frames in the given *Adavu* video.
- **Second:** Recognize the KP using trained CNN
- **Third:** Mark the duration in which the given KP occurs
- **Fourth:** Validating the predicted annotation with the ground truth.

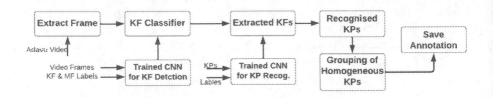

Fig. 2. Work Flow of Annotation Tool

4.1   Video Segmentation

This section solves the first subproblem, where a given RGB video is given as input and converted to its corresponding gray frames. In this, we need to differentiate the frames that are associated with the *elementary posture* frame from the motion frames. We use a simple approach [3] for this task. We adopt an Ex-OR operation between two consecutive frames to distinguish these frames, considering only three MSBs. Considering MSBs is to ensure the significant changes that only affect the MSBs, not LSBs. If Fr_i and Fr_{i+1} are two consecutive frames then $d_i(x,y) = Fr_{i+1}(x,y) \oplus Fr_i(x,y)$. Here d_i is the resultant intensity value after the Ex-OR operation. (x,y) denotes the pixel position of a gray video frame where $1 \le x \le 480$ and $1 \le y \le 640$. EX-OR technique helps to detect the changes between two consecutive frames. If no change is encountered between Fr_i and Fr_{i+1}, then $d_i(x, y)$ will have zeros in most of the pixel positions. It implies Fr_i is a posture frame (PF). Otherwise, it is a motion frame (MF). CNN [3] takes this feature (d_i of each frame) to classify a frame as PF or MF.

After CNN marks the video frames as 1 or 0, we apply the majority voting technique to reduce false positives and negatives in this binary classification result. We count zeros (C_0) and ones (C_1) in a five-window frame. If $C_1 \geq C_0$, then we update the 3rd frame to one in the given five-window frame. The window floats across frames in a given video, and the same process is applied. This process helps in increasing the contentiousness of PF occurrences. The given CNN detects the KF with an accuracy of 87.15%.

4.2 Posture Recognition

After segmenting the video to detect the elementary posture frames, the next task is to label the posture frames. This section deals with the posture recognition part and solves the second subproblem. Here, we use CNN as shown in Fig. 3.

The CNN model comprises two convolutional (CV) layers and three fully connected (FC) layers. The first CV layer has 32 channels, and the second has 64 channels, both with the necessary padding in the input. The feature normalization is carried out using layer normalization, and max-pooling is performed with a 2×2 window and stride two. The output of each CV layer is illustrated in Fig. 3.

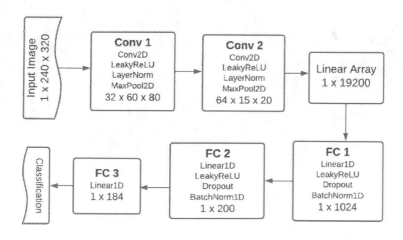

Fig. 3. KP Classification Using CNN

The operations involved in each FC layer are shown in Fig. 3. To avoid overfitting, dropout regularization is applied, and the number of epochs is limited to 15. These techniques prevent the CNN model from memorizing the data and help it to learn better. The number of epochs is determined by analyzing the train-test accuracy.

Finally, the output of the last FC layer comprises 182 feature arrays that correspond to 182 KP classes. These features are transformed into class scores using the softmax layer, and the unknown KPs are labeled accordingly.

Unlike the papers [21, 23, 25] on posture recognition, our CNN can handle a large data set with an accuracy of 98.39%. The average training and testing time (in seconds) per sample is 0.233 s and 0.0070 s, respectively. The proposed CNN can classify 182 postures, where 139 postures score 100% accuracy. Table 2 shows the accuracy of the rest of the 43 classes. The column named, *Wrongly Predicted* follows a template $P'\#(n)$, where $P'\# =$ posture class that has been mispredicted with a given class P and $n =$ number of miss predicted samples. For example, posture class 8 ($P = 8$) has test samples 414. Of these 414 samples, 7 ($n = 7$) has been mispredicted as class 173 ($P' = 173$). So, *Wrongly predicted* column represents 173(7).

Except for two postures (#36, #67), most postures' recognition accuracy is above 90% or 95%. The accuracy of classes 36 and 37 are 55.56% and 50%, respectively. This bad accuracy may be due to the low training samples compared to the rest of the classes.

Table 2. Posture Classes having Accuracy <100%

Class Labels	Training Samples	Test Samples	Wrongly Predicted	Accuracy (%)	Class Labels	Training Samples	Test Samples	Wrongly Predicted	Accuracy (%)
3	4556	1139	173(13), 94(1), 48(10), 11(1)	97.81	58	116	29	47(1)	96.55
5	700	175	1(2), 173(1)	98.29	59	636	159	47(1), 50(1), 55(1), 1(1)	97.48
8	1656	414	173(7)	98.31	60	452	113	74(1)	99.12
11	1680	420	1(1), 5(2)	99.29	66	100	25	144(2)	92
14	164	41	15(6)	85.37	67	16	4	60(2)	50
15	116	29	14(3)	89.66	69	20	5	46(1)	80
27	908	227	173(1), 139(1), 100(1), 3(1)	98.24	73	32	8	180(1)	87.5
28	216	54	173(6)	88.89	74	76	19	60(1)	94.74
36	36	9	173(4)	55.56	76	312	78	78(1)	98.72
42	68	17	46(1)	94.12	78	244	61	76(1)	98.36
43	172	43	48(1)	97.67	84	176	44	173(2)	95.45
44	432	108	50(1), 3(1), 48(1)	97.22	89	28	7	142(1)	85.71
45	428	107	46(1), 3(1)	98.13	92	28	7	3(1)	85.71
46	720	180	3(1), 49(1)	98.89	93	104	26	27(1)	96.15
48	656	164	49(1), 3(4)	96.95	100	764	191	173(1)	99.48
49	388	97	45(1)	98.97	103	572	143	100(1)	99.30
51	88	22	44(1)	95.45	139	268	67	173(3)	95.52
52	200	50	46(1), 59(1)	96	156	204	51	144(1)	98.04
54	116	29	47(1)	96.55	163	68	17	173(1)	94.12
55	240	60	3(1)	98.33	181	60	15	87(1)	93.33
56	200	50	55(1)	98	182	64	16	87(1)	93.75
57	240	60	52(1)	98.33					

4.3 Generating and Validating the Annotation File

After recognition of the postures in a given *Adavu* video, we club the similar KFs in that video, marking its start and endpoints as shown in the Table 1(b). The same is saved as a *.csv* file. The file name is similar to the *Adavu* name for which the annotation is done automatically.

We compare the manually annotated file with the predicted one and compute the accuracy. We take a boundary threshold of three frames. If both $|Ac_{Start} - Pr_{Start}| \leq 3$ and $|Ac_{End} - Pr_{End}| \leq 3$, then we consider the predicted one as the correct annotation. Otherwise, it is treated as wrong. Here, Ac_{Start} and Ac_{End} = starting and ending frame number of actual annotations. Similarly, Pr_{Start} and Pr_{End} = starting and ending frame number of predicted annotations. By following this criterion, we achieve an overall accuracy of 75.46% with the proposed automatic annotation tool. Table 3 shows the annotation accuracy of each *Adavu*.

Table 3. Annotation Accuracy of each *Adavu*

Adavus	Test Accuracy (%)	*Adavus*	Test Accuracy (%)
Joining	83.56	Sarika	66.66
Katti-kartari	82.14	Tatta	89.91
Mandi	75.00	Tattal	74.84
Mettu	63.01	Tei-Tei dhatta	76.56
Natta	85.41	Trimana	60.01
Nattal	67.34	Utsanga	79.16
Paikkal	80.75	Overall	75.46

4.4   Annotation Tool

We developed a Graphical User Interface (GUI) for this annotation tool. It takes an *Adavu* video and the depth information of that video as input through `Browse` button. Pressing `Generate Annotation` generates the annotation file in `.csv` format.

5   Conclusions

The paper presents the process of developing an annotation tool, from segmenting the video & posture detection to generating an annotation file. It achieves an accuracy of 87.15% in detecting PF and MF and 98.39% in posture recognition, which are very impressive with 182 classes. The posture recognition accuracy outperforms the earlier version of CNN [21,23], where they only try a few classes. The proposed tool can annotate *Bharatanatyam Adavus* videos with 75.46% accuracy. As we can see, there is a scope to increase the accuracy.

Automatic Annotation of dance videos will remove various obstacles for ICD researchers and help build applications like tutoring systems, dance transcription, preserving cultural heritage digitally, motion & posture recognition, dance simulation, and many more. Research on automatic annotation of dance videos is limited, especially in Indian classical Dance forms. As highlighted in the research gap, no earlier work was done in duration tracking in the annotation of dance videos. The proposed tool is capable of this.

The paper leaves the following work as future work.

– The current work heavily relies on depth data to subtract the background. So, another technique may be applied to remove the background for non-Kinect data.
– The current work only considers posture annotation. However, with the availability of motion data, we may go for motion annotation along with the KP.
– The proposed technique is yet to be evaluated against other dance data sets.
– We may use the audio information for this segmentation.

References

1. Aich, A., Mallick, T., Bhuyan, H.B.G.S., Das, P.P., Majumdar, A.K.: *NrityaGuru*: a dance tutoring system for *Bharatanatyam* using kinect. In: Rameshan, R., Arora, C., Dutta Roy, S. (eds.) NCVPRIPG 2017. CCIS, vol. 841, pp. 481–493. Springer, Singapore (2018). https://doi.org/10.1007/978-981-13-0020-2_42
2. Bhuyan, H., Das, P.P.: Recognition of *Adavus* in *Bharatanatyam* dance. In: Singh, S.K., Roy, P., Raman, B., Nagabhushan, P. (eds.) CVIP 2020. CCIS, vol. 1378, pp. 174–185. Springer, Singapore (2021). https://doi.org/10.1007/978-981-16-1103-2_16
3. Bhuyan, H., Das, P.P., Dash, J.K., Killi, J.: An automated method for identification of key frames in Bharatanatyam dance videos. IEEE Access **9**, 72670–72680 (2021)
4. Bhuyan, H., Dhaipule, R., Das, P.P.: Sequence recognition in Bharatnatyam dance. In: Gupta, D., Bhurchandi, K., Murala, S., Raman, B., Kumar, S. (eds.) CVIP 2022. CCIS, vol. 1776, pp. 390–405. Springer, Cham (2022). https://doi.org/10.1007/978-3-031-31407-0_30
5. Bhuyan, H., Roy, M., Das, P.P.: Motion classification in *Bharatanatyam* dance. In: Babu, R.V., Prasanna, M., Namboodiri, V.P. (eds.) NCVPRIPG 2019. CCIS, vol. 1249, pp. 408–417. Springer, Singapore (2020). https://doi.org/10.1007/978-981-15-8697-2_38
6. Bianco, S., Ciocca, G., Napoletano, P., Schettini, R.: An interactive tool for manual, semi-automatic and automatic video annotation. Comput. Vis. Image Underst. **131**, 88–99 (2015)
7. Cunha, B.C., Machado Neto, O.J., Pimentel, M.d.G.: MoViA: a mobile video annotation tool. In: Proceedings of the 2013 ACM Symposium on Document Engineering, pp. 219–222 (2013)
8. Dantone, M., Gall, J., Leistner, C., Van Gool, L.: Human pose estimation using body parts dependent joint regressors. In: Proceedings of the IEEE Conference on Computer Vision and Pattern Recognition, pp. 3041–3048 (2013)
9. Dollie, K.: Exploration of dance annotation tool representation models and searchability of annotations. Submitted to Department of Computer Science University of Cape Town South Africa (2020)
10. Dutta, A., Zisserman, A.: The via annotation software for images, audio and video. In: Proceedings of the 27th ACM International Conference on Multimedia, pp. 2276–2279 (2019)

11. El Raheb, K., Ioannidis, Y.: Annotating the captured dance: reflections on the role of tool-creation. Int. J. Perform. Arts Digit. Media **17**(1), 118–137 (2021)
12. El Raheb, K., Kasomoulis, A., Katifori, A., Rezkalla, M., Ioannidis, Y.: A web-based system for annotation of dance multimodal recordings by dance practitioners and experts. In: Proceedings of the 5th International Conference on Movement and Computing, pp. 1–8 (2018)
13. El Raheb, K., Papapetrou, N., Katifori, V., Ioannidis, Y.: BalOnSe: ballet ontology for annotating and searching video performances. In: Proceedings of the 3rd International Symposium on Movement and Computing, pp. 1–8 (2016)
14. Gayathri, B., Vedavyas, R., Sharanya, P., Karthik, K.: Effectiveness of reflective learning in skill-based teaching among postgraduate anesthesia students: an outcome-based study using video annotation tool. Med. J. Armed Forces India **77**, S202–S207 (2021)
15. Guo, F., Qian, G.: Dance posture recognition using wide-baseline orthogonal stereo cameras. In: 7th International Conference on Automatic Face and Gesture Recognition (FGR06), pp. 481–486. IEEE (2006)
16. Johnson, S., Everingham, M.: Learning effective human pose estimation from inaccurate annotation. In: 2011 IEEE Conference on Computer Vision and Pattern Recognition (CVPR), pp. 1465–1472. IEEE (2011)
17. Kale, G., Patil, V.: Bharatnatyam adavu recognition from depth data. In: 2015 Third International Conference on Image Information Processing (ICIIP), pp. 246–251. IEEE (2015)
18. Khoshelham, K.: Accuracy analysis of kinect depth data. Int. Arch. Photogramm. Remote. Sens. Spat. Inf. Sci. **38**, 133–138 (2012)
19. Lagrue, S., et al.: An ontology web application-based annotation tool for intangible culture heritage dance videos. In: Proceedings of the 1st Workshop on Structuring and Understanding of Multimedia heritAge Contents, pp. 75–81 (2019)
20. Leung, K.C., Shek, M.P.: Adoption of video annotation tool in enhancing students' reflective ability level and communication competence. Coaching: Int. J. Theory Res. Pract. 1 11 (2021)
21. Mallick, T.: A framework for modeling, analysis and transcription of Bharatanatyam dance performances. Ph.D. thesis, CSE, IIT Kharagpur, India (2017)
22. Mallick, T., Bhuyan, H., Das, P.P., Majumdar, A.K.: Annotated Bharatanatyam data set: online (2017). http://hci.cse.iitkgp.ac.in
23. Mallick, T., Das, P.P., Majumdar, A.K.: Posture and sequence recognition for Bharatanatyam dance performances using machine learning approach. arXiv preprint arXiv:1909.11023 (2019)
24. Microsoft: Tracking users, with kinect skeletal tracking (2010). https://msdn.microsoft.com/en-us/library/hh438998.aspx
25. Mohanty, A., et al.: Nrityabodha: towards understanding Indian classical dance using a deep learning approach. Signal Process.: Image Commun. **47**, 529–548 (2016)
26. Monda, L.G.: Digital dance writing. A teaching tool to support the understanding of digital choreography. Int. J. Perform. Arts Digit. Media **17**(1), 102–110 (2021)
27. Ning, H., Xu, W., Gong, Y., Huang, T.: Discriminative learning of visual words for 3D human pose estimation. In: 2008 IEEE Conference on Computer Vision and Pattern Recognition, CVPR 2008, pp. 1–8. Citeseer (2008)
28. Rabiner, L.R.: A tutorial on hidden Markov models and selected applications in speech recognition. Proc. IEEE **77**(2), 257–286 (1989)

29. Ribeiro, C., Kuffner, R., Fernandes, C.: Virtual reality annotator: a tool to annotate dancers in a virtual environment. In: Ioannides, M. (ed.) Digital Cultural Heritage. LNCS, vol. 10605, pp. 257–266. Springer, Cham (2018). https://doi.org/10.1007/978-3-319-75826-8_21

30. Samanta, S., Purkait, P., Chanda, B.: Indian classical dance classification by learning dance pose bases. In: 2012 IEEE Workshop on the Applications of Computer Vision (WACV), pp. 265–270. IEEE (2012)

31. dos Santos, A.D.P., Loke, L., Martinez-Maldonado, R.: Exploring video annotation as a tool to support dance teaching. In: Proceedings of the 30th Australian Conference on Computer-Human Interaction, pp. 448–452 (2018)

32. Shailesh, S., Judy, M.: Automatic annotation of dance videos based on foot postures. Indian J. Comput. Sci. Eng. Eng. J. Publ.-ISSN **976**, 5166 (2020)

33. Sharma, A.: Recognising Bharatanatyam dance sequences using RGB-D data. Ph.D. thesis, IIT Kanpur, India (2013)

34. Shek, M.M.P., Leung, K.C., To, P.Y.L.: Using a video annotation tool to enhance student-teachers' reflective practices and communication competence in consultation practices through a collaborative learning community. Educ. Inf. Technol. 1–24 (2021)

35. Stancliffe, R.: Training the analytical eye: video annotation for dance. Theatre Dance Perform. Train. **10**(2), 273–288 (2019)

36. Suh, J., Gallagher, M.A., Capen, L., Birkhead, S.: Enhancing teachers' noticing around mathematics teaching practices through video-based lesson study with peer coaching. Int. J. Lesson Learn. Stud. (2021)

37. Tian, Y., Zitnick, C.L., Narasimhan, S.G.: Exploring the spatial hierarchy of mixture models for human pose estimation. In: Fitzgibbon, A., Lazebnik, S., Perona, P., Sato, Y., Schmid, C. (eds.) ECCV 2012. LNCS, vol. 7576, pp. 256–269. Springer, Heidelberg (2012). https://doi.org/10.1007/978-3-642-33715-4_19

38. Yousef, A.M.F., Chatti, M.A., Danoyan, N., Thüs, H., Schroeder, U.: Videomapper: a video annotation tool to support collaborative learning in MOOCs. Proceedings of the Third European MOOCs Stakeholders Summit EMOOCs, pp. 131–140 (2015)

Enhancing Face Emotion Recognition with FACS-Based Synthetic Dataset Using Deep Learning Models

Shiwangi Mishra[1,2](✉)[iD], P. Shalu[1,2], and Rohan Singh[2]

[1] Asterbyte Software Systems Private Limited, Thalassery, Kerala, India
shiwangi@trymph.com
[2] Imentiv AI, Cupertino, CA, USA
https://imentiv.ai/
https://asterbyte.com/

Abstract. In our study, we propose an innovative approach for facial emotion recognition that employs both transfer learning and deep learning techniques. Our methodology allows automatic detection of visual cues linked to various facial emotions. The approach is highly consistent and effectively addresses the challenge of detecting seven fundamental human emotions, which include anger, disgust, fear, happiness, sadness, neutral, and surprise. Additionally, we introduce a new dataset named EMOTE-2023, which is developed using Unreal Engine and the Maya platform. Also, the proposed approach is analyzed on other existing datasets, such as FER2013 and CK+. To enhance the accuracy of our emotion classification, we have used multiple deep learning models VGG, ResNet, MobileNet to verify the effectiveness of our Facial Emotion Recognition system. Our proposed approach achieved the highest accuracy of 72.49%, 96.97%, and 97.97% using the ResNet18 model for FER2013, CK+ and EMOTE-2023 respectively. Our work involves leveraging transfer learning techniques that use pre-trained neural network layers and trained on larger datasets that are commonly employed in computer vision applications.

Keywords: Emotion Recognition · Deep Learning · FER · VGG · emotions

1 Introduction

In today's world, digital imaging and image processing are rapidly evolving fields of study with numerous applications. Image processing, in particular, has gained significant attention due to its wide range of applications in various areas [8]. One of the most significant applications of image processing is facial expression recognition (FER). In interpersonal communication, facial expressions play a crucial role in conveying emotions. Facial expressions represents non-verbal communication that involves the use of facial muscles to express emotions. As

H. Kaur et al. (Eds.): CVIP 2023, CCIS 2009, pp. 523–531, 2024.
https://doi.org/10.1007/978-3-031-58181-6_44

a result, FER has become an essential component of artificial intelligence (AI) and robotics [1].

Developing an accurate emotion recognition system requires the ability to detect and classify faces accurately, which is a challenging task. Facial emotion recognition systems are capable of working under different ambient lighting conditions, with individuals wearing eyeglasses, or different facial hair styles. While traditional computer vision systems were initially developed and deployed, deep learning frameworks have proven to be more accurate and faster. Deep learning networks use end-to-end learning which is helpful in overcoming problems associated with other traditional methods [12]. However, deep learning methods require vast amounts of training data. The performance of deep learning models depends on the size of training dataset, necessitating larger datasets [9]. Researchers are exploring different techniques, such as data augmentation, translations, cropping, and scaling, to increase the size of the dataset. In this context, our work proposes a new dataset, EMOTE-2023, that consists of basic human emotions. Existing datasets, such as FER, focus on seven basic emotions anger, disgust, fear, happiness, sadness, neutral, and surprise. Our dataset includes three additional emotions: contempt, boredom, and joy. We also propose a new approach to synthetically build emotion datasets using automated tools such as the Unreal Engine and the Maya platform. We demonstrate the validity of this dataset by training multiple deep learning models VGG-16, VGG-19, ResNet-18, MobileNet to verify performance on new emotions dataset as well. In conclusion, our research proposes a new emotion dataset that will enable the development of more robust and accurate emotion recognition systems. Utilizing multiple datasets, including FER2013, EMOTE-2023, and CK+, allows us to analyze the performance of the FER system comprehensively.

2   Related Works

Gray-Level Co-Occurrence Matrix (GLCM), Local Directional Patterns (LDA), Gabor wavelets, and other conventional techniques are available for extracting geometric and texture aspects from facial features. However, in recent times, deep learning has emerged as a highly effective and successful method due to its capacity for automatic feature extraction and categorization. Convolutional Neural Networks (CNN) and Recurrent Neural Networks (RNN) are examples of such architectures [14]. Researchers have invested substantial efforts in developing deep neural network architectures that have yielded satisfactory results in this domain. Over the past decade, advances in deep learning techniques have revolutionized the field of facial emotion recognition, resulting in significant improvements in accuracy, robustness, and efficiency. Deep learning models can automatically learn and extract meaningful features from high-dimensional facial images, enabling them to outperform traditional machine learning approaches in this task. These models are particularly well-suited for handling large, complex datasets with a high degree of variability and noise, which are inherent in facial emotion recognition. Furthermore, deep learning-based facial expression identification offers a wide range of useful applications across various industries, including healthcare, education, marketing, and entertainment.

Sun et al. (2017) [19] performed reduction of within-class distances by using a unique reduction strategy and a state-of-the-art classifier. Komala et al. (2020) [10] suggested applying Viola-Jones algorithm to more accurately identify the emotions in real-time webcam or photos. Minaee et al. (2021) [13] suggested a deep neural net approach based on an artificial neural network (ANN) to emphasise the important areas of the human face, outperforming earlier models on multiple datasets. In another study, Khaireddin et al. (2021) [7] fine-tuned the hyperparameters of the VGGNet architecture and tested several optimization techniques. Sureddy et al. (2021) [20] proposed the MF-MLP Classifier to address facial appearance identification challenges and conducted extensive tests on both constrained and uncontrolled datasets, demonstrating its effectiveness. Gaddam et al. (2022) [4] introduced a network for classifying human face expressions from still images using ResNet50. Sreevidya et al. (2022) [18] created a multi-modal system with an older target that integrates data from audio and video modalities. Chahak et al. (2023) [5] investigated the application of feature extraction techniques such as HOG and SIFT in combination with CNNs. They conducted performance assessments on two datasets, CK+ and JAFFE, to experiment the efficacy of their methods. In Wasi et al. (2023) [22], they introduced ARBEx, an innovative attentive feature extraction framework employing the Vision Transformer with reliability balancing for FEL. ARBEx incorporates data preprocessing, cross-attention ViT, and the use of learnable anchor points with multi-head self-attention to enhance label predictions. They also propose the use of Anchor loss to improve label classification.

3   Our Proposed Dataset

Emotion theories propose that emotions can be categorized into three types: physiological, cognitive, and neurological. According to these theories, emotions arise as a result of specific physiological responses that occur before, during, or after an emotional experience. These emotional experiences can then be expressed through facial expressions. Emotion models can be broadly classified into categorical and dimensional models. The categorical model proposes that there are basic emotions such as anger, fear, sadness, happiness, surprise, and disgust, as proposed by Ekman et al. [2,3]. In contrast, the dimensional model, describes emotions in terms of two dimensions, arousal and valence, or adds a third dimension, power, to the two dimensions. To better understand a person's true emotional state, the Facial Action Coding System (FACS) is utilized. FACS systematically categorizes facial muscle movements that align with specific displayed emotions. It is a comprehensive and useful system for determining emotions based on facial expressions. Within the FACS [15], there exist 32 fundamental facial muscle activities referred to as Action Units (AUs). Additionally, there are 14 supplementary Action Descriptors (ADs) that encompass various actions, including head attitude, gaze direction, and movements such as

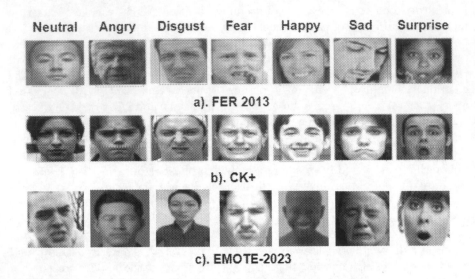

Fig. 1. Images from Facial Emotion Recognition datasets a) FER2013, b) CK+ c) EMOTE-2023

jaw thrust, blow, and bite. Overall, emotion theories and models, along with the FACS system, provide a framework for understanding and identifying emotions based on physiological responses and facial expressions. Keeping this theory in mind, we propose the new dataset EMOTE-2023.

For computer applications to recognize emotions, Deep Learning models must undergo training on datasets. There are publicly available datasets, such as CK+ and FER2013, that focus on seven primary emotions experienced by all individuals: happiness, sadness, anger, disgust, fear, surprise, and neutrality. However, we propose a novel dataset, EMOTE-2023. Details about these datasets are provided below:

FER2013 (Facial Expression Recognition 2013): The FER2013 dataset was introduced at the ICML 2013 Challenges in Representation Learning conference. [6]. The database includes 28,709 training images, 3,589 validation images, and 3,589 test images labeled with seven expression categories.

CK+ (Cohn-Kanade+): The CK+ database includes 593 video sequences from 123 individuals, with varying durations of frames, showcasing a progression from a neutral facial expression to the peak expression [11]. CK+ is a widely used dataset that contains 327 image sequences from 118 subjects having facial expressions, ranging from neutral to seven basic emotions. The dataset also includes intensity labels, action unit annotations, and demographic information for each subject.

Our proposed dataset, EMOTE-2023, is a novel dataset consisting of 4826 synthetic images generated using the powerful 3D computer graphics engines, Unreal Engine (UE) and Maya Platform. Unreal Engine, developed by Epic

Games, is a gaming engine used for 3D computer graphics, while Maya is a popular application used for 3D animation, simulation, modeling and rendering. Our approach leverages the mapping of emotions to FACS Action Units (AUs) to create realistic facial expressions in UE and Maya. We then apply these emotions to a variety of metahuman avatars in diverse lighting and environmental conditions. Figure 1 shows images showing different emotions for each dataset. While existing Face emotion datasets are low resolution (for example, 48×48 for FER), EMOTE-2023 contains high resolution images (256×256). The development of the proposed dataset also contributes significantly to the expansion of the emotional spectrum in facial emotion recognition research. By introducing novel emotions such as contempt, boredom, and joy, this dataset provides a more comprehensive understanding of human emotional expressions. It enables the training and evaluation of FER models under diverse and realistic conditions, ultimately enhancing the field of facial emotion recognition.

4   Methodology

The methodology proposed for this study comprises five key steps: (a) preprocessing of facial images, (b) face detection and region selection, (c) transfer learning using network, and (e) Training and Cross-validation.

4.1   Pre-processing

For improving performance of the FER, the initial step is to arrange and preprocess the data. Sample data from the datasets are depicted in Fig. 1. Preprocessing of images involves several steps, including face detection, cropping, and resizing to a standardized size of 256 * 256 pixels.

4.2   Face Detection and Region Selection

Face detection, which is also referred to as face registration, involves identifying the area of interest (i.e., the face) within an image. For this task, we utilize the OpenCV haarcascade-frontal face-default approach. Once the face has been detected, we crop the image to isolate the face and subsequently resize it to 256 * 256 pixels.

4.3   Transfer Learning and Model Training

Transfer learning is a technique in machine learning where a pre-trained model is used as a starting point for a new task. The idea behind transfer learning is that the pre-trained model has already learned relevant features twhich can be useful for the new task. This approach saves a lot of time and computational resources as the pre-trained model is not trained from scratch, and also it can be fine-tuned on the new data. In transfer learning, the pre-trained model is usually trained on a large dataset. After pre-training, the model's weights are saved, and the model is then re-used for a new task, typically with a smaller dataset. To fine-tune the pre-trained model for the new task, the model is trained on the new dataset. Transfer learning has many benefits, including faster training times, better performance on small datasets, and improved accuracy. It is widely used in image and text-based tasks, such as object detection, sentiment analysis, and language translation.

In our work, the process of transfer learning involved two main steps. Firstly, Pre-training on a large dataset is performed, our deep learning networks are trained on a large dataset, ImageNet, to learn general features that are useful for many different tasks. Then, fine-tuning on a target dataset is performed through additional training on smaller target datasets FER2013, CK+, and EMOTE-2023 respectively. The deep architectures used in our work are discussed below:

1. VGG: The VGG (Visual Geometry Group) network is a deep convolutional neural network that was trained on ImageNet. It consists of multiple convolutional layers followed by fully connected layers [16].
2. ResNet: The ResNet (Residual Network) is a deep neural network that uses skip connections to address the vanishing gradient problem. It has many layers and was also trained on ImageNet [21].
3. MobileNet: The MobileNet network is a lightweight deep neural network that was designed to run efficiently on mobile devices. It uses depth wise separable convolutions to reduce the number of parameters [17]. In our work, emotion classification task, the pre-trained model trained on ImageNet are fine-tuned based on emotion datasets.

4.4   Model Testing

The dataset consists of FER 2013, CK+ and EMOTE-2023 images. These datasets are divided into training and testing dataset. The different versions of VGG, ResNet and MobileNet are used for transfer learning. The trained model is then used to identify different emotions.

5   Results and Discussion

Table 1. Face Emotion Recognition System performance on FER2013 dataset

Deep Learning Model	Accuracy	Precision	Recall
VGG-16	70.93%	68.65%	68.90%
VGG-19	69.85%	73.23%	69.85%
MobileNet	68%	69%	68.90%
ResNet-18	72.49%	70.50%	69.35%

Table 2. Face Emotion Recognition System performance on CK+ dataset

Deep Learning Model	Accuracy	Precision	Recall
VGG-16	96%	78.65%	78.90%
VGG-19	93.94%	80.32%	89.85%
MobileNet	92.02%	75.60%	76.30%
ResNet-18	96.97%	80.50%	79.35%

Table 3. Face Emotion Recognition System performance on Emote-2023 dataset

Deep Learning Model	Accuracy	Precision	Recall
VGG-16	96.97%	80.10%	79.80%
VGG-19	94.94%	85.60%	90.13%
MobileNet	93.45%	76.52%	78.51%
ResNet-18	97.97%	84.86%	86.88%

The methodology of our research involves using transfer learning technique to train a deep learning model to perform face emotion recognition. We used a pre-trained convolutional neural network, including different versions of VGG, ResNet, and MobileNet, which were initially pre-trained on the ImageNet dataset, as our starting point.

To adapt the pre-trained model for our specific task, we trained the model on new datasets. We fine-tuned the model using three datasets: FER2013, CK+, and our newly introduced EMOTE-2023 dataset. The proposed model is trained using the stochastic gradient descent optimizer with a learning rate of 0.001. The training process was performed on a GPU for faster computation. We employed the cross-entropy loss function to measure the error between the predicted and actual emotions. The model was trained for 60 epochs, and the batch size is set to 128. After training, performance of our model was tested on various FER datasets. After training, we evaluated the model's performance on various FER datasets, including VGG, ResNet, and MobileNet models. Performance of the system is evaluated based on accuracy, precision, and recall metrics of the model. Our results show that the fine-tuned VGG16, VGG19, ResNet18, and MobileNet models achieved accuracy scores of 70.93%, 69.85%, 72.49%, and 69%, respectively, on the FER2023 dataset, as summarized in Table 1. On the CK+ dataset, these models achieved accuracy scores of 96%, 93.94%, 96.97%, and 92.02%, respectively, as shown in Table 2. Additionally, on the EMOTE-2023 dataset, they achieved accuracy scores of 96.97%, 94.94%, 97.97%, and 93.45%, respectively, as summarized in Table 3.

Our findings demonstrate that transfer learning is a powerful technique for emotion recognition tasks, particularly when dealing with small datasets like EMOTE-2023 and have also yielded promising results with the proposed three emotions (Joy, Boredom, Contempt). Overall, our methodology highlights the effectiveness of transfer learning and model training in achieving high accuracy in emotion recognition. As shown in Table 2, among the different deep learning model, the ResNet model outperformed other existing models, demonstrating its superior performance on all the three datasets.

6   Conclusions

In this research, we introduced a novel synthetic dataset, EMOTE-2023, consisting of 4826 images of different emotions generated using Unreal Engine and Maya with FACS Action Units mapping for emotions. We evaluated the performance of our dataset by training a facial emotion recognition system using transfer learning with several deep learning models, including VGG-16, VGG-19, ResNet-18, and MobileNet. The pre-trained network architecture's weights are initially trained on a large dataset, ImageNet. Subsequently, the complete network is fine-tuned using input datasets: FER 2013, CK+, and EMOTE-2023. The emotions covered by our dataset include Happy, Sad, Neutral, Fear, Disgust, Surprise, and Anger. Our transfer learning approach achieved the highest accuracy of 72.49%, 96.97%, and 97.97% using the ResNet-18 model for FER2013, CK+, and EMOTE-2023 respectively. Overall, our research demonstrates the effectiveness of synthetic datasets and transfer learning for emotion recognition tasks. Our results also highlight the potential of our approach for developing more accurate and robust emotion detection systems for a range of applications, including healthcare, gaming, and education.

References

1. Arshid, S., Hussain, A., Munir, A., Nawaz, A., Aziz, S.: Multi-stage binary patterns for facial expression recognition in real world. Clust. Comput. **21**, 323–331 (2018)
2. Ekman, P., Friesen, W.V.: Facial action coding system. Environ. Psychol. Nonverbal Behav. (1978)
3. Ekman, P., et al.: Basic emotions. Handb. Cogn. Emot. **98**(45–60), 16 (1999)
4. Gaddam, D.K.R., Ansari, M.D., Vuppala, S., Gunjan, V.K., Sati, M.M.: Human facial emotion detection using deep learning. In: Kumar, A., Senatore, S., Gunjan, V.K. (eds.) ICDSMLA 2020. LNEE, vol. 783, pp. 1417–1427. Springer, Singapore (2022). https://doi.org/10.1007/978-981-16-3690-5_136
5. Gautam, C., Seeja, K.: Facial emotion recognition using handcrafted features and CNN. Procedia Comput. Sci. **218**, 1295–1303 (2023)
6. Goodfellow, I.J., et al.: Challenges in representation learning: a report on three machine learning contests. In: Lee, M., Hirose, A., Hou, Z.-G., Kil, R.M. (eds.) ICONIP 2013. LNCS, vol. 8228, pp. 117–124. Springer, Heidelberg (2013). https://doi.org/10.1007/978-3-642-42051-1_16
7. Khaireddin, Y., Chen, Z.: Facial emotion recognition: state of the art performance on FER2013. arXiv preprint arXiv:2105.03588 (2021)
8. Khan, S.A., Hussain, A., Usman, M.: Facial expression recognition on real world face images using intelligent techniques: a survey. Optik **127**(15), 6195–6203 (2016)
9. Ko, B.C.: A brief review of facial emotion recognition based on visual information. Sensors **18**(2), 401 (2018)

10. Komala, K., Jayadevappa, D., Shivaprakash, G.: Human emotion detection and classification using convolution neural network. Eur. J. Mol. Clin. Med. **7**(06) (2020)
11. Lucey, P., Cohn, J.F., Kanade, T., Saragih, J., Ambadar, Z., Matthews, I.: The extended Cohn-Kanade dataset (CK+): a complete dataset for action unit and emotion-specified expression, pp. 94–101 (2010)
12. Mellouk, W., Handouzi, W.: Facial emotion recognition using deep learning: review and insights. Procedia Comput. Sci. **175**, 689–694 (2020)
13. Minaee, S., Minaei, M., Abdolrashidi, A.: Deep-emotion: facial expression recognition using attentional convolutional network. Sensors **21**(9), 3046 (2021)
14. Ng, H.W., Nguyen, V.D., Vonikakis, V., Winkler, S.: Deep learning for emotion recognition on small datasets using transfer learning, pp. 443–449 (2015)
15. Rosenberg, E.L., Ekman, P.: What the Face Reveals: Basic and Applied Studies of Spontaneous Expression Using the Facial Action Coding System (FACS). Oxford University Press, Oxford (2020)
16. Sengupta, A., Ye, Y., Wang, R., Liu, C., Roy, K.: Going deeper in spiking neural networks: VGG and residual architectures. Front. Neurosci. **13**, 95 (2019)
17. Sinha, D., El-Sharkawy, M.: Thin MobileNet: an enhanced MobileNet architecture, pp. 0280–0285 (2019)
18. Sreevidya, P., Veni, S., Ramana Murthy, O.: Elder emotion classification through multimodal fusion of intermediate layers and cross-modal transfer learning. Signal Image Video Process. **16**(5), 1281–1288 (2022)
19. Sun, Y., Wen, G.: Cognitive facial expression recognition with constrained dimensionality reduction. Neurocomputing **230**, 397–408 (2017)
20. Sureddy, S., Jacob, J.: Multi-features based multi-layer perceptron for facial expression recognition system. In: Chen, J.I.-Z., Tavares, J.M.R.S., Iliyasu, A.M., Du, K.-L. (eds.) ICIPCN 2021. LNNS, vol. 300, pp. 206–217. Springer, Cham (2022). https://doi.org/10.1007/978-3-030-84760-9_19
21. Targ, S., Almeida, D., Lyman, K.: Resnet in resnet: generalizing residual architectures. arXiv preprint arXiv:1603.08029 (2016)
22. Wasi, A.T., Šerbetar, K., Islam, R., Rafi, T.H., Chae, D.K.: ARBEx: attentive feature extraction with reliability balancing for robust facial expression learning. arXiv preprint arXiv:2305.01486 (2023)

Fusion of LSTM and RNN for Abnormal Activity Detection from CCTV Camera Feeds

Vijay Ukani$^{(\boxtimes)}$ and Pritam Prajapati

Department of Computer Science and Engineering, Institute of Technology, Nirma University, Ahmedabad 382481, India
{vijay.ukani,21mcec08}@nirmauni.ac.in

Abstract. Video surveillance is widely utilized in both public and private settings for observation and monitoring purposes, making it a prominent application of computer vision technology. It resulted in less human work put towards oversight. Homes, workplaces, hospitals, malls, parking lots, etc. places can use smart video surveillance systems. Due to its many uses, including identifying criminal behavior, traffic accidents, and unlawful activities, abnormal detection in video surveillance is a well-liked study topic in computer vision. Abnormal activity means any behavior or event that is not considered normal in a particular situation. For example, in CCTV footage, abnormal activity could include unusual or suspicious actions like theft, vandalism, or violence. The definition of abnormal activity can change based on the surveillance system's context and objectives. In this paper, we conducted a literature survey on abnormal activity detection. We experimented with detecting violence in videos using a convolutional neural network on the Real-Life Violence Situations(RLVS) dataset. Here, we have implemented three model architectures incorporating spatial and temporal features for violence detection. The first model combines MobileNetV2 with an RNN layer, while the second model employs an LSTM layer instead. The third model uses their strengths to represent a fusion of LSTM and RNN.

Keywords: LSTM · RNN · Fusion · RLVS · Spatio-temporal features · Violence Detection

1 Introduction

Machine learning research has exploded in popularity during the previous two decades [7]. Moreover, deep learning has gained significant popularity compared to other machine learning algorithms in the past decade. This trend highlights the expanded scope of machine learning, specifically deep learning, in terms of its applications. In deep learning, most commonly employed models are Multilayer Perceptron's (MLP), Convolutional Neural Networks (CNN), and Long Short Term Memory(LSTM). CNN is frequently utilized in computer vision [13] and

H. Kaur et al. (Eds.): CVIP 2023, CCIS 2009, pp. 532–543, 2024.
https://doi.org/10.1007/978-3-031-58181-6_45

natural language processing [14]. MLP has numerous uses, including applications in domains line health, athletics, finance, etc. LSTM is mostly used in sequential data, such as text [20], sound [5], and video [8].

Abnormal activity detection in CCTV footage is an emerging field of research that aims to develop automated methods for identifying unusual events in video footage captured by surveillance cameras. The main objective is to send notifications on time and stop security breaches, crimes, or other possible hazards. The requirement for precise and effective abnormal activity detection expands with the global proliferation of security cameras. The creation of powerful machine learning approaches that can precisely discern between normal and abnormal actions in video data has attracted much study attention. Deep learning strategies have demonstrated a lot of potential in this field. Using cutting-edge neural network designs, it is feasible to effectively identify anomalous activity by extracting spatio-temporal information from video data. These methods have the potential to completely transform the surveillance industry by allowing for the timely, accurate, and reliable identification of anomalous activity. Creating algorithms that can precisely discriminate between normal and abnormal activity is one of the major issues facing this subject. In order to do this, advanced machine learning methods that can identify patterns in video material must be used. CNNs and Recurrent Neural Networks (RNNs)have shown a lot of promise in this field.

Abnormal activity refers to any behavior or event that deviates from what is considered normal or expected in a given context. In the context of CCTV footage, abnormal activity could refer to any behavior or event that is unusual or suspicious, such as theft, vandalism, or violence. Abnormal activity can vary from surveillance system target and depend on the application.

Abnormal activities in public places can include a wide range of actions that deviate from what is considered normal or acceptable behavior. Some examples of abnormal activities in public places can include theft, violence, accidents, vandalism, fighting, chain snatching, crime, and other suspicious activities. There have been proposals for computer vision-based systems that can efficiently detect abnormal activities happening in public places.

When any abnormal activity is detected from surveillance video, a warning can be sent to the appropriate law enforcement agency or security officials to take prompt action. In the current era of digital advancements, the widespread availability of video content has brought forth a range of possibilities and obstacles. Among these challenges, one crucial task is accurately identifying and categorizing violent content. The detection of violence in videos has gained significant importance across multiple fields, including security, surveillance, and content moderation. The development of automated models capable of efficiently analyzing video content and discerning between violent and non-violent scenes holds immense potential for bolstering public safety measures and refining content filtering procedures.

The remainder of the article is structured as follows. A literature review highlighting the state of the art in the domain is described in Sect. 2. Based on the observations in the literature review, three models are proposed, which are described in Sect. 3. Results of the three proposed models are discussed in Sect. 4. The article ends in Sect. 5 with a conclusion and future remarks.

2   Literature Survey

Abnormal activity detection from live surveillance video is an interesting study area that many people have been researching. However, due to the complex nature of the problem itself, the required level of accuracy could not be achieved. However, interest has recently increased in utilizing powerful deep-learning algorithms for this problem.

Pathade's proposed method used deep features and hand-crafted features for detecting crowd abnormal events [11]. If people are walking coherently, and freely roaming, significant movement between the people is considered as a normal event. Merging and sudden dispersion events are considered abnormal events. The author uses handcrafted features in their proposed method. These features consisted of three spatial measures: "the average distance from the crowd's centroid", "the rate of change in the average distance from the centroid", and "the rate of change in average density". Additionally, two motion features, "the average magnitude of motion" and "the rate of change in magnitude of motion" are also used. For deep feature extraction, authors used pre-trained GoogleNet with 12 layers [17]. Fusion of hand-crafted features and deep features authors got 1029×1 vector which helps classify into a normal event, abnormal event using SoftMax layer. PETs get 97.2 AUC and UMN gets 99.2 AUC [11].

The authors in [9] used a variational autoencoder for the abnormal event detection. The authors explained how to train a model using normal samples to find and discover anomalous video events. The method uses partially labeled data, where only the normal samples are labeled, rather than fully labeled training data. This pattern aids the model's comprehension of typical behavior in the video. It is less likely for the model to fit into the Gaussian distribution pattern of normal samples when it encounters an abnormal event. The algorithm can identify and pinpoint the anomalous event in the video because of that change in pattern. The model is based on variational autoencoder (VAE) and for experiments, they use the UCSD dataset and Avenue dataset. VAE have two part: one is the encoder, and another is a decoder. Each point in the latent space represents a potential encoding of the input data, and the encoder transforms the input data into a lower-dimensional representation within the latent space. Convolutional or fully connected layers of neural networks are frequently used in the encoder for lower-dimensional representation within the latent space. The decoder maps points in the latent space to the initial input data space. Additionally, it frequently includes several layers of neural networks that gradually upscale the latent representation to the original data space. The final layer of the decoder usually employs an activation function such as sigmoid or softmax to produce the output data. During training, the VAE model optimizes a loss function comprising two terms: a reconstruction loss, which calculates input data and the output difference, and a regularization term, which encourages the learned latent space to follow a specific prior distribution. In the model used, the encoder and decoder have four hidden layers. The first and second layers have 500 neurons, the third layer has 2000 neurons, and the last layer has 30 neurons. They resized images in 160 × 120. In the UCSD Ped1 dataset, the proposed method achieved results in the frame-level AUC of 92.3%, 71.4% AUC at the pixel-level, and in the avenue data set, the frame-level AUC of 82.1% [9].

Ullah et al. [18] proposed abnormal event detection for live surveillance networks. The model uses a sequential learning approach to accurately identify aberrant behaviors in a video stream. The authors used a pre-trained MobileNetV2 model on an ImageNet dataset for feature extraction from the video frames. The features are learned from the pre-trained model for the abnormal event detection task. The author used the attention-based LSTM concept for the sequential learning method. The residual attention mechanism plays a crucial role in identifying the key areas of the input frames that are significant for anomaly detection. It enables the model to pay more attention to the relevant features while disregarding irrelevant details, ultimately enhancing its performance. The suggested model is able to successfully learn temporal information and identify abnormal activity in the video stream by utilizing a residual attention-based LSTM. Additionally, compared to the typical LSTM network size, the adoption of a residual attention-based LSTM reduces the number of learnable parameters by more than 10%, making the model lighter and more computationally efficient. To evaluate the proposed model, the author used a UCF-Crime dataset that contains various anomalous activities in outdoor scenes. UFC crime data set contains 13 abnormal events, but in the experiment, they tried to detect abnormal events like assaults, explosions, fighting, and road accidents. The use of fifty videos from each of the five classes divided the records into 50% as training, 30% as validation, and 20% as testing. For the UCF crime data set, they are able to achieve 78.3% accuracy, and for the avenue and UMN data set their proposed model achieves 98.30% accuracy and 98.29% accuracy respectively.

Biradar et al. [3] proposed a method that used two types of features: appearance-based features and flow-based features. For appearance-based features, the author uses the pre-trained model VGG-19 on image-net. For flow-based features, they use optical flow between two successive frames. The image is then resized into the 227 × 227, and for motion feature extraction, they used FlowNet [4], which was trained on UCF 101. The data proportion used for training, validation and testing was 50:30:20. Authors could achieve 76.66% detection accuracy.

An approach for predicting violence in videos was proposed by Halder et al. in [6] which uses a CNN-BiLSTM model architecture. For analyzing the sequential flow of the frame author proposed this model. The video is initially divided into frames, and the information contained in every frame is extracted using a CNN. This allows the network to identify and isolate relevant features in the video. It uses three layers of CNN followed by max pooling layer, each consisting of 64 units. After extracting the spatial features from each frame, the information is fed into a Bidirectional LSTM layer. For comparing ongoing frame information with previous and upcoming frames, this layer is used. By comparing the information in this way, the network can recognize any sequential flow of events that may indicate violent actions. The classification is done by using a dense layer consisting of 64 and 32 units of two layers and a final layer with two neurons that classify the event as violent or not. The CNN-BiLSTM architecture provides a comprehensive approach to analyzing videos for violent actions. Overall, this proposed approach offers a promising method for identifying violent actions in videos. For experimentation, they used Hockey fight, Movies fight dataset, Violent-Flows dataset. They resize all images into 100×100 pixels. 90% of data was used for training while the remaining 10% for testing. The proposed model could achieve 99.27% accuracy on the hockey fight data set, 100% accuracy in movie fights, and 98.64% for the violent flow dataset.

Authors in [19], used Mobile-net as an encoder and make Unet like a model for the spatial feature extraction and for the temporal feature extraction author uses LSTM. The classification was achieved by using two layers of fully connected dense layers. In the proposed model, the author made architecture like the Unet model using Mobile-net as an encoder in the model. For the experiment, they used 1600 videos from the RWF-2000 dataset, 200 from the Movie Fights dataset, and 500 videos from the Hockey Fights dataset. They were able to achieve $82.0 \pm 3\%, 96.1 \pm 1\%$, and $99.5 \pm 2\%$ accuracy respectively.

3D Convolutional Neural Networks (CNNs) is an effective tool for spatiotemporal feature extraction from videos, including detecting violent events. However, these models still suffer from limitations, such as generating false positives for friendly gestures or fast movements, such as hugs or high-fives. To overcome this problem, the author proposed a new data set called the AIRTLab dataset [15]. The dataset used in the study comprises 350 MP4 videos. The average duration of the video is 5.63, and videos are in the range of 2 to 14 s long. Videos have frame rate of 30 fps and the resolution is 1920×1080 pixels. Data set is divided into non-violent and violent classes. The authors test the dataset on three different deep-learning-based model. They used 3D CNN for feature extraction from the videos and SVM for classifying the clip, which was able to achieve 96.1% accuracy. Same 3D CNN is used in the second model for feature extraction, but they use two fully connected dense layers for the classification. This model was able to achieve 95.62% accuracy. ConvLSTM was used in the last model, and 97.15% accuracy was achieved. These models show promise in reducing false positives and improving the accuracy of violence detection.

Detecting abnormal events in videos presents significant challenges, primarily because "abnormality" is subjective. Unfortunately, accurate event classification using large, complex datasets is difficult to achieve with current deep-learning techniques. Creating novel architectures that can quickly identify and categorize abnormal events in surveillance scenes is crucial.

Violence is one of the abnormal events incurred by the human. This research aims to develop an architecture that performs better, is more accurate, and is more effective when identifying and classifying events as violence or non-violence.

Article	Model Used	Features Extraction	Dataset	Results
Pathade et al. [11]	Fusion of deep and handcrafted features	Googlenet for feature extraction	PETS and UMN	PETs get 97.2 AUC and UMN gets 99.2 AUC
Ma et al. [9]	Variational autoencoder	single-class SVM	UCSD Ped1and Avenue	AUC of 92.3% for UCSD and AUC of 82.1% for Avenue
Ullah et al. [18]	Attention-based LSTM	MobileNetV2 for feature extraction	ImageNet, UCF-Crime, Avenue, UMN	Accuracy of 78.3% for UCF, 98.30% for Avenue and 98.29% for UMN dataset
Biradar et al. [3]	Pre-trained VGG-19 and FlowNet	pretrained light-weight CNN	UCF 101	76.66% detection accuracy
Halder et al. [6]	CNN-BiLSTM	CNN	Hockey fight, Movies fight, Violent-Flows	Accuracy of 99.27% on hockey fight, 100% on movie fights, 98.64% for violent flow dataset
Vijeikis et al. [19]	Similar to Unet model with Mobile-net as encoder	Unet and LSTM	RWF-2000, Hockey fight, Movies fight	Accuracy of 82.0 ± 3%, 99.5 ± 2%, and 96.1 ± 1% for 3 datasets
Sernani et al. [15]	3D CNN+SVM, ConvLSTM	3D CNN for feature extraction	AIRTLab	96.1% accuracy using CNN+SVM and 97.15% using ConvLSTM
Accattoli et al. [2]	3D CNN and SVM	3D CNN for feature extraction	Sport-1M, Hockey fight, Crowd Violence	98.51% on the Hockey fight and 99.29% on crowd violence dataset

3   Methodology

In the proposed model, we use MobileNetV2, a pre-trained model, RNN and
LSTM. The model seeks to capture the visual context and the temporal dynamics inside the movies, enabling reliable violence classification. It extracts spatial
features using MobileNetV2 and temporal features using RNN or LSTM. The
Real-Life Violence Situations 1 (RLVS) data set is used for the experiment.
It comprises of 2000 clips with uniform distribution of violent and nonviolent
classes. Three different model architectures that incorporate spatial and temporal features for violence detection are proposed in this work. The first model
combines MobileNetV2 with an RNN layer, while the second model employs an
LSTM layer instead. The third model represents a fusion of LSTM and RNN
and uses the strengths of both LSTM and RNN.

3.1   Data Pre-processing

The Real-Life Violence Situations 1 (RLVS) datasets include movies that are
collected from several categories and have a wide range of genders, ethnicities,
and ages. The videos contain violence and depicts fight happening in different
places including street, prison, school, etc. In contrast, the non-violence videos
showcase a range of activities involving people, like playing football, basketball,
tennis, talking, running, dancing, etc. [16].

The average video clip duration is five seconds, with a minimum length of three seconds and a maximum length of seven seconds. The data set contains a video with different resolutions ranging from 224×224 to 1920×1080. Sixteen frames from each video are extracted and resized into 100×100 pixels. The frame's RGB values are normalized and labeled with violence and non-violence. We use 90% data for the training and 10% data for the testing. 20% of data from the training set was used for validation. 200 videos were used for testing, 1440 videos for training, and 360 for validation (Fig. 1).

(A)   (B)

Fig. 1. Example of (A) Violence and (B) Non-Violence scenario from RLVS dataset [16]

3.2 MobileNetV2 with RNN Model

In the first model for the temporal feature extraction, we use RNN as shown in Fig. 2. The data is first fed into the pre-trained model MobilenetV2. The input size is $16 \times 100 \times 100 \times 3$, where 16 represents the number of frames per video, 100×100 is the size of frames, and 3 is the RGB value of the frame. The output of the pre-trained model is fed into the RNN layer, which contains 64 units of neurons. The output of RNN serves as input to two dense layers with 64, 32 fully connected neurons. The final layer has two neurons, classifying the frame into violence and non-violence classes. The softmax activation function is used at the last output neuron to get probabilistic output.

3.3 MobileNetV2 with LSTM Model

This model for the temporal feature extraction uses LSTM. The data first feed into the pre-trained model MobilenetV2. For temporal feature extraction, LSTM is used instead of RNN. The rest of the architecture is the same as the first model.

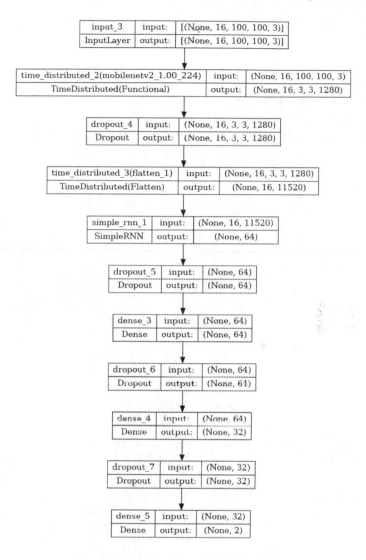

Fig. 2. MobileNetV2 with RNN Model

3.4   LSTM and RNN Fusion Model

The third model is the fusion of LSTM and RNN as illustrated in Fig. 3. The data
is passed as input to the pre-trained MobilenetV2. The output of MobilenetV2
is passed into two layers of LSTM as well as two layers of RNN. LSTM and RNN
both have a first layer with 64 neurons and a second layer have 32 neurons. The
output of RNN and LSMT are added and fed into two fully connected dense
layers with 64 and 32 neurons. The final output layer has two neurons that
classify the date into violence and non-violence classes.

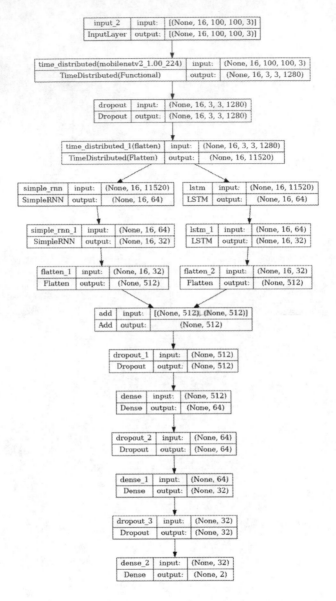

Fig. 3. Model summary of LSTM and RNN fusion

4   Results and Discussions

A classification report is used for analyzing the violence detection models. A classification report includes precision, recall, and f1-score. The precision score evaluates how accurately the model predicted each class. The recall score, also called sensitivity, indicates how well the model captures the favorable instances of each class. The F1-score is a measurement that combines recall and precision into a single number. It offers a general evaluation of the model's effectiveness for each class.

In RNN based model, the precision for the non-violence class is 0.95, meaning that 95% of the instances classified as non-violence were accurate. The precision for violence is 0.86. Recall for non-violence is 0.84, which indicates that 84% of the actual occurrences of non-violence were correctly identified. 96% of the actual instances of violence were correctly identified, according to the recall for violence, which is 0.96. The F1-score for non-violence is 0.89, indicating a performance that balances recall and precision. The F1-score for violence is 0.91, which indicates a comparable balance. 90% of the instances in the dataset were correctly classified according to the classifier, which has an overall accuracy of 0.90.

In MobileNetV2 with LSTM Model, the Precision for the non-violence class is 0.99, while for violence, it is 0.93. Recall for non-violence is 0.92, and violence class is 0.96. The F1-score for non-violence is 0.95, and violence is 0.96. And overall accuracy is 95%. The LSTM-based model achieved an impressive accuracy of 95%, surpassing the RNN model's performance. This suggests that the LSTM architecture was more effective in capturing the temporal dynamics of the videos, leading to improved classification results.

Finally, the third model, which fused LSTM and RNN architectures, demonstrated the highest level of performance among the three models. Precision for the non-violence and violence class is 0.97 and 0.98, respectively. Recall for non-violence is 0.98, while for the other class it is 0.97. The F1-score for non-violence is 0.97, for violence is 0.98. Its overall accuracy is 97%, showcasing its superior capability in accurately classifying violence and non-violence in videos. The fusion of LSTM and RNN seemingly enhanced the model's ability to capture spatial and temporal features, resulting in improved accuracy.

Table 1. Tabular summary of results of three models

Model	Accuracy	Precision	Recall	f1-score
RNN	90%	91%	90%	90%
LSTM	95%	96%	95%	95%
LSTM+RNN	**97%**	**97%**	**98%**	**97%**

Based on the evaluation of the violence detection models, the fusion of LSTM and RNN seems to outperform the other two models in terms of accuracy and other measures. Table 1 illustrates this comparison. The proposed approach was compared with previously published work in terms of accuracy in Table 2. The RNN-LSTM fusion model demonstrated the potential of using spatial and temporal features to classify violent and non-violent videos effectively. These results highlight the importance of selecting appropriate model architectures and feature extraction techniques for accurate violence detection in videos.

Table 2. Comparison of RNN+LSTM fusion model with other published work

Model	Accuracy
Soliman et al. [16]	88.20%
Traor'e and Akhlouf [10]	90.25%
Rathi, K. [12]	94.00%
A. R. Abdali [1]	96.25%
LSTM and RNN Fusion Model	**97.50%**

5   Conclusions and Future Scope

Video surveillance has significantly increased deployment in public and private spaces. By anomaly detection using machine learning and deep learning, we can reduce the human intervention for surveillance. The main objective is to send notifications on time and stop security breaches, crimes, or other possible hazards. In this paper, we conducted a literature survey on abnormal activity detection and experimented with detecting violence in videos on the Real-Life Violence Situations 1 (RLVS) dataset. Three different model architectures were implemented that incorporate spatial and temporal features for violence detection. The first model combines MobileNetV2 with an RNN layer, while the second model employs an LSTM layer instead. The third model uses a fusion of LSTM and RNN, leveraging the strengths of both architectures. Of the three models for violence detection, the fusion of LSTM and RNN outperformed the other two models in terms of accuracy. This model can be examined on a complex data set. In the future, the fusion of audio and video data can be an interesting challenge for abnormal activity detection, as audio provides additional information that may be critical in classifying the activity.

References

1. Abdali, A.R.: Data efficient video transformer for violence detection. In: 2021 IEEE International Conference on Communication, Networks and Satellite (COMNET-SAT), pp. 195–199. IEEE (2021)
2. Accattoli, S., Sernani, P., Falcionelli, N., Mekuria, D.N., Dragoni, A.F.: Violence detection in videos by combining 3D convolutional neural networks and support vector machines. Appl. Artif. Intell. **34**(4), 329–344 (2020)
3. Biradar, K., Dube, S., Vipparthi, S.K.: DEAREVSt: deep convolutional aberrant behavior detection in real-world scenarios. In: 2018 IEEE 13th International Conference on Industrial and Information Systems (ICIIS), pp. 163–167. IEEE (2018)
4. Dosovitskiy, A., et al.: FlowNet: learning optical flow with convolutional networks. In: Proceedings of the IEEE International Conference on Computer Vision, pp. 2758–2766 (2015)
5. Ertam, F.: An effective gender recognition approach using voice data via deeper LSTM networks. Appl. Acoust. **156**, 351–358 (2019)

6. Halder, R., Chatterjee, R.: CNN-BiLSTM model for violence detection in smart surveillance. SN Comput. Sci. **1**(4), 201 (2020)
7. Hao, K.: We analyzed 16,625 papers to figure out where AI is headed next (2020)
8. Lu, N., Wu, Y., Feng, L., Song, J.: Deep learning for fall detection: three-dimensional CNN combined with LSTM on video kinematic data. IEEE J. Biomed. Health Inform. **23**(1), 314–323 (2018)
9. Ma, Q.: Abnormal event detection in videos based on deep neural networks. Sci. Program. **2021**, 1–8 (2021)
10. de Oliveira Lima, J.P., Figueiredo, C.M.S.: A temporal fusion approach for video classification with convolutional and LSTM neural networks applied to violence detection. Intell. Artif. **24**(67), 40–50 (2021)
11. Pathade, M., Khambete, M.: Recognition of crowd abnormal activities using fusion of handcrafted and deep features. Indon. J. Electr. Eng. Comput. Sci. **28**(2), 1076–1087 (2022)
12. Rathi, S., Sharma, S., Ojha, S., Kumar, K.: Violence recognition from videos using deep learning. In: Mahapatra, R.P., Peddoju, S.K., Roy, S., Parwekar, P. (eds.) Proceedings of International Conference on Recent Trends in Computing. Lecture Notes in Networks and Systems, vol. 600, pp. 69–77. Springer, Singapore (2023). https://doi.org/10.1007/978-981-19-8825-7_7
13. Ravichandran, K., Arulchelvan, S., PeriyaKannan, K.: Perception of medical awareness of media analyzed by multilayer perceptron. J. Media Commun. Stud. **10**(10), 118–127 (2018)
14. Rawat, W., Wang, Z.: Deep convolutional neural networks for image classification: a comprehensive review. Neural Comput. **29**(9), 2352–2449 (2017)
15. Sernani, P., Falcionelli, N., Tomassini, S., Contardo, P., Dragoni, A.F.: Deep learning for automatic violence detection: tests on the AIRTLab dataset. IEEE Access **9**, 160580–160595 (2021)
16. Soliman, M.M., Kamal, M.H., Nashed, M.A.E.M., Mostafa, Y.M., Chawky, B.S., Khattab, D.: Violence recognition from videos using deep learning techniques. In: 2019 Ninth International Conference on Intelligent Computing and Information Systems (ICICIS), pp. 80–85. IEEE (2019)
17. Szegedy, C., et al.: Going deeper with convolutions. In: Proceedings of the IEEE Conference on Computer Vision and Pattern Recognition, pp. 1–9 (2015)
18. Ullah, W., Ullah, A., Hussain, T., Khan, Z.A., Baik, S.W.: An efficient anomaly recognition framework using an attention residual LSTM in surveillance videos. Sensors **21**(8), 2811 (2021)
19. Vijeikis, R., Raudonis, V., Dervinis, G.: Efficient violence detection in surveillance. Sensors **22**(6), 2216 (2022)
20. Wei, D., et al.: Research on unstructured text data mining and fault classification based on RNN-LSTM with malfunction inspection report. Energies **10**(3), 406 (2017)

Interval Valued Data Representation for Gender Classification of Celebrity Cartoon Faces

S. Prajna[1]([✉]) [iD], D. S. Guru[1] [iD], D. L. Shivaprasad[1] [iD], and N. Vinay Kumar[2] [iD]

[1] Department of Studies in Computer Science, University of Mysore, Manasagangotri, Mysuru 570009, India
prajna.s63@gmail.com, dsg@compsci.uni-mysore.ac.in
[2] NTT Data Services, Bangalore, India

Abstract. In this paper, we address the problem of recognizing the gender of celebrities in cartoons images. We propose a method of representing celebrity cartoon faces by the use of interval-valued features and suitable symbolic classifier for gender classification. The FaceNet architecture which is recommended for Face recognition is adopted to extract features for cartoon faces. In each class, the similar looking celebrity cartoon images are clustered using K-means clustering algorithm. The approach is carried forward to preserve the intra-class variation present in each cluster corresponding to each class using a vector of interval-valued data is empirically evident. Thus, a cluster of gender cartoon faces is represented in the form of a vector of intervals. Further, a method of reducing the dimensionality of interval-valued features is employed to reduce considerably the number of interval-valued features for compact representation to have efficient yet effective classification with a minimal number of feature set by reducing computational burden is add on in our proposed methodology than the contemporary models. However, based on gender celebrity cartoons identification and facial expression prediction is kept beyond the scope of this paper as it is our future target. For experimentation purpose, we have used IIIT-CFW Celebrity Cartoon Face database. The results show that the proposed model outperforms the other existing models with respect to F-measure.

Keywords: Deep features · partitional clustering · Interval Valued Data Representation · Symbolic Classifier · Celebrity cartoon gender classification

1 Introduction

In the domain of cartoon face recognition [1] cartoon character face recognition is more commanding than celebrity faces in cartoons. Cartoon faces are the most prominent form of appealing art that is used regularly in our day-to-day life. Cartoons are a form of non-realistic or semi-realistic image that elevate hilarious context/situational interpretations of real-world circumstances. In the area of entertainment, education, advertising, etc., cartoons play vital roles and have a wide range of applications. Generally, cartoon images of celebrities pose high intra-class variations and heterogeneity in terms of their features. Hence the detection and recognition of faces of celebrities in cartoon images

H. Kaur et al. (Eds.): CVIP 2023, CCIS 2009, pp. 544–553, 2024.
https://doi.org/10.1007/978-3-031-58181-6_46

are demanding. In this direction, categorizing the gender using the recognized cartoon images is still more expecting, thus it motivated us to take up the work in the view of diminishing the search complexity in the space of recognition.

Classification of gender is a binary class problem, which carries a highly distinguished information concern to gender specific. It aims to recognize the gender of a person based on the characteristics that differentiate between masculinity and femininity. With this motivation we address the problem of recognition of gender of celebrities in cartoons images. In literature, we can find a couple of works carried out on detection and recognition of faces of cartoon characters. In [2] face detection of cartoon characters were explored using primitive features such as skin color regions and edges which are extracted from the given cartoon character images. Subsequently region segmentation is performed to extract the face regions. Then, based on two criteria such as jaw contour and symmetry of face, the resulting regions are considered as facial regions of cartoon characters. The elementary features such as skin color, hair color and quantity are extracted and represented in a feature vector. The extracted features are then compared against the features of cartoon images in the database and their similarities are determined. Based on the similarity it infers that when the distance value is small, the similarity of two faces is high. Meanwhile it is hard to perform recognition using facial features.

In this direction we found a work carried out towards celebrity cartoon face recognition [3] demonstrate that the face detection and recognition techniques which work for conventional face detection and recognition may not work well for cartoon images. By incorporating the Multi-task Cascaded Convolutional Network (MTCNN) architecture they have compared the performance of the network with that of conventional methodologies of face detection using features like Haar and Histogram of Gradient (HOG). Substantially it infers that deep learning techniques. Work well for detection and recognition of cartoon faces of celebrities. To the best of our knowledge, no concrete work has been reported, except a few works in literature on detection and recognition of faces of celebrities in cartoon images. In this brief survey on cartoon character and celebrity cartoon recognition we understand that no work has been carried out towards representing the celebrity cartoon face as interval-valued symbolic features to preserve intra class variations among them.

In (See Fig. 1.) illustrates celebrity cartoon images of both male and female class. However, we know that the class should exhibit less intra-class variation with the class and high inter class variations between the class for correct classification. Having more intra-class variation may lead to the misclassification of cartoon face concern to gender specific. To avoid such misclassification a method which can take care of preserving the intra-class variations present in classification of gender in celebrity cartoon images is needed. One such method is interval valued data representation [5]. Symbolic data appear in the form of continuous ratio, discrete absolute interval and multivalued, multivalued with weightage, quantitative, categorical, etc.

The concept of symbolic data analysis has been extensively studied in the field of cluster analysis [6] and it has been proven both theoretically and experimentally that the clustering approaches based on symbolic data outperform conventional clustering techniques. More details and applications of symbolic data can be found in [7]. A symbolic representation model for 2D shapes has been proposed and it is also shown that

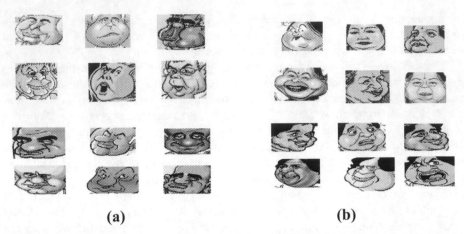

(a)   **(b)**

Fig. 1. Illustration of celebrity cartoon gender images exhibiting high intra-class variation (a) celebrity cartoon image of male class and (b) celebrity cartoon image of female class.

symbolic representation effectively captures shape information, and the corresponding retrieval methodology outperforms conventional representation techniques. In symbolic data analysis, the interval representation of data can take care of intra class variations of features which help in classification [9] clustering [10] and regression [11] of data. As classification of gender in celebrity cartoon face is two class problem [20], it is better to group the similar looking cartoon faces according to it specific gender. Which indeed results in the class containing the gender specific celebrity cartoon face images with lesser variations within the class. It further helps in representing them in symbolic interval form. In the literature, there exist some symbolic classifiers [5, 10, 12].

To the best of our knowledge, no work has been reported in the literature which uses symbolic representation of celebrity cartoon faces for classification of gender. With this backdrop, we made an initial attempt toward application of symbolic data concepts for representing the celebrity cartoon face for classification of gender. Further, extensive experimentations are conducted to evaluate the performance of the proposed methods by selecting the most contributing features. The results of the experimentations reports that the proposed model outperforms. The overall contribution of this work is that we adopt an interval-valued feature representation for celebrity cartoon faces for classification of gender.

The major contributions of this paper are as follows:

1. Explored interval-based representation for genders in celebrity cartoons.
2. Interval Feature selection technique is explored for reducing the number of interval valued features.

The rest of this paper is structured as follows: In Sect. 2, a brief introduction of the proposed methodology is presented. In Sect. 3, the details of experimentations along with results are summarized. A comparative study is presented in Sect. 3.4 Finally, Sect. 4 follows with conclusions.

2   Proposed Methodology

In this section, a brief introduction to the proposed model (see Fig. 3) is given. The model comprises of different stages viz., Feature extraction, class-specific clustering, symbolic representation, and symbolic classifier designed for gender classification.

2.1   Deep Feature Extraction

FaceNet is a well-known architecture (see Fig. 2) for general face recognition of adults. It is a 22 layers deep pre-trained architecture for real face images showing remarkable margin of performance [12] on face recognition. Thus, here in our work, we recommend adopting the FaceNet architecture [4] for representing celebrity cartoon faces also. We train the pre-trained network using celebrity cartoon faces to extract $d = 128$ dimensional unique embeddings. FaceNet learns face images by the use of triplet loss function and extracts d number of features for images such that the images of the same class have less distance than images of different classes.

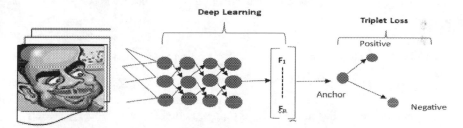

Fig. 2. FaceNet Architecture adopted for celebrity cartoon gender face recognition.

2.2   Class-Specific Clustering

The basic idea of the proposed model is to cluster the similar cartoon images of same gender, so that instead of having a single larger higher space representation for a class, it is to have split multiple sub-higher spaces of same dimension. This could help later to preserve effectively the intra-class variations. Let there be 'N' number of samples putting together say N_1 number of samples of male class (C_1) and N_2 number of samples of female class(C_2).

We recommend clustering of the N1 samples of male class into K_1 clusters and N_2 number of samples of female class into K_2 clusters using K-means clustering. The K_1 and K_2 are fixed empirically by varying K so as to optimize the performance of the proposed gender classification method.

2.3   Interval Valued Cartoon Face Representation

In this stage, the clustered cartoon gender face images are represented in the form of a vector of interval-valued data, a representation which preserves the intra-class (cluster) variations [14].

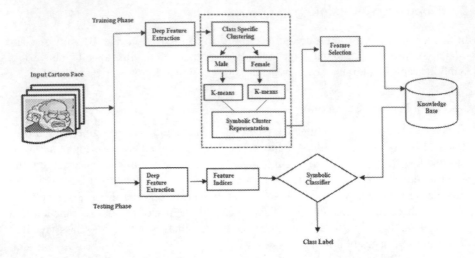

Fig. 3. Architecture of Symbolic-based Approach for gender classification in celebrity's cartoon face images.

Consider the jth cluster where the interval valued representation is given by Eq. (1).

$$IR_j = [I^1, I^2, I^3, I^4, \ldots\ldots\ldots, I^d] \quad \forall_j = (1\ldots, K_1 + K_2) \tag{1}$$

For i^{th} feature of the jth cluster, the interval representation is given by Eq. (2) where.

$$I^i = [f_i^-, f_i^+] \tag{2}$$

where $f_i^- = {}_j\mu^i - {}_j\sigma^i$ and $f_i^+ = {}_j\mu^i + {}_j\sigma^i$

${}_j\mu^i$ and ${}_j\sigma^i$ are calculated are given below, where ${}_jx_s{}^i$ represents i^{th} feature s^{th} samples of jth cluster

$$_j\mu^i = \left[\frac{1}{M}\right]\sum_{s=1}^{M} {}_jX_s^i \qquad where\ i = 1, 2, \ldots, d \tag{3}$$

$$_j\sigma^i = \left(\frac{1}{M}\sum_{s=1}^{M} ({}_jX_s^i - {}_j\mu^i)^2\right)^{1/2} \tag{4}$$

Similarly, we compute the interval representation for all d features. The obtained mean and standard deviation of the cluster is used for interval-valued representation. The lower limit is the difference between mean and standard deviation and the upper limit is the sum of mean and standard deviation. It preserves the internal variations present within the samples of each cluster [9].

2.4   Symbolic Interval Feature Selection

Chi-square [16] is used to assess two types of comparison: tests of goodness of fit and tests of independence. In feature selection it is used as a test of independence to access if the class label is independent of a particular feature. Here, the degree of independence of a feature is a function of relevancy of a feature. In our proposed model we have adopted feature selection technique based on ranking criterion which is suitable for interval valued features [15, 18]. The ranking criterion computes a relevancy score associated with feature. Based on the relevancy score, the features are ranked from the highest relevant feature to the lowest relevant feature. The interval chi-square score (ICS) for a ith interval-valued feature with u unique values and C different classes is defined as:

$$ICS^i = \sum_{a=1}^{u} \sum_{b=1}^{C} \frac{(Iw_{ab} - I\mathcal{X}_{ab})^2}{I\mathcal{X}_{ab}} \tag{5}$$

where Iw_{ab} is the number of interval samples with a^{th} interval feature value in class C_b, and $I\mathcal{X}_{ab} = \frac{n_b Iw_{a*}}{K}$.

Here Iw_{a*} is the number of interval samples with the ath interval feature value corresponding to ith feature, n_b is the number of interval samples Cb, and K is the total number of interval samples. After computing the interval chi-square score for all interval features, they are sorted. Subsequently, the top d' (d' ≪ d) features are selected and preserved in the knowledge base for further consideration during classification.

2.5 Symbolic Classifier

Since the proposed representation of cartoon images is based on interval valued vectors, no conventional classification algorithms can be used for the purpose of gender classification. Hence, we make use of a symbolic classifier proposed in [4] for classification. Initially we consider a test sample $S_q = \{s_1, s_2, \ldots s_d\}$, with d number of features, and subsequently we selected d' number of features based on the indices of the features selected during training, thereby, we obtain $S_{q'}$ it is subset of S_q with d' number of features (d' < d). The test sample $S_{q'}$ needs to be classified as a member of any one of the two classes. To keep a track of the number of features of a single valued feature lie within the corresponding reference interval valued features, a counter called acceptance count (A_c) is used. If the feature of a test sample (s_v) lies within the corresponding interval valued feature of the reference $([f_v^-, f_v^+])$, then the acceptance count is incremented by 1. Similarly, the (A_c) between $S_{q'}$ and all remaining samples are computed. If $S_{q'}$ said to be a member of any one of the two classes, then the value of acceptance count A_c of a class is greater.

The acceptance count A_c is defined as:

$$A_c = \sum_{v=1}^{d'} Sc\left(s_v, [f_v^-, f_v^+]\right) \tag{6}$$

$where, Sc(s_v, [f_v^-, f_v^+]) = \begin{cases} 1 & if\ s_v \geq f_v^-\ and\ s_v \leq f_v^+ \\ 0 & otherwise \end{cases}, i = 1, 2, \ldots, m, j = 1, 2, \ldots, k,$

$and\ \forall s_v \in S_{q'}$

3   Experimentation

3.1   Dataset

We have evaluated our model using the existing dataset which we refer as IIIT cartoon faces in the wild (or IIIT-CFW in abbreviation) [19]. The dataset consists of 8928 cartoon faces of 100 public celebrity figures in that 6565 are male celebrity cartoon and 2073 are female celebrity cartoon face respectively. It is observed through the facts that dataset is highly imbalanced with respect to their classes.

3.2   Experimental Setup

During the stage of feature extraction FaceNet architecture, which is suggested for real face is adapted for extracting features. Using this pre-trained architecture, we extract 'd'-dimensional embeddings. We recommend class specific clustering as explained in the above Sect. 2.2. Here, K_1 and K_2 values are fixed empirically by varying from 2 to 50 to fix up the suitable number of cluster value it is observed in Table 1 under varying train-test ratio. Obtained clusters are represented in the form of interval-valued data as clearly explained in Sect. 2.3. The resultant interval matrix yields huge reduction in sample space and reduce the complexity. For classification, a symbolic classifier is adopted. Subsequently, complete experimentation the results are evaluated for different trails (T = 10). During testing the performance of the system is evaluated using F-Measure. In addition to this the interval feature selection technique is explored to reduce the number of interval-valued features as explained in above Sect. 2.4.

Table 1.   Depicts the k-value under varied train-test ratio using IIIT-CFW

IIIT-CFW DATASET		
Train/Test Split	Gender	K-Value
60:40	Female	35
	Male	30
70:30	Female	36
	Male	30
80:20	Female	35
	Male	29

3.3   Results

The performance of the proposed system is evaluated using F-measure computed by confusion matrix [17]. It is evident from Table 2 that the performance under varying train test ratio without feature selection and with feature selection, the results without feature selection are not prominent. While the results after feature selection the performance is improved. Further it works with using a few numbers of features.

Table 2. Symbolic representation for gender in celebrity cartoon faces using symbolic classifiers under varying percentage of train and test ratio on IIIT-CFW dataset after Feature selection.

Train/ Test Ratio	IIIT-CFW Dataset			
	Without Feature Selection (F-Score)		With Feature Selection F-Score	
	Minimum	Maximum	Minimum	Maximum
60:40	37.66 (128)	49.63 (128)	87.87 (16)	89.02 (20)
70:30	29.39 (128)	46.14 (128)	86.16 (17)	89.51 (26)
80:20	20.53 (128)	27.93 (128)	85.59 (17)	87.60 (16)

3.4 Comparative Analyses

The proposed model is compared against the existing model [3]. We know that from the literature no attempt is carried out to preserve the intra class variation in cartoon images through interval representation towards the gender classification: The Existing model [3] uses InceptionV3 architecture with SVM classifier yielding F1-measure of 91% for 2048 features on balanced dataset. It is evident from the table that our proposed model is on-par with the existing model by achieving 89.5% for 26 features on unbalanced dataset. It is observed that there is a huge reduction in the number of features in our model than the existing model which in turn reduces the computational complexity shown in Table 3.

Table 3. Depicts Comparative analysis of existing models.

Model	Dataset	Precision	Recall	F1-score	Attempt for Balancing Data
Existing Models					
HCNN (Jha et. al., 2018)	IIIT-CFW	90.4 (100)	82.7 (100)	86.4 (100)	YES
INCEPTION V3 + SVM (Jha et. al., 2018)	IIIT-CFW	92.7 (2048)	89.4 (2048)	91.0 (2048)	YES
Proposed Symbolic Model	IIIT-CFW	89.4 (26)	89.5 (26)	89.5 (26)	NO

4 Conclusion

In this paper, we made a successful attempt towards classification of gender based on the interval valued representation of celebrity cartoon images. We have adopted a clustering method to group suitable cartoon face images of same gender. For each cluster of cartoon face images, a vector of interval valued data is computed as representation. Subsequently, an interval valued feature selection method is employed for reducing the number of features. Since our representation is based on interval valued data, a suitable symbolic classifier is adapted for classification. The added advantage of the proposed method is that it has effective and efficient representation of gender cartoon faces is represented in the form of a vectors of intervals and noticed that using this representation there is a huge reduction in the number of features in-turn reduces the computational complexity. An extensive experimentation has been conducted to demonstrate the effectiveness of the proposed approach and a comparative study reveals that the proposed approaches superiors other existing contemporary models.

References

1. Li, Y., Lao, L., Cui, Z., Shan, S., Yang, J.: Graph jigsaw learning for cartoon face recognition. IEEE Trans. Image Process. **31**, 3961–3972 (2022)
2. Takayama, K., Johan, H., Nishita, T.: Face detection and face recognition of cartoon characters using feature extraction. In: Image, Electronics and Visual Computing Workshop, vol. 48 (2012)
3. Jha, S., Agarwal, N., Agarwal, S.: Bringing cartoons to life: towards improved cartoon face detection and recognition systems. arXiv preprint arXiv:1804.01753 (2018)
4. Schroff, F., Kalenichenko, D., Philbin, J.: Facenet: a unified embedding for face recognition and clustering. In: Proceedings of the IEEE Conference on Computer Vision and Pattern Recognition, pp. 815–823 (2015)
5. Guru, D.S., Prakash, H.N.: Online signature verification and recognition: an approach based on symbolic representation. IEEE Trans. Pattern Anal. Mach. Intell. **31**(6), 1059–1073 (2008)
6. Giusti, A., Grassini, L.: Cluster analysis of census data using the symbolic data approach. Adv. Data Anal. Classif. **2**, 163–176 (2008)
7. Jain, A.K., Dubes, R.C.: Algorithms for Clustering Data. Prentice-Hall, Inc. (1988)
8. Sinaga, K.P., Yang, M.S.: Unsupervised K-means clustering algorithm. IEEE Access **8**, 80716–80727 (2020)
9. Billard, L.: Symbolic data analysis: what is it?. In: Compstat 2006–Proceedings in Computational Statistics: 17th Symposium Held in Rome, Italy, pp. 261–269. Physica-Verlag HD (2006)
10. de Barros, A.P., de Carvalho, F.D.A.T., Neto, E.D.A.L.: A pattern classifier for interval-valued data based on multinomial logistic regression model. In: Proceedings of the 2012 IEEE International Conference on Systems, Man, and Cybernetics (SMC), pp. 541–546. IEEE, October 2012
11. Duda, O.R., Hart, E.P., Stork, G.D.: Pattern Classification, 2nd edn. Wiley-Interscience (2000)
12. Fagundes, R.A., De Souza, R.M., Cysneiros, F.J.A.: Robust regression with application to symbolic interval data. Eng. Appl. Artif. Intell. **26**(1), 564–573 (2013)
13. Silva, A.P.D., Brito, P.: Linear discriminant analysis for interval data. Comput. Statistics **21**, 289–308 (2006)

14. Ding, C., Tao, D.: Robust face recognition via multimodal deep face representation. IEEE Trans. Multimedia **17**(11), 2049–2058 (2015)
15. Guru, D.S., Prakash, H.N.: Online signature verification and recognition: an approach based on symbolic representation. IEEE Trans. PAMI **31**(6), 1059–1073 (2009)
16. Guru, D.S., Vinay Kumar, N.: Interval Chi-Square Score (ICSS): feature selection of interval valued data. In: Abraham, A., Cherukuri, A.K., Melin, P., Gandhi, N. (eds.) ISDA 2018 2018. AISC, vol. 941, pp. 686–698. Springer, Cham (2020). https://doi.org/10.1007/978-3-030-16660-1_67
17. Liu, H., Setiono, R.: Chi2: feature selection and discretization of numeric attributes. In: 1995 Proceedings of the International Conference on Tools with Artificial Intelligence, pp. 388–391. https://doi.org/10.1109/TAI.1995.479783
18. Guru, D.S., Vinay Kumar, N., Suhil, M.: Feature selection of interval valued data through interval feature selection. Int. J. Comput. Vis. Image Process. **7**(2), 64–80 (2017)
19. Mishra, A., Rai, S.N., Mishra, A., Jawahar, C.V.: IIITCFW: a bench- mark database of cartoon faces in the wild. In: European Conference on Computer (2016)
20. Prajna, S., Vinay Kumar, N., Guru, D.S.: Classification of gender in celebrity cartoon images. In: International Conference on Computer Vision and Image Processing, pp. 525–537. Springer International Publishing, Cham, December 2021. Vision. Springer, 35–47. https://doi.org/10.1007/978-3-031-11346-8_45
21. Powers, D.M.W.: Evaluation: from precision, recall and F-measure to ROC, informedness, markedness, and correlation. J. Mach. Learn. Technol. **2**(1), 37–63 (2011)

Polyphonic Sound Event Detection Using Modified Recurrent Temporal Pyramid Neural Network

Spoorthy Venkatesh[(✉)] [ID] and Shashidhar G. Koolagudi[ID]

National Institute of Technology Karnataka, Surathkal 575025, India
{spoorthyv.187co007,koolagudi}@nitk.edu.in

Abstract. In this paper, a novel approach to performing polyphonic Sound Event Detection (SED) is presented. A new deep learning architecture named "Modified Recurrent Temporal Pyramid Neural Network (MR-TPNN)" is introduced. The input features fed to the network are spectrograms generated from Constant Q-Transform (CQT). CQT spectrograms provided better sound event information in the audio recording than the Short Time Fourier Transform (STFT) and Fast Fourier Transform (FFT) methods. The temporal information is an essential factor for detecting the onset and offset of events in an audio recording. Capturing the temporal information is ensured by fusing Temporal pyramids and Bi-directional long short-term memory (LSTM) recurrent layers in deep learning architecture. Extensive experiments are carried out on three benchmark datasets, and the results of the proposed method are superior to those of the existing polyphonic SED systems.

Keywords: Polyphonic Sound Event Detection (SED) · Constant Q-Transform (CQT) · Deep learning · Modified Recurrent Temporal Pyramid Network

1 Introduction

In audio processing, the task of identifying the onset and offset, along with their corresponding class label, is termed Sound Event Detection (SED). Sound events can refer to any sound with a specific meaning, such as a car honk, a human voice, a barking dog, or a musical instrument. SED has many practical applications, including environmental noise monitoring [8], acoustic quality control [6], audio surveillance [15], human-computer interaction [4], and so on. SED is challenging because sound events are highly variable, and different events can overlap in time and frequency. The diversity of sounds that can occur in a given environment also makes it difficult to develop robust and accurate SED systems [7]. Developing efficient and accurate SED systems requires advanced signal processing and machine learning techniques that can process and analyze large volumes of audio data.

© The Author(s), under exclusive license to Springer Nature Switzerland AG 2024
H. Kaur et al. (Eds.): CVIP 2023, CCIS 2009, pp. 554–564, 2024.
https://doi.org/10.1007/978-3-031-58181-6_47

Sound events can be monophonic, where only one sound source produces the sound, or polyphonic, where multiple sound sources produce the sound simultaneously. Monophonic and polyphonic SED differ in the number of sources involved and the complexity of the task. Monophonic sound event detection involves identifying and categorizing sound events generated by a single sound source, such as a dog barking or a car horn honking. Monophonic SED can be relatively straightforward, as there is only one sound event to detect and classify, and the detection can be performed using simple algorithms. However, monophonic SED can still be challenging in certain situations, such as when there is a lot of background noise or when the sound event is similar to other sounds in the environment. Polyphonic sound event identification entails identifying and categorizing sound events brought on by various sound sources that overlap in frequency and time. Examples of polyphonic sound events include a group of people talking, music with multiple instruments, and a noisy construction site. Polyphonic SED is more complex than monophonic SED, as it requires identifying and separating multiple sound sources and classifying each sound source's corresponding sound event.

Polyphonic SED typically involves using advanced signal processing and machine learning techniques, such as non-negative matrix factorization, machine learning, and deep learning [3]. These techniques can separate the different sound events in the audio signal, extract the features, and classify each corresponding sound event. Developing efficient and accurate monophonic and polyphonic SED systems is an important research area in audio processing with numerous applications. While monophonic SED is relatively straightforward and can be performed using simple algorithms, polyphonic SED is a more challenging task that requires advanced signal processing and machine learning techniques. The goal of ongoing research in this field is to develop tools and algorithms that will increase the performance and efficiency of monophonic and polyphonic SED systems.

This work aims to develop an effective polyphonic SED system that can accurately identify the sound events' start (onset) and end (offset) points and their corresponding class label. The proposed system includes feature extraction from input audio recordings and a newly introduced deep learning architecture that performs SED tasks. The features used to feed the neural network are CQT spectrograms. The CQT spectrogram features provide better event information than log Mel band energies. The key contributions of this work are:

- A new deep learning architecture named 'Modified Recurrent Temporal Pyramid Neural Network (MR-TPNN)' is proposed in this work to perform polyphonic SED.
- Extensive result analysis is performed on three benchmark SED datasets.
- Existing polyphonic SED systems are evaluated and compared to the proposed system's performance analysis.

The remaining part of the paper is structured as follows: Sect. 2 provides a brief overview of the existing systems that have been proposed for the SED task. A detailed discussion of the proposed method is presented in Sect. 3. The implementation details of the proposed method are provided in Sect. 4. The performance obtained from the proposed method is discussed in Sect. 5. The proposed work's conclusions are stated in Sect. 6.

2   Related Work

This section briefly reviews the current approaches proposed for the polyphonic SED task. In the past decade, researchers have shown much interest in detecting overlapped sound events in a given audio recording. The current methods proposed for this task are developed using various deep-learning architectures. The deep learning models have proven to perform better by learning discriminative features from the input features [23,24]. They have used CapsNets to handle the polyphonic SED task, where several sound events occur simultaneously. They recommended using the capsule units to represent a set of distinctive characteristics for each sound event. The capsule units are connected using dynamic routing, which encourages learning part-to-whole relationships and improves detection performance in a polyphonic context. An in-depth analysis of three publicly accessible datasets is presented in their work, demonstrating how the CapsNet-based algorithm not only performs better than conventional CNNs but also outperforms them in terms of state-of-the-art algorithms [25]. Their work proposes to extract hidden state feature representations using convolutional recurrent neural networks (CRNNs). In addition, they have developed a technique for self-attention that uses a symmetric score function to remember long-term relationships between the features that the CRNNs collect. Then, a plan for methods for adaptive memory-controlled self-attention is suggested. Finally, the suggested adaptive memory-controlled model performed on par with a fixed attention breadth model is demonstrated. According to experimental findings, the suggested attention mechanism can enhance sound event detection [26]. The other works in which deep learning methods used for polyphonic SED are Convolutional Neural Networks [2], Feed Forward Neural Networks (FFNN) [1], Recurrent Neural Networks [18], CRNN [3], etc. This work proposes a modified Recurrent Temporal Pyramid Neural Network to perform polyphonic SED tasks.

3   Proposed Polyphonic SED Method

3.1   Overview

The schematic diagram of the proposed polyphonic SED system is shown in Fig. 1. The system is divided into two important phases, namely, feature extraction and detection of sound events using neural network architecture. The features used to identify different sound events are spectrogram features extracted using CQT. The CQT-based spectrograms are fed as input to the neural network architecture. The network proposed to identify and detect sound events is the Recurrent Temporal Pyramid Network. The network uses a temporal pyramid pooling layer to get relevant information from the input frames. The recurrent layer used in the network is Long-Short Term Memory (LSTM). Detailed information on each method is given in the below subsections.

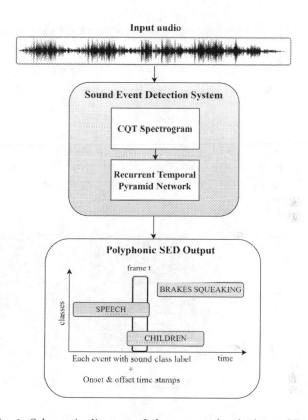

Fig. 1. Schematic diagram of the proposed polyphonic SED

3.2   Feature Extraction

The log Mel-band energies are the features that have been employed in the baseline system for the DCASE 2017 challenge [11]. The spectrogram generated in the baseline system uses the Fast Fourier Transform (FFT) as the transform function. The feature extraction in this work is similar to that of the baseline system except for the variation in the transformation function. The transformation function used in this work is Constant Q-Transform (CQT), which is a time-frequency representation in which all frequency bins have the same Q-factors (ratios of their center frequencies to bandwidths). The frequency bins are geometrically spread out in the CQT. Due to the fact that the CQT is essentially a wavelet transform, low frequencies are better for frequency resolution, and high frequencies are better for time resolution [22].

The transform can be viewed as a series of filters, where each filter f_y has a spectral width δf_y that is a multiple of the filter f_y that came before it as given in Eq. 1:

$$\delta f_y = 2^{\frac{1}{n}} \cdot \delta f_{y-1} = (2^{\frac{1}{n}})^y \cdot \delta f_{min} \tag{1}$$

where δf_y is the bandwidth of the yth filter, f_{min} is the lowest filter's central frequency, and n is the number of filters per octave [19,27]. The feature extraction in this work is carried out by transforming the input audio recordings using CQT instead of the conventional STFT or FFT technique. Figure 2 shows the spectrogram obtained from STFT and CQT algorithm for given input audio recordings chosen from the DCASE 2017 Challenge Task 2 dataset. The circled region in the figure indicates the sound activity in the audio recording. The Mel spectrogram has captured the sound event activity. However, while observing, the circled region of the CQT-based spectrogram shows a better intensity region than the former feature.

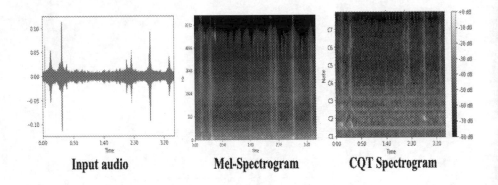

Input audio   **Mel-Spectrogram**   **CQT Spectrogram**

Fig. 2. Illustration of Mel spectrogram and CQT spectrogram for an audio recording chosen from DCASE Sound Events 2017 development dataset

3.3   Neural Network Architecture

An MR-TPNN architecture is proposed in this work to perform polyphonic SED. The neural network architecture of the proposed MR-TPNN is shown in Fig. 3. The network consists of convolutional layers for representation learning of input CQT spectrogram features, an average pooling layer for retaining the relevant information from the feature map, a temporal pyramid layer to convert the input into fixed dimensional vectors, bi-directional LSTM provides the flow of sequence information in both forward and backward direction, at last, the fully connected layers are used convert the output matrix into a vector. One of the modifications of the neural network architecture is adapting the linear Swish activation function for hidden layers in the network. The mathematical computation of the Swish activation function is given in Eq. 2:

$$swish(a) = a.sigmoid(\beta a) = \frac{a}{1 + e^{-\beta a}} \qquad (2)$$

where β is a trainable parameter or a constant depending on the requirement of the model. Unlike the Rectified Linear Unit (ReLU) activation function that thresholds all negative weights to zero, the Swish activation function allows a small number of negative weights to be propagated through. It is a necessary property to achieve a non-monotonic smooth activation function for better learning in deep neural networks [20]. The usage of the Swish activation function is done along with hidden layers, that is, convolutional layers in the proposed network.

Temporal Pyramid Pooling: The output resulting from the convolutional layers is usually varying in nature. In order to achieve a fixed-dimensional feature and extract information from the different temporal scales, in this work, we utilize a Temporal Pyramid pooling approach inspired by various computer vision solutions [10,28]. The windows used for pooling operation are adaptive instead of other pooling operations such as Max pooling or average pooling. A pyramid level consisting of n number of bins, the max-pooling window is traversed across the feature map through time, where i^{th} bin is related to the feature map within $\left[\left\lfloor \frac{i-1}{n}L \right\rfloor, \left\lceil \frac{i}{n} \right\rceil L \right]$, where L is the row dimension of the input feature map obtained from the predecessor convolution layer [28]. The number of levels in the temporal pyramid pooling layer depends on the input feature map. After obtaining the pooling values of different pyramid levels, the values are concatenated to obtain a fixed-dimensional vector for further process. The primary usage of TPP is to convert a variable-length feature map into a fixed-length output. This layer helps in aggregating information of different temporal scales and captures the temporal information of various sound event activities in the audio recording.

4 Implementation Details

The implementation details of the techniques used for developing the proposed system are provided in this section.

Features: Spectrogram features are extracted using CQT and are provided as input to the proposed neural network architecture. To extract the spectrogram features, the window's length is set to 40 ms, and the overlap length is set to 20 ms.

Neural Network: There are several layers in the MR-TPNN that have been proposed. The convolutional layers' kernel sizes range from 3 to 5. The pooling layer's kernel is set to a size of 3. With a learning rate of 0.001, Adam is the optimizer used to train the network. The activation functions used in the hidden layer and final layer are Swish and Softmax, respectively. The number of levels

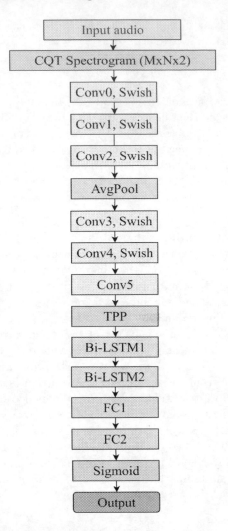

Fig. 3. Neural network architecture of the proposed MR-TPNN (Conv: Convolution, AvgPooling: Average Pooling, TPP: Temporal Pyramid Pooling, Bi-LSTM: Bi-directional Long Short Term Memory layer, FC: Fully-Connected layer)

provided for the Temporal Pyramid Pooling layer is 3 (Fig. 4). The training and testing sets of the datasets are used as per the DCASE challenge evaluation setup. The loss function used is weighted focal loss [21] as it is a multiclass classification. The computation of the weighted focal loss is given in Eq. 3:

$$FL(A_t) = -\sigma(1 - a_t)^\gamma log(a_t) \tag{3}$$

where FL represents weighted focal loss, A_t is the estimated probability of the model for different classes, which ranges from [0,1], a modulating factor γ is added to the cross entropy loss function with tunable parameter $\gamma > 0$ [9], and σ is the weight factor added.

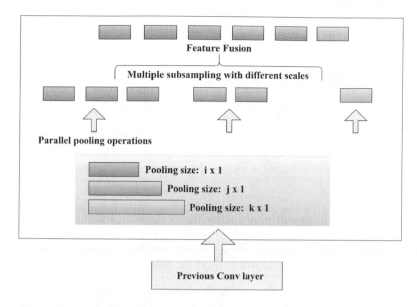

Fig. 4. Working of Temporal Pyramid Pooling Layer

Dataset: Three datasets are used to evaluate the proposed method: TUT Sound events Synthetic dataset 2016 [12], TUT Sound events 2016 development dataset [13], and TUT Sound events 2017 development dataset [11]. The TUT Sound Events 2016 development set consists of sound events that were captured in two different acoustic scenes, namely a home (indoors) and a residential area (outdoor). The recordings of street acoustic scenes with varying traffic levels and other activities are part of the TUT Sound Event 2017 development set. The equipment used for recording is the same as the one used for collecting the 2016 dataset.

5   Results and Analysis

We evaluated our proposed method on three datasets based on DCASE challenges, including the sound event synthetic dataset (DCASE 2016), the sound event real-life dataset (DCASE 2016), and the sound event dataset (DCASE 2017). The audio recordings in the dataset are of varying lengths. For each dataset, we used a single channel that was randomly picked. The performance measures used to evaluate the proposed method are Error Rate (ER) and F-measure as per DCASE challenge evaluation [14]. The results obtained from the log-Mel energies and CQT-based spectrogram fed as input to the proposed method are presented in Tables 1 and 2. It can be observed that a significant improvement has been observed in the performance rate in both the metrics, ER, and F-measure for CQT spectrograms. DCASE synthetic dataset, an improvement of 4% has been observed in the F-measure score, and a decrease in ER is observed as well.

Table 1. Performance obtained for the proposed method on log mel energies and MR-TPNN

Dataset	ER	F-measure
TUT synthetic 2016 (Dev.)	0.53	72.0%
TUT Sound events 2016 (Dev.)	0.64	48.2%
TUT Sound events 2017 (Dev.)	0.63	47.9%

Table 2. Performance obtained for the proposed method on CQT based spectrograms and Modified Recurrent Temporal Pyramid Neural Network

Dataset	ER	F-measure
TUT synthetic 2016 (Dev.)	**0.49**	**76.1%**
TUT Sound events 2016 (Dev.)	0.60	52.7%
TUT Sound events 2017 (Dev.)	0.58	51.8%

The proposed approach is compared with the existing polyphonic SED systems. The methods considered are baseline system of 2016 challenge dataset [13], CNN [5], CRNN [3], DNN-driven feature learning [16], and Transpose Convolutional Recurrent Neural Network (TCRNN) [17]. The performance of these methods, along with the proposed method, is shown in Table 3.

Table 3. Performance comparison of the proposed MR-TPNN with the existing polyphonic SED systems evaluated on DCASE 2016 Sound Events Development Dataset

Method	ER	F-measure
Baseline	0.91	23.7%
CNN	1.09	26.4%
CRNN	0.95	30.3%
DNN-driven feature learning	0.71	44.5%
TCRNN	0.92	38.7%
Proposed method	**0.60**	**52.7%**

6   Conclusion

This work proposes a deep learning model that learns the temporal information from the given input features to identify the onset and offset times of various sound events along with their class labels. The proposed MR-TPNN used a pyramid pooling approach to get a fixed-dimensional feature vector, and the use of a Bi-directional LSTM layer helps in retaining the temporal sequence information of the input. This, in turn, improved ER and F-measure performance for the polyphonic SED task. The experiment results on three benchmark datasets demonstrate that the proposed approach performed better than existing polyphonic SED systems.

References

1. Cakir, E., Heittola, T., Huttunen, H., Virtanen, T.: Polyphonic sound event detection using multi label deep neural networks. In: International Joint Conference on Neural Networks (IJCNN), pp. 1–7. IEEE (2015)
2. Cakir, E., Ozan, E.C., Virtanen, T.: Filterbank learning for deep neural network based polyphonic sound event detection. In: International Joint Conference on Neural Networks (IJCNN), pp. 3399–3406. IEEE (2016)
3. Cakır, E., Parascandolo, G., Heittola, T., Huttunen, H., Virtanen, T.: Convolutional recurrent neural networks for polyphonic sound event detection. IEEE/ACM Trans. Audio Speech Lang. Process. 25(6), 1291–1303 (2017)
4. Ge, S., Yu, Z., Yang, F., Liu, J., Wang, L.: Human-machine collaboration based sound event detection. CCF Trans. Pervasive Comput. Interact. 4(2), 158–171 (2022)
5. Gorin, A., Makhazhanov, N., Shmyrev, N.: Dcase 2016 sound event detection system based on convolutional neural network. In: IEEE AASP Challenge: Detection and Classification of Acoustic Scenes and Events, pp. 1–3 (2016)
6. Grollmisch, S., Abeßer, J., Liebetrau, J., Lukashevich, H.: Sounding industry: challenges and datasets for industrial sound analysis. In: 27th European Signal Processing Conference (EUSIPCO), pp. 1–5. IEEE (2019)
7. Heittola, T., Mesaros, A., Eronen, A., Virtanen, T.: Context-dependent sound event detection. EURASIP J. Audio Speech Music Process. 2013(1), 1–13 (2013)
8. Imoto, K., Tonami, N., Koizumi, Y., Yasuda, M., Yamanishi, R., Yamashita, Y.: Sound event detection by multitask learning of sound events and scenes with soft scene labels. In: International Conference on Acoustics, Speech and Signal Processing (ICASSP), pp. 621–625. IEEE (2020)
9. Lin, T., Goyal, P., Girshick, R., He, K., Dollár, P.: Focal loss for dense object detection. In: Proceedings of the IEEE International Conference on Computer Vision, pp. 2980–2988 (2017)
10. Ma, Q., Lin, Z., Chen, E., Cottrell, G.: Temporal pyramid recurrent neural network. In: Proceedings of the AAAI Conference on Artificial Intelligence, vol. 34, pp. 5061–5068 (2020)
11. Mesaros, A., et al.: DCASE 2017 challenge setup: tasks, datasets and baseline system. In: Proceedings of the Detection and Classification of Acoustic Scenes and Events Workshop, pp. 85–92 (2017)
12. Mesaros, A., et al.: Detection and classification of acoustic scenes and events: Outcome of the DCASE 2016 challenge. IEEE/ACM Trans. Audio Speech Lang. Process. 26(2), 379–393 (2018)
13. Mesaros, A., Heittola, T., Virtanen, T.: TUT database for acoustic scene classification and sound event detection. In: 24th European Signal Processing Conference (EUSIPCO), pp. 1128–1132 (2016)
14. Mesaros, A., Toni, H., Virtanen, T.: Metrics for polyphonic sound event detection. Appl. Sci. 6(6), 162 (2016)
15. Mnasri, Z., Rovetta, S., Masulli, F.: Anomalous sound event detection: a survey of machine learning based methods and applications. Multimed. Tools Appl. 1–50 (2022)

16. Mulimani, M., Kademani, A.B., Koolagudi, S.G.: A deep neural network-driven feature learning method for polyphonic acoustic event detection from real-life recordings. In: International Conference on Acoustics, Speech and Signal Processing (ICASSP), pp. 291–295. IEEE (2020)
17. Mulimani, M., Koolagudi, S.G.: Segmentation and characterization of acoustic event spectrograms using singular value decomposition. Expert Syst. Appl. **120**, 413–425 (2019)
18. Parascandolo, G., Huttunen, H., Virtanen, T.: Recurrent neural networks for polyphonic sound event detection in real life recordings. In: International Conference on Acoustics, Speech and Signal Processing (ICASSP), pp. 6440–6444. IEEE (2016)
19. Patil, A.T., Khoria, K., Patil, H.A.: Voice liveness detection using constant-q transform-based features. In: 30th European Signal Processing Conference (EUSIPCO), pp. 110–114. IEEE (2022)
20. Ramachandran, P., Zoph, B., Le, Q.: Searching for activation functions. In: Proceedings of the 6th International Conference on Learning Representations (ICLR), pp. 1–13 (2018)
21. Qin, R., Qiao, K., Wang, L., Zeng, L., Chen, J., Yan, B.: Weighted focal loss: an effective loss function to overcome unbalance problem of chest X-ray14. In: IOP Conference Series: Materials Science and Engineering, vol. 428, p. 012022. IOP Publishing (2018)
22. Schörkhuber, C., Klapuri, A.: Constant-q transform toolbox for music processing. In: Proceedings of the 7th Sound and Music Computing Conference, Barcelona, Spain, pp. 3–64 (2010)
23. Mulimani, M., Koolagudi, S.G.: Acoustic scene classification using deep learning architectures. In: 2021 6th International Conference for Convergence in Technology (I2CT), pp. 1–6 (2021). https://doi.org/10.1109/I2CT51068.2021.9418177
24. Venkatesh, S., Koolagudi, S.G.: Device robust acoustic scene classification using adaptive noise reduction and convolutional recurrent attention neural network. In: Prasanna, S.R.M., Karpov, A., Samudravijaya, K., Agrawal, S.S. (eds.) SPECOM 2022, vol. 13721, pp. 688–699. Springer, Cham (2022). https://doi.org/10.1007/978-3-031-20980-2_58
25. Vesperini, F., Gabrielli, L., Principi, E., Squartini, S.: Polyphonic sound event detection by using capsule neural networks. IEEE J. Sel. Top. Signal Process. **13**(2), 310–322 (2019)
26. Wang, M., Yao, Y., Qiu, H., Song, X.: Adaptive memory-controlled self-attention for polyphonic sound event detection. Symmetry **14**(2), 366 (2022)
27. Wang, M., Wang, R., Zhang, X., Rahardja, S.: Hybrid constant-q transform based CNN ensemble for acoustic scene classification. In: Asia-Pacific Signal and Information Processing Association Annual Summit and Conference (APSIPA ASC), pp. 1511–1516. IEEE (2019)
28. Yu, Z., Xu, X., Chen, X., Yang, D.: Temporal pyramid pooling convolutional neural network for cover song identification. In: Proceedings of the 28th International Joint Conference on Artificial Intelligence (IJCAI), pp. 4846–4852 (2019)

Egocentric Action Prediction via Knowledge Distillation and Subject-Action Relevance

Snehasis Mukherjee[1]([✉])[iD] and Bhavay Chopra[2]

[1] Shiv Nadar Institute of Eminence, Delhi NCR, Greater Noida, India
snehasis.mukherjee@snu.edu.in
[2] VIT University, Vellore, India
bhavay.chopra2019@vitstudent.ac.in

Abstract. Egocentric action prediction aims to predict the future actions of the performer wearing the camera, given a partial video segment. The challenge in egocentric action prediction tasks (over action recognition) is the lack of context. The definition of an egocentric action as a noun-verb combination helps to obtain the context information from the video. However, the lack of training data to train two sequential deep-learning models to detect nouns and verbs remains a challenge. We propose a model involving two sequential GAN architectures where the first one determines the noun (based on the frames), and the next determines the verb (based on the optical flow). Each of these GAN architectures consists of a teacher and a student architecture. The teacher architectures are much deeper CNNs (pre-trained on a large dataset) compared to the student architectures. We further reduce the search space for the verb by applying the Reduced Verb Space Generator (RVSGen) algorithm between the noun prediction and verb prediction processes. RVSGen helps in proposing the most suitable verbs corresponding to the noun obtained by the noun predictor. Experimentation carried out on a benchmark dataset shows the efficacy of the proposed model compared to the state-of-the-art.

Keywords: Egocentric action prediction · GAN · RVSGen · Knowledge distillation

1 Introduction

Due to the growing popularity of wearable sensors and their numerous practical uses, egocentric activity analysis is becoming an emerging area of research in computer vision and robotics. Analyzing videos captured by wearable cameras is useful in several real-life applications such as child and elderly monitoring, robot navigation, extreme sports, and many more.

Analyzing egocentric videos is challenging due to the sudden abrupt camera motion and extreme camera jerk. Spatial and motion information extracted from

H. Kaur et al. (Eds.): CVIP 2023, CCIS 2009, pp. 565–573, 2024.
https://doi.org/10.1007/978-3-031-58181-6_48

egocentric videos often affects the recognition process due to the unusual motion inherent in the egocentric videos. Traditional methods for egocentric activity recognition generally rely on techniques to stabilize the jerk present in the egocentric video frames [1,2]. However, motion due to the abrupt head movement still remained an unsolved problem. Kahani et al. proposed a correlation-based approach to reduce the effect of head movement on the recognition process [3].

After the introduction of deep learning models, efforts have been made to apply 3D CNN models to extract the spatio-temporal features from the egocentric videos, for classification [4]. However, abrupt and sometimes no camera motion still remains a problem in egocentric activity recognition. After the phenomenal work by Damen et al. the definition of egocentric actions is changed [5]. According to the new definition of egocentric action, an action is a combination of a noun and a verb. Hence, the problem of egocentric activity recognition is defined as a combination of two smaller research problems: Noun prediction (brings down to object detection) and verb prediction (temporal feature analysis).

Based on the noun-verb definition of egocentric action, Kazakos et al. proposed a parallel CNN architecture, where one architecture predicts the noun and the other architecture predicts the verb [6]. The problem in such parallel architecture is that the model assumes that nouns and verbs are independent, which is wrong in reality. For example, the verb "open" or "close" cannot be associated with the noun "door". Prabhakar et al. proposed a sequential architecture to first predict the noun, followed by the verb [7]. Further, they introduced a reduced verb space generator (RVSGen) algorithm to reduce the search space for the verb predictor, based on the predicted noun.

Despite a few attempts to recognize actions in egocentric videos, predicting future actions in egocentric videos is a relatively unexplored area of research [8]. Recently knowledge distillation approaches are being used for predicting future actions by training the teacher model with the whole video, and the student model with a part of the video [9,10]. Zheng et al. used a GAN-based model to transfer the knowledge from the teacher network to the student network using an adversarial training [10] procedure. However, Zheng et al. proposed a parallel prediction of nouns and verbs, affects the recognition process.

Motivated by the success of [10], we propose a knowledge distillation-based approach for egocentric activity prediction. Unlike [10], we propose a sequential architecture for the nouns and verbs prediction, where both noun prediction and verb prediction are done using two GAN architectures, each comprising a teacher and a student model. Further, we apply the RVSGen algorithm [7] to reduce the search space for the verbs, based on the predicted noun. This paper has the following major contributions:

- We propose a sequential architecture comprising two GANs where the first one predicts the noun and the second one predicts the verb.
- We reduce the search space for the verb predictor, by applying RVSGen algorithm.

Next, we make a survey of literature in the related area of research.

2   Related Works

Analyzing egocentric videos and recognizing actions has become a popular area of research in computer vision and robotics during the last few years [11]. Traditional methods for egocentric activity recognition focused on the camera jerk. They used to apply various techniques to reduce the motion information (typically obtained due to camera jerk) at the background pixels in video frames [1,2]. Vinodh et al. point-wise multiplied the optical flow matrix and the gradient matrix of each frame, to obtain the gradient weighted optical flow (GWOF) feature [1]. This method reduces the motion information from the smooth background (due to almost zero gradient). However, for cluttered or textured backgrounds, [1] fails to reduce the unnecessary motion. Sai Suma et al. [2] extracted the GWOF features only from the spatio-temporal interest points obtained from STIP feature [12], to obtain GF-STIP feature. However, abrupt camera motion due to head movement remains a challenge.

Kahani et al. attempted to reduce the effect of abrupt head movement by a correlation-based approach [3]. They represented the per-frame spatial features in a time series and modeled the inter and intra relationship between the features to find the dynamics of the scene. This method reduced the effect of abrupt camera motion but faced challenges in analyzing egocentric videos with high inter-class similarity (such as EGTEA+ dataset [13]).

Deep learning models have become popular in egocentric activity recognition during the last few years, due to the ability to extract meaningful features automatically [11]. Efforts have been made to apply 3D CNN, to extract the spatio-temporal features for egocentric action recognition [4]. Furnari et al. proposed an LSTM-based technique to handle the temporal information and the challenges due to abrupt camera motion [14]. Li et al. extended the method of [14] model the relation between the objects and the body parts of the wearer [15]. However, in most of the egocentric datasets such as EGTEA+, body parts are not much visible in the video.

The observation of Damen et al. changed the definition of egocentric actions, where the action is considered a combination of nouns and verbs [5]. This new definition of egocentric actions simplifies the task of action recognition by dividing the task into two parts: predicting the noun and predicting the verb. Based on this noun-verb definition of egocentric actions, Kazakos et al. proposed a pipeline of two parallel CNNs; one predicting the noun and the other predicting the verb [6]. Kazakos et al. assumed that nouns and verbs as independent of each other, which is not true in reality. To address this problem, Jaisurya et al. proposed a pipeline with a noun predictor followed by a verb predictor [7]. Further, they introduced RVSGen algorithm preceding the verb predictor, to reduce the search space for the verb.

Predicting egocentric action is a less studied area of research [8]. Mascaro et al. proposed a multi-layered Perceptron (MLP) mixer to extract the high-level and low-level human intention from the video [16]. Then they proposed a variational autoencoder (VAE) network to predict action from initial frames. The concept of knowledge distillation (KD) is recently becoming popular for video prediction tasks including egocentric action prediction [9,10]. Huang et al. proposed a graph network to model the global relations between the past and future frames by distilling the knowledge from the past to the future information [9]. Zheng et al. made use of the noun-verb definition of egocentric actions and applied a GAN-based model to transfer the knowledge from the teacher network to the student network using an adversarial training [10] procedure. However, the interdependency between the nouns and verbs of egocentric actions is ignored in [10]. We propose to redesign the parallel KD architecture proposed in [10] by proposing a sequence of two KD-based GAN networks; the first one predicting the noun and the next predicting the verb. We further apply the RVSGen algorithm [7] preceding the verb predictor, to reduce the search space for verbs, based on the predicted noun.

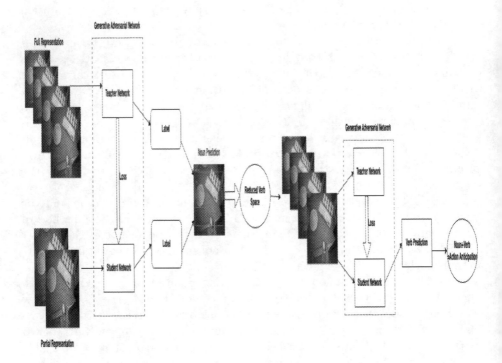

Fig. 1. The overall diagram of the proposed method for egocentric action recognition. The teacher model is trained on the whole video, whereas, the student model is trained on the initial parts of the training video.

Next, we illustrate the proposed method for egocentric action anticipation.

3   Proposed Method

In the proposed egocentric action recognition paradigm, the information from RGB frame and optical flow can be considered as two different modalities. The proposed model makes use of the RGB frame for noun prediction, and the optical flow for verb prediction, to accomplish task-oriented fine-grained motion information extraction while avoiding the pre-computation of optical flow during the inference period, which requires a lot of computation time. The motion information is extracted after the object information.

We use two KD architectures in the proposed method to predict the nouns and verbs separately. The individual KD architectures for noun and verb prediction are influenced by [10], with two major differences. First, unlike [10], the proposed KD architectures are sequential. Second, we do not use a common discriminator for noun and verb prediction, as done in [10]. Rather, we use the same discriminator architecture in both GANs. The overall procedure for the proposed model is illustrated in Fig. 1.

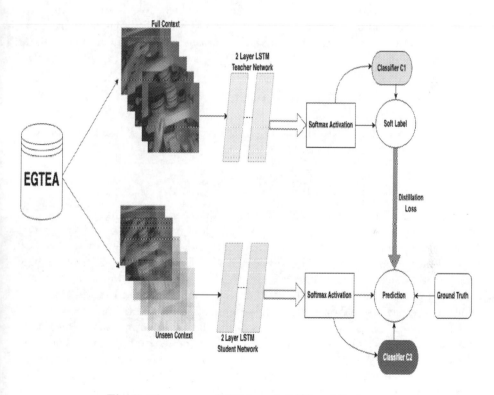

Fig. 2. The proposed KD-based GAN architecture.

The teacher network consists of two LSTM networks, the first one extracts features from the early frames of the video sequence, whereas the next LSTM module extracts features from the later frames. The student network for both the KD-based GANs consists of only one LSTM analyzing the early frames of the video sequence. We apply a softmax classifier for the classification of videos.

While adversarial training with the KD networks, we use two regularization techniques following [10]: Discriminative Knowledge Regularization (DKR) to make the student network learn more discriminative features from the teacher model and Latent Knowledge Regularization (LKR) to make the student model learn more latent features from the video sequences. Figure 2 illustrates the proposed KD-based GAN architectures.

After the noun prediction, we apply the RVSGen algorithm following [7] to reduce the verb space, before feeding the optical flow matrices to the proposed verb predictor. RVSGen ranks the most likely verbs that may occur with the predicted Noun, based on a likelihood score obtained from the empirical probability of the verbs to occur given the predicted noun. There are a total of 53 nouns and 19 verbs present in the EGTEA+ dataset, providing a total of $53 \times 19 = 1007$ possible combinations of noun-verb pair (possible actions). Out of all the possible noun-verb pairs, we prune out some pairs which do not make sense. We prune out such pairs according to the empirical probability of noun-verb pairs in the training data. Next, we discuss the dataset and experimental details of the proposed method.

4   Dataset and Experiments

We first describe the dataset used for validation of the proposed method, followed by the implementation details.

4.1   Dataset

EGTEA Gaze+ is a large-scale dataset for first-person actions and gaze [13]. It includes HD videos (1280 × 960), audio, gaze tracking information, frame-level action annotations, and hand masks at pixel-level samples of the frames. Specifically, 86 different sessions involving 32 subjects totaling 28 h of cooking activities are included in EGTEA Gaze+. Additionally, hand masks and human annotations of actions (human-object interactions) have been made available. For our project, we make use of the videos and action annotations.

The action labels in the EGTEA Gaze+ dataset are present in verb-noun pairs with each verb having one or more possible noun combinations. There are three divides made from the full dataset. Each split has its own train/test set (mutually exclusive). Each video was made to go through a 2-channel optical flow computation and individual frame (RGB channels) extraction. We use the whole dataset for evaluation.

4.2   Experimental Settings

The teacher network and student network for both the GANs (noun and verb predictors) are 2 layer LSTMs that take input sizes (224,224,3). The models also have a dense layer which has 64 units with ReLU activation function. The final dense layer has 11 units with a softmax activation function. Each teacher network was set to train for 100 epochs whereas each student network was set to train for 150 epochs. The learning rate for the teacher network was 0.01 whereas for the student networks, it was 0.0001. The distillation loss is calculated as,

$$Loss = (\alpha * studentloss) + (1 - \alpha) * distillationloss, \qquad (1)$$

where α was set to 0.1 and temperature to 3. Next, we discuss the results.

5   Results and Discussions

The results of the proposed egocentric activity predictor compared to the state-of-the-art are provided in Table 1. As the proposed method does not use gaze data, for a fair comparison, we compare the results obtained by the proposed method against the state-of-the-art methods that do not use gaze data. We observe that the proposed method outperforms the state-of-the-art with a significant margin of around 5%. We further observe that the sequential implementation of KDGAN architecture for the noun and verb predictors increased the accuracy from 54.12% to 57.72%, even without implementing the RVSGen algorithm. Implementation of the RVSGen algorithm further increases the accuracy by a significant margin of around 1.5%.

Table 1. Results obtained by the proposed method on EGTEA+ dataset, compared to the state-of-the-art. The results are shown by analyzing the first 50% of the test videos.

Methods	Published	Percentage of accuracy
Prabhakar et al.	IJCNN'22	53.66
Huang et al.	ACM Multimedia'21	37.80
Zheng et al.	ACM Trans. MCAP'23	54.12
Mascaro et al.	WACV'23	53.89
Proposed method without RVSGen	–	57.72
Proposed method with RVSGen	–	59.37

Moreover, we observe that the proposed student network, when tested on the full (100%) video, is providing 66.67% accuracy on the EGTEA+ dataset, which is much higher than the current state-of-the-art ego-centric action recognition performance of 64% accuracy. Hence, the proposed model can be used for action recognition as well.

We further compare the prediction accuracy of the proposed method against the state-of-the-art, when different percentages of the test video are provided to the ego-centric action predictor (student network) for predicting the action. The results are shown in Table 2, where the proposed method is observed to perform significantly better compared to the state-of-the-art.

Table 2. Results obtained by the proposed method on EGTEA+ dataset, compared to the state-of-the-art, in terms of % of accuracy. The results are shown by analyzing the first x% of the test videos, where x takes the value as 12.5, 25, 37.5, 50, 62.5, 75, 87.5, and 100.

Methods	12.5	25	37.5	50	62.5	75	87.5	100
Prabhakar et al.	39.36	46.54	49.86	53.66	56.24	58.81	60.59	62.04
Zheng et al.	42.20	48.83	52.04	54.12	55.87	56.93	57.54	58.06
Mascaro et al.	41.89	47.67	51.27	53.89	55.74	56.51	57.12	57.39
Proposed method without RVSGen	41.34	47.49	52.87	57.72	60.81	63.08	64.32	64.97
Proposed method with RVSGen	42.96	49.18	54.31	59.37	62.48	62.91	65.17	66.67

6   Conclusions

We propose a method for predicting human activity in egocentric videos. The proposed method applies adversarial training between a teacher and a student network in a knowledge distillation setup. Experimental results show that the sequential implementation of noun and verb predictors enhances the efficacy of the KD-based GAN architecture. Further, we include a reduced verb space generator algorithm to further reduce the search space for the verbs for the predicted noun. The inclusion of RVSGen could enhance the efficacy of the proposed method significantly. In the future, the proposed adversarial KD architecture can be used in other video prediction tasks such as predicting future frames. Further, using the Gaze and audio information available in the EGTEA+ dataset, as additional two modalities with additional two GAN architectures, can surely improve the accuracy.

References

1. Buddubariki, V., Tulluri, S.G., Mukherjee, S.: Event recognition in egocentric videos using a novel trajectory based feature. In: Proceedings of ICVGIP 2016, pp. 76:1–76:8 (2016)
2. Sai Suma, K., Aditya, G., Mukherjee, S.: Activity recognition in egocentric videos using bag of key action units. In: Proceedings of ICVGIP 2018, pp. 9:1–9:9 (2018)
3. Kahani, R., Talebpour, A., Mahmoudi-Aznaveh, A.: A correlation based feature representation for first-person activity recognition. Multimed. Tools Appl. **78**(15), 21673–21694 (2019). https://doi.org/10.1007/s11042-019-7429-3
4. Singh, S., Arora, C., Jawahar, C.V.: Trajectory aligned features for first person action recognition. Pattern Recogn. **62**, 45–55 (2017)
5. Damen, D., et al.: Scaling egocentric vision: the epic-kitchens dataset. In: Proceedings of ECCV (2018)
6. Kazakos, E., Nagrani, A., Zisserman, A., Damen, D.: Epic-fusion: audio-visual temporal binding for egocentric action recognition. In: Proceedings of ICCV (2019)
7. Prabhakar, M., Mukherjee, S.: First-person activity recognition by modelling subject-action relevance. In: Proceedings of IJCNN (2022)

8. Rodina, I., Furnaria, A., Mavroedis, D., Farinella, G.M.: First-person activity recognition by modelling subject-action relevance. Comput. Vis. Image Understanding **211**, Article number 103252 (2021)

9. Huang, Y., Yang, X., Xu, C.: Multimodal global relation knowledge distillation for egocentric action anticipation. In: Proceedings of ACM Multimedia (2021)

10. Zheng, N., Song, X., Su, T., Liu, W., Yan, Y., Nie, L.: Egocentric early action prediction via adversarial knowledge distillation. ACM Trans. Multimed. Comput. Commun. Appl. **19**(2), Article number 59 (2023)

11. Núñez-Marcos, A., Azkune, G., Arganda-Carreras, I.: Egocentric vision-based action recognition: a survey. Neurocomputing **472**, 175–197 (2022)

12. Willems, G., Tuytelaars, T., Van Gool, L.: An efficient dense and scale-invariant spatio-temporal interest point detector. In: Forsyth, D., Torr, P., Zisserman, A. (eds.) ECCV 2008. LNCS, vol. 5303, pp. 650–663. Springer, Heidelberg (2008). https://doi.org/10.1007/978-3-540-88688-4_48

13. Li, Y., Liu, M., Rehg, J.M.: In the eye of beholder: joint learning of gaze and actions in first person video. In: Proceedings of ECCV (2018)

14. Furnari, A., Farinella, G.M.: Rolling-unrolling LSTMs for action anticipation from first-person video. IEEE Trans. Pattern Anal. Mach. Intell. **43**(11), 4021–4036 (2021)

15. Li, H., Zheng, W.S., Zhang, J., Hu, H., Lu, J., Lai, J.H.: Egocentric action recognition by automatic relation modeling. IEEE Trans. Pattern Anal. Mach. Intell. **45**(1), 489–507 (2023)

16. Mascaro, E.V., Ahn, H., Lee, D.: Intention-conditioned long-term human egocentric action anticipation. In: Proceedings of WACV (2023)

Enhancement of Screening Mammograms Using Dual-Tree Complex Wavelet Transform

Annie Julie Joseph$^{(\boxtimes)}$, Farah Naz, and P. N. Pournami

National Institute of Technology Calicut, Kozhikode, Kerala, India
annie_p180094cs@nitc.ac.in

Abstract. Breast cancer has become one of the most common cancers worldwide. It is also one of the leading causes of death in women. Early detection of breast cancer is the need of the hour as it offers increased treatment options, better survival chances, and improved quality of life. The most economical technique is screening mammograms to promote breast cancer identification at an early stage. This paper proposes an enhancement strategy for screening mammograms based on Dual-Tree Complex Wavelet Transform (DTCWT). The DTCWT yields six directionally selective high-pass sub-bands on multiple scales. The reconstruction from the decomposed bands produces a resultant image with enhancement in directional edges. Thus, edge details are enhanced, improving the visualisation of mass boundaries inside the breast tissues. The proposed method offers PSNR values of 54.3612, 46.043, 48.8719 and SSIM is 0.9977, 0.9869, 0.9916 for the MIAS, DDSM and Inbreast datasets respectively. The proposed DTCWT-based mammogram enhancement can be used as an efficient preprocessing technique in a computer-aided diagnosis system to detect breast cancer in its early stages. The comparison of the proposed method with many of the recent algorithms depicts the overall dominance of its performance, with minimum error and good signal enhancement.

Keywords: Breast cancer · Computer aided diagnosis · Dual-tree complex wavelet transform · Image enhancement

1 Introduction

Cancer is the uncontrolled growth of cells in a specific human body location. It is one of the leading reasons for death worldwide, accounting for one in six deaths globally. Among the cancers in women (i.e. lung, colon, rectal, prostate, skin cancer, stomach, and liver), breast cancer is the most common Cancer (24.2%

Mammograms, especially screening mammograms, are used to diagnose malignant (cancerous) tissues in the breast. A mammogram is a specific X-ray image of the breast. The primary views are from top to bottom, craniocaudal (CC), and the side view is the mediolateral oblique (MLO) view. Mammogram

H. Kaur et al. (Eds.): CVIP 2023, CCIS 2009, pp. 574–585, 2024.
https://doi.org/10.1007/978-3-031-58181-6_49

image analysis involves studying mammogram images to identify any abnormality in the breast tissue.

The most common abnormality visible in a mammogram is called a mass. The masses in mammograms are either malignant (cancerous) or benign (noncancerous) type. A normal mammogram is one with no masses or benign masses. The distinction between benign and malignant masses is difficult due to the low quality of the mammogram, and recent advances in computer-aided diagnosis(CAD) systems help radiologists accurately identify the abnormality in breast masses. A reliable CAD system improves the malignant tissue from benign or normal breast tissue in mammograms. The CAD system for digital mammogram breast tissue classification involves (1) preprocessing of the mammogram, (2) segmentation of the region of interest (ROI), (3) feature extraction from ROIs, (4) feature reduction and (5) classification of breast tissue. The preprocessing step is the most fundamental and essential requirement for mammogram image analysis. In screening mammograms, the low beam X-rays are passed to the breast. Due to the movement of plates and other noises during image acquisition, the resultant screening mammogram image could be better quality. The image preprocessing step involves the removal of label artefacts and noise signals from the mammogram. The enhancement techniques help to highlight the relevant breast tissues.

The primary contributions of this paper are:

- Mammogram enhancement using DTCWT is carried out in the three publicly available datasets.
- The qualitative and quantitative performance assessment parameters indicate the overall dominant performance of the DTCWT based mammogram enhancement scheme.
- The importance of introducing DTCWT as a preprocessing step of mammography image analysis is also amply demonstrated by comparing the DTCWT-based enhancement scheme with other cutting-edge approaches.

The paper's outline is structured as follows. Section 2 focuses on the related works in the literature for mammogram enhancement. Section 3 describes the research technique. Section 4 presents and discusses experimental outcomes. Section 5 concludes the work and its main findings.

2 Related Works

It is evident from the published research that mammogram preprocessing involves noise reduction such as label and artefact removal, mammogram segmentation for breast border extraction and pectoral muscle suppression [1], and mammogram enhancement. Many investigators have performed image enhancement based on various approaches, which include unsharp masking, histogram, wavelet transform and machine learning/rule-based techniques. Each method has its own merits and demerits. Among these, unsharp masking, histogram-based, and wavelet-based methods are the most widely used despite some limitations of these methods.

Conventional unsharp masking (CUSM) is a straightforward conventional method used in mammogram image enhancement. It reduces the low-frequency details but amplifies high-frequency components. As alternatives to the CUSM, many improved unsharp masking techniques are also proposed. Ramponi et al. [2] developed a cubic unsharp masking method for contrast enhancement to avoid excessive overshoot in the detail areas and noise amplification in the conventional unsharp masking technique. This method can reduce noise sensitivity. A novel method of optimum wavelet-based masking (OWBM) using Enhanced Cuckoo Search Algorithm is developed by Daniel and Anitha [3] for contrast improvement of the mammograms.

Histogram-based methods usually modify the image histogram and accordingly improve the contrast. Among the various histogram-based approaches, Contrast Limited Adaptive Histogram Equalization (CLAHE) [4] is the most widely used method. CLAHE uses a clip limit to the histogram to obtain an optimum image enhancement without overamplifying noise in the image [5]. The main limitation of the clipped histogram equalisation techniques is the manual setting of the plateau level of the histogram. Sheeba Jenifera [6] has suggested a recent, fuzzy-clipped contrast-limited adaptive histogram equalisation method. In this method, the clip limit is automatically selected using a fuzzy algorithm, thus overcoming the limitations of the CLAHE.

Wavelet transform is inevitable in image enhancement, segmentation, compression and feature extraction. It can perform multi-dimension, multi-resolution, multi-scale, and multi-level image analysis. DWT analyses mammogram images in space and frequency domain [7]. One of the limitations of DWT is shift variance, which means it suffers from image energy between levels of a multi-scale decomposition varied significantly. A shift in an image degrades the performance of DWT and causes poor resolution/directional selectivity as its high-frequency sub-bands orient only three spatial orientations (0, 45 and 90°). It could have performed better at higher dimensions (2- or 3-dimensions) and levels.

Among the variants of the wavelet transforms, more advanced wavelet transforms are proposed by the research community [8,9]. The dual-tree complex wavelet transform (DTCWT) is a widely used variant, which yields better performance than the other standard wavelet transforms [10]. Applying the DWT and DTCWT-based methods includes classifying MR images, pathological brain detection, abnormal brain detection, hearing loss detection, dendrite spine detection, etc. These methods have proven very valuable because they are advanced tools and helpful in sharpening and filtering off the noise in the images. DTCWT is near shift-invariant and has improved directional selectivity, facilitating better results in denoising and characterising textures more accurately. A retinal image enhancement algorithm using DTCWT and morphology-based methods method is proposed by Li et al. [11]. They concluded that the performance of DTCWT is better than the histogram-based methods. In mammogram studies, DWT and

DTCWT variants for image classification are used. However, DWT and DTCWT applications for mammogram preprocessing are rarely available; hence, further exploration is highly desirable. The radially oriented edges present in the mammogram can be better inspected by applying enhancement for directional edges. DTCWT, an improved wavelet transform of DWT can retrieve more directional sub bands and enhance.

3   Methodology

In the present study, a systematic contrast enhancement strategy is proposed which uses Dual-Tree Complex Wavelet Transform (DTCWT) and its performance is evaluated qualitatively and quantitatively using three publicly available standard datasets.

3.1   Data and Data Sources

1. MIAS Dataset [12]
   The publicly available MIAS The Mammographic Image Analysis Society (MIAS) database (v1.21) [12] contains 322 digital mammograms.
2. DDSM Dataset [13]
   The Digital Database for Screening Mammography (DDSM) is a database of digitised film screen mammograms with associated ground truth information. It contains mammography screening exams of 2620 patients. Each mammogram includes four standard views (mediolateral oblique and craniocaudal) from each breast. The DDSM dataset contains a total of 10,480 (2620 * 4) images.
3. Inbreast Dataset [14]
   This dataset contains 910 mammograms. It includes screening mammograms, diagnostic mammograms, and follow-up mammograms. It has 90 patients' MLO and CC images of each breast and 25 mammograms of patients who had undergone mastectomy. For such cases, only two views of one breast are available.

3.2   Mammogram Enhancement Using 2D DTCWT

In preprocessing, diagnostically significant features of mammograms are to be enhanced and the concealed characteristics are to be recovered. Preprocessing techniques include manipulation of contrast and intensity, noise reduction, background removal, sharpening edges, and filtering.

DTCWT is an advancement over the DWT method. It is also multidimensional, multi-resolution, and multi-level, similar to DWT. It overcomes the problems of the standard DWT. The DTCWT provides approximate shift invariance with redundancy of 2:1 for 1-D or $2^d : 1$ for the d-dimensional images, which is substantially lower than the DWT, improves angular resolution, allows perfect reconstruction and reduced aliasing [15]. DWT, the basis is real-valued

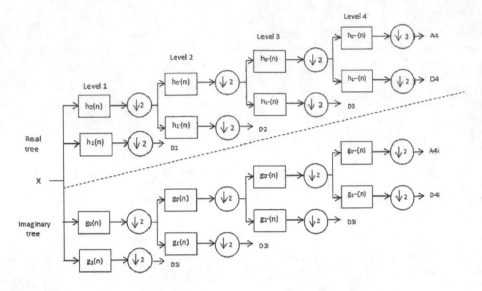

Fig. 1. 2D DTCWT image decomposition [16]

oscillating wavelets. The DTCWT basis is complex-valued oscillating wavelets. The DTCWT yields six directionally selective high-pass sub-bands at ±15, ±45, and ±75° and two low-pass sub-bands in 2-D. But, DWT yields three real high-pass sub-bands and one real low-pass sub-band at each level oriented at 0, 45 and 90°. Figure 1 depicts the decomposition process of 2-dimensional standard DTCWT up to two levels. The DTCWT is implemented in two distinct wavelet trees. A separate tree of independent filters computes the complex wavelet coefficients' real and imaginary parts. The real part is obtained from the upper tree, while the imaginary part is obtained from the lower tree.

2-dimensional DTCWT decomposes an image using a complex shift, dilated mother wavelet, and scaling function. A complex scaling function $\varphi(x)$ and wavelet $\psi(x)$ are defined as in Eqs. (1) and (2) respectively [8].

$$\varphi_c(x) = \varphi_h(x) + j\varphi_g(x) \tag{1}$$

$$\psi_c(x) = \psi_h(x) + j\psi_g(x) \tag{2}$$

where $\varphi_c(x)$ is the complex scaling function, $\psi_c(x)$ is the complex wavelet, $\psi_h(x)$ is the real and even part of the complex wavelet, and $\psi_g(x)$ is the imaginary and odd part of the complex wavelet, $\varphi_c(x)$ is the real and even part of the scaling function, and $\psi_g(x)$ is the imaginary and odd part of the scaling function, j is the imaginary function as $j = \sqrt{-1}$.

The scaling, $\varphi_{(}x)$ and wavelet, $\psi_{(}x)$ functions are defined similar to 1D DWT as given in Eqs. (3) and (4) respectively.

$$\varphi(x) = \sqrt{2} \sum_{n=0}^{L-1} h(n) \, \varphi(2x - n) \tag{3}$$

$$\psi(x) = \sqrt{2} \sum_{n=0}^{L-1} g(n) \, \varphi(2x - n) \tag{4}$$

In 2D, DTCWT decomposed of scaling functions that are defined as per Eq. (5) given in [17].

$$\varphi(x, y) = \varphi(x) \, \varphi(y) \tag{5}$$

Three 2D wavelet functions are defined in Eqs. (6), (7) and (8).

$$\psi^{II}(x, y) = \psi(x) \, \varphi(y) \tag{6}$$

$$\psi^{V}(x, y) = \varphi(x) \, \psi(y) \tag{7}$$

$$\psi^{D}(x, y) = \psi(x) \, \psi(y) \tag{8}$$

where $\varphi_c(x, y)$ is scaling function of the LL frequency sub-band, $\psi^H(x, y)$ is a horizontal wavelet function of the low-low (HL) frequency, $\psi^V(x, y)$ is a vertical wavelet function of the low-low(HL) frequency sub-band, and $\psi^D(x, y)$ is a diagonal wavelet function of the high-high (HL) frequency sub-band.

The expression for 2-D of the diagonal function of the HH pass-band is given in the Eq. 9.

$$\psi^{D}(x, y) = \psi(x) \, \psi(y) = \psi_h(x) \, \psi_h(y) - \psi_g(x) \, \psi_y(y) + j \left[\psi_h(x) \, \psi_g(y) + \psi_g(x) \, \psi_h(y) \right] \tag{9}$$

The sum of two separable wavelets is obtained when the real part of this complex wavelet is considered as given in Eq. (10).

$$Real \; part \; [\psi(x, y)] = \psi_h(x) \, \psi_h(y) - \psi_g(x) \, \psi_g(y) \tag{10}$$

Applying both of the separable transforms to the same 2-D data gives a total of six sub-bands: two HL, two LH, and two HH sub-bands with approximately shift-invariant and oriented at $\pm 15°$, $\pm 45°$, and $\pm 75°$ and two LL bands. The 2-D DTCWT using the bio-orthogonal and ba-ba-filters decomposes mammogram images similarly to the DWT. The 2D DTCWT yields six directionally selective high-pass sub-bands at ± 15, ± 45, and $\pm 75°$ and two low-pass sub-bands for both the real and imaginary parts, in contrast to the DWT.

The procedure for implementing the Dual-Tree Complex Wavelet Transform (DTCWT) to mammograms is given in Algorithm 1.

Algorithm 1. Mammogram Enhancement using Dual-Tree Complex Wavelet Transform(DTCWT) method

---

[!htbp] **Input:**Mammogram Image, I(x, y)
Output: Enhanced Mammogram Image, $I_{DTCWT}(x, y)$

1: **procedure** DTCWTEnhancementProcedure($I(x, y)$)
2:      Decompose mammogram input image, $I(x, y)$ in standard DTCWT domain by applying a low-pass filter, $h(x, y)$ and high-pass $g(x)$ filters to the rows of the image and then columns of the resultant image.
3:      Obtain the low-frequency information after $h(x, y)$ and the high-frequency information after filtering with $g(x, y)$.
4:      Downsample the low-frequency and the high-frequency response function by a factor of two($\downarrow$).
5:      Obtain six directional sub-bands that are wavelets oriented at $\pm 15°$, $\pm 45°$, $\pm 75°$.
6:      The decomposed approximate two low-pass filter coefficients obtained is the new image, I, and further decomposed by repeating steps 1 to 3.
7:      Obtain two approximate low-pass filter coefficients and six detail (high-frequency coefficients) at the second level.
8:      Reconstruct the image, using two low pass coefficients (approximate coefficients) and six directional subband details (high-frequency coefficients) at the second level by applying an inverse dual-tree complex wavelet transform.
9:      Reconstruct the final enhanced image, $I_{DTCWT}(x, y)$ by applying inverse dual-tree complex wavelet transform using the reconstructed image from step (7) and six directional subband details (high pass coefficients) from the first level.

---

4 Results and Discussion

Evaluation Metrics
Numerous enhancement quality assessment methods exist for qualitative and quantitative [18] analysis. The qualitative evaluation checks the image's visual quality, which is very subjective. In this study, the evaluation metrics used are Absolute Mean Brightness Error (AMBE), Mean Square Error (MSE), Root Mean Square Error (RMSE), Peak Signal Noise Ratio (PSNR), Universal Image Quality Index (UIQI), Structural Similarity Index Measure (SSIM), Edge Contents (EC) and Feature Similarity Index Measure (FSIM) for comparing the performances of the mammogram enhancement methods. The technique with the highest PSNR, UIQI, SSIM, EC and FSIM values and the lowest values for AMBE and RMSE is considered the best.

The proposed DTCWT-based enhancement algorithm is applied to the three datasets - MIAS, DDSM and Inbreast. The performance of our proposed technique is compared with Conventional Unsharp Masking (CUSM), CLAHE and DWT algorithms using qualitative and quantitative measures. From the radiologist's and observer's viewpoint, the visual quality also plays a vital role in the contrast enhancement of mammograms for their analysis to diagnose Cancer. For the qualitative comparison, three sample mammogram images, each belonging to normal (Image mdb003.pgm), benign (mdb001.pgm), and malignant (Image mdb023.pgm) cancer categories are randomly selected from the mammograms of the MIAS dataset and visually analysed.

The normal, benign, and malignant images and their corresponding enhanced images are given in Fig. 2(a–e). This illustration visually compares the original mammograms and their corresponding enhanced mammograms by the four enhancement techniques. From Fig. 2(a–e), we observe that all three mammograms preprocessed by the CUSM yield very noisy, and it is difficult to diagnose the abnormality masses in mammograms. However, enhanced images by the CLAHE method produced perfect quality images as the contrast is increased in CLAHE yielded images. It can be observed that the processed images through the proposed DTCWT enhancement methods are nearly identical to the original mammogram images, with enhanced edges.

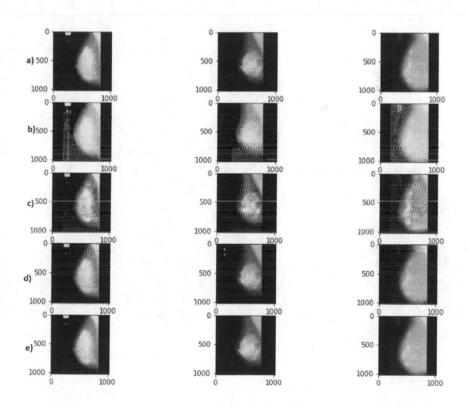

Fig. 2. A visual comparison of the original and enhanced images with normal, benign and malignant mammogram categories by different enhancement techniques: (a) original images, (b) enhanced images by CUSM, (c) enhanced images by CLAHE, (d) enhanced images by DWT, (e) enhanced images by DTCWT

The proposed DTCWT-based mammogram enhancement technique is subjected to quantitative analysis as the next step. Seven quantitative measures are employed to compare the preprocessing methods' performances. The quantitative measures are absolute mean brightness error (AMBE), root means square error (RMSE), peak signal-to-noise ratio (PSNR), universal image quality index (UIQI), structural similarity index metric (SSIM), edge contents (EC) and feature similarity index measure(FSIM). Their respective formulas calculate the value of these measures, and calculated values for the AMBE, RMSE, PSNR, UIQI, and SSIM are reported in Table 1. The quantitative measures AMBE, RMSE, and PSNR measure errors, which indicate the net differences between the original and the enhanced image grey level values. Meanwhile, UIQI and SSIM are much better indicators of overall image quality and structural similarity. It is evident from Table 1 that the image enhancement through the DTCWT method has the lowest errors in terms of AMBE and RMSE, followed by the DWT method.

Table 1. Quantitative Statistics of Different Mammogram Enhancement Techniques

Mammogram Enhancement Techniques				
Evaluation Metric	CUSM	CLAHE	DWT	DTCWT (Proposed)
MIAS Dataset				
PSNR	12.7765	25.5939	35.7864	**54.3612**
SSIM	0.4855	0.6421	0.9630	**0.9977**
UIQI	0.7788	0.4457	0.9613	**0.9978**
RMSE	0.2317	0.0536	0.0165	**0.0019**
AMBE	21.2057	4.7102	0.0431	**0.0011**
DDSM Dataset				
PSNR	9.0825	22.5939	32.5404	**46.0423**
SSIM	0.0826	0.8583	0.9397	**0.9869**
UIQI	0.4764	0.8745	0.9790	**0.9975**
RMSE	0.3531	0.0750	0.0235	**0.0053**
AMBE	43.6466	10.8299	0.3319	**0.0180**
INbreast Dataset				
PSNR	20.0689	28.5429	37.4200	**48.8719**
SSIM	0.6653	0.5507	0.9621	**0.9916**
UIQI	0.9641	0.3271	0.9727	**0.9911**
RMSE	0.1020	0.0383	0.0137	**0.0036**
AMBE	10.9725	2.2946	0.0608	**0.0128**

Finally, the performance of DTCWT is compared with the advanced mammogram image enhancement algorithms recently published using the MIAS dataset. The comparative results are given in Table 2.

Table 2. Comparison of MSE and PSNR values of Recent Mammogram Enhancement Techniques

Publication	Method	RMSE	PSNR
Abhijith et al. 2021 [19]	Rolling Ball Algorithm and Huang's Fuzzy Thresholding	2.3741	46.57
Suradi et al. 2021 [20]	FADHECAL	2.28	26.843
Dabass et al. 2019 [21]	ENTROPY and CLAHE Based Fuzzy	2.01	22.4759
Iswardani et al. 2018 [22]	Digital Image Processing Techniques	44.8	31.7
Gupta et al. 2017 [23]	Digital Image Processing Techniques		18.9
Hashmi et al. 2022 [24]	CNN based mammogram enhancement	17.34	29.37
Proposed Method	**DTCWT**	**0.0019**	**54.3612**

The proposed method is also compared with recently published works in mammogram enhancement [19–23]. The recent work of Pawar et al. in 2021 [25] proposed local entropy maximisation-based image fusion for mammogram enhancement. They used Edge Contents (EC) and FSIM (Feature Similarity Index Measure) to compare the method's performance.

Table 3. Performance Evaluation of Different Mammogram Enhancement Techniques on MIAS Dataset

Evaluation Metric	Original	Pawar et al. [25]	DTCWT (proposed)
FSIM	1	0.96	**0.99**
EC	0.35	0.72	**0.86**

In the MIAS dataset, the edge contents of the enhanced image are improved by 0.37 [25], while the proposed method has an improvement of 0.51. FSIM measure on average is 0.96 in [25] whereas the proposed method has the FSIM value of 0.99. This comparison is given in Table 3. The proposed method's enhancement is a high similarity preserving mammogram enhancement method, confirmed by the experimental results.

5   Conclusion

In the present study, an efficient preprocessing step that will enhance the mammogram image is presented. The suggested DTCWT based method outperformed the conventional unsharp masking, CLAHE and DWT techniques when applied to digital mammograms from the MIAS, DDSM and Inbreast databases. The modification of DTCWT-based enhancement together with other filtering methods will help to highlight the lesions present in mammograms more accurately.

References

1. Bhateja, V., Misra, M., Urooj, S.: Non-linear polynomial filters for edge enhancement of mammogram lesions. Comput. Methods Programs Biomed. **129**, 125–134 (2016)
2. Ramponi, G.: A cubic unsharp masking technique for contrast enhancement. Sig. Process. **67**(2), 211–222 (1998)
3. Daniel, E., Anitha, J.: Optimum wavelet based masking for the contrast enhancement of medical images using enhanced cuckoo search algorithm. Comput. Biol. Med. **71**, 149–155 (2016)
4. Zuiderveld, K.: Contrast Limited Adaptive Histogram Equalization. Academic Press, Cambridge (1994)
5. Nayak, D.R., Dash, R., Majhi, B.: Discrete ripplet-II transform and modified PSO based improved evolutionary extreme learning machine for pathological brain detection. Neurocomputing **282**, 232–247 (2018)
6. Jenifer, S., Parasuraman, S., Kadirvelu, A.: Contrast enhancement and brightness preserving of digital mammograms using fuzzy clipped contrast-limited adaptive histogram equalization algorithm. Appl. Soft Comput. **42**, 167–177 (2016)
7. Rowe, A.C.H., Abbott, P.C.: Daubechies wavelets and mathematica. Comput. Phys. **9**(6), 635–648 (1995)
8. Kingsbury, N.: Complex wavelets for shift invariant analysis and filtering of signals. Appl. Comput. Harmon. Anal. **10**(3), 234–253 (2001)
9. Kingsbury, N.: Rotation-invariant local feature matching with complex wavelets. In: 2006 14th European Signal Processing Conference, pp. 1–5. IEEE (2006)
10. Li, D., Zhang, L., Sun, C., Yin, T., Liu, C., Yang, J.: Computer-aided diagnosis of breast microcalcifications based on dual-tree complex wavelet transform. Biomed. Eng. Online **11**, 96 (2012)
11. Li, D., Zhang, L., Sun, C., Yin, T., Liu, C., Yang, J.: Robust retinal image enhancement via dual-tree complex wavelet transform and morphology-based method. IEEE Access **7**, 47303–47316 (2019)
12. Bowyer, R.M.K., Kopans, D., Kegelmeyer, W.P.: Mammographic image analysis society (MIAS) database v1. 21. In: Proceedings of the Fifth International Workshop on Digital Mammography, pp. 212–218 (2001)
13. Heath, M., Bowyer, K., Kopans, D., Moore, R., Kegelmeyer, P.: The digital database for screening mammography. In: Proceedings of the Fourth International Workshop on Digital Mammography (2000)
14. Moreira, I., Amaral, I., Domingues, I., Cardoso, A.J.O., Cardoso, M.J., Cardoso, J.S.: Inbreast: toward a full-field digital mammographic database. Acad. Radiol. **19**(2), 236–248 (2012)
15. Daubechies, I.: Ten Lectures on Wavelets, vol. 61. SIAM (1992)
16. Bhan Singh, B., Patel, S.: Efficient medical image enhancement using CLAHE enhancement and wavelet fusion. Int. J. Comput. Appl. **167**(5), 1–5 (2017). ISSN: 0975-8887
17. Vyas, A.: Multiscale Transforms with Application to Image Processing (2018)

18. Yang, Y., Tong, S., Huang, S., Lin, P.: Dual-tree complex wavelet transform and image block residual-based multi-focus image fusion in visual sensor networks. Sensors **14**(12), 22408–22430 (2014)

19. Beeravolu, A.R., Azam, S., Jonkman, M., Shanmugam, B., Kannoorpatti, K., Anwar, A.: Preprocessing of breast cancer images to create datasets for deep-CNN. IEEE Access **9**, 33438–33463 (2021)

20. Suradi, S.H., Abdullah, K.A., Mat Isa, N.A.: Improvement of image enhancement for mammogram images using fuzzy anisotropic diffusion histogram equalisation contrast adaptive limited (fadhecal). Comput. Methods Biomech. Biomed. Eng. Imaging Vis. **10**(1), 67–75 (2022)

21. Dabass, J., Arora, S., Vig, R., Hanmandlu, M.: Mammogram image enhancement using entropy and CLAHE based intuitionistic fuzzy method. In: 2019 6th International Conference on Signal Processing and Integrated Networks (SPIN), pp. 24–29 (2019)

22. Iswardani, A., Hidayat, W.: Mammographic image enhancement using digital image processing technique (2018)

23. Tiwari, M., Gupta, B.: A tool supported approach for brightness preserving contrast enhancement and mass segmentation of mammogram images using histogram modified grey relational analysis. Multidimension. Syst. Signal Process. **28**, 1549–1567 (2017)

24. Hashmi, A., et al.: Contrast enhancement in mammograms using convolution neural networks for edge computing systems. Sci. Program. **2022**, 1882464 (2022)

25. Pawar, M., Talbar, S.: Local entropy maximization based image fusion for contrast enhancement of mammogram. J. King Saud Univ. Comput. Inf. Sci. **33**(2), 150–160 (2021)

Actor-Centric Spatio-Temporal Feature Extraction for Action Recognition

Kunchala Anil[1]($\boxtimes$) (iD), Mélanie Bouroche[2] (iD), and Bianca Schoen-Phelan[1] (iD)

[1] Technological University Dublin, Dublin, Ireland
D20125529@mytudublin.ie, bianca.schoenphelan@tudublin.ie
[2] School of Computer Science and Statistics, Trinity College Dublin, Dublin, Ireland
melanie.bouroche@tcd.ie

Abstract. Action understanding involves the recognition and detection of specific actions within videos. This crucial task in computer vision gained significant attention due to its multitude of applications across various domains. The current action detection models, inspired by 2D object detection methods, employ two-stage architectures. The first stage is to extract actor-centric video sub-clips, i.e. tubelets of individuals, and the second stage is to classify these tubelets using action recognition networks. The majority of these recognition models utilize a frame-level pre-trained 3D Convolutional Neural Networks (3D CNN) to extract spatio-temporal features of a given tubelet. This, however, results in suboptimal spatio-temporal feature representation for action recognition, primarily because the actor typically occupies a relatively small area in the frame.

This work proposes the use of actor-centric tubelets instead of frames to learn spatio-temporal feature representation for action recognition. We present an empirical study of the actor-centric tubelet and frame-level action recognition models and propose a baseline for actor-centric action recognition. We evaluated the proposed method on the state-of-the-art C3D, I3D, and SlowFast 3D CNN architectures using the NTURGBD dataset. Our results demonstrate that the actor-centric feature extractor consistently outperforms the frame-level and large pre-trained fine-tuned models. The source code for the tubelet generation is available at https://github.com/anilkunchalaece/ntu_tubelet_parser.

Keywords: action detection · action recognition · untrimmed action detection in extended videos

1 Introduction

The widespread availability of cameras, combined with the recent advancements in convolutional neural networks, has attracted significant interest among

This work was conducted with the financial support of the Science Foundation Ireland Centre for Research Training in Digitally-Enhanced Reality (d-real) under Grant No. 18/CRT/6224.

researchers in computer vision. In particular, action understanding has emerged as a crucial task due to its numerous applications across diverse fields, such as security, autonomous vehicles, smart cities, and human-computer interactions.

Action understanding comprises of the recognition and detection of spatio-temporal actions across multiple people in a given video. *Action recognition* involves identifying the specific action being performed, while *action detection* involves localizing the spatial and temporal extent of the action. The introduction of 3D Convolution Networks (CNNs) as a natural extension of 2D CNNs with a temporal domain has significantly improved the performance of action understanding models [22]. To extract spatio-temporal features from videos, 3D CNNs are employed as backbone models for action detection [3,8,11,12,17,20] and classification tasks [2,6,7,22], owing their robust ability to representing spatio-temporal features. For action recognition, these features are fed to classifiers such as SVM or MLP to predict the action label. These models are trained with trimmed videos of specific activities, where each frame may contain more than one person, and the classifier predicts the single or collective action (e.g., handshake, hugging). Kinetics [2] and UCF101 [21] are popular datasets used in action recognition models.

Action detection is usually carried out in two stages: (i)feature extraction & (ii) individual proposal generation and action classification. The feature extraction stage involves extracting spatio-temporal features for a given video, and the proposal generation consists of locating and generating the spatio-temporal features of individuals. Finally, these features are used to predict the action class label for the individual. In literature, two types of individual spatio-temporal feature extraction methods are prevalent:

1. key-frame-based methods (cuboids): a detector is used to detect the individuals in the keyframe image, and the detected bounding boxes are used to extract the spatiotemporal features for all the sampled frames.
2. tracker-based methods (tubelets): a tracking algorithm is used to extract the detection of each individual for sampled frames, and tracking bounding boxes are used to extract the spatiotemporal features.

Cuboids are predominately used for atomic action detection [4,7,8,12]. The most popular datasets used for atomic action detection are AVA [12] and UCF101 [21]. These datasets generally consist of trimmed or untrimmed videos of one or two people performing a single action. In these videos, the actor is in the foreground, occupying a large area in the image. Cuboid-based aggregation fails in the case of large movements where a person's movement in sampled frames is not matched with the keyframe [20]. To overcome this limitation, tubelet-based action detection has been introduced to extract the tubelets by employing the tracker for sampled frames [3,17,20]. A tracking algorithm is used to extract the person-tracking bounding boxes of the individuals within the sampled frames. Unlike cuboids, tubelets have varying lengths and shapes based on a person's activity. Tubelet-based methods are prevalent in untrimmed extended video detection [3,9–11,16,17].

Fig. 1. Comparison of full frames (top) to actor-centric tubelets (bottom). A person detector is used to detect and extract the individual from the frame to generate tubelets. Images are taken from the NTURGBD [15] dataset.

Conventional activity detection in trimmed videos [7,8] achieved state-of-the-art performance with the introduction of large action detection datasets such as AVA [12]. However, most of the data available in the real world is in untrimmed extended video format (such as surveillance videos), and conventional activity detection methods based on cuboids are not suitable for real-world applications [3,16]. Several works [3,9,11,16,17] explore tubelet-based action detection for extended videos.

For both action recognition and spatio-temporal detection, a 3D CNN backbone is used to extract the frame-level features for the given video. In contrast to action recognition, action detection is used to classify the activities at the individual level. The general approach for spatio-temporal action detection is to initialize the 3D CNN model pre-trained on a large action recognition dataset(ex Kinetics [2]) and fine-tune the model with actor-centric tubelets [3,10,11,16]. We argue that utilizing the action recognition backbone trained using full-frame features for individual action recognition leads to suboptimal feature extraction and restricts action detection performance. Indeed, the person who is the primary subject of interest, as shown in Fig. 1, typically occupies a relatively small area within the frame (for ex., in extended videos). The full-frame features consist of broader scope and are not specifically optimized to capture discriminative features for individual actions. The resulting individual diluted features limit the system's ability to recognise and differentiate between various actions accurately. We hypothesize that actor-centric spatio-temporal feature extractors can significantly improve classification accuracy and serve as the optimized backbone for action detection. To this end, we conducted an extensive empirical comparative study of existing state-of-the-art (SOTA) 3D CNN classification models for both frames and action-centric tubelets. Due to the lack of existing datasets for actor-centric action recognition, we generated the derived actor-centric action recognition dataset using the NTURGBD dataset [15] using SOTA MobileNet [13] object detector. The source code to generate tubelets is available at https:// github.com/anilkunchalaece/ntu_tubelet_parser. The NTURGBD dataset consists of a collection of videos capturing single and multi-person videos across a range of activities. For the proposed work, we selected a subset that specifically focuses on single-person videos from relevant daily action classes. The original frame-based dataset is used to compare the action recognition performance with the derived tubelet dataset. The contributions of this paper are as follows:

1. We conducted an extensive comparative study of frame-based and actor-centric tubelet-based feature extraction for action classification.
2. We propose an actor-centric tubelet-based backbone that enhances spatio-temporal feature extraction for action classification and detection compared to the existing frame-level models.

The remainder of the paper is organized as follows: Sect. 2 explores the related work in action recognition and detection. Section 4 describes the actor-centric features and motivation for the actor-centric feature extractor for action recognition and detection. Section 5 presents the experimental setup followed by results. Finally, Sect. 6 concludes the proposed work and delineates the potential future work.

2   Related Work

The strong representational power of CNNs, coupled with the availability of large video understanding datasets, has led to significant advancements in action recognition and spatiotemporal action detection [2,8,12]. This section discusses the existing literature, focusing first on action recognition, followed by spatio-temporal action detection.

2.1   Action Recognition

Action recognition networks extend image recognition networks by including temporal dimensions while preserving spatial properties. Traditionally, image-based 2D models are adapted and extended for video action detection. One popular approach for these are so-called two-stream networks, where recurrent neural networks (RNNs) are added on top of 2D CNNs. The introduction of 3D CNN resulted in the paradigm shift from 2D to 3D CNN for video analysis. 3D CNNs expand the capabilities of 2D image recognition models for action recognition. The C3D is the first to propose a 3D CNN architecture for action recognition that extracts spatio-temporal features from video frames. It has been shown to outperform 2D CNNs and two-stream networks on various benchmark datasets [2,12,21]. The impressive performance of 3D CNNs led to the introduction of variants of 3D CNNs to learn spatio-temporal features to address different challenges in action recognition, such as long-term dependencies [2] and temporal dynamics [7].

2.2   Spatio-Temporal Action Detection

Spatio-temporal action detection is used to localise and recognise the actions temporally. Action detection models are developed on top of action classification, where the major focus is proposal generation and processing instead of spatio-temporal feature optimization. Generally, backbone 3D CNN classification networks are used to extract features in action detection. The majority of the state-of-the-art in action detection focuses on foreground action detection on trimmed videos [2,7,8], trained using datasets such as AVA [12] and UCF101 [21]. However, most of the visual data in the real world are comprised of extended untrimmed videos. In recent years, there has been an increasing interest in action detection in extended videos [3,11,16,17]. These studies have delved into the challenging task of accurately detecting activities in extended video sequences. The offline tracking algorithms are utilized to extract the bounding box detection of individuals across the sampled frames, and these detections are then combined and processed to generate the tubelets for classification.

A common characteristic shared by all these approaches is their reliance on existing action classification backbones that utilize frame-level features. Notable works include [3,16,17], which use offline trackers such as [1] to extract the tubelets from the VIRAT dataset [18] for spatio-temporal action detection. These tubelets are classified using 3D CNN architectures pre-trained using Kinetics-400 action classification dataset [2]. We believe the following are the major reasons behind the trend:

1. The lack of existing studies exploring the advantages of tubelet spatio-temporal features compared to the frame-level features for action classification
2. The lack of actor-centric tubelet datasets and the absence of a dedicated 3D CNN backbone for feature extraction have resulted in a heavy reliance on frame-level feature extractors.

To this end, we conducted an extensive empirical study to compare actor-centric tubelet-level features using popular 3D CNN networks to the frame-level features for action recognition. Since there are no datasets available for actor-centric tubelets, we generate a derived actor-centric dataset for action classification using the NTURGB [15] dataset.

It is also worth noting that classification models used in spatio-temporal action detection are primarly focused on individual action only. This is mainly because both cuboids and tubelets consist of only individual spatio-temporal features without any background context information. In recent works, background subtraction [16] or Graph Convolution Networks [17,23] have been proposed to extract and incorporate background context information inorder to model object relationships. The same limitation is also inherited by the proposed actor-centric recognition network, as it relies solely on spatiotemporal features for action recognition.

3   Overview of Action Detection Networks

A prevalent approach for action detection is to utilize an action classifier on top of local actor features pooled from an intermediate feature map of the 3D CNN backbone. Figure 2 depicts the overview of spatio-temporal action detection

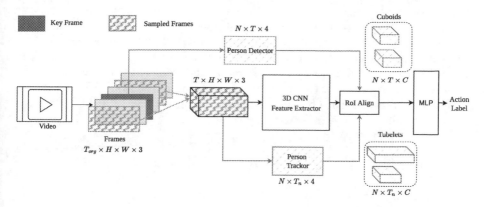

Fig. 2. Overview of spatio-temporal action detection methods. Both key-frame-based (highlighted in red) and tubelet-based (highlighted in blue) methods pool actor features using 3D CNN frame-level feature maps. T number of frames are sampled from T_{org} video frames. Key-frame-based methods utilize a person detector to extract the cuboids ($N \times T \times C$), whereas a tracker is used to generate tubelets ($N \times T_n \times C$) for tubelet-based action detection. Where N is the total number of persons, T_n is the length of the n'th person tubelet, and C is the number of features. (Color figure online)

methods for both key-frame-based methods (highlighted in red) and tubelet-based methods (highlighted in blue).

Key-frame-based methods are primarily used to detect atomic actions in trimmed and untrimmed videos, where the actor is usually in the foreground occupying most of the area in the frame. Cuboids with fixed shapes are extracted using an offline person detector or region proposal network [12] on the keyframe. The bounding boxes of the person detections in the key frame are utilized to extract the region of interest features from all sampled frames for that person. The key assumption of these methods is that actors' positions do not vary significantly across the sampled frames in order to aggregate cuboid features. However, cuboid-based aggregation is ineffective for extended videos, where the actor's position may vary significantly. Furthermore, most extended videos involve multiple actors performing diverse actions simultaneously in the background in varying spatio-temporal settings. Recently, tubelet-based methods have been proposed for extracting tubelets for individual actors by using an offline tracker. Unlike cuboids, tubelets are extracted by tracking individual persons in all sampled frames, where tubelets may have a different length, depending on the individual frame's presence and length of action being performed. The tubelet-based methods are predominately used to detect activities under large motion [20] and extended videos [3,16,17].

In both keyframe and tubelet-based models, as depicted in Fig. 2, a 3D CNN backbone network is used to extract spatio-temporal features, and it is usually pre-trained using frame-based action recognition datasets (ex, Kinetics-400). These frame-level features are pooled for each person as cuboids or tubelets. However, pooling actor-centric features from frame-level intermediate feature maps leads to sub-optimal feature aggregation, specifically when there are multiple people in the frame with significant spatio-temporal variations. This is prevalent in extended videos (ex, surveillance videos) where actors are mostly in the background and limited to a small area in the frame. When multiple people are present in the frame, actor-centric feature extraction can potentially enhance the model's ability to learn the discriminative features to detect complex actions at spatio-temporal scale variations.

4   Actor-Centric Spatio-Temporal Features

Our approach aims to optimize actor-centric spatio-temporal feature representation for action recognition. Figure 3 depicts the proposed actor-centric action recognition model. In contrast to existing recognition networks, we first extract the actor-centric tubelets for a given video using a person detector and use a 3D CNN to extract the features to predict the action labels. The actor-centric spatio-temporal feature representation allows for a better understanding of the action performed by the person, leading to more accurate recognition, and provides a better baseline for spatiotemporal action detection compared to the frame-based action recognition baselines.

4.1   Actor-Centric Action Recognition

Tubelet-based methods have shown promising results in action detection tasks, as they capture the spatio-temporal information of the actions more efficiently compared to cuboid-based methods. However, these methods depend on frame-level features to pool the actor-centric tubelet features as depicted in Fig. 3a, leading to sub-optimal feature extraction in extended videos in which actors occupy a small area in the frame. The proposed actor-centric spatio-temporal features are a promising alternative to overcome this limitation. Figure 3b depicts the proposed action recognition network to extract actor-centric spatio-temporal features. For an input video of T_{org} frames with shape $T_{org} \times H \times W \times 3$, T frames are sampled, where H, W are the height and width of frames containing 3 colour channels. A person detector is used to detect the person bounding boxes of shape $T \times 4$, where each frame contains a single person, represented by a bounding box of length 4. These detections, along with sampled images, are used to extract actor-centric crop images on a temporal scale with the shape of $T \times H_t \times W_t \times 3$ where $H_t \leq H$ and $W_t \leq W$ is the height and width of actor-centric images respectively. These actor-centric temporal images are then used to train the network. The network is optimized to extract actor-centric action features without considering the complete frame information, focusing solely on relevant spatio-temporal features. The proposed model can be easily adapted for multiple people per frame by simply replacing the detector with a tracker, where individual tracks per actor can be separated and aggregated based on the activity.

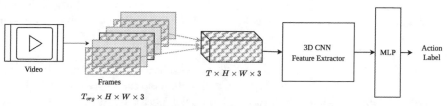

(a) Overview of existing action recognition networks.

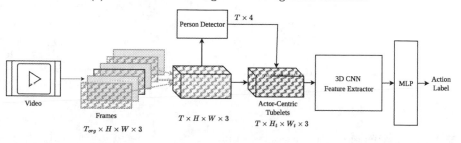

(b) Proposed actor-centric action recognition network

Fig. 3. Overview of proposed actor-centric tubelet action recognition network compared to existing frame-based action recognition networks. T frames are sampled from an input video of $T_{org} \times H \times W$ frames, where H and W are the height and width of frame. A person detector is used to extract the bounding boxes $T \times 4$. These bounding boxes are used to extract tubelets of shape $T \times H_t \times W_t \times 3$ where H_t and W_t are the height and width of person in frame t

5 Experimental Evaluation

In this section, we first introduce the dataset used, followed by baseline models. Finally, we present the results of the proposed method and critically discuss our findings.

5.1 Dataset

Although there are a plethora of state-of-the-art datasets available for action classification (such as Kinetics-400 [2], Sports-1M [14], and UCF101 [21]), these are not directly applicable to our proposed model as they contain multiple actors per video and focus on overall action recognition rather than actor-centric action recognition. Therefore, we generated a dataset derived from the NTURGBD [15] dataset with actor-centric tubelets. NTURGBD consists of 120 action classes with 57,600 video samples, where action classes are divided into daily actions, medical conditions, and mutual actions. Within the available classes, we opted for seven daily action classes (sit down, stand up, hand waving, phone call, playing with the phone or tablet, taking a selfie, and running on the spot with approximately 1000 samples per class) due to their relevance in extended video action detection. The NTURGBD dataset was selected due to the availability of single-person videos at frame level across the selected classes, which makes it suitable for training and evaluating action recognition models using frames and tubelets.

MobileNet [13] is used as an object detector to extract the person bounding boxes for tubelet extraction in a given video. In contrast to existing tubelet-based detection methods, our proposed model's performance evaluation does not involve any post-processing of the generated tubelets. The reason for this choice is two-fold: firstly, using raw tubelets allows us to generalise the results, facilitating comparisons across existing tubelet-based detection methods. Secondly, this approach allows flexibility for future improvement and adaptation to diverse application use cases. Unless otherwise indicated, all experimental results are reported on the NTURGBD validation dataset for the selected classes.

5.2   Baseline Models

The proposed model (tubelets) is compared with frames and two fine-tuned models as described in Table 1. For both pt-large and pt-frames models, the dataset is reduced by 50% for fine-tuning to provide a valid comparison between fine-tuned and trained-from-scratch models. Due to their strong representational power at both image and video levels, pt-large models are able to achieve better performance compared to other baseline models.

Table 1. Baseline methods and their description

Model	Description
frames	model trained from scratch with frames and evaluated using frames
tubelets	model trained from scratch with tubelets extracted from the dataset and evaluated using tubelets
pt-large	model pre-trained using large action classification dataset, fine-tuned and tested using tubelets
pt-frames	pre-trained frames model, fine-tuned and tested using tubelets

5.3   Experimental Setup

The proposed method is evaluated using widely popular and state-of-the-art 3D CNN architectures for action recognition (C3D [22], I3D [2] and SlowFast [7]). The selected models represent common approaches for modelling spatio-temporal features in videos. Through a comparative evaluation of these models, our aim is to assess both the relative performance and generalisability of the proposed tubelet-based action recognition model.

All the experiments are performed using a batch size of 240 and trained for 45 epochs[1]. Table 2 depicts the sampling strategy used in each architecture. The dataset is split into training and testing groups using the cross-subject evaluation from NTURGB [15]. Furthermore, centre-crop data augmentation is removed for actor-centric tubelets training in each model.

Table 2. Sampling strategy for 3D CNN models

Architecture	Sampling Strategy
C3D	$16 \times 1 \times 1$
I3D	$32 \times 2 \times 1$
SlowFast	$8 \times 8 \times 1$

5.4   Results

To determine the effectiveness of the proposed method, we evaluated the action recognition performance of a model trained with tubelets and compared it with a model trained with frames from scratch (frames), fine-tuned model with a large action recognition dataset (pt-large) and frames (pt-frames). Table 3 presents the results for proposed and baseline methods across three popular and widely used 3D CNN architectures, specifically C3D [22], I3D [2] and SlowFast [7]. The results show that our proposed approach outperforms the frames-only model and is able to match the performance of fine-tuned pre-trained models trained on the SOTA large benchmarking dataset. Moreover, it is evident that SlowFast models outperform C3D and I3D models due to their improved network architecture, allowing for better modelling of spatio-temporal features. We can also notice that the proposed tubelet-based performance is consistent across all architectures, highlighting the generalisability of the model across both simple(C3D) and complex(I3D, SlowFast) architectures.

It can be observed that a tubelet-based training model is able to achieve improved accuracy across all architectures without any tubelet postprocessing. We can also notice that the tubelet trained-from-scratch model is able to match the performance of the fine-tuned model with large action recognition datasets. This demonstrates that tubelet-based training with large actor-centric tubelet datasets is able to achieve superior performance for action recognition extended videos by learning optimized spatio-temporal features. Furthermore, it can also serve as a better alternative for existing action detection models in extended videos where a frame-based action classification backbone is widely utilized. Note however that the proposed method is restricted to individual action recognition

---

[1] https://github.com/open-mmlab/mmaction2.

Table 3. Action recognition results on NTURGBD [15] frames and derived tubelets dataset. Comparison of the action recognition performance for state-of-the-art 3D CNN (C3D, I3D and SlowFast) architectures across both trained-from-scratch(frames, tubelets) and fine-tuned(pt-large, pt-frames) models. The proposed tubelet-based method (tubelets) is able to achieve improved performance by efficiently modelling actor-centric spatio-temporal features for action recognition across all architectures.

3D CNN	Model	Resolution	Pretrain	Top 1	Top 3	mAcc
C3D	frames	112×112	✗	0.720	0.967	0.678
	tubelets		✗	**0.910**	**0.987**	**0.897**
	pt-frames		frames*	0.842	0.968	0.818
	pt-large		sports-1M	0.909	0.994	0.895
I3D	frames	224×224	✗	0.871	0.982	0.851
	tubelets		✗	**0.919**	**0.992**	**0.906**
	pt-frames		frames*	0.910	0.987	0.896
	pt-large		Imagenet + kinetics-400	0.958	0.997	0.952
SlowFast	frames	224×224	✗	0.926	0.997	0.914
	tubelets		✗	**0.951**	**0.997**	**0.943**
	pt-frames		frames*	0.942	0.992	0.934
	pt-large		kinetics-400	0.968	0.996	0.963

*frames model trained from scratch is used as the pre-trained model for finetuning the pt-frames model

like any other tubelet-based recognition methods [3,11,16,17] compared to the frame-level recognition methods [7,14,22].

The C3D [22] and I3D [2] models are pre-trained using the sports-1m [14] and Kinetics-400 [2] datasets, respectively, whereas the I3D models are pre-trained using both the Imagenet [19] and Kinetics-400 [2] datasets. It can be noted that due to their strong representation power at both image and video levels, large pre-trained models are able to achieve slightly better performance compared to tubelet-based methods. This performance difference is significant for I3D, where the model is pre-trained using both Imagenet and Kinetics-400 datasets. Nevertheless, this observation emphasizes the model's ability to acquire spatiotemporal representations through actor-centric tubelets. Surprisingly, even when trained with a limited dataset, the model achieves competetive performance to a fine-tuned model using a large SOTA dataset pre-trained model.

Model performance with different sizes of images is crucial for extended video action recognition and detection applications since a person usually takes up a very small area. Figure 4 presents the model performance for SlowFast (Fig. 4a) and I3D (Fig. 4b) across different input image sizes for both pre-trained and tubelet models. The tubelet models, trained from scratch, outperform pre-trained models at lower input sizes, i.e. for images lower than 64×64. This suggests that training tubelet models from scratch may be more effective for tasks that require the processing of small input images. This is the case of action

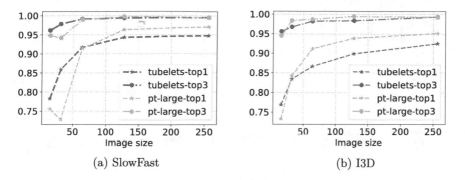

(a) SlowFast

(b) I3D

Fig. 4. Model performance comparison for the SlowFast and I3D across various input image sizes. Input image is scaled to specified size before applying to 3D CNN.

detection in extended videos. Additionally, the performance gap between pre-trained and tubelet models decreases as the input image size increases, indicating that existing pre-trained models are more suitable for larger input sizes, i.e. frame-level classification.

6 Conclusion and Future Work

This paper presents a comprehensive empirical evaluation study of frame-level and actor-centric action recognition models using state-of-the-art 3D CNN architectures. We demonstrated that the actor-centric recognition model outperforms both frame-level and fine-tuned large pre-trained models by efficiently modelling spatio-temporal features. Furthermore, we propose an actor-centric backbone for action detection for untrimmed extended videos. The results show that the proposed actor-centric backbone performs significantly better for small image sizes (below 64px), making it ideal for extended video activity recognition and detection.

Future work will consider proposing a large actor-centric tubelet action recognition dataset by combining and processing existing extended video action detection datasets (such as VIRAT [18] and JRDB-Act [5]). Furthermore, we plan to release 3D CNN backbones pre-trained using the proposed large-scale action recognition dataset to be used for action detection for extended videos.

References

1. Bewley, A., Ge, Z., Ott, L., Ramos, F., Upcroft, B.: Simple online and realtime tracking. In: 2016 IEEE International Conference on Image Processing (ICIP), pp. 3464–3468. IEEE (2016)
2. Carreira, J., Zisserman, A.: Quo vadis, action recognition? A new model and the kinetics dataset. In: Proceedings of the IEEE Conference on Computer Vision and Pattern Recognition, pp. 6299–6308 (2017)

3. Dave, I., Scheffer, Z., Kumar, A., Shiraz, S., Rawat, Y.S., Shah, M.: Gabriellav2: towards better generalization in surveillance videos for action detection. In: Proceedings of the IEEE/CVF Winter Conference on Applications of Computer Vision, pp. 122–132 (2022)
4. Duan, H., Zhao, Y., Chen, K., Lin, D., Dai, B.: Revisiting skeleton-based action recognition. In: Proceedings of the IEEE/CVF Conference on Computer Vision and Pattern Recognition, pp. 2969–2978 (2022)
5. Ehsanpour, M., Saleh, F., Savarese, S., Reid, I., Rezatofighi, H.: JRDB-act: a large-scale dataset for spatio-temporal action, social group and activity detection. In: Proceedings of the IEEE/CVF Conference on Computer Vision and Pattern Recognition, pp. 20983–20992 (2022)
6. Feichtenhofer, C.: X3D: expanding architectures for efficient video recognition. In: Proceedings of the IEEE/CVF Conference on Computer Vision and Pattern Recognition, pp. 203–213 (2020)
7. Feichtenhofer, C., Fan, H., Malik, J., He, K.: Slowfast networks for video recognition. In: Proceedings of the IEEE/CVF International Conference on Computer Vision, pp. 6202–6211 (2019)
8. Girdhar, R., Carreira, J., Doersch, C., Zisserman, A.: A better baseline for ava. arXiv preprint arXiv:1807.10066 (2018)
9. Gkountakos, K., Touska, D., Ioannidis, K., Tsikrika, T., Vrochidis, S., Kompatsiaris, I.: Spatio-temporal activity detection and recognition in untrimmed surveillance videos. In: Proceedings of the 2021 International Conference on Multimedia Retrieval, pp. 451–455 (2021)
10. Gleason, J., Castillo, C.D., Chellappa, R.: Real-time detection of activities in untrimmed videos. In: Proceedings of the IEEE/CVF Winter Conference on Applications of Computer Vision Workshops, pp. 117–125 (2020)
11. Gleason, J., Ranjan, R., Schwarcz, S., Castillo, C., Chen, J.C., Chellappa, R.: A proposal-based solution to spatio-temporal action detection in untrimmed videos. In: 2019 IEEE winter conference on applications of computer vision (WACV), pp. 141–150. IEEE (2019)
12. Gu, C., et al.: Ava: a video dataset of spatio-temporally localized atomic visual actions. In: Proceedings of the IEEE Conference on Computer Vision and Pattern Recognition, pp. 6047–6056 (2018)
13. Howard, A.G., et al.: MobileNets: efficient convolutional neural networks for mobile vision applications. arXiv preprint arXiv:1704.04861 (2017)
14. Karpathy, A., Toderici, G., Shetty, S., Leung, T., Sukthankar, R., Fei-Fei, L.: Large-scale video classification with convolutional neural networks. In: Proceedings of the IEEE Conference on Computer Vision and Pattern Recognition (CVPR) (2014)
15. Liu, J., Shahroudy, A., Perez, M., Wang, G., Duan, L.Y., Kot, A.C.: Ntu rgb+ d 120: a large-scale benchmark for 3D human activity understanding. IEEE Trans. Pattern Anal. Mach. Intell. **42**(10), 2684–2701 (2019)
16. Liu, W., et al.: Argus: efficient activity detection system for extended video analysis. In: Proceedings of the IEEE/CVF Winter Conference on Applications of Computer Vision Workshops, pp. 126–133 (2020)
17. Mavroudi, E., Bindal, P., Vidal, R.: Actor-centric tubelets for real-time activity detection in extended videos. In: Proceedings of the IEEE/CVF Winter Conference on Applications of Computer Vision, pp. 172–181 (2022)
18. Oh, S., et al.: A large-scale benchmark dataset for event recognition in surveillance video. In: CVPR 2011, pp. 3153–3160. IEEE (2011)
19. Russakovsky, O., et al.: ImageNet large scale visual recognition challenge. Int. J. Comput. Vision **115**, 211–252 (2015)

20. Singh, G., Choutas, V., Saha, S., Yu, F., Van Gool, L.: Spatio-temporal action detection under large motion. In: Proceedings of the IEEE/CVF Winter Conference on Applications of Computer Vision, pp. 6009–6018 (2023)
21. Soomro, K., Zamir, A.R., Shah, M.: UCF101: a dataset of 101 human actions classes from videos in the wild. arXiv preprint arXiv:1212.0402 (2012)
22. Tran, D., Bourdev, L., Fergus, R., Torresani, L., Paluri, M.: Learning spatiotemporal features with 3D convolutional networks. In: Proceedings of the IEEE International Conference on Computer Vision, pp. 4489–4497 (2015)
23. Zhang, B., Wan, J., Zhao, Y., Tong, Z., Du, Y.: Multi-actor activity detection by modeling object relationships in extended videos based on deep learning. Eng. Appl. Artif. Intell. **114**, 105055 (2022)

Author Index

Printed in the United States
by Baker & Taylor Publisher Services